T0114417

Praise for

Napoleon in Egypt

"In *Napoleon in Egypt*, Paul Strathern has written both a gripping adventure story and a sobering morality tale."
—*The Wall Street Journal*

"*Napoleon in Egypt* is undoubtedly the finest account of the Savants and their contribution to date. . . . Strathern has woven an illuminating account of the long-neglected scientists and artists who accompanied him. . . . The breadth of his findings on the secondary characters in this empirical venture do make *Napoleon in Egypt* a necessary addition to any Napoleonic shelf." —*The Christian Science Monitor*

"Those looking for an exciting, comprehensive narrative history of the whole expedition are advised to hunt down . . . *Napoleon in Egypt*."
—TOM REISS, author of *The Orientalist*,
The New York Times Book Review

"Nonfiction author and award-winning novelist Strathern turns up plenty of surprises in an enthralling history of the first of Napoleon's world-class debacles. . . . Stories of powerful men making disastrous decisions have an endless fascination, and Strathern makes the most of it in this entertaining account." —*Publishers Weekly* (starred review)

"Strathern's skillful use of memoir and other primary sources brings to life one of the most fascinating campaigns in military history."
—*Library Journal* (starred review)

"Strathern, a prize-winning novelist as well as a historian, has probed Napoleon's complex personality, both the megalomania for which he is vilified and the military prowess for which he is admired, and has in the process created a highly readable lesson in the rhymes of history."
—*BookPage*

NAPOLEON IN EGYPT

NAPOLEON in EGYPT

PAUL STRATHERN

BANTAM BOOKS TRADE PAPERBACKS

2009 Bantam Books Trade Paperback Edition

Copyright © 2007 by Paul Strathern

Published in the United States by Bantam Books,
an imprint of The Random House Publishing Group,
a division of Random House, Inc., New York.

BANTAM BOOKS and the rooster colophon are registered trademarks
of Random House, Inc.

Originally published in hardcover in Great Britain by Jonathan Cape,
an imprint of The Random House Group Ltd., London, in 2007
and subsequently published in hardcover in the United States by Bantam Books,
an imprint of The Random House Publishing Group,
a division of Random House, Inc., in 2008.

Strathern, Paul, 1940–
Napoleon in Egypt / Paul Strathern.
p. cm.
Includes bibliographical references and index.
ISBN 978-0-553-38524-3 (pbk.) 1. Egypt—History—French occupation,
1798–1801. 2. Napoleon I, Emperor of the French, 1769–1821.
3. Civilization—Egyptian influences. 4. France—History—1789–1815. I. Title.

DC225.S77 2008
962'.03—dc22   2008028135

www.bantamdell.com

147429898

Text design by Catherine Leonardo
Maps by Reginald Piggott

To Matthias

CONTENTS

ILLUSTRATIONS

General Bonaparte at the Bridge of Arcole, 17 November 1796, by Antoine-Jean Gros (© *Photo RMN/Gérard Blot*).

Pauline Fourès (© *Photo RMN; all rights reserved*).

The Battle of the Pyramids, painting by Louis François Lejeune (© *Photo RMN/Gérard Blot*).

Andoche Junot (© *Photo RMN/Jean-Gilles Berizzi*).

Louis-Joseph Maximilie Caffarelli du Falga (© *Photo RMN; all rights reserved*).

Gaspard Monge, painting by Jean-Baptiste Mauzaisse (© *Photo RMN/Gérard Blot*).

Claude-Louis Berthollet, by André Dutertre (© *Photo RMN/Jean-Gilles Berizzi*).

Nicolas Jacques Conté, engraving by Louis-Pierre Baltard de la Fresque (© *Photo RMN/Gérard Blot*).

Déodat de Dolomieu (© *Photo RMN; all rights reserved*).

Joachim Murat (© *Photo RMN; all rights reserved*).

Jacques-François Menou, charcoal portrait by André Dutertre (© *Photo RMN/Franck Raux*).

Jean-Baptiste Kléber, painting by Antoine Jean Joseph Ansiaux (© *Photo RMN/Jean Schormans*).

Louis-Charles-Antoine Desaix, painting by Andrea Appiani (© *Photo RMN/Gérard Blot*).

Sheik El-Bekri, painting by Michel Rigo (© *Photo RMN/Daniel Arnaudet*).

Murad Bey, from *Costumes and Portraits of "Description of Egypt,"* vol. 2, 1822, engraved by Nicolas Ponce after André Dutertre (*Stapleton Collection/Bridgeman Art Library*).

Savants measuring the Sphinx, from *Voyage en Égypte* by Dominique Vivant Denon, 1802, engraving after Jules Alfred Vincent Rigo (*Archives Charmet; private collection/Bridgeman Art Library*).

The remains of the temple at Edfu, engraving by J. Pass after Denon (*Mary Evans Picture Library*).

French graffiti on the temples of Upper Egypt.

Napoleon visits the plague victims at Jaffa, painting by Antoine-Jean Gros (© *Photo RMN; all rights reserved*).

Sir Sidney Smith at the siege of Acre, engraving by Cook after Eckstein (*Mary Evans Picture Library*).

Napoleon's return from Syria (© *Photo RMN/Daniel Arnaudet*).

MAPS

AUTHOR'S NOTE

Napoleon was of course merely General Bonaparte at the time of his invasion of Egypt. However, he remains for the most part better remembered in history as Napoleon. In accord with this popular conception, I have referred to him as Napoleon throughout (as indeed he did himself in his third-person memoirs of this period).

ACKNOWLEDGMENTS

Once again, I am particularly glad to acknowledge the meticulous and perceptive editing of Jörg Hensgen of Jonathan Cape. I am also indebted to Will Sulkin of Jonathan Cape, who believed in the idea of *Napoleon in Egypt* and encouraged it. However, none of this could have come about but for my indefatigable agent, Julian Alexander of LAW, who as ever played such a leading role in the conception of this book.

Europe is a molehill. . . . Everything here is worn out. . . . Tiny Europe has not enough to offer. We must set off for the Orient; that is where all the greatest glory is to be achieved.

Napoleon

The time I spent in Egypt was the most delightful of my life because it was the most ideal.

Napoleon

I saw the way to achieve all my dreams. . . . I would found a religion, I saw myself marching on the way to Asia, mounted on an elephant, a turban on my head, and in my hand a new Koran that I would have composed to suit my needs. In my enterprises I would have combined the experiences of the two worlds, exploiting the realm of all history for my own profit.

Napoleon

NAPOLEON IN EGYPT

PROLOGUE:
THE SONG OF DEPARTURE

THE invasion of Egypt by Napoleon in the summer of 1798 was the first great seaborne invasion of the modern era. At the time, it may well have been the largest ever launched in the Western world—at least on a par with Xerxes' vast Persian fleet which attacked Athens at the Battle of Salamis in 480 BC, and certainly double the size of the sixteenth-century Spanish Armada which attempted to invade Elizabethan England. Yet unlike these predecessors, Napoleon's invasion involved a long sea voyage of almost 2,000 miles. His armada consisted of 335 ships, ranging from towering battleships and fast frigates to lowly transports, from those bearing a cargo of just forty tons to those carrying over 400 tons. Each of these ships carried full crews, and in all the fleet was loaded with 1,200 horses, 171 field guns and an official roll-call of 35,000 soldiers. In fact, the number of soldiers was almost certainly nearer 40,000: Napoleon exploited the opportunity provided by four separate main embarkation ports—Toulon and Marseilles in France, Genoa and Civitavecchia in Italy—to surreptitiously increase the quota allowed him by the five-man Directory which ruled revolutionary France at the time.

Yet these were not the only unofficial additions to the expedition: as many as 300 women are also thought to have traveled aboard the fleet. A good number of these would have been the washerwomen and seamstresses who normally accompanied the French army at this time, but there were certainly many others smuggled aboard, contrary to Napoleon's orders. These were mainly the wives of junior and middle-ranking army officers, who were hustled up the gangways dressed in officer's uniform, their figures disguised by cloaks, their tresses swept up under military caps. As we shall see, these women would prove more than mere supernumeraries, and two in particular would achieve fame: one as Egypt's new Cleopatra, the other spiritedly opposing a Napoleonic insult to women.

It took little time for Napoleon to become aware that these extra women had been smuggled aboard: he always made it his business to be well supplied with intelligence by spies, as much amongst his own ranks as amongst the enemy. Far from disconcerting him, this discovery meant he felt less compunction about initiating his own covert plan for female company. As arranged, after four days at sea he dispatched the frigate *Pomone* to collect his wife Josephine from Naples—a mission which proved fruitless because Josephine had capriciously decided not to travel to southern Italy.

After the convoys from the separate ports had combined at sea and begun sailing for the eastern Mediterranean, the invasion armada swelled to cover almost five square miles, often reduced to traveling at the stately speed of one knot. Each afternoon all soldiers were paraded for inspection on the wide decks of the ships of the line. Military bands, their brass instruments glinting in the June sunlight, played stirring marches, while Napoleon watched from the bridge of the aptly named flagship *L'Orient*.

Napoleon cut a surprisingly unimpressive figure at this early stage in his career. He was thin as a rake and only five foot three inches tall.[1] His gaunt, hard-eyed features, sullen in repose, were framed by long sideburns and lank shoulder-length hair. He was just twenty-eight years old. Yet this was very much a young man's expedition, and some of his generals were even younger. Promotion came fast to men of ability in the revolutionary army, and their sallow-skinned young Corsican leader was an inspiration to both his officers and his men. He had already conducted a brilliant campaign in Italy, putting the powerful Austrians to flight and defeating the pope. The men of the Army of Italy were all too willing to follow their leader on this expedition into the unknown. To improve morale, Napoleon encouraged the soldiers parading on deck to sing patriotic songs, and each afternoon their voices would ring out across the sunlit Mediterranean, taken up by other soldiers from ship to ship through the fleet. Their favorites were "La Marseillaise" and the stirring "Chant du Départ" ("Song of Departure"):

Inspiring victory leads us through all barriers,
Liberty guides the footsteps of us warriors,
And from the north to the Midi we all
Hear the war-like trumpets call.
Tremble you enemies of France,
Our blood stirred with pride we advance.
The sovereign people are victorious,
All true patriots call on us:
A Frenchman must never ask why
For his country he must live or die![2]

Napoleon himself was a bad sailor, and in order to overcome seasickness he had ordered a special bed with casters attached to its legs to be installed in his cabin. This was intended to compensate for the rolling of the sea, and astonishingly it appears to have worked. Napoleon spent much of the voyage in bed, drawing up his plans for the invasion; this was his opportunity to emulate his hero, Alexander the Great. As he had confided to his secretary Bourrienne, prior to departure: "Europe is a molehill. . . . Everything here is worn out. My glory is slipping from my grasp, tiny Europe has not enough to offer. We must set off for the Orient; that is where all the greatest glory is to be achieved."[3] Napoleon's choice of words here was particularly revealing: he spoke of the Orient, not just Egypt. Although the Directory was under the impression that he intended to invade Egypt, Napoleon harbored dreams of following in the footsteps of Alexander the Great, and marching all the way to India. When he had revealed to the Directory this extension to his plans, they had reluctantly assented to it, for the most part because they did not believe in it: this was merely the fantasy of a man intoxicated by ambition, and would prove impossible on the ground. In fact, as we shall see, Napoleon had already made detailed plans for the realization of this "Oriental fantasy."

Even the approved, more realistic aims of Napoleon's invasion of Egypt were highly ambitious. His primary purpose was to liberate the Egyptians from the oppressive rule of the Mamelukes. But this was only the beginning. Along with his soldiers he had brought with him a team of 167 hand-picked "savants"; these consisted of the young intellectual cream of France, comprising many of the country's finest mathematicians, scientists, artists, writers and inventors. The contemporary French historian Dominique Arago, with an ingenuousness that remains resonant to this day, characterized the aim of the invasion as being:

"to offer a succoring hand to an unhappy people, to free them from the brutalizing yoke under which they have groaned for centuries, and finally to endow them without delay with all the benefits of European civilization."[4] The Egyptians were to be freed from tyranny; they were to be shown the light of reason, provided with the advantages of popular government, and instructed in the latest scientific advances. (Napoleon had been insistent that the expedition should include one of the latest Montgolfier balloons, an impressive new technology which he felt sure would inspire wonder in the native population.)

Yet this was not to be an entirely one-sided undertaking. Napoleon felt that there was also much for the expedition to learn from Egypt itself. The Sphinx and the pyramids were already known to Europe, but travelers had returned with tales of huge statues and amazing temples standing in the desert on the edges of the Nile valley in Upper Egypt. These appeared to be the remains of a mysterious civilization that had preceded the ancient Greeks, and in exploring these ruins the expedition would be seeking to discover the lost origins of Western civilization.

Each morning Napoleon would decide upon a question for discussion that evening between himself, the senior savants and the generals traveling with him aboard *L'Orient*. Seated around a table, their faces dimly illuminated by lanterns, this collection of young ambitious soldiers and brilliant minds would discuss their leader's chosen topics. These included "Is there life on other planets?," "How will the world end?" and "How old is the earth?" (Ironically, the findings of the expedition would completely transform all previous knowledge of this latter subject.)

Amongst those who played a leading role in these nightly debates were the mathematician Gaspard Monge, the inventor of descriptive geometry; the chemist Claude-Louis Berthollet, who discovered the foundations of chemical reaction; the portly Italian engineer General Louis Caffarelli, who had a wooden leg and was the most popular general with the soldiers; Napoleon's young friend and aide Andoche Junot; and of course Napoleon himself, who in this intellectual forum insisted upon being heard as an equal, though in practice his voice stilled all others.

The debates would continue beneath the vast dome of the starlit heavens, as the ghostly looming canvases of the sails above them filled and slackened in the breeze.[5] From the darkness all around came the shush of the passing waves and the creaking of the ship's timbers as it shifted in the swell. The officer on the bridge would ring the bell to mark the passing of the watch, calling to the lookouts, their distant voices replying from the prow and from the crow's nest high in the darkness of the masts.

Occasionally Napoleon and his assembled staff and savants would listen to readings from various classic texts, which in turn would inspire their own topics for discussion. A reading from the Bible describing Joseph's dream provoked a debate on whether dreams had meanings that could be interpreted. And after hearing a passage from Rousseau's *Discourse on the Origin of Inequality*, there followed a debate lasting three nights on the social advantages and disadvantages of property. The spirit of the Revolution lived on, even amongst the generals: despite the setbacks of Robespierre's Terror and the evident corruption of the current Directory, the shipboard debaters felt free to propose all manner of idealistic questions. Nothing was sacred— even property. Inspired by Rousseau's stirring words, Caffarelli declared: "I maintain that the laws which sanctify property sanctify usurpation and theft." He even went so far as to propose a form of communism to replace the laws of property. The savant Regnault demanded to know how a society could possibly function without such laws. The following evening Caffarelli pulled from the breast pocket of his uniform the speech he had prepared in reply to Regnault. As he paced back and forth, his wooden leg knocking hollowly against the planks of the deck, he outlined his solution. With regard to property, society would be divided into two classes: there would be those who owned property, and their tenants, who would be the future owners. After twenty years of working for the profit of the owners, the tenants would in their turn become the owners of the property, and would take on their own tenants. This unique system would thus exist in perpetuity.

As the invasion fleet sailed east across the Mediterranean, Napoleon would lie in bed reading and dictating to Bourrienne. His principal reading was from the Koran. Like Alexander the Great before him, he intended to absorb the religion of the people over whom he would rule. He insisted that, if necessary, he himself was willing to become a Muslim—an intention that, at least initially, he would show every sign of wishing to fulfill. However, it should also be noted that in Napoleon's shipboard library the Koran was shelved under "Politics."

At the same time, he also busied himself with dictating his "proclamation" to the Egyptian people.

In the name of Allah the merciful ... People of Egypt, you will have been told that I come as an enemy of Islam. This is a lie ... I have come to restore your rights and punish those who oppress you. ... I worship God more than your oppressors; I respect Mohammed his prophet and the holy Koran. ... The French are also true Moslems. The proof of this can be seen in the fact that they have marched against Rome and destroyed the throne of the Pope, who constantly incited the Christians to make war on all Moslems ...[6]

Prior to arrival, this proclamation would be translated into Arabic by one of the Orientalists amongst the savants and printed on the Arabic printing press which Napoleon was carrying on board *L'Orient*. (He had scoured Europe for an Arabic printing press; ironically, the only one he had managed to find was at the Papal Propaganda Office in Rome.) On arrival, he intended that his proclamation should be distributed amongst the Egyptians, and it was hoped that this would overcome the need for armed conflict. Such was to be the first step in the creation of his Oriental empire. As Napoleon later put it, when describing his feelings at this time: "I saw the way to achieve all my dreams. ... I would found a religion, I saw myself marching on the way to Asia, mounted on an elephant, a turban on my head, and in my hand a new Koran that I would have composed to suit my needs. In my enterprises I would have combined the experiences of the two worlds, exploiting the realm of all history for my own profit."[7]

On June 30, 1798, six weeks after setting out from Toulon, the French fleet approached the shore of Egypt. In the third century BC the Pharos of Alexandria, the 400-foot lighthouse that had been one of the Seven Wonders of the Ancient World, could be seen on a clear day from thirty-five miles out to sea, and on a clear night the radiance of its mirror-aided light was reputed to have been visible from below the horizon for up to eighty miles. But this wonder had long since crumbled into the harbor. As the leading ships of Napoleon's armada approached land, all that could now be seen was a smudge on the horizon of the flat African coastline, with the solitary ruin known as Pompey's Pillar forming the landmark for the once great city of Alexandria.

I

The Origins of the Egyptian Campaign

SINCE earliest times, Egypt had been a source of wonder to the European eye. The ancient Greek historian Herodotus, visiting the country in the mid fifth century BC, encountered the following scene: "During the flooding of the Nile only the towns are visible, rising above the surface of the water like the scattered islands of the Aegean Sea. While the inundation continues, boats no longer keep to the channels and rivers, but sail across the fields and plains. On a journey far inland you can even sail past the pyramids." [1] Less than two centuries later, the Macedonian Greek Alexander the Great conquered Egypt, completing this task in a matter of months, but remaining long enough to found the city of Alexandria, whose site he selected in 331 BC at what was then the western mouth of the Nile delta. After this, in what appeared to be a characteristic act of hubris, but was in fact an attempt to win over the local priesthood, Alexander sacrificed to the sacred bull Apis and had himself crowned pharaoh. He then set off east on his campaign of conquest against the Persians, during which he planted the seeds of Greek culture across a great swath of Asia. Eight years later, having extended his conquests to the limits of the known world, Alexander died after a drinking bout in Babylon, and his body was brought back to Alexandria to be buried in a magnificent tomb, made of gold and glass, whose site has since been lost.

In Roman times, Egypt would become the granary of the Mediterranean world, providing over a third of the grain supplies for the entire Roman Empire. During the first century BC Alexandria would become the focus of stirring events which changed the fate of that empire, when the charms of Cleopatra, queen of Egypt, proved irresistible first to Julius Caesar and then to Mark Antony, while rivalry between these two ambitious men plunged the Roman Empire into civil war.

Under the Greeks, and then the Romans, Alexandria would become the intellectual capital of the Western world, the city that produced Euclid and educated Archimedes, its celebrated library a respository of all knowledge. It was here that Eratosthenes calculated the circumference of the earth and its distance from the sun. For the latter, he used the known fact that on a certain day the sun could be seen at the foot of a deep well in Aswan 500 miles to the south, and was thus directly overhead. He then measured the length of the shadow cast by a pole in Alexandria, and thus the angle of the sun's rays there; using trigonometry, he then calculated the distance of the sun within around 5 percent of the accepted modern figure. Such was the reach and achievement of Alexandrian learning at its prime. When its library burned down in two disastrous fires, the last of which was started by zealot Christians in AD 391, the ancient world lost over half a million scrolls, and with these much as a quarter of the knowledge and cultural heritage of Western civilization vanished forever.

French interest in Egypt began with the Seventh Crusade in the thirteenth century, led by Louis IX (who partly on account of this became known as St. Louis). In 1248 the king and over 30,000 men disembarked from 100 ships near Damietta on the Nile delta. Here they encountered the full might of the Mameluke cavalry, which inflicted on them a crushing defeat, capturing Louis and holding him to ransom.

The Mameluke cavalry was arguably the greatest war machine of the period, certainly superior to any European militia. In 1260, just ten years after the debacle of the Seventh Crusade, the Mameluke cavalry would encounter the Mongol hordes of Genghis Khan's successor at the Battle of Ayn Jalut, just north of Jerusalem. Here they put the Mongol cavalry to flight, thus destroying for the first time the myth of their invincibility. Had the Mamelukes lost this battle, the Mongols could have pressed on across North Africa into Spain, encircling Europe. Not for nothing has this victory been reckoned as one of the great turning points of history, though it passed unnoticed in the medieval world it rescued. Meanwhile, to the European mind Egypt remained for the most part a land of Biblical legend: the setting of the plague of frogs, the Nile turning to blood, and Moses' parting of the Red Sea.

Four hundred years later, the German philosopher Leibniz would approach Louis XIV with a meticulously detailed plan for a French

invasion of Egypt, including details of a Suez canal to facilitate trade
with the Indies. Despite such lofty foresight, Leibniz's motive was in
fact down to earth and devious: his employer, the Elector of Mainz,
wished to divert the Sun King from invading the German states. But
Louis rejected Leibniz's idea, informing him that "since the days of St.
Louis, such expeditions have gone out of fashion." The papers detailing
the scheme would gather dust in the archives at Hanover after Leibniz's
death. It has been suggested that Napoleon might have been inspired by
these plans, but it is now certain that he had no idea of their existence
until he passed through Hanover in 1803, some years after his Egyptian
expedition. When they were drawn to his attention, he remarked crypti-
cally: "This work is very curious."[2] Nonetheless, Leibniz's plans remain
relevant; his scheme represented a trend that would flourish recurrently
during the ensuing centuries: namely, the European habit of exporting
internal conflicts to the territories of other continents.

Despite the rejection of Leibniz's scheme, during the ensuing century
France expanded its colonial empire to Canada, Louisiana, the West
Indies and India. Other European powers were engaged in similar enterprises, and this soon resulted in conflict, most notably between Britain
and France. Britain's growing economic and maritime power eventually tipped the balance, with rapid and disastrous effect on the French
colonies. In 1761 France lost Pondicherry and trading posts on the
east coast of India; in 1762–3 it was forced to cede the Louisiana
Territory to the Spanish and the British; and in 1763 it lost sovereignty
over its Canadian colonies to Britain.* France's valuable sugar-producing
colonies in the West Indies—Martinique, Guadeloupe and Saint-
Dominique (Haiti)—now looked particularly vulnerable. Mindful of
this state of affairs, Louis XV's foreign minister, the Duc de Choiseul,
came up with a scheme to take over Egypt in 1769, the very year
Napoleon was born. Given Egypt's climate and its plentiful cheap labor,
it was ideal for sugar plantations, and could easily supplant if
not exceed France's imports from the West Indies. The fact that Egypt
was nominally part of the Ottoman Empire, a long-term ally of France,
could easily be overcome by the simple expedient of buying it from

---

* Although the kingdoms of England and Scotland formed a union in 1707 to
become Great Britain, the French continued to refer to the British as *Anglois* or
Anglais (i.e., the English); for reasons of consistency I have referred to Britain, the
British, the British navy (which flew the Union Jack), etc., throughout.

the Turks. The following year the aging Louis XV took the courtesan Madame du Barry as his mistress, de Choiseul fell from favor, and his planned introduction of retail theory into foreign policy was shelved.

Yet France's colonial situation remained under threat, and in 1776 the idea of turning Egypt into a French colony was resurrected, when the Ministry of the Navy decided to dispatch an envoy there. The man chosen was Baron François de Tott, a Frenchman of Hungarian descent who had lived in the eastern Mediterranean for several years and had much experience of Levantine affairs. Yet this experience would prove of little avail. On his arrival in Cairo, de Tott was immediately escorted to the Citadel, the city's fortress, where he had an audience with the pasha "surrounded by all the pomp of his Vizirate." De Tott described how "the Pasha sent away the crowd which filled the hall of the Divan, [whereupon] he confided to me that there was a fermentation amongst the beys (a sure sign that a revolution was about to take place)." No sooner had de Tott arrived at the French consul's house than a revolt duly erupted and he found himself barricaded in for his own safety "while the ruling beys took possession of the Citadel, forcing the Pasha with a pistol under his throat to issue an order banishing the revolters into exile . . . but the rebels, despising such vain formalities, began firing at their enemies. . . . After several days of blasting their guns, with more noise than effect, the ruling beys fled from the Citadel into Upper Egypt . . . and a new group of beys declared themselves to be in charge."³ Such chaos had now become a regular feature of life in Egypt, with the pasha, who was nominally the Ottoman ruler, reduced to a mere figurehead at the mercy of the beys, the ruling provincial chieftains, all of whom were members of the warrior caste of Mamelukes.

The Mamelukes had a long history in Egypt. They were originally brought into the country around 1230 by the ruling Ayyubite sultan al-Malik, who purchased 12,000 youths from Turkey to strengthen his army. The word *Mameluke* derives from *mamluk*, the Arabic for "slave" or "bought man," though in this case the latter is closer to the actuality. In a remarkably short time the imported Mamelukes had molded themselves into the fearsome fighting force encountered by Louis IX and the Seventh Crusade in 1248. Ten years later they became the major power in the land, murdering al-Malik's successor and establishing their own dynasty. At this stage they appear to have been largely

Turkic—non-Arab and non-Muslim in origin, often barely understanding Arabic. Yet curiously it was under this new dynasty that Egypt became established as the center of Arabic culture in the Muslim world, with the great Al-Azhar mosque as a beacon of learning, its medical and mathematical knowledge far outshining anything in medieval Europe. This was mainly due to the influx of refugee scholars from such places as Baghdad and Damascus, fleeing in the face of the Mongol hordes. Had the Mamelukes not defeated the Mongols at the Battle of Ayn Jalut in 1260, the Muslim world, much like medieval Europe, would not have survived.

Yet just twenty years later this invincible force would begin a long decline. Initially this was because its ethnic origins changed. From now on, the imported youths were of Caucasian origin—Georgians and Circassians from remote mountain villages who had had little contact with civilization. As a result, the Mamelukes became more tribalized and disorganized.

In 1517 Egypt was overrun by the Turks and became part of the expanding Ottoman Empire. Egypt was now ruled from Constantinople by the distant Sublime Porte, the Turkish administration under the sultan's vizier. A pasha was installed in Cairo, and the country was obliged to pay annual tribute (*miry*) to the Turkish sultan. But in fact, the power of the beys who ruled over the various regions, each with their company of young, freshly imported Mamelukes, remained largely unchanged. The Porte in faraway Constantinople was not concerned, as long as there was a semblance of peace and the sultan received his *miry*. Over 200 years later, this had degenerated into the farcical situation encountered by de Tott. Each time a new pasha was sent from Constantinople, he would be greeted ceremoniously by the ruling beys and escorted to the Citadel, where he would be installed in some style. Here he would remain under virtual house arrest with little power to do anything but issue the occasional imperial decree (*firman*), whose contents and effectiveness were entirely under the control of whichever group of beys held the upper hand. Should any pasha attempt to interfere with this arrangement, a request would be sent to the Porte for a replacement, and one would duly be sent.

The Mamelukes maintained their social position and ethnic purity by the simple expedient of not recognizing mixed offspring. Although their chieftains, the ruling beys, frequently kept harems of local Egyptian women, occasionally including darker Nubians or Abyssinians from the south, they only took wives of Mameluke stock, who were imported from the Caucasus for this purpose. These seldom produced children, owing to their habit of aborting themselves when pregnant, as they believed that not giving birth helped maintain their youth, beauty and attractiveness to their husbands.

The Mamelukes thus relied upon youths imported from the Caucasus region to keep up their population, which usually stood at between 10,000 and 12,000. When these youths arrived in Egypt, they were usually of prepubescent age, sometimes as young as eight years old, and were immediately subjected to a fierce disciplinary regimen aimed at instilling the warrior virtues of the Mamelukes. Only when a Mameluke reached a certain military rank, and took command of other warriors, did he achieve the status of a free man, whereupon he was allowed to grow a beard. From this time on, the mounted Mameluke was attended by two Egyptian *serradj*, attendants on foot, who accompanied him into battle, bearing his extra arms.

By the late eighteenth century, Egypt was divided into around two dozen regions, each ruled by its own Mameluke bey, assisted by what was virtually his own private Mameluke army, whose duties remained purely military. No Mameluke ever stooped to labor in the fields or gather the harvest. The beys kept a firm hold over the *fellahin*, the local peasantry of their own region, extracting taxes and maintaining a regime that kept the *fellahin* downtrodden and allowed little development of any sort—economic, social or cultural. The territory outside a bey's immediate domain was of little interest to him, which meant that the fierce nomadic Bedouin tribesmen had free rein over the extensive wilderness and desert regions of the country, thus further hindering the development of trade along the routes that passed through these regions.

The beys themselves formed groups of allegiance, creating a hierarchy that supported the two senior sheiks, who ruled from Cairo. One of these was the Sheik el-Beled (chief of the country), who took control of the Ottoman pasha and ensured that the necessary annual tribute was collected and dispatched to Constantinople. The other held the title of Emir el-Hadj (leader of the annual pilgrimage to Mecca), an important post, as the large numbers of pilgrims required protection from the Bedouin and other predators. In general, there were two great pilgrimages during this period. From the west came pilgrims from as far afield as Niger and Morocco, converging on Cairo. From the north, as many as 40,000 pilgrims accompanied by anything up to 35,000 camels converged on Damascus. These pilgrimages then joined up and made their way to Mecca. The organization of the Cairo pilgrimage involved considerable power and military resources, requiring widespread cooperation amongst the beys, a situation which was often placed under considerable strain by unruly Mameluke behavior.

De Tott's arrival in Cairo in 1777 had coincided with one of the frequent shifts of power in the Mameluke hierarchy. However, his eventual report to the French Ministry of the Navy was determinedly optimistic. Despite the little difficulty he had encountered in Cairo, he could see, or chose to see, no problem whatsoever in mounting an invasion, which would result in "the peaceful occupation of a defenseless country." This report was gratefully received in Paris, where it met with the fate of so many such reports: it was duly filed and ignored.

The next important French visitor to Egypt would prove the most crucial to Napoleon and his invasion. Constantin Volney was born in 1759 near Angers in the Loire valley. At school he showed exceptional promise whilst studying the classics, particularly admiring Herodotus and his method of immersing himself in all knowledge concerning the countries through which he traveled. Volney moved to Paris at the age of seventeen, where he was deeply influenced by the Enlightenment *philosophes* who were producing the *Encyclopédie*, the multi-volume work intended to contain all rational, artistic and scientific knowledge. This project inspired Volney, who dreamt of producing a "science of man"—a dream which pre-dated the birth of sociology by almost a century.

On his coming of age, Volney inherited sufficient income to allow him to travel, and decided that "Egypt offered scope for the sort of political and social observation I was interested in making." He was not physically robust, but he realized that his trip might involve him in considerable hardship, so he embarked upon a strict training regimen. This included prolonged periods without food, journeys on foot lasting several days, climbing walls, and leaping water-filled ditches such as he expected to find in the Nile delta—much to the bemusement of his rural spectators.[4] He then set off alone, a pack on his back containing a change of clothes, a musket slung across his shoulder, and a leather belt around his waist with 6,000 francs in gold coins.

Volney arrived in Egypt in 1783, and would remain in the region for three years, adopting native dress and learning Arabic well enough to be accepted amongst the Arabs. A year after his return he published his *Voyage en Egypte et en Syrie*, which revealed every aspect of contemporary Egyptian life as never before, in a wealth of detail. He described how "each year there arrives in Cairo a caravan from Abyssinia bringing from 1,000 to 1,200 black slaves, as well as elephants' teeth, gold powder, gum, parrots and monkeys."⁵ He listed the local ethnic populations—Mamelukes, Copts (Christian Egyptians), local Arabs, Iraqi Arabs, Yemenis, Greeks, Jews, etc.—as well as French residents (around sixty, mainly traders, living in Cairo, Alexandria, Rosetta and Damietta). These conducted their trade through Marseilles, exporting cotton, linen, coffee and rice, and importing silk from Lyons, cloth from Provence and beaten metal for pots. The French traders were forced to live in *funduks*—fortified compounds within whose walls were living quarters and warehouses. Volney even dared to investigate the legendary beauty of the mysterious Mameluke wives, "who remain even more invisible than the local women." Making use of a female informant, he discovered that their beauty was something of a myth, conforming as it did to the Turkish notion of pulchritude, which admired whiteness of skin and largeness: "Her face is like the full moon, her hips are like cushions."

According to Volney, the indigenous population consisted of poverty-stricken *fellahin* and city-dwellers living in squalid slums, a small class of wealthy merchants, and the religious community, whose senior scholars, the *ulema*, were responsible for the administration of Islamic law. The religious community centered on the Al-Azhar mosque and university in Cairo, which was a shadow of its former self: in place of the widespread learning of old there was now little more than narrow religious teaching, encouraging fanaticism amongst the young students, who had no other outlet for their intellect, or indeed social prospects, amongst a society which had fallen into decay under the near-anarchic rule of the Mamelukes. In consequence, Volney warned of the difficulty facing any invasion: "If the French dare to disembark there, Turks, Arabs and peasants will arm themselves against them. . . . Fanaticism will take the place of skill and courage."⁶

Yet he was not entirely pessimistic, offering an enticing cultural prospect: "If Egypt fell into the hands of a nation interested in culture, it would yield material to further our knowledge of antiquity such as can be found nowhere else in the world." The ruins in the Delta region were largely destroyed, "but in the less populated region of Upper Egypt and at the less frequented edges of the desert, several monuments remain intact. They are buried in the sand, stored ready for future generations to discover." Years later Napoleon would read these words with keen interest. Indeed, his regard for Volney's *Voyage en Egypte* was such that he took a copy with him to Egypt and used it as his constant reference work. His chief of staff, Berthier, would record that this was "the sole work that never led us astray."

The French were not the only Europeans trading with Egypt during the years of Volney's visit. Having made inroads into France's empire in the Americas and India during the previous decade, the British now began to challenge French commercial dominance in Egypt. In January 1775 two British ships approached the port of Suez, one laden with merchandise, the sole purpose of the other being to lead the way into the port, taking soundings of the channel as it went. Two months later a full commercial treaty was signed between "the most serene and powerful prince Mohammed-Abou-Dahab [the ruling Mameluke sheik in Cairo] and the honourable Warren Hastings president and governor for the British nation in Bengal."[7] This was followed by the arrival at Suez of a group of British commercial agents and "geographers" (cartographers and surveyors). There could be little doubt concerning British expansionist motives, and news of these developments was quickly relayed by the worried French consul in Cairo to the foreign ministry in Paris and the Porte in Constantinople, causing some consternation in both capitals. In the following year, with the encouragement of their French allies, the Porte issued a *firman* forbidding access at Suez to ships from India.

The British simply ignored this. By now they had already established a communications link carrying messages from India to Suez, overland to Alexandria, and from here by sea to Trieste—rather than the more normal route through Marseilles—and thence to London, thus circumventing France altogether. The French consul reported that the British even had "a man called Baldwin, resident in Cairo, especially charged with overseeing this correspondence."[8]

During the 1780s, French traders began to suffer increasing harassment, as the authorities showed preference for the British. In fact, the Mamelukes had initially offered a trading treaty to the French, but the French government had realized that it could not sign any such treaty without damaging its close relationship with the Porte. The French traders now protested, demanding that their government take action to prevent this harassment, but once again the French government felt powerless to act as long as the Ottoman sultan remained titular ruler of Egypt. Then everything changed.

The storming of the Bastille in Paris on July 14, 1789, marked the start of a new era in Europe, heralding the French Revolution, the overthrow of the *Ancien Régime*, and the proclamation of the Rights of Man beneath the republican tricolor. But "liberty, equality and fraternity" soon gave way to the Terror, led by the fanatical Jacobin leader Robespierre, during which thousands were sentenced to the guillotine and "heads fell like slates from the roofs." In 1794 Robespierre was overthrown and himself went to the guillotine. A reaction against such extremism saw the appointment in 1795 of a five-man Directory to rule the country; this attempted to steer a course between the Jacobins and the Royalists, but soon revealed itself as both ineffective and corrupt, working hand in hand with the profiteers who were exploiting the economic freedom following the collapse of the old system.

By now rulers throughout Europe had become fearful of French revolutionary ideas, and had sought to exploit the chaotic state of affairs which prevailed in France. As early as 1792 Prussia had invaded France; the following year Britain declared war, and France soon found itself confronted by a coalition of every major power in Europe, its borders threatened by Spain, Holland and Austria. In 1794 Britain seized Martinique, and in the following year consolidated its hold on India by taking over from the Dutch the Cape of Good Hope, which commanded the sea route to the East. In the same year the young Napoleon Bonaparte was appointed commander of the Army of the Interior and put down a revolt on the streets of Paris. A year later, in 1796, he took command of the Army of Italy, and began inflicting a series of spectacular defeats on the Austrians. Requisitioned treasure from this campaign helped to fill the depleted French exchequer, enabling the Directory to continue its ramshackle regime. With the revolutionary armies away fighting in Italy and on the Rhine, the Directory was safe. So long as the country remained at war, they would remain in power.

It was now that the idea of a French invasion of Egypt was resurrected. The man responsible for this was Charles-Maurice de Talleyrand-Périgord, the most able and devious politician of this devious era. Talleyrand was born in Paris in 1754, the second son of an aristocratic but somewhat impecunious family. A childhood accident left him with a limp, and instead of joining the army, he entered the Church, from which he was expelled for keeping a mistress, though his silver tongue and ready wit soon convinced the king to appoint him a bishop. By a series of characteristically deft and devious moves, he survived the Revolution and was appointed envoy to London, until he was expelled to America. After the Directory took power, he returned in 1796 to France, where he began scheming for high office, soon gaining the support of Paul Barras, the most influential (and corrupt) member of the Directory. The decisive moment came when Talleyrand delivered a paper before the prestigious Institute of France for the Sciences and the Arts (L'Institut de France) on 15 Messidor Year V (July 3, 1797).[9]

Entitled "On the advantages to be derived from new colonies under the present circumstances," Talleyrand's speech outlined before the assembled members of the Institute the case for French colonial expansion. Everyone had "long been aware that the West India colonies will one day separate themselves from the mother country. . . . Disastrous measures have carried devastation into our colonies."[10] With some aptness, he quoted Machiavelli: "Every change lays the foundation for another." Talleyrand admitted that what he was suggesting had earlier been proposed by de Choiseul—namely, that France should occupy Egypt. This was classic Talleyrand tactics: skilfully, he succeeded both in making his daring proposal, and at the same time placing responsibility for it with another.

It is unclear how serious Talleyrand was about the Egyptian idea at this juncture. His primary aim was to impress the audience with his knowledge of foreign affairs, and this he duly succeeded in doing. Accordingly, two weeks later he was appointed to the coveted post of foreign minister. As such, he received a letter dated September 13, 1797, from the commander of the Army of Italy; in it, he was astonished to read Napoleon's declaration that: "We must seize Egypt. This country has never belonged to a European nation. . . . In order to take it, we would need to set out with 25,000 men, escorted by eight or ten ships of the line. . . . I would be pleased, citizen minister, if you could arrange in Paris some meetings so that I can know what the reaction of the Porte would be to such an expedition to Egypt."[11]

At a stroke, an idea had taken on the flesh and blood of reality, complete with a leader.

II

"The Liberator of Italy"

NAPOLEON has long been credited with having an "Oriental complex": a dream of making great conquests in the East and setting up an Asiatic empire. The origins of this dream are profound and obscure. As early as eleven years old, whilst studying at the military college in Brienne, he had read of Alexander the Great and his campaign of Oriental conquest. As a result, this supreme military genius of the Hellenic world became the young Napoleon's hero and model. Despite this precocious self-identification, Napoleon did not stand out amongst his fellow pupils. After gaining acceptance at the prestigious École Militaire in Paris when he was fifteen, he shared a desk with the aristocratic Louis-Edmond Phélippeaux, who much to Napoleon's chagrin invariably topped the class. The best Napoleon would be able to manage was third, and as a result he and Phélippeaux developed a robust rivalry, which involved much surreptitious kicking of each other's shins beneath the desk during classes. Napoleon's final examination report spoke of his "pride and boundless ambition," yet his results were uneven, and only in mathematics did he shine.

Napoleon was subsequently commissioned in the artillery, considered socially inferior to the cavalry or the smart guards regiments. Yet this would prove the making of him. Artillery was becoming the key to modern warfare; it also required a knowledge of logistics and geography. Guns and ammunition came in varying strength and mobility, knowledge of terrain and weather was vital, and consequently more things could go wrong. Napoleon used his mathematical knowledge to calculate such matters mentally, and at speed. He was becoming adept (in theory) at the new kind of warfare which would supplant the incalculable vagaries of infantry deployment, the cavalry charge and the artillery barrage, with the tactics of technology and speed. As a result, he would develop an exceptional ability when confronted with a situation: he learned to consider *all* the options—not just the obvious ones—and to retain these in his mind. "Act first, and then wait to see what happens" became one of his trusted maxims. His ability to retain options that others had long since disregarded, or not even considered, would leave him master of situations far beyond the battlefield.

Young Lieutenant Bonaparte of the artillery quickly became bored with the boisterous activities of his fellow junior officers, and spent much of his leisure time reading. Science, politics, history, geography—all were grist to the mill of his avaricious mind. The only subject he balked at was philosophy; he was developing the view he later expressed as "History is the only true philosophy." The man in command, the one who made history, was the only one whose thoughts were worth considering.

Napoleon was the second son, who even in infancy had dominated his older brother. He had won the tough love of his powerful mother Letizia, who punished his wrongdoings mercilessly when she could trick her increasingly willful child into her grasp, but who according to Napoleon "instilled in me pride." This led to a self-belief which crossed into the superstitious: luck and destiny became tenets of faith. (Later, when he was thinking of employing a general, he would inquire: "Is he lucky?")

Alexander the Great had set out on his conquests at the age of twenty; and in the revolutionary year of 1789, at the age of nineteen, Napoleon read for the first time Volney's *Voyage en Égypte*, which had been published two years previously. He was enthralled, not least by Volney's apparently prosaic, almost statistical approach to such a poetical subject. The romantic who was inspired by the deeds of Alexander and Caesar also had the mind of a mathematician. As he put it himself: "My dreams are measured with the callipers of reason."[1] Then in 1792, whilst on a trip home to Corsica, he was introduced to Volney, who had come to the island to buy an estate where he intended to grow cotton, much as he had seen growing in Egypt. Napoleon was delegated to show Volney around the island, and soon became fascinated by the brilliant mind of this middle-aged traveler, questioning him in detail about his knowledge of Egypt. During this brief interlude Napoleon must also have made a lasting impression upon Volney, who was quick to discern the huge ambition of the apparently insignificant young lieutenant, and would remark a few years later with some apprehension: "Given half a chance, he'll become the head of Caesar on the shoulders of Alexander."[2]

Although Napoleon had received a military education, his widespread reading had led him to a belief in Enlightenment ideas; as a result, he initially welcomed the Revolution, though later events would cause him to modify his views. On August 10, 1792, he was in Paris and witnessed the mob storming the Tuileries, putting Louis XVI to flight, and then tearing the palace courtiers limb from limb. His experience of the mob led him to call them "the vilest rabble," yet he equally despised the king for his indecision and his willingness to let himself be humiliated, declaring: "In politics an act that degrades can never be lived down."[3]

Napoleon's great opportunity would come in the following year. In the summer of 1793 the Royalists seized the main Mediterranean naval port of Toulon, and were supported from the sea by the British navy under Rear-Admiral Hood. Napoleon was rushed in from a nearby training camp at Valence, and given charge of the artillery barrage ranged against the all but impregnable fortifications of the city. The commander of the siege of Toulon was General Doppet, an appointed revolutionary who had previously been a mesmerist doctor; his tactics consisted of little more than fruitless frontal assaults, which came to nothing owing to the bombardment from the British fleet. The twenty-three-year-old Napoleon suggested to his commander a daring plan: instead of attacking the fortifications, they should seize some high ground to the south and bombard the British fleet. The plan soon began to prove successful, and Napoleon himself showed exceptional bravery in leading his men in the final assault on the city. In the course of this charge he received four wounds, including a pike thrust that nearly resulted in his leg being amputated in the field. According to Hood's twenty-nine-year-old second-in-command, the brave young maverick sailor Sir Sidney Smith, the fleeing British and Royalist troops "crowded the water like the herd of swine that ran furiously into the sea possessed of the devil."[4] However, Smith managed to deprive the French of complete victory by spectacularly detonating the arsenal and setting ablaze the ships that were being left behind. This would not be the last time that Smith encountered Napoleon and thwarted the French army; as we shall see, this brilliant if eccentric sailor would play a crucial role in Napoleon's Egyptian campaign. Coincidentally, two other men present at Toulon would also play leading roles in Egypt.

Napoleon's aide at this siege was a young Burgundian sergeant called Andoche Junot, who stuck to his side throughout the fiercest of the fighting. At one point Napoleon had just finished dictating an order paper to Junot when a British salvo landed close by, nearly killing them both and showering the order paper with earth. Junot merely remarked, "Good, now I won't have to sand the ink."⁵ Napoleon was pleased to recognize a man as fearless as himself. Another future hero of the Egyptian campaign who fought at Toulon was the twenty-seven-year-old Louis-Charles Desaix, whose military brilliance whilst serving with the French army on the Rhine had led to him being promoted from sub-lieutenant to brigadier general in just seven months. During the turbulent years following the Revolution, men of merit as well as mesmerist doctors could achieve unprecedented advancement.

In December 1793 Napoleon was promoted to brigadier general—his ascent had been even more meteoric than that of Desaix: he had risen from captain to general in just four months. He had already taken part in some minor post-Revolution engagements, but Toulon had been his true baptism of fire, and he had proved himself a heroic leader, inspiring fervent loyalty amongst his men, the cannoneers. The rough conscripted troops under his command, illiterate peasants and the Revolutionary underclass of the city slums, knew that he was always with them; no matter the conditions, he ate and drank with them, swore with them and encouraged them. When necessary he rode on his horse, leading from the front, a gesture which also stirred his junior officers and hardened NCOs. He appeared fearless under fire, and even General Doppet noticed that he was always at his post: "If he needed rest he slept on the ground wrapped in his cloak, he never left his batteries."⁶

After Toulon, le général Napoleone Buonaparte, as he was then known, was recognized as a rising star; as a result, he would be befriended by the powerful Paul Barras, who had been one of the two government commissioners (political officers) overseeing the siege. Barras was a corrupt former Royalist officer who had inveigled himself into power with Robespierre's Jacobins, and then played a major role in Robespierre's execution when he fell, emerging as commander of the Army of the Interior and the police. A dangerous and unsavory character of considerable hauteur and presence, Barras stood out amongst the grasping mediocrities who were rising to the top in post-Revolution politics. He enjoyed his power, using it for personal enrichment as well as widespread seduction of prominent Parisian beauties and even some of the young men they attracted. He also had considerable political acumen, and it was this that caused him to befriend Napoleon, the young up-and-coming general. Napoleon had traveled to Paris, the center of power, in the hope of obtaining an active command, only to find himself balked by political maneuvering, forced to live in impecunious circumstances on half-pay. His connection with Barras would change his life.

By October 1795 Barras was a leading member of the ruling but unruly National Convention, the elected assembly which had proved so unpopular that it had succeeded in uniting the three opposing factions—the remnant Jacobins, the increasingly vocal Royalists, and even the so-called moderates. All these finally took to the streets in the thousands in an uprising on October 4 (now better remembered by its revolutionary date, 13 Vendémiaire). In desperation, Barras sent for Napoleon, who with the aid of "a whiff of grapeshot" and a dashing cavalry major called Joachim Murat put the mob to flight.

After 13 Vendémiaire Barras dramatically announced to the Convention: "The Republic has been saved!" By the end of October, the Convention had been replaced by an elected five-man Directory, with Barras manipulating the vote so that he became one of the directors. He then managed to persuade the Directory to appoint the twenty-six-year-old Napoleon commander of the Army of the Interior. He is said to have got his way by telling his fellow Directors: "Promote this man or he will promote himself without you." Barras evidently understood the extreme nature of Napoleon's ambition—at a time when even Napoleon himself does not appear to have fully articulated his own aims. Napoleon, for his part, would remember the role played in these events by the young cavalry major Murat: another man he would take to Egypt.

Barras was also responsible for one more major development in Napoleon's life. Around this time, he introduced Napoleon to a thirty-two-year-old widow called Rose de Beauharnais; she had been born in Martinique and had been lucky to live through the Terror, when her husband had been guillotined and she had been briefly imprisoned. Despite having two children, she had managed to survive after this through having a number of liaisons with high-ranking officers and rich businessmen. Eventually she had become the mistress of Barras, who had set her up in a "pavilion-house in the Greek style" on the Rue Chantereine, paying the 4,000-franc rent as well as the wages of her maidservants, chef, groom and gardener.

Rose's experiences had transformed her from a provincial innocent with a Caribbean accent into a woman of sophistication and hard realism, but the uncertainties of her position had taken their psychological toll, inclining her to extravagance and promiscuity. The bloom of her youth was beginning to fade, and she had such bad teeth ("like cloves") that rather than open her mouth to laugh, she maintained a tight-lipped smile whilst snickering through her nose, and went out of her way to avoid eating in company.

By now Barras was beginning to tire of Rose de Beauharnais, and indicated to her that she should attach herself to the young Napoleon— thus giving Barras a certain hold over his protégé, as well as providing him with privy access to any plans Napoleon might mention.

Napoleon was no sexual innocent, but he was not emotionally sophisticated: his life was far too dedicated to ambition to leave much time or energy for attentive devotion to women. He came across as gauche, and referred to himself as "unlucky in love." In a friendly fashion, Rose began encouraging him to improve his toilette so that it was in keeping with his new commander's uniform, allowing him to blend in with the Parisian society in which he now found himself. As a result, the rough young Corsican former artillery officer now began brushing his hair and sprinkling himself with eau de Cologne.

In no time Napoleon was in love. A mere seven months after they had first met, he suggested to Rose that they should get married. She hesitated, but gave in when Barras persuaded the Directory to appoint Napoleon commander of the Army of Italy. Here was a young man who was going places—she was unlikely to find a better catch, especially at her age. Ostensibly as a mark of affection, and perhaps unconsciously as a mark of possession, Napoleon changed Rose's name, calling her Josephine. Curiously, it was also at this time that he formalized his own name, dropping the more Italianate elements to become plain Napoleon Bonaparte. With Barras as his best man, on March 9, 1796, Napoleon married Josephine in a civil ceremony.

Two days later, he left for Nice to take up his command, dispatching passionate love letters at every stage along the way. Josephine remained in Paris, promising to join him as soon as she could. The main reason for Napoleon's appointment had been for him to launch an invasion of northern Italy, which was at present occupied by the Austrians. Yet when the twenty-six-year-old commander arrived at his headquarters he found himself confronted by 38,000 raggedly uniformed troops, mainly rough Gascon and Provençal conscripts and disillusioned officers, who were owed pay and were hungry and mutinous. With a mixture of bluff admission and stirring challenge, he appealed to these men of the Revolution:

Soldiers, you are naked, ill-fed; though the Government owes you much, it can give you nothing. Your patience and courage . . . have yet to bring you glory, fame has not yet shone upon you. I want to lead you into . . . rich provinces, where great cities can become yours; you will find honor, glory and riches. Soldiers of the Army of Italy, will you lack courage and determination?[7]

The men believed him, and soon believed *in* him: here was the man to lead them from misery to victory. After just days to instill discipline, Napoleon marched his army across the Alps to face 55,000 superior, disciplined Austrian and Piedmontese troops. Yet within fifteen days he had gained six victories and conquered most of Piedmont. The rabble he had inherited was transformed into a motivated, if bloodthirsty, force, of sufficient bravery to overcome a determined enemy. They were to remain motivated by their leader throughout the campaign. Spurred on by a combination of Republican fervor and high rewards, they were willing to march through the night over vast tracts of countryside, storm bridges and cross mountain passes in order to execute the swift surprise tactics with which their commander again and again put the enemy to flight. It is no exaggeration to say that Napoleon was inventing a new type of warfare, a new type of battle even. Instead of formalized slogging matches, involving the tactical deployment of infantry, cavalry and artillery, he introduced the elements of speed and surprise: "Act first, and then wait to see what happens. . . . Consider all options."[8] His soldiers were enthused by victory, motivated by the indomitable combination of reawakened revolutionary belief and lust for booty instilled in them by their commander.

In November 1796, the Army of Italy won a great victory at Arcola, where Napoleon had his horse shot from under him in the midst of the battle. He fell into a swamp, stuck up to his shoulders in mud, with the Austrians on the point of charging. On the spur of the moment, his brother Louis and a young officer named August Marmont rushed forward under enemy fire and managed to pull him free, rescuing him from certain death. Another great victory followed at Rivoli on January 14, 1797. There appeared to be no stopping

Napoleon. In February he occupied the Papal States, and began seizing vast amounts of treasure, sending it back to the cash-strapped Directory. But the Directory were becoming increasingly worried about him taking things into his own hands. Without their authority, he embarked upon negotiations with the Austrians at Campo Formio, dictating the terms of the peace treaty. Austria would cede all her northern Italian territories, recognizing the "independent" republics established there by the French (in fact ruled by puppet governments favorable to the French). On top of this Austria would cede to France the Austrian Netherlands (now Belgium).

For the first time, Napoleon had become more than a mere general, for besides setting up these new republics he even supervised the writing of their constitutions. This was his first taste of political power, and he resisted all attempts by the Directory to interfere. He appears to have decided from the start that political power involved deception: revolutionary France was intended to be seen not as a conqueror but as a liberator. This tenet would be fundamental to his Egyptian campaign.

Despite all this activity, from the outset of his Italian campaign Napoleon still found time to write to Josephine every day, imploring her to join him, pouring out his love for her with candid abandon: "a thousand kisses on your lips, your eyes, your tongue, your cunt."[9] But Josephine was unimpressed: her sexual sophistication may have bewitched Napoleon, but the fact was that she did not return this love. Within days of Napoleon leaving Paris, she began an affair with a young officer of the Hussars called Hippolyte Charles, who was described as having a "pretty face and the elegance of a hairdresser's assistant."

As March passed into April, and then May, Napoleon's letters from Italy became more insistent, demanding to know why she had not joined him. The few letters he received from her were little more than casual scraps; to Napoleon's outrage, one of them even addressed him formally as "*vous*." Eventually the dashing Murat was dispatched to Paris, bearing a frantic note from Napoleon: "A kiss on your heart, then a little lower, *much lower*"—the last two words were underlined so many times and with such fervor that Napoleon's pen had torn through the paper.

Finally, after four months of prevarication, Josephine set off from Paris, accompanied by Hippolyte Charles, for whom she had secured an appointment as aide to General Leclerc, one of Napoleon's commanders in Italy. Traveling in the same party was at least one "financier": Josephine was betraying not only Napoleon, but also his army. Making use of her closeness to Barras, and her position as the wife of the commander of the Army of Italy, she was ensuring that army supply contracts were awarded to certain dubious businessmen she knew, who rewarded her accordingly.

Josephine finally arrived at Milan on July 13, whereupon to her surprise she was granted a mere forty-eight hours of Napoleon's attention before he rushed back to the front. His campaign was at a vital juncture, and this was all he could spare her. This pattern was repeated, and each time a relieved Josephine would return to the arms of Hippolyte, whilst Napoleon would send her delirious letters from the front, promising "to strip from your body the last film of chiffon, your slippers, everything, and then as in the dream I told you about . . ." When he was able to return for longer periods, Josephine was proudly displayed at balls in Milan, at the opera, at gala dinners. Napoleon was immensely proud of his new wife, seemingly blind to her faults (which had quickly become apparent to members of his staff).

Josephine, for her part, became increasingly disappointed with Napoleon, and what she considered to be his crude habits. So much attention has been paid to him, and to his exceptional personality, that we now know even the most intimate details of his life. How he was in the habit of masturbating before a battle, in order to calm his nerves. How he gobbled his food, and could be equally impatient with other physical matters, declaring that neither meals nor lovemaking should last more than a quarter of an hour—practices which hardly endeared him to the languid, sensual Josphine.

It would seem to be no coincidence that the young Napoleon conducted his first brilliant campaign in a blaze of erotic awakening. At times his energy and willpower seemed almost a delirium. Nothing appeared impossible to him. Yet his character, like his military tactics, remained unfathomable to all around him: his enemies, his aides, his generals, Josephine, the Directory, none were able to predict his next move. However, there was no mistaking the evolving power of the intelligence behind these moves, and there was no doubting that the Italian campaign marked a major stage in this evolution. As Napoleon himself recalled, it was in Italy that he first became aware of the full extent of what he could achieve. It was here for the first time that "I saw the world recede beneath me, as if I were being borne up into the sky."[10] What had before been barely articulated ambition, inspired by heroes such as Alexander, Hannibal and Caesar, was now beginning to take on a more distinct and particular form.

On April 9, 1797, Napoleon invited to dinner Raymond Verninac, the French ambassador to the Ottoman Porte at Constantinople, who was on his way back to Paris. During his tour of duty, Verninac had dispatched a French commissioner to Egypt, who had returned with a firsthand report on the sad state of the country under Mameluke rule, the inroads the British were making, and the harassment of French merchants. Verninac was convinced that the Ottoman Empire was on the point of falling apart, and suggested to Napoleon that the French should consider invading Egypt, possibly as a prelude to taking over the whole of the Ottoman Empire. If France did not seize this opportunity, it would be taken by another power better placed geographically to do so—such as Austria. Europe would then be faced with a revitalized Austrian Empire stretching from the Elbe to the Nile.

This meeting had an electrifying effect upon Napoleon, stirring his dreams of following in the footsteps of Alexander the Great. He found himself remembering Volney's *Voyage en Égypte*, and how he had conversed with this wise, avuncular figure during their travels together in Corsica. In no time he became obsessed with the idea of mounting an expedition to Egypt. According to his secretary Bourrienne "he spoke of it daily when conversing with his generals." On August 16 he even went so far as to write to the Directory, revealing to them his plan: "The time is not far off . . . when it will be necessary for us to take Egypt."[11] But the Directory ignored this: indeed, all the evidence suggests that the letter may even have remained unread.

But Napoleon was not to be put off. In November he dispatched Citizen Poussielgue, the civilian financial administrator of the Army of Italy, on what was described as a tour of inspection of the ports of the Levant. It was in fact a mission to spy out the defenses of Malta, an island whose strategic importance would be vital to any French invasion of Egypt. By now the Directory had appointed Talleyrand as the new foreign minister. Unaware that Talleyrand had gained office by proposing the colonization of Egypt, Napoleon now wrote to him outlining his own plans for an invasion of the country. A publicly floated idea and a private obsession became one.

The following month, on December 5, 1797, Napoleon returned to Paris, where he received a rapturous welcome. Grand balls were thrown to mark his return, and he was showered with honors. The upheavals of the Revolution and its bloody aftermath, followed by the vicious and muddled rule of the Directory, had left France in need of a hero: here was someone of whom its citizens could be proud, a leader who had achieved great victories and planted the ideals of the Revolution in Italy. "*Vive le libérateur de l'Italie!*" was on everyone's lips. When Napoleon took up residence at Josephine's house in Rue Chantereine, crowds gathered outside, hoping to catch a glimpse of the man of the moment, and in his honor the Parisian authorities renamed the street Rue de la Victoire.

However, precisely because of his popularity these were dangerous times for Napoleon, and he went in very real fear of his life. A number of powerful cliques were covertly scheming to take power; meanwhile, Barras was doing his utmost to protect the shaky rule of the Directory. Several sources remark on the fact that during this time Napoleon never removed his spurs, and he is said to have kept a horse permanently saddled and ready in the stable at the back of 6 Rue de la Victoire. His faithful old schoolfriend Bourrienne, who had accompanied him to Italy as his secretary, recorded receiving a note from a woman warning Napoleon that he was to be poisoned. When the woman was traced, she was found with her throat cut. After this, when Napoleon appeared at public functions he employed someone to taste his food. The finger of suspicion points to the Directory.

Napoleon now turned to the one person he felt he could trust: Talleyrand. During the course of his regular correspondence from Italy, he had established a deep rapport with the new foreign minister. He was soon revealing in confidence what sort of government he thought France should have, and he quickly made it plain that he despised the Directory, describing them contemptuously as "just blatherers and lawyers."

Talleyrand, for his part, exercised his supreme diplomatic skills, which quickly enabled him to gain an insight into Napoleon's difficult character. It was mostly through Talleyrand's influence that Napoleon was elected to the prestigious Institute of France, whose elite membership was limited to the country's top intellectuals and scientists. This honor, which purported to recognize Napoleon's intellect rather than his military or political skill, pleased him above all the others he received at this time. He even began placing it above his military rank, and from now on took to signing himself "Bonaparte, Member of the Institute of France and General-in-Chief." Talleyrand understood the real way to flatter him.

Yet Napoleon also knew how to put such things to good use. In his speech of acceptance at the Institute, he went out of his way to make a favorable impression on his fellow members, declaring: "The real conquests, those that leave behind no regrets, are those made over ignorance." If he was to make his Egyptian expedition something more than a mere campaign of conquest, if it was to be comparable with Alexander the Great's mission to "hellenize" the Eastern world, then like Alexander he would need to bring the philosophers of his civilization with him. The Institute of France was where he wished to recruit the savants for his expedition to Egypt.

In the midst of all this, domestic life at Rue de la Victoire took a dramatic turn for the worse when (not for the first time) Napoleon's suspicions concerning his wife's fidelity were confirmed, this time by her maid. Josephine's affair with Hippolyte Charles had continued on their return to Paris. As on at least one previous occasion in Italy, Napoleon had probably suspected the truth, but only when he was unavoidably confronted with it would it appear to affect him: he would rage at her, threaten her, and almost certainly beat her. (On occasions when he lost his temper he was liable to become violent, as his subordinates, servants and aides knew all too well.) Josephine would weep hysterically, protesting her innocence, denying everything; she would beg him on her knees, cajoling him, pretending to faint when all else failed. There is no doubt that he enjoyed humiliating her, especially when he was aware that she was attempting to manipulate him. Indeed, she was manipulating him just as his mother used to do when she sought to entice him into her grasp so that she could thrash him. All the evidence points to there being a strong undercurrent of sado-masochism in the relationship between Napoleon and Josephine, for despite her infidelities, and his beatings, they remained together. Her need for humiliation must have been as great as his need to humiliate her, and her suspected infidelities must have acted as a necessary humiliation for him. Or so it would appear—for we know what he suspected, and we know her behavior. But as long as neither would admit to the truth, the self-deception could continue. Only when someone brought it to Napoleon's attention would he confront Josephine, and even then her fervent protestations of innocence were enough to satisfy his need to believe her, as well as his need to deceive himself.

We can only speculate how much this nexus of self-deception and unconscious behavior derived from Napoleon's relationship with his mother, though its resemblance is uncanny. And without any resort to psychology, it is also easy to see how such a maternal relationship makes for ideal training for a battle commander: the slightest mistake is liable to bring devastating punishment.

But the marital upsets of Napoleon and Josephine were contained within the privacy of their home; in public, they managed a suitable façade. At the grand ball staged in their honor by Talleyrand on January 4, 1798, amidst the glittering surrounds of the Hôtel Gallifet, the young couple appeared in icy splendor beneath the chandeliers. Such was their poise that they appeared to many like royalty.

Napoleon had come to Paris with the idea of joining forces with Talleyrand to put before the Directory his plan for the invasion of Egypt. The Directory needed a nation at war in order to ensure their survival, and it had soon become clear that they felt threatened by Napoleon's popularity; they wanted him out of the way, and an invasion of Egypt appeared to fulfill the wishes of all concerned. Consequently, it came as a shock to both Napoleon and Talleyrand when their Egyptian plan was turned down. Instead, the Directory ordered Napoleon to take command of the Army of England and prepare for an invasion of France's sole remaining powerful enemy.

Napoleon went through the motions, and on February 8, 1798, he set off on a tour of inspection of the Channel ports from Boulogne to Antwerp. Two weeks later he returned to Paris, declaring against any invasion: "It's too chancy. I don't intend to put France at risk on the throw of a dice."[12]

But the Directory were less easily persuaded when Napoleon appeared before them to put his renewed case for an invasion of Egypt. A stormy scene ensued, during which two members of the Directory—Reubell and Larevellière-Lépeau—made no secret of their contempt for the young upstart general. Napoleon for his part eventually lost his temper and threatened to resign. Reubell seized the opportunity and with a dramatic gesture exclaimed: "Here is a pen. We await your letter." Barras at once realized the seriousness of the situation: if the unpopular Directory appeared to have dismissed the hero of the hour, this could well provoke a popular uprising which they might not survive. Eventually he succeeded in smoothing ruffled feathers and Napoleon was asked to go away and provide a memo outlining his plans.[13]

In fact, Napoleon was not exactly the innocent victim in this confrontation, which may well have concealed his first attempt at a bid for power. He knew that his popularity in Paris was fading ("nothing lasts long here"). At the same time, he knew that there were others who were considering a coup against the Directory. If he could not leave Paris and regain popularity by leading his Egyptian campaign, he needed to stake his claim to become ruler at once. What better way than to appear to have been dismissed by the Directory? But the moment had passed; Barras had sensed which way the wind was blowing and had foiled him by patching up his relations with the Directory. Even if Napoleon had been forced to resign from his command of the Army of England, he would probably have retained its loyalty. At the same time, he could certainly have relied upon the loyalty of the Army of Italy, where he was still regarded as a hero. Such strong backing from two of the armies of the Republic would probably have swayed the rest of the army to rally behind him, and in this way he could have staged a coup, coming to power as a military dictator with considerable popular backing.

This would have been a big step on to the larger stage, and when the moment arose Napoleon appears to have had stage fright: he did not yet feel sufficiently confident in himself to call the Directory's bluff. Even so, it seems to have been a much closer-run thing than is usually acknowledged, and its failure to materialize will account for many of Napoleon's subsequent actions. As he confided to Bourrienne when they were passing through the streets of Paris in an open carriage: "I ought to overthrow them and make myself king; but the time has not come. I would be alone. I want to dazzle the people once more. . . . We will go to Egypt."[14] He realized that he could well have lost his opportunity. It was at this time that he famously declared: "My glory is slipping from my grasp, tiny Europe has not enough to offer. . . ."

Yet again, Napoleon presented to the Directory his plans for an invasion of Egypt. These were nothing if not ambitious. He would require 30,000 men and 3,000 horses, mainly drawn from the Army of Italy; the cavalry would in fact require 10,000 horses, but as it would not be possible to transport so many, the extra number would be made up from Arab mounts to be captured in Egypt, though all cavalrymen would bring their own saddles. He would also need to take 1,500 artillerymen, and the requisite number of artillery pieces. The invasion fleet would embark from at least four separate ports, where supplies would be loaded in a particular sequence, to facilitate the immediate requirements of the first troops ashore, spearheading the invasion. The details went on and on, each aspect of the expedition meticulously accounted for. As Napoleon continued, the full extent of his intentions gradually became clearer: having conquered Egypt, he would then mount an expedition to India, where he would attack the British. This force would require 60,000 men, 30,000 of whom would be recruited and trained from amongst the Egyptians; it would take 10,000 horses and 50,000 camels, sufficient to carry supplies for sixty days and water for six. Other provisions would be sequestered on the march, which would take four months to reach the Indus. In India he would link up with the forces of Tippoo Sahib, the ruler of Mysore who had risen against the British and sworn allegiance to French revolutionary ideals. Napoleon concluded by announcing that the entire expedition would cost between eight and nine million francs.

The Directory was aghast: they simply did not have such money. Similarly, they could not afford to lose as many as 30,000 experienced men from the Army of Italy, who might be called upon to defend the territory they had occupied. On the other hand, the Directory knew that if they were to remain in power it was imperative to get rid of Napoleon. So they struck a bargain: Napoleon could have 25,000 men in total, but he would have to raise the money to pay for the expedition himself. Also, there was no question of him marching on to India: his expedition was to be limited solely to the conquest of Egypt, and he was expected to return in six months. Meanwhile Talleyrand would be dispatched to Constantinople to reassure their Turkish allies that the French harbored no aggressive intent against the Ottoman Empire. Napoleon would merely overthrow the Mamelukes and restore order to the country, so that French traders could go about their business unmolested. Afterwards the Directory and the Porte would come to an arrangement about how the country should best be governed.

Napoleon accepted the Directory's terms with a suspicious rapidity and lack of bargaining, but the Directory were not worried. He was agreeing to leave France and mount an expedition at no cost to themselves; what he might or might not decide to do after he reached Egypt was another matter altogether. When he once more brought up the benefits of marching on India, the Directory gave the impression that they acquiesced, leaving the matter up to him.

The Italian campaign, followed by Napoleon's protracted treaty negotiations and his marital problems, had left him exhausted. Even before his return to France he had written to his brother: "My health is ruined. . . . I can barely get into the saddle and need two years rest." Yet no sooner had the Directory agreed to his invasion on March 5, 1798, than he launched himself into a delirium of activity, prompting even Bourrienne to comment: "He worked night and day on this project. I never saw him so active."[15] The first requirement was money, and Napoleon knew that the only way to raise this was by looting from the exchequers of the countries France had "liberated" for the Revolution. Here he proved as ruthless as in his military campaigning: nothing would stand in the way of his "glory." He dispatched his chief of staff Berthier to Rome to ransack the Vatican; General Joubert, whose military prowess had proved vital to the success of the Italian campaign, was sent to Holland; and General Brune, who had already established himself as a notorious looter in Italy, was ordered to Berne, where he sent back to Napoleon what amounted to the entire Swiss exchequer, a sum equivalent to three million gold francs.

Napoleon soon had more than enough to finance his expedition to Egypt, though an indication of his further ambitions is seen in the fact that he had also covertly budgeted to take on further assets. Around this time he received a report from his former financial administrator Poussielgue about his spying mission to Malta, where according to intelligence sources the treasury of the resident Knights of St. John contained relics, valuables and bullion worth several millions. The taking of Malta would have more than strategic value for the Egyptian expedition.

III

The Cream of France

NAPOLEON now set about recruiting the most talented commanding officers he could muster. Loyalty, bravery and leadership were the qualities he most prized. Many of those he chose had already served with him, and thus he had witnessed their abilities firsthand on the battlefield.

For his chief of staff he chose the forty-four-year-old General Louis Berthier, who had proved both loyal and highly efficient in this demanding post during the Italian campaign. Berthier was from a military family and had fought in the American War of Independence under Lafayette, whose forces had played such a vital role in thwarting the British. He had been cited for bravery at Philipsburg, but had fallen from favor with the Jacobins after the Revolution. Later he had been reinstated, and in 1793 at the outbreak of the serious Royalist uprising in the Vendée (which coincided with the Royalist seizure of Toulon and threatened the entire Revolution), he had served with distinction. He had been quick to recognize Napoleon's exceptional qualities, and had volunteered to become his chief of staff in the Army of Italy. He often bore the brunt of his commander-in-chief's volatile temperament, but nevertheless at all times maintained the smooth running of Napoleon's staff. Berthier was as meticulous in his military dress as he was in his administrative duties; despite this, he presented an odd figure: even shorter than Napoleon, he had an oversized head, wiry hair, a hesitant, nervous manner, and his nasal voice had a stutter. Napoleon had been impressed by his bravery in the field, particularly at the Battle of Lodi, where he had led his men under heavy fire across a vital bridge. In Italy the bachelor Berthier had fallen in love with a certain Contessa Visconti, who had been attached to Josephine as a lady-in-waiting, but with some reluctance he decided that his loyalty to Napoleon came before this late flowering of his love life.

Also on Napoleon's staff, amongst his aides, was the fearless Junot, who had fully justified Napoleon's faith in him during the Italian campaign, and whose likeable qualities had led to him being one of the few men to become close to Napoleon. Other aides included Napoleon's favorite brother, Louis, still just twenty-one, and the young officer August Marmont, who together had risked their lives pulling Napoleon from the mud at the Battle of Arcola. The youngest aide of all was the seventeen-year-old Eugene Beauharnais, Josephine's son, whom Napoleon had taken under his wing with the affection he might otherwise have given to the son Josephine seemed incapable of providing for him.

However, Napoleon's second-in-command was a more problematic figure, whose loyalty could not be assumed. General Jean-Baptiste Kléber was a big, bluff Alsatian, the son of a peasant, who had trained as an architect and risen through the ranks on exceptional military prowess alone. He was forty-five years old and considered himself, with some justification, to be at least Napoleon's equal as a commander; not only this, but he reckoned his seniority should have entitled him to the command of the Egyptian expedition. He too had gained recognition in the Vendée, helping to save the Revolution. Despite this he had been dismissed by the fanatical Jacobins in 1793 when he had refused to slaughter in cold blood 4,000 prisoners taken at St. Florent. Reinstated under the Directory, he had distinguished himself serving in the Army of the Rhine, winning the Battle of Fleurus and taking Frankfurt in 1794, after which he had retired. Napoleon brought him out of retirement to join the Egyptian expedition because he admired his exceptional ability. He also admired Kléber for the charismatic figure he cut, which was in many ways the equal of his own. As Napoleon would later remember in admiration: "Kléber! He was the god Mars in uniform!"[1] However, this admiration was not fully reciprocated. Kléber prided himself on being a soldier's soldier: he believed in commanding his men with some panache, and also with some compassion. He resented Napoleon's youth, disliked his political ambitions, and although he could not help admiring Napoleon's tactical brilliance and daring, this did not extend to his often brutal military methods. Kléber claimed that Napoleon "was the kind of general who required an income of 10,000 men a month."[2] He nonetheless remained a proud professional soldier, and as such took his orders without question.

The only other man Napoleon chose for the Egyptian expedition whose military brilliance came close to his own was General Louis-Charles Desaix, who although only a year older than Napoleon had already risen to the rank of general before they met at the siege of Toulon. Desaix had been born into a family of impecunious nobility in the mountainous Auvergne region in central France. At the age of eight he had entered military college, but had proved such an inept cadet that on graduating at the age of fifteen he had decided to join the navy, only to be turned down. On the outbreak of the Revolution he had been a lowly twenty-one-year-old sub-lieutenant, but had elected to remain in the revolutionary army rather than flee into exile along with his fellow aristocrats (and many of his family). Not until he went into active service with the Army of the Rhine did he reveal his brilliance and achieve rapid promotion in an army which had lost so many of its aristocratic higher-ranking officers. In 1796 Desaix more than justified his position as the youngest general in the French army when instead of surrendering he held out for two months against vastly superior Austrian forces at the strategic fortress of Kehl, guarding the Rhine crossing. By the end of the campaign his military renown was on a par with that of Napoleon, but this nearly proved to be his undoing: the political commissioners of the Directory ordered his arrest on the spurious charge that he was an aristocrat. Fortunately his loyal troops got wind of this, and when the commissioner arrived to arrest General Desaix he was sent on his way by armed soldiers with fixed bayonets, whereupon the matter was dropped.

Desaix had an overriding interest in military tactics, of both the great battles of history and contemporary conflicts. In pursuit of this he would travel four months later to Italy to make a firsthand study of the battlefields where Napoleon had achieved his spectacular victories. Here he also encountered Napoleon in person, and was immediately impressed. The feeling was mutual, despite their disparate characters. Desaix retained a certain aristocratic manner, though his appearance by this stage was far from refined. His ugly face was further disfigured by a long scar from a slashing sabre, he had a drooping, undistinguished moustache, and long straggly hair hung down from beneath his cap. Yet despite this unattractive appearance, his enthusiasm for women was such that the variety and quantity of his conquests were legendary, even by French military standards. Napoleon's regard for Desaix meant that he was one of the first to be accorded the privilege of listening to Napoleon's Italian evening reveries on following in the footsteps of Alexander the Great and achieving glory in the Orient. Soon Desaix too had been gripped by this dream, and moved heaven and earth to make sure that he was allowed to join the Egyptian expedition.

So far, the motives behind Napoleon's choice of senior generals appeared evident, yet this was certainly not the case with General Jacques Menou, who according to a colleague "was without any sort of military talent, but was not lacking in bravery." Menou had a bad military record, and the slovenliness of his appearance was a source of constant irritation to Napoleon, who remarked of his uniform, "he wears it all wrong and can't even do it up properly." At forty-nine, Menou was the oldest of Napoleon's commanders, and certainly looked it. The years had not treated him kindly—he was bald and fat, and contemporaries remarked on the fact that he had the stance and bearing of a waiter, rather than a general. Yet surprisingly, he was the scion of an ancient aristocratic family. Prior to the Revolution, the young Baron de Menou had followed in the footsteps of many a young aristocrat and become an army officer, where his lineage had assisted in his election to the Constituent Assembly, in which he advocated reform of the army.

In 1789, like a number of progressively minded aristocrats, Menou welcomed the Revolution, and miraculously survived the ensuing Terror which cost so many of his friends their lives. He then left Paris to take part in the campaign against the Vendée uprising. Here his ineptitude on the battlefield was such that it led to a charge of treason, instigated by no less a person than Robespierre. Astonishingly he survived his trial, was then appointed general, and in the ensuing upheavals ended up as commander of the Army of the Interior. His indecisiveness in this post was instrumental in allowing the 13 Vendémiaire insurrection in Paris to get out of hand, when Barras replaced him with Napoleon, and the "whiff of grapeshot" saved the day. After this, Menou was forced into well-deserved retirement, until Napoleon's remarkable decision to place him in command of a division on the Egyptian expedition. No plausible reason has been put forward for this decision (which was to have its ramifications in Egypt); the unusual, but most likely, explanation is that Napoleon never forgot anyone who helped him in his career, and his reason for recalling Menou was in fact gratitude for the opportunity Menou's incompetence had given him.

Other notable figures in Napoleon's military entourage included his giant mulatto chief of cavalry General Alexandre Dumas (future father of the novelist), whose physical prowess was such that it was said he could grasp a beam in the stables and lift his horse between his clenched legs. He was supported in the cavalry by the swashbuckling thirty-year-old General Murat, whose swift action had so helped Napoleon on 13 Vendémiaire.

However, of all Napoleon's generals the one closest to him personally was the forty-two-year-old Louis Caffarelli, who had lost a leg serving with the Army of the Rhine and now had a wooden one. Descended from a noble Italian family which had emigrated to France just over a century previously, he had entered the college of military engineering at Mezières, where he had studied under the great French mathematician Gaspard Monge, who was quick to recognize his exceptional mathematical ability. After a brave and distinguished military career in the engineers, Caffarelli had settled in Paris, where he had been elected to the Institute of France. It was here that he had met Napoleon, who had been so charmed by his easy manner and evident intellectual brilliance that he had persuaded him out of retirement to command the engineering corps for the expedition to Egypt. Napoleon also entrusted Caffarelli with the task of recruiting the members of the Commission of Arts and Sciences, the so-called savants, who were to accompany the expedition. A list of the different professional groups included amongst the savants gives an indication of the sheer scale of this civilian aspect of the expedition: it was to comprise architects; artists and composers; astronomers; botanists; chemists and physicists; surgeons and doctors; geometers; printers; naval engineers; geographical engineers (including cartographers); constructors of bridges and highways; men of literature, economists and antiquarians; mechanical engineers; mineralogists; Orientalists; pharmacists; and zoologists. The Commission of Arts and Sciences would eventually include no fewer than 167 members, who would be augmented by a number of junior professionally qualified assistants and administrators.

Caffarelli was also instructed to requisition or purchase all the necessary equipment required by these savants—this would include everything from astronomical telescopes to ballooning equipment, from chemical apparatus to Latin, Arabic and Syraic printing type. As if this was not enough, he was also briefed by Napoleon personally on the library that would be required for the expedition, a collection that would include over 500 books. These represented nothing less than a compendium of French, European and world culture, including such works as the many volumes so far produced of the *Encylopédie*, which had been assembled throughout the eighteenth century by the leading French philosophers, intellectuals and scientists of the Enlightenment, with the intention of including "all knowledge." The library to be taken to Egypt also included the works of Voltaire; a political section, into which category fell such disparate tomes as the Koran, Montesquieu's *The Spirit of Laws*, the Hindu Vedas and the Bible; the writings of pioneering travelers in the Orient, such as Volney; and the latest maps put together by the great geographer D'Anville, covering any regions into which the expedition might venture, ranging as far afield as Hindustan (India) and Bengal. These maps give a hint of the true nature of the expedition: its unique blend of meticulous planning and sheer fantasy.

One of Caffarelli's chief assistants in his recruitment of savants was his former professor Gaspard Monge, another of the brilliant figures who had been able to rise from nowhere owing to the fluid social circumstances of the revolutionary era. Monge had been born the son of an itinerant knife-grinder in Burgundy in 1746. At fifty-two he was one of the older members of the Egyptian expedition, and was already regarded as one of the most distinguished mathematicians in Europe. His crowning achievement had been the conception of descriptive geometry, which enabled a three-dimensional object to be represented on a two-dimensional surface such as a page, by use of plane and elevation, thus allowing the dissemination of blueprints for the design of the machines that brought about the Industrial Revolution. At the time France believed in employing its finest minds in an administrative capacity, and in 1792 Monge was appointed Minister of the Navy. In the following years, when the Revolution was blockaded by France's enemies, he played a major role in national defense by producing a pamphlet describing a process that enabled small-scale iron producers all over the country to manufacture steel. Together with the chemist Claude-Louis Berthollet he also invented a method for extracting saltpeter from the soil, thus giving a huge boost to France's ailing munitions industry. In 1795 he was one of the originators of what became the Institute of France, which was intended to nurture France's leading scientific and creative intellectuals. In the same year, he was also appointed as the first director of the elite engineering École Polytechnique, which would become a model for scientific higher educational establishments throughout Europe.

In 1797, Monge and his friend Berthollet were dispatched by the Directory to Italy, where they were instructed to seek out and requisition works of art in the territories "liberated" by Napoleon. During the course of this work they would ship back to Paris many of the paintings that nowadays form the Renaissance collection in the Louvre, as well as several of Leonardo da Vinci's notebooks. It was during this time that Monge first met Napoleon, who was immediately drawn to the middle-aged mathematician with the big bullish face yet unexpectedly kind manner. Monge's combination of simple living, good-heartedness and mathematical genius quickly endeared him to the young commander-in-chief. It is difficult to exaggerate the warmth and suddenness of the distant Napoleon's feelings for Monge, who soon found himself occupying the role of respected father-figure—a role that Napoleon's actual father had never occupied, on account of his perceived weakness.* In Milan, when Napoleon had been distraught over Josephine's behavior, it was to Monge that he turned, pouring out his heart, and from then on his relationship with Monge was such that he always wished to have the mathematician amongst his close entourage.

During his time in Italy, Monge also became close to his scientific companion, the fifty-year-old Berthollet, who was now the foremost figure in the emerging science of chemistry. Berthollet had already successfully collaborated with Monge on such projects as the saltpeter process, though his attempt to use potassium chlorate as a substitute for saltpeter in gunpowder had merely resulted in the invention of colored fireworks. For many years Berthollet sought an underlying theory which would explain all chemical reactions—the basis of chemistry itself—and

---

* Napoleon always suspected that his father was not his real father, unconsciously at first, but more openly later. He certainly discovered that his mother, Letizia, had had an affair prior to his birth, a revelation that had a profound if enigmatic effect on his psychology. This probably played a part in his deep and difficult relationship with Josephine, but what effect it had on his ambition and his need to assert his willpower remains a matter of speculation.

his thinking on this subject had reached a crucial stage when he joined Napoleon's expedition. His findings in Egypt would prove vital to this theory, which would become his major contribution to science.

Other leading scientists who would join Napoleon's savants included the mathematician Joseph Fourier, whose theoretical researches in Egypt would lead to his conception of the Fourier series, which he used to describe the flow of heat, and consequently how the earth had cooled to its present state. The savants would also include leaders in technological fields, such as the forty-seven-year-old mineralogist Déodat Dolomieu, the discoverer of dolomite, which is named after him, along with the range in the Italian Alps formed out of this rock. Dolomieu had lived a hectic early life, which was destined to catch up with him when the expedition reached Malta. In his youth he had joined the Knights of Malta, and at seventeen had been sentenced to life imprisonment for killing a fellow knight in a duel, only to be pardoned by the Grand Master on condition he left the island forever.

Another savant whose name remains familiar was the forty-three-year-old inventor Nicolas Conté, who had made his fortune as a society portrait painter. Only after the Revolution, when aristocratic sitters were in short supply, did he turn to invention, a pursuit at which his ingenious mind proved highly adept. During the Revolutionary Wars against England, when refined Cumberland graphite had become unavailable for making pencils, Conté was given the task of coming up with a substitute, which he duly produced within forty-eight hours. This used coarse local graphite mixed with clay, and became known as the Conté pencil, which would in time earn his descendants a fortune. A man of indefatigable energy, with a genius for practical improvisation, he was also instrumental in the development of the balloon, which had been pioneered by the French Montgolfier brothers just a few years previously, in 1783. Conté was the first to realize the military potential of the balloon as a means of spying behind enemy lines, and was asked to bring along kits for assembling balloons in Egypt. Ironically, Napoleon had disregarded the balloon as a means for long-distance observation of enemy troop movements, and only wanted this latest scientific wonder in Egypt as a demonstration of France's technological superiority. Conté's main role on the expedition was to be as an inventor, using his ingenious skills to improvise any devices that might be required.

Here again we have another clue as to the true nature of the Egyptian expedition, and its purpose as Napoleon saw it; the sheer range, quantity and caliber of the savants hints at a further aspect of his fantasy. These assembled scientists, men of literature, architects, economists, legislators, Orientalists and what have you were to be something more than just a cultural mission for the dissemination of Western civilization: they in fact represented nothing less than an embodiment of French culture itself. The purpose of these savants was far more than education; their constitution was of sufficient size and multiplicity for them to evolve independently, of their own accord, a culture quite separate from that which had produced them. Monge and Fourier had played a major role in the establishment of the Institute of France and the elite École Polytechnique, which were simultaneously both ornaments of French culture and foundation stones of the new revolutionary order. The purpose of these two sages on the expedition would be to establish similar institutions in the Orient. Similarly, Conté's role as an inventor and balloonist could spearhead independent technological advances to be made there, in case circumstances—in Europe or elsewhere—led to a rupture between France and its new colony. There are indications that from the very outset Napoleon foresaw that his Eastern empire might indeed become independent of France, much as the American colonies had recently become independent of their mother culture in Britain. Only when this is understood will some of Napoleon's more bizarre actions and sayings in Egypt become clear. As he constantly reminded himself: "Consider all the options." One of the options for the Egyptian expedition—and certainly not a minor one, indeed one for which it was well prepared—was the foundation of an America of the East, with the new Alexander as its president.

All this remained very much Napoleon's private dream. Indeed, even the officially designated destination of the expedition remained a closely guarded secret, known only to a chosen few. Napoleon's confidants Monge and Berthollet certainly knew, as did the Directory and Talleyrand (and the Prussian ambassador, to whom Talleyrand had blurted it out, though this was dismissed as a ruse). Even the Minister of War, Schérer, had been led to believe that the destination of the expedition led by the commander of the Army of England, still Napoleon's official title, was England. As a result, several older members of the Institute of France turned down Napoleon's invitation, some because they thought it would be too cold in England, others because they could foresee no use for their Orientalist talents there. Also in on the secret were Napoleon's senior aides, as well as his senior generals, but no one else. Kléber recorded that, in all, only around forty people in the entire country knew that Egypt was the destination of Napoleon's expeditionary force.

The reason for such secrecy was obvious. The British navy had to be kept guessing to prevent any attack on such a large and vulnerable armada, which although it would be escorted by a strong contingent of ships of the line would also contain a host of slow, indefensible transport vessels. With flotillas now being assembled in Toulon, Marseilles, Genoa, Civitavecchia and Ajaccio, British spies quickly ascertained that the French were preparing for a major expedition of some sort. When this intelligence began reaching London early in April 1798, Pitt the Younger summoned the British cabinet and they considered the potential invasion targets. Portugal or Sicily were agreed to be possibles, but the most likely option was the most dangerous. It looked as if the French Mediterranean fleet would attempt to break out via Gibraltar, join up with the French Atlantic fleet at Brest, and then launch an invasion of Britain or Ireland. Invasion panic swept Britain, with *The Times* demanding "Barricadoes for each street, to be defended by the inhabitants of the street" and "All obnoxious foreigners be sent out of the country."[3]

Meanwhile preparations for the French expeditionary force continued apace in the Mediterranean. However, although most of those gathering at the ports had no idea where they were going, not even those few who were in on the secret knew how long they would be away. Napoleon had assured the Directory that he would be back in six months, a hollow assurance at best. He was a little more frank, if equally unreassuring, when his secretary Bourrienne asked him how long they were liable to be away: "A few months, or six years. It all depends on the course of events. I shall colonize that country. I shall import artists, workmen of all kinds, women, actors, etc. We are only twenty-nine years old;* we'll be thirty-five then. Six years will be enough for me, if all goes well, to go to India."[4] In other words, nothing was certain—though despite the incoherence of Napoleon's plans, every eventuality was being prepared for. The idea of marching to India may have belonged in the realms of fantasy, but Napoleon continued with preparations towards this end, sending word to the Directory on April 14: "I would like to take with

---

* He was in fact twenty-eight.

me Citizen Piveron, who was for many years the king's agent at the court of Tippoo Sahib. We should try to get him through to India, so that he can send us intelligence of the situation there."[5]

Astonishingly, one member of Pitt the Younger's cabinet, the Minister of War, Henry Dundas, had guessed correctly that Napoleon was planning to invade Egypt and then march overland to attack the British in India. This view was reinforced when intelligence arrived in London from Udney, the British consul in Leghorn (Livorno), saying he had received word that Napoleon's destination was Egypt. All this was dismissed by Pitt as unlikely. However, in order to appraise the situation, a message was sent on May 2 from Earl Spencer, First Lord of the Admiralty, to Admiral St. Vincent, who was besieging the Spanish fleet off Cadiz. This message informed St. Vincent that at the risk of weakening the British fleet, "the appearance of a British squadron in the Mediterranean is a condition on which the fate of Europe may at this moment be stated to depend."[6] St. Vincent was ordered to dispatch Admiral Sir Horatio Nelson to fulfill this role. In fact, on the previous day St. Vincent had upon his own initiative sent Nelson into the Mediterranean with a squadron containing three battleships, two frigates and a sloop "to endeavour to ascertain the real object of the preparations in the making by the French."[7]

Napoleon supervised the assembly of his expeditionary force from Paris. He would complete this complex international operation, involving the loading of almost 40,000 men, their military equipment, supplies and artillery onto hundreds of vessels at six different ports, in just ten weeks, using methods which are now seen as forming the basis of modern logistical theory. Having accomplished this mammoth task, he hurried south to Toulon, planning to set out within days of his arrival, in order to reach Egypt well before the annual flooding of the Nile halted any military campaigning over a wide area of the country. He arrived in Toulon, accompanied by Josephine, early on the morning of May 9. Immediately he embarked on an extensive inspection of the fleet, his arrival aboard each warship being greeted with a two-gun salute that resonated throughout the harbor, echoing from the hills above—the very spot where he had gained his first triumph as a young artillery captain just five years previously. That night military bands played in the squares of the city, the public buildings were illuminated in his honor, and the streets were thronged with soldiers. Several eyewitnesses commented on how the entire city was filled with an almost unbearable frisson of anticipation. Ahead lay an unknown yet undoubtedly historic undertaking, and all knew that while some might be returning as heroes, others would not be returning at all.

Next day Napoleon reviewed his troops, many of whom had fought bravely and victoriously under him in the Italian campaign, accumulating modest fortunes from booty in the process. In an unprecedented measure, he had ensured that the booty captured by his soldiers during the Italian campaign was sent safely home. This had prevented it from being lost, gambled away or stolen; it had also ensured that his soldiers were not impeded by unnecessary baggage on their forced marches. Such a move made for enhanced discipline in the ranks: there was a lack of drunkenness (booty could not be sold for wine), less fighting over gambling losses, and the soldiers' morale was increased by the thought of what awaited them when they returned. Although they had not yet managed to get home to enjoy these savings, almost all of those present had good reason to be grateful to the charismatic young commander who had led them to heroic victories. This, as much as any other reason, explains why they were so willing to follow him into the unknown. Amidst the hurried assembly of so many men at so many disembarkation points there was ample opportunity for desertion, but although desertions are known to have taken place, these were no more than usual under normal circumstances.

After inspecting the troops, Napoleon addressed them:

Soldiers of the Army of the Mediterranean!

You are now a wing of the Army of England. You have campaigned in the mountains, in the plains and before fortresses; but you have yet to take part in a naval campaign. The Roman legions that you have sometimes rivaled, but have yet to equal, fought Carthage on this very sea ... Victory never forsook them. . . . Europe is watching you. You have a great destiny to fulfill, battles to fight, dangers and hardships to overcome. You hold in your hands the future prosperity of France, the good of mankind and your own glory. The ideal of Liberty that has made the Republic the arbiter of Europe will make it also arbiter of distant oceans, of faraway countries.[8]

He went on to promise that if they succeeded, each man would be awarded a bounty of six acres of land. Such an appeal went to the heart of all rural Frenchmen—though they remained blissfully ignorant of the location of their promised six-acre plots, which were seemingly part of Napoleon's covert plan to establish a permanent military presence loyal to his command in his new Oriental empire.*

Two days later, on the eve of May 12, the embarkation of all troops from their barracks and camps into the waiting vessels was complete. The commander of the Mediterranean fleet, Vice-Admiral Brueys, informed Napoleon that the fleet was in full readiness to weigh anchor and sail on the morrow.

By now Nelson and his squadron had taken up position off Toulon, and were riding at anchor several miles out to sea, just below the horizon. One of Nelson's frigates intercepted an unwary French corvette; the crew were interrogated, and Nelson learned that at Toulon "fifteen sail of the line are apparently ready for sea."[9]

---

* The six acres of land is not mentioned in the official version of Napoleon's speech, though there is overwhelming evidence that he did make this promise. Some sources quote it as follows: "I promise every soldier that, upon his return to France, he shall have enough money to buy himself six acres of land" (Saintine and Reybaud, *Histoire scientifique et militaire de l'Expédition Française en Égypte*, Vol. 3, pp. 43–4). However, there is much evidence that the soldiers themselves understood the promise to mean an allocation of six acres of land at their destination, for when they first saw the Egyptian wilderness they coined an ironic catchphrase: "*Voilà*—the six acres of land they promised us" (Denon, *Voyages dans la Basse et la Haute Égypte pendant les campagnes de Bonaparte*, Vol. 1, p. 21), a saying which quickly gained currency throughout the expeditionary army.

IV

Outward Bound

OVERNIGHT on Saturday, May 12, a strong wind blew up, in the form of the notorious mistral. By morning this had developed into a raging storm, forcing Vice-Admiral Brueys to postpone the sailing of the expeditionary fleet from Toulon. The chilling mistral continued to howl down from the mountains for another seven days, until finally in the early hours of May 19 the storm abated, and at six A.M. the waiting ships received the order from *L'Orient* to depart.*

According to plan, the ships in Toulon harbor weighed anchor and made their way under sail towards the open sea, each ship lowering its colors in salute as it passed beneath the towering decks of *L'Orient*, which was at the time easily the largest and most powerful warship in the world, with its 120 cannons mounted on three decks. In all, the Toulon convoy of the Egyptian expedition was made up of 180 ships, consisting of thirteen ships of the line, nine frigates, twenty-three corvettes, sloops and smaller armed vessels, as well as 135 transport

---

* *L'Orient* had previously been named *Sans-Culotte*, after the revolutionary mob of Paris, and later the extreme Republican faction. Yet the sans-culottes had now fallen from favor, and Napoleon "renamed [the ship] to give it a name more in line with the aim of the expedition" (Benoist-Méchin, *Bonaparte en Égypte*, p. 327, n. 6). But when exactly did this renaming take place? Had it been done during the preparations in Toulon, this would surely have given away the expedition's destination. On the other hand, Napoleon first refers to *L'Orient* as such in his dispatches for May 17, two days prior to sailing, heading his dispatches for the 19th itself "On board *L'Orient*." Whether this renaming had actually happened at this stage, or had happened and was not made public, or was simply Napoleon's intention, or was perhaps inserted by the later editors of the *Correspondance*, remains unclear.

vessels of various sizes. For much of the day, Napoleon stood on deck watching as they passed. Regimental bands played from the passing ships, cannons thundered from the forts in the hills, the crowds on the quayside waved and cheered—the procession took no less than eight hours to clear the port.

Napoleon was aware that his expeditionary force might be sailing into danger from the British navy, but he dismissed this, writing to the Directory on the very day of his departure: "Four Spanish frigates arrived yesterday from Minorca . . . it appears that there are a number of English warships in the lower Mediterranean, but it doesn't look as if they will bother us."[1] In fact, he was to be a lot luckier than he realized. The very storm that had prevented him from sailing had driven Nelson and his waiting squadron from their station, the offshore gale being so strong that it carried them far to the south, in the process dismasting Nelson's ship *Vanguard*. Against all advice, Nelson effected repairs off the southwestern tip of Sardinia, and then proceeded to sail the 300 miles back north; but amidst the storm he had become separated from his two fast frigates, and these had returned to Gibraltar, assuming that he had done likewise. This meant that he was now deprived of the "eyes" of his squadron, which could carry out reconnaissance over a wide area. On May 27 Nelson and his reduced squadron arrived back at their station off Toulon. The following day they intercepted a neutral merchantman out of Marseilles, which informed them that Napoleon's fleet had sailed nine days previously for an unknown destination.

By now Napoleon's Toulon convoy had long since joined up with the Marseilles convoy, which was carrying troops under the command of Jean-Louis-Ebenezer Reynier, as well as the Genoa convoy carrying troops under Menou, and together they had all proceeded east and then southwards along the Italian coast. The convoy from Civitavecchia carrying troops under Desaix had not materialized at the appointed rendezvous, and after a brief wait Napoleon ordered Vice-Admiral Brueys to continue south. A day later Napoleon dispatched the frigate *Pomone* for Naples to pick up Josephine.

Josephine had traveled with Napoleon to Toulon on the understanding that she would be accompanying him to Egypt. All the indications are that she had not really wanted to go, but had felt it would best suit her purpose if she made a show of being willing. Napoleon was similarly ambivalent, but for very different reasons. He could not bear the thought of being separated from her, but evidently he had taken the sighting of British warships a little more seriously than he had indicated in his note to the Directory, and felt that the fleet might be in some danger immediately after it left Toulon. As a result, he arranged that Josephine should travel overland to Naples, where he would send the *Pomone* to pick her up when the danger was past. Josephine, however, appears to have "misunderstood" how long it would take her to travel to Naples, and instead set off north, missing her appointment with the *Pomone*, and eventually returning to Paris and the arms of Hippolyte Charles. Deeply disappointed at the return of the empty frigate, Napoleon continued on his way, finally effecting a successful rendezvous with Desaix and the Civitavecchia flotilla off Malta on June 9.

Malta had been in the possession of the Knights of Malta, an ancient crusading order, for over 250 years, resisting all who sought to dislodge them. The large harbor at Valletta was protected by the most formidable fortress in Europe, which had walls that were ten feet thick and defended by 1,500 cannon. But when Poussielgue had reported to Napoleon on his return from his spying mission, he had revealed that the fortress was in fact in a dilapidated condition, its guns largely rusted and in disrepair. The knights themselves had fallen into a similar state of decay: of the 327 resident knights, fifty were too ancient to fight, and of the rest around 200 were French and unwilling to bear arms against their compatriots. Further intelligence had revealed that the 10,000 conscripted Maltese who made up the garrison were in no mood to lose their lives defending their unpopular masters.

The appearance of Napoleon's vast fleet off Malta caused consternation amongst the population. According to one astonished eyewitness: "Never had Malta seen such a numberless fleet in her waters. The sea was covered into the far distance with ships of all sizes whose masts resembled a huge forest."[2] The Grand Master of the Knights of Malta, an aging and weak Prussian called Ferdinand von Hompesch, decided to send a message asking Napoleon his intentions: a somewhat superfluous move, for Napoleon had already landed armed men who had taken over the unfortified parts of the main island with hardly a shot fired. Napoleon dispatched ashore his savant Dolomieu, in the hope that the former Knight of Malta would be able to reach an agreement with von Hompesch. Dolomieu undertook his mission with extreme reluctance. He had no experience whatsoever of negotiating, and he knew that the Knights would be within their rights to seize him and execute him for returning to Malta. To make matters worse, Napoleon insisted that he be accompanied by Poussielgue, who would immediately be recognized as having been a spy. Confronted with this delegation, von Hompesch dithered. For twenty-four hours there was a tense standoff, whilst that night, under cover of darkness, the alleyways of Valletta descended into mayhem, with bands of Maltese conscripts bearing torches roaming the alleyways and setting upon any Knights they could find.

On June 11 von Hompesch surrendered, in return for an annual pension of 300,000 francs from the French government. During the course of the following week the Knights of Malta were sent into exile, with each awarded a modest pension dependent upon his length of service. Napoleon now established his headquarters ashore and set about transforming a medieval anachronism into an island with the trappings of a modern state. His energy all but defies belief. During the ensuing seven days he issued 168 reports, orders and dispatches: these abolished all feudal privileges, reformed the monasteries, and guaranteed equal rights to Christians, Jews and Muslims. At the same time he freed 2,000 Turkish and Moorish slaves from their shackles in "the disgusting galleys."[3] He reformed the education system, establishing fifteen schools to teach "the principles of morality and of the French constitution," and also making provision to send sixty promising pupils for free education in France (echoing the system that had enabled him to leave Corsica and study at the military college in Brienne).

Yet he also took as much as he gave. He dispatched his two senior savants, Monge and Berthollet, to fulfill the role they had performed so successfully for the Directory in Italy: with their expert eye, they sought out the valuables in the island's monasteries, churches, knightly residences and treasuries. Within a week, seven million francs' worth had been "deducted" from Malta's exchequer. At the same time, so many valuables (mainly in the form of gold plate and jewelry) had been seized that there was not sufficient time to evaluate them, though Napoleon was reliably informed (probably by Monge) that their worth too certainly ran into millions. Napoleon ordered a generous portion of the cash to be sent to France to keep the Directory happy, but kept the rest to bolster the finances of the Egyptian expedition.

Once again he insisted upon being far more than just a conquering general; equally important to him was his civilian role as a legislator, administrator and reformer. He had first tried his hand at this—and discovered how much he enjoyed doing it—in Italy, but in Malta he went much further, changing the country beyond recognition. As we shall see, this was but a dress rehearsal for all the more sweeping reforms he had in mind for his empire in Egypt.*

Whilst Napoleon worked into the early hours, and Monge and Berthollet scoured the island's treasuries, others disembarked to sample the pleasures of Malta, whose women were renowned throughout the Mediterranean for their beauty. The officers of the French expedition were welcomed ashore by the French contingent amongst the Knights of Malta, many of whom would volunteer to join Napoleon. Like all the Knights they had taken a vow of chastity; however, this did not prevent them from providing such hospitality as was expected of them by their compatriots. According to one young cavalry officer: "All of them have mistresses who are ravishingly beautiful and charming, concerning whom they are neither possessive nor jealous."⁴ Meanwhile the lower ranks enjoyed themselves along the docks of Valletta, whose taverns and bordellos were said to contain more prostitutes than any other port in Europe.

All too soon the order came to re-embark, and on June 19 the last of the Egyptian expeditionary force returned to their ships, carrying in their pockets all they had managed to pick of the local oranges. Napoleon left behind General Vaubois and a garrison of some 4,000 French soldiers. But the expedition was far from being seriously depleted: he had taken with him 2,000 troops from the Malta garrison, along with 34 French Knights of Malta who had volunteered to join him, and many of the liberated "Turkish and Moorish" slaves, a large number of whom were in fact Egyptian. The latter were intended largely as a propaganda weapon: when Napoleon arrived in Egypt he wished to be seen as the liberator of Egyptians, as well as a friend of the Turks. However, crammed onto the transports, these men may have begun to have second thoughts about this "liberation." As one young French military officer, Captain Vertray, recorded in his journal: "I suffered from seasickness the whole time. Combat on land was nothing compared

---

* The apotheosis of this role would of course come with the establishment of the Napoleonic Code in France, and in the European territories that Napoleon conquered. The code remains to this day the basis of much law throughout Europe. As with surprisingly many features of the Egyptian expedition, here once again we can see Napoleon's future being worked out in embryo.

to the tortures suffered by those not accustomed to sailing for any length of time, especially in such frail craft as those in which we put to sea."[5] Conditions belowdecks throughout the fleet were appallingly overcrowded, and as a result soon became almost unbearably fetid, vermin-ridden and squalid. None of the peasant soldiers had ever put to sea before and many were prostrated with seasickness. Their non-commissioned officers, many of whom lived in makeshift "cabins" erected on deck out of planks, fared little better, getting in the way of the sailors. Relations between army and navy personnel of all ranks deteriorated—each regarding themselves as the senior company, each blaming the other for the cramped and increasingly unhygienic conditions. Even aboard Brueys' flagship *L'Orient*, where Napoleon had his own personal quarters, equipped with a library and his bed on rollers, conditions belowdecks must have been seriously overcrowded. The normal ship's company was 1,000 men, living in cramped conditions at the best of times, but according to Bourrienne *L'Orient* was "like a village from which women have been excluded . . . a village of two thousand inhabitants."[6] If the flagship had double its quota, one can but imagine the situation on lesser ships and the transports.

After a week at sea, the provisions on board several vessels were found to have become spoiled. Wine casks had leaked, salt beef and water barrels had become tainted, and hard tack (ship's biscuit) was becoming worm-eaten; even the fresh animals intended for the officers (chickens, pigs, sheep) were soon in short supply, with cockroaches and fleas getting everywhere. As one of the savants commented drily, "The animals which we were to eat were disappearing, while those which ate us began multiplying a hundred-fold."[7] The men groused as they were put through their morning inspection and drill on deck, rallying only when the bands played and the singing began in the afternoon. Napoleon would stand on the bridge of *L'Orient* waving his arms like a conductor as he encouraged the men in their intership choruses of the "Chant du Départ" and "La Marseillaise."[*]

Napoleon was not entirely unaware of the state of morale amongst the men, but he considered this a mere setback which would soon be

---

[*] This latter, the most rousing of all anthems, had been composed overnight by Rouget de Lisle, a young officer in the engineers, just six years previously, and was originally known as "The War Song of the Army of the Rhine." It gained its current name because of its popularity with the units from Marseilles, many of whom were now members of the expeditionary force. Ironically, it would later be banned by Napoleon when he became emperor, because of its revolutionary associations.

put right on arrival at their destination. Similarly difficult relations prevailed amongst the generals, senior naval officers and leading savants aboard *L'Orient*; even Vice-Admiral Brueys had to share his stateroom with Monge.

Napoleon was genuinely interested in higher learning, especially scientific and quasi-philosophical topics; he saw no conflict between this and his role as a military leader, and he appeared to take it for granted that his staff officers would feel the same. Indeed, he often seemed more at home amongst his leading savants, especially Monge and Berthollet, than he did amongst his generals. Most of the generals and naval commanders, with a few notable exceptions such as Caffarelli, were much more traditional in their tastes, maintaining a hearty contempt for the "donkeys"—their disparaging term for the savants, with their braying intellectual accents. Matters were hardly improved by the fact that the generals and commanders even had to dine alongside these intellectuals, with their unmilitary attitudes, lack of respect for rank, and ridiculous uniforms.* Yet worse was to follow after dinner, when Napoleon insisted that his staff officers and commanders should accompany him and the savants in their nightly discussions on deck under the stars. This particularly irritated Napoleon's favorite aide Junot, who made a point of appearing to fall asleep during the learned conversations, only rousing himself to make the occasional pointed remark—such as the suggestion that General Lannes was surely qualified to become a member of the savants on account of his name (*l'âne* being French for donkey). Junot was eventually exempted by Napoleon from having to attend these meetings, because of his inability to enter into the spirit of the proceedings.

As the vast French expeditionary fleet continued east across the Mediterranean, Napoleon's nightly discussions with his senior officers and savants ranged across such topics as the nature of electricity, whether there was life after death, and what infinite mysteries might still remain for mankind to discover. Sometimes, when these grand debates were finished and the others had retired to their cabins, Napoleon would continue walking the deck with Monge and Berthollet, discussing his

---

* The savants had been provided with their own uniforms, designed by Napoleon himself, which were a plain version of those worn by celebrated members of the Institute in Paris. These uniforms were the object of much contempt and derision amongst all ranks of those who wore "proper" military or naval uniforms.

ideas. Although he grew close to both the mathematician and the chemist, as Bourrienne recorded, "it was easy to see that he preferred Monge, whose imagination may have been devoid of precise religious principles, but had a propensity towards religious ideas which was in harmony with Napoleon's own view of this subject."[8] Berthollet's cold chemist's imagination was inclined to mock such things, tending towards the kind of materialism Napoleon always deplored. Yet regardless of Napoleon's forcefully expressed opinions, Berthollet stuck to his guns. In exasperation, Napoleon at one point gestured towards the stars, demanding of the obstinate materialist, "If that is the case, then tell me who made all this?"

Napoleon's attitude towards religion was ambivalent; his deepest belief appears to have been in the idea of destiny, most notably his own. This had grown out of a natural youthful self-conviction, allied with strong ambition, which evolved to metaphysical proportions with his meteoric rise. Nonetheless, this evolution had remained tinged with reality. Experience, particularly on the battlefield, had made him come to see that destiny also included the lesser, and less predictable, notion of luck. All this represented a deep internal conviction, with which he was so filled that it often spilled over into his pronouncements. On the other hand, his external view of religion itself was at the same time less spiritual and less favorable. According to Bourrienne, "As he frequently said to me, his principle was to look upon religion as the work of man, but to respect it everywhere as a powerful means of government."[9]

Pacing the deck with Monge and Berthollet, Napoleon was in a sense merely attempting to immerse himself deeper in his self-inspired sense of destiny. As the fleet sailed up under the lee of Crete, with its high barren mountain peaks visible to the north, in his daytime conversations with Bourrienne

his imagination became exulted as he expounded with enthusiasm on ancient Crete. . . . He spoke of the decadence of the Ottoman Empire which so little resembled the fabulous land of history, a country so many times bathed in the blood of men. He began thinking of the ingenious fables of mythology, giving his words a poetic quality, which became further inspired . . . leading him to reason about the best laws to govern mankind . . . people's need for religion . . .[10]

However, beyond the immediate darkness of night and Napoleon's nebulous philosophical speculations, there did indeed lurk destiny—in the all too real form of the British fleet.

Even before Napoleon had reached Malta, he had received further information about the British ships that were searching for him. Writing to the Directory, he had described how a French sloop from the fleet had chased an English brig, forcing it to beach on Sardinia, where it had been burned: "The crew of this vessel repeatedly spoke of an English squadron, which I believe at the most boils down to five or six warships."[11] Even so, should such a squadron have surprised the huge and extended French fleet it could still have inflicted considerable damage, which was why Brueys and Napoleon had come to the conclusion that it was better to travel under the lee of Crete, deviating by well over 100 miles from the direct route to Egypt. Even if this meant losing valuable time, they would at least avoid the British squadron if it had guessed their destination and was searching along the direct route to Alexandria.

What Napoleon did not know was that Nelson's small and depleted squadron had on June 7 been reinforced, so that it now had thirteen ships of the line, precisely the same number as Brueys had under his command. Nelson's orders from St. Vincent had also changed. His appointed mission was no longer to spy on the enemy, in order to discover its strength and destination, but "to proceed in quest of the armament preparing by the enemy at Toulon . . . [and] use your utmost endeavours to take, sink, burn or destroy it."[12]

British naval intelligence was behind the times: by now Nelson had known for two weeks that Napoleon had sailed from Toulon. The fact that St. Vincent off Cadiz remained in ignorance of this event gives just an inkling of the problems of communication involved during this period. In fact, trans-Mediterranean communications and their difficulties were from now on to play a major role in both the successes and failures of the Egyptian expedition, as well as of those who sought to oppose it. Seaborne communications beyond flag-reading distance relied entirely upon messages carried aboard ships, which were dependent upon the wind, and at the mercy of currents and storms. Added intelligence could be extracted from passing ships, though this was not always reliable. Most important, any seaborne intelligence was always open to being intercepted by enemy naval vessels, who might put it to their own uses. As with St. Vincent's communication to Nelson, messages usually took weeks rather than days, and were frequently out of date by the time they arrived, leaving much to the initiative of the individual commanders. And few of these had more initiative than Rear Admiral Sir Horatio Nelson.

Nelson was just thirty-nine years old, young indeed for an admiral in the ultra-conservative British navy, but he had already demonstrated exceptional talent. He was a battle-scarred veteran, having lost his right eye leading his men ashore at Corsica, and had his right arm shattered in an assault on Tenerife, the latter resulting in an amputation from which he had only just recuperated, leaving him physically frail. In fact, he had always suffered from a weak physique, and upon entering the navy at the age of twelve had been lucky to survive the tough conditions which then prevailed on board, where, according to a hoary British naval saying, "the ships were made of wood, and the men were made of iron." Nelson's will to survive had over the years deepened into a driving ambition; as a consequence, he took command of his first ship at the age of just twenty, making him the youngest captain in the entire fleet. Later, he saw action at the siege of Toulon, which the ambitious young Napoleon had played such an important part in ending. Yet there was a significant difference between the similarly powerful ambition of these two young men. Nelson was a man of deep religious conviction, in a traditional Christian sense; his dislike of the French Revolution, which he saw as an irruption of godlessness, led him to hate the French and all things French with an all-embracing fervor. The self-aggrandizement and lust for glory which so characterized Napoleon were thus sublimated into a certain selflessness in Nelson, who came to see himself as God's instrument in this war against His enemy.

Just a year previously, in 1797, the low pay, brutal discipline and appalling conditions prevailing in the British navy had led to serious mutinies at the home ports of the Nore and Spithead. Nelson had always sought to temper these conditions, and the men who served under him loved him for it. The verb is not too strong: just as Nelson was driven by his sense of duty, so he instilled it in his men, who were willing to follow the example of their frail, savagely wounded, but fearless commander. However, on this particular occasion in the summer of 1798, he would begin by leading them on a wild goose chase. Having missed the French fleet as it slipped out of Toulon, Nelson and his reinforced squadron were now faced with the task of hunting down a prey that had nine days' start on them and could have been anywhere in the Mediterranean—a stretch of water over 2,000 miles long and 500 miles wide, with several extensive arms and gulfs, together with many islands large and small which could provide cover for any size of fleet.

As soon as Nelson received his reinforcements and new orders, he set sail on June 8 from his station off Toulon, following what he rightly assumed had been the French fleet's course east and then southwards along the Italian coast, all the time trying to work out Napoleon's likely route and intentions. By June 15 he was writing to First Sea Lord Spencer: "The last account I had of the French fleet was from a Tunisian cruiser, who saw them on the 4th, off Trapani, in Sicily, steering to the eastward. If they pass Sicily, I shall believe they are going on their scheme of possessing Alexandria, and getting troops to India—a plan concerted with Tippoo Saib [*sic*], by no means so difficult as might at first view be imagined."[13] Imagined by Nelson, that is. Ironically, whereas Napoleon planned to march in Alexander the Great's footsteps across 3,000 miles of desert and hostile territory, Nelson envisioned a far more practical and well-organized scheme. He assumed that Napoleon had already sent French ships ahead, around the Cape of Good Hope, which would arrive at Suez and then ferry his army to India. He was not to know that Napoleon's plans, executed in haste and inspired by glory, remained lacking in such practicalities.

Two days later, on June 17, Nelson and his squadron arrived off the Bay of Naples, where he sent inquiries to his friend the British ambassador Sir William Hamilton and his wife Emma, and picked up word that the French fleet had been sighted on June 8 off Malta, seemingly on the point of invading the island. Nelson at once set off on the 400-mile voyage through the Straits of Messina, at the same time working out the tactics he would employ if he encountered the French fleet. He decided that he would split his squadron into three: two groups would engage the French battleships, whilst the third would do its utmost to destroy as many of the French transports as possible. Had this happened, it could well have resulted in sprigs of cypress for Nelson rather than the laurel wreath he coveted. The first two groups would have been outgunned by the French, and the French transports would certainly have scattered, making it difficult for Nelson's few chasing ships to destroy a significant number. However, although Nelson's quixotic bravery might well have resulted in his own destruction, and that of his entire squadron, it would probably have wreaked sufficient damage and dispersal to have put an end to any immediate French invasion of Egypt. Nelson's estimate of the situation may have been reckless, but it was certainly closer to effective reality than that of Napoleon, who would later declare: "If the English had really wanted to attack us during the voyage we should have easily beaten them."[14]

More pertinently, Nelson reasoned that if after leaving Malta the French fleet sailed north, it would be to invade Sicily; if it sailed east, it would be heading for Alexandria. And early on June 22, as Nelson was sailing past Cape Passaro, the southeastern tip of Sicily, he received the news he had been waiting for. His squadron encountered a Genoese merchantman which informed them that the French had conquered Malta on June 15 and departed the next day, sailing in an easterly direction. Napoleon was definitely bound for Alexandria. Nelson set off in hot pursuit.

It is no exaggeration to say that had this information, shouted early one summer's morning from one passing ship to another off a lonely Mediterranean cape, proved correct, it would have changed the course of world history. Napoleon's expedition to Egypt would probably have been thwarted, leaving his career in ruins. But the voice calling across the water from the Genoese merchantman had been misinformed. In fact, Napoleon had only set sail from Malta on June 19, but Nelson, under the misapprehension that the French had six days' start on him, now turned his squadron east on a direct course for Alexandria, making haste with all sail. Later that same day the weather became misty and the blurred shapes of what appeared to be three frigates appeared in the distance. Nelson ordered the brig *Mutine* to investigate, and when it returned at dusk its captain reported that he had identified the three as French. Nelson decided to allow the ships to disappear into the misty darkness; he reasoned that he could not afford to split his squadron on a wild goose chase after three lone frigates. His objective was the entire French fleet, which he calculated was by now several hundred miles to the southeast.

Nelson's decision proved an unfortunate and colossal blunder. The three French frigates were in fact the outriders of the French fleet, which lay just over the horizon, having left Malta only three days previously, traveling in a northeasterly direction towards Crete. And so, during the misty night of June 22/23, the paths of the two fleets actually crossed within a few miles of each other, the French listening in silence as the guns of Nelson's squadron boomed dully through the pitch darkness at regular intervals.*

Next morning, as dawn broke, the two fleets each found themselves surrounded by an empty horizon: their courses had crossed and they

---

* In the dark and under misty conditions, British squadron procedure was to sound guns at regular intervals, enabling ships to stay in contact, and by following the direction of the sound to maintain relative position.

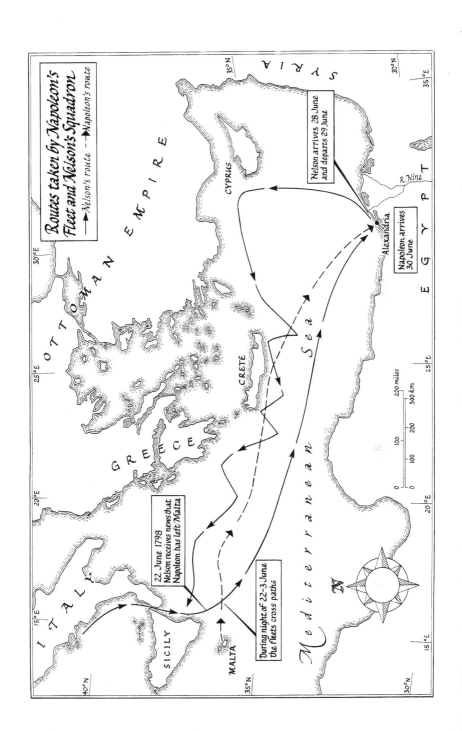

Routes taken by Napoleon's Fleet and Nelson's Squadron

→ Nelson's route   → Napoleon's route

Nelson arrives 28 June and departs 29 June

Napoleon arrives 30 June

22 June 1798 Nelson receives news that Napoleon has left Malta

During night of 22-3 June the fleets cross paths

OTTOMAN EMPIRE

SYRIA

CYPRUS

CRETE

GREECE

ITALY

SICILY

MALTA

Alexandria

R. Nile

EGYPT

Mediterranean Sea

200 miles

300 km

200

100

100

0   0

N

30°N

35°N

30°N

35°E

35°E

30°E

25°E

20°E

15°E

25°E

20°E

15°E

40°N

35°N

30°N

were now divergent, Nelson bound southeast direct for Alexandria in pursuit of a chimera, Napoleon bound northeast for Crete on his odyssey in pursuit of destiny.

Making over a hundred miles a day, Nelson managed to reach Alexandria in just six days. To his consternation, he found no sign of the French fleet. He dispatched Captain Hardy aboard the brig *Mutine* ashore for intelligence: in the harbor was just one ancient Turkish warship, and a few merchant vessels. Amongst the curious Egyptian spectators drawn to the quayside there were no French uniforms or any suggestion of an invading army. The local *sherif* knew of no French fleet.

Nelson was plunged into despair. In his extremity he would shift the responsibility for his failure to the inadequacies of his squadron: "I have again to deeply blame my want of frigates, to which I shall ever attribute my ignorance of the situation of the French fleet,"[15] he wrote back to his immediate superior, Admiral St. Vincent, who had placed so much trust in him. Nelson had no idea where the French fleet could be. Had it sailed north to invade Sicily after all? Or, worse still, had it headed west for the Straits of Gibraltar, to join up with the French Atlantic fleet for an invasion of England or Ireland? These questions would, over the following days, bring Nelson to the brink of a nervous breakdown. He had blundered badly, and he knew it. When the news of his failure reached London, it was greeted with outrage. In Parliament it was denounced by the future cabinet minister George Rose as "the most extraordinary instance of the kind I believe in the Naval History of the World."[16] The newspapers soon took up the chorus of disbelief, one declaring: "It is a remarkable circumstance that a fleet of nearly 400 sail, covering a space of so many leagues, should have been able to elude the knowledge of our fleet for such a long space of time."[17]

After waiting just twenty-four hours off Alexandria, Nelson set sail north on the morning of June 29.

V

"A conquest which will change the world"

AT dawn on the very morning that Nelson's squadron set off north, the French frigate *La Junon*, sailing ahead of the French fleet, caught its first sight of the African shoreline. Astonishingly, neither *La Junon* nor Nelson's squadron noticed one another. Almost equally astonishingly, Napoleon's cumbersome fleet had covered a greater distance than Nelson's squadron and had taken only a couple of days longer.

La Junon had been sent ahead to reconnoiter the coast and pick up the French consul in Alexandria, so that he could apprise Napoleon of the situation. The report from consul Magallon made for uncomfortable listening. Nelson's emissary ashore, Captain Hardy, had informed the *sherif* of Alexandria, Mohammed El-Koraïm, that he was in pursuit of a large French fleet which was intending to invade Egypt. According to the chronicle of events written by Nicolas Turc, a poet of Greek extraction who was living in Egypt at the time, El-Koraïm had been frankly distrustful of the British. "It is not possible that the French are thinking of coming to our country. What would they do here?" he demanded. He had denied the British permission to put ashore for fresh water and victualing, adding: "If the French arrive here with hostile intentions, it will be for us to see them off."[1]

In fact, El-Koraïm's answer was certainly disingenuous. The Egyptians had initially mistaken Nelson's ships for a French fleet; as it happened, they were already expecting the French. But how could they possibly have been aware that the French were planning to invade Egypt? Some suggest that El-Koraïm had been informed by a merchantman from Malta about Napoleon's occupation of the island, and that he had guessed the next target would be Egypt. Napoleon had put an embargo upon any ships leaving Malta during his occupation, yet news of his invasion had certainly spread, if only in inexact form—witness what Nelson had learned from the Genoese merchantman off Sicily. However, much more likely is that El-Koraïm and the Egyptian authorities had already received official word from the Porte in Constantinople warning of a French invasion. Although Napoleon's destination had remained a tightly kept secret, with even the British only picking up the vaguest of rumors, the Porte had learned that the French intended to invade Egypt almost as soon as the decision had been taken. Greek intelligence agents working for the Turkish embassy in Paris had discovered the truth as early as March, the very month in which the Directory had initially sanctioned Napoleon's idea. This news had been conveyed speedily overland to Constantinople, and in April the Turkish ambassador in Paris had received instructions to confront Talleyrand, demanding to know if the French fleet being assembled at Toulon was in fact preparing to invade Egypt. Talleyrand had remained his inscrutable, imperturbable self, pointing out that the French were close allies of the Porte, and as such could not possibly have aggressive intentions towards any territory under direct Turkish rule, a slippery answer which gave him sufficient space to maneuver. Whether Egypt was under *direct* Turkish rule was an open question—a point recognized at once by the Turkish ambassador. Typically, Talleyrand decided not to pass on to Napoleon the full details of this diplomatic encounter, which certainly failed to convince the Porte. News of French intentions was probably conveyed to Egypt at least by early June, doubtless causing some consternation. Even so, as we shall see, there is abundant evidence that nothing much was done about this, and the matter appears to have been forgotten. The arrival of Nelson's squadron had jolted it back into mind. Even so, El-Koraïm appears to have been reassured by Nelson's willingness to depart, for he still undertook very little in the way of defensive preparations.

The French consul ended his report to Napoleon by revealing that Captain Hardy had delivered a secret note to the British representative, with instructions that this be conveyed forthwith via Suez to India. Napoleon now knew that Nelson's squadron was in close proximity and searching for him, and that the Egyptians were forewarned of the French arrival. He also knew that his dream of creating an Eastern empire, dismissed by so many as fantasy, had been taken seriously at least by Nelson. His bold strike in the footsteps of Alexander would be lacking the element of surprise: the British would be waiting for him.

As if all this potentially disastrous news was not bad enough, a strong northeasterly wind had now begun to blow, and was soon whipping up the waves and driving the fleet towards the shore. In the words of the savant Denon, who was present at the meeting between the French consul and Napoleon: "The English could have arrived at any instant. The wind was so strong that the warships were becoming mixed up with the transport convoy, and amidst the confusion we would have been assured of the most disastrous defeat if the enemy had appeared." Despite everything, Napoleon remained unmoved, and when the consul had finished his report, Denon observed: "I was not able to detect the slightest expression on his features, and after several minutes of silence he ordered the disembarkation to begin."²

Napoleon had decided against any disadvantageous landing amidst the shallows and enclosed harbors of Alexandria, in case he faced determined resistance. Instead he chose to land at the fishing village of Marabout, some five miles west of Alexandria. Owing to the underwater reefs along this part of the coast, it was not possible to stage a widespread simultaneous landing, so the disembarkation was limited to a narrow stretch of coastline and thus likely to take at least three days. Vice-Admiral Brueys immediately protested in the strongest possible terms: attempting even a limited landing amidst shoals in such weather was far too dangerous. Napoleon refused to argue: "Admiral, we have no time to lose. Fortune has given me three days, if we do not take advantage of this we are lost."³

Brueys had no alternative but to concede, though he refused to allow the fleet under his command to anchor any closer than three miles offshore, owing to the constant danger from the uncharted shoals and the strengthening onshore wind. Disembarkation began at midday on July 1, but such were the conditions that the first men did not reach the shore until late afternoon, and did not begin arriving in larger numbers until dusk. Fortunately, their landing was unopposed.

It quickly became clear that the expedition was equipped with insufficient longboats to row the men ashore. Since the expedition's destination had remained unknown at the time when equipment was being loaded at the ports, few had given thought to the actual circumstances of the invasion, and this oversight had not come to light during the dress-rehearsal invasion of Malta, when comparatively few troops had been put ashore.

As darkness fell and the swell increased, the overloaded longboats began capsizing. Most of those plunged into the water were not able to swim, but were quickly located by their screams through the sound of the waves as they clung to the upturned boats in the darkness. In Napoleon's subsequent report to the Directory, he would state that twenty-nine men died in this operation; most firsthand sources suggest that this was a considerable underestimate, and that around three times this amount may have perished. Some of the crowded longboats took as long as eight hours to row through the storm until they managed to beach amidst the rollers, and a few were unable to make it back against the wind. Groggy with seasickness, the men assembled on the beach in the darkness in their sodden uniforms, clutching their muskets, attempting to dry out their kit and rations.

At the outset, Napoleon had watched the disembarkation from the quarterdeck of *L'Orient*. In the middle of the afternoon his dismay had turned to horror when an approaching warship had been spotted on the horizon. Fearful that this was the vanguard of Nelson's squadron, he paced up and down the deck, crying out: "Am I now to be abandoned by Fortune? Can you not be merciful and grant me just a few more days?" In the event, the ship was soon identified as the French frigate *La Justice*, which had followed on from Malta. Napoleon then boarded a Maltese galley, which rowed him closer to the shore, so that he could see what was happening on the beach.[4]

At one A.M. on the morning of July 2, Napoleon finally jumped into a launch and was rowed ashore, accompanied by his chief of staff General Berthier, his close friend General Caffarelli, and General Dommartin, commander of the artillery. He had appointed Menou, Kléber and Bon as commanders of the three prongs of the initial invasion force; while Desaix's forces were to defend the beachhead, enabling the landing to continue. Napoleon waded ashore through the surf to find that Menou and Kléber had successfully landed with their advance forces (1,000 men each), whilst Bon had so far disembarked only a few of his men. Meanwhile Desaix and his contingent were still out in the water, trying to make it in against the waves. Napoleon supervised the defenses of the beachhead, and then lay down to sleep for an hour on the sand. Those safely landed soon followed suit, though the atmosphere that night on shore is best evoked by an entry in Captain Vertray's journal: "I snatched some sleep until a false alarm, caused by several drunken soldiers, awoke the entire camp."[5] Such was the chaotic situation for the men: having suffered misery for weeks at sea, they were now plunged into the darkness of an unknown land far from home, with the prospect of fighting for their lives. Not surprisingly, some resorted to the bottle, which only made things worse. When Napoleon awoke at three A.M., the beach was bathed in the light of a brilliant half-moon, with a warm wind now blowing in from the desert. The men paraded, while Berthier tallied their numbers: there were still fewer than 4,000 men ashore. These had limited rations, one canteen of water apiece, and sixty cartridges each. They were supported by neither artillery nor cavalry, as it was still impossible to land horses or field guns. Despite this, Napoleon was determined to press on and occupy Alexandria, so that he could secure the harbors there for the major unloading as quickly as possible.

As dawn rose across the desert ahead, the columns of men began tramping forward towards the silhouette of Alexandria and its minarets looming against the pink glow of the horizon. When the sun rose in the sky the heat quickly became insufferable; the men had soon emptied their canteens of water, and the few wells they came across could hardly quench the thirst of so many. At the head of the columns marched Napoleon, the wooden-legged Caffarelli gamely keeping pace at his side. Accompanying them were "Dumas, commander of the cavalry, without a horse; and Dommartin, commander of the artillery, without a gun."[6]

At five A.M. the first Bedouin appeared out of the desert on the army's flanks. There were around 400 or 500 of them on horseback, "from the Henady tribe, the most ferocious of the desert Arabs, almost naked, black and scrawny."[7] Their wild hair made them appear like warriors from another age. They were armed with lances, and seeing that the French had no cavalry they began charging between the columns, screaming their terrible cries, harassing any stragglers. As Napoleon was forced to concede: "If these 500 Arabs had been Mamelukes, they would have achieved a great success in this opening encounter."[8] But they turned out to be more cowardly, and were seen off with little difficulty. Even so, they managed to take a dozen French prisoners, "who excited their vivid curiosity. The Arabs marveled at their white skin, and the prisoners who were returned some days later gave grotesque details of the horrible practices to which they were subjected by these men of the desert."[9]

At six A.M. Napoleon arrived at Pompey's Pillar, which stood on a promontory southwest of Alexandria. By now even he and his staff were suffering from severe thirst, but there were no nearby wells. One of his officers produced some oranges which he had brought with him from Malta, and offered them to his commander. Napoleon accepted one, immediately tore it open and began sucking at it greedily. From his vantage point, he looked out over Alexandria. The city which had once been second only to Rome in the Roman Empire, famed for its library and its 400 temples, palaces and monuments, with a population of over a quarter of a million, was now reduced to 24,000 inhabitants.* In the words of Captain Vertray: "Alexandria which from afar appeared a superb city, was now seen to be little more than a heap of ruins."[10] Even so, it had its defenses. Napoleon described how he looked out over "the castellated walls of the Arab fortress . . . beyond which were the minarets of the city and the masts of the Turkish warship moored in the port."[11] It could be seen that the walls and towers of the city were lined with people, including women and children.

The arrival of the vast French fleet off Alexandria at dawn on July 1 had proved an awesome sight for the local population. According to Nicolas Turc, "When the inhabitants of Alexandria looked to the horizon they could no longer see the sea, only the sky and ships. They were seized by a terror beyond imagination."[12] As soon as El-Koraïm had seen the fleet, he had immediately sent a message to Murad Bey, the Mameluke leader in Cairo: "My lord, the fleet which has arrived here is immense. One can see neither its beginning nor its end. For the love of God and His Prophet send us fighting men to protect us."[13] Throughout that day and the following night he had dispatched a further dozen messengers to Cairo, begging for help. But Murad Bey remained undaunted. He demanded of one messenger: "Are they on horseback?" When he learned that the French army was on foot, he replied: "My men will destroy them and I will slice open their heads like watermelons in the fields."[14] Such bravado was of little use to the people of Alexandria. The few guns which were dragged up onto the ramparts were evidently useless, and only one barrel of gunpowder could be found. As for the city's defensive forces, these consisted of an Egyptian garrison of fewer than 500 men and a detachment of just twenty Mameluke cavalry.

---

* Estimates vary, with some authoritative sources claiming the population was down to 6,000. However, the evidence suggests that 24,000 was more likely, of which around 800 were Jews, 100 Greeks, and 100 other Europeans, mainly French and British traders.

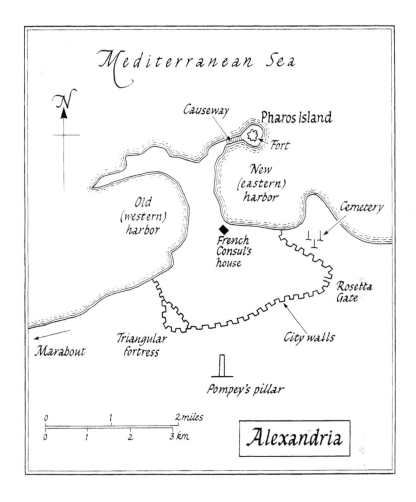

Napoleon hoped to occupy the city without armed conflict, and to this end he had dispatched a message for El-Koraïm as soon as the fleet arrived off Alexandria: "The beys [Mamelukes] have been harassing our merchants, and I have come to demand reparation." This was the official French government reason for the invasion, the one which Talleyrand had agreed with Napoleon should be conveyed to the Porte in Constantinople. "I will be in Alexandria tomorrow," Napoleon went on in his message. "You need have nothing to fear. We French are great friends of the Sultan of Turkey, and you should conduct yourself as you would towards his ally. However, if you commit the least hostility against the French army I will treat you as an enemy, and you will regret it, though it is far from my heart's desire to do such a thing."[15]

This letter received no reply, and according to Nicolas Turc, as the day progressed "the citizens fell into the greatest agitation, passing a night of such terror as to make the hairs of infants at their mothers' breasts turn white in the blink of an eye."[16] In the early hours news reached El-Koraïm that the French had established a beachhead and were marching towards the city, whereupon he rode out of the city at the head of his twenty Mamelukes. At daybreak he encountered a French scouting party, operating beyond the flanks of the advancing forces. "He charged them, cut off the head of the captain commanding them, and paraded it in triumph through the streets of Alexandria. This sight electrified the population."[17]

The contemporary Egyptian historian El-Djabarti, an educated man and a senior member of the Muslim community, who provided the most authoritative account of the French invasion, described how that morning the inhabitants of Alexandria saw "the French scattered around the outskirts of the city like a swarm of locusts."[18]

El-Koraïm's attack on the French scouting party made Napoleon realize that he would have to take the city by force. Standing with his generals beneath Pompey's Pillar, he reiterated his plan of action: Bon was to force his way in through the eastern Rosetta Gate to their right, Kléber was to scale the walls directly ahead, Menou was to attack the triangular fortress overlooking the old western harbor to the left. The three French divisions took up their positions out of cannon range under the silent gaze of the population lining the walls. According to a young French lieutenant: "All of a sudden the men, women and children burst into hideous screams, and at the same time there was a discharge of artillery fire from the walls." Napoleon ordered the bugles to sound for the charge: "The screams doubled in intensity, our soldiers rushed forward with their generals at their head. Despite the gunfire from the defenders and the hail of stones that they threw down at us, we began fearlessly scaling the walls."[19] The city walls were in such a state of disrepair that in some places they had crumbled, allowing the French to gain access with comparative ease. Menou was the first to break through and led his men into the city itself, receiving no fewer than seven wounds in the process, none of which proved capable of halting him in his intrepid charge. Not so lucky was Kléber, who led his grenadiers on the frontal assault to scale the walls and "was hit on the forehead by a musket-ball, which knocked him to the ground."[20] Though serious, this did not prove fatal. Meanwhile, Bon found his way through the Rosetta Gate barred, but a detachment led by General Marmont "hacked down the gate with axes, under fire from the walls" and burst into the city.[21]

The bravery of the French soldiers under fire is indisputable, though their motive may not have been such as to inspire their commander. "In confidence I can assure you," a young French officer wrote in a letter home, "it was thirst which drove our soldiers in the capture of Alexandria. Such was our state, it was either find water or die—we had no choice."[22] After the men had slaked their thirst with water from the wells and water jars they found in the nearby houses, the French army gradually moved through the streets, facing occasional sniper fire, which resulted in a few savage reprisals. Only El-Koraïm and his household guard offered any concerted resistance, eventually retreating up the causeway to Pharos Island, site of the ruined ancient lighthouse, where they barricaded themselves in the fort and refused to surrender. Napoleon finally entered the city around midnight, making his way through the narrow streets. "As he turned a corner, a shot from a window shaved the boot on his left leg. His guardsmen scrambled onto the rooftops and entered the house, where they found a single Turk barricaded in a room with six rifles, and killed him on the spot."[23]

Napoleon quickly set up his headquarters in the house of the French consul, on the seafront overlooking the new eastern harbor and Pharos Island, where El-Koraïm remained under siege. Negotiations continued throughout the early hours and into the morning, when El-Koraïm finally saw that his position was hopeless and surrendered. Given safe conduct to Napoleon's headquarters, he prostrated himself before his conqueror, swearing that he was now his slave.

Napoleon knew that "anarchy is the greatest enemy that a conqueror has to dread, above all in a country so different in language, customs and religion."[24] After consulting with the French consul Magallon, he decided to stabilize the situation with a bold stroke: he entrusted to El-Koraïm the task of policing the city. El-Koraïm responded by "re-establishing order, ensuring that the citizenry were disarmed, and procuring for the army all it required."[25] The French had taken the city at a cost of "between thirty and forty men killed, and eighty to a hundred wounded."[26] Egyptian fatalities were reckoned at between 700 and 800, indicating that a sizable number of civilians must have been killed, and even more wounded. How many of these were armed, and thus technically combatants, remains unknown.

Napoleon had given strict instructions to his soldiers that the local people were to be treated with respect, and before landing, copies of a proclamation to this effect had been distributed to all personnel throughout the fleet. This document gives a deep insight into Napoleon's state of mind at this juncture, and what he was doing, or thought he was doing:

Soldiers!
You are about to embark upon a conquest which will change the world. Its effect upon civilization and world trade will be incalculable. You are about to inflict upon England the most certain and telling blow she can suffer, until the day comes when you can deliver the blow that finishes her off.[27]

Although he was careful not to spell out the full extent of his ambitions, there can be no doubt that he had in mind here his campaign to India, and the effect upon Britain resulting from the loss of its Indian empire. During his vast reading as a young officer, he had absorbed the ideas of the physiocrats, who had been the prevailing economic theorists in France at the time. The physiocrats held that ultimate economic wealth lay in land, of which France had so much more than Britain, whose disproportionate wealth appeared to stem from the added land of its colonies. If the British were driven from India, this was liable to result in an economic collapse in Britain itself. In fact, the physiocrats had not yet fully accepted the ideas of Adam Smith, whose *Wealth of Nations*, with its deeper understanding of how economics actually worked, had only recently been translated into French. They had also misunderstood the significance of the Industrial Revolution, which was taking place in Britain at the time but was only just beginning in largely rural France. However, although Napoleon's ambitions were certainly colored by physiocrat ideas, they were not reliant upon them. What he sought was empire and power, and economic might was merely a consequent factor. Rather than relying upon Adam Smith or the physiocrats, for theoretical guidance he turned to Alexander the Great and the manner in which he had conducted his campaign of conquest. Alexander's intention had been absorption, rather than annihilation; he had believed in respecting the ways of the people he conquered, and Napoleon was determined that his army should behave in a similar fashion. In his proclamation to his soldiers he specifically informed them that:

The people amongst whom we are going are Mahommedans. Their first article of faith is: "There is no god but God, and Mohammed is his prophet." Do not contradict them. Act towards them in the same way as we acted on the Italian campaign towards the Jews and the Italians. Show respect for their muftis and their imams, just as you have respected the rabbis and the bishops. Show the same respect for the ceremonies prescribed by the Koran for use in the mosques, as you have shown towards convents and synagogues, towards the religion of Moses and the religion of Jesus Christ. The Roman legions protected all religions.[28]

It is worth noting that Napoleon addressed his soldiers as fellow atheists, in the required post-Revolution manner. Like all French armies during this period, the Army of the Orient, as it now became known, had no chaplains and held no religious services; the only requirement was that all soldiers should adhere to republican principles. To this end the Directory had introduced a good number of spies into all ranks and all regiments to make sure that no politically suspect views were expressed, the main fear being that the army, which had many former aristocrats amongst its officers, might become a hotbed of Royalist sympathizers.

Napoleon went on to make clear how he expected his men to behave:

You will find amongst these people customs which are unlike any to be found in Europe. You will have to become accustomed to these. The people in the countries where we are going treat their women very differently from the way we do; however, in all countries any man who rapes a woman is a monster.

Looting enriches only a few. It dishonours us, destroys our resources, and makes enemies of the very people whom it is in our interest to have as friends.

The first city we shall see was built by Alexander the Great. At each step on our way we will find evidence of feats fit to inspire the emulation of Frenchmen.[29]

These encouraging words were backed by a number of forceful and explicit orders which made their commander's intention more immediately plain to all ranks:

No individual soldier is authorized to make requisitions or raise contributions from the local populace without specific authorization from his commander-in-chief acting on direct orders from the general-in-chief himself. . . . All silver or gold which comes into the possession of the army must be deposited within

twelve hours in the lock-up of the divisional cashier. . . . Those who contra-
vene these orders will be stripped of all their possessions and clapped in irons
for two years.[30]

Napoleon was quick to back up his words with deeds, when an opportunity presented itself whilst he was receiving a delegation of local
Muslim dignitaries. According to an eyewitness: "A French soldier was
brought before him, charged with stealing a dagger from an Arab who
was going about his business in a peaceful fashion. The truth of the
charge was quickly confirmed, and the soldier was shot on the spot."[31]

The Arab delegation appear to have been suitably impressed by
Napoleon's evenhandedness. The message was clear: French and
Egyptians alike would be expected to obey his orders. Napoleon was
willing to go to great lengths to encourage the Egyptian authorities to
adopt a friendly attitude towards the French; to this end, he also
dispatched a message to Pasha Abu Bakr, the nominal Ottoman ruler
in Cairo:

The Directory of the French Republic has already sent several messages to the
Sublime Porte requesting them to punish the Mameluke beys of Egypt who
continue to harass the French merchants operating here.

The Sublime Porte has decided that the willful and avaricious beys have
ignored the principles of justice. The Sublime Porte has not authorized these
outrages perpetrated upon their good and ancient allies the French, and in
consequence it has withdrawn its protection from the beys.

The French Republic has thus decided to send a powerful army to put an
end to this piracy by the beys. You, who ought to be master of the beys, yet
are held by them in Cairo deprived of power and authority, must surely
welcome my arrival. You are no doubt already informed that I have no intention
of doing anything against the Koran or against the Sultan. Therefore I invite
you to come and meet me, so that together we can curse these ungodly beys.[32]

Napoleon was being devious here. Although he hinted that the sultan
and the Porte were in favor of this action by their French allies, he
knew they had not yet authorized such action. This part of the message
was doubtless intended to persuade the pasha to support him. He knew
that his message would be passed on to Constantinople, where its
favorable attitude towards the sultan, and its assumption of his
blessing, might aid Talleyrand in his mission to persuade the Porte that
the French had no aggressive intentions towards their ancient ally the

Ottoman Empire, or indeed towards any Muslims. It is difficult to see how the Porte, even at its most lackadaisical, could have regarded the French action in Egypt as anything other than an invasion of their territory, but it appears that Napoleon believed his flimsy excuse regarding the overthrow of the Mamelukes, and hoped his letter would reinforce it. In fact, it mainly served to reinforce this myth in his own mind.

He also knew that this letter would be intercepted by the beys, and wished them to understand that they faced the combined might of the Ottoman Empire and the French Republic, whose armies had been victorious in Europe. As he knew all too well, one of the first principles of the art of war is to convince your opponent that he cannot win.

Alexandria was now little more than a backwater of Mameluke Egypt. Its importance as a port had long since been eclipsed by Rosetta and Damietta, the ports at the end of the western and eastern navigable channels of the Nile delta, which linked them directly to Cairo. The canal linking Alexandria to the Nile delta had silted up, was no longer navigable, and was barely producing sufficient fresh water to supply the city's wells. The educated French officers may have been disappointed to find Alexandria a shadow of its former glorious self, but others found it exotic enough. According to Citizen Joubert in a letter home:

You can see for sale in the bazaar sheep, pigeons, tobacco, and above all there are the barbers, who put the head of their customer between their knees, and look more as if they are about to decapitate them than shave them. They are however very dexterous. I also saw several women, dressed up in long robes which completely mask their bodies and reveal only their eyes, almost like the outfit worn by religious penitents in our southern provinces.[33]

The women darkened their eyes with kohl, and the children ran around the unpaved streets completely naked. Private Millet described the Egyptian men:

They shave their head, wearing on it a small red hat, known in Arabic as a *tarboush*, with a turban wound around it five or six times. They wear several large robes, made of silk or cloth, one on top of the other, all very long, falling to their heels, like a cassock. Their legs are bare, and often their feet are too; they have long beards which gives the old men a majestic look and makes them respected by the young.[34]

Joubert goes on to describe how amongst "the heap of ruins one sees houses built of mud and straw leaning up against the sections of fallen granite columns," and later mentions "the obelisk called Cleopatra's Needle."* The only sign of vegetation was "several date palms, sad trees, which from afar resemble pine trees whose stem has been stripped almost as far as the top." On the edges of the city he found "an atmosphere, a way of life which has been unknown to us for ages." Others came across more bizarre sights. Captain Vertray described how "there were cases of the plague in one of the quarters of this unhappy city, and during our stay we witnessed a terrible sight. A plague-stricken woman, holding in her arms a child similarly stricken with this horrific disease, was carried to a cemetery, and under the eyes of more than forty of us French onlookers was buried alive."[35]

Meanwhile the French fleet had now occupied the port and was rapidly unloading in the eastern and western harbors. First men and horses, then rations and supplies, and next artillery: the majority of this was off the ships as early as July 3. Food was soon in short supply in the overcrowded city. Unfortunately Vice-Admiral Brueys had not taken the precaution of blockading the western harbor as his ships entered, thus allowing a large number of boats bringing fish, tomatoes, melons and other fresh local produce from along the coast to flee. Napoleon was furious and reprimanded Brueys, but he remained even more concerned with defending the fleet against Nelson's squadron, which could still have appeared at any moment. The eastern harbor was large enough to shelter a fleet, no matter how large, but parts of the entrance channel appeared to be no more than five fathoms deep, too shallow to allow in the larger seventy-four-gunners. On July 3 Napoleon sent word to Vice-Admiral Brueys: "The admiral will send a report tomorrow informing the general-in-chief whether the fleet can enter the port of Alexandria, or if not whether it would be able defend itself against a superior enemy fleet whilst anchored in Aboukir Bay." This wide bay provided a good anchorage along the coast fifteen miles east of Alexandria. Napoleon went on: "In case neither of these possibilities is feasible, the admiral should, having disembarked all artillery, set sail for Corfu." He was to leave behind in Alexandria only sufficient ships for its defense.[36]

Amongst the equipment unloaded was the Arabic printing press,

---

* Now on the Thames embankment in London.

which was immediately put into action printing copies of Napoleon's proclamation to the people of Egypt. An indication of the undeveloped state of Egypt at the time is the fact that this was the first printing press in the country. Napoleon's proclamation went out of its way to reassure the people of Egypt that he came as a friend of Islam, intent upon freeing them from the dictatorship of the Mamelukes:

In the name of God, ever clement and merciful; there is no God save Allah; He has no son and shares His power with no one.

Commander-in-chief of the French Armies General Bonaparte to the people of Egypt:

For too long this bunch of slaves bought in Georgia and the Caucasus has tyrannized the most beautiful country in the world. In the eyes of God all men are equal, so what entitles the Mamelukes to all that makes life comfortable and pleasant? Who own all the great estates? The Mamelukes. Who have all the loveliest slaves, the most splendid horses and the finest houses? If Egypt truly and rightfully belongs to them, let them produce the deeds by which God gave it to them. Once you had great cities, large canals and prosperous trade. What has destroyed all this if not the greed, iniquity and tyranny of the Mamelukes?[37]

He promised them that once the Mamelukes had been defeated, "Egyptians will be able to occupy all public offices, so that the country will be governed by virtuous and educated rulers, and the people will be happy. Let the Kadis, Sheiks, Imams, and Tchorbadjis [i.e. the religious and civil leaders and men of eminence in the community] inform the people of Egypt that the French are true Moslems; they come as the enemy of the Christian enemies of Islam. Happy, thrice happy, will be those Egyptians who side with us. They will prosper in fortune and rank." But lest there be any misunderstanding, he warned: "Let those who take up arms on behalf of the Mamelukes beware, and thrice beware, for them there shall be no salvation. They are beyond hope; they will perish."

This point was reinforced by a number of practical edicts concerning the future campaign:

1. All villages within ten miles of the route taken by the French army will send delegations submitting to the commanding general, informing him that they are flying the flag of the French army, which is blue, white and red.
2. Any villages that take up arms against the French army will be burnt to the ground.
3. All villages that have submitted will, beside the flag of the French army,

fly the flag of our friend the Ottoman Sultan (may God grant him a long reign!).

4. The local sheiks will ensure that all houses, goods, and properties belonging to the Mamelukes are sealed, and will make it their business to ensure that nothing is removed from them.

5. The sheiks, kadis and imams shall remain in their posts and continue to exercise their functions in the community. All inhabitants shall remain in their homes and prayers continue as usual. All Egyptians shall render thanks unto God for the destruction of the Mamelukes, proclaiming in a loud voice: "Glory to the Ottoman Sultan! Glory to his friend the French Army! May God curse the Mamelukes and bestow happiness upon the Egyptian nation."[38]

Napoleon ordered his chief of staff Berthier to have copies of this proclamation in French, Arabic and Turkish put up on the streets of Alexandria. It was also read out by town criers so that it could be understood by the largely illiterate general population. At the same time he ordered the release of the 700 galley slaves who had been brought from Malta. Many of these were Egyptians, who were encouraged to return home, taking with them copies of the proclamation. In this way, word of Napoleon's intentions spread ahead of him through the villages of the delta, to the people of Cairo, and even into Upper Egypt. These galley slaves had originally been sailors on ships captured by the Knights of Malta, and by the time of their release they had been reduced to half-starved, dehumanized wretches clad only in filthy rags. During their period with the French fleet they had been properly fed and given decent clothes. Many of them came from other parts of the Arab world, some from as far afield as "Tripoli, Algiers, Tunis, Morocco, Damascus and Syria, Smyrna [Izmir] and even Constantinople"[39] and these were given sufficient funds to enable them to reach their homes. Besides being a humanitarian gesture, this was good propaganda for Napoleon and his expedition. As in the Italian campaign, it was intended to show the indigenous people at large that the French came as benefactors, inspired by their revolutionary beliefs in the liberty, equality and fraternity of mankind.

Last of all to be disembarked were the savants, who had been largely forgotten during the rapid unloading of soldiers and essential equipment. They had simply been left to fend for themselves on their ships, sleeping on deck, begging moldy ship's biscuit and putrid water from the grudging sailors. Eventually the frigate *Montenotte* had been dispatched to make a round of the anchored fleet, picking up groups of savants from the various ships. Around sundown they were unceremoniously dumped ashore with their luggage, beyond the city walls at the dilapidated end of the eastern harbor whose quays "consisted only of a rubble of granite and marble columns."[40] From here they made their way into the city as best they could. According to one of them, "We arrived in riotous disorder, after blundering through the frightful ruins of the Arab quarter, a huge wasteland of tombs, and some stretches of arid sand with a few palm trees, fig trees and saltwort."[41] The fifty-one-year-old Vivant Denon fared even worse:

Braving the spirits of the dead, I crossed the cemetery. When I arrived at the first habitation of the living I was assailed by packs of wild dogs, which came at me from the doorways, the streets, the rooftops, their cries reverberating from house to house, from family to family . . . in order to escape the clamor of the dogs and follow a route where I wouldn't get lost, I left the streets and tried to cling to the shoreline, but the battlements and the rubble which went down to the sea barred my way. I jumped into the sea to get free of the dogs, and when the water became too deep I scaled the walls themselves. Finally, soaked to the skin, covered in sweat, overcome with fatigue and frightened out of my wits, I reached the soldiers on guard at midnight, convinced that the dogs were the sixth and most terrible of the Biblical plagues of Egypt.[42]

This must have been quite an ordeal for the aging artist, especially after weeks of seasickness.

Eventually a number of the savants made their way to the headquarters of General Caffarelli, who was meant to be in charge of them. But Caffarelli was in the throes of trying to set up the engineering corps and organize the unloading of their equipment; he simply had neither the time nor the space for the savants. His soldiers were preparing for the march on Cairo, and were having to make do as best they could amongst the ruins. He suggested that the savants do the same. By now the soldiers had occupied all the habitable spots and commandeered the wells for themselves. The savants were reduced to begging moldy rejected rations, and occasional gulps of water from the canteens of their compatriots. The lucky ones were able to hire local lodgings at inflated prices, where they slept on the floor a dozen or so to a room. The others simply lay on the ground beside their trunks and bundles, where they spent sleepless nights being devoured by mosquitoes. In order to earn some food they took to acting as messenger boys and scribes for the various army units, and volunteering as orderlies at the makeshift hospitals. This was hardly what the scientists, writers, artists and Orientalists had been led to expect.

Only the distinguished senior savants found themselves properly accommodated. Monge and Berthollet, Napoleon's favorites, were lodged in his headquarters; others, such as Dolomieu and Conté, became involved in unloading the scientific equipment that came ashore with the printing presses, to which Napoleon had given priority, along with the artillery and essential engineering gear. When Dolomieu belatedly learned of the plight of his colleagues, he set off to the French consulate to protest to Napoleon. As a result, the savants were accorded the temporary rank of private soldiers, which entitled them to rations and such shelter as could be provided. This may not have protected them from the mosquitoes, but with guards standing on duty at least their possessions were safe from the nimble-fingered local sneak-thieves who operated under cover of darkness.

Despite Denon's ordeal, he was determined to fulfill his purpose as one of the expedition's artists. Having made it into the city, next day he presented himself at Napoleon's headquarters, where he was permitted to make sketches of his commander-in-chief at work. Here he was able to sit in on a meeting between Napoleon and El-Koraïm, observing with the eye of an artist that the Egyptian

had the physiognomy of a man of intelligence, but there was something about his face which spoke of dissimulation. He had been shaken by the turn of events, but was not overwhelmed by Napoleon's loyalty and generosity towards him. He appeared to be unsure as to whether or not his defeat had been brought about by some kind of trick. Only when he saw that the French had landed 30,000 troops and columns of artillery did he definitely commit himself to Napoleon and remain loyally beside him in his headquarters.[43]

Later Denon set out on a sketching tour of the city itself, visiting the sights such as Pompey's Pillar and Cleopatra's Needle, the fresh-water reservoir and a ruined Christian church. He noticed that soldiers had taken over the public baths to do their laundry, and that the main mosque was in a sad state of disrepair. As he wandered amongst the remnant stones which had once been ancient buildings, he speculated on their age. Finally he came to the quarter by the Rosetta Gate:

Here I had an encounter which provided the most striking of contrasts. I came across a young French woman, dressed in white with her skin as pink as a rose, seated on a block of stone still covered with blood from the fighting, around her the debris of battle and dead bodies still lying about unburied. She was like the angel of the resurrection. Moved by compassion, I expressed my surprise at finding her here all alone. She replied with a touching naïveté that she was waiting for her husband so that they could go and sleep in the desert. She spoke as if she was simply going to a new home to sleep. From this you can see the quality of the women to whom love had given the courage to follow their husbands on the expedition.[44]

In fact, her husband would have been taking her "to sleep in the desert" amongst the French forces camped outside the Rosetta Gate. Had they slept alone in the desert they would certainly have fallen victim to the marauding Bedouin.

Dolomieu also found time to undertake some exploration. He sought out the ancient church of St. Athanasius, which had been converted into a mosque, and here discovered a seven-ton stone sarcophagus covered in hieroglyphs which he took to be the long-lost tomb of Alexander the Great. This find was indicative of the architectural riches which had yet to be discovered in Egypt, but it also hinted at the contemporary state of knowledge concerning Egyptian history: it was highly unlikely that Alexander the Great would have been buried in a tomb covered with ancient Egyptian hieroglyphs. Several decades later this sarcophagus would be identified as that of Nectanebo I, king of Egypt during the fourth century BC, who died some thirty years before Alexander conquered Egypt.

The citizens of Alexandria had been ordered to hand in their weapons, but otherwise were free to go about their business much as usual. In order to demonstrate their loyalty to the French, they were ordered to wear on their headdress a tricolor cockade such as the French revolutionaries had worn in their caps. As a mark of their rank, sheiks, kadis, imams and other dignitaries were allowed to keep their weapons, and were ordered to wear a tricolor sash across their chest, such as those worn by French mayors. Soldiers on guard duty outside the French headquarters were ordered to salute these dignitaries when they came for meetings with Napoleon. At the same time the city merchants were required to deposit varying sums of money with the French exchequer, a forced loan to raise local currency to pay for immediate requirements; this was to be repaid out of customs revenue from goods passing through the port. To raise larger amounts of cash, Napoleon exchanged quantities of the gold bullion seized from Malta. In a repeat of his frenetic activity in Malta, Napoleon now began issuing a whirlwind of orders, decrees and directives. For the artillery: setting up of a barracks, construction of an arsenal and a powder magazine. For the engineers: setting up of a barracks, construction of machine shops and tool depots. For the administration: offices for the different sections, hospitals (one for the wounded, one for diseases), prisons (civil, military, and for prisoners of war). For the navy: barracks, arsenal, quarantine station. The mapping of the city; the excavation and opening up of the freshwater canal to the Nile; "the names of men of the French army who were killed in the taking of Alexandria to be engraved on Pompey's Pillar" . . . And so the constant stream of orders and decrees continued to flow from headquarters, morning, noon and night.[45]

Initially, Napoleon was unwilling to delegate. He appeared to be able to attend to the smallest details, yet at the same time keep in mind the larger picture. He knew precisely what he wanted. Only when the foundations of this were laid, and he was on the point of leaving, did he appoint Kléber as governor of Alexandria. Kléber was very much a campaigning general, and expressed his disappointment at being given what he considered to be a desk job. However, taking into account the seriousness of Kléber's head wound, Napoleon insisted that his decision was final. Kléber's role as governor was to oversee the implementation of all Napoleon's projects; as far as the local population was concerned, he was merely to supervise the rule of El-Koraïm. Napoleon's instructions were clear: "To maintain as far as possible good relations with the Arabs; and to show the greatest consideration for the muftis and the principal sheiks of the country." He characterized his intentions: "We must gradually accustom these people to our outlook and way of life, and meanwhile we must allow them plenty of latitude between themselves in their internal affairs; above all, we must not interfere with their judicial system, which is founded on the divine law and keeps entirely to the Koran."[46]

VI

The March on Cairo

NAPOLEON planned to begin his march on Cairo as soon as possible. Desaix's division, which had secured the beachhead at Marabout and had not taken part in the assault on Alexandria, had afterwards advanced and camped on the outskirts of the city.

As early as the evening of July 3, just a day after the fall of Alexandria, Desaix was ordered to set out for Damanhur, forty miles to the southeast, the first stage of the 150-mile march to Cairo. Before he left, Napoleon advised him: "If attacked, screen your cavalry, show the enemy only your infantry platoons. Do not use light artillery. It is necessary to save this for the great day when we shall have to fight four or five thousand enemy horse."[1] At this stage, such advice was superfluous. The unloading of the fleet was still under way in the port, and Desaix was forced to leave with no artillery, and minimal cavalry support. Even this small contingent was in no fit state to embark upon a long march across the desert, let alone take part in a battle; the horses had not yet recovered from their long sea journey, and according to Desaix, in a vain appeal to Napoleon, "we have only two days' supply of oats for the horses, and no other fodder."[2] The men each had just four days' supply of dry biscuits, and their individual canteens of water.

Initially, the route followed the dried-up bed of the canal linking Alexandria to the Nile. Despite the state of the canal, Desaix's Bedouin guide assured him that there would be sufficient wells at the villages on the way, and that Damanhur itself was a highly civilized city four times larger than Alexandria.

Two days later, Reynier's division marched from Alexandria along

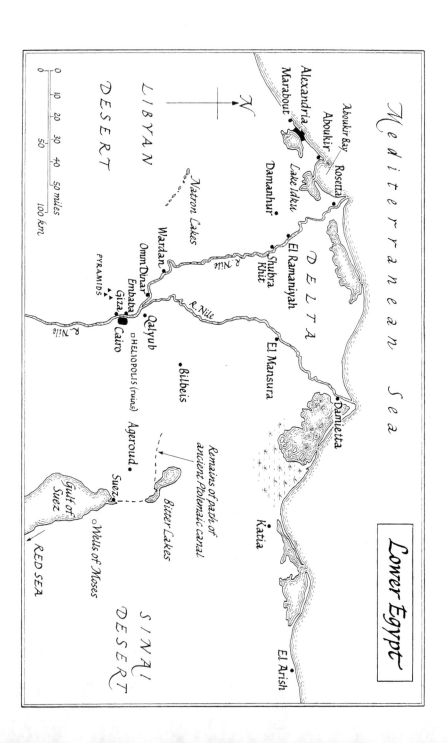

Lower Egypt

the same route, to be followed by two more divisions on the subsequent days. Meanwhile a fifth division under General Dugua left for Rosetta, some thirty miles along the coast to the east, at the entrance to the western navigational channel of the Nile. In parallel with Dugua's division, a flotilla under Captain Perrée set off for Rosetta by sea. This consisted of over a dozen gunboats and ships with a draft of less than five feet, with a complement of 600 sailors. Once Rosetta was taken, Desaix's division was to march south and rendezvous with the other four divisions at El Ramaniyah. Perrée's flotilla, augmented by captured river boats from the port at Rosetta, would transport bulk supplies of rice, lentils and other provisions down the Nile to victual all the divisions converging on El Ramaniyah.

On July 5 Napoleon held a meeting in Alexandria with thirteen local Bedouin chieftains, organized for him by El-Koraïm. These were the very men who had harassed Napoleon during his advance on Alexandria, but he succeeded in persuading them that he came as a supporter of Islam, and as such was their true friend. He assured them that the sole purpose of his presence in Egypt was to rid the country of the Mamelukes, and that once he had done this he would return to the Bedouin the land from which they had been dispossessed by the Mamelukes. The Bedouin chieftains agreed to sell Napoleon 300 good horses for use as cavalry, and 500 riding camels, as well as allowing him to hire a further 1,000 pack camels along with their minders for transport duties. They also supplied him with spies, who would travel ahead of his army during its march on Cairo, seeking out information about the Mamelukes' military movements.

For a payment of 100 piastres, the Bedouin also agreed to release the thirteen French prisoners they had taken during the advance on Alexandria. According to Bourrienne, these were duly returned and brought before Napoleon, who sought to obtain from them intelligence about life amongst "these semi-savages."[3] He asked one of the returned prisoners, "How did they treat you?" whereupon the man dissolved into tears.

"Why are you crying?" demanded Napoleon.

Between sobs, the man explained that they had been subjected to what Bourrienne tactfully describes as "the treatment so well known in the Orient."

"You big booby," remonstrated Napoleon. "That's not too bad. Serves you right for falling behind the column. You should thank heaven for having come out of it so lightly. Now stop blubbing and answer my question." But as Bourrienne drily observed, "the little time that he had spent amongst the Arabs, and the way they had treated him, had prevented him from making the least observation, and he was unable to tell his commander anything at all."

News of what had happened to these prisoners quickly spread through the ranks, leaving them with no illusions about the consequences if they were captured and their lives spared. Although this was more than half a century before the Geneva Convention (of 1863), in Europe historic practice had established various rules of war concerning the treatment of prisoners; these were on occasion violated, by mistreatment or even slaughter, but the French soldiers were unprepared for this particular violation.

In the event, the return of these prisoners was to be the only part of the agreement the Bedouin fulfilled. When the chieftains returned to their tribes they received word from Cairo that the grand mufti (the chief expert in Muslim law) had decided that the French should be placed under a *fetfa*, or *fatwa,* a decree declaring that all true Muslims should take up arms against them. In one fell swoop, Napoleon had not only lost his promised transport, but the wilderness through which his army was marching had been transformed once more into hostile territory.

Among the first to become aware of this were the columns of Dugua's division, who were forced to fend off Bedouin attacks as they made their way up the coast, then along the narrow sand spit separating the brackish Lake Idku from the sea. Only when they were halfway along the spit did they discover that their maps had not taken into account a recent change in the ever-shifting geography in and around the Nile delta. The small channel linking the lake to the sea had become wider and deeper. Dugua now found himself trapped, with the Bedouin waiting behind him at the entrance to the spit, while his entire division could muster less than half a dozen vessels, each capable of transporting only fifteen men at a time across the water. Fortunately Dugua managed to signal to Captain Perrée, whose flotilla was keeping up with them, just off the coast, and the flat landing craft came inshore and assisted in carrying the men across the channel. In an attempt to speed up this painfully slow operation, the horses and requisitioned pack camels laden with equipment were coaxed into swimming alongside the craft;

despite this, the entire operation lasted from first light until well into the night. The forty-mile march to Rosetta, which should have taken less than three days, ended up taking almost twice as long, with Dugua's division not sighting the minarets of the city until the morning of July 8.

But time was made up when they reached Rosetta, which offered no resistance. At the approach of the French the hated Mameluke governor Selim Bey had called upon the local population to slam closed the gates and take to the walls in defense of their city. But already several copies of Napoleon's declaration to the people of Egypt had reached Rosetta, and the population was in no mood to respond to Selim Bey's call to arms. Quickly sensing the situation, he and his attendant Mamelukes had fled the city.

In contrast to the dusty ruins of Alexandria, the French soldiers found Rosetta "surrounded by gardens filled with palms and orchards containing dates, lemons, oranges, figs, apricots and all manner of other fruit."⁴ The town itself had well-built modern houses belonging to European merchants along the quayside bordering the Nile. The inhabitants stood at the doorways of their houses watching as the columns of French troops marched past, some of the locals even coming out to offer bread, fruit and water to the soldiers. Soon the plentiful market reopened and the soldiers were able to replenish their rations of dry biscuit with fresh fruit (at only slightly exaggerated prices). According to the journal kept by Dugua's chief of staff, Colonel Laugier, Rosetta "was the first pleasant impression we have experienced since our arrival in Egypt."⁵ The troops were similarly impressed.

In line with Napoleon's orders to all his commanders to "make friends and respect the mosques," Dugua quickly summoned the local dignitaries, making plain to them his peaceful intentions and his respect for Islam. He assured them that all promissory notes issued by the French army in payment for provisions would be honored by the paymaster-general in Alexandria. As a result he was able to start purchasing in bulk the rice and lentils to be transported by Perrée's flotilla down the Nile. But this pleasant interlude would not last long. Just over twenty-four hours after Dugua's arrival, he received a messenger from Napoleon, who had assumed that Dugua had already arrived at his rendezvous thirty miles down the Nile at El Ramaniyah. It looked as if Dugua was now in danger of holding up the entire advance on Cairo; there was nothing for it but to secure Rosetta and set off up the Nile at once.

As per instructions, Dugua proceeded to garrison Rosetta, leaving behind Menou, who was still recovering from the wounds he had received in the taking of Alexandria, as military governor of the city. Shortly after midnight on July 10, his division began the march south, with Perrée's flotilla following them up the Nile. As dawn broke, the marching French columns were greeted by the timeless sight of the lush Nile delta. Colonel Laugier recorded, "We followed the main channel of the Nile, passing through cultivated fields criss-crossed by irrigation ditches filled with water. The local peasants stood beside the road to welcome us and watch us pass. They seemed prosperous enough and had a proud almost majestic air. Their women were joyful and greeted us with soft cries which uncannily resembled the cooing of doves."[6] The soldiers gathered watermelons to supplement their rations, with their officers under strict orders that these should be paid for. On July 11 the advance columns of Dugua's division began arriving at El Ramaniyah, where they linked up with the divisions led by Desaix and Reynier, and the two following divisions, which had marched overland from Alexandria. By contrast with Dugua's men, these four divisions were in a pitiful state.

Desaix's men had departed from Alexandria during the night of July 3–4. As night faded and the sun rose over the vast arid wilderness, the soldiers began to experience the debilitating heat and privations of the Egyptian desert, conditions for which they were particularly ill-prepared. In the interests of secrecy at the embarkation ports, the men had been issued with no equipment suitable for the desert. Their woolen uniforms, intended for campaigning in Europe, soon proved all but unbearable as the heat rose to 35°C (95°F) and beyond. Their individual water canteens were quickly emptied, and there were no water wagons to replenish them. The men soon began to suffer from extremes of thirst and the debilitating effects of dehydration, and as if this was not enough, the increasingly bedraggled columns trudging across the sand now faced the *khamsin*, or "poisoned wind." According to Lieutenant Thurman, "in the midst of a fine morning the atmosphere became darkened by a reddish haze, consisting of infinitely many tiny particles of burning dust. Soon we could barely see the disc of the sun. The unbearable wind dried our tongues, burned our eyelids, and induced an insatiable thirst. All sweating ceased, breathing became difficult, arms and legs became leaden with fatigue, and it was all but impossible even to speak."[7] Since time immemorial the fierce hot *khamsin* from the hinterland desert had been the curse of Egypt, its dust and grit finding its way into every-thing—penetrating the eyes and the nostrils, getting into bread and all food, to such an extent that teeth were ground down during eating. This is particularly noticeable in the ancient Egyptian mummies, whose teeth were sanded so smooth that some of the first archaeologists specu-lated that they belonged to an earlier evolutionary stage in our dental development.

In time the leading columns of Desaix's division began to come across a number of remote villages. These typically consisted of "makeshift dwellings just four feet high with walls made of earth or sometimes mud bricks baked in the sun. They differed in size according to the size of the families which lived in them. You could only enter them bent low, and inside you couldn't stand upright."[8] When Desaix's columns came to the first villages, the soldiers broke ranks and besieged the wells, quickly drinking them dry. At word of the advancing French army, the villagers had fled, taking their livestock with them. The villages themselves were eerily deserted, with no sign of food, which meant there was no opportunity to supplement the soldiers' meager rations of dried biscuits, many of which had become worm-eaten during the long sea voyage. As the men pressed on, they found that the village wells had been filled with stones and refuse, which the sappers labored to clear. According to the savant Denon, "at the bottom of these wells they would find just a little brackish muddy water, which they would scrape up with cups and distribute amongst the men in small mea-sures like shots of brandy."[9] By now there was no mistaking the fact that they were traveling through territory that was more than just geographically hostile, and once again lines of mounted Bedouin began harassing the flanks, threatening to carry off any stragglers.

Reports differ, but it seems that despite such hardships the men, at least at the outset, retained a measure of resilience. In the words of the ever-observant Denon, "This was the first foray of our troops into another part of the world. Though separated from their homeland by seas infested with enemy ships, and passing through deserts a thou-sand times more dreadful still, such foreign circumstances dampened neither their courage nor their good spirits."[10]

But this was only the beginning, and soon the French would begin finding themselves in even more "foreign circumstances." Nicolas-Philibert Desvernois, a twenty-seven-year-old lieutenant in a cavalry regiment of Desaix's division, recounted how he supervised the 200 men of his platoon in setting up their camp, and then set off with a military patrol to reconnoiter the surrounding desert.

I hadn't covered a kilometer before I came across an encampment of 150 Arab tents made of brown and black wool. They were deserted, but while cautiously searching amongst them I came across an old Arab with an old woman, both stark naked, lying on a mat. In order to allay their fears, I gestured my peaceful intentions and tossed them a Spanish gold piastre. The old man sat up and began gesticulating towards the desert. I understood that his fellow tribesmen who had departed during the night were going to return and attack us.[11]

Soon after Desvernois returned to his camp, he noticed "a great cloud of dust rising on the horizon." Sure enough, this was the tribesmen coming to attack him, but he and his men were waiting for them, and soon drove them off.

Denon records an even more bizarre encounter. On their second day out from Alexandria, several soldiers came across an upsetting sight in the midst of the desert some way off from a village: a woman, her face covered in blood, carrying a newborn baby, was wandering blindly across the sand. The soldiers were curious, and summoned the column's Arab guide, who also acted as an interpreter. They learned that the woman's plight was the result of the jealous rage of her husband; she didn't dare beg for mercy on her own account, but prayed that they might save the innocent child, who was the cause of her husband's rage. The soldiers were deeply moved, and forgetting their own needs began pressing on her their rations and precious water. Then they saw an angry man approaching them from across the desert. He came up to the woman and dashed the food and water from her hand. "Stop!" he cried. "She has betrayed her honor and blackened my name. This child has brought about my disgrace, he is the son of a crime." When the soldiers tried to oppose him, his jealous fury was rekindled, where-upon "he pulled out a dagger and stabbed the woman to death, then seized the child and smashed it to the ground. Stupefied with anger, he stood immobile, gazing fixedly at the soldiers surrounding him, daring them to avenge what he had done."[12]

As a consequence of this incident, Denon gained from their interpreter a curious insight into the Egyptian way of life. Apparently, for a Muslim this man's behavior would have been regarded as evil not because he had stabbed the woman to death, but because he had not allowed the will of God to run its course, "for if God had not wished her to die, at the end of forty days in the desert the unfortunate woman could have been taken in and looked after by charity."[13] The full extent of the French incomprehension of Egypt was gradually being revealed: first had been the men's incredulity at Egyptian behavior (the woman buried alive with her child in Alexandria, the old man and his wife abandoned naked in the Bedouin camp); now it was their inability to understand the Egyptian way of thinking. They were in another continent: here it was not just the climate and the landscape, or the appearance and language of the people, which was different from Europe. *Everything* was different.

As the columns of Desaix's division marched further across the desert, the soldiers found themselves undergoing another weird experience. When they marched forward each morning, "soon after the rising of the sun the objects ahead became distorted to the point where they were no longer recognizable ... distant villages appeared as if surrounded by flood waters from the Nile, which seemed to spill over the entire landscape." The men had never before experienced mirages, which at first perplexed them, and then began filling them with superstitious misgivings when "what at one moment appeared to be a sheet of water vanished as they advanced and became transformed into the utterly parched and arid ground of the desert."[14] The very world itself appeared to be falling apart, and many of the soldiers began regarding such mirages as a kind of fatal omen.

Desaix's leading division finally made it to the town of Damanhur on July 7; their forty-mile march had taken four days. The sight of Damanhur at the edge of the wilderness, with its domes and minarets poking up through the green palm trees, had initally encouraged the men, but as they marched into the town itself, this prospect too appeared to have been something of a mirage. Damanhur hardly lived up to the fulsome praise of the guide. Apart from the mosques and a few houses belonging to rich cotton merchants, the town consisted mainly of alleyways lined with primitive baked-mud dwellings. But it was not all disappointment. In the market the soldiers found meat, fruit, bread and dried beans for sale. They had little money to bargain for extra rations, but soon found that the Arab vendors were willing to accept the shiny brass buttons from their uniforms as currency, and in no time a rapid trade was established.

Reynier's division, which was following Desaix on the march to

Damanhur, fared far worse. Unlike most of the expeditionary force, who came from the Army of Italy, these were men from the Army of the Rhine, who had not fought under Napoleon before, had not experienced his charismatic leadership, and felt little loyalty towards a man whom they regarded as no more than an upstart young Corsican. The soldiers, and officers, of the Army of the Rhine were notorious for their indiscipline and unwillingness to obey orders with which they disagreed. This was after all the army that had adopted that most revolutionary of anthems, "La Marseillaise," as its battle song:

> Liberty, beloved Liberty,
> Fight alongside her defenders!*

It was the soldiers of the Army of the Rhine who had resisted the Directory's attempt to have Desaix arrested. When a good general gained their loyalty they stood by him, taking their lead from his example. And this was certainly the case with their commander in Egypt, the twenty-seven-year-old Swiss-born Jean-Louis-Ebenezer Reynier, a highly intelligent and brave soldier who had also earned their respect by looking after them. However, much like his men, Reynier was also a willful individualist, liable to act on whim when the spirit so moved him, and quick to pick an argument with anyone who questioned his decisions. He tended to treat staff officers with disdain, and simply disregarded any higher orders he considered wrongheaded. The Revolution had certainly produced a new breed of young generals, and a new breed of fighting men, who together were capable of defeating any army in Europe when they believed in what they were doing. Such men had been released from a social hierarchy where superiors were simply obeyed; their strength now came from their self-belief. Over the years, the revolutionary mob had begun to evolve into individual citizens who held their own opinions and acted accordingly.

It did not take General Reynier long to find fault with his orders after leaving Alexandria. With some justice, he complained that his men were insufficiently rested after their long sea voyage. Compared

---

* In fact, a later verse in this song specifically refers to the invading German army which the Army of the Rhine had faced:

> Do you hear in the countryside
> The roar of those savage soldiers
> Who come to . . . cut the throats of our sons, our comrades.

to most of the others, his division had been lucky: they had not been involved in the assault on Alexandria, and had merely guarded the beachhead alongside Desaix's division. But there was no denying that Napoleon's haste to move on Cairo had resulted in some lapses in organization. For the first leg of the march from Alexandria he had made no adequate provision for supplies—a not uncommon failing with Napoleon, who as an artillery officer had never fully grasped the needs and limits of infantry on the move. In Italy this had not proved a serious failing: his army had lived off the land. In Egypt, this had proved possible for Dugua moving south from Rosetta along the cultivated edges of the Nile delta, but in the desert there was simply nothing to live off. Even Desaix, whose men were the first to enter the villages, quickly found that they had been deserted, all livestock gone, their stores of food all vanished. Only occasionally did one of his more resourceful officers discover some small concealed cache of dried lentils or dates, which hardly went far amongst the men. Likewise, the assurance of the local guides that there were wells along the route to Damanhur was only true in the most literal sense. There were indeed a few village wells, but not sufficient to water a division of 4,600 soldiers. Desaix's men had quickly drunk almost all the water available, with the result that the men of Reynier's following division soon ran out. Their general's open criticism of this state of affairs filtered down to the men, who were reduced to a demoralized and pitiful state. First the heat, then the lack of water, began to take a terrible toll. The ranks of marching soldiers started disintegrating into broken groups, a number of which soon fell into disarray. Some of the men began running after the mirages; others stumbled and fell to the ground, so enfeebled that they were unable to rise; others strayed off into the desert, where they fell prey to the Bedouin or were simply never seen again. One member of Reynier's division described how, after blundering over burning sands towards visions of water that always disappeared,

all of us were overcome with despair. My sadness isolated me from the sufferings of others. I was dumb to the cries and groans of my companions in misfortune who implored our assistance as they lay dying. Too much suffering closes the heart to all feeling for humanity, and drained of all emotion I saw them fall at my feet. Each man followed his own path in mournful silence. We barely looked with compassion at the mutilated bodies we encountered at every pace. . . . When finally Damanhur appeared before us, we felt the same joy as sailors seeing a rainbow after a storm.[15]

As indicated by the reference to mutilated bodies above, the Bedouin continued to harass the outer columns of the advancing divisions, picking off stragglers, isolated soldiers, or even occasional messengers. According to Denon: "Adjutant-general Galois was killed carrying an order from the general-in-chief [Napoleon]" and "Adjutant Delanau was taken prisoner just a few paces from the army whilst crossing a ravine: the Arabs demanded a price for his ransom, then disagreed amongst themselves whilst sharing this out, and to put an end to the dispute, blew out the brains of this fine young man." Denon also recalled how "Mireur, a distinguished officer, who was suffering from a bout of melancholic distraction and did not respond when called to come closer, was assassinated 100 paces from an outpost."[16] In fact there are several versions of this particular incident, involving the cavalry commander General Mireur. According to his fellow officer Desvernois, the incident happened later at Damanhur, where Mireur angrily confronted Napoleon. During the course of this encounter he blamed Napoleon for the suffering of his men on the march from Alexandria, denouncing him in no uncertain terms for his ineptitude over supplies, even going so far as to condemn the entire expedition as a reckless adventure which was doomed from the outset. In Mireur's stated opinion, the sole purpose of the expedition appeared to be nothing more than to gratify Napoleon's personal quest for glory. Napoleon apparently heard him out in silence, and then simply turned on his heels and left. Whereupon Mireur, realizing that his career was at an end, fell into a deep depression. According to Desvernois, "The following morning before daybreak he mounted his horse, rode out into the desert, and then committed suicide by shooting himself in the head."[17] Desvernois even claims to have found Mireur's body, still holding the pistol in his hand. However, several contemporary memoirs cast doubt on this suicide, and there is some evidence that Desvernois's account may all have been hearsay. The official version resembled Denon's account, stating that the general had been murdered and robbed by Bedouins.

Whatever the case, there is no doubting that a number of soldiers on the grueling march from Alexandria to Damanhur did commit suicide. Adjutant General Boyer, in a letter to his father, expressly states that "some, seeing the suffering of their comrades, blew their own brains out."[18] Corporal François also states in his memoirs that "many soldiers who were unable to get water killed themselves."[19] Such sensational stories would inevitably have spread like wildfire through the army, and one could easily have become attached to General Mireur's death. Precisely how many men took their lives during the course of this forty-mile march through unforgiving desert without adequate supplies remains a vexed question. Such lurid events are always prone to exaggeration; on the other hand, it is hardly surprising that men were reduced to ultimate despair in such alien circumstances—the maddening *khamsin*, the mirages, the delirium of heat and thirst, the marauding Bedouin, and the sight of their dying comrades. Even the more reliable sources tend to split on this matter, and not always along expected lines. The French historian La Jonquière, who often favored Napoleon, claimed that men even took to committing suicide in front of their generals, whereas the twentieth-century Egyptian historian Shafik Ghorbal regarded such reports as "grossly exaggerated."[20] Most modern sources now tend to agree that "a few hundred men"[21] amongst the four divisions that marched on Damanhur (around 18,000 men in all) were lost on the way—either died of privation, committed suicide, or were killed by the Bedouin. Many thousands of others must have suffered dreadfully, for it is known that the leading two divisions were forced to leave Alexandria without medical supplies, as the vessel carrying much of the medicine and hospital equipment had accidentally been sunk in the harbor during the rapid unloading of the fleet. Only after the departure of Desaix and Reynier was it possible to equip six field ambulances. Even Napoleon in his memoirs, written in exile on St. Helena, when he tended to adopt a rather rose-tinted view of his former exploits, conceded in a somewhat flimsy gloss: "No water could be found anywhere on the way from Alexandria [to Damanhur]. The army was not equipped to march over such terrain. It suffered a great deal from the heat and the sun and the absence of any shade or water. It developed a dislike for those vast deserted plains, and especially for the Bedouins."[22]

Napoleon himself remained in Alexandria until July 7. The day before he left, he dictated a note to the French chargé d'affaires in Constantinople: "We are marching on Cairo. You must convince the Porte of our firm resolution to keep them fully informed of what we are doing. An ambassador is to be appointed [in Constantinople], and will not be long in arriving."[23] If nothing else, this would seem to indicate that Napoleon still believed the Turkish Porte would not regard his invasion of Egypt as a warlike act against what was at least nominally part of the Ottoman Empire—and that he believed Talleyrand would soon arrive in Constantinople to resolve any problems that arose. On this optimistic note he then departed from Alexandria late on the afternoon of July 7, accompanied by his savant friends Monge and Berthollet, together with the French consul Magallon as his adviser. Riding swiftly through the night with his staff, Napoleon soon overtook the columns of the last two divisions, reaching Damanhur the following morning to join up with Desaix and Reynier. Throughout that day and the following night the last two divisions continued arriving at Damanhur.

Napoleon was to remain for two days in Damanhur, during which he held a council of war with his generals. It proved to be a stormy affair. Whether or not it was Mireur who confronted him, there is no doubt that the twenty-eight-year-old commander-in-chief faced some heavy criticism from his generals, who were furious that their men had been forced to undergo such an ordeal without supplies or backup of any kind. The twentieth-century English historian P. G. Elgood, who had some experience in such matters, having been a senior military officer in Egypt, blamed Napoleon's shortcomings on his staff. They were the ones who had naively accepted the local guides' assurances that there were sufficient wells en route, without troubling to investigate the actual situation. But it is difficult to see how they could have done this: they had no time to check their information, and any scouting party would have been picked off by hostile Bedouin. This said, there is no doubt that there were deficiencies amongst Napoleon's staff. His chief of staff, Berthier, had certainly proved his merit on the Italian campaign, but according to Elgood, amongst the "headquarters staff of 142 officers . . . the quality of some of its members was uncertain. Influence in Paris played a part in the appointments."[24] Although the generals for the expedition were all picked by Napoleon himself, there is no doubt that the Directory had a hand in other, more cushy appointments. However, all are agreed that one of the main factors, if not the leading one, in the debacle of the march on Damanhur was Napoleon's haste to reach Cairo. His thinking was evident: he was banking on a quick, decisive victory, which would present the Porte with a fait accompli, rather than a longer campaign with large enemy loss of life, which was liable to antagonize them.

Years later, during his exile in St. Helena, Napoleon admitted, "It would be difficult to give an idea of the disgust, the discontent, the melancholy, the despair of that army during its first weeks in Egypt."[25]

And he recalled his council of war at Damanhur: "The generals and officers gave voice to their discontent with even greater force than the men."[26] Some admission: his generals were a tough, campaign-hardened, and in many cases foul-mouthed lot, who were not known for mincing their words. But the young, diminutive Napoleon evidently stood his ground. Nothing was resolved at this meeting. Napoleon remained adamant in his insistence upon haste, and the generals remained furious. The chief discontents seem to have been amongst the cavalry. One officer remembered "seeing his most distinguished generals, Lannes and Murat, in a fit of rage flinging their braided hats to the sand and stamping on them, in the presence of their men."[27] This was the dashing Murat who had served with such loyal devotion in Italy. The army was in open disarray, a situation which so angered Napoleon that on one occasion "he strode up to a group of discontented generals, confronted the tallest amongst them, and told him vehemently: 'What you are saying is sedition. Watch out, or I'll have you on a charge. Don't think your five foot ten inches will prevent you from being hauled in front of a firing squad in a couple of hours.'"[28] This tall general was almost certainly the charismatic mulatto cavalry commander Dumas, who had from the outset made it clear that he had little respect for Napoleon, and quickly became a focus of opposition to him (perhaps the reason why discontent was greatest amongst the cavalry).

Ironically, it was Napoleon's insistence upon haste, as much as anything, which now held the disparate parts of his army together, uniting them in their dissatisfaction with their commander. The divisions of Desaix and Reynier had less than forty-eight hours' rest before they were ordered to continue; the others had even less. Throughout the night of July 9–10, the four divisions departed from Damanhur. It was just fifteen miles from Damanhur to the rendezvous with Dugua and the supply flotilla on the Nile at El Ramaniyah. The terrain on this stretch of the march was much less forbidding, there were even stretches showing signs of remnant cultivation, and the men were motivated by the prospect of proper rations. Even so, the wells remained for the most part inadequate, or sabotaged, and once again the men were soon suffering from the effects of severe dehydration.

The first columns reached the banks of the Nile on the afternoon of July 10 (22 Messidor). Although the river had sunk to its lowest level since the annual flood just under a year previously, it nonetheless proved an inspiring sight. According to Desvernois, "When the soldiers caught sight of the Nile they broke ranks, rushed forward, and threw themselves into the water. Some leapt in fully clothed, complete with their rifles, others took time to undress before running and plunging in, and they remained bathing in the water for several hours. Some even drank themselves to death with so much water."[29] On the banks of the river the soldiers came across fields of watermelons and began gorging themselves; the men quickly christened 22 Messidor "The Feast of St. Water Melon."

The excessive diet of watermelons would soon wreak its effect on the weakened digestive systems of the soldiers. Within two days, diarrhea was so rife that after consulting with his chief medical officer Napoleon issued orders that "commanders will instruct their soldiers to eat very little of the fruit they call pumpkins or watermelons unless these are cooked: only then are they healthy and nourishing."[30]

The following day Dugua's division arrived from Rosetta, but to Napoleon's fury it was not accompanied by Perrée's flotilla on the Nile. In his effort to reach the rendezvous at El Ramaniyah on time, Dugua had disobeyed orders and gone ahead of the slow-moving flotilla. The original flotilla had been augmented by a number of craft requisitioned at Rosetta, most of which were *chebeks* (three-masted Levantine sailing craft, which could also be rowed), so that the flotilla now numbered sixty vessels, of which twenty-five were armed. This unwieldy group had encountered considerable difficulty in navigating the Nile channels. These were now at their lowest, and at several bends in the river some of the flotilla's craft became grounded on sandbanks, taking time and considerable maneuvering to drag them free. Then there was trouble with the wind, which frequently dropped, or changed direction. It would be over twenty-four hours later before the flotilla finally arrived at El Ramaniyah.

By this time Napoleon's scouts, aided by their Arab guides, had learned that the fearsome Mameluke leader Murad Bey had set out from Cairo, heading north along the west bank of the Nile with a force of 3,000 Mameluke cavalry and 2,000 attendant infantry. According to Napoleon,[31] he himself had a force of 20,000 men. Most of these were foot soldiers, although he did by this stage have limited cavalry properly horsed and some extra artillery unloaded from Perrée's flotilla. Napoleon now took the opportunity to address his troops, and ordered a full-scale review of all five divisions for the afternoon of July 11. The refreshed troops spent all morning polishing their boots, cleaning and brushing their uniforms, bathing and shaving, checking their equipment, their packs and their rifles. This was intended as a timely exercise in re-establishing discipline and military pride. The men of each regiment were stirred by marching before their colors, each in their distinctive uniforms.*

By mid-afternoon, the five divisions of the Egyptian expedition were drawn up outside El Ramaniyah. At three P.M. the drum-roll sounded, and Napoleon appeared on horseback before his men; he and his cavalcade of staff officers now passed in review along the lines of the five divisions, stopping before each one to call forward its senior officers, to whom he gave a rousing address, intended to be relayed on to the men. In this he informed them that their sufferings were at an end; perhaps as early as the morrow they would be confronting the Mamelukes, and the veteran heroes of the Army of the Rhine would triumph gloriously over these barbarians. There would be victories to be won and deserts to cross, but "after this we will arrive in Cairo where we will have as much food as we want!"[32] Vertray recalled: "This speech had a great effect. It looked as if [Napoleon] had at last convinced us all of the purpose and greatness of his plans. Each commander proclaimed to his soldiers that we would soon be going into battle. The news filled the whole army with enthusiasm, and after they were dismissed and broke ranks they began meticulously checking their rifles, sharpening their bayonets, testing their firing flints, at the same time breaking into song."[33] Other firsthand sources suggest that not all the men were quite so easily won over. Napoleon evidently went out of his way to address some smaller groups of soldiers directly, and here the men who had survived their ordeal in the desert gave him a somewhat less rapturous reception. At the end of one badly received speech a soldier called out: "Well, general, are you going to take us to India?" "I wouldn't set out on such a journey with soldiers like you," replied Napoleon dismissively.[34] This indicates that by now the men had got wind of the fact that Egypt was not intended as the expedition's final

---

* As the great German military theorist Clausewitz perceptively noted, a distinctive uniform plays an essential role in a soldier's life: it makes him identify with the glorious traditions of his regiment, and at the same time its very distinctiveness renders him noticeable, making it difficult for him to desert—for better or for worse, he is identified with his regiment.

destination. Other generals found themselves facing similar insubordination when they passed on the gist of Napoleon's speech to their men.
Engineer General Caffarelli, who had lost his leg on the Rhine, was
heckled by a wit: "It's all right for you, general, you've still got one foot
in France." Caffarelli took this in good humor, and the men responded
with cheers as he stomped off.[35] Caffarelli was a popular figure; indeed,
the generals closer to their men, such as he and Desaix, appear to have
played an important role in winning over many of those not convinced
by Napoleon's charismatic oratory. (It is noticeable that in his speech
Napoleon specifically appealed to the men from the Army of the Rhine;
he could be more sure of the men who had fought with him in the Army
of Italy.)

Napoleon now gained intelligence that Murad Bey and his Mamelukes
were preparing to make a stand at the village of Shubra Khit, on the
Nile some nine miles upstream on the direct route to Cairo. Desaix
was ordered to advance along the western bank of the Nile, with his
men formed into squares in order to resist any attack from Mameluke
cavalry. These squares usually consisted of lines of men three deep;
when attacked they took up their positions: the outer rank kneeled,
the second rank crouched, the inner rank remained upright. All had
their bayonets at the ready and were also able to open fire. As long
as the men held steady, such a line was sufficient to deter all but the
most determined heavy cavalry attack. Few horses could be induced
to plunge into a three-deep barrier of steel bayonets. This square formation had the effect of giving the men solidarity, both material and
psychological; it also made retreat or flight all but impossible. Like the
men's uniforms, this military item had its double edge.

As Desaix's division moved forward, it caught sight of some advanced
units of Mameluke cavalry.* Initially these consisted of just a few scouts,
reconnoitering the advancing French vanguard, but they were soon
joined by a larger group around 300 strong. These charged diagonally
across the French line of advance, apparently with the aim of driving
between Desaix's left flank and the Nile. Noting this, Desaix ordered
his men to halt, fix bayonets, and take up their positions in a stationary
square. At the same time he ordered his small detachment of cavalry,
which included General Murat, to try and cut off the Mamelukes' line

---

* Sources differ as to the precise timing of this encounter, which may well have
happened *before* Desaix arrived at El Ramaniyah.

of retreat. The Mamelukes quickly realized what was happening and fell back. This particularly disappointed Murat, who was hell-bent on glory. Indeed, his lust for glory and women had now led him to engrave his cavalry sword with the slogan *l'honneur et les dames* (honor and women). Murat may have flung down his hat in disgust at Napoleon's conduct of the campaign, but he was not about to miss an opportunity for heroism. When he saw the Mameluke cavalry retreating, he set off alone at full gallop in pursuit. After a while they turned to confront him, whereupon he halted and called for them to send out their best man to fight him in single combat. The Mamelukes stood their ground uncertainly; although they did not understand Murat's words, his actions were plain enough. But they had no tradition of single combat taking place between an assembly of two confronting foes, and suspected that Murat's action was part of some deceptive tactic. Ignoring his taunts, they turned on their heel and rode back to rejoin their main force at Shubra Khit.

Napoleon now ordered his main force to advance along the west bank of the Nile; at the same time Captain Perrée's flotilla of sixty craft was to proceed in parallel upstream. The twenty-five vessels forming the armed vanguard of the flotilla served the purpose of protecting the French flank against attack from an enemy flotilla, which Napoleon had learned was advancing downstream from Cairo. The other thirty-five vessels would enable him to transfer troops quickly across the Nile if he needed to confront the enemy on the far bank.

For safety, and to prevent any hindrance to his fighting troops, Napoleon transferred some of his pack animals as well as all non-combatants onto Perrée's flotilla. These his secretary Bourrienne, the officers' wives and women, who were no longer traveling incognito, as well as Monge, Berthollet and the accompanying savants. However, some of the pack donkeys and non-combatants must have been left behind, for it was now that the presence of the savants began to attract the suspicions of the soldiers, who noticed them making observations, gathering plant samples, and writing down notes as the army advanced. Denon, in particular, was always conspicuous, making his sketches. Rumor soon spread that these "braying donkeys" were in fact the reason for the entire expedition. They were the ones who had persuaded Napoleon to embark upon this madcap scheme, in the course of which good soldiers were suffering and dying. The growing distrust and positive dislike for the savants was only partly alleviated when the officers made public fun of them: as the troops lined up in their formation squares ready to begin their advance the officers would call out, to the widespread merriment of the soldiers, "Donkeys and savants into the middle!"

During the evening of July 12, the remaining four divisions—commanded by Reynier, Vial, Bon and Dugua—set off behind Desaix. The close presence of the Nile reassured the soldiers that this was not to be another desert ordeal, and they covered the nine miles to the outskirts of Shubra Khit under cover of darkness with revived spirits, despite the arduous business of being made to maintain line and march in squares. On arrival each division took up its position in a square six deep, rather than the usual three, with artillery stationed at each corner. Napoleon had decided upon this extra defensive mode as a precaution against any unforeseen Mameluke tactics.

The fact was, neither he nor anyone else really knew what to expect from the Mamelukes. They retained a forbidding historic reputation, largely on account of their crushing victory over St. Louis' crusade in the thirteenth century, when they had been the most formidable fighting force known to the Western world. French military tactics had made great advances during the ensuing five centuries, to the point where *they* were now the most formidable fighting force known to the Western world; yet no one knew whether the Mamelukes had made their own similar advances. Napoleon had read Volney's description in *Voyage en Égypte* of their fearless but chaotic cavalry charges, but these had been their tactics (or lack of them) in their small-scale disputes amongst rival groups. What would they do when they united to form an army, and came face to face with a foreign enemy? It was known that they now possessed artillery, and if their battle tactics had improved over the centuries as much as those of the French, they might well prove invincible.

Napoleon allowed his soldiers a short snatched sleep at their stations, before having them roused at sunrise by the stirring sound of military bands playing "La Marseillaise." The men took up their battle positions, their choruses ringing out through the sunlit desert air from division to division:

> *Aux armes, citoyens!*
> *Formez vos bataillons . . .*
>
> (To arms, citizens!
> Form your battalions . . .)

Meanwhile the Mamelukes appeared out of the desert before them in battle formation, standing in one long line. According to cavalry officer Desvernois, presumably with the aid of a telescope:

It was a magnificent sight. In the distance, the desert beneath the blue sky, before us these beautiful Arab steeds, sumptuously harnessed, snorting, neighing, prancing lightly and gracefully beneath their martial riders, who were covered with dazzling arms inlaid with gold and jewels. They were clad in varied brilliantly-colored costumes, some wearing turbans bedecked with egret feathers, others wearing golden helmets, armed with sabers, lances, maces, spears, rifles, axes and daggers, each with three double-barreled pistols, two attached by cord to the twin pommels of their saddle, the other tucked into a belt on the left side of their stomach.[36]

Years later, at the end of his life, Napoleon would remember how "the sun touched their helmets and coats of mail, making their fine line glimmer in all its brilliance."[37] According to Desvernois: "The novelty and richness of this spectacle dazzled our soldiers," but not in the sense that they were intimidated; far from it, for "from then on they began to dream of pillage."[38]

The line of Mameluke cavalry extended west in one long sweep from the bank of the Nile out into the desert, outflanking the French squares. Murad Bey's Mameluke force had by now been joined, in a rare display of solidarity amongst such independent chieftains, by the beys and their men from the various delta regions they controlled. Assorted Bedouin groups could also be seen riding about in the desert to the west of the French squares. Behind the line of Mamelukes was a mixed force of Egyptian foot soldiers and armed attendants of the Mamelukes; estimates vary, but most sources agree that the French force of 18,000 men, with 2,000 held in reserve, now probably faced an almost equal number of Mamelukes and attendant infantry. The French squares were in fact oblongs, extending 300 yards or so at the front and back, and fifty yards at the sides. These contained thirty-six artillery pieces ranged at their corners, allowing each to fire over a 180° arc, yet also allowing the front eighteen to focus their fire on any particular point at the same time. But to Napoleon's irritation, his left flank remained exposed: he could see no sign of Perrée's flotilla beyond the palm trees lining the banks of the Nile.

As the sun rose in the sky, the opposing forces remained warily watching one another amidst an uncanny silence. This state of affairs went on for a seemingly unending hour, during which the tension rose to an all but unbearable pitch amongst the French ranks. Then the French soldiers became aware of cries and movement along the Mameluke line, various horsemen galloping wildly up and down in front of the others, brandishing their arms, with no apparent purpose except presumably to encourage their men. After this a number of individuals, and then some seemingly disordered groups, began charging down towards the French squares, pulling up in the face of the gleaming bayonets, then turning and galloping between the squares, and around the back, apparently seeking a way into this porcupine of steel, finally riding back between the squares to their own lines. The French sharpshooters opened fire whenever the charging Mamelukes came within range, and a few of them fell.

Suddenly, amidst this sporadic gunfire came the sound of artillery to the west. Captain Perrée's flotilla had at last arrived, but it had seemingly overshot the French line and sailed into an ambush consisting of Murad Bey's armed flotilla and a number of concealed gun batteries on the river banks. There was nothing Napoleon could do but watch from a distance. His forces were too far away and committed to their squares, as the charges from the Mameluke line now began increasing in ferocity and number.

A charging Mameluke was indeed an impressive sight. At full gallop he could fire his carbine with some accuracy, and he would follow this by discharging his pistols at closer range. Next he used his *djerid*, a short, light spear, flung like a javelin, and in closer hand-to-hand combat he wielded his razor-sharp scimitar with deadly accuracy and power, capable of slicing off a human head with one blow. Some Mamelukes could even slash with scimitars in both hands, whilst holding their horse's reins between their teeth. As Napoleon himself observed with some admiration: "The Mamelukes displayed all their skill and courage. They were at one with their horses, which appeared to sense their every wish ... having fired their six weapons they would outflank the line of sharpshooters and pass between the squares with marvelous dexterity."[39] But all this quixotic heroism was to no avail. When the Mamelukes eventually made a concerted grand charge they were met with barrages of artillery fire, grapeshot and more general rifle fire from the French squares. After ineffectually swirling about in a vain quest for a weak spot, they rode back to their positions, leaving over 300 dead scattered over the sandy wilderness before and behind the French squares. During what appeared to be a hurried conference between Murad Bey and the other Mameluke leaders on a hillock overlooking the field of battle, there was a thunderous explosion from the direction of the river, where Perrée's flotilla was still trying to fight its way out of the ambush. A few moments later the entire Mameluke force turned and galloped away across the desert, simply abandoning the nine guns they had set up on the outskirts of Shubra Khit. Napoleon watched impotently: he had only 200 operational cavalry, and could not risk sending them in pursuit. His tactic of concentrating his men in defensive squares had been vindicated, and his soldiers had experienced for themselves their ability to withstand the dreaded Mameluke cavalry. Yet the undeniable fact remained: most of the enemy had lived to fight again. As soon as it became plain that the Mamelukes would not return, Napoleon hastened to the river to discover what had happened to Perrée's flotilla.

The previous day, after embarking from El Ramaniyah, the flotilla had kept alongside the advancing land army, but during the night they had lost contact with the forces onshore and apparently become becalmed. Not until eight in the morning, well after sunrise, had the favorable north wind arisen, allowing them to proceed down the Nile. In the words of Lieutenant Laval Grandjean, who was aboard the flotilla, "We did not know whether the army was ahead of us or behind us. We therefore sailed on with the idea of stopping at the first village we came across, to find out whether or not the army had passed."[40] Partly because of an increasingly strong north wind, and partly because they had no idea of the French army's position, Perrée's flotilla had then sailed ahead of the land forces and run into the ambush.

Murad Bey's flotilla was commanded by his naval adviser, a Greek called Nikola, an expert Nile sailor who knew the strengths and weaknesses of all the vessels capable of navigating the river. His flotilla consisted of a dozen or so vessels, half of which were heavily armed and manned by experienced Greek, Egyptian and black Nubian crews. Nikola had stationed his armed vessels just upstream from where the channel narrowed and flowed through an embankment at Shubra Khit; he had then positioned a battery of nine-pounders on the embankment on either shore: a perfect spot for an ambush.

Captain Perrée was on his command ship, the *chebek Le Cerf*, which also had on board Napoleon's secretary Bourrienne, as well as the senior savants Monge and Berthollet. Along with the rest of the vanguard, three gunboats and a galley, this unwittingly sailed straight into the ambush, and was soon under heavy fire from Nikola's gunboats and the batteries on either shore. The gunfire attracted attention in the village of Shubra Khit. According to Lieutenant Grandjean, "The Mamelukes, Arabs and peasants ran out in a crowd, swarming towards us with hideous cries, some began hauling their boats down from the bank, others threw themselves into the water, all coming to attack us on board."[41] Those remaining on shore fired rifles at Perrée's stalled flotilla; and some of the Bedouin even had small guns mounted on their camels.

Nikola's vessels came alongside two of the French gunboats and the galley. According to Bourrienne, "Soon several of our ships had been boarded by the Turks [as the French called the enemy], and before our eyes they began massacring their crews with barbaric ferocity, holding aloft their decapitated heads by the hair."[42] In no time the Nile was awash with bodies, as Le Cerf and the remaining gunboat did their best to pick up the survivors who had dived into the Nile. One of the vessels in Perrée's convoy was carrying several hundred cavalrymen, who had no horses, and these began valiantly repelling the boarders with their sabers. Amidst the chaos, Perrée did his best to direct operations, suffering a gunshot wound in his left arm in the process. The mathematician Monge, despite his fifty-two years, began helping to reload the guns, whilst the fifty-year-old chemist Berthollet adopted a more stoic stance. According to a fellow savant, "He began filling his pockets with stones, much to the indignant astonishment of his companions who had found better things to do at this juncture; he explained that this was so that he could sink more quickly if things became mortally dangerous, enabling him to escape the savagery of the Mamelukes. But he was eventually persuaded to take up arms and join in the defense of the group."[43]

Bourrienne remembered how "towards 11 o'clock, Perrée informed me that things weren't getting any better, that the Turks were inflicting more damage on us than we were on them, and that we were going to run out of ammunition."[44] But the situation was to be suddenly and dramatically relieved. One of the guns on Le Cerf scored a direct hit on the commanding Mameluke gunboat, just at the point where its ammunition was stored. The result was a huge explosion. "As it exploded the men flew up into the air like birds," recorded Nicolas Turc (who could not have been present, but was almost certainly repeating the picturesque phrase of an Arab eyewitness).[45] There was an immediate panic amongst the Arabs, Mamelukes and Greeks. Those on shore ran away, those in boats made for the shore, and Nikola's remaining flotilla beat a hasty retreat upstream. This was the detonation heard by Murad Bey and his cavalry commanders as they were conferring after the first concerted Mameluke charge, and it seems to have played its part in the Mameluke abandonment of the battlefield and final flight. Whether this flight resulted from Murad Bey's order or was spontaneous is not clear; what *is* clear is that the Mamelukes could not have known for certain that it was one of their own gunboats that had blown up.

Napoleon now hastened to the rescue of Perrée's flotilla and his savant friends, but arrived to find that the engagement was all but over. Captain Perrée's heroism was rewarded with promotion to rear-admiral. The skirmish at Shubra Khit on July 13 had resulted in no French casualties on land, while according to Perrée's report to his commander Vice-Admiral Brueys, "twenty of my men were wounded, and several were killed. I lost my sword and a piece of my left arm."[46] This was a considerable understatement, judging from the eyewitness descriptions and the fact that the engagement lasted from nine A.M. until twelve thirty P.M., during which in all over 1,500 artillery shells were fired. More realistic estimates concur that there were more than 300 French casualties (killed and wounded), the majority of these being sailors. On the other hand, Napoleon's unavoidably tardy move to rescue the flotilla seems to have resulted in something of an overstatement; his secretary Bourrienne records how Napoleon later reproached him: "In order to save you, Monge, Berthollet and the others on the flotilla, I had to move to the left towards the Nile, rather than to the right, around Shubra Khit, a move which would have cut off the Mamelukes and prevented any of them from escaping."[47] This was sheer wishful thinking, as only cavalry could have spearheaded this move with sufficient swiftness. Napoleon's frustration at his lack of cavalry, at least in part due to his own haste, led him to seek scapegoats. In his mind he was doubtless already composing the official version of events he would be sending in his future report back to the

Directory. Meanwhile, he had more pressing problems. This first large-scale encounter with the Mamelukes had been inconclusive, and the men soon reverted to their old disgruntled ways. They were far from home, and they were far from happy; and the farther they marched from home, the unhappier they became. Napoleon was convinced that what they needed to boost their morale was a glorious victory.

VII

The Battle of the Pyramids

THE French army was still less than halfway to Cairo, which lay some eighty miles upstream on the Nile. Napoleon remained intent on reaching this destination as soon as possible, and the men were allowed just a few hours' rest at Shubra Khit before setting forth once more in the late afternoon of July 13. In order to make up time, Napoleon decided that the army should not follow the curves of the Nile, but instead should head direct for Cairo across the hinterland. This was land that had been cultivated after the flooding of the Nile during the previous year but was now utterly dried up. Fields had become tracts of cracked earth, the banks of the irrigation channels had become baked mud ruts, and the larger irrigation canals were reduced to dry ditches. All these proved difficult obstacles for the artillery, each piece of which had to be dragged by six horses, with wheels frequently coming off and axles breaking.

The men now began suffering terribly from flies, and many appeared to have caught a mysterious eye disease, which had been noticeable amongst the Arab population in Alexandria, where there was an unusually high proportion of people who were blinded in one or both eyes. As the men continued marching dumbly through the wilderness, many found that their eyes became red, irritable and swollen, with discharges of pus. Some even complained that they were going blind. The senior medical officers decided that this was a particularly severe Egyptian strain of ophthalmia, but since they had no medical equipment to examine the men properly, or medicine with which to treat them, any effective prophylactic measures would have to wait until they reached Cairo.

Supplies were now running low, but Napoleon had calculated that the leading divisions of Desaix and Reynier would rejoin the Nile in three days, where they could replenish their supplies from Perrée's flotilla. But on July 15 the flotilla became grounded on sandbanks. The river was too low for anything but boats of the shallowest draft to continue, which in practice meant only *djermes* (Nile sailing boats with large triangular lateen sails, similar to feluccas). These could do little other than transport important passengers (such as Monge, Berthollet and Bourrienne, who were reduced to living off watermelons), as well as pick up a few of the worst invalids. Officers and men all realized that there was no going back, and the leading divisions were forced to march on without supplies. As a result, discipline soon began to break down. The groups of Bedouin which had continued to shadow the outer columns began picking off stragglers, and on July 16 Napoleon reissued the order forbidding groups to separate from their main divisional force. Amongst the rear divisions, still camping at night on the banks of the Nile, the men were now plagued with mosquitoes, to such an extent that more than one senior officer began to suspect there was an outbreak of smallpox.

Meanwhile, those crossing the dried-up fields, which soon gave way to desert, had their own problems. During the day, the heat became all but unbearable, and the men grew desperate. According to young Corporal François, "As we crossed dunes of burning sand, some were dying of suffocation. All the time it felt as if we were passing in front of the mouth of a raging furnace. Several soldiers committed suicide."[1] The men became increasingly uncontrollable. When they arrived at a village they would simply fall upon it, ransacking all they could, their officers turning a blind eye to what was going on. Corporal François recorded: "The inhabitants of one village ganged together and refused even to let us buy any food, firing at us. . . . We scaled the walls and set fire to the place . . . we grabbed all we could find, goats, donkeys, horses, eggs, cows, sheep." François claimed that they killed "around 900 men, as well as women and children."[2] Other firsthand sources indicate that this was a wild exaggeration, but there is no doubting that serious atrocities occurred. Colonel Laugier described coming upon a village being looted by French soldiers: "There was a frightful noise from the men wailing and the women weeping. The women climbed onto the rooftops, and when they saw an officer riding by called out to him in distress, flapping their shawls in their hands and breaking into a hideous howling lamentation." Though Laugier noticed that as soon as senior officers managed to control the situation "the inhabitants became transformed, turning from fear and despair to trust and even happiness, so that the troops received unleavened bread, rice and meat."[3] Again, this too would seem to contain its element of exaggeration, while conveying something of what must have occurred.

Later, things deteriorated still further, judging by Laugier's outraged military sensibilities: "One could not conceive of such an undisciplined army. Our division was only able to complete the ruin of the villages through which we passed, because the preceding divisions had left nothing to carry off or destroy. Sometimes even the harvest in the fields was on fire, so that when we arrived we couldn't even find straw or barley for the horses."[4] It is difficult to assess precisely how widespread such incidents were. Several sources appeared to find nothing remarkable about this stage of the march. The observant artist Denon, for instance, simply commented that "our march along the Nile became less difficult, though we did not follow the river all the time."[5] Yet there is no doubt that conditions were in general hard, and that the men were not happy. Even Napoleon comments laconically in his memoirs: "The army was overcome by a vague collective melancholy that nothing could overcome; it was an attack of spleen; several soldiers threw themselves in the Nile in order to have a quick death." He mentions how whenever possible the men would bathe in the Nile at the beginning of the day: "On leaving the Nile the soldiers would begin their barrack-room politics, exasperating themselves and lamenting their unfortunate lot, exclaiming, 'What have we come to do here? The Directory has deported us!'" Napoleon insisted that the men did not blame him for their predicament, because they saw that he was living just as they did, and that "the dinner for the generals consisted often of just a plate of lentils."[6]

When, on July 18, the leading divisions reached Wardan, some sixty-five miles up the Nile from Shubra Khit, Napoleon decided that the men needed a rest for forty-eight hours. By now the scavenging troops had built up their supplies, and for the next day or so the wilderness around Wardan began filling up with troops. Their hundreds upon hundreds of campfires burned into the night, roasting whole sheep and goats, as well as haunches of cow, on spits the soldiers had improvised from their rifle ramrods. The entire army was exhausted, and all made do as best they could, through the damp chill of the night and the burning heat of the day, with the men and officers stretched out together amongst the tethered donkeys, transport camels, pack and cavalry horses. Such an encampment of over 20,000 men—with the soldiers washing themselves in the Nile, hanging out their scrubbed uniforms to dry, cleaning their equipment, checking their rifles and sharpening their bayonets, some muttering, some singing, others prostrate with fatigue—must have made quite a sight. Yet in no time it was gone. Orders came to march, and the leading divisions set off, arriving on the evening of July 20 at Omm-Dinar, the village at the head of the delta where the Nile divides into its two main navigational channels, just eighteen miles downstream from Cairo.

Meanwhile Napoleon was making plans for the great victory with which he intended to "revive the spirits" of his army—and gain glory for himself. His scouts reported that the Mamelukes were entrenched before Cairo, with Murad Bey commanding an army on the western bank of the Nile directly in front of him, and Ibrahim Bey commanding one across on the eastern bank, before the walls of the city itself.

Murad Bey and Ibrahim Bey were the joint Mameluke rulers of Egypt, with Murad Bey as Emir el-Hadj (leader of the pilgrimage to Mecca) and Ibrahim Bey as Sheik el-Beled (chief of the country). Technically Ibrahim Bey ruled the whole of Egypt, under the puppet Turkish pasha Abu Bakr, but in fact his rule was centered on Cairo, with only certain beys in the delta and the hinterland remaining strictly loyal to his rule. Murad Bey also had his loyal beys, mainly in Upper Egypt. All the local beys collected taxes from their peasants, the *fellahin,* over whom they ruled like feudal lords, with Ibrahim Bey and Murad Bey being paid their dues by their loyal beys. A small fraction of this would then be passed on, in the name of the puppet pasha, to Constantinople.

Ibrahim Bey and Murad Bey ruled in uneasy partnership. Murad Bey was loath to set foot in Cairo, which was very much Ibrahim Bey's domain, but he had built himself a palace on the west bank of the Nile at Giza, near the Pyramids. Although Murad Bey was now probably in his fifties (his precise age was unknown, even to himself), he remained a powerful figure, in both mind and body. Legend had it that with one mighty swing of his scimitar he could decapitate an ox. He retained a thick-set, powerful build, whilst his pale-skinned face had fierce eyes and a large, bushy blond beard. His arrogance and cruelty were legendary, and it was said that his anger was sufficient to make even the bravest of his Mameluke deputies tremble in his presence. Murad had been born in a poor mountain village in the Caucasus and sold into slavery, merchants bringing him to Egypt around the age of eight. Here he received strict military training, learning horsemanship and leadership, being instilled with a ferocious pride in his Mameluke status. Yet at the same time he remained the property of his Mameluke master, who was in the habit of venting his lust on the better-looking boys in his possession. Only when a young Mameluke was appointed a military leader, often at puberty, did he become free to grow a beard and take on slaves of his own. He often had children by the time he was fourteen. From this time on he owed feudal allegiance to his former master. In this way the Mamelukes established a network of loyalties amongst the constantly squabbling beys. Murad was in the service of Ali Bey, who ruled Egypt from 1763. During the power struggle after Ali Bey's death in 1773, he quickly rose to power, even marrying the rich and formidable Setty-Nefissa, widow of his former master. It was at this time that he emerged as Emir el-Hadj.

An interesting light is shed on Murad Bey by the evenhanded and perceptive obituary of him written a few years later by the contemporary Egyptian historian El-Djabarti, who spoke of his "fearsome loud voice and face criss-crossed with scars from saber slashes. He was cruel and unjust, enterprising and conceited, but he respected the *ulema* [the religious scholars responsible for interpreting Islamic law], listened to their advice and gave way to their pleas. . . . He liked to play chess and music. His finest qualities were his energy and his generosity. He left no children."⁷ Between his bouts of furious energy, Murad Bey delighted in a life of luxurious idleness, in one of the several palaces which he had built in his fiefdoms throughout the country with the fortune he had accumulated from taxes. However, according to El-Djabarti, "He liked to have about him men who were hard, brave and cruel." In his clashes with unruly beys it was said that "his rash bravery sometimes bordered on madness, yet at other times he showed cowardice."⁸ His only real contribution to the country as a whole was his establishment of a fleet on the Nile, which he entrusted to his Christian henchman, the Greek known as Nikola.* The ships for this fleet were constructed by artisans and craftsmen conscripted from Turkey, and the gunboats were exact copies of those in the Turkish navy.

★ Most sources say he was Greek, although El-Djabarti identifies him as Armenian.

Murad Bey's fellow ruler Ibrahim Bey was in many ways his opposite. Where Murad Bey was passionate and extravagant, Ibrahim Bey
was more cautious and devious. Although he was capable of dismissing
one pasha after another, almost at whim, whenever they displeased
him, and dispatching them back to Constantinople, he also made sure
that the annual tribute, the *miry*, was sent to Constantinople without
fail. Where Murad Bey acted on impulse, Ibrahim Bey was a calcu-
lating realist. On occasion, he would attempt to restrain his fellow
ruler from his worst excesses, but only when these resulted in indignant delegations of merchants or beys descending upon Cairo, or a
further flight of *fellahin* to Syria. Even so, his interventions had little
effect. Between the two of them they were ruining a country which
had already sunk into a sorry state of neglect. The chaotic rule of
the Mamelukes seriously hampered trade, as even the European traders
found it difficult to meet the whimsical tariffs demanded by the beys.
And beyond the cultivated regions of the Nile valley and the delta,
the wilderness territory had fallen to the Bedouin tribes, who had to
be bribed to ensure safe passage.

The Mameluke "taxes"—in effect little more than demands for money
with menaces—had reduced the *fellahin* to penury. The Mamelukes
claimed possession of the land, only allowing the *fellahin* to rent out
plots, and extracting a tithe at every harvest. In recent years there had
been several "bad Niles," when the annual flooding had been insufficient to water more than the fields nearest to the irrigation channels
of the Nile valley and the delta, and the *fellahin* were more wretched
than ever. The harvest was gathered in May, and from then on the
land lay uncultivated, becoming increasingly parched by the unrelenting
sun until the Nile flooded once more in August, covering much of the
delta in water, leaving a similar sight to that observed by Herodotus
over twenty centuries previously.

Under Mameluke rule there was no provision for improving the
irrigation canals and saving water, or even for basic maintenance of
the water systems upon which all agriculture depended. As a result,
the *fellahin* lived much as they had done in Herodotus' time; indeed,
much as they had done during the time of the pharaohs well over
three millennia previously, when things had in fact been much better
organized. The crops remained the same as they had been since time
immemorial: a rotation of wheat, barley, beans and lentils, with rice
as a staple and flax for mats and building materials. The lack of social

stability, which had lasted through much of the five centuries of Mameluke rule, meant that there was no possibility of progress. The country that had once built the pyramids had yet to see the introduction of the wheelbarrow. Its most technically complex method of raising water from one level to another, a process upon which its very survival depended, remained the Archimedes Screw.*

The administration of the country, such as it was, remained incorrigibly corrupt and unsystematic. The law rested on the judgment of the kadis, who turned to the Koran for their authority; outside the teachings of the Koran there was no legal code as such. Life for the impoverished downtrodden *fellahin* was a long, hard daily toil, with only the occasional grim and dangerous distraction, as their Mameluke masters fought amongst themselves. The historian Christopher Herold admirably evokes the scene:

> The peasants, glancing up from their labours, would observe [the Mamelukes'] gleaming cavalcades, all aglitter with steel and resplendent in multi-coloured turbans and flowing silken gowns, galloping toward their equally glittering foes, skirmishing for a while, then either entering the capital victoriously or tearing south at a lightning gallop toward Upper Egypt, where they would lie low until there arose an opportunity to fight another day.[9]

The historic stasis of the countryside also extended into the towns and cities it enveloped. Cairo's era of greatness had reached its pinnacle during the early fourteenth century, when it had a population of almost half a million, making it larger than any city in Europe or the Middle East. And this greatness extended to far more than just its size: culturally no city outside China could match it. Profiting from the influx of Islamic scholars fleeing the Moguls during the previous century, along with the decline of Baghdad and Damascus, Cairo's Al-Azhar mosque and university had become the major center of religious teaching throughout the Islamic world, a region that

---

* In this instance, usually a makeshift wooden cylinder wrapped in a spiral around a central axle, inclined at 45° with its foot in water. When the axle is turned, water is carried up from twist to twist of the cylinder, eventually disgorging at a higher level. Although this ingenious device may in fact not have been invented by Archimedes, it certainly dates from his time—that is, some 2,000 years previously.

extended from Morocco to the Philippines. This wealth of learning extended into mathematics and the sciences, as well as medicine, knowledge of which subjects far exceeded that in medieval Europe. Such intellectual wealth was supported by the more tangible wealth of the spice trade between the Far East and Europe, whose sea route passed up the Red Sea, then overland to the Mediterranean. Almost all of Cairo's great religious, and to a lesser extent secular, architecture dated from this period.

However, after the initial stability brought about by Mameluke rule, there were increasing periods of decline, caused by a nexus of calamitous circumstances: the devastation wreaked by the Black Death in 1348, the consequent inability of the rulers to control the Mamelukes, and the collapse of the spice-trade sea route monopoly after Vasco da Gama pioneered the route around Africa to India in 1497. The Ottoman conquest of Egypt in 1517 merely confirmed Cairo's status as a provincial backwater, and the two ensuing centuries witnessed the city's decline into cultural aridity—maintained by chaotic rule, fundamentalist religious teaching appropriate to a seventh-century desert society, and a majority population of illiterate and dispirited peasantry.

Revolutionary France saw itself as the liberator of mankind. Its army had defeated kings and princes in Europe, and even the pope, in the name of freedom. Age-old ruling dynasties quailed at the approach of its idealistically inspired soldiers. Even during the reign of the Directory this remained much how the French army liked to see itself, and Napoleon too subscribed to this fading myth, though very much for his own purposes. The French had come to Egypt to liberate the downtrodden Egyptians from their Mameluke tyrants, to bring to a backward people the benefits of European civilization and culture. Who could resist the chance of such enlightenment? As such, the French expected that they would be welcomed, once the initial suspicions of the people had been overcome. Their oppressive Mameluke masters would soon be put to flight.

But the reality was to hold some unexpected surprises. When news first reached Cairo that the French invasion fleet had arrived off Alexandria, "the beys and their henchmen let out cries of joy; Cairo was lit up in celebration. 'It will be like slicing open watermelons,' they cried. 'Every Mameluke will vow to bring back a hundred heads.' " Or so the story goes. These words appear in Napoleon's memoirs, and seem to be confirmed by very similar words in the memoirs of several French officers.[10] Nicolas Turc paints a somewhat different picture: "When Murad Bey learned [of the invasion] he threw the letter to the ground and called for his soldiers with a roar. His eyes became red and fire devoured his entrails. He ordered his horse to be brought and arrived at the residence of Ibrahim Bey in a passionate state. Soon news of the infidel invasion spread through the city, where it caused strife and confusion, the inhabitants pouring out of their houses filled with consternation and anxiety."[11]

Ibrahim Bey and Murad Bey called a *divan*, a council of state that was attended by the pasha Abu Bakr, as well as the senior beys, sheiks and *ulema*. Murad Bey immediately confronted the pasha: "The French could only have arrived here with the consent of the Porte, and being their representative here you must have known of this. Destiny will aid us in our struggle against you and against them."

The pasha rejected this accusation, adding: "Be courageous and steadfast, rise up like the brave men you are, prepare to fight and resist with force, before placing your fate in the hands of God." Some of the beys and *ulema* insisted: "We must exterminate the Christians in our midst before marching against the infidels." Already the mob had begun to desecrate Christian churches and was threatening houses in the European quarter, crying out, "Cursed infidels, your last hour has arrived. We are now allowed to kill you and ransack your houses." But the word of Ibrahim Bey and Pasha Abu Bakr prevailed. Ibrahim Bey ordered that the European quarter be sealed off, and its inhabitants were escorted to the Citadel for their own safety, while at the same time a collective fine of 20,000 francs was imposed on them for good measure. Later they were given shelter in the palace of Ibrahim Bey's wife, a woman renowned for her piety and charity, who saw no anomaly in offering hospitality to the compatriots of the very people her husband might soon be fighting against.

The duplicitous letter that Napoleon sent to Pasha Abu Bakr from Alexandria, claiming that the Porte had "withdrawn its protection from the beys," and inviting the pasha to come and meet him, evidently did not reach its intended recipient. The pasha summoned Bardeuf, the leader of the French community in Cairo, for an explanation of the French invasion, but he too said that he knew nothing about it, though significantly he did suggest that the French army might perhaps be on its way to India. Meanwhile Murad Bey assembled a force of around 6,000 Mamelukes, 15,000 armed Egyptians and 3,000 Bedouin, and set forth from Cairo, heading north. According to El-Djabarti, "As soon as Murad Bey left Cairo a mood of sadness and fear descended on the city. . . . At sunset the crowd deserted the streets. Seeing this state of affairs, Ibrahim Bey ordered the cafés to stay open during the night and ordered the inhabitants to light lanterns in front of their houses and shops."[12] This perhaps accounts for the reports which reached Napoleon of the city being lit up in rejoicing at the prospect of defeating the French. El-Djabarti also records how, "after the departure of Murad Bey from Cairo the *ulema* gathered every day at the El-Azhar mosque and read the Holy Books for the success of the Egyptians; the sheiks of the main sects also assembled in their mosques and called upon God, while the holy scholars did the same in their schools."[13]

By the time Murad Bey and his forces returned after the indecisive encounter at Shubra Khit, Ibrahim Bey had assembled a force on the eastern bank of the Nile at Boulac outside the gates of Cairo. Again, estimates vary as to its strength, but it seems he certainly had at least 1,000 Mameluke cavalry, along with their attendants. (Each Mameluke took into battle as many as three or four attendants; during a charge the riders would fire their pistols and then simply toss them over their shoulders to be gathered up by their attendants, who would also, occasionally, be used as infantry support.) Ibrahim Bey's force also included a number of artillery pieces, as well as several thousand separate infantry. Perhaps as many as half of these would have been trained militia; the rest would have been conscripts, *fellahin* and the urban poor, most of whom would only have been armed with sticks and the like. These in turn were accompanied by a throng of women, children and spectators, amongst whom were musicians playing tambourines and flutes, as well as others chanting—all of whom had come along to watch the battle against the infidels. Sources indicate that this gave something of a holiday atmosphere to the proceedings, though others mention that this procession also chanted fervent prayers for victory. Judging from the previous consternation on the streets of Cairo, many in this procession would certainly have been frightened and fearful of what might happen to them if the infidels from faraway Europe prevailed.

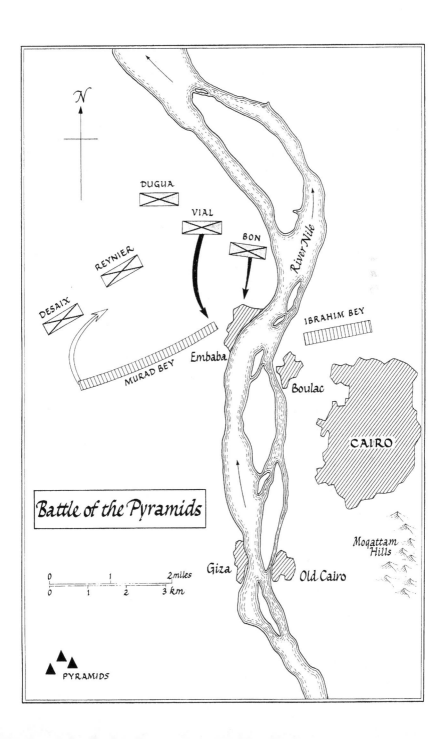

N

DUGUA

VIAL

BON

REYNIER

DESAIX

River Nile

IBRAHIM BEY

MURAD BEY

Embaba

Boulac

CAIRO

Battle of the Pyramids

0   1   2 miles
0   1   2   3 km

Giza

Old Cairo

Moqattam
Hills

▲ PYRAMIDS

Meanwhile Murad Bey and his forces took up their positions across the Nile at the village of Embaba. Nikola and his boats were ordered to blockade the Nile, then dig in and mount artillery around the village itself. When Napoleon was informed that the Mameluke forces were split in two, he could hardly believe his luck. This tactical blunder was probably due to the headstrong Murad Bey. Had he crossed the river and joined forces with Ibrahim Bey outside the city walls, not only would this have consolidated the Mameluke fighting strength, it would also have forced Napoleon to make a river crossing if he was to take Cairo. Such an operation would have left him highly vulnerable, especially from cavalry attack and the artillery of Nikola's flotilla.

By the evening of July 20, Napoleon's five divisions were assembled at Omm-Dinar, at the head of the Nile delta, where they were allowed but a few hours' rest. At one in the morning the drums began sounding through the darkness, wakening the men and beating the call to arms; an hour later the men were ready to depart on the final leg of their march on Cairo. One by one the divisions moved away into the darkness in battle formation. Just over two hours later, as first light broke over the eastern horizon, the French soldiers were greeted by a spectacular sight, the like of which not even the hardiest of well-traveled veterans had seen before. To the left of them, across the Nile, they could see the myriad domes and mosques of Cairo rising against the pink dawn. Dominating this skyline were the castellated walls of the Citadel, which dated from the time of the great warrior Saladin, the scourge of the Crusaders, who had retaken Jerusalem in 1187. According to Napoleon, his soldiers greeted their first sight of Cairo with "a thousand cries of joy":[14] they had at last arrived at their destination. As the sun rose above the low Moqattam hills to the east, its rays passed over the expanse of the flat plain to the west of the Nile, and the soldiers could see in the distance the triangular mounds of the Pyramids, their stone flanks turning golden in the sunlight. Gradually, as they marched towards the three pyramids, their solid stone forms began to shimmer and melt in the heat haze, and across the floor of the plain could be distinguished a long arc, which glinted like jewels in the sunlight, stretching between the banks of the Nile and the pyramids, a distance of some eight miles. This, the soldiers soon realized, was the line of Murad Bey's Mameluke cavalry with its attendants and accompanying infantry.

According to Napoleon in his memoirs, Murad Bey's forces consisted of "20,000 Janissaries,★ Arabs and militia from Cairo" all dug in at Embaba "with forty pieces of cannon."[15] At the same time, stretched out across the desert was a line of "12,000 Mamelukes, agas, sheiks and other Egyptian notables, on horseback and each having three or four men on foot to serve them, forming a line of 50,000 men." This was also supported by "8,000 Bedouin Arabs . . . all in a line which stretched three leagues [i.e., around nine miles]." Meanwhile "the Nile, stretching from Embaba to Boulac, as far back as Old Cairo, was barely sufficient to contain their flotilla, whose masts appeared like a forest." All other sources indicate that these figures are exaggerated. In the effort to build up his reputation in history, Napoleon wished to stress that his 25,000 men of the Army of the Orient faced a greatly superior force in this epic battle. There is no denying that the combined Egyptian force was superior in number—it probably had at least half as many again as the French—but the caliber of some of its conscripted men cannot be compared with that of the French. When it came down to professional soldiers and trained fighting men the numbers probably favored the Egyptians by a mere few thousand.

The five French divisions arrived in front of Embaba at around two P.M., in the very heat of the day, and settled down for a brief respite amidst the fields of watermelons which were growing in profusion along the banks of the Nile. Despite Napoleon's previous orders, this was hardly the time and place to start boiling the fruit, and they were simply gulped down raw by the thirsty troops, which only served to worsen an already bad situation. Afterwards, Colonel Savary wrote: "The whole army has diarrhea."[16]

But Napoleon now had his mind on higher matters. This was the moment he had been waiting for: the battle that would decide the fate of Egypt. As always at such moments he was filled with a sense of destiny. He called together his commanders, and after outlining his battle plan delivered a speech: "You are going into a battle which will be engraved upon the memory of mankind. You will be fighting the oppressors of Egypt." Gesturing to the distant pyramids, he uttered the

★ The Janissaries were the Ottoman garrison officially under the command of the Turkish pasha, but were in practice commanded by the Mamelukes. They were trained infantry, and were mainly Albanian in origin. It is unclear precisely how many of them were garrisoned in Egypt at this time, but a figure of a few thousand is most likely. Napoleon, and other French sources, often used this name loosely to describe any Egyptian troops.

memorable words: "Soldiers, forty centuries of history are looking down on you."[*17]

Napoleon's battle plan was similar to that which he had adopted at Shubra Khit: his five divisions would form into defensive squares, with strategically placed artillery and sharpshooters. His continuing lack of sufficient cavalry left him with little other option. However, as his squares were six deep, this allowed for the first three ranks to march forward in a column of attack, whilst he still retained his main force in defensive squares capable of resisting cavalry attacks. He knew that this would be no inconclusive minor skirmish such as he had encountered at Shubra Khit: this time the Mamelukes would be riding into battle to defend all that they stood for, their centuries of heroic tradition, and would be liable to fight to the last man. Napoleon's main worry was that on this occasion, confronted with the full force of the determined Mameluke cavalry, the men might break ranks. He realized that his soldiers were weakened by their long march, as well as being debilitated by hunger, eye disease and diarrhea, which had left them for the most part dispirited—a situation which was not conducive to obeying orders that went against their natural inclination. During their many campaigns in Europe, the French revolutionary army had prided itself on its charges: the men taking the battle to the enemy and sweeping all before them. Such bravery and enthusiasm had required spirit rather than instilled discipline; their belief in France and the revolutionary cause had been enough. It had only been possible to enforce stricter discipline after the initial chaos and fervor of the post-revolutionary years had died down, and this had been achieved with varying success (as could be seen with Reynier's division). Napoleon was well aware that he was taking a risk in ordering his men to adopt a passive role in a major battle. Even he was not entirely certain that they would hold their line, and their fire—under massed frontal attack from brave and experienced cavalry—until the enemy were at point-blank range, and the order to fire was given.

Napoleon's force was still arrayed in five divisions, under Desaix,

---

* There are several versions of this speech: the version I have given collates some of Napoleon's more characteristic phrases. On the other hand, many reliable sources claim that he never in fact made the speech, simply inserting it into his memoirs to add to his legend. However, the fact that he did make the speech was confirmed in a recently published letter by Bernoyer, written on the day after the battle. (This letter was only made public in 1976 with the posthumous publication of Bernoyer's *Avec Bonaparte en Égypte*, where it appears on p. 59.)

Reynier, Dugua, Bon and Vial. Bon's division was deployed directly beside the Nile in front of Embaba, with Vial's division to his right. To the right of Vial, but held back in reserve, was Dugua's division, where Napoleon himself set up his command headquarters. Approximately a mile separated the two front lines at this point, but Colonel Laugier describes how General Murat "wanted to go right up to the point where he could reconnoiter the enemy, so I joined him, and followed him. We pursued our reconnaissance to within cannon range of the Mameluke camp. We could very distinctly see their tents, and see them mounting their horses in preparation for battle."[18] Murad Bey soon came forth from his brightly colored tent, riding his prancing steed down the line before his men, greeting each bey in turn, instilling in them courage for the battle ahead: this was a fight for the Mameluke heritage of Egypt, for Muslims against the infidel invaders, who would be driven from their shores just as the Crusaders had been forced to flee Saladin (who had himself been technically a Mameluke).

The right wing of Napoleon's forces consisted of Reynier's division, and beyond this, further forward, Desaix's division, which was moving towards a position where it could outflank the Mamelukes if they charged, and then cut off their retreat. Murad Bey quickly realized what was happening, and Napoleon watched as he "dispatched one of his bravest beys with an elite corps of 7 or 8 thousand horses, who charged with the speed of lightning"[19] towards Desaix's division. This was having some difficulty maintaining its square as it progressed through clumps of palm trees and stumbled down into the hollowed-out beds of dried-up navigation canals. As the leading soldiers began emerging from yet another canal bed, their line in some disarray, they saw that the charging Mameluke cavalry was almost upon them. According to Savary, "The last stragglers were not yet in their ranks when the line began firing on the Mamelukes, who were 200 paces away."[20] Desaix at once ordered his officers to close up their lines. As the Mameluke cavalry thundered over the plain towards the French square, a number of the soldiers were hit by the Mamelukes furiously discharging their rifles and pistols ahead of them, but the rest of the line held firm. Not until the order was given did the men fire their muskets, slicing down the Mamelukes as their horses rode right up to the line of bayonets then reared in panic, turning on their hind legs. A few riderless horses toppled over into the French line as the men followed the command to reload.

Wave upon straggling wave of Mameluke cavalry emitting blood-curdling screams, their brandished scimitars glinting in the sun, now broke against the line of Desaix's division. Some groups swerved to their right to avoid the falling horses and men, charging towards the uncluttered line of Reynier's division. This was tightly aligned, with kneeling bayoneteers and lines of riflemen holding steady until the order was given to fire, and more screeching Mameluke riders fell from their horses.

The fact is, neither Murad Bey nor the Mamelukes had any conception of an ordered, concerted cavalry charge, such as might have broken through the French ranks. No sooner was the order to charge given than they simply rode forward as fast as they could, each man keener than the next to be first into the fray, each intent upon individual glory more than any collective victory. Instead of a charge, it became more of a race, the line rapidly becoming uneven and ragged as they approached the French positions. Even so, they presented an awesome and unnerving sight, as Corporal François recalled:

They threw themselves forward in a mad charge. Our order was not to move! We hardly breathed; brigade commander Marmont had ordered us not to fire until he gave the command. The Mamelukes were almost upon us. The order was finally given, and it was real carnage. The sabers of the enemy cavalry met the bayonets of our first rank. It was an unbelievable chaos: horses and cavalrymen falling on us, some of us falling back. Several Mamelukes had their [silk] clothes on fire, set alight by the blazing wads from our muskets. I was by the flag and I saw right beside me Mamelukes, wounded, in a heap, burning, trying with their sabers to slash the legs of our soldiers in the front rank. We were closed in such tight rank that they must have believed we were joined together. I have never seen men more brave and more determined.[21]

Captain Vertray, who was with Reynier's division, remembered:

The number of corpses which lay all around us was soon considerable. The clothes of the dead and wounded Mamelukes burned like tinderwood . . . the flaming wads from our rifles penetrated their exotic uniforms, which floated in the air like gauze embroidered with gold and silver . . . they all wore chiffon chemises and cloaks of silk, with their weapons encrusted with ivory and finely cut gemstones . . . It was imperative for troops such as us to resist these fearsome charges by the enemy. Our brigade was at this time composed almost exclusively of battle-hardened warriors accustomed to victory; besides, we knew that it was all or nothing.[22]

General Reynier was full of praise for his division: "I have never known officers and men, holding themselves in line, who have conducted themselves better."[23]

With their ensuing charges disrupted by panicking riderless horses, the Mamelukes swerved to charge between the divisions, some even continuing on as far as Dugua's division, many now falling victim to crossfire and sharpshooters. On the French right flank, the battle was becoming a rout, and the majority of the remaining Mamelukes turned their horses and galloped back towards their own line in the direction of the pyramids.

Seeing this, Napoleon made his move. "I seized the opportunity and ordered General Bon's division, which was by the Nile, to launch an attack on where the enemy was dug in [at Embaba]."[24] Vial's division also advanced, covering Bon's flank. Seeing this, Murad Bey dispatched the unused right wing of his cavalry, which galloped forward, discharging their muskets, firing their pistols, then brandishing their gleaming scimitars above their heads. As they charged towards the French line the air was filled with the piercing screams of their battle cries.

The advancing French divisions quickly took up their positions in defensive squares, with the commanders and the few cavalry taking their place in the center, followed by the order for the pack animals and the savants to follow suit (the latter order now reduced to a mere "Donkeys in the middle!"). Once again the Mameluke charge broke against an impenetrable wall of French soldiers as the men of Bon's division held their line. But this time, as the Mameluke cavalry turned, they found their way partially blocked by Vial's division, which had swept round to cut off their retreat. Many of the cornered Mamelukes rode through the cannons and fortifications on the outskirts of Embaba, taking refuge in the village as Bon's division continued their advance along the Nile.

Bon and Vial then gave the orders for the front lines of their division squares to break forward into columns of attack, and these began advancing towards the entrenched positions at the edges of Embaba. The young cavalry officer Desvernois relates a memorable incident which now took place:

A distinguished Mameluke bey with a fine long beard paraded himself before the front line of Bon's division. At the sight of this insolent enemy I was overcome with anger and bringing my magnificent Arab steed to the gallop I broke out like lightning from the ranks of our divisional square and joined battle with this audacious bey. Bullets rained around us, but we did not heed them. With a pistol shot I knocked him from his saddle. He fell from his mount and approached me on hands and knees. Seeing him, with his white beard, coming in this way towards me, slicing the ground from right to left with his sword, I understood that he wished to beg clemency from me, and trying to make him understand that I wished him no ill, I placed my sword under my left elbow, point to the rear, handle protruding, and reached out to him with my arms.[25]

But Desvernois had underestimated his enemy. The bey continued forward, attempting to slice the legs of Desvernois's horse. When Desvernois reined to one side to avoid these blows, the bey leapt to take cover under the horse's neck, then "with the speed of a serpent" seized the reins with his left hand, and with his right slashed furiously at Desvernois with his sword. At the same time Desvernois's horse reared, and instead the bey's sword hit the horse's forehead.

But, quick as lightning, I struck at my enemy with two vigorous blows, one on the arm and the other on the hand which had seized the reins, then two or three other blows on his head and his other arm. Even then, severely wounded but not disarmed, the bey continued on his knees to try and give me more of the same game. But I'd had enough of this type of game, and I leaned over him and smashed open his head.[26]

Whereupon several soldiers broke ranks, rushed towards the bey and finished him off with their rifle butts, "causing his yellow cashmere turban to come off, revealing a red felt skullcap into which were sewn more than 500 gold coins."

Meanwhile, on the other bank of the Nile, Ibrahim Bey—along with his Mamelukes, *fellahin* militia and crowd of spectators—had been watching the battle unfold. As the French lines closed in on the outskirts of Embaba, he began ordering his artillery to fire salvos at the far bank and beyond the village, in an attempt to halt the enemy advance. By now the crowd of spectators, which according to some sources consisted of the entire population of Cairo, had worked themselves up into a frenzy. El-Djabarti, who was amongst them, describes how they all "began to scream at the top of their voices, crying 'Oh God, Oh God' and other imprecations of this kind . . . howling and barking like dogs."[27] The clamor was so great that it soon became impossible for Ibrahim Bey to make his shouted orders heard by his men. Even so, according to El-Djabarti, at this point "a large number of emirs and soldiers from the forces on the Cairo bank of the river decided to cross the river to aid their fellows on the other shore. Amongst these was Ibrahim Bey himself. There was a great confusion amongst the men because there were only a few rowing boats."[28]

At the same time, on the far bank the lines of the advancing French weathered a further chaotic Mameluke charge and soon began storming the defensive positions at the edge of Embaba. Initially, the Janissary infantry and artillerymen attempted to hold their positions, with various groups of Mameluke cavalry continuing to charge and cannons firing at the advancing French from across the Nile, but to little avail. According to Private Millet, one of the French soldiers who stormed the defenses of Embaba: "We cut off a group of the enemy so that they had to throw themselves in the Nile where many of them drowned and those that we reached were bayoneted. . . . This resulted in a frightful carnage. The corpses of men and horses presented a hideous spectacle, so bloody was the carnage."[29]

As the French breaking into Embaba began bayoneting their way through the Janissaries and the garrison, the *fellahin* militia simply panicked and ran en masse for the Nile, where other soldiers were already piling into the few boats. Mameluke cavalry were plunging into the water, amidst the fleeing soldiers and *fellahin*, in a general chaos and confusion. In mid-stream, these boats became mixed up with the boats attempting to reach Embaba from the Cairo side, while the French soldiers began firing at them from the bank. According to El-Djabarti, things became even more chaotic when, "at that moment a violent wind blew up, so that the surface of the river became rough; the sand blown up by the wind beat against the faces of the Egyptians, and no one was able to open their eyes." He then added, with more patriotism than conviction: "The wind came from the enemy shore and was also one of the causes of the defeat of the Egyptian army."[30]

The spectators on the Cairo shore gazed in horror at what was happening. According to Nicolas Turc: "The population was in anguish, maddened by the infernal noise of incessant thunderous gunfire." When they realized that the battle was lost, "the people sobbed and slapped their own faces, yelling: 'What evil has befallen us! Now we will become prisoners of the French.'"[31] Amidst scenes of hollering terror, the spectators scrambled back towards Cairo.

The battle was now all but over. According to Turc: "The combat had lasted more than two hours—but two hours of indescribable horror."[32] Others claim it did not last even this long. As far as the vanquished were concerned, it was now every man for himself. Those of Murad Bey's Mameluke cavalry who had escaped the carnage, possibly as many as seven or eight thousand, simply galloped back to their lines, and then continued on in flight towards their domains in Upper Egypt. Murad Bey himself rode back to his palace at Giza; here he ordered that Nikola's entire flotilla and any other boats on the Nile should be set on fire, in an attempt to impede the French in their crossing of the river to take Cairo. As the sun set, he too galloped off with his squadron of loyal beys in the direction of Upper Egypt. From the distance, Napoleon could only watch; he had insufficient cavalry to give chase to any of the fleeing Mamelukes. In the dark, in countryside that he knew, Murad Bey would have been in his element. It would have taken more even than the likes of the dashing Murat, Desvernois or the formidable mulatto General Dumas to catch and destroy the large force of Mamelukes that had eluded Napoleon's grasp, and would now live to fight another day.

On the Cairo side of the river, Ibrahim Bey galloped back towards Cairo, scattering the stream of wailing citizens in his path. Once in the city, he sought out Pasha Abu Bakr, and then fled eastwards towards Sinai, taking his remnant Mameluke cavalry and the pasha with him. Whether or not Abu Bakr went willingly is disputed; Nicolas Turc even claims that he was with Ibrahim Bey and his forces at Boulac. Either way, the pasha's absence represented a serious setback to Napoleon's plans; he had intended to make his peace with the Ottoman viceroy, and use his considerable charm to win him over as his friend. Napoleon had intended that Abu Bakr should retain his position as the titular ruler of Egypt, giving him a much more public role than he had occupied under the Mamelukes. He believed that this would lend a considerable air of legitimacy to the French presence in Egypt, and would help smooth over any difficulties between the French government and the Porte when Talleyrand's promised diplomatic mission arrived in Constantinople (if it had not already done so).

That night, Napoleon and his staff took up residence in Murad Bey's magnificent palace on the banks of the Nile at Giza. As Napoleon remembered it:

None of his slaves or servants had remained behind. Nothing of its interior decor remotely resembled a European palace. However, the staff officers were delighted to move into a house so well furnished with divans upholstered with Lyons silk and golden tassels, and other such dizzying luxuries of European craftsmanship. The garden was full of beautiful trees; there was a great trellis covered with vines from which hung bunches of excellent grapes, which proved a precious discovery. Word of this spread through the camp, attracting crowds of soldiers, and the harvest was soon over.[33]

But not all the French were so interested in grapes. Many soldiers left the camp on the pretext of seeking out any remaining French wounded. Moving through the darkness of the battlefield with lanterns, they began poring over the bodies of the Mameluke fallen, looting them of the gold coins secreted amongst their charred satin jerkins, sewn into their silk cloaks and hidden in money belts. Napoleon himself described the scene in his memoirs:

The divisions camped at Embaba had a field day. They found the luggage left behind by the beys and their warriors, containers of jam and sweets, carpets, porcelain, silverware in great abundance. All through the night, the minarets of Cairo were lit up by the swirling flames from the burning flotilla on the Nile, their glimmer reflected on the walls of the pyramids. During the days following the battle, the soldiers busied themselves fishing in the Nile for bodies, many of which had two or three hundred gold pieces on them.[34]

According to Marmont, who also mentions this looting: "Soon many bayonets were plunging into the Nile, and there was fine fishing. Some soldiers deposited as much as thirty thousand francs with their regimental cashier."[35] At last the morale of the troops was restored.

Across from the battlefield, amidst the darkened streets and alleyways of Cairo, chaos reigned as the terrified population loaded up their possessions and attempted to flee. They could see the flames and the glow in the sky from Nikola's burning ships on the Nile; many even thought that the French had entered the city itself and were burning it down. In a delirium of tribulation, men threw dust upon their heads and beat their breasts, while women howled, raising their arms to the flickering sky. Others began breaking into the deserted palaces of the beys, looting them and setting them on fire. Ibrahim Bey's palace was one of the first to be set alight. At the same time the mass of the population streamed towards the eastern gates of the city, driving overladen donkeys, camels and mules before them through the clamorous streets and alleyways. Once outside, in the darkness beyond the city walls, the

Bedouin were waiting for them; with hideous cries they began setting on the screaming refugee columns, ransacking them of anything valuable, tearing necklaces and bracelets from the women, cutting through the clothes of the men to discover hidden pouches of valuables, stripping others naked in their frenzied greed. As El-Djabarti put it, summing up the day's experience: "Never before had Egypt seen such horrors. Never have we seen such things in the history of humanity; you may hear my words, but you can never imagine what they described."[36]

History drily records the fact that on July 21, 1798, the French army won what came to be called the Battle of the Pyramids. These "monuments of destiny," as Napoleon liked to call them, were in reality almost ten miles from the main battlefield. Cairo was of course closer, as well as being the ultimate object of the battle, but Napoleon rightly understood that this name did not have quite the same ring to it, and to call such a conflict the Battle of Embaba, which was where it actually took place, would have been an act of military diffidence quite alien to its victor. In his report back to his nominal masters the Directory, written three days later on 6 Thermidor Year VI (July 24, 1798), Napoleon estimated "the loss of 2,000 elite Mameluke cavalry, with a large part of the beys wounded or killed. Mourad [sic] Bey has been wounded in the face. Our losses amount to 20 or 30 killed and 120 wounded."[37] Later, in his memoirs of the campaign, he estimated "enemy losses, killed, wounded, drowned or taken prisoner, as many as 10,000 Mamelukes, Arabs, Janissaries, Azabs,* etc."[38] Compared with the estimates in some contemporary memoirs, these figures appear high. Yet the nature of the fighting, and its scale, would suggest that casualties must have approached such figures. However, even though the Battle of the Pyramids may have been a rout, it had not been the comprehensive victory Napoleon had been hoping for: too many Mamelukes had escaped.

---

* I have been unable to identify this group; indeed there is a strong possibility that it is either a word coined by Napoleon (which appears nowhere else in the French language) or a misprint which runs through all editions.

VIII

Cairo

NAPOLEON was up at dawn on July 22, ready to embark upon yet another whirlwind of administrative activity. Desaix had been dispatched five miles up the Nile to construct defenses in case Murad Bey's Mamelukes returned to threaten the French forces as they attempted to cross the Nile; but Napoleon's main problem was to find sufficient river transport to enable him to accomplish this. Perrée's flotilla was still stuck at a low-water point further down the Nile, and Nikola's flotilla was now destroyed beyond repair. Fortunately a scouting party from Vial's division discovered several craft further up the Nile, but by the end of the day these had only managed to transport 300 men across the river.

Early on the same day, Napoleon had dispatched a message to the *ulema* and sheiks* of Cairo, who he learned had gathered at the Al-Azhar mosque. He assured them that he came in peace: "There is no need to worry, for no one desires to contribute more to your happiness than myself."[1] Despite this somewhat unconvincing message from the commander of the 25,000-man invading army camped across the river, a delegation of two *ulema* was sent to negotiate with the infidel conqueror. Napoleon was not impressed, and demanded to know why all the others had not come. The two *ulema* duly returned with the reassuring message that Napoleon wished to set up a *divan* of local dignitaries to rule the city. Deciding to take him at his word, most of the *ulema* and sheiks crossed the river to meet with him. Bardeuf, the leading French resident in Cairo, was by now at Giza with Napoleon, acting as his interpreter

---

* Napoleon used this title loosely to refer to leading religious, and sometimes civic or tribal, dignitaries.

and go-between; together with the consul Magallon, he had drawn up a list of all the most powerful notables of Cairo, so that when the larger delegation arrived Napoleon could check who was missing. When Napoleon demanded of the delegation why the *cadi*, the high judge, and Sheik Said Omar were not present, the delegates were suitably impressed and disconcerted at his knowledge; they replied that both men had fled. Napoleon informed the delegation that there was no need for anyone to flee, for he came as a liberator of Egyptians and a friend of Islam. The delegation duly promised to supply provisions for Napoleon and his men, as well as transport to enable his army to cross the river; there were still a large number of local boats drawn up in the creeks on the Cairo shore which had escaped the conflagration of Nikola's flotilla.

That day, even before the major crossing of the Nile was under way, Napoleon appointed General Dupuy as governor of Cairo, along with a temporary ruling commission of five officers, and ordered him to proceed into the city accompanied by 200 of the soldiers who had crossed the river. As night fell, this small force marched in through the Boulac Gate to take possession of the city, which at that time probably still contained over a quarter of a million inhabitants. In the words of Captain Malus, one of the young officers who accompanied Dupuy: "We departed for Cairo at night. . . . Hardly had we penetrated the cramped and torturous alleyways than the flicker and glimmer of flames above the rooftops made us realize that parts of the city were on fire . . . . We met not a single person on our way. Only the frightened ululuing of the women locked inside their harems made us realize that the city was inhabited."[2] As the columns of Frenchmen wound their way through the streets in the dark, they were preceded by soldiers beating drums. According to one soldier, "this unusual noise inspired terror in the inhabitants,"[3] although another claimed that the sole purpose of the drummers was in fact to prevent the soldiers at the back of the column from losing their way in the maze of darkened, deserted streets. In the end, even their Egyptian guide got lost, and Dupuy was unable to lead his men to their intended destination in the European quarter. After wandering about aimlessly, they eventually found themselves outside the gates of what appeared to be an abandoned Mameluke mansion. Dupuy ordered his men to break in, the mansion proved to be deserted, and the troop camped out in the large empty courtyard.

During the following days, four of the French divisions began crossing the Nile, guarded by Desaix's division upstream. On July 24 Napoleon

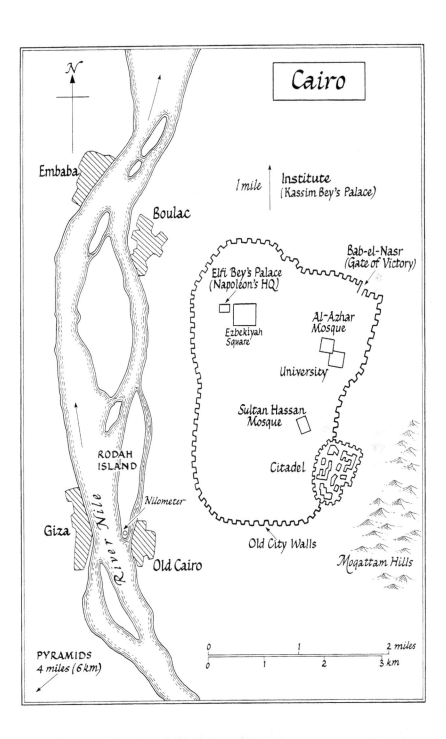

N

Cairo

Embaba

Boulac

1 mile | Institute
(Kassim Bey's Palace)

Bab-el-Nasr
(Gate of Victory)

Elfi Bey's Palace
(Napoleon's HQ)

Al-Azhar
Mosque

Ezbekiyah
Square

University

Sultan Hassan
Mosque

RODAH
ISLAND

Citadel

Nilometer

Giza

Old City Walls

River Nile

Old Cairo

Moqattam Hills

PYRAMIDS
4 miles (6 km)

0   1   2 miles

0   1   2   3 km

himself crossed the river and reviewed before the walls of Cairo those men of the four divisions who were already across. Before them was drawn up a delegation of sheiks and *ulema* offering the keys to the gates of the city in an act of symbolic submission. After a short ceremony the trumpets sounded a fanfare, there was a roll of drums, and Napoleon rode into the city at the head of a column of grenadiers. This time the streets were lined with spectators, all curious to catch a glimpse of the infidel conqueror.

Napoleon established his headquarters in the deserted palace of Elfi Bey on the northwestern edge of the city. This was in fact the most modern and luxurious residence in Cairo, having been recently completed at great expense for its powerful owner, who had long been a favorite of Murad Bey, and who had fled with his master into Upper Egypt. Elfi Bey's palace was set amidst extensive beautiful gardens with cypress and orange trees. Its grand front terrace, complete with marble pillars and polished Aswan granite floor, looked out over the large open park known as Ezbekiyah Square, which for part of the year was flooded by the waters of the Nile and became a lake. The front hall of the palace contained a large ornamental fountain and each of its main rooms was decorated in lavish style, with gilt mirrors, damask curtains and silk-woven Persian carpets, as well as divans and sofas. Unusually for a Mameluke palace, it also had chairs, and sunken baths on both floors.*

Cairo was during this period regarded as the second city of the Ottoman Empire; its permanent population consisted of an estimated 500,000 inhabitants (almost a fifth of the Egyptian population), making it larger than Paris. It was a renowned trading center, with large seasonal caravans, consisting of hundreds of camels, arriving from as far afield as Aleppo, Mecca, Darfur in the Sudan, and Timbuktu 2,000 miles away on the other side of the Sahara. Within the precincts of Cairo there were more than 300 mosques, from whose minarets the voices of the muezzins would ring out over the rooftops of the city day and night with the regular calls to prayer. The post of muezzin was traditionally occupied by blind men, allegedly so that when they looked down from the minarets they could not see into the exposed private rooms of the houses below. Whether or not this was the case, the muezzins in Cairo would have seen little at certain times of day, when

---

* In the following century this would become the site of the celebrated Shepheard's Hotel.

the atmosphere was blighted by a pall of brown smog from the house-hold cooking fires, many of which used dried dung for fuel. They would also have needed strong voices, to make themselves heard over the barking of the rabid dogs which roamed the alleyways in packs; these were liable to break into a cacophonous racket at the slightest distur-bance, in the process setting off any other dogs in the vicinity. It was said that throughout the country the number of wild dogs may well have outnumbered the population of Egyptians, which had sunk to just two and a half million, a third of its size at the height of pharaonic times over three millennia previously.

Many of Napoleon's generals were billeted in deserted Mameluke palaces, and even the leading savants Monge and Berthollet took up residence in a fine mansion on Ezbekiyah Square. Other officers, as well as the men, had to make do with lesser accommodation throughout the city, with the soldiers often camping out in courtyards. Up until now, most members of the French expeditionary force had barely come into contact with the indigenous population; and when first they ventured beyond the walls of their billets into the teeming streets of Cairo, they were in for a deep culture shock. The reaction of Major Detroye of the engineers is typical, infused as it is with the prejudices of his race and era:

On entering Cairo, what do you find? Narrow streets, unpaved and filthy, shadowy houses often in ruins, even the public buildings seem like dungeons, shops are nothing better than stables, the air is filled with dust and the reek of garbage. You see men with one milky eye, others totally blind, men in beards, clothed in rags, swarming through crowded alleyways, or smoking pipes, squatting like monkeys before the entrance to their caves. And as for the women—nature's masterpiece elsewhere in the world—here they are hideous and revolting, hiding their emaciated faces behind reeking threadbare veils, their naked pendulous breasts showing through their torn robes, their children yellow and skinny, covered in suppurating sores, surrounded by flies. Hideous smells come from the filthy interiors, and you choke on the risen dust together with the odor of food being fried in rancid oil in stuffy bazaars.[4]

After his "sightseeing tour," Detroye would return to his Cairo abode, which was evidently not in one of the Mameluke palaces:

A place devoid of human comforts, or proper living space. The flies, the midges, a thousand insects of all sorts, waiting to pounce on you in the night.

Soaked in sweat, prostrate with exhaustion, instead of resting you spend the time boiling and itching. In the morning you get up in a foul temper, your eyes swollen, sick in your stomach, your skin covered in bites which have by now been scratched septic. And so another day begins, no different from the last.[5]

Memoir after memoir lists the complaints of the occupying soldiers in these unfamiliar surroundings far from home. But reactions were not always entirely negative: young Captain Malus, with exemplary pragmatism, commented, "In the face of all this, one realized that it was necessary to renounce our European behavior, and to behave as they did. Unfortunately, during the first days we experienced all that was despicable in their Turkish [sic] behavior and none of the delights."[6] Surprisingly, it was the aging artist Denon who was the first to discover these delights, though even he was not totally enamored. He watched some belly dancers performing, accompanied by two male musicians on accordion and hand-drum, and some singers with tinkling finger-cymbals. Of the dancers he commented:

The way in which they twist their bodies lends an infinite grace to the move-ments of their wrists and fingers. At first their dancing appears beautifully voluptuous, but it soon descends into lasciviousness, becoming no more than the expression of a crude and indecent sensuality, and what is most disgusting about the show is that even when the dancers are performing with delicacy and restraint, one of the musicians will begin leering like a coarse buffoon, turning the whole thing into a drunken debacle.[7]

Denon noticed that these women

drank the local firewater in big glasses as if it was lemonade, so that although they might have been young and pretty they soon became tired and withered, except for two whose beauty and manner were as striking as any two famous beauties in Paris, their purely natural grace suggestive of the caresses and sweet voluptuousness that they doubtless reserved for those upon whom they lavished their intimate favors.[8]

The Egyptian reaction to the French occupation was similarly double-edged. El-Djabarti records his wonder at the soldiers "walking about the streets of the city unarmed and not molesting anyone. They joked with our people and in the bazaars bought whatever they wanted. . . . They went on buying bread, no matter how high the prices rose. The bakers, to increase their profits, reduced the size of their loaves and

mixed in dust with the flour."⁹ More perceptively, Nicolas Turc noted
how the French "easily pardoned their enemies, showing themselves
open and indulgent, observing justice, making good rules and passing
good laws. However, in spite of all these efforts, they were not able
to win over the hearts of the people. The Muslims hid their hatred for
these people."¹⁰

Despite such ambiguities, the truth of the situation was simple
enough. For all the good- and ill-will, these two so different people
were divided by a gulf of incomprehension. And nowhere was this
more apparent than in the *divan* which Napoleon set up to rule Cairo.
This was established on the day after his entry into the city, and consisted
of nine sheiks, with a French commissioner appointed to sit in on the
proceedings, and two Arabic-speaking savants to translate for him. The
divan was to meet every day, and was expected to ensure the smooth
running of the city in matters ranging from policing to the burial of
the dead. The first French commissioner appointed to the *divan* was
Poussielgue, Napoleon's former financial administrator and spy, who
was expected to advise the members when necessary and to report back
to his commander-in-chief on the day's proceedings.

From the outset, there was to be no meeting of minds here. Napoleon's
covert intention was clear, as he later confided in a long letter to Kléber
in Alexandria: "By winning over the opinions of the leading sheiks of
Cairo, one has the support of all the people of Egypt and any chieftains these people might have. None are less dangerous to us than the
sheiks, who are timid, have no idea how to fight, and like all priests
inspire fanaticism without being fanatics themselves."¹¹ The sheiks for
their part resisted all attempts to make them take any responsibility
for administering the city. This was in part because they feared the
return of the Mamelukes and the reprisals which might then take place;
worse still, the sheiks suspected that they would be made responsible
for the arrest of the remaining Mamelukes who were known to be still
in hiding in the city. However, there was a deeper problem than this:
the sheiks simply did not understand either the concept or the function of such a ruling council. The power of any previous *divan* had
been severely limited. Egypt had for so long been ruled on the whim
of the autocratic Mameluke beys that the give and take of discussion
was unknown to the sheiks. When the Cairo *divan* was inaugurated
under French rule, no sheik had any intention of revealing his ideas
about administrative matters, let alone discussing them. One by one

they insisted to Poussielgue that such decisions as he required of them should be referred to the Mamelukes or the Turks, not themselves. When Poussielgue said that this was no longer the case, the sheiks persisted in the view that such matters were nothing to do with them, pointing out that they were in fact the province of the government— it did not occur to them that this was precisely what *they* were meant to be! Even if this was not in reality fully the case, Napoleon had at least intended that the *divan* should be a conduit for public opinion. At best it would enable the French to act in concert with the wishes of the Egyptian people; it would play its part in initiating popular rule throughout the country, under the benign progressive ideas of the French. Yet here lay the deepest misunderstanding of all: there was no such thing as collective public opinion in a country which had no notion of the concept of democracy, amongst a people who had for centuries been deprived of any liberty whatsoever. The only collective public inclination—hardly a debatable opinion—was an instinctive suspicion, or worse, of all foreigners and infidels, a reservoir of ill-will whose potential was just waiting to be exploited.

The *divan* continued to meet on a daily basis, and its proceedings were duly reported to Napoleon, but nothing of any consequence was decided. The ruling of the city thus remained in the hands of Dupuy, who proceeded as best he could to administer Napoleon's wishes in consultation with the expert local advice of Magallon and Bardeuf, who drew on their knowledge as long-term residents. Magallon suggested that the policing of the city was best placed in the hands of a European resident of Cairo called Barthelemy. According to El-Djabarti, Barthelemy was "a Greek Christian of the lowest class" whom the Egyptians called "Fart-el-Roumman, or grenadine pip"[12]—the former said to be an Egyptian onomatopoeic rendering of Barthelemy, rather than an insult, though the latter was definitely intended as such, its sense being akin to "pipsqueak." Barthelemy was in essence a colorful, unscrupulous adventurer: a marketplace bully with an overbearing demeanor, who was known for his flamboyant appearance, habitually dressed in a large white turban and traditional gold-embroidered Greek costume, with baggy trousers and a scarlet sash around his waist. He took to his new responsibilities with characteristic panache, immediately recruiting a troop of around 100 low-life Greek and Moorish cronies as his fellow police officers, and requisitioning a Mameluke palace as his headquarters, at the same time appropriating the former occupier's harem and slaves.

Prior to the French occupation, Cairo had been policed in its own rather lackadaisical manner. The city was divided up into a number of separate walled and gated quarters, each of which was presided over by its own sheik, who was expected by the Mamelukes to maintain some semblance of public order, though that was liable to be disturbed at any moment by the Mamelukes themselves. Napoleon saw this division of the city as a threat to the French authority, and therefore ordered Barthelemy to make breaches in the walls which sealed off the quarters, and to destroy the gates.

Barthelemy took to riding around Cairo on a donkey with a large scimitar dangling from his side, at the head of his similarly mounted troop. The scimitar was not for display purposes, and malefactors (or even those simply suspected of crimes) were liable to be beheaded on the spot. Napoleon was now willing to tolerate such behavior; after his initial attempts to ingratiate himself with the people of Cairo, he had quickly become exasperated at the lack of respectful response—from the devious sheiks on the *divan* to the distrustful ordinary citizens. In a report to the Directory, he concluded: "Cairo, which has more than 300,000 inhabitants, has the most villainous population in the world."[13]

From the outset, Magallon had advised him that the Egyptians regarded compassion in a ruler as a sign of weakness, advice that Napoleon had initially been unwilling to follow. He was determined that the French should demonstrate their progressive ideas by sympathetic example. Just as in Alexandria, he gave orders to all commanders that soldiers who committed an offense against the local people—whether it be theft, lack of respect for Islam, or rape—should be clapped in irons and even executed. But now that he realized progressive ideas could not be instilled in the Egyptians overnight, he began applying to them a similar regime to the military discipline he imposed upon his own men. Advising Menou at Rosetta, he wrote: "The Turks* can only be ruled with the greatest severity; every day I have five or six heads cut off in the streets of Cairo . . . We must adopt a manner which makes these people obey us; and for these people, to obey means to fear."[14] Although he was still intent upon introducing progressive ideas, he now had no qualms

---

* The French soon began regularly referring to *all* the inhabitants of Egypt as "Turks," possibly a reflection of the fact that the country was part of the Ottoman Empire.

about using traditional Oriental methods to impose them. The irony of this appears to have escaped him.

At the same time, he continued to proclaim his sympathetic attitude towards Islam, informing a senior Muslim cleric that his aim was "to unite all the wise and learned men of the country, and establish a proper overall government, founded upon the principles of the Koran, which alone are true and which alone can bring happiness to mankind."[15] He was conciliatory in his approach to the muftis and religious leaders of the Al-Azhar mosque, even going so far as to proclaim his own belief in the principles of Islam, and attempting to demonstrate his deep understanding of the Koran. This last was not quite so laughable as it sounds. In his history El-Djabarti dismisses Napoleon's proclamations to the Egyptians, with their Islamic pretensions, ridiculing their awkward and un-Koranic Arabic; but in fact the faulty Arabic is entirely due to Napoleon's Oriental scholars who translated his original French. Several modern Arabic scholars have remarked on the fidelity of the Koranic tone in Napoleon's original French versions, a fidelity which he had acquired during his intense study of the Koran on his journey across the Mediterranean.

Once again, Napoleon saw himself as following in the footsteps of his great hero:

When Alexander arrived in Egypt, they ran to him, greeting this great man as a liberator. When he marched for fifteen days into the desert, from Alexandria to the Temple of Ammon, and was declared the son of Jupiter by the priestess, he demonstrated that he understood these people: he played on their deepest inclination, which was for their religion. This did more to assure his conquest than if he had built twenty castles and brought in 100,000 Macedonian troops.[16]

Likewise, Napoleon had understood from the outset that he could only rule Egypt with the aid of Islam. He too had come as a liberator, but initially at least, the success of his conquest would depend upon his adherence to Muslim principles, as well as leaving the Islamic structure of society untouched. And this would have to be seen to be the case: in other words, he would have to gain the blessing of the muftis. Napoleon was willing to go to great lengths to acquire this seal of legitimacy for French rule, and for this reason he approached the muftis with immense tact, using all his considerable charisma and intelligence in an effort to win them over to his cause. In no time his charm offensive began to bear fruit. Napoleon remembered in his official memoirs (in which he was in the habit of referring to himself in the third person):

The sheiks were old men, worthy of great respect for their morals, their knowledge, their riches and even their noble birth. Every day, at the setting of the sun, they and the *ulema* of the Al-Azhar mosque made a habit of calling at the palace of Elfi Bey, before the hour of prayer. Their entourage stretched all the way across Ezbekiyah Square: they arrived on their richly harnessed mules, surrounded by their servants and a great many attendants armed with sticks. The French soldiers on guard would present arms, according them full military honors. When they arrived in the salon, they would be received with the utmost respect by the staff officers and interpreters, and would then be served with sherbet or coffee. A few moments later the general-in-chief himself would enter and sit down amongst them on the same divan. He would seek to gain their trust by discussing with them the Koran, asking them to explain to him principal passages and revealing his great admiration for the Prophet. When they left they went on to the mosques, where the people were assembled, and here they spoke to them of all their hopes, calming the mistrust and fears of the entire population.[17]

Napoleon recounts the arguments and flatteries by which he sought to win over the wise men and *ulema* of the Al-Azhar mosque. No approach was too shameless. He softened them up with a blatant appeal to their patriotism:

Why has the Arabic nation submitted to the Turks? How come that fertile Egypt and holy Arabia are under the domination of a people from the Caucasus [i.e., the Mamelukes]? If the prophet descended from the heavens today where would he go? Mecca? This would not be at the center of the Muslim empire. Constantinople? This is a profane spot where there are more infidels than believers: here he would be amongst his enemies. No, he would prefer the blessed waters of the Nile, he would come to live at the Al-Azhar mosque.

At this, the venerable old men nodded in approval, exclaiming: "How true, how true!"[18] Or so Napoleon would have us believe in his memoirs. However, the evidence suggests that something similar must indeed have taken place, though perhaps without quite such a thoroughly acquiescent audience. As if all this was not preposterous enough, Napoleon now tried to persuade the assembled worthies of the Al-Azhar mosque that he was "destined" to arrive in Egypt, something that would not have been quite so difficult as it sounds, due to the fact that he certainly believed this himself. Soon, "their fondness for Napoleon was evident, and already they accepted that in principle he was a true Moslem." Napoleon proceeded to elaborate his argument: "The French would never have been able to conquer you people of the true faith, if their leader had not been under the special protection of the Prophet; the Mameluke army was invincible, the bravest in all the Orient. . . . This great revolution [the French victory] was written in several passages of the Koran."[19]

As a result of these arguments, Napoleon became known by the muftis as Sultan El-Kebir, the great ruler. He was flattered, though the degree of irony in this usage is unclear. The muftis eventually agreed to issue a *fatwa* recognizing the French as the legitimate rulers of Egypt, on condition that Napoleon and the French army converted to Islam. Napoleon, for his part, had no objection to this, and felt that with a little persuasion he could sell this to his army as a mere formality. After all, his men could hardly object on religious grounds as they were not practicing Christians. But the muftis insisted that such a move should be more than a formality: the French would all have to be circumcised and swear to abstain from alcohol. At this stage Napoleon was forced to concede that such a move was impossible: no French soldier would ever swear to abstain from alcohol. Even so, he continued to press the muftis at his afternoon meetings, until finally they found their way to a suitably devious concession: because the French were not Christians, although they were not Muslims they could be recognized as allies of the Muslim religion.

Napoleon appeared to have won his point. But what precisely *was* his point? In his long letter to Kléber, he would later write: "We must lull to sleep this fanaticism before we can eradicate it."[20] Despite all his claims to respect Islam, his dealings with it were cynical—more so than perhaps he could admit to himself at this stage, when he still saw himself as following the example of Alexander the Great, who at least partially sought to assimilate his army to the ways and customs of the countries it conquered. Yet despite himself and all his overweening ambition, Napoleon's agenda was more than power, more even than the establishment of an empire. Concomitant with all this was his seemingly benevolent wish to "civilize" Egypt, to introduce the latest progressive Western ideas. But was this combination of aims in any way compatible?

During his first few weeks in Cairo, Napoleon set in motion an extensive program of reform. He was faced with a city where piles of rubbish lay festering in all open spaces (waiting to be carried away by the annual flooding of the Nile), where one in five of the population had at least one sightless milky eye, where the dead were buried in open spaces, their graves desecrated by the packs of scavenging dogs. Both the conditions and the physical state of the population harked back to that of medieval times, a world which had largely disappeared from Europe 300 years previously.

On the very day of his entry into the city, Napoleon ordered the establishment of four hospitals, capable of treating 600 patients, "all to be ready in eight days."[21] New baking ovens and bakeries were constructed. Soon burial was no longer permitted within the walls of Cairo, and the engineers were set to work mapping the entire city. According to Nicolas Turc, "Each house door was ordered to have an illuminated lantern hanging outside it at night, and if the night patrols found one without a lantern they would hammer a nail in the door, so that next morning a punishment could be inflicted on the owner."[22] Once the streets were illuminated, a concerted operation was launched against the packs of rabid dogs, which in the course of one night were all poisoned—a move which bemused the locals. El-Djabarti was convinced that this was simply an act of revenge against the dogs for the lack of respect they showed the French, "because when they passed through the streets at night the dogs followed them barking."[23] Meanwhile, further public health measures were taken: military doctors identified the Egyptian eye disease as a virulent indigenous strain of ophthalmia. At the same time efforts were made to render the streets more hygienic, and the dumping of refuse inside the city was only permitted at allotted spots, which were cleared daily.

All this was just the beginning. Yet such a program required money, and this was soon in short supply, though it is difficult to account for precisely why this should have been so. Assuming that Napoleon had spent all the three million francs he had initially received from the Swiss exchequer in Berne, as well as the sums purloined from other European exchequers, on outfitting his expedition before it set out, there was still the seven million francs (plus quantities of gold and silver plate) he had taken from Malta. Despite this, there is no denying that he soon claimed to be short of cash in Cairo, and all the indications are that this claim was genuine. During the Italian campaign Napoleon had always been able to requisition treasures from

local cities and castles, but in Cairo he found that the Mamelukes had
long since drained the exchequer dry. Meanwhile, the army's wage bill
amounted to one million francs a month, a bill it appears he could
not pay. (The soldiers' main currency in the bazaars continued to be
their buttons.) Fortunately food was plentiful, and suppliers were issued
promissory notes for rice, beans, lentils and vegetables, as well as
sheep and goats brought in from outside the city. Napoleon sent an
urgent message to Kléber in Alexandria, ordering him to issue
promissory notes and redeem all the gold that had been issued to local
merchants; this was to be dispatched to Cairo, where it would be
minted into coins. Meanwhile, in an effort to raise some immediate
cash, he ordered a tax on all wealthy merchants. Barthelemy's local
knowledge was used to assess how much individual merchants could
afford, then he and his brigade of "policemen" were simply dispatched
to collect it. Napoleon even felt that this move might increase his popularity amongst the downtrodden urban poor, who resented the wealth
of these fellow countrymen whom they felt to be living at their expense.

When Napoleon heard that the wives of many of the wealthy
Mamelukes were still roaming the countryside outside Cairo in camel
caravans, abandoned by their masters and preyed on by the Bedouin,
he issued an armistice allowing them to return to their palaces in
Cairo. But for this privilege each of them would be required to pay
a large "ransom": in this way he hoped to gain access to the treasures
which he knew had been concealed in the Mameluke palaces and elsewhere. When Setty-Nefissa, Murad Bey's wife, arrived back at her
palace, Napoleon's young aide Eugene Beauharnais, the son of his
wife, Josephine, was sent to pay a courtesy call, and at the same time
to inform her of the sum she would be required to pay. Setty-Nefissa
was a powerful woman, having been married to the great Mameluke
ruler Ali Bey before she became Murad Bey's wife. Besides being
extremely rich, she was also respected throughout Cairo, and even in
these difficult times she continued to maintain Murad Bey's numerous
household, which included "a harem containing fifty women of all
countries and all colors." Napoleon reports that when Sub-Lieutenant
Beauharnais arrived at her palace, "all the slaves and servants wanted
to see the fine young Frenchman. Setty-Nefissa received the messenger
from Sultan El-Kebir [Napoleon] with dignity and grace. She led him
into the harem, treated him with great kindness, did him the honor
of serving him with a superb meal, and gave him a very valuable

ring."[24] Yet all this sumptuous hospitality proved of no avail, and Setty-Nefissa was still required to pay 600,000 francs.

Napoleon knew that these enforced levies could only be a temporary measure. At the same time, he realized that he could expect little in the way of regular financial support from the Directory back in France. They would be the first to point out that a colony was expected to send goods back to the mother country, rather than be a drain on its resources. With this in mind he planned to send to France regular convoys containing large amounts of expensive coffee, sugar and cotton, as well as other Egyptian products such as rice and dried beans. He also had high hopes of creating a lucrative trade in spices and other luxury goods from the Far East. However, as he explained in one of his regular reports to the Directory, before such trade could be inaugurated he first had to establish a French colony, and this would require further military support, especially cavalry. But it is his list of other items he wished to be sent from France that is most revealing:

1. A troupe of comedians.
2. A troupe of ballerinas.
3. At least two or three puppeteers.
4. 100 French women.
5. The wives of all those who are stationed out here.
6. 20 surgeons; 30 pharmacists; 10 physicians.
7. Some iron foundrymen.
8. Some liqueur makers and distillers.
9. 50 gardeners with their families, and seeds of all types of vegetables.
10. Each convoy must bring 200,000 pints of eau-de-vie [alcoholic spirits] and a million pints of wine.
11. To be sent with these, 300,000 lengths of blue and red flag cloth.
12. To be sent with these, soap and oil.[25]

Such were deemed the necessities of a French colony, without which it would be impossible to lay down the foundations of civilization. Indicatively, Napoleon had chosen to bring with him intellectuals for the pursuance of his own grandiose vision, rather than entertainers for his soldiers.

However, despite the lack of comedians and ballerinas, Napoleon still found opportunity for diversion, and one day not long after his arrival in Cairo he set out with his entourage on a trip to the pyramids. These huge 4,000-year-old monuments (to this day the most massive stone buildings in the world) had been a source of awe and mystery to visiting Europeans since classical times, when they had been seen as one of the Seven Wonders of the Ancient World. Later, medieval visitors had speculated that they might be Joseph's granaries, as mentioned in the Bible. Despite the erosion inflicted by the desert winds and sandstorms, the summit of the Great Pyramid was still almost five hundred feet above ground level, and proved so impressive that Napoleon suggested his companions should take part in a race to the top. He is said to have been highly amused at the sight of his staff officers and savants scrambling up the crumbling slabs of the steep stone slope beneath the stupefying heat of the Egyptian sun. Berthier, who was lovesick for his Italian *contessa*, soon lost the will to continue, and gave up halfway. Surprisingly, it was the fifty-three-year-old mathematician Monge, with a gourd of reviving eau de vie attached to his buttonhole, who was first to the summit. Lieutenant Desvernois, who climbed to the top some weeks later, described the view:

At the top you look down to see a vast sweep of countryside, a spectacle more imposing than you could possibly dream. To the west, the view stretches into the immensity of the bare arid desert, while to the east the fertile valley of the Nile, all green with vegetation, rolls away into the far distance. Compared with the enormous mass of this mountain of stones, the people far below at its feet appear like crawling insects. . . . Around rise other pyramids, one of them . . . still covered to around 150 feet from the summit with slabs of red granite which are smooth and polished like a mirror, making it impossible to climb.[26]

As the other members of Napoleon's staff reached the summit, Monge offered each of them a reviving slug of eau de vie. Far below they could see Napoleon, standing alone, lost in thought. When they descended, it became clear that he had not been preoccupied with the timeless wonder of the Great Pyramid, but with the more mundane facts of its construction. He informed Monge that the stone blocks used to erect it would be sufficient to build a wall three meters high and one meter wide around France; the great mathematician thought for a moment, and then confirmed that he was correct.*

---

* Though some historians have cast doubt on these figures, mathematicians I have consulted assure me that they are indeed correct (personal conversations with Howard Martin and Mark Strathern). In some sources Napoleon is quoted as saying this wall around France would be "ten feet high and three feet wide." It is not clear which system of measurement he actually used. The exact proportions of the metric system were not decided until 1797, and thus only came into use during the year before the Egyptian expedition set out. As is evident from the memoirs and official correspondence of the expedition, many continued to use, and think in terms of, the older system.

Other members of the Egyptian expedition would later attempt to explore the inside of the Great Pyramid, which had only been opened up again a few years previously. The French traveler Savary was one of the first to penetrate the interior, and most vividly evokes the atmosphere inside the pyramid at this time:

We left our coats at the entrance to the passage which led into the interior, and began to descend, each holding a burning torch. Towards the bottom, we had to wriggle on our bellies like snakes in order to gain access to the inner passageway. . . . We scrambled up this on our knees, at the same time pressing our hands against the sides. Had we not done this, we risked slipping backwards, and the slight grooves on its surface would not have been able to stop us from sliding all the way down to the bottom. About halfway up we fired a pistol shot whose deafening noise echoed away forever through all the distant recesses of the immense edifice. This awakened thousands of bats, which hurtled down, striking us on our hands and face and extinguishing several of our torches.[27]

As night fell, Napoleon's officers had their tents erected at the foot of the Great Pyramid. It was noticed that Berthier had two tents, and Napoleon discovered that inside one of these he had erected a little shrine to the Contessa Visconti. As they sat around their campfire in the desert, Napoleon could not resist poking fun at Berthier over this.[28] However, events which have since come to light indicate that Napoleon's attitude towards Berthier and his pining for his great love were more complex than his outer badinage would suggest. Similarly, it seems likely that Napoleon's preoccupation at the foot of the Great Pyramid was concerned with more than just mental arithmetic. We now know that prior to this he had received some personal news that had left him an emotionally broken man.

IX

"Josephine! . . . And I am 600 leagues away!"

NAPOLEON'S tactical brilliance at the Battle of the Pyramids, together with his whirlwind of activity during the first weeks in Cairo, is rendered all the more remarkable by the single-mindedness with which he put aside a revelation that had devastated him. A couple of days before the battle, he was walking on the edge of an oasis with his loyal aide Junot at his side, his secretary Bourrienne and his staff entourage following a few paces behind.¹ Some time prior to this he must have been boasting to his officers, as was his habit, about how lucky he was to have the love of a good woman—namely his wife, Josephine. By this stage, her infidelities had become common knowledge amongst his senior officers. Junot must have noticed their exchange of scoffing looks when Napoleon spoke of his feelings for his wife, and must have wished to put his master straight on this matter to avoid Napoleon humiliating himself any further. This is of course conjecture, but something must surely have taken place along these lines—for there is no doubting Junot's loyalty, and it is difficult to imagine why else he might have chosen to bring up such a painful subject at this particular, highly inopportune moment.

At any rate, as Napoleon and Junot were walking on the edge of the desert, Junot revealed that Josephine had persisted in her affair with Hippolyte Charles, giving precise details of their liaison and even showing Napoleon a letter that confirmed these details, which according to Junot were the talking point of all Paris. On hearing this news, Napoleon went into a state of shock: his limbs began moving in an involuntary spasmodic fashion, all the blood drained from his already pale face, turning it quite white, and he slapped his hand to his forehead several times. Then he turned to Bourrienne and Berthier behind him, demanding to know if this was all true, and if so, why they had not told him. When Berthier confirmed the truth of what Junot had said, Napoleon flew into a rage. "Josephine! . . . And I am 600 leagues away! . . . I have no wish to be the laughingstock of all those useless Parisians. I will publicly divorce her." According to Bourrienne, in his rage he kept repeating the word "divorce" again and again.[2]

Inevitably, Josephine's son Eugene Beauharnais soon got to hear of what had happened. Five days later he wrote to his mother, informing her of what Napoleon had been told, and adding hopefully that he was sure all this gossip had been invented by her enemies. The following day Napoleon wrote a letter to his elder brother and confidant Joseph in Paris, in which his extreme rage and despair are all too evident. "I am weary of human nature. I need solitude and isolation. Greatness no longer interests me. All feeling in me is dried up. My thirst for glory has faded at the age of twenty-nine. I am completely worn out."[3] This was July 25: in the intervening period he had fought the Battle of the Pyramids, made his triumphal entry into Cairo, and begun his "revolution" of the affairs of Egypt. The supreme effort of will involved in putting such emotional turmoil out of his mind can only be marveled at. In his letter to his brother he also wrote: "I can be in France in two months. Have a country house ready for me when I return, either close to Paris or in Burgundy. I count on locking myself up and spending the winter there." In the midst of his triumph he wished to give it all up; yet paradoxically, at the same time he continued laying the foundations of his "Oriental empire."

This letter in which Napoleon poured out his soul ("The veil is torn . . . the same heart is torn by such conflicting feelings"), and the letter from Eugene Beauharnais revealing the precise details of why Napoleon was in such a state, were dispatched from Cairo to Alexandria, and thence by sea for France. Unfortunately, before they could reach their destination they were intercepted on the high seas by the British navy, and transmitted to London. The British seized on this opportunity to inflict a propaganda victory on the French, and the letters were published amidst much merriment in the *Morning Chronicle* of London on November 24, 1798; French spies soon relayed this information back to Paris, where Napoleon truly became a laughingstock.

But why had Napoleon reacted in such an extreme fashion to what Junot had told him? This was hardly the first time he had heard about

Josephine being unfaithful to him; Junot had merely given voice to what he must surely have suspected, as he had on previous occasions. Many explanations have been put forward for Napoleon's violent outburst this time. Junot had confirmed—in the presence of others— what had previously only been a suspicion: a private fear had been made public. This had caused Napoleon to look a fool in the eyes of others, something he could not abide. It had also forced him to act against Josephine, something he was only willing to do when things reached an unavoidable crisis point. Previously he had been able to confront Josphine, to humiliate her sadistically, and then effect an emotional reconciliation: the sadomasochistic element that bound their relationship had thus been reinforced. But this time she simply was not there, and was not likely to be in the near future—hence his cry of anguish: "Josephine! ... And I am 600 leagues away!" This unbridgeable absence, amongst the nexus of contributory circumstances, may well have been what tipped the balance. Yet in the end, one can only speculate.

It has been claimed that this crisis marked both a physical and an emotional turning point in Napoleon's life, and there is some evidence to support this view. From now on the thin, rakish figure with long, unkempt hair would gradually become transformed into the suave, plump man of legend. Whether this was through compensation for emotional deprivation or due to purely glandular effects is unclear, but there is no doubting that Napoleon underwent a physical transformation, and that this certainly showed its first manifestations around the time of his Egyptian expedition. The mental transformation is equally difficult to pinpoint. In his youth, Napoleon cut a dashing, heroic figure, driven by dreams of glory, but at some pivotal stage in his career these more positive qualities were gradually transmogrified into the cold, ruthless and often blind ambition which led him to his greatest honors and his greatest disasters. There had always been a cruel, heartless element in Napoleon's character, but it was only in Egypt that this would begin to appear as a ruling characteristic. As he concluded in his letter to his brother Joseph: "There is nothing left for me but to think only of myself."[4] Whatever the effects of this crisis upon Napoleon, one thing is certain: from this time onwards Junot fell from grace. The fearless sergeant who had stood by the youthful Napoleon at the siege of Toulon would continue to prosper, but he would no longer remain Napoleon's faithful confidant—someone had to take the blame. As for

Napoleon himself: once he had given vent to his extreme emotions, he seemed miraculously capable of putting them from his mind, consciously committing himself to the task at hand with ever-renewed vigor and single-mindedness. At the same time, these ignored elements would continue to play their own souring role, independent of conscious control.

Meanwhile the situation in Egypt as a whole remained unresolved. Napoleon had taken Alexandria, driven his troops down through the delta, defeated the Mamelukes in a set-piece battle and marched into Cairo. He had expected that the taking of Cairo would secure Egypt under French rule, but it had not. As long as Murad Bey and Ibrahim Bey remained at large, even with depleted Mameluke forces, French rule remained a temporary measure in the eyes of the Egyptian population. It was evident that they feared a return of the Mamelukes far more than they feared even the most severe measures imposed by the French.

By now the Nile waters were beginning to rise, and Desaix reported from Giza that the flooding of the banks upstream meant that it was impossible for him to mount any effective pursuit of Murad Bey immediately. Napoleon decided upon a different tack, and on August 1 dispatched the Austrian consul Carlo Rosetti to Upper Egypt to meet with Murad Bey, whom Rosetti had come to know as a personal friend during his years in Egypt. Napoleon instructed the neutral consul to negotiate a peace settlement, giving him full powers to make Murad Bey the generous offer of the governorship of Girga province in Upper Egypt if he was willing to accept French rule.

Ibrahim Bey was another matter. News soon reached Napoleon that he had halted his flight towards the safety of the Sinai desert at Bilbeis, just thirty miles northeast of Cairo. Here he had intercepted the annual pilgrimage on its return from Mecca, and plundered it of camels and provisions for his journey. Sensing his chance, Napoleon immediately dispatched Reynier after Ibrahim Bey with a hastily assembled force, including some 350 cavalry (his mounted forces now augmented with horses requisitioned in Cairo). The French infantry were reluctant, and Reynier's progress was slow. Impatient at this news, Napoleon decided to take command himself, and quickly rode out into the field to effect more speedy progress.

Napoleon and the advance cavalry unit surprised Ibrahim Bey as he was camped in a stand of palm trees on the outskirts of El Saliyeh, at the edge of the Sinai desert; but the tables were quickly turned as the French found themselves confronted by 500 Mameluke cavalry and 500 Arab infantry. In the ensuing skirmish the French suffered thirty casualties, and Napoleon himself was saved only by the timely arrival of Reynier's troops, whereupon the 500 Arabs switched sides, and the French at last tipped the scales. Even so, Napoleon could only watch impotently as Ibrahim Bey and his camel caravan of wives and treasures escaped into the distant desert.

Napoleon now learned from one of the Arab deserters that he had also been close to capturing Pasha Abu Bakr, who was still with Ibrahim Bey. In a switch of tactics, he immediately dispatched a conciliatory message to Ibrahim Bey, offering him peace terms: "You have been driven to the edges of Egypt and are now faced with the prospect of crossing the desert. You will find in my great generosity the good fortune and happiness that will transform your present circumstances. Let me know soon of your intentions. The Pasha of the Turkish Sultan is with you: send him to me with your reply. I willingly accept him as a go-between."[5]

Ibrahim Bey was not for one moment deceived by Napoleon. He had no intention of sending Abu Bakr as an intermediary—whereupon he would certainly have been detained by Napoleon, who would have used him to validate his claims of legitimacy with the Porte. Napoleon now sent out patrols to make contact with the scattered remnants of the caravan from Mecca, which he ordered to be escorted to Cairo under armed French protection.

Napoleon remained for two days at El Saliyeh, organizing the French administration of the delta. By now Vial had taken Damietta, where he was established as governor; Reynier was appointed governor of the eastern delta region at Bilbeis; and Murat became governor at Qalyub, in the delta region north of Cairo. Each military governor was ordered to establish a provincial *divan*, its members drawn from amongst local sheiks and *ulema*, which was to deal with the everyday running of their district. Although this was hardly democracy, any more than it represented a truly liberated Egypt, it is worth noting that it was the nearest thing to popular rule the country had experienced throughout its five millennia of history.

On August 13 Napoleon set off back for Cairo. Before he reached

Bilbeis he was met by a military courier who had left Alexandria thirteen days previously, but whose speed had been hampered by his need for a military escort through the countryside of the delta, which remained treacherous. The courier delivered to Napoleon some catastrophic news which would transform his entire Egyptian expedition.

X

The Battle of the Nile

AFTER sailing from Alexandria on June 29, Nelson's squadron had set off north in search of Napoleon's expeditionary armada. Although Nelson had mentioned to his officers the possibility that he had arrived ahead of Napoleon, in his agitation he chose to forget this: evidently Napoleon's destination had not been Egypt after all. Nelson now surmised that the French fleet was in fact heading for Turkey, but after five days' sailing he changed his mind again and turned west. By now, the heady atmosphere which had enthused the squadron during its chase to Alexandria had entirely dissipated, and an air of despondency prevailed— especially amongst the officers on board the *Vanguard*, Nelson's flagship, where alcohol began to flow more freely over the dinner table. Records show that during the first week in July alcohol consumption peaked, with Nelson, his captain and his dozen or so officers managing to get through twelve bottles of port, nine of sherry, six of claret and twenty of porter (and this does not include the private stocks which most officers maintained for their own personal consumption on board).[1]

Turning west off Cyprus, Nelson began zigzagging his way under the lee of Crete, up the Mediterranean, in the hope of catching sight of the French fleet, but to no avail. The horizon remained empty. They were off the main shipping routes, and there wasn't even the occasional passing merchantman to give them any news: the huge French fleet had seemingly vanished. Nelson remained perplexed, at the same time showing increasing signs of anxiety, summoning his captains to frequent meetings aboard the *Vanguard*, at which they would again and again fruitlessly discuss all likely possibilities. After Napoleon had taken Malta, had he sailed north to take Sicily? Or worse still, had he headed west for the Atlantic, where he might by now be mounting an invasion of England, or Ireland, or even Brazil? Once again Nelson's nerves appeared at breaking point. After nearly three weeks' sailing, the British squadron of thirteen ships of the line arrived off Sicily, putting into Syracuse on July 20. The local populace lined the quayside to gaze at the British fleet, as the first longboat was rowed ashore. Nelson learned that Napoleon had not invaded Sicily, and also received news that he had not sailed west for Gibraltar either. The French were still somewhere in the Mediterranean.

Nelson remained four days in Syracuse, taking on supplies. Limited shore leave, together with fresh provisions—including vegetables, lemons, haunches of beef, and 100-gallon butts filled with water from the legendary Fountain of Arethusa—bolstered the morale of the squadron, and on July 23 Nelson noted, "The fleet is unmoored, and the moment the wind comes off the land, shall go out." [2] The offshore evening breeze filled the slack sails of the British ships of the line, and Nelson's squadron headed once more for the eastern Mediterranean. He still had no clear idea what to do, but prior to departing he had left a message for dispatch to his superior, Admiral St. Vincent, off Cadiz: "It is my intention to get into the mouth of the Archipelago [Aegean Islands], where, if the enemy are gone towards Constantinople, we shall hear of them directly: if I get no information there, to go to Cyprus, when, if they are in Syria or Egypt, I must hear of them." [3] These words show all the signs of being written in hope rather than expectation: evidence with which to defend himself before the expected Admiralty inquiry. But then Nelson had a lucky break: after five days' sailing he found himself off Coroni, at the southwest tip of the Greek Peloponnese, where he dispatched ashore Captain Troubridge on the *Culloden* to seek out any local intelligence. Here Troubridge heard that the local Turkish governor had been informed by the Porte in Constantinople that Napoleon had invaded Egypt. This news was confirmed with the capture of a French brig bound for Egypt loaded with wine, which was taken in tow by the *Culloden*.

Nelson at once set sail, though he remained uncertain of what to do when he arrived; Napoleon's fleet would doubtless be safely moored in harbor, well out of harm's way. All he could do was blockade the French, until such time as his shipboard supplies ran low and he was forced to leave. Meanwhile Napoleon would probably be well on his way to India. Nelson knew that in the eyes of the Admiralty his initial blunder was only liable to be compounded by further ineffective action, such as a temporary blockade. But what else could he do? It now looked as if he would be held responsible for the loss of the British Empire's most valuable possession, no less.

On the morning of August 1, the *Alexander* and the *Swiftsure*, sent ahead by Nelson, appeared off Alexandria. Observing through their telescopes, the British made out the French tricolors flying from the forts and towers. In the port there were all kinds of craft, including two French ships of the line and several frigates, but no sign of the main French battle fleet, and this news was duly signaled back to Nelson. The *Zealous* and the *Goliath* were dispatched on a search east along the coast. Eight miles down the coast, at two-thirty P.M., the masthead lookout on the *Zealous* spotted, beyond the curving sand spit which protected Aboukir Bay, a forest of masts: the French fleet was lying at anchor in the bay. At two-forty-five, Captain Hood aboard the *Zealous* signaled by flags, "Sixteen sail of the line at anchor, bearing East by South."[4] The news was greeted by a burst of cheering from the British sailors, which soon began resounding from ship to ship around the squadron.

Aboukir Bay lay at one of the ancient mouths of the Nile, which had long since silted up. It provided a fine anchorage, its vast sweep protected by a peninsula, with a fort at its end, as well as shoals and a rocky islet beyond. Inside the peninsula and islet were further shoals and shallows, close to which the French fleet was anchored in line. It consisted of thirteen* ships of the line, their strongest guns mounted on their offshore side—a classic defensive position—with the French flagship *L'Orient* anchored in the middle of the line. The British squadron still did not quite match the French, especially in gunpower, and if it went on the attack it would have to sail towards a line of enemy ships with over 500 guns mounted to starboard, with the French crews having nothing else to do but concentrate upon firing these guns. Meanwhile the British sailors would have to sail their ships as well, while they maneuvered themselves into a position where they could fire at the enemy. And even then they would only be able to fire half their guns—those mounted on the side facing the French fleet.

When the British sails had first been sighted by the lookouts of the French fleet at around two P.M., many crew members had been ashore

---

* The earlier signal from the *Zealous* had been inaccurate.

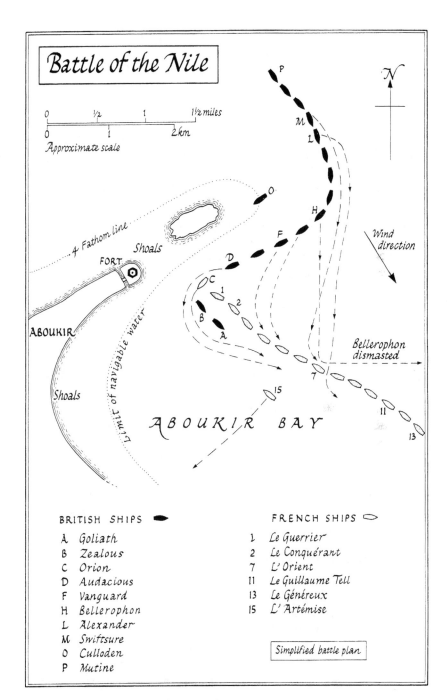

Battle of the Nile

0 — ½ — 1 — 1½ miles
0 — 1 — 2 km
Approximate scale

N

4 Fathom line
Shoals
FORT
ABOUKIR
Shoals
Limit of navigable water

Wind direction

Bellerophon dismasted

ABOUKIR BAY

BRITISH SHIPS		FRENCH SHIPS	
A	Goliath	1	Le Guerrier
B	Zealous	2	Le Conquérant
C	Orion	7	L'Orient
D	Audacious	11	Le Guillaume Tell
F	Vanguard	13	Le Généreux
H	Bellerophon	15	L'Artémise
L	Alexander		
M	Swiftsure		
O	Culloden		
P	Mutine		

Simplified battle plan

digging wells in the sand for fresh water, together with their armed escorts, to guard against the hostile Bedouin who roamed the dunes. Alarm flags were raised on the masts of the French fleet, and the men ashore began making their way back to the boats, but with no particular urgency: the source of the alarm, the British sails approaching from the horizon, remained blocked from their view by the peninsula. The men began rowing the three miles from the beach across the shallows to the line of French warships swinging at anchor. Even when these crews were on board, many of the French ships remained undermanned, as several hundred men had been sent with the available sloops to Alexandria and Rosetta to bring back spare rigging, together with much-needed supplies of rice, beans and vegetables.

It has been estimated that some ships of the French fleet may have been lacking as many as a third of their crew; and even those on board were not exactly battle-hardened sailors. In the rush to crew up the French fleet at Toulon, all manner of local fishermen, dockside loafers, and even jailbirds had been press-ganged to make up the numbers. In consequence, much of the French fleet was manned by an undisciplined rabble. (As governor of Alexandria, Kléber had already had cause to order all shore leave canceled after several incidents between sailors and the locals. Napoleon's strict orders to his men concerning conduct towards the Egyptians had been ignored by the sailors, who as naval men did not consider themselves bound by army orders.)

From the quarterdeck of *L'Orient*, Vice-Admiral Brueys gazed through his telescope at the approaching British sails. By four P.M., as the shadows started to lengthen, the British ships of the line were still making their way along the coast in a following wind in no particular formation, spread over miles. It appeared that they would take up their battle stations when they anchored for the night, in preparation for an attack on a morning onshore breeze. Only gradually did it become clear to Brueys that the British seemed intent upon an immediate attack. He could hardly believe his eyes: they would be sailing in failing light into shallow waters for which they had no charts, and as darkness fell during the engagement they would be liable to mistake their own ships for the enemy.

Nelson had his reasons for such precipitate action: the steady northwest wind which was blowing gave his ships the advantage of a following wind as they entered Aboukir Bay. If he anchored overnight, the French would have time to prepare, and the wind was liable to change; the French might even use this to slip away under cover of darkness, and then he would have to begin the chase all over again. Now at last he knew where they were, even if their defensive anchorage meant that they were in a stronger position. He was also undeterred by the fact that his squadron was scattered and not in any close battle formation: his captains could be relied upon to remedy this of their own accord. The frequent meetings which Nelson had called with his captains during the previous weeks, when he had sought their advice, had not just been exercises in shifting the blame for his lack of success; they had also been used to rehearse battle plans in case they did happen upon the French fleet. Nelson placed great trust in his captains: he had implicit faith in their seamanship, their bravery, and most of all their initiative. These were the qualities which had enabled him to achieve success in battle and rise above commanders who stuck to the traditional methods of engagement at sea; and Nelson looked for such innovative qualities in his captains. In his view, "the boldest moves are the safest," and his guiding principle was to always "engage the enemy more closely." This required a steady nerve, amidst the mayhem and death of close-range encounter, but it often ensured a quick, decisive victory.

At three P.M. Nelson issued his orders, and the *Vanguard* ran up the signal: "Prepare for battle." His squadron continued before the wind, moving at around four knots, and an hour or so later, before the ships were rounding the point to enter the bay, he issued a further order: "Prepare to anchor with the sheet cable in abaft and springs, etc."★⁵ This order would be acted upon when the British ships came alongside the line of anchored French ships. The British could anchor in parallel with the French, but the "springs" would give them a certain maneuverability, so that they could direct their fire at the weakest parts of the enemy ships, such as the bows and the sterns. Then it would become a slogging match, with the ships of both sides firing their cannons, blasting each other at short range, with much splintered timber and carnage amidst the cannon smoke and collapsing rigging. There was no rigid preconceived battle plan and Nelson would issue only the minimum of simple commands; his captains would know what was required, and how to act in concert, or seize the initiative.

Nelson took dinner early, along with his officers. Raising his glass

---

★ The sheet anchor was the largest on board, and was least likely to drag. The springs were attached to the anchor cable, enabling the vessel to swing to one side or the other.

in a toast, he promised them that the morrow would see him bound for the House of Lords or Westminster Abbey: made a lord or given a hero's burial—there was no thought of defeat. Meanwhile, above their heads the sailors' bare feet padded over the decks and scampered up the rigging in well-rehearsed drill as they prepared for battle. As with his captains, there was little need for orders: by now every man had spent many long months (or even years) at sea, and each knew his task—their seamanship was second nature. (Years later, when Napoleon was being taken into exile aboard the *Bellerophon*—which also happened to be one of Nelson's squadron at Aboukir—he would comment on the silence and minimum of shouted orders as the ship got under way: this was not the way it was done in the French navy.)

The qualities of seamanship amongst the British "jack tars," with their deck-hardened feet, rope-hardened hands and tarred pigtails, may have been encouraged by Nelson, but such qualities were also enforced by strict discipline. Nelson's men may have felt deeply for their brave and compassionate leader, but order was maintained nonetheless with a heavy hand in many of his ships, where conditions could sometimes be as harsh as those prevailing before the Nore and Spithead mutinies. In such cases the jack tars belowdecks often hated and feared their officers more than they did their enemy. Any man who stepped out of line faced the lash: a vicious public whipping whose screams of agony and flayed flesh were compulsorily witnessed by the entire crew, as a horrific warning. On the very morning the squadron sighted Alexandria, three men aboard the *Bellerophon* were given twelve lashes apiece for drunkenness. Yet things were not all that they appeared belowdecks: lessons had been learned from the mutinies, and conditions were not entirely harsh—for instance, it is known that several ships in Nelson's squadron had women aboard. And these were not officers' wives. A seaman aboard the *Goliath* mentions there being several women: "the gunner's wife . . . one woman belonging to [i.e., from] Leith, [another] belonged to Edinburgh" and others.[6]

After Nelson had finished his early dinner he retired briefly to his cabin. He was suffering from a severe toothache, and he wished no one to mistake his state for pre-battle nerves, which would by now have been afflicting every man (and woman) in every crew throughout the squadron. Nelson may not have been willing to contemplate defeat, but he had been willing to anticipate his own death: naval battles involved much slaughter and maiming, and such was the nature of the conflict that no man's fate lay in his own hands. The dead were in many ways lucky; the wounded or maimed frequently died in agony or under the attentions of the harassed shipboard surgeon, who operated as best he could amidst the mayhem. (For obvious reasons, naval surgeons were popularly known as "sawbones.") In view of this atmosphere of universal trepidation, all hands were kept especially busy before an engagement, to keep their minds off what lay ahead.

As Nelson stood in his cabin all but whimpering with pain, across the squadron the men completed the order to "clear decks for action." Belowdecks bulkhead partitions were taken down and livestock removed to clear the way for the smooth operation of the guns, while above decks nets were rigged to protect the crew from falling masts and rigging. Sand was scattered across the well-scrubbed planks to prevent feet from slipping in the blood, and four lighted lanterns were hung in a line from the mizzen mast to identify the ship after dark as British.* As the ships turned to enter Aboukir Bay, the marine drummers "beat to quarters," calling the men to drop all tasks and run to their battle stations. A sailor on board one of the leading ships vividly recalled: "The sun was just setting as we went into the bay, and a red and fiery sun it was."[7]

Nelson mounted to the deck of the *Vanguard*, and passed his glass slowly along the line of French ships riding at anchor in the bay ahead; as an eyewitness remembered it: "The enemy's line presented a most formidable appearance."[8] Nelson noted that the ships in the French van, at the head of the line, appeared to be the least prepared for action, though they were heavily reinforced by the awesome three gundecks of the flagship *L'Orient* in the middle of the line. There was now only need for two further orders: at four P.M. *Vanguard* ran up the signal "I mean to attack the enemy's van and centre"; half an hour later Nelson flagged the second order: "Form line of battle as convenient."[9]

The official plan of the battle shows the British squadron forming in line for the attack: the reality was slightly different. Both Nelson and his captains were keen to engage the enemy before nightfall, so

---

* Nelson must also have given an order which strictly contravened British naval practice. He was "Admiral of the Blue," which meant that he and his ships sailed under the blue ensign. But at the Battle of the Nile his squadron fought under the red ensign, whose most distinctive feature was a red cross on a white background. He reasoned that the whiteness of this large flag would further assist the British ships in recognizing one another in the dark.

there was no waiting for the slower ships to catch up and form a proper line. The *Culloden* had earlier been towing a captured French merchantman, which had made her lag some seven miles behind, before she was ordered to cut free her prize tow and try to catch up with the others.

As the British ships that had entered the bay raced to engage the French, a single brilliant observation passed simultaneously through the mind of Nelson and that of Captain Foley aboard the *Goliath*, which was ahead of the others and already in musket range of the *Guerrier*, the leading ship of the French line. Nelson realized that "where there was room for an enemy's ship to swing, there was room for one of ours to anchor."[10] In plain terms, he saw that the French ships were anchored in line by the bow, which allowed them to swing in an arc, with the wind or the current. This meant that there must have been a deep passage beyond them, on their shore side, so that they did not ground on the shoals when they swung at anchor. There was thus room for British ships to pass, and anchor, *inside* the French line as well as outside it, allowing it to be fired on from both sides. Since the French were unprepared for attack from the shore side, their guns were liable to be unmanned and unprepared, and it soon transpired that the gun ports on the shore side of the *Guerrier* were not even open. In fact, the lower deck guns were heaped over with storage boxes and other stowed lumber.

But seeing all this was one thing: acting upon it was another matter altogether. Nelson watched from the *Vanguard* as the sun sank behind the fort at the end of the Aboukir peninsula, observing the *Goliath* glide forward across the bow of the *Guerrier* on the light breeze, moving slowly towards the line of waves breaking against the shallow rocks of the shoals. There was no need for communication, even had this been possible in the rapidly growing dimness. Nelson was fully aware of the brave and dangerous nature of what Foley was undertaking. According to one member of the squadron: "No one in the fleet had the least knowledge of the bay; nor was any known chart of it existing, except an ill-drawn plan found on board the [French] vessel captured on 29 June, which had been presented to the Admiral [Nelson], but from that nothing could be made out."[11] Foley had to guess at the width of the deep passage beyond the French line: a single mistake as he navigated his course, and he would run his ship aground on the underwater rocks.

In the rapidly gathering darkness of the Egyptian night, which fell with tropical suddenness, the *Goliath*, followed by four other British ships of the line, made for the inside channel. The skilled leadsman at the bow of each ship took soundings with his leadline, his voice singing out through the darkness at regular intervals, calling the depths. As their sails guided them, their sheet anchors astern held them on their curving course, preventing their sterns from swinging round on to the shoals. Had the French guns been manned and run out through the ports on the shore side of the *Guerrier*, the *Goliath* would now have been a sitting target as it swung, its own guns not yet aligned for attack. But Foley's gamble had paid off—at least as far as the enemy's guns were concerned. The *Goliath* swung, and fired a broadside at the *Guerrier*'s flank, receiving no reply. At this point Foley's luck broke: the *Goliath*'s sheet anchor dragged, and he could do nothing to stop his ship drifting up to the second French anchored ship, the *Conquérant*. Yet this was no longer of consequence to the overall maneuver. It was now clear there was a way through, and three of the following British ships—the *Zealous*, the *Orion* and the *Audacious*—soon passed along the inside channel. The move had taken the French completely by surprise: even their shore batteries were not manned. It seems a French frigate anchored in the shallows did manage to fire at *Orion*, but fire was returned by the *Goliath* and "in a moment she went to the bottom, and her crew were seen running into the rigging."[12]

Only one of the British ships, the *Culloden*, failed to negotiate a passage into the channel, running ashore on shoals close to the island beyond the peninsula, leaving Captain Troubridge and his crew as spectators of the ensuing battle. Even so, they were able to serve some purpose. The squadron had two stragglers, the *Swiftsure* and the *Alexander*, which had earlier been sent ahead to reconnoiter Alexandria harbor and were now attempting to catch up and rejoin the squadron. These were able to use the lights of the stranded *Culloden* as a beacon to guide them around the shoals into the bay, where they sailed forward to join Nelson.

As the *Goliath* rounded the van of the French line, Nelson led his main squadron towards the seaward side of the line; these ships now executed a turn so that they fell into line with the French. Nelson's ships furled their sails and cast anchor, taking up their stations in close range of the enemy and firing their first broadsides. The leading French ships now found themselves caught between two lines of British ships, and the slugging match began, cannon for cannon, broadside for broadside, wreaking hideous damage.

But it quickly became clear that all was not going according to plan for the British. Amongst Nelson's line, the *Bellerophon* had dropped anchor too late, so that it came to a halt directly opposite the French flagship *L'Orient*. The *Bellerophon*'s two gundecks, with more than thirty cannon overall, were no match for the towering three decks and more than sixty cannon of *L'Orient*. The *Bellerophon*'s masts and cables, decks and gunports were quickly being blown to smithereens by the French firepower. In the midst of the darkness, smoke, blinding flashes, cannon roars, and cries of men, a third of the *Bellerophon*'s 600 crew were soon put out of action: dead, dying or seriously wounded.

By now the last light of day had faded from the western horizon and the bay was shrouded in darkness. Despite the fact that there was a bright moon, none of its light could penetrate the thick pall of smoke from the guns and the fires. The deafening uproar of the battle itself was fitfully illuminated by the garish flashes of gunfire on all sides and the flickering flames from burning rigging. By around eight p.m. the massive firepower of *L'Orient* had completely dismasted the *Bellerophon*, which now had just three splintered stubs sticking up from its decks, most of its guns silenced, and only one remaining officer on the quarterdeck, young Lieutenant Cathcart. He gave the order to cut her cables, allowing her battered hulk to drift free, away from the French line and any further carnage. But the danger was not over. By now the latecomers—*Alexander* and *Swiftsure*—were bearing down under press of sail, racing to join in the fray; they were both heading for the center of the French line and *L'Orient*. The *Alexander* intended to break through the French line and take up a position on the shore side of *L'Orient* whilst the *Swiftsure* engaged her on the seaward side. Amidst the chaos and clamor of battle, Captain Hallowell aboard the *Swiftsure* saw the dismasted *Bellerophon* drifting away from the French line and mistook her for a fleeing French ship. The four lanterns which would have distinguished her as British had long since been shot away with her mizzen-mast. "Supposing that she was an enemy, he felt inclined to fire into her; but as that would have broken the plan he had laid down for his conduct, he desisted."[13] The *Bellerophon* had had a lucky escape. A few minutes later the *Swiftsure* anchored just ahead of the spot which had previously been occupied by the *Bellerophon*, and began firing into the vulnerable bows of *L'Orient*.

By now conditions aboard *L'Orient* itself were beginning to deteriorate. Part of the ship was on fire, and the French commander Brueys had been struck by a cannonball which had taken off his left leg (or, according to some sources, both legs). The ships were now so close that each of the crews could easily observe across the narrow gap of water what was happening in the flickering light of the enemy ship at which they were firing. The eleven-year-old midshipman John Lee aboard the *Swiftsure* would later remember: "The brave Bruyes [*sic*], the French commander-in-chief, having lost both his legs, was seated with tourniquets on the stumps, in an armchair facing his enemy, and giving instructions for extinguishing the fire, when a cannon ball from the western side of the *Swiftsure* put a period to his gallant life, by nearly cutting him in two."[14] Amidst such hellish action, none was safe— friend or foe, cabin boy or commander. Around this time, "Admiral Nelson received a very severe wound in his head and was obliged to be carried off the deck."[15] In fact, it is now known that he had been struck by some flying metal, such that the sliced skin of his forehead hung down from the wound and covered his left eye, rendering him sightless; as he subsided in the arms of Captain Berry beside him, he exclaimed: "I am killed," and was immediately carried down below to be attended by the ship's surgeon.

Conditions amidst the hurtling cannonballs, flying debris, musket fire and collapsing rigging on deck were bad enough, but belowdecks it was even worse. The spaces between decks were cramped at the best of times. Even given the short stature of most men of this period, it was impossible to stand upright, and the only outside air and light came from the gun ports. When the cannons fired they clattered back on their wheels, which could crush the unwary amidst the deafening noise, smoke, confusion and howls of the wounded, and there was the ever-present prospect of death by direct hit or by being flung into the sea to drown.

The most powerful cannons were thirty-six- and twenty-four-pounders (the figure relating to the weight of the cannonballs they fired). A thirty-six-pounder had a barrel almost nine feet long, weighed nearly four tons and required fifteen men to operate it, each of whom was drilled to play his part in an elaborate routine—hauling and powdering the guns, heaving the cannonballs, firing the powder, all men coordinated, following bellowed orders in the smoky, sweating, panicky darkness. The well-rehearsed preparations required before a shot could be fired meant that a good gun crew took around two minutes between shots; others often took as much as eight minutes. Such weapons were extremely powerful, especially at the close range at which Nelson encouraged his ships to engage the enemy. A thirty-six-pound cannon-ball fired from 200 feet could penetrate a ship whose oak hull was almost three feet thick. Often at close range a cannonball would pass through one side of a ship and out the other, causing hideous damage to the swarm of men in the dim, cramped conditions in between. A British tar called John Nicol, who was a member of a gun crew belowdecks on the *Goliath*, recalled the battle. His terse description bespeaks the bravery of men amidst such conditions: "In the heat of the action a shot came right into the magazine, but did no harm, as the carpenters plugged it up, and stopped the water rushing."[16] The women, too, seem to have held their nerve, as Nicol thankfully records: "I was much indebted to the gunner's wife, who gave her husband and me a drink of wine every now and then, which lessened our fatigue much." He records: "There were some of the women wounded, and one woman belonging to Leith died of her wounds." Astonishingly: "One woman bore a son in the heat of the action. . . . We never ceased firing."

By now two of the French ships towards the van of their line were in a similar crippled state to the *Bellerophon*, but the battle still hung in the balance. There remained an ever-present danger to the British from the powerful French battleships at the rear of the French line— most notably the *Généreux* and the *Guillaume Tell*, the latter carrying Brueys' young and ambitious second-in-command Rear-Admiral Villeneuve. Had Villeneuve taken his own initiative he could have upped anchors and led these two powerful ships forward towards the main action around *L'Orient*. Here they could have given the British a taste of their own medicine, by outflanking Nelson and his ships on the seaward side, thus sandwiching them between two lines of French battleships and subjecting them in turn to a murderous crossfire. However, he did not attempt this—either because he had not received orders to do so, or because he faced a headwind that would have rendered this a difficult (though not impossible) maneuver. Unlike Nelson's captains, the French naval commanders were not encouraged to use their initiative. They were expected to follow their orders to the letter, and remain at their station until commanded otherwise.

The battle now underwent a decisive development. In the middle of the French line, it became evident that fire had once again broken out on board *L'Orient*. As young Midshipman Lee saw it: suddenly the smoke cleared and "the cold, clear, placid light of the moon formed a striking contrast with that of the burning ship, and enabled the lines of the hostile fleets to be, for the first time, clearly distinguished."[17] This time the fire aboard *L'Orient* took hold and Lee on board the *Swiftsure* noticed how it "soon ran up the rigging, along the yards and decks."[18]

The French historian La Jonquière, drawing on firsthand accounts from aboard *L'Orient*, described what happened next: "By now everything was contributing to the confusion. The incendiary pump was found to be broken; the fire hatchets were buried beneath piles of debris; the buckets that were meant to be kept in the fo'c'sle were scattered all over the ship, so that some even had to be brought up from the hold."[19]

By this stage, according to Lee, the intense heat of the fire could be felt from across the water: "The *Swiftsure* was so near the burning *L'Orient* the pitch ran out of her seams in streamlets down the side."[20] Cooper Willyams, the ship's chaplain aboard the *Swiftsure*, now watched how several officers and men aboard *L'Orient*,

seeing the impracticability of extinguishing the fire . . . jumped overboard; some supporting themselves on spars and pieces of wreck, others swimming with all their might to escape the dreaded catastrophe. Shot flying in all directions, dashed many of them to pieces; others were picked up by boats of the fleet, or dragged into the lower parts of the nearest ships; the British sailors humanely stretched forth their hands to save a fallen enemy, though the battle at that moment raged with uncontrolled fury.[21]

It was becoming obvious to all that *L'Orient* was on the point of blowing up. Nelson had by now been treated by his ship's surgeon, who had removed the flap of skin from his eye and succeeded in persuading him that he was not dying: "Forgetting his sufferings, [Nelson] hastened on deck, impelled by the purest humanity and gave directions that every exertion should be made to save as many lives [from the crew of *L'Orient*] as possible." The compassion and absurdity of the scene were seemingly plain to everyone: "Above seventy men were saved by the exertions of those so lately employed in their destruction."

Casabianca, the Corsican captain of *L'Orient*, had by this stage been struck on the head and carried below. His son, a midshipman who was two years younger even than Lee, was left standing on the quarterdeck. Urged by his crewmates to save himself and jump overboard, the boy refused to leave the ship without his father, and remained on the burning deck.*

Just before ten P.M. the inevitable happened. Willyams aboard the *Swiftsure* remembered: "The fire communicated to the magazine, and *L'Orient* blew up with a crashing sound that deafened all around her."[22] Lee, also aboard the nearby *Swiftsure*, recalled: "It was like an earthquake, the air rushing along the decks and below with inconceivable violence, and creating a tremulous motion in the ship, which existed for some minutes, and was awfully grand."[23] Even ships further away felt the devastating blast. According to Nicol, belowdecks: "The *Goliath* got such a shake, we thought the after-part of her had blown up, until the boys told us what it was."[24] *L'Orient* had a full ship's company of over 1,000 men, though many fewer than this would have been aboard at the time—of these it was estimated "a few score were saved." Others claim the figure for those saved was higher. Either way, when *L'Orient* exploded, the bodies of many hundreds of men were blasted into the heavens above Aboukir Bay.

According to Captain Berry aboard the *Vanguard*, after the explosion, "An awful pause and death-like silence for about three minutes ensued, when the wreck of the masts, yards, &c., which had been carried to a vast height, fell down into the water, and on board the surrounding ships."[25] This silence, during which all ships on both sides ceased firing, is remarked upon by many witnesses. Some say it lasted as long as twenty minutes. Its uncanniness, after the hours of deafening noise, may well have made it seem that long, though Berry's estimate does seem a little short, for reasons which will become clear. Some put the silence down to the men's wonder at the sheer force, size and spectacle of the detonation. However, although doubtless there was a feeling of wonder amongst many of those present, this was not enough to stop a battle; men do not cease fighting (nor are they allowed to do so) through a sense of wonder alone. It is Berry who points to

* This incident was witnessed by several French survivors, and passed on to Napoleon, who mentioned it in his consequent report to the Directory. It would later give rise to the popular verse by the American poet Felicia Hemans:

> The boy stood on the burning deck
> Whence all but he had fled;
> The flame that lit the battle's wreck,
> Shone round him o'er the dead . . .

the real reason why every cannon throughout both fleets was silenced for several minutes. Debris from the exploded *L'Orient* was flung high into the air and came down over a very wide area, and this was more than just the scattered splinters of a ship blasted to smithereens by its exploding magazine. Recently, naval archaeologists diving in Aboukir Bay discovered a cannon from *L'Orient* weighing two tons which had been hurled over 400 yards from the site of the explosion. With such debris raining down out of the night sky, there would have been little time for wonder: with one accord, all those on deck would have fled below for cover. Yet no sooner would they have found safety than they would have been ordered back on deck regardless, together with many of the belowdecks gun crews. Much of the debris falling from the sky was burning, and began setting the surrounding ships on fire. All hands were soon required to put out the blazes which now broke out on deck and in the riggings. Meanwhile the debris continued to fall through the darkness. Besides cannons and rigging, cadavers and limbs, there would also have been over a million francs' worth of gold bullion, and much of the historic jewel-encrusted plate seized from the Knights of Malta, which was known to have been aboard *L'Orient*. Napoleon's precious financial reserves, upon which the future economy of his colony depended, had also been blown sky high.

The sound of the battle had been heard from the outset as far away as Alexandria, fifteen miles to the west, and Rosetta, twenty miles to the east. Many members of the French expedition had taken to the rooftops to observe the flashes and detonations of what all must have realized was a historic encounter, upon which their fate probably hung. Poussielgue, Napoleon's financial controller, was on a high terrace in Rosetta and witnessed the explosion of *L'Orient*:

The sound of cannon-fire was very heavy until a quarter past nine, when we saw through the darkness an immense light, which made us realize that a ship was on fire. Around this time the sound of cannon-fire redoubled in intensity; at ten o'clock the ship which was on fire blew up with an almighty explosion, which we heard at Rosetta; between the sight of the explosion, and the hearing of it, took about two minutes. After this there was utter darkness and complete silence for about ten minutes. Then the firing restarted again, and lasted without a break until three in the morning.[26]

Later, the firing gradually died down once more, and then all but petered out for a couple of hours. The gunners on both sides were by this stage utterly exhausted. Drained of all adrenaline by the frenzy and terror of the night-long battle, they simply slumped where they stood, falling into a deep slumber, not even roused by the kicks of such officers as wished them to continue firing. Then, at five in the morning, according to Poussielgue, the cannon fire "restarted with more force than ever," lasting until the morning, when he heard another large explosion. This was the French frigate *Artémise* blowing up: an incident which caused some controversy, owing to the actions of her commander, Captain Estandet. The *Artémise*, "having no means of escape, struck her colours"[27] and the British sent boats to take possession of the surrendered French ship, "her officers and crew having previously left in their boats for the shore." Whereupon the *Artémise* "burst into flames . . . and in about half an hour she blew up." The firing of his ship by Captain Estandet contravened the accepted rules of naval engagement, and "aroused the indignation of Nelson and all on board the fleet, for having so dastardly burnt the ship, after her colours had been hauled down." This incident gives an indication of the deep cultural difference between the French and the British at this time. Such rules of naval engagement were not enshrined in anything other than convention: the British adhered to tradition, whereas the French, having undergone a revolution, no longer felt themselves obliged to honor any such gentlemanly agreements.

The morning sun rose into the sky above a ghastly scene. Nicol remembered: "When we ceased firing, I went on deck to view the state of the fleets, and an awful sight it was. The whole bay was covered with dead bodies, mangled, wounded and scorched, not a bit of clothes on them except their trowsers."[28] Here Nicol was in fact drawing a veil of modesty over the scene; several eyewitness accounts remark on the fact that many French sailors who were rescued after their ship exploded were stark naked, having had all their clothes blown off them by the blast.

Nelson's squadron had not lost a single ship, but most of them were in a sorry state, with two (including the *Bellerophon*) severely damaged and out of action, three more completely dismasted, and six partially dismasted. But there was no doubt about who were the victors. The French fleet was reduced to a far worse state: *L'Orient* and *Artémise* were blown to smithereens, six other ships had struck their colors, and four others were still flying their colors but were beached or grounded and had abandoned firing. Of the entire French fleet, the only ships to remain in full fighting trim were a few frigates and the two battleships at the rear of the French line, namely the *Guillaume Tell* and the *Généreux*. Rear-Admiral Villeneuve aboard the *Guillaume Tell* had officially been in command of the French fleet after Brueys was killed aboard *L'Orient*, but there had been no means of communicating this fact to him. Neither of the two French battleships at the rear of the line had taken any part in the action, and only late in the morning did they make their first move. Taking advantage of the offshore breeze, the *Guillaume Tell* and the *Généreux* headed away from the British ships and out of the bay, whereupon two French frigates, the *Justice* and the *Diane*, cut their cables and followed them. Nelson ordered ships in pursuit, but they soon proved to be in no fit condition to give chase. As a result, Villeneuve and his battleships escaped into the open sea.

Yet this would do Villeneuve little good—for it would mean that Napoleon now had a scapegoat. In his memoirs, he would place most of the blame for the defeat upon "the bad conduct of Rear-Admiral Villeneuve," launching into a long tirade against him: "The opinion of the sailors of both fleets is unanimous. Villeneuve could have turned this into a French victory at any time: he could have done this at eight in the evening; he could have done it at midnight, after the loss of *L'Orient*; and it was once again within his power at daybreak."[29] Despite Napoleon's evident bias, there nonetheless remains an element of truth in what he says. The two fleets were fairly evenly matched, though the French had the greater firepower. However, two major factors contributed to Nelson's victory: firstly, his decision to attack at once; and secondly, the masterly seamanship and initiative shown by his captains, which enabled them to take advantage of the gap they had spotted on the shore side of the French. Had Villeneuve acted decisively—especially after the *Bellephoron* was dismasted, forced to cut her lines and drift away from the combat—he might have sandwiched Nelson's ships between two lines of French ships. Yet such a move, sailing into the wind, would have required even greater seamanship; and it would also have required Villeneuve to act on his own initiative. The Revolution may have changed the French attitude towards the rules of naval engagement, but not towards its conduct: here Nelson was the true revolutionary.

The first few days following the Battle of the Nile were largely devoted to treating the wounded and burying the dead. Many were buried at sea in traditional fashion, their bodies sewn into a hammock or sailcloth, weighted down with two cannonballs, and slid over the side; others, including those who died as a result of their wounds, were buried on the island at the head of Aboukir Bay. British figures state that Nelson had 895 casualties, of whom 218 were killed; the French dead were estimated at 1,200 or thereabouts. Over 3,000 French sailors were taken prisoner, but Nelson found himself unable to cope with so many, especially as a large number were wounded. Consequently he shipped most of these ashore on parole, once they had sworn that they would not take up arms against the British, a condition that both sides must have known would not be observed. Only senior French officers and men deemed to be of value were retained as prisoners. Nelson now set about rendering all the ships of his squadron seaworthy and ready for action, salvaging gear and timbers from many of the incapacitated French ships, whilst taking the rest of them in tow as prizes.

Before Nelson departed from the Egyptian coast he was joined by two British frigates which had been dispatched somewhat tardily by St. Vincent from Cadiz. These were now ordered to remain behind, along with the *Swiftsure, Zealous* and *Goliath*, all under the command of Captain Hood of the *Zealous*, to enforce a blockade of French-occupied Egypt, maintaining a constant patrol between Alexandria, Rosetta and Damietta. Nelson's victory meant that links between Napoleon and France had now been severed, though the French were not at once fully aware of this: as late as August 8 a ship sailed from Alexandria bound for France. That same day it was intercepted, and found to be "containing despatches from Bonaparte, and thousands of letters from the French army, to their friends in France, which gave the English a true description of the nature of their expedition, and the deprivations which those who composed it were then suffering."[30] This was how news of Napoleon's cuckolding reached the *Morning Chronicle* in London.

Nelson had been one of the few who had always taken Napoleon's dream of invading India seriously, and after his victory at the Battle of the Nile he wrote a note to the governor of Bombay, telling him that there was no fear of Napoleon moving on India now. (As we shall see, Napoleon thought otherwise.) The officer bearing Nelson's note— Lieutenant Duval of the *Zealous*, who had volunteered to undertake the hazardous overland journey to India—was put ashore on the

Turkish coast at Alexandretta, in the northeastern corner of the Mediterranean. From here, dressed in Arab clothes and traveling by camel, he made his way to Baghdad and then on to the port of Basra, where he took ship for Bombay, arriving on October 21—in fact, just two weeks after news of Napoleon's invasion of Egypt reached India by means of a ship traveling from England round the Cape of Good Hope. Such delays, and time differences between different means of communication, would now begin to play a major role in the fate of Napoleon's expedition.

Nelson also dispatched both the battleship *Leander* and the brig *Mutine* separately to carry news of his victory to England, which still remained largely isolated from the European mainland, and fearful of French invasion. Sending both ships proved a wise precaution, as the *Leander* was intercepted off Crete—ironically by the *Généreux*, one of the ships that had managed to escape with Villeneuve.* Word of Nelson's great victory at what came to be known as the Battle of the Nile would only reach England via the *Mutine*, which put in at Naples, where Emma Hamilton fainted when she heard what had happened, the first public hint of her feelings for Nelson. The news then passed overland via Austria and Germany to beleaguered England, where it arrived on October 2. Here it was greeted with the ringing of church bells and the firing of cannons, with London bedecked in illuminations. Nelson's name was on everyone's lips, and just as he had hoped, he was elevated to the House of Lords—becoming Lord Nelson of the Nile.

Weeks after the battle was over, the artist Denon described what he witnessed at Aboukir Bay:

At midnight, we arrived at the sea. The rising moon illuminated an unprecedented scene; twelve miles of shoreline covered with the debris of our fleet gave us the measure of what had taken place in the battle. All along the coast wandering Arabs, in search of nails or bits of iron, were burning masts, gun carriages, boats, much still as good as when it recently left our ports. Even the debris seemed like treasure to those who lived in this place so bereft of anything. The thieves fled at our approach; there remained only the bodies of

---

* However, Nelson would have the last word in this personal contest: seven years later he would meet Villeneuve, now commander of the French fleet, at the Battle of Trafalgar. After this loss Villeneuve would commit suicide rather than face Napoleon's wrath once more.

the unfortunate victims, brought in by the sea and deposited on the sand, which now more than half covered them, so that they appeared more sublime than frightful. Gradually such deathly sights made my spirits sink into a somber melancholy; I avoided these horrifying specters, their frozen gestures preventing me from looking at them . . . at the fate that had awaited what were now just effigies on a foreign shore, desiccated by the burning sun, their skulls already blanched. . . . What is this stripped skeleton? . . . Only a few months ago, I had seen these boys, young, full of life, of courage and hope . . . held in the embrace of their mothers, their sisters, their lovers, the feeble grasp of their young children. . . .[31]

XI

"We are now obliged to accomplish great things"

NEWS of the destruction of the French fleet did not reach Napoleon until almost a fortnight later, on August 13, as he was returning from El Saliyeh and his unsuccessful attempt to capture Ibrahim Bey. All witnesses agree that he received the news with his customary sangfroid, "without a flicker of emotion passing over his features."[1]

Although he was not directly responsible, this was his first taste of defeat: the myth of his invincibility was destroyed—and would be regarded as such throughout Europe. Napoleon sensed this, but refused to accept it. From the outset he was determined that no one should see this defeat as his fault. Although he blamed Villeneuve for his inaction, the main blame for the loss of the fleet was placed on the French naval commander Vice-Admiral Brueys; and there is no denying that there was some justification for this.

After the unloading of the French fleet at Alexandria, Napoleon had given explicit orders to Brueys before departing for Cairo: if the channels did prove too shallow for the French fleet to be safely anchored in the port at Alexandria, it should be anchored at Aboukir Bay—but only if "it would be able to defend itself against a superior fleet."[2] If not, Brueys was to sail for Corfu. In the event, the harbor channels proved too shallow for the large French ships of the line, and Brueys sailed down the coast to Aboukir Bay. Brueys and Napoleon now sent several messages to one another, but most of these did not get through, as their couriers were ambushed by Bedouin en route. This failure of communication led to misunderstandings. Napoleon thought, or claims he thought, that Brueys had sailed for Corfu. Brueys, on the other hand, did not act upon what he took to be a mere suggestion from

Napoleon; he did not wish to be seen as abandoning Napoleon and his army in Egypt. Whatever Brueys' intentions, it was undoubtedly the inept anchoring of his fleet that led to his downfall. All remembered his exceptional bravery during the battle, and his refusal to give up his command despite his legs having been shot away, and Napoleon would pay generous tribute to this bravery in his letter to Brueys' widow, as well as in his official report to the Directory: "If he made mistakes, he expiated them by a glorious death." But he left no doubt that there had been mistakes, and serious ones at that: Brueys had disobeyed orders, and anchored his fleet without sufficient precaution.[3] Napoleon's verdict was: "He did well to die."[4] Someone had to take the blame, and it was not going to be Napoleon.

In the eyes of the British, the Battle of the Nile was the turning point for Napoleon's expedition to Egypt. Nelson reported: "The French army is in a scrape. They are up the Nile without supplies. The inhabitants will allow nothing to pass by land, nor [the British blockade] by water. Their army is wasting with the flux [dysentery], and not a thousand men will ever return to Europe."[5] Many still see the Battle of the Nile as the beginning of the end for Napoleon; however, this was not how Napoleon saw it, and there is much to support his view. The British claimed to control the sea, but they only had Nelson's squadron in the entire Mediterranean, and the blockade imposed by Nelson on Alexandria and the Nile ports would be very difficult to maintain with so few ships under such treacherous local weather conditions. Even if the British did control the sea, Napoleon's aim was to build an empire on land, and the news from Aboukir only served to reinforce this aim. Napoleon recalled how he addressed his downcast officers and men:

So, we are now obliged to accomplish great things, and accomplish them we will. We are obliged to found a great empire, and found it we will. The sea, of which we are not masters, separates us from our homeland; but no sea separates us from either Africa or Asia. There are plenty of us here: we will not be lacking in men who can be recruited to run the place, and we will not be lacking in munitions which if necessary can be manufactured by [the savants and the engineers].[6]

These are the words that Napoleon puts into his own mouth in his memoirs, which often rewrite reality in his favor. However, both their tone and their content is confirmed by several of the memoirs of those present. Marmont has him saying: "We are perhaps destined to change the face of the Orient, and place our names beside those that are recalled with most brilliance from ancient history."[7] Desvernois recalls him declaring: "We must remain in these lands or leave them having become as great as the men of ancient times."[8]

These were to be the most revealing words that Napoleon uttered during his entire stay in Egypt—psychologically it is no accident that such truths should surface at his time of greatest stress. This speech hinted at grandiose ideas which he had certainly thought out in considerable detail, the full extent of which he had not even revealed to his closest confidants. His primary aim in coming to Egypt was to found an empire—one that would extend to encompass Asia, but would also include Africa. Egypt stood at the crossroads of three continents. These ideas had originated with Leibniz's suggestion to Louis XIV, but their multicontinental implications of world domination had since been disregarded, or glossed over as too fantastic. The ruler of Europe, Asia and Africa would have become the ruler of the world—the undeveloped Americas would soon have fallen to such a power.

According to Napoleon, his officers and men were inspired by his speech: "Their spirits were electrified. They ceased complaining. . . . They encouraged one another to be worthy of the destiny that lay before them."[9] This was in fact pure wishful thinking, saying more about his own reaction than that of his troops. According to Bourrienne, who had eyes for the world beyond staff headquarters: "Any illusions about the expedition had disappeared from the outset. There remained nothing more than the reality, which was sad indeed. The bitter complaints that I heard from Murat, Lannes, Berthier . . . and so many others . . . endless unrestrained complaining which often bordered on sedition, affected Napoleon deeply." Indeed, he insists that "from the moment the army set foot in Egypt, almost everyone was overcome with disgust, disquiet, discontent, and homesickness."[10] Many speak of this depression, which gradually took hold amongst all ranks; in short, the expeditionary army became afflicted with that peculiarly French malaise that came to be known as *cafard*—a blend of nostalgia, melancholy, blues and general fed-upness, which is said by etymologists to have first acquired its name some years later amongst the homesick French colonial army in North Africa. In fact, it almost certainly originated amongst Napoleon's army in Egypt: the word *cafard* derives from the Arab word *kafr*, which means infidel. At the heart of this malaise was the understanding that they were alien to these people.

The army's morale was hardly improved by the news that now reached Cairo from El-Mansura, a small town on the eastern navigational channel of the Nile, some eighty miles downstream from Cairo. General Vial had occupied El-Mansura, and had left behind a garrison of 120 men, before moving on to secure the port of Damietta forty miles downstream. But the inhabitants of El-Mansura were incensed by this occupation, and on the very next day they stoned to death the sentry standing on duty outside the local barracks, which the French had taken over. A few hours later two other soldiers were assassinated. A couple of days after this, the barracks was surrounded by an angry crowd bearing various weapons, who attempted unsuccessfully to set fire to the building. Fighting continued throughout the day, during the course of which eight French soldiers were killed. After the angry crowd dispersed, the officer in charge decided to abandon the post, but as the French column retreated through the streets they came under fire from nearby houses. By the time the soldiers made it into open countryside they were being pursued by a mob firing at them, whilst other men were seen running off to nearby villages to get reinforcements. As darkness fell, the French soldiers headed south along the Nile, with the aim of making it to Cairo. Throughout the night they were pursued, suffering heavy losses. At daybreak there were only twenty to thirty of them left, with the enemy closing in on all sides. Private Mourchon, who had received a bullet through his thigh during the night, had an astonishing tale to tell:

By now we had run out of ammunition, and were forced to defend ourselves with our weapons as best we could. In the end, the ten of us who were wounded preferred to drown ourselves rather than fall into the hands of the enemy. We were now down to just fifteen soldiers in all, and a mass of enraged peasants threw themselves upon us, tearing our clothes from our bodies, massacring us, bludgeoning my comrades and me with clubs. I threw myself naked into the Nile with the intention of drowning myelf, but because I knew how to swim sheer instinct prevented me from drowning and I swam to the far bank of the river.[11]

Here he struggled towards a village, hardly aware of what he was doing, when:

I saw coming towards me seven armed Egyptians on horseback, and threw myself into the Nile again. Having noticed that two of them were signaling for me to come to them, I returned to the shore. One of the two fired his rifle at me point blank, but it jammed. The other gestured to me that he did not wish me any harm and placed me in the hands of two peasants, each armed with a double-barreled rifle, who tied me up and led me to the village by a path through thorns where I suffered greatly being barefoot and wounded. When we arrived at the village the inhabitants untied me, took care of me, fed me, and showed me great kindness. . . . I must mention that the person who took most care of me was an eight-year-old boy who secretly brought me boiled eggs and bread.

After several days, the villagers told him that a barge carrying French soldiers was passing along the river. On board was Lieutenant Thurman, who takes up the tale:

As we reached the village, we heard a voice calling out in our own language: "Come and save me, I am French." We saw appear a poor unfortunate, dragging himself along, bareskinned, with just some ragged shorts to cover his nakedness. After his first rapturous delight at seeing his fellow countrymen again, he begged Colonel Laugier to give him some money to pay back the peasants of the village for the care they had given him, assuring the colonel that he was the only person who had escaped the massacre of the entire garrison at El-Mansura.[12]

Outside the garrisoned towns, the delta region was to remain a dangerous place for the French, to such an extent that they were still barely able to maintain a courier route between Cairo and Alexandria.

Despite the widespread low morale amongst the French army, Napoleon would write in his report to the Directory: "Everything is perfectly fine here. The country is under control and the people are becoming accustomed to our presence. . . . I am awaiting news from Constantinople. I will not be able to return to Paris in October, as I promised you, but this will only be delayed a few months."[13] It is difficult to know what Napoleon really meant by this last remark about his return; presumably he made it without any regard for truth, but merely to pursue his customary policy of keeping all his options open.

Regardless of what was taking place in the rest of the country, Napoleon was determined that things should remain as normal as possible in Cairo. One of the main events of the Cairo year was the Nile ceremony, which was celebrated when the waters of the Nile rose to a certain level, signaling the beginning of the agricultural cycle when crops could be planted once more. The waters were measured by the famous Nilometer, a large permanent stone structure which stood at the upstream end of Rodah Island. There had been a Nilometer here since pharaonic times, though the current one dated from AD 861, some two centuries after the Arab-Muslim conquest. The signal for the Nile ceremony was when the water at the Nilometer rose to 16 cubits (just over 8½ meters). If the river rose significantly above this level there would be widespread flooding, reminiscent of the scene Herodotus had witnessed, whereas if it remained below this level it signaled a drought, crop failures and even famine. The chaotic circumstances of Mameluke rule meant there was no widespread provision for lean years, so a low Nile often led to much suffering and even starvation. In consequence, the Wafa el-Nil (Abundance of the Nile) was greeted with universal and heartfelt rejoicing, along with a time-honored ceremony which was attended by joyous crowds.

This time Napoleon himself presided, and later recorded how just before sunrise on August 18 "the Sultan El-Kebir left his palace, leading the procession, with El-Bekri, descendant of the Prophet on his right, and El-Sadat, descendant of Hassan* on his left. They were accompanied by the general staff, four muftis, *ulema*, grand sheiks, *sherifs* and members of the Cairo *divan*." The general staff were all in full dress uniform, while the Egyptian dignitaries with their beards and turbans wore their ceremonial robes. This colorful procession made its way to the river where "200,000 spectators covered both banks of the Nile," while on the water were "several thousand rafts and other crafts covered with flags and banners."[14] Once the dignitaries had assembled themselves on the balcony above the Nile, the bands began to play, the thudding drums and blaring brass of the French military bands clashing discordantly with the high-pitched wailing quarter-tones of the Egyptian wind instruments. Below them the soldiers began digging at the earthen dyke that kept the waters of the Nile from spilling into the Khalidj canal, which ran around the city. A contemporary print depicts the French soldiers wearing aprons to protect their uniforms, and carrying away the earth in wheelbarrows, one of the first public appearances of this novel technical device in Egypt.

When the waters finally burst in a torrent through the breached dyke, a cheer arose from the watching populace, and the French batteries on the shore and aboard the Nile flotilla began firing a barrage of cele-

---

* The venerated grandson of the Prophet.

bration. As the waters filled the canal, there took place a ceremony that had been observed since time immemorial: an effigy of a young virgin was cast into the stream—in pharaonic times this had been an actual virgin, chosen for her exceptional beauty, sacrificed to the Nile god as his annual bride. This ritual, at least in its token version, had continued through the Greek era, where it had no significance amongst the gods of Mount Olympus; the Christian era, when it was one of the few pagan ceremonies to survive the fanatical anti-heresy persecutions; and finally through to the Muslim era, when its timeless aptness continued to be recognized by all the people of Cairo: the Muslims, the Jews, the Coptic, Syrian, and Greek Christians, and now the French post-Revolution atheists.

After Napoleon had delivered a speech praising Allah for his bountifulness, coins were thrown into the canal, and the men on the first boats through the dyke began diving into the water to retrieve them. The French contingent then marched back to Napoleon's palace in Ezbekiyah Square, whose open space would normally have been flooded by the waters spilling from the Khalidj canal, but was now protected by a low embankment. (The French had turned the wide expanse of Ezbekiyah Square into an artillery park and a parade ground where Napoleon would inspect his troops.) All French firsthand sources agree that the Nile ceremony was a huge success, especially the fireworks afterwards. Napoleon placed great faith in the propaganda value of firework displays, and had even included a treatise on fireworks by the great French *pyrotechnicien* Frézier amongst the library he brought with him to Egypt. However, the spectacular display in the night sky above the minarets and domes of Cairo on Wafa el-Nil on August 18, 1798, does not seem to have achieved quite the effect that he had hoped. It may have been a success for the French, but El-Djabarti in the privacy of his journal was scornful of these celebrations, declaring: "That night the Christians, Syrians, Copts and long-term European residents of Cairo came out, but there was not a single Muslim amongst them."[15] This may well be an exaggeration attributable to anti-French spleen, but there can be no doubt that many Muslim Egyptians felt resentful at the French taking over their local ceremony and using it for propaganda purposes, in an attempt to demonstrate that all was well between the Egyptians and the French.

During the following days the river continued to rise, with the promise of a good season ahead. According to El-Djabarti, "This year the flooding of the Nile was exceptional; all the country was flooded and communications came to a halt. The whole of Egypt was reduced to a vast swamp."[16] Goods imported from Syria and Libya shot up in price, whilst there was a glut of local produce and prices at the Cairo markets fell accordingly. Such instabilities were endemic, but inevitably the local population turned its irritation on the French. Ironically, Napoleon was already searching for ways to overcome such financial fluctuations, though by this stage his own financial plight was hardly a model of stability.

The Nile ceremony also marked the beginning of the Egyptian tax year. It meant that the *miry* could now be assessed for each farmer, on the likely size of his crop—a welcome prospect of some much-needed income for Napoleon's administration. The *miry* was theoretically the tribute paid to the Ottoman authorities in Constantinople, but a heavy percentage of this had always found its way into the pockets of the local Mameluke beys and the tax collectors themselves. The French intended to use this money to finance their administration and its reforms of Mameluke practices. However, all this income remained very much a prospect, for the *miry* was not collected until after the harvest, when many of the smallholders paid in kind, involving further transactions before this could be converted into actual financial assets. So far the chief financial administrator Poussielgue and his paymaster-general Estève had managed to keep the finances of the French administration afloat by creating a "Compagnie de Commerce," which sold and auctioned off all requisitioned Mameluke property and treasures. But this could only be a temporary measure, and in an attempt to raise further cash they issued bonds on the mint, in exchange for gold and silver. These bonds were rendered all the more attractive by making them redeemable with interest in the exceptionally short period of three months, an indication of how strapped the French administration was for cash. Even so, they were still regarded with suspicion, and in many cases wealthy merchants were virtually compelled to buy them, turning the bond issue into something of an enforced loan. This was particularly the case amongst the Coptic, Jewish and Greek communities, which were largely sympathetic towards the French, and had benefited from their presence through the cessation of discriminatory practices. Poussielgue maintained a tight hold on the finances whilst the administration's income remained low, and this meant that Estève was only able to pay the army with token handouts, which nonetheless served to stimulate the economy in the bazaars.[17]

An indication of the French administration's situation can be gleaned from the accounts that Poussielgue was even now drawing up for the end of the year (that is, the revolutionary year, which ended in September). These showed that the total expenditure of the expedition so far had been 8 million francs; meanwhile assets for the same period—which included spoils from Malta and the remnant assets of the Berne bank—stood at 9.3 million.* This left a theoretical balance of just 1.3 million. Although this was no mean sum, it was not large compared with the Egyptian agricultural economy as a whole, for which Poussielgue drew up some general figures. According to these, the total tax revenue gathered from the *fellahin* in previous years had amounted to the equivalent of around 63 million francs per annum. Out of this:

  8 million was retained by the Coptic tax collectors
12 million went towards local administration of one form or another
  6 million was sent to local landlords by way of the local mayors (who also took their cut)
  4 million went direct to the local Mameluke governors
  9 million was paid to the Bedouin as protection money
6.4 million was dispatched as *miry* to Constantinople

In practice, this left a figure of around 17.3 million for the authorities in Cairo (the fact that these figures do not add up is very much in keeping with the Egyptian economy of the period); but all these figures (such as they were) meant nothing until the taxes could be collected. For the time being the French administration had to soldier on as best it could, on the hunt for cash whenever and wherever it could be found. At times, this would even enter the realms of the comic: the new fiscal year would open with Napoleon dispatching the following advice to Poussielgue: "General Dumas has news of a bey's mansion where there is hidden treasure. See that you join forces with him in the necessary digging hunt for this treasure."[18]

Napoleon now noticed that no preparations were being made to celebrate the Birth of the Prophet, the major event of the Muslim year. This was due to take place a few days after the Nile ceremony, and was customarily marked by festivities stretching over a four-day period. When Napoleon summoned Sheik El-Bekri and asked him why nothing was being done about the celebrations, the sheik prevaricated, suggesting

* It is unclear whether this figure included those assets which now lay at the bottom of Aboukir Bay with *L'Orient*.

that it was not right for Egyptians to celebrate during such difficult times. In fact, the main reason for suspending these celebrations was because the Egyptians were in no mood to rejoice, filled as they were with increasing resentment against the French. According to El-Djabarti: "The sheik wished to invoke as an excuse the crisis which was affecting the country. But the general would not accept this reason, and gave the order to celebrate the feast. He also gave the sheik 300 ecus to help pay for the expenses."[19]

Despite such heavy-handedness, Napoleon was determined to show that he came as an understanding friend of Islam. He promised El-Bekri that he would attend the holy ceremonies and celebrations in person, and he sent word to Kléber in Alexandria and Menou in Rosetta, ordering that they should organize and take part in their own local celebrations for the Birth of the Prophet. On the appointed day, Napoleon duly attended the ceremonies at the residence of El-Bekri, where prayers were said and the family tree of the Prophet was read out: a seemingly endless list of his genealogy extending from the seventh century to the present. According to some sources, Napoleon even went so far as to attend these ceremonies in Arabic dress. He himself makes no mention of this, and neither does El-Djabarti, who would have been present. However, the story of Napoleon adopting Arabic dress is not entirely mythical: he certainly wished to do so, and Bourrienne describes how one day he turned up at dinner with his staff wearing some kind of Oriental dress: "he entered in his new costume; scarcely was he recognized than he was greated with great bursts of laughter. He took his place calmly: but he cut such a poor figure in his turban and oriental robe, looked so gauche in his unsuitable costume, that he very soon retired to take it off, and never since did he feel tempted to make a second appearance in this masquerade."[20]

No matter how he was dressed, Napoleon certainly attended the great banquet held at El-Bekri's residence, later recalling "that it was served on fifty small tables, each set with five places. In the midst of this was Sultan El-Kebir and Sheik El-Bekri." If not dressed in the native style, Sultan El-Kebir at least dined in the same manner as his hosts, seated on a cushion and eating with his hand. Afterwards he discovered the joys of smoking a *nargileh* (oriental water pipe) and sipping sweet muddy Turkish coffee.

A French military band was ordered to play outside El-Bekri's residence day and night throughout the celebrations, and at night "each mosque, each palace, each bazaar, each market was picked out in illuminations." Napoleon also recalled how "the army played its part in the rejoicing and happiness of the inhabitants,"²¹ yet how far this extended beyond the inevitable fireworks, which one officer at least found "a pathetic display," and the "military exercises which took place at Ezbekiyah Square" mentioned by El-Djabarti, remains a moot point. The Egyptians were quite capable of enjoying themselves without French military assistance, although their manner of doing so often left the French somewhat bewildered. The prickly Major Detroye once more manifested his astonishment and prejudice at "men bearing aloft flaming torches or vast chandeliers containing more than forty lamps, others singing ornate outlandish songs, accompanied by even more ornate outlandish music, such was the procession which paraded throughout the town the whole night through, crying out, howling, making an infernal din." Things reached their climax on the fourth day when "the public places were filled with little sideshows, featuring dancing bears, trained monkeys, male and female singers enacting tableaux, women chanting poems, jugglers who made live snakes disappear in containers, children performing the most lascivious dances, wrestlers taking part in single combat. Toward evening the fakirs appear: the people regard with the utmost veneration these fanatics, who have long hair and are dressed in the most skimpy garb."²² These holy men greatly intrigued the French, who studied their habits in some detail. According to Malus: "These are the saints of Egypt: their life is lived in a state of perpetual ecstasy and they are permitted to do anything they want. At various times of year, several of them run through the streets, naked as monkeys."²³ Malus cites a study of them made by the savants, which viewed such "holy men" with a distinctly jaundiced scientific eye: "It seems that nothing is beyond the cynical behavior of these so-called saints, above all on the days of religious festivals. They are granted complete license. The women esteem it a great blessing when any amongst them are chosen by a fakir for the exercise of his sexual desires, and they form around the couple a protective circle."²⁴

In Alexandria, Kléber dutifully mounted his own festival for the Birth of the Prophet, but his heart was not in it. According to one of his officers he was "sullen and upset [and] only reluctantly took part in this religious farce."²⁵ On the occasion when he was invited to dine with the local *divan* he appeared distinctly unimpressed by the fact that the rice had been dyed red, white and blue in honor of the French. Later, when the local dignitaries came in turn to receive hospitality at his headquarters, he made sure that he and his officers were seated at a separate table where they were served wine. On the other hand, in Rosetta Menou entered into the spirit of things with some zeal, transforming the main street into a large reception hall, complete with tents, carpets and lanterns, where dancers accompanied by musicians entertained the guests until dawn.

Napoleon had grasped that the Islamic world was in many ways a cohesive whole, which extended across national borders; the key to this lay in the annual pilgrimage to Mecca. He now sought to capitalize on his pro-Islamic policy in Egypt by writing to three of the leading Islamic figures in the Arabic world: the Bey of Tripoli, the Pasha of Damascus and the Sherif of Mecca, all of whom had responsibility for the Mecca pilgrimage.* He reminded them how he had gone to the rescue of the returning pilgrims who had been attacked by Ibrahim Bey, and promised that "the journey through Egypt of the pilgrims to Mecca and Medina will continue to be protected as in the past," adding, as if by constant repetition it would come to be believed: "We are friends of Muslims and of the Prophet and we desire to do all we can to please you and be favorable to your religion."[26] Napoleon's aim was to gain pan-Islamic acceptance of his rule, but in this he was to be disappointed. The Pasha of Damascus and the Bey of Tripoli did not even deign to reply.

Word had spread throughout the Levant and North Africa of Nelson's destruction of the French fleet, and it was now widely assumed that the French were a spent force, who would soon be gone. In fact, Napoleon seems to have been one of the last in the region to hear the news of the British victory, which had spread far more quickly through the desert network of Bedouin tribes than it had via the French couriers with their armed escorts. Ibrahim Bey almost certainly knew what had happened by the time he raided the Mecca pilgrims and Napoleon set out after him, and even Murad Bey in Upper Egypt knew of these events by the time the Austrian consul Rosetti arrived with Napoleon's peace deal, in which he had generously offered Murad Bey the governorship of an entire province. After greeting his old friend Rosetti, Murad Bey dispatched him back to Cairo with a contemptuous message, indicating that he now felt he had the upper hand and could afford to

---

* Each of these figures resided within the confines of the Ottoman Empire, though by this period the further regions of the empire maintained varying degrees of autonomy. Libya, for instance, was virtually independent under the Karamanlis.

be generous: "Tell the commander-in-chief to assemble all his troops and return to Alexandria. I shall pay him 10,000 purses of gold coins to cover the expenses of his army. By doing this, he will spare the lives of his soldiers and save me the trouble of fighting him."[27] On receiving this message, Napoleon immediately ordered Desaix to prepare to march into Upper Egypt, with the aim of hunting down Murad Bey and his Mamelukes until they were finally eliminated. On August 25 Desaix and his division began heading south up the Nile.

Napoleon knew that Ibrahim Bey had taken refuge across the Sinai in Syria,* and in order to head off any threat from this eastern quarter he dispatched one of his staff officers, Major Beauvoisin, with a letter to Ahmed Pasha, the governor of Acre. In this, Napoleon informed him:

Since my arrival in Egypt I have reassured the people and protected the muftis, the imams and the mosques. The Mecca pilgrims have never been welcomed with more care and friendship than I have shown for them, and the festival of the Prophet has just been celebrated with more splendor than ever.

I send you this letter through an officer who will make known to you in his own words my intention to achieve a good understanding between us . . . because the Muslims have no greater friends than the French.[28]

Ahmed Pasha was a formidable figure, better known as Djezzar ("The Butcher"), a name he had earned with some gusto during his long rule in Acre. Though notorious for his cruelty, greed and general cantankerousness, he was also possessed of considerable political acumen. He had been appointed several years previously by the sultan's vizier, and never forgot his loyalty to his masters: his *miry* was always paid promptly and in full. This rare state of affairs ensured him considerable prestige in Constantinople, where he was regarded as a model governor and allowed to rule as he pleased. Christians were his favorite object of persecution, and his habit of having malefactors bricked into the walls of the cities over which he ruled earned him widespread renown. Such a man was unlikely to respond favorably to Napoleon's overtures, and this proved the case. He refused even to meet Major Beauvoisin, and when the contents of Napoleon's letter were read out to him "he flew into a violent rage, and told the translator: 'Return

---

* During this period the name *Syria* was used to denote the entire region east and north of Sinai, as far as Turkey, including modern Palestine, Israel, Jordan and Lebanon, as well as the territory now known as Syria.

to the infidel and make him leave. If he continues to set foot in this country I will have him thrown into a fire.'"²⁹ Despite Beauvoisin's diplomatic status, he was lucky to escape with his life; other emissaries would be cast into the dungeons, or simply executed.

However, when Beauvoisin returned he was able to report circumstances of which Napoleon had not been aware: the French arrival in Egypt had apparently caused widespread consternation in Syria, and the Porte had subsequently increased Djezzar's authority by appointing him military governor of the entire region. All that Beauvoisin had seen had led him to believe that the whole of Syria was in a state of ferment.

Napoleon was not too disconcerted by this news. He was relying upon the Directory's promised diplomatic initiative to iron out any difficulties with the Porte, and was confident that even now these matters were being resolved. As early as August 19, in his regular report to the Directory, he had asked, "Is Talleyrand in Constantinople?"³⁰ In his report of August 30 he had written: "I imagine Talleyrand is in Constantinople," and on September 8 he wrote: "I await news from Constantinople." He was confident that at least some of his messages were managing to beat the English sea blockade, but he informed the Directory: "Since our departure, I have received no letter from you, nor from any ministry, nor from any relevant authority. My dispatches have without doubt been more lucky than yours. I have sent them to you by way of Malta, Tripoli, Ancona, and Constantinople; I have used all ways open."³¹

The start of the New Year, according to the new French revolutionary calendar, was I Vendémiaire (which fell on September 22, 1798). This was the beginning of Year VII, and Napoleon was determined that it should be commemorated by a great festival. Here was a chance to show the Egytians some French culture, as well as an opportunity to improve morale amongst the troops.

The celebrations centered on Ezbekiyah Square, where a wooden Arc de Triomphe was erected, on which the artist-savant Rigo had been commissioned to paint a scene depicting the Battle of the Pyramids. At the other end of the square was another ceremonial arch, on which was painted in large gold letters, in French and in Arabic, "There is no god but God, and Muhammad is his prophet." All around the square flew French tricolors crossed with Turkish flags to denote the friendship of the two nations, whilst in its midst stood a seventy-foot-high obelisk inscribed with the battle honors, together with the names of the fallen, of the Army of the Orient. During the morning, bands played and there was a military parade, after which a senior officer read out a proclamation by Napoleon:

Soldiers! You are assured of a fine destiny because of what you have achieved and the great esteem in which you are held. You will die with honor, like the heroes whose names are inscribed on this pyramid,★ or you will return to your country covered in laurels and the admiration of the world. In the five months that we have been far from Europe, our fate has been a matter of constant concern to our compatriots. Today, forty million of your fellow citizens will be thinking of you. . . .[32]

The New Year celebrations attracted large crowds, but for the most part the Egyptians seem to have remained unimpressed, if El-Djabarti's observations are anything to go by: "The music played unceasingly . . . finally the soldiers gathered around the mast and one of their high priests read to them some writing in French. None of us could understand it. The speech seemed to be pieces of advice or a sermon. . . . [Afterwards] the French placed guards around the mast because they pretend it is a symbol of their victories and the grandeur of their country."[33] And Nicolas Turc had this to say: "They constructed a long column covered in gold, painted with a portrait of their sultan and of his wife who had died in Paris [sic]. The French said that this column was the tree of liberty; but the Egyptians replied that it was if anything the stake upon which they were impaled and the emblem of the conquest of their country."[34] The Egyptians were encouraged to enjoy the festival, but General Desgenettes, Napoleon's chief medical officer, noted that "these festivals . . . meant little to the inhabitants of Cairo, in spite of their magnificence."[35] Another French officer noticed: "It would be absurd to believe that the Egyptians invited to our festival totally shared in our full-blooded enjoyment. In spite of all their efforts to disguise how they felt, we easily perceived their unhappiness."[36]

Napoleon's proclamation was followed by a cantata composed by the musician-savant Rigel, to words by the poet-savant Parseval-Grandmaison, whose interminable verses proved equally incomprehensible to soldiers and Egyptians alike. After this there were races between riders on French and Egyptian horses, followed by a banquet for senior

★ What was erected in the center of Ezbekiyah Square is variously described as an obelisk, a column, a pyramid, and even a mast, depending largely upon how impressed the spectator was by this monument.

French officers and Egyptian dignitaries at Napoleon's headquarters in the palace of Elfi Bey. This time, in accordance with French custom, guests sat on chairs, and were expected to eat with knives and forks. On each table was a centerpiece incorporating a cap of liberty and a crescent, whilst the napkin beside each place contained concealed within it a scroll inscribed with the Rights of Man and another with sayings from the Koran. At the end of the dinner there was a series of toasts, beginning with Napoleon raising his glass to the future and the three hundredth anniversary of the Revolution, and ending with Monge raising his "to the perfection of the human spirit and the progress of reason."[37]

Once again, French technological expertise was embodied in a fireworks display, which apparently lasted for two hours. Napoleon had hoped that on this occasion his engineer-savant Conté might lay on a demonstration balloon ascent, but Conté was unable to construct a balloon in time. The original balloon which Napoleon had insisted upon importing from France now lay at the bottom of Alexandria harbor, along with much scientific equipment and instruments, having gone down in the ship carrying medical supplies which was accidentally sunk in the rush to unload in case Nelson's squadron reappeared. Conté was doing his best to construct this pioneering aeronautical device, of which the French were so proud, using only locally available materials and machinery which he had assembled from scratch. Yet despite his indefatigable ingenuity, it was proving a far more difficult and lengthy task than he had foreseen. The French were in many ways like Robinson Crusoe on his island. Defoe's book, which had been published earlier in the century, had captured the imagination of Europe, spawning many similar books in France, and several of the scientist-savants in Egypt would come to see themselves in a similar role to the shipwrecked sailor. They had arrived armed with their theoretical knowledge, but they would now be forced to start their science afresh, using only the most basic local ingredients occurring in nature.

Many of the conflicts and contradictions inherent in the celebrations of the revolutionary New Year, along with the Robinson Crusoe role occupied by the savants, were emblematic of the central problem which now faced Napoleon: precisely what kind of colony did he intend to establish? In this, as in so much else, he saw himself following in the footsteps of Alexander the Great, the pioneer of European colonization on the grand scale. Just as Alexander had sought to hellenize the Eastern world, Napoleon saw himself as the harbinger of a superior European culture. Yet his cultural, commercial and technological aspirations were in many ways more in line with the model of the Roman Empire, whose very nature had ensured its survival on a more permanent basis than Alexander's empire of conquest, which began to fall apart on the death of its founder. These ancient exemplars still inspired the European empire builders nearly one and a half millennia later, but had given rise to a number of different interpretations.

At the end of the eighteenth century, the concept of a colony had not yet been fully realized amongst the European powers, who had only started to embark upon the imperial project which would in the following century see them colonizing almost the entire globe. Each power had begun the enterprise in its own characteristic fashion. The Spanish emphasis in South America had been on the export of gold and the enforced import of Christianity; whilst the British and the French in North America had simply driven out the indigenous population and brought in their own pioneers, who had attempted as far as possible to build a society based on the European model. Much the same had happened in the Caribbean, with the importation of African slaves coming in the wake of the pioneers, and the establishment of an elite European society as dependent upon slavery as ancient Greece and Rome. An alternative model was provided by the British in India and the Dutch in the East Indies, where these two commercial nations had seen their colonies as little more than business enterprises—protected, then reinforced and expanded, by military strength.*

Egypt did not fit easily into any of these categories. It was hardly virgin territory, having been the locus of a civilization which far preceded any in Europe; on the other hand, although it may already have been a colony, it was only part of the Ottoman Empire in the loosest sense. At the same time, it had an indigenous population which was neither savage nor sophisticated, who identified closely with a thousand-year-old highly spiritual yet xenophobic religion. The existing European colonial models were not appropriate, and it is now clear that from the very outset Napoleon had no wish to follow any such path: his idea of an Egyptian colony was both ambitious and unique at the time.

* The British settlement in Australia, and the French settlement in Guyana which was consciously modeled upon this, could not at this time be taken seriously as colonial exemplars, being nothing other than penal colonies or dumping grounds for those considered socially undesirable.

French culture would play a leading role, if necessary evolving independently of the mother culture—just as the United States was
beginning to do in America. If the link with Europe remained severed,
Napoleon could foresee himself expanding eastwards into India,
becoming if necessary the emperor of an independent Eastern empire
entirely free from the political domination of a distant Europe. He
would create nothing less than a United States of Asia; and the indications are that he felt this empire might even be based upon a quasi-
Muslim religion ("I saw myself marching on the way to Asia . . . in my
hand a new Koran," etc.)[38] Napoleon had meditated upon these ideas
at some length, as is shown in his memoirs, where he sets out his vision
for the future of Egypt in more detail:

After fifty years of prosperity and good government . . . emigrants from the
depths of Africa, from Arabia, Syria, Greece, France, Italy, Poland and Germany
would have quadrupled the population;* and by sheer force of circumstance
the commerce from the Indies would have returned to its ancient route . . . a
colony as powerful as this would not be long in proclaiming its independence.
Without doubt a great nation, as in the time of the Pharaohs and the time of
the Ptolemys, would occupy this land which is so desolate today. Through its
right hand it would support the Indies, and through its left it would support
Europe; if local circumstances alone ought to decide the prosperity and greatness of cities, Alexandria, more than Rome, Constantinople, Paris, London,
or Amsterdam would have been and will again be called the center of the
universe. . . . After fifty years of this, civilization will have spread through
the interior of Africa, where several great nations will enjoy the benefits of the
arts, sciences and the religion of the true God, because it is through Egypt
that the people of central Africa must receive enlightenment and happiness.[39]

Here undeniably lay the beginnings of a world empire such as history
had not yet seen: no man before Napoleon had ever thought on such a
grand scale, or had even conceived of such a vision.

* This list includes countries which were at war with France at the time, such as
much of Germany. What is perhaps more interesting is the countries that are *not*
on the list—such as Britain, America, Spain (an ally at the time) and Austria (also
an ally). The new Egypt was evidently envisaged as a largely continental European
affair, free from any Anglo-Saxon influence. It would also have no Hispanic or
Dutch input. In other words, it would not include those countries that already
had large empires beyond Europe. Now it was France's turn, and the empire based
on her culture was intended to dwarf all others.

XII

The Institute of Egypt

CENTRAL to Napoleon's dream was to be the creation of an Institute of Egypt in Cairo. This was to be modeled upon the Institute of France in Paris, of which Napoleon was so proud to have become a member that even in Egypt he still headed his dispatches "Member of the Institute and Commander-in-Chief"—in that order. Indeed, it is his pride on becoming a member of the Institute in Paris that may well have crystallized his vision of himself as more than just a general, more even than a conqueror of foreign countries; rather as a bringer of civilization.

The Institute in Cairo was created by a decree issued as early as August 22—that is, just ten days after Napoleon had heard that his fleet had been destroyed and his army was stranded in Egypt. Its proclaimed objectives were:

1. Progress and the propagation of enlightenment in Egypt.
2. Research, study and the publication of natural, industrial and historical facts concerning Egypt.
3. To give advice on the different questions on which its members will be consulted by the government.[1]

Intellectuals were thus to play a central role in the creation of the new Egypt from the very outset. The Institute would consist of four sections: mathematics, physics, political economy, and culture (literature and the arts). Each of these was to have a maximum of twelve members, not all of whom would be drawn from amongst the ranks of the savants. This was partly because Napoleon did not wish the Institute to be seen as something separate from his military administration, yet also because some of his senior military officers were genuinely interested in learning, and had sufficient knowledge to contribute to the proceedings. Thus, the mathematics section contained Monge and Fourier, both major mathematicians of their time, as well as the astronomers Nouét and Quesnet, but also Napoleon himself, Horace Say, chief of staff of the engineers (and brother of the renowned economist after whom Say's Law is named), General Andréossy, and the twenty-three-year-old Captain Malus of the engineers, who was in fact already a scientist in his own right through his original studies of light. The physics section included members of all but the most mathematical of sciences,* such as the major chemist Berthollet, the renowned geologist Dolomieu, the pioneer biologist Geoffroy Saint-Hilaire, the engineer and balloonist Conté, as well as the army's chief medical officer General Desgenettes. The political economy section inevitably included Poussielgue (though pointedly not the unfortunate paymaster-general Estève, despite the fact that six positions in this section remained vacant: someone had to be scapegoat for the lack of wages being paid to the army). Also in this section was the one-legged engineer General Caffarelli, presumably on the strength of his "communist" speech on the voyage out.

Another place in the political economy section was filled by Citizen Jean-Lambert Tallien, one of the more desperate characters to emerge in the aftermath of the Revolution, whose life history provides an exemplar of unscrupulous survival at all costs during this turbulent period. As such, he was something of a rarity on the Egyptian expedition, whose members for the most part were decent men who had not been party to the excesses and corruptions of recent French political life. Tallien, on the other hand, had played a leading role in these proceedings: after sending many to the guillotine during the Terror, he had conspired with Barras to overthrow Robespierre and then accused many of his former colleagues of being Royalists, having them thrown into prison. Later, he married the aristocratic Madame Cabarrus, who like Napoleon's Josephine had also been a mistress of the omnivorous Barras. In the end, he had fallen from grace simply because no one would trust him, and he only managed to inveigle himself a place on the Egyptian expedition

---

* Physics was of course by now becoming a very mathematical science, so ironically this section of the Institute did not include what we would call physicists, who were instead in the mathematics section. The naming of the physics section was in line with the French scientific nomenclature of the period, where *physique* would perhaps be better translated as "physical sciences," i.e., the study of all physical matter.

after Napoleon and the fleet had sailed. He traveled across the Mediterranean on *Le Vif*, a courier ship that evaded the British naval blockade and reached Alexandria on August 13. Suprisingly, Tallien appears to have earned Napoleon's respect, and thus his membership of the prestigious Institute, by being the only one bold enough to persuade the commander-in-chief not to repeat his foray into Oriental dress.

The literature and arts section of the Institute contained another mixed bag: this included the aging but ever-industrious painter Denon, the portraitist Dutertre (whose sketches would preserve for posterity the faces of so many savants, generals, emirs and even Mamelukes), as well as the poet Parseval-Grandmaison and the musician Rigel (the duo responsible for the interminable New Year cantata), and a member simply listed as "a Greek priest."[2] This was a certain Don Raphael de Monachis, a Greek Orthodox priest who was the only member of the Institute not to be part of the French expedition. A later addition to this section would be the muralist Rigo, appointed as a reward for privately completing a fashion plate of Napoleon in plumed turban and Oriental robes.

According to a proclamation issued by the French headquarters, the first meeting of the Institute of Egypt was held at seven A.M. (i.e., before the heat of the day) on 6 Fructidor Year VII (August 23, 1798) at the palace of the departed Mameluke Hassan-Kachef Bey, in his vacated harem. At this meeting, Monge was elected president, Napoleon became vice-president, and Fourier was made secretary. In the event, Fourier would become the leading organizer—though it quickly became clear during the proceedings who was the leading voice in the Institute. When Napoleon spoke, as he frequently did, often interrupting the individual speakers to seek clarification of some point he did not understand or agree with, most others fell silent. The only two who stood up to him were Berthollet, whose chemist's materialism saw no place for Napoleon's quasi-metaphysical worldview in a scientific institution, and Desgenettes, whose insistence upon medical priorities frequently grated with Napoleon's more ambitious schemes. During a discussion of the Institute's scientific program, Napoleon became so exasperated with both of them that he exclaimed: "Chemistry is just cookery for physicians, and medicine the science of murderers." "In which case," replied Desgenettes witheringly, "how would you define the science of generals?"[3]

Yet Napoleon's contribution was far from always being intrusive or negative; he may have had a slightly overblown view of himself as a mathematician, but he was genuinely interested in science, and frequently sought to fill the gaps in his learning—to such an extent that he even asked Berthollet to give him chemistry lessons while he was in Cairo. All this in the midst of the grueling daily program he had imposed upon himself. Napoleon's exceptional qualities, which even now continued to develop, appear to have been driven to evolve by the exceptional quantity of work he undertook during these early weeks in Cairo. Daily he would be at his desk before dawn, working in full uniform through the heat of the day, administering his army and Egypt's internal affairs almost singlehandedly, at the same time putting together a full-scale reform program. Meanwhile he was also doing his best to maintain a foreign policy towards the outside world whilst deprived of almost any reliable information about what was happening there. Certainly he was now learning to delegate, yet all major policy decisions remained his, as can be seen from the relevant volumes of his *Correspondance*—which include orders of the day, civil and military decrees, as well as dispatches to his military governors and generals, communications with foreign potentates, and extensive regular progress reports to the Directory. And in the midst of all this he still found time for serious study of "chemical cookery."

Napoleon may have gathered some of the finest French scientific minds in his Institute, and encouraged their theoretical discussions, but he was insistent that this collection of geniuses, generals and assorted oddballs should also address themselves to mundane practical matters. Illustrative of this are the six questions he personally posed at the end of the first meeting:

1. Can the ovens used for the baking of bread for the army be improved upon, and if so how?
2. Can we brew beer in Egypt with something other than hops [which were not available]?
3. What are the ways commonly used for clarifying and rendering potable water from the Nile?
4. Given the conditions in Cairo, which is the most practical—watermills or windmills?
5. Does Egypt have any resources for the manufacture of gunpowder, and if so what are they?
6. What is the situation in Egypt with regard to jurisprudence, civil and criminal law, and education? What possible improvements can be made in these fields which would be in accord with the wishes of the people?[4]

These questions were not raised merely with the aim of provoking intellectual debate. In each case a commission of Institute members was designated to come up with answers, to be produced at the next or subsequent meetings, which would take place every five days. For instance, regarding the all-important matter of the second question (hopless beer), the relevant commission included members from the mathematics section, the physics section and the political economy section, headed by none other than the foremost chemical genius in Egypt, Berthollet.

Besides such immediate matters, the Institute soon became involved in long-term investigations, drawing up feasibility studies in the manner of a modern think-tank. The subjects of these reports included agricultural improvements and the introduction of new crops (was it possible, for instance, to provide by selective breeding a new species of hops which could withstand the rigors of the Egyptian climate?), as well as a medical report on the prevention of contagious diseases. They would later include a survey for the construction of a canal linking the Mediterranean and the Gulf of Suez.

In keeping with its model, the Institute in Paris, the activities of the Institute in Cairo also included the pursuit of scientific and cultural knowledge, as well as technological know-how, with projects initiated to study the historical monuments and arts of Egypt, the region's geological structure, and the flora and fauna of the country. Members even pursued theoretical learning purely for its own sake. At a subsequent meeting Fourier would deliver a talk, to the bemusement of all but Monge, on his latest work in linear partial differential equations. Similarly, Berthollet would propose a theory explaining the fundamental nature of the chemical reaction. In Cairo, lasting contributions would now be made to the advancement of human knowledge for the first time in over half a millennium. Amidst heat, poverty and primitive conditions which would have been recognizable to citizens of ancient Athens, a small patch of Cairo was being turned into something resembling Plato's Academy.

The Institute was housed two kilometers from Ezbekiyah Square, on the outskirts of Cairo in the palaces of Hassan-Kachef Bey and Kassim Bey, both of whom were with Murad Bey in Upper Egypt. The palaces themselves were surrounded by an extensive garden complex, which was enclosed by walls, providing the members and their savant colleagues with one of the most pleasant spots in the city. The Institute would soon include all manner of facilities, including an extensive library consisting largely of the books Napoleon himself had selected to bring with him on the expedition: a core compendium of Western literature and knowledge. At the other end of the scale was the foundry and workshop established by Conté, where he set about reconstructing as far as possible all the scientific instruments and equipment that had been lost in Alexandria harbor, as well as the further losses in one of the ships sunk in Aboukir Bay at the Battle of the Nile. A meridian line was marked out along the floor of the main corridor of the Institute building, recording the precise number of degrees by which Cairo lay east of the Paris meridian, which was at the time used by the French as the marker for 0° when measuring longitude.

Halls and loggias in the two Mameluke palaces were adapted for use as chemistry laboratories and study rooms, and cellars were soon being used to house the scientific collections that were already being made by the savants. As soon as the printing presses arrived by camel from Alexandria, they were set up at the Institute (the only other printing presses in the entire Levant were at Constantinople and a Maronite Christian convent in Lebanon). These printing presses would become a source of some concern to the *ulema* and sheiks of the Al-Azhar mosque, who insisted that the only font of true knowledge was the Koran, of which they alone were the rightful interpreters. Without such authority any book could only be the devil's work. However, it seems the wise men of the Al-Azhar mosque were being somewhat disingenuous here, for one of the French savants who befriended a sheik discovered that his library did in fact contain a number of non-religious works—including a treatise on love, an anthology of sayings and poems, a book of historical curiosities, instructions for the drawing up of marriage and divorce contracts, and a manual of sexual techniques.

Outside the palaces, the extensive gardens of the Institute would gradually be transformed into botanical gardens for the study of indigenous plants, and a small menagerie of birds, monkeys and snakes would be assembled. The savants would regularly meet in these gardens in informal assembly, as one of them remembered:

We had at the side of the palace of Hassan-Kachef Bey the vast garden of Kassim Bey where we would gather for our evening promenade. The conversation of Fourier contributed great charm to these meetings; sometimes Monge would expand on his views of the future of Egypt, sometimes on his skeptical

ideas, sometimes on his latest ideas regarding his beloved descriptive geometry. He spoke with such enthusiasm that it colored his entire imagination.
The beauty of the night sky, the scent of the orange trees, the sweet and
pleasant airs, all added to the ambience of our meetings, which went on into
much of the night.[5]

But Cairo was not the only center of intellectual activity: a number
of savants remained at Rosetta under the charge of the governor,
General Menou. According to one of them: "All twenty of us live
together in a house, where we share everything in common, including
rations and fresh water. We are looked after by three Maltese former
slaves and a local Frenchman, whom several of us ganged together to
take on."[6] The most industrious of these savants was the precocious
twenty-seven-year-old biologist Etienne Geoffroy Saint-Hilaire, who at
twenty-one had delivered the first lectures on zoology at the university in Paris, a year later being appointed to the first chair in this
subject. In his own words: "It is my good fortune to have the encouragement and protection of General Menou . . . who has given me an
armed escort so that I can go deep into the delta and hunt there safely.
I have found a number of interesting birds; I have observed their habits,
described them zoologically and anatomically, stuffed them and mounted
their skeletons."[7] Geoffroy Saint-Hilaire would also initiate a project
for the study and classification of the fish in the Nile, whose different
species would be expertly drawn and colored by the flower-painter
Redouté, whom Monge and Berthollet had had the foresight to recruit
as a savant. Geoffroy Saint-Hilaire's work in assembling these collections, and the insights that they enabled him to gain into different
species, would allow him to correct certain mistakes made by Linnaeus,
the great Swedish naturalist and founder of biological classification.
He would also undertake a study of ibises, comparing his modern specimens with those which had been mummified by the ancient Egyptians;
his findings here would assist the great French biologist Lamarck in
his pioneering theory of evolution.

Other savants at Rosetta were similarly industrious, even if they did
not produce quite such groundbreaking results. The engineer Jollois
busied himself hiking along the coast with his shotgun, shooting any
seabirds he could find, and bringing back the remains to add to Geoffroy
Saint-Hilaire's collection. Meanwhile others studied the many ruins in the
district, which were deemed to be mainly attempts at ancient pyramids,

dating from an early pharaonic dynasty, while the ubiquitous Denon continued sketching birds, flowers, buildings and even the ruins (enabling them to be correctly identified at a later date as the remains of centuries-old Mameluke fortifications).

Menou was only too pleased to have such men working at Rosetta, and would enjoy listening to their intellectual conversation after dinner at his headquarters. Sadly for him, almost all his savants would soon be summoned to Cairo, where they would become involved in the various projects started by the Institute.

One of the first papers to be read out at the regular meetings of the Institute was Monge's "Explanation of the Optical Phenomenon Called a Mirage." A simplified version of this paper would be circulated throughout the French army in Lower Egypt, so that this phenomenon could be explained to the soldiers, thus dissipating as far as possible the irrational fears the mirages had induced. Other talks ranged from Berthollet's paper on "The Process Followed in Egypt for the Manufacture of Indigo," to Geoffroy Saint-Hilaire's "Observations on the Wing of the Ostrich." Even a number of Napoleon's senior officers soon became enthusiastically involved in the savants' various projects; so much so that chief of staff Berthollet found time to dispatch to the Institute "one hundred birds' mummies preserved and sealed in sandstone pots"[8]— the very find that would enable Geoffroy Saint-Hilaire to study the development over three millennia of the Egyptian ibis.

All manner of new science was soon being introduced to Egypt. A leading light in this enterprise was chief medical officer Desgenettes, who organized the printing of manuals in French and Egyptian outlining treatment for smallpox and bubonic plague. He also sent a circular letter to all medical officers attached to the French army, reminding them that Egypt had been one of the birthplaces of medicine, and that elements of this early medicine probably survived in contemporary Egyptian medical practice. They were to record any instances of this they came across, partly for the benefit of medical history, and partly in case some of these timeless practices forgotten by European medicine remained efficacious. Desgenettes also set in process the daily recording of deaths in Cairo, with these classified under separate columns for men, women and children, listing where possible the cause. The tables would later be used to monitor the rise and fall of contagious diseases in the city, as well as to compare seasonal and annual variations. This was the first use in Egypt of statistical analysis, a science which was barely under way in Europe. Desgenettes also read a paper to the Institute on ophthalmia, the eye disease which affected so many Egyptians and was now beginning to spread amongst French soldiers. Other civil projects included the mapping of Cairo, whose labyrinthine streets were pinpointed by theodolite readings taken by two astronomer-savants, Nouét and Mechain; Conté's construction of an experimental windmill at the northern end of Rodah Island, to catch the wind that blew up the Nile valley; and a study regarding the feasibility of building a Nile barrage.

Amongst its cultural activities, the Institute produced its own journal, *La Décade*, which appeared every ten days, i.e., once every revolutionary week. The first edition was dated 10 Vendémiaire Year VII (October 1, 1798), and came out under the editorship of Tallien, who prudently promised in its prospectus that it would contain "no news or political discussion," but would instead be devoted to the sciences and the arts. This prospectus gives yet another indication of how the French continued to see their role in Egypt—or, more pertinently, how their commander-in-chief viewed this role, for there can be little doubt that Tallien's text was written in the closest possible collaboration with the "vice-president" of the Institute.

We no longer live in times when conquerors only knew how to destroy what they had taken by force of arms, when the lust for gold dictated all their actions, when devastation, persecution and intolerance accompanied them wherever they went. Today, by contrast, the French respect not only the laws, the customs, the habits, but even the prejudices of the people whose territory they occupy. They leave it to time, reason, and education to introduce the changes that philosophy and the enlightenment of the present century have brought about, whose implementation becomes each day ever closer.[9]

Despite the attitude of the Egyptian people, their widespread mistrust and suspicion of the French, even the violent opposition in the countryside, nothing appeared to have changed in the French attitude since they had first set foot in Egypt. Indeed, it appeared that nothing had changed since the day the expedition had been conceived thousands of miles away in France. Time and reason would bring about the inevitable enlightenment of the Egyptian people, who would eventually begin to behave and see the world as if they were Frenchmen.

Contributions to the first issue of *La Décade* ranged from an article by General Andréossy on how to manufacture gunpowder with local materials, to "A Fragment taken from the 17th song of Jerusalem," an extract from the poet-savant Parseval-Grandmaison's epic work-in-progress. A further fragment of this work would appear in a later issue of *La Décade*, featuring such immortal lines as:

> The dawn was lit by the fires of day
> The mountains shone with its golden ray
> Renaud's helmet reflected this light
> As he breathed an air more pure and bright . . .[10]

Ensuing issues of the journal would include translations from the Koran, and from the journals of Egyptian travelers, as well as astronomical observations, analyses of Nile water and tests on Egyptian soil samples. Such a wide-ranging intellectual magazine would have been the envy of most provincial cities in Europe, and even a few of its capitals.

The founding of the Institute aroused much curiosity amongst the leading Egyptian intellectuals, as is illustrated by El-Djabarti's description:

The French installed in one of the houses a large library with several librarians who guarded the books and gave them to readers who needed them. This library was open every day from two hours before midday. The readers gathered in the big hall beside the one where the books were kept. They sat in chairs ranged around the large tables and set to work. Even ordinary soldiers came to work in the library. If a Muslim wished to come into the library he was not in any way prevented, on the contrary he was welcomed in a friendly manner. The French were most pleased when a Muslim visitor appeared interested in the sciences; they immediately made themselves available to him, showing him all sorts of printed books, with designs representing certain parts of the terrestrial globe, animals and plants. . . . I have had occasion to visit this library several times and remain constantly astonished at the sight of all these beautiful things.[11]

Such naïve astonishment, especially coming from a learned man and one who was no admirer of the French, is revealing. This was the reaction of a man who was not only deprived of secular learning, but also had never encountered a world in which such learning was freely available, and open to all. Five hundred years previously, this might have been the reaction of a French medieval scholar entering the Al-Azhar mosque and university, where the study of mathematics, chemistry and medicine was far in advance of anywhere in Europe.

El-Djabarti goes on to describe how the French had "many Moslem books which had been translated into their language," including the Koran, and how some were "learning verses of the Koran by heart." He also observed how "they applied themselves night and day to learn the Arabic language." And evidently not all the French scientific instruments lay at the bottom of Alexandria harbor or Aboukir Bay, for El-Djabarti goes on to admire "astronomical instruments of great precision . . . telescopes which opened out and could be reclosed so that they fitted into little boxes. These were used to observe the stars and determine their distances, their volume, their conjunctions and their opposites." Visiting the painters' atelier, he marveled at the artists: "Among them was Arago [evidently Rigo] who made portraits; he was so skilled that on seeing his portraits one might have said they were in relief [i.e., three-dimensional] and on the point of speaking."

El-Djabarti's greatest wonder was reserved for the scientists: "When an animal or a fish unknown in France is discovered, they put it in a liquid which preserves it indefinitely without alteration." Later he visited the chemistry laboratories, where one of the assistants "took a flagon containing a certain liquid and poured part of it into an empty glass; then he took another flagon of liquid and poured it into the same glass. This gave off a colored smoke and when this smoke disappeared the liquid had turned solid and remained a yellowish color. I touched this solid and found that it was as hard as stone. The same experience was repeated with other liquids, and they produced a blue stone, while a third produced a red stone like a ruby." He was also shown a certain machine: "If a person touched it, his body received an instant shock, which made the bones of his shoulders and his arm crack."

The bathos of such schoolboy experiments astonishing a learned Egyptian makes depressing reading indeed. This was the land where over 3,000 years previously, *chymia*, the art of embalming, had been the first chemistry known to humanity, and had even given the science its name. This was the region where Arabic *al-chemia* had become alchemy, nursing the techniques which had given birth to modern chemistry. It is arguable that the modern rational sciences arising out of such knowledge had played a significant role in enabling the French to overcome the obfuscations of their religion, yet at the same time, it seems, causing them to forget the universal compassion which this very religion had preached. As a result, they felt no compunction about imposing themselves upon the Egyptians, who had done nothing to deserve such attentions. On the other hand, just as surely, the increasing orthodoxy of Islam had overcome the Arabic love of learning, causing the Egyptians in turn to forget all that Islam had taught them. Islam had originally instructed its followers: "To know the world is to know God"; now they had encountered a nation that knew the world but no longer knew God. Mutual incomprehension—from the most trivial scientific experiments and social practices to the most fundamental assumptions of their different civilizations—was perhaps inevitable.

Despite this, the sheiks of Al-Azhar did in fact attend some of the first open meetings of the Institute, but what they made of the learned scientific papers read out by the members is difficult to assess. When Geoffroy Saint-Hilaire finished his paper describing the many new fish that he had discovered in the Nile, he was asked by a sheik in the audience why he bothered himself with such futility, when it was known that the Prophet had settled all these matters ten centuries previously— saying that God had created 30,000 different types of animal, 10,000 of them to live on the land and 20,000 of them to live in water. Unlike El-Djabarti, the leading sheik of the Cairo *divan*, El-Bekri, declared himself unimpressed by the things he had seen at the Institute, and assured the savants that such things were unlikely to impress any Egyptian. When asked why, he replied that Egyptians believed in sorcery: how could the accomplishments of the scientists and artists of the Institute be compared with the wondrous conceptions of any sorcerer, who could conjure up scenes from the heavens, or with the wizardry of even the most ordinary djinns?

El-Bekri even challenged Berthollet on this matter, asking the great chemist if his science was able to make him be in two places at the same time—so that he could appear in both Cairo and Morocco simul- taneously. Berthollet did not deign to answer, merely shrugging his shoulders. El-Bekri took this to be an admission of failure and mocked Berthollet, telling him that despite all his science he was still no sorcerer.

Monge decided to adopt a more positive approach to this culture gap, and attempted to gain the sympathy of the Egyptians by charming them with music. He arranged for an orchestra, made up of musicians from amongst the savants and the regimental bands, to assemble at Ezbekiyah Square and play to the public. This soon attracted a vast crowd. First of all Monge asked the band to play a number of simple tunes, but the audience did not respond in the slightest. After this he tried them with some military marches, then a series of stirring fanfares, "but to no avail, during this magnificent concert the Egyptians all remained completely impassive, all as immobile as the mummies in their catacombs."[12] Monge became exasperated, and turning to the musicians exclaimed: "They're not worth the effort you're making. Just play them 'Marlborough,'* that's all they deserve." According to Monge's contemporary and biographer Arago, when the orchestra launched into "Marlborough," "immediately thousands of people became animated and a wave of joy ran through the crowd. Within a moment young and old launched themselves into the spaces in the crowd and began dancing, filled with hectic gaiety." Monge was intrigued by this result, and repeated the experiment several times, each time with the same result. He tried playing them pieces of Haydn, and pieces of Mozart, with no reaction; yet as soon as the orchestra struck up the sentimental strains of "Marlborough," the crowd went wild. In the end, he concluded that this only showed the Egyptians' complete lack of taste. They simply were not up to appreciating anything so civilized as Western music, except in its most debased popular form.

Some years later the truth behind this peculiar episode would emerge, and Monge would be proved wrong. A nineteenth-century French musicologist discovered that the tune of "Marlborough" was in fact based upon an Arabic song dating from the Middle Ages. This had first arrived in Europe in the thirteenth century with the soldiers returning from the Crusade of Louis IX, and was thought to tell the tale of a legendary mixed-race Franco-Arab called Mabrou. Later the name of the great English general Marlborough, who defeated the French, had somehow replaced that of the obscure Mabrou; though according to Arago this "only came about through a gross blunder." Either way, it is evident that the Egyptians certainly knew what sort of music they liked: their own.

---

* A vulgar sentimental tune, popular in the low taverns of Paris.

XIII

Life in Exile

LA *Décade* was not the first journal to be issued by the French army in Egypt; it was preceded by a four-page news-sheet intended for more general readership called *Le Courier de l'Égypte*,★ whose first edition was dated 12 Fructidor Year VI (August 29, 1798). Its editorship was initially offered to the poet Parseval-Grandmaison, but he refused to dirty his hands with mere journalism, and instead the first few issues were edited by the mathematician-savant Costaz, after which Fourier took over. Despite being run by mathematicians, *Le Courier* was no dry, abstract publication, and the appearance every five days of this four-page news-sheet proved a welcome diversion for the officers as well as the men. (Those who could not read would have the paper read out to them by their friends.) However, from the outset *Le Courier* was forced to scrape the barrel for news, limited as it was to such scraps as reached Egypt: "On 24 Prairial [June 14—i.e., nearly two months previously] the government was overthrown by a revolution in Batavia [Indonesia]"; "Vizier deposed in Constantinople," etc. Little wonder that Fourier would soon be reduced to filling out the double-columned pages with letters from soldiers in various outlying garrisons, as well as "News from Cairo," "Anecdotes" and so forth.

The opening edition of *Le Courier* carried a riveting report, worthy of any French provincial newspaper, covering the festival of the Birth of the Prophet: "After attending a magnificent dinner served in the local manner,

---

★ Most sources amend this spelling to the correct *Le Courrier*, but the bound copies in the British Library show that the magazine itself obstinately retained this anachronistic military misnomer throughout all editions.

the Commander-in-chief retired to his residence. There followed a display of fireworks made by local craftsmen which was a huge success."[1] Napoleon was to take a keen interest in *Le Courier*, and viewed this report on the huge success of the festival as a huge success in its own right, even going so far as to write that very day to Kléber in Alexandria about it: "You will find enclosed with this letter the first issue of *Le Courier*, which has just appeared here in Cairo. If you still have an Arabic printing press in working order, have the article about the Festival of the Prophet printed in Arabic and distributed throughout the Levant. Send me 400 copies."[2]

Kléber was not impressed by what he read, and wrote back to Berthier: "The editing of your journal from Cairo is insufficiently engaging for you to hope to attract many subscribers. At least you should make sure it is written in proper French."[3] In fact, the style of *Le Courier*—like the political content—was quite correct; Kléber was probably referring to the misprints. However, *Le Courier* soon got into its stride and began featuring topics of genuine interest to its readers, such as an article about "Oriental customs with regard to women." This piece described how a Muslim woman's veil was "the last nudity which she grants to the curiosity and caresses of her lover," and went on to tell how the women of Cairo "take much pleasure in visiting the public baths, where they learn all the news about what is going on in the city, and compare how liberated their husbands are. If the behavior of a husband is such that they all disapprove, then an almighty racket breaks out."[4]

In fact, *Le Courier* was much more revealing about the French themselves in Cairo, rather than the habits of the locals. Unlike *La Décade*, one of *Le Courier*'s declared aims was to report on politics; though in the event its coverage of such matters was distinctly propagandistic, as doubtless Napoleon intended. Even so, some of the fulsome poems in praise of the commander-in-chief go beyond the bounds of credulity:

> As on land, so on the sea,
> Bonaparte is covered in glory,
> Braving the English fleet,
> He lays victory at our feet[5]

This poem may ostensibly have been about the taking of Malta ("Gaily they ate the oranges / from the Knights of Malta's bushes"), but its propaganda can hardly have been apposite, let alone convincing, after the Battle of the Nile.

A far more genuine reflection of French life in Cairo can be found amongst the personal notices which began appearing in *Le Courier*: "On the night of the 12th a portfolio of papers was lost. The person who lost them set off from Rue Petit-Houards to go to Old Cairo. Anyone who finds it is requested to take it to the shop in Old Cairo"; "Citizen Baudeuf informs all citizens that the raffle for a watch which was to take place on 29 Vendémiaire has been postponed until 10 Brumaire. There are still a lot of tickets to be had."[6] Even more informative are the advertisements: "Factory producing all kinds of liqueurs and syrups. Citizens Faure, Nazo & Co, place Birket-el-Fil, near Hospital No. 2. All at good prices"; "French baths, at the house of Radhcwan Kâchef, Malafar quarter, residence of the commandant of the First Section, behind place Birket-el-Fil." This last would have fulfilled a genuine need, as the presence of French soldiers in the local baths had so upset the Egyptians that they had soon been placed off limits for army personnel. "The French hatmakers announce to their fellow citizens that they have set up their factory behind the post office." This indicates that there were enough officers' wives, amongst the 300 French women who had traveled with the expedition, to support such an establishment, i.e., probably several score rather than a few dozen. "French manufacturer of tobacco of all kinds, maison Mehemet-Kâchef, Rue Petit-Thouars, opposite the Milanese restaurant." This shows how the French soon moved on from having points of reference (e.g., "near Hospital No. 2"), and began using their own names for the streets, which were signposted accordingly—a creeping colonization which after the first three months had "changed the entire look of this country, so new to civilization, so that if the Army has anything to do with it Cairo will become a little Paris."[7] There is no denying that they were leaving their mark, though all other indications point to this judgment being more than a little overenthusiastic, not to say premature. As the French historian Charles-Roux pointed out: "These exaggerations merely point up the contrast between the little bits of France which grew up here and there in Cairo, and the vast oriental city which engulfed them."[8]

These pioneer European inroads into the Cairo retail economy were allowed to develop in their own way, in true free-market fashion; however, they had in fact been purposely initiated by Napoleon himself. Around the same time as he launched *Le Courier*, he also sent a message to Kléber in Alexandria, ordering him to dispatch to Cairo an armed convoy containing any spare savants, civilian administrators and other expedition members who remained without gainful employment in the city. This he knew would include the various enterprising characters who, like the officers' wives, had contrived to get themselves smuggled aboard the fleet before it sailed. Kléber expressed himself only too pleased to be rid of "these innumerable vermin who follow our armies like sharks follow ships, which no words are sufficient to describe."[9] In fact, this company of unemployed "vermin" dispatched from Alexandria also seems to have included a group of redundant balloonists, as well as a number of freed Malta slaves of various nationalities, ranging from Moroccans to Armenians, who had chosen not to return to their homelands.

The arrival of this mixed group of freebooters and camp-followers in Cairo quickly enlivened the social scene. The more enterprising amongst them opened a number of cafés and restaurants, as well as tailors' shops, furniture makers, and leather merchants for harnesses, saddles and boots. As Napoleon had hoped, all this helped to dispel the *cafard* which continued to afflict his army. Many of these establishments were new to Cairo, and were greeted with some curiosity and bemusement by the locals. Here is El-Djabarti's description of a French restaurant:

The cooks of these places bought meat, vegetables, and fish, as well as honey, sugar and so forth, and prepared dishes in the manner of their country. Each establishment had a sign on the door indicating the nature of its business. If passers-by wished to eat they entered these establishments, where they found places of different categories, each with its own sign showing the prices charged there.★

In the middle of the establishment was a wooden table on which places were set, around the table were chairs on which they sat; waiters carried dishes to the customers. Thus each person ate, and each person paid what he owed, no more, no less.[10]

The notion of fixed prices, with no bargaining, was evidently an innovation to the Egyptians. These restaurants seem to have been established mainly by Greeks, Italians and local French residents, largely employing their own kind as waiters and cooks. The freed Malta slaves opened cafés and refreshment bars. El-Djabarti describes the behavior he

★ This would seem to indicate that they had different classes of dining areas, with corresponding menus; presumably this ensured the separation of the officers, the NCOs and the men.

observed—apparently over some time and with some curiosity—at a café
opened by a freed slave who came originally from Aleppo in Syria:

People met in this café and spent part of the night here. . . . The local population of the entire quarter would gather outside to observe their amusing
behavior, because such people are always drawn to foolishness and idle pleasure.
Such also is the nature of the French. At these gatherings in the café, people
chatted, joked and laughed. One officer used to bring along his wife, who was
very cheerful and was Egyptian.[11]

Relations between French men and Egyptian women were inevitably
a touchy subject, filled with all manner of ambiguities and misunderstandings. El-Djabarti, doubtless echoing the response of many in Cairo,
took a close if somewhat disdainful interest in this matter: "Many French
asked notables of Cairo for permission to marry their daughters, and
some consented to these alliances, either through greed, or to ensure
that they had protectors in the French army. It was a simple matter for
the French, for all they had to do was make two professions of faith,
which cost them nothing because they didn't believe in religion anyway."[12]
These two professions of faith involved simply repeating, "I declare that
there is no god but God" and "I declare that Muhammad is his prophet."

It is not clear precisely how many French soldiers actually "married"
Egyptian women in this fashion, but there is no doubt that Napoleon
was in favor of the practice. Alexander the Great had forced his
generals to take local wives, but Napoleon refrained from going this
far. When General Menou, the governor of Rosetta, eventually became
a genuine convert to Islam and went through a more formal wedding
ceremony with a local Egyptian woman, it was certainly of his own
free will. This act would receive Napoleon's enthusiastic endorsement:
here was concrete evidence for the *ulema* of Al-Azhar that the French
were willing to convert to Islam. Menou's fellow officers proved less
enthusiastic. Many claimed that Menou's new wife, Zobeida, was the
daughter of a common bathhouse-keeper who had beguiled the forty-
eight-year-old bachelor with her sexual charms and made a fool of
him. Others said that she came from one of the richest families in
Rosetta, and that Menou was only after her money. Menou himself
insisted that Zobeida came from the most illustrious stock, being directly
descended from the Prophet on both sides of her family. Whatever the
truth, he seems to have found himself lonely in the evenings after being
deprived of his intellectual after-dinner conversations with the savants.

He converted to Islam, and then participated in a full Muslim marriage ceremony, even taking on the name Abdullah—though he was apparently excused from undergoing the circumcision ceremony on account of his age and rank. It is difficult to gauge the precise nature of his commitment: regarding his marriage, he wrote enigmatically to his close colleague General Dugua, "I believe this measure will be in the public interest."[13]

The reaction of most of his fellow generals was perhaps best exemplified by his friend General Marmont of the cavalry, who wrote to him from Alexandria: "You are right when you say that your marriage astonished so many of us. For my part, my dear general, I see it as a mark of great devotion to the interests of the French army." From irony, Marmont moved on in his next letter to downright impertinence, inquiring: "Would it be indiscreet, my dear general, to inquire how you find your new married state? I am impatient to know if Madame Menou is pretty, and if you intend, in the manner of the country, to give her any companions in the form of a few more wives?"[14] One can almost hear Marmont reading out his letter, amidst widespread guffaws, to his fellow cavalry officers in the mess at Alexandria. Menou's reply was apparently serious, though it is difficult to judge whether or not he too is indulging in some irony here: "I shall not be taking up the permission granted by Mohammed to have four wives, not including concubines that is. Moslem women have a vehement appetite; one is more than enough for me." In answer to Marmont's more inquisitive inquiries, he replied:

My wife, of whom you speak so kindly, is large, strong and good enough in all respects. She has very beautiful eyes, the complexion of an Egyptian, with long and extremely black hair; she has a fine temperament, I find that she has much less repugnance than I expected for my French habits, and above all she has little or no superstition. Although she sticks very punctiliously to her religious observances, she believes that all other religions are also good.

I have not yet urged her to let herself be seen unveiled in the company of other men; that will come little by little. I told her that you have asked me to pass on a thousand felicitations to her, and she replied to me in Arabic: "Salam kétir ou maroul fi sari Askir men Skenderie." Which means: "A great many salutations and greetings to the general in Alexandria."[15]

This would indicate that Menou had learned how to speak Arabic, at least enough to communicate with his wife, and probably more. The local dignitaries were certainly impressed with him, and appear to have been willing to overlook his habitually scruffy appearance, which so irritated Napoleon. Yet Menou was certainly the exception. Despite all Napoleon's promises to the *ulema* with regard to Islam, and his claims to be a regular reader of the Koran, he learned little Arabic beyond the meaning of his grandiose title, Sultan El-Kebir. Even his regular reading of the Koran (in French translation), which he may well have developed as an instructive habit in order to try and comprehend the Egyptian way of thinking, would hardly have impressed the sheiks and *ulema* of Al-Azhar. For the true believer, the Koran existed in Arabic, and Arabic alone.

El-Djabarti's disapproving observations confirm how much Menou was the odd man out: "Moslem women who married the French immediately adopted French habits and dressed in the European manner; they walked alongside the men and busied themselves in their affairs. Guards armed with canes walked in front of them, clearing a way for them through the crowd and treating them as if they were a governor."[16] Although the ordinary soldiers wandered the streets freely, exchanging the usual badinage and more-or-less good-natured insults with the street-sellers, El-Djabarti makes clear that the French authorities did not endear themselves to the shop-owners: "They ordered them to clear the goods from in front of their shops, under the pretext of making it easier for the carts to pass along the street, but in reality to get rid of anything the people might use to make a barricade in case of a revolt.... The traders were seriously inconvenienced by all this, because it meant that they had to remain inside their shops, like mice in their holes."[17] This quaint image, with its subtle overtones of oppression and humiliation, only emphasizes the deteriorating situation: both the French and the Egyptians were now aware that a revolt might take place.

As ever, it was the behavior of the women that continued to grate with the Egyptians: worse than the Muslim women who fraternized with the French were the French women themselves. As El-Djabarti observed: "The French women who arrived with the army went about the streets with their faces unveiled, wearing all kinds of colored clothes and silk scarves. They rode on horseback or on donkeys with cashmere wrapped around their shoulders; they galloped through the streets laughing and joking with the leaders of their mounts and the locals of the lowest class."[18] Such behavior seems to have struck a chord with the local women, if not the men. Within weeks of the French arrival, they too were behaving in this outrageous fashion. El-Djabarti's ever-watchful eye noted: "At the Nile ceremony, the women threw all shame to the winds, abandoning any restraint to their desires. They got into boats with the French, dressed seductively and covered with jewels, they devoted themselves day and night to dancing, to orgies and to singing. The local boatmen, heads filled with hashish, made all sorts of grimaces, imitating the French language and adding their befuddled cries to the singing of the women and the music."[19] This paints a vivid picture—though how much of it is due to El-Djabarti's inflamed imagination and how much to any actual bacchanalian revels is difficult to judge. The public "orgies" can definitely be discounted, and the confusion inspired in El-Djabarti's mind by the sight of men and unveiled women mingling publicly at a shipboard party may well account for the rest. On the other hand, the mimicking behavior of the hash-doped boatmen rings all too true. Egyptians at various levels of society may have responded in their different ways, but there is no doubting the bewilderment, moral vertigo and shock which such libertine scenes provoked.

El-Djabarti describes how such behavior spread: "This indecent liberty encouraged the badly brought-up women of Cairo, and as the French pride themselves on their submission to women, as well as lavishing on them gifts and presents, the women began to enter into relationships with them." The Egyptians were frankly baffled by the French behavior towards women. "This licentiousness spread rapidly throughout the entire city; many women attracted through a love of luxury or the gallantry of the French, imitated the example of the French women. In fact, the French had all the money of their country to hand and always gave way to women, even when these women beat them with their slippers." The effect of such gallantry on the women of Cairo soon reached epidemic proportions: "The black women, seeing the love of the French for women, climbed the walls of the houses where they were servants and went out looking for them in groups. They introduced the French soldiers into the houses of their masters and showed the riches that were hidden there."[20] This seems to be a reference to the black slaves and servants left behind in the Mameluke palaces. The officers who were billeted in many of these palaces often found that concubines as well as servants had been abandoned, and Admiral Perrée wrote home to a naval colleague: "The beys have left us several pretty Armenian and Georgian women, whom we have requisitioned for the good of the nation."[21] As the historian Christopher Herold remarked: "One wonders what Madame Perrée thought of this when she read it in the collection of intercepted letters published by the English."²²

However, what most baffled the Egyptians was the French predilection for women in the first place. Most Egyptians preferred to indulge their extra-marital appetites with young boys, a custom which had been widespread throughout the Levant since earliest times. (It has been claimed that this practice—amongst otherwise heterosexual men—accompanied the spread of Oriental learning and mathematics to ancient Greece, resulting in the foundation of Western philosophy as well as the behavior described in some of Plato's philosophical dialogues.)

In fact, many French soldiers did make use of locally available young men and boys, but not for sexual purposes. When the French soldiery discovered the slave market at the bazaar, they were at first drawn by curiosity. Black Nubian slaves and other tribal captives, as well as children sold into slavery, were imported on the trade caravans from the south, as well as being shipped up the Red Sea. Later, some soldiers took advantage of this market. Small groups—men rather than officers—would pool their resources and buy a slave, whom they employed to perform the more menial tasks in their barracks. As a result of French military cameraderie, as well as the revolutionary outlook amongst the soldiers, most of these slaves were treated far better than they would have been in Egyptian houses; though there was undeniably a certain amount of racist bullying, and the inevitable sadism which comes with absolute power. Such a slave may not have been paid, but the men would share their food with him, and generally looked after their new possession, often regarding him as a kind of human mascot.

The buying of slaves by soldiers was of course forbidden by the French military authorities, but in practice officers tended to turn a blind eye. In mitigation, it is worth remembering that many labor practices in western Europe during this period still remained little better than slavery: in England, women and children in rags were paid a pittance for crawling on all fours dragging carts along cramped coal-mine galleries, and the French navy still made use of wretched prisoners condemned to the unimaginable misery and degradation of the galleys. Outside Europe, the Atlantic slave trade continued to ship slaves by the hundreds, literally packed like sardines, to work the plantations of the Americas, a practice that would not be banned for another thirty-five years. By comparison, the ancient Arab routes shipping slaves up to Egypt by sea from Zanzibar and overland from the Sudan were almost humane.

The French soldiery did of course also resort to local prostitutes, and these too were frequently smuggled into barracks, where they were supported by the men to whom they had become attached. There were in fact many more of these kept women than there were slaves, but not all such covert occupants of the French barracks were prostitutes— many were escaped servants, especially the black women mentioned by El-Djabarti. These women all thought they would be better treated by the French soldiers than they had been by their Egyptian masters, and judging by El-Djabarti's disapproving observations on the French behavior towards women, this was probably the case. However, in general the French soldiers found the local Egyptian women unattractive. The prevailing French and Egyptian notions of female beauty differed widely, the Egyptians tending to favor squat, broad-hipped, heavily proportioned women—hence their popular expression of esteem: "She was so beautiful she could not fit through the door."*

Inevitably, many French soldiers also went looking for prostitutes outside their barracks, but such forays into the crowded maze of back alleyways could prove hazardous. According to Nicolas Turc: "In Cairo and around, the soldiers were attracted to the local prostitutes in great numbers; without mercy their throats were cut and their bodies thrown into pits in order to erase all traces of the crime. This is how so many disappeared. Many amongst them also suffered the pernicious effects of venereal disease, an illness which was very widespread in Egypt."[23] It is difficult to distinguish between Nicolas Turc's disapproval and the actual occurrence of these murders. It would seem that such disposal of French soldiers was very far from being as widespread as he suggests; on the other hand, French medical records indicate that venereal disease became increasingly prevalent amongst the soldiers.

As a result of this, the presence of women in the barracks became a recurrent problem for the military authorities, who took to rounding them up and simply expelling them. Such action was not quite so humane (or ineffective) as it sounds; according to Egyptian law, Muslim women who had sexual relations with Christians were sentenced to

---

* This saying was apparently once prevalent throughout the Levant, particularly within the confines of the Ottoman Empire, but in my experience it is now fondly recalled only in more remote parts of modern Turkey.

be sewn into a sack and thrown into the Nile. Many of the women expelled from the French barracks were soon subjected to this local practice. It seems that the French military authorities became aware of this, but made little attempt to intervene; indeed, as venereal disease became more prevalent, and the evictions of soldiers' women more thorough, there is evidence that this murderous practice was condoned, and even encouraged, though perhaps not at the highest level. As General Dugua wrote to Napoleon: "The men's quarters are infested with these women of the streets. To get rid of them it would be necessary to drown those who are found in the barracks."[24] Napoleon summoned the *agha*, the local Egyptian official charged with enforcing Islamic law, and

insisted that he put an end to this disordered state of affairs, which was responsible for the spread of venereal disease. The *agha* bowed respectfully before the general and promised that his orders would be carried out. And so they were. Within no time four hundred unfortunate women suspected of liaisons with French soldiers were arrested by the henchmen of the Cairo police. When the high command later asked the *agha* what had happened to these prisoners he replied, in the manner of a man who believed he had faithfully accomplished his task, that on that very night they had all been decapitated, stuffed into large sacks and thrown into the Nile. He felt sure that he had understood his orders correctly, but Napoleon did not see it this way at all. He was furious at this news, believing that one could hardly achieve solidarity with the Egyptians by means of such cruelties.[25]

Napoleon again summoned the *agha* and began angrily berating him. According to the same eyewitness, the conversation went as follows:
    "What has happened to the women I entrusted to your supervision?" Napoleon demanded.
    "They are in the Nile," replied the *agha*.
    "In the Nile!" cried the general, rousing himself into a fury and banging his hand on the table in front of him. "You're nothing but a wretch, a brigand! Is this how you go about the art of reconciliation? I should shoot you like an assassin."
    The *agha* remained silent.
    "Answer me! Answer me!" repeated Napoleon. "What on earth made you commit this act of insane cruelty?"
    "It is the custom," replied the *agha* calmly. "I simply carried out the law of the Prophet."

Once again, the chasm of mutual incomprehension seemed insurmountable.

Napoleon ensured that all soldiers with venereal disease were treated in the military hospitals which he had set up in Cairo and the main provincial cities of Lower Egypt under French rule, such as Alexandria, Rosetta and Damietta. The running of these hospitals was contracted out to French civilians, mostly drawn from members of the administrative personnel brought to Egypt on the expedition, although the medical staff were all military doctors under the command of physician-in-chief Desgenettes and surgeon-in-chief Larrey. The British blockade and the lack of cash meant that supplies were short; only seriously ill and wounded men were guaranteed beds, but the wards had soon become badly overcrowded. Those whose health had succumbed during the march from Alexandria to Cairo, as well as the wounded from the Battle of the Pyramids, Shubra Khit and the various recurrent skirmishes in the delta, quickly occupied the field hospitals established on the outskirts of Cairo. But as these were released, victims of disease—particularly ophthalmia—quickly took their place; this was the case in Cairo, as well as in the provincial hospitals. Figures for all French military personnel in Egypt indicate that on August 18, 1798, 10 percent of them were in hospital—in other words, well over 3,000 men. But things soon began to deteriorate: in two months this figure had swollen, mostly through disease, to 15 percent—i.e., possibly as many as 5,000 men. The overworked military doctors did their best under difficult conditions. The entire French army remained afflicted by periodic bouts of *cafard*, but morale in the hospitals was even lower: many of the men thought they were dying and would never see their homeland again. Desgenettes protested constantly to Napoleon that more resources should be diverted to his hospitals, but the commander-in-chief refused to be sidetracked from his ambitious schemes for his colony, which were already hard pressed. The fact remained that there was simply not enough in the budget to go round. Instead, Napoleon ordered all military bands to put on regular daily concerts at the field hospitals and in the courtyards of the buildings requisitioned for inner-city hospitals. Uplifting marches, along with popular tunes such as "Marlborough," were all that could be offered to the flyblown patients languishing amidst the unbearable heat in their beds.

Outside the hospitals, the able-bodied men raised their spirits as best they could. A popular pastime amongst off-duty soldiers was donkey-riding. Donkeys were plentiful in Cairo, their owners using them as beasts of burden, as well as a means of personal transport. They could also be hired, at a very low cost, as the soldiers found to their delight. El-Djabarti recorded how the French soldiers "loved riding on the donkeys, and were willing to pay generously to hire them. Several would continue riding around all day on donkey-back; others joined together in groups and went around singing and laughing. The donkey-minders joined in with them in their pleasures."[26]

Others took part in excursions to the pyramids and the ancient ruins at Giza—where evidence of these visits remains to this day, in the form of soldiers' names and other graffiti carved into the upper stones of the pyramids, inside the burial chambers, and on other ruins. In his journal, young Corporal François recalled: "I inscribed my name, my place of birth, my rank . . . in the royal chamber, on the right of the sarcophagus, in the second pyramid."[27] Such behavior was still commonplace amongst Europeans abroad, and would not generally be regarded as vandalism for several years to come. (Two decades later, Lord Byron would happily carve his name on several ancient ruins as he traveled around Europe.) The myth persists in Egypt to this day that Napoleon's soldiers actually disfigured some of these ruins, and are even said to have used the Sphinx as target practice for their cannons, shooting off its nose. This last is a calumny: it is known that the Sphinx was defaced as early as the eighth century by the Sufi iconoclast Saim-ed-Dahr,[28] and was further damaged in 1380 by fanatical Muslims prompted by the Koran's strictures against images. During these early times the Sphinx was not regarded as a precious historical object, but instead inspired fear: through the centuries it became known to the Egyptians as Abul-Hol (Father of Terrors), and would only begin to be regarded more favorably when it became a tourist attraction in the later nineteenth century.

For the most part, the French responded with romantic wonder to the sight of the Sphinx. Denon and several other artists sketched this mysterious ancient figure, though a number of the savants responded in more prosaic fashion, embarking upon a project to measure its vast features with the aid of plumb lines and calipers. (They discovered that from forehead to chin it measured thirty feet, whilst its width was fourteen feet between the ears.) Even so, these intrepid statisticians could only speculate upon the proportions of its body, for during this period the Sphinx remained buried up to its neck in sand blown in over the centuries from the surrounding Libyan desert.

Another desert activity indulged in by the French soldiery which helped to boost their morale was ostrich-hunting; this was carried out in groups, without the aid of firearms, in order not to waste precious ammunition. The object of the exercise was to catch an ostrich, overpower it, and pluck its spectacular hind feathers. This was no mean feat, as many soldiers learned the hard way. Ostriches might not be able to fly, but they can run very fast, and struggle with some vigor, their knobbly protuberances striking savage blows. Despite such difficulties, these hunts appear to have achieved a high success rate. Several memoirs confirm that within a matter of months most of the French soldiers in Cairo sported magnificent ostrich feathers in their caps. In the interests of morale this practice was tolerated, except during full-dress inspections by senior generals or the commander-in-chief himself. Indeed, judging from Napoleon's memoirs, he seems to have had only a hazy idea of what an ostrich actually looked like, describing it as having, "in its own sort of way, a resemblance to a camel."[29]

Proudly sporting their ostrich plumes, the off-duty French soldiery would roam the streets and the souks in groups, occasionally joining some of their colleagues at one of the buffet-canteens that had opened up. Standing at the makeshift buffets the soldiers would quaff shots of the cheap, locally distilled hooch and watch the natives going about their business. Like the cafés where the officers openly drank alcohol, these buffet-canteens were mainly confined to the French quarter, where so many new shops, outfitters and distillers had opened to meet the needs of the French army that the district became known as "Little Paris." However, the quarter was certainly not confined to Europeans, and the Egyptians were able to watch the Europeans drinking alcohol, as we have seen from El-Djabarti's observations of the cafés and restaurants. In a center of Islam such as Cairo, alcohol had officially been forbidden for many centuries. However, as Denon had observed, it was nightly available in the belly-dancing dens. Also, the Christians, most of the Mamelukes, and even some of the sheiks regularly drank alcohol in private. Indeed, according to El-Bekri's favorite young Mameluke catamite Roustam Raza, who would later become Napoleon's faithful manservant, Sheik El-Bekri put himself to sleep each night by consuming a bottle of wine mixed with a bottle of the local firewater.[30] As with so many drinking tales, this may well be an exaggeration: even so, it would seem to indicate that El-Bekri, the head of the Cairo *divan*, was at the very least a regular heavy drinker. But all this was done behind closed doors, and the sight of the French soldiers publicly flouting the ban would certainly have been deemed by the general population an insult to Islam. Gossip concerning this practice would have spread quickly throughout the city, generating further widespread disapproval. Gathered together at their buffet-canteens, the French soldiers from the various regiments also exchanged their own versions of the latest gossip. During September a rumor did the rounds that Desaix had captured Murad Bey in Upper Egypt (this turned out to be false), and later word spread that Sheik El-Bekri had offered his sixteen-year-old daughter to Napoleon (as we shall see, there was more truth in this). Drunkenness amongst the depressed and homesick French soldiers was surprisingly rare—mainly through shortage of money, lack of any palatable drink, and the threat of heavy punishment. As El-Djabarti observed: "Usually the French only drank to become happy, and if one amongst them drank too much he did not leave his barracks, because if he went out and committed any disorder he was punished."[31] Disorderly behavior, especially in public, was liable to severe punishment; in line with Napoleon's early proclamation, he was determined that as far as possible his troops should not upset local sensibilities. When a small group of impecunious soldiers took matters into their own hands and embarked upon a burglary, after which they were soon apprehended, their punishment was exemplary. El-Djabarti records how a public notice regarding this appeared on the walls of Cairo: "The general-in-chief has punished the soldiers who broke into the house of Sheik Mohammed el Djohari: he had two of them executed in the Place Karamidan, several others were disgraced and stripped of their ranks."[32] El-Djabarti may have dutifully recorded such announcements, as did his fellow commentator Nicolas Turc, but his whole tone indicates that he remained unimpressed. Both these observers—who understood the mood of the local population—sensed growing resentment throughout the city.

XIV

The Perils of Diplomacy

ON October 5, 1798, Napoleon convened a general *divan* in Cairo containing delegates from all the provinces in Egypt then under French rule. Each delegation consisted of three sheiks versed in Islamic law, three local merchants, and three representatives of the local people—one from the *fellahin*, one of the local mayors, and a Bedouin tribal leader. Although these delegates were in fact chosen by the French governors, the *raison d'être* of the *divan* was democratic. According to Napoleon: "The purpose of the Divan is to accustom the notables of Egypt to the ideas of assembly and government."[1] In order to facilitate this, he appointed Monge and Berthollet as "commissioners" to the *divan*, in the hope that they would encourage the delegates to engage in democratic debate.

The first function of the general *divan* was to attempt a widespread reform of the unmanageable tax system and the ancient property laws. But what was to be proposed in their place? With regard to the property laws, Napoleon found himself in a quandary. The more revolutionary amongst his advisers were all for a radical redistribution of land amongst the downtrodden *fellahin*, who made up over 90 percent of the rural population. The advisers pointed out that a reform along these lines would be relatively easy to effect, as most of the Mameluke landlords had already fled their properties. Others were against such a reckless move. They reminded Napoleon of his promise to reward all of his soldiers with six acres of land—this would be impossible if he had already given it all away to the local *fellahin*. He would also be unable to reward any of his deserving officers with estates, or have anything available to give to the French colonists whom he intended to import. Napoleon decided to bide his time, and see what ideas the *divan* might come up with.

At the opening session of the general *divan*, which was held at one of the palaces on Ezbekiyah Square, Napoleon's opening message was read out in Arabic by his interpreter, the fifty-three-year-old Jean-Michel de Venture, the foremost Orientalist amongst the savants. El-Djabarti, who was one of the delegates, recorded some of this speech, in which Napoleon assured them that

The sole desire of the French is to put the affairs of Egypt in order . . . to protect the weak against the strong, so as to reconcile the sympathies of the people. It is thus better for the Egyptians to renounce their ideas of revolt and to display friendship towards the French. The delegates who have arrived from all over the country will bring order to the affairs of Egypt. These are wise and knowledgeable people, and when they are questioned they must reply with sincerity, so that the general-in-chief will know what to do.

El-Djabarti commented that nothing pleased him so much in Napoleon's speech as when he spoke of "the government of ignoramuses and fools."[2] He was of course being sarcastic—pretending to believe that Napoleon was referring to his own government, when he knew perfectly well that he was in fact referring to previous rulers of Egypt.

The proceedings of such an assembly were a novelty to the delegates. When the opening speech was finished, the interpreter proposed that they should choose a president. Several of the delegates proposed Sheik El-Charkawi, the chief of the *ulema*, custodians of Islamic tradition and law at the Al-Azhar mosque and university. But the French commissioners dismissed this, insisting that there must be a vote—so a secret ballot was held, and once again the same sheik obtained the majority of votes. It was evident to the French that the delegates would have to be instructed in even the most basic of democratic procedures; meanwhile, it was equally evident to the delegates that such proceedings were an irrelevant farce. El-Djabarti's description of the ensuing meetings was peppered with telling comments: "The question was discussed . . . and it was decided that nothing should be changed"; "After a long discussion it was found that the question was too complicated"; "Nothing was decided with regard to this subject and the meeting rose"; " 'How did you arrive at this?' [asked one of the French commissioners.] 'From the Koran,' they replied, and cited several verses concerning this question."[3]

Although the delegates saw no reason to change anything, Monge and Berthollet did eventually manage to steer through a number of reforms, including a new sliding-scale tax on town houses and shops: homes that were rented for less than one talari a month were exempted, while dwellings, inns, bathhouses, olive-oil presses and shops were to be taxed between thirty and forty talaris, depending upon their size. Engineers were then drafted in to make a tour of inspection and assess the categories of all houses; at the same time copies were made of these regulations which were distributed throughout the provinces, and also put up in all the main streets of Cairo. According to El-Djabarti, "When the inhabitants learned of these regulations most of them said nothing, simply bowing to their fate, while others gathered together in groups muttering amongst themselves."[4] It was clear that the householders of Cairo were as little inclined to change as the delegates who were meant to be representing them at the *divan*, but Napoleon knew that some unpopular measures were unavoidable if he was to raise sufficient money to keep his administration going and pay for the upkeep of his army. He had sought to win over the common people by exempting them from such taxes, and placing the burden on their oppressors, the landlords and the merchants. Yet there was little sign that his strategy was succeeding.

Likewise, Napoleon's original proclamation to the people of Egypt, which had been circulated throughout the country, also seemed to have won over few hearts. The massacre of the garrison at El-Mansura, whose details had been recounted by its one miraculous survivor, Private Mourchon, had been followed by several similar incidents, though on a lesser scale. After severe reprisals, including beheadings and the burning down of the villages involved, these incidents had stopped and the delta region had appeared pacified. The couriers between Cairo and the coastal cities were still accompanied by armed escorts, but were now rarely molested by Bedouin sorties. Menou in Rosetta felt it quite safe to allow Geoffroy Saint-Hilaire deep into the delta with an armed escort to search out the local wildlife. These scientific sorties proved a great success, with Geoffroy Saint-Hilaire collecting a vast number of specimens, and even receiving help in his quest from local villagers. As a result, Menou decided in mid-September to mount a larger scientific expedition into the delta, led by himself, and accompanied by several distinguished savants, including the geologist Dolomieu, the musician Villoteau, and the artists Denon and Joly.

Protected by a cavalry escort of 200 men under General Marmont, and led by a team of native guides, the expedition pressed on into the flooded regions of the eastern delta, invariably receiving a friendly welcome as they passed from village to village. At one point Menou rode ahead from the main group, accompanied only by a few of the savants and some of the guides. In Menou's words, at this point "we heard some shouting from a nearby village, and a swarm of armed men rushed out and confronted us. In spite of the efforts of our native guides to appease them, they began firing a few shots at us. On account of our small number, and our lack of armed escort, we felt it necessary to fire back, at first just a few warning shots, and then a little more seriously."[5] They found themselves facing 200 angry villagers in the midst of flooded terrain, which was only fordable by means of certain narrow embankments. Then they became aware that some of the villagers were running behind them to cut off their escape route. In order to beat a hasty retreat they were forced to charge through the mob. Denon, Dolomieu and Villoteau made use of their swords and pistols to break through, but Menou reported that "one of the artists who was with us, Citizen Joly, having totally lost his head, threw himself from his horse, screeching in terror. . . . Circling about him we all shouted, imploring him to get back on his horse, or jump on the back of one of ours." According to Marmont, "Joly had got off his horse, apparently from fear of falling off it . . . but became witless with terror, and finally fell to the ground as if struck by epilepsy."[6] The enemy was now upon them and they were forced to flee, leaving Joly to the fury of the mob.

By the time Menou's armed escort arrived on the scene, the attackers had all returned to their village, where they had barricaded themselves in behind the fortified mud-brick walls. The French attacked the village, and a fierce engagement continued throughout the afternoon and into the night, with bursts of heavy fire exchanged on both sides. When at midnight the village went quiet, the French discovered that the villagers had managed to escape under cover of darkness. Marmont recalled in his *Mémoires*: "We lost twenty soldiers, killed or wounded; and General Menou had his horse shot from under him. The unfortunate Joly had had his head hacked off, we later found his mutilated body."

September also saw a rise in the Bedouin harassment of the French lines of communication. Back in Cairo, Napoleon doubled the armed escorts for his couriers and took punitive measures wherever possible, which ensured that most of the couriers reached their destination. However, the British naval blockade meant that Napoleon and his army were all but cut off from the outside world. Yet at least one communication from the Directory in France did manage to get through, though not without some difficulty.

The Directory's message had been dispatched from Paris on July 6, carried by courier Lesimple, who embarked from Toulon on July 17 aboard the sloop *L'Anénome*, under the command of Captain Garibou. *L'Anénome* made its way along the Italian coast, calling in at Civitavecchia to pick up General Camin and several other military personnel bound for Egypt, before finally departing Malta on August 26, by which time they had been informed of the British blockade of Egypt. With the aid of a good following wind, Captain Garibou arrived off the African coast near Marabout, five miles to the west of Alexandria, in the early hours of September 2. Here he waited for a few hours, intending at daybreak to navigate the coastal shoals and sneak into Alexandria harbor, but at five A.M. *L'Anénome* was spotted by some of the British warships maintaining the blockade. Owing to the freshness and direction of the wind, escape proved impossible, so Captain Garibou put Lesimple ashore with a small armed escort, and then beached his ship, with the aim of unloading his passengers, together with the arms and ammunition he had on board, so that they could make their way along the coast to Alexandria. Unfortunately, the sea was so rough that in the course of this exercise the ammunition became soaked, rendering it useless for any defense against the Bedouin who were known to infest this region.

The group began making their way as best they could along the shore, carrying some of the luggage and bearing a large French flag in the hope that they might be spotted by a French patrol. In no time the first few Bedouin appeared. They gestured for the French to follow them inland, but the French insisted upon continuing on their way towards Alexandria. When a larger group of mounted Bedouin appeared on the dunes, the French soon found themselves under attack. As they fled, abandoning their luggage, the Bedouin leapt on it, leaving the French under the impression that they were only interested in robbing them of their possessions. So when the Bedouin continued to pursue them, the French reasoned that they must be after their clothes and whatever they might be carrying in them. One of the passengers, Devouges, described what happened next:

I stripped myself stark naked, imagining this was the only way to avoid being killed. General Camin was also stripping off beside me, but unfortunately he removed neither his cap nor his shirt nor his pants. . . . a Bedouin chief on horseback galloped up to him, taking aim with his rifle. The general sank to his knees asking for his life to be spared, turning aside the butt of the rifle which was already pointing at his chest. Then he raised himself once more and staggered back a few paces, but the pitiless Moor blasted him back onto the sand and he was stripped of his clothes.[7]

Whilst the others were being attacked around him, Devouges made a run for it, stark naked, plunging into the sea even though he could not swim. Here he came across General Camin's adjutant Bella, and together the two of them struggled vainly against the high wind-driven breakers which were forcing them back towards the shore. Bella took his hand, as much a gesture of farewell as to hold out against the force of the waves, and they clung to each other in terror, watching as their comrades were murdered on the beach.

Then our turn came. Two of the brigands waded into the sea up to their waists. The first aimed at Bella, who was in front of me, and his shot hit Bella, going in through one side of his neck and out the other. "I am lost, my friend," he cried to me, letting go of me to raise his hands to his wounds. Two streams of blood ran down his shoulders. For a moment the sea separated us. The second brigand was taking aim at me, but before his finger could pull the trigger I plunged into the sea.

Somehow Devouges escaped, and later "I felt a body beside me, floating alongside two others. I raised its head: it was Bella. The body of a poor little twelve-year-old child was floating beside him."

The Bedouin eventually rounded up those of the group who had managed to escape—around twenty in all, including Lesimple, who was still clinging to the remnants of his dispatches from the Directory— and they were held to ransom. As soon as this news reached Kléber in Alexandria, he paid the ransom, and then sent Lesimple under escort to Cairo. On September 8 Lesimple finally arrived at his destination and presented his dispatches from the Directory to Napoleon. All that was left was a message congratulating Napoleon on the taking of Malta.

As it happened, Napoleon had that very day been completing the latest of his regular reports for the Directory. This was the one in which he had blithely informed his political masters: "Everything is perfectly fine here. The country is under control and the people are becoming accustomed to our presence. The rest is just a matter of time: all the institutions which can speedily bring this about are in place. . . . Mistress of Egypt, France will before long be mistress of the Indes." Beneath these breathtaking claims, he now added a brief note: "Courier Lesimple has just this moment arrived. His ship was beached before Alexandria, and he could only save part of his dispatches. All he had was a letter from you dated 18 Messidor [July 6]. . . . He was probably carrying others which have been lost."[8]

Two vital points arise from this tale. Firstly it demonstrates not only the hazardousness, but also the sheer length of time dispatches took to reach Cairo from Paris—over two months, with no guarantee of delivery. And secondly, this confirmed to Napoleon that he was now entirely his own master, free to act as he pleased. More even than in Italy, he alone now ruled the territory nominally under his command. He was able to introduce reforms, found institutions, make Egypt into anything he pleased. Here, as a result of its shambolic political structure and historical stasis, was a *tabula rasa* upon which he could write anything he wished. Any orders the Directory might send him would be out of date, and therefore liable to be irrelevant, by the time they arrived in Egypt. Napoleon was thus free to dream of "France [becoming] mistress of the Indes," as he tactfully put it. In fact, if the situation remained as it was, with the British navy controlling the Mediterranean, he realized that he alone could be master of the Indes—France would have no say in the matter.

There was only one small cloud on the horizon of this blue-skied geopolitical fantasy. And this was not the present reality of Egypt, which remained barely under control: becoming complete master of Egypt was "just a matter of time." There remained the question of how the Turkish authorities had reacted to his invasion of what was, nominally at least, their sovereign territory. Had Talleyrand managed to convince the Porte that France had no hostile intentions towards its long-time ally the Ottoman Empire? Even in his optimistic letter assuring the Directory "everything is perfectly fine," Napoleon still felt the need to remind them that "I am waiting on news from Constantinople."

As we have seen, Napoleon had written as early as August 19 to the Directory asking, "Is Talleyrand in Constantinople?"[9] Three days later, taking matters into his own hands, he wrote to the Turkish sultan's chief minister, the grand vizier: "The French army, of which I have the honor to be commander, has entered Egypt to punish the Mameluke beys for the insults that they have ceaselessly inflicted upon French business interests." Working on the assumption that Talleyrand had not yet arrived, he informed the grand vizier: "Citizen Talleyrand, minister of foreign affairs in Paris, has been named on behalf of France as the ambassador to Constantinople. . . . He is furnished with powers and instructions to negotiate, conclude and sign any agreement which will remove any difficulties arising from the occupation of Egypt by the French army, and to consolidate the ancient and vital friendship which should exist between our two powers."[10]

Napoleon's further pleas during the following weeks concerning Talleyrand's whereabouts received no reply. Then, early in October, General Marmont, who had taken over from Kléber as governor of Alexandria, informed Napoleon in Cairo that the blockading British squadron had been joined by a number of warships flying the Turkish flag. Marmont had consequently interviewed the captain of a Turkish caravelle which had put into Alexandria harbor, and told Napoleon: "The Turkish captain is deeply convinced of the friendship which the Porte has for us, he did not believe there was any hostility, and he claimed that the Turkish naval ships off Alexandria had been rounded up in the Aegean islands by the British, and were at present under their control."[11] The Turkish captain had also revealed some interesting background information: "He told one of our officers that he had received news of the sensation caused in Constantinople by our entry here; that at first there had been much anger, but that when the official note arrived opinion had changed, and that the Sultan had dispatched everywhere small warships bearing orders to respect the French." This "official note" may have been the letter sent by Napoleon, soon after his arrival, to Pasha Abu Bakr, the sultan's representative in Egypt, informing him that "I have no intention of doing anything against the Sultan."[12]

However, soon after Marmont's report from Alexandria, the French got wind of a rumor circulating in Cairo that the Porte had declared war on France. Napoleon refused to believe this, and on October 30 he dispatched the interpreter Bracevich and Ibrahim-agha, a local dignitary of Turkish extraction, to Alexandria, where they were instructed to sail out to the blockading fleet on a ship flying the Turkish flag, thus indicating that the French authorities in Egypt still recognized Turkish sovereignty. Bracevich and his party were to go aboard the commanding warship, on the pretext of conducting a neutral parley, and "to try and pick up all possible intelligence concerning our position with the Porte."[13]

The French boarding party were received with due civility, as well as some amused astonishment that they should be sailing under the Turkish flag. Bracevich was informed by the British commander Commodore Hood that Turkey had declared war upon France, news that was reinforced by the presence of the venerable Turkish naval commander of Rhodes, Hassan Bey. This was duly relayed back to Napoleon, although General Marmont in Alexandria remained unconvinced. He informed Napoleon that "during the last four days the enemy has begun firing at our fort at Aboukir, but quite uselessly and with no other effect than the death of one man." However, he had observed the Turkish warships taking part in this operation and had noticed "never does a Turkish ship approach one of our batteries without being followed by a British ship . . . one remains persuaded that these ships are not an expedition coming from Constantinople, but a few warships, found cruising or at Rhodes, and rounded up by the British."[14]

Napoleon was inclined to agree. Rumors of a Turkish declaration of war continued to circulate in Cairo, but he remained convinced that this was all part of a British attempt to undermine French rule in Egypt. In order to confirm his suspicions, he decided to send a second mission to the blockading fleet, and on November 16 he briefed Lieutenant Guibert, a promising young officer in the Guides, for this delicate mission. Napoleon's briefing to Guibert is highly revealing:

You will let drop, in the course of the conversation, that I often receive news from Constantinople overland. . . . You will also say to them, as if inadvertently, with a lack of reticence that will easily be attributable to your youth, that since the first days of September I have daily dispatched a courier to France . . . if they ask from where they have departed, just say you don't know. . . . You will say to them that I am at present at Suez, letting drop casually that you believe a large number of battleships have arrived there from the Isle de France [Mauritius]. . . . You will also say that if they are having difficulty with supplies of fresh water or anything else which they need to make life bearable, you know that I am quite willing to provide them with such things.[15]

It is evident from this that Napoleon suspected the British were just as much in the dark as himself, and that he was in a better position to bluff than they were. After all, Turkey was France's ally, and Talleyrand was due to sort things out with the Porte. The British communications were stretched to their very limits, and they may well have felt threatened by the prospect of a French fleet arriving to relieve the blockade. Yet if this was the case, they were giving nothing away. Lieutenant Guibert was received coldly but politely by Commodore Hood, who allowed him to talk freely with those on board. As Guibert later reported back to Napoleon:

Hassan Bey spoke to me of the war that the Sublime Porte had declared against us, and said to me that Russia and Britain, now allied with Turkey, were going to attack us. I replied in Italian: "Do you think that the Porte would ever become allied to Russia, your natural enemy, who has unceasingly sought to expand into your territory?" I repeated to him that you have frequent correspondence with Constantinople by way of Syria, and that the Sultan was well aware of what was happening. The Turk who accompanied him then said to me, in a tone of some ferocity, that at Rhodes 140 Frenchmen had been clapped in irons and that similar measures had been taken in provinces throughout Turkey.[16]

In short, there was no meeting of minds. Commodore Hood insisted that Turkey was at war with France, but Lieutenant Guibert remained unconvinced: "It didn't even have the appearance of truth. In general, despite the ostensible friendliness and warmth that they affected towards the old pasha of Rhodes [Hassan Bey] and his attendants, the British appeared to me to be in little sympathy with them, and were above all very discontented with the Arabs."[17] Guibert revealed that one British captain had told him how Hassan Bey "had appeared very astonished to see the sociable manner of the discussions between the French and the British, he pointed out that in Turkey such envoys were in danger of losing their lives. Whereupon the British officer could not refrain from telling him: 'We are not barbarians like you.' "

The full import of this latter exchange would have been all too clear to the French diplomatic representative in Constantinople, who was at that very moment languishing in the notorious Yedikule dungeons. Despite the apparently deceptive signals Napoleon had received in Cairo, and the similarly deceptive messages he had sent from Cairo to Constantinople, the entire situation had been transparently clear to the Porte for some time.

As we have seen, news had probably reached Constantinople of Napoleon's intention to invade Egypt by early May 1798, owing to some highly skilled espionage work by Greek agents working for the Turkish embassy in Paris. At the time, French affairs in Constantinople were being handled by Citizen Ruffin, a junior diplomat of little experience. The ambassador appointed to replace Verninac—who had so inspired Napoleon in Italy on his journey home—had died. As soon as news of Napoleon's expedition reached Constantinople, Citizen Ruffin was hastily summoned before the Turkish foreign minister Reis Effendi.* Despite Reis Effendi's insistence, Ruffin was unable to offer any explanation: all he could do was insist that he knew nothing whatsoever of any invasion plans, and assure the minister that he was certain France harbored no aggressive intent against its long-term ally. This was also the position adopted, rather more disingenuously, by Talleyrand when he was confronted by the Turkish ambassador in Paris. Even when news of the actual invasion first reached Paris, ironically via Constantinople, Talleyrand continued to assure the ambassador that France had no hostile intentions.

As Ruffin wrote in his report to Talleyrand: "There is an old Turkish proverb: 'When an Ottoman hunter goes after a hare, he starts out in a horse and cart.' This aptly captures the prudent tardiness of the Porte."[18] Here, at least, Ruffin knew what he was talking about. Just as he predicted, in the customary manner of the Ottomans Sultan Selim III decided to bide his time and see what would happen. The far-flung and ramshackle Ottoman Empire was now coming to be regarded as "the sick man of Europe," with European powers casting covetous eyes upon its territory. During a ruinous five-year war, which had only ended six years previously, Russia had seized the Crimea, and Austria had expanded into the Balkans. France was virtually the only European power that Selim III could rely upon, and he had no wish to end this alliance by any precipitate action. This lenient attitude towards France also received encouragment from an unlikely source—the sultan's favorite wife, Sultana Velideh, a Frenchwoman who had arrived at her present position as a result of a remarkable adventure. Aimée du Buc de Rivery had been born in Martinique and by a curious coincidence was in fact a cousin and childhood friend

---

* Reis Effendi was the official title of the Porte's foreign minister, who at the time was Asif Ahmed; however, many contemporary reports refer simply to Reis Effendi (seemingly mistaking this for his actual name), and I have thus retained this usage to avoid confusion.

of Napoleon's Josephine. When she had been sailing home to Martinique after her convent schooling in France, her ship had been attacked by pirates, who had taken her captive and sold her in Algiers. The sight of this impeccable white virgin had attracted the attention of the sultan's representative, who had sent her to Selim in Constantinople, where her beauty, vivacity and intelligence had quickly established her as the sultan's favorite. However, Sultana Velideh's influence could do little to aid the hapless Ruffin, who remained in ignorance in the French Embassy. His uncomfortable situation was further worsened when news of Napoleon's great victory at the Battle of the Pyramids reached Constantinople.

With feelings running high throughout Turkey, Ruffin was summoned to Reis Effendi and informed that no Frenchman resident in the Ottoman Empire was to appear in public, and also that from now on he himself was banned from the foreign ministry. If he wished to deliver any diplomatic communication to Reis Effendi, he was only permitted to call at his private residence after dark. Although Reis Effendi assured him "that these were simply practical measures, to avoid any angry incidents,"[19] Ruffin had sufficient diplomatic expertise to understand the subtleties of what was happening. As he explained in his report to Talleyrand: "Before I took my leave of him, he made no attempt to offer me either sherbet, perfume or a scented handkerchief, and I concluded from the absence of these traditional marks of hospitality that this had not been a diplomatic meeting but had in fact been a diplomatic reprimand."

Meanwhile, behind the scenes the British had been doing their utmost to persuade the Porte of the seriousness of the French invasion of Egypt, suggesting that this could well be the prelude to a full-scale offensive against the Ottoman Empire, with Napoleon marching up through Syria to threaten Constantinople itself. The British did not in fact take such an outlandish idea very seriously, although ironically Napoleon did, believing that it was a realistic alternative: he had informed Talleyrand that if he was prevented from marching overland to India, he would "return home via Constantinople."[20] In order to protect the territory of its empire, the Porte would be best advised to form an alliance with the British, according to their persuasive minister plenipotentiary Charles Spencer Smith, brother of Sir Sidney Smith, the maverick sailor who had played a decisive role at the siege of Toulon. Spencer Smith even went so far as to suggest that the Porte should forget its differences with its traditional enemy, Russia, and instead form a triple alliance with Russia and Britain against the French. The Porte took cognizance of this astonishing advice, but continued to bide its time.

When news of Nelson's victory at the Battle of the Nile and the destruction of the French fleet reached Constantinople, the Porte belatedly stirred into action. On September 2 Ruffin and his two official interpreters were summoned to the sultan's residence at Topkapi Palace to present themselves at the seraglio.* The French delegation was received in stony silence. Ruffin recorded that in accordance with etiquette and the local tradition of hospitality, "coffee was served, and afterwards, when the chargé d'affaires had set down his cup, Reis Effendi made a speech."[21] In the course of this, he referred to

the ancient and sincere friendship which for so long and so happily united our two powers. The Porte had only been able to view with the saddest astonishment the invasion that the aforesaid republic had allowed itself to embark upon, in the midst of peace, against Egypt. This was the most precious province of the Ottoman Empire, which could be seen as nothing less than the navel of Islam, by reason of its proximity to the two revered and noble cities of Mecca and Medina.

Immediately this speech was over, the French delegation was placed under arrest. It was then marched out of the palace and through the streets of Constantinople by a detachment of Janissaries of the Imperial Guard. According to one of the delegation, they passed "through a

---

* This hall was not actually within the confines of the sultan's seraglio (or harem), but attached to it, and served as the council chamber of the cabinet (the *divan*). Here the grand vizier and his ministers would sit in order of rank on the low couches at the sides of the room (the original divans from which all such councils took their name). During meetings of the *divan* the sultan would sit hidden above the chamber behind a grille, listening to the discussions. He would rap his cane against the grille to signify the start and finish of these meetings, but would take no part in them. Afterwards, the grand vizier and other ministers might in turn be summoned to private audiences with the sultan to give account of what they had said. Unsatisfactory explanations could lead to serious consequences. During the earlier reign of Selim the Grim, seven grand viziers had been executed in eight years. Such government did not make for precipitous decisions; but by the same token, once a decision was made, and approved by the sultan, it was not lightly rescinded.

crowd of curious onlookers from all walks of life, who crammed the streets, the shops and the crossroads, without uttering a single shout or manifestation of aggression."²² Ruffin and his colleagues were taken to the Yedikule, the Castle of Seven Towers, the notorious dungeons in the ancient Byzantine walls of the city, which stood next to the so-called Well of Blood into which the heads of executed prisoners were cast. Despite these medieval conditions, Ruffin manfully prepared his report for Talleyrand on what had happened. Meanwhile, on September 9 the Porte issued a declaration of war against France, which was duly conveyed to Paris under the good offices of the Spanish ambassador. At the same time, French nationals throughout the Ottoman Empire were rounded up and thrown into jail. This almost certainly involved some thousand or more men, women and children, although precisely how many is impossible to determine. The identity of any foreigner was difficult to establish in this age before passports, and many zealous local authorities simply picked up anyone they suspected of being French. Ruffin reported that 200 were arrested in Constantinople, including "businessmen, artists, writers, citizens and 'protégés' [as well as] rajas of various nations and even returned Turkish emigrés."²³ At least a quarter of these ended up as galley slaves.

By now Charles Spencer Smith had convinced the Porte to sign a treaty with Britain; at the same time the Porte had been persuaded to ally itself with Russia, in what has been called "one of the most improbable alliances in the history of international relations."²⁴ Within weeks, a Russian fleet was sailing down the Bosphorus on its way to join with the Turkish fleet in the Mediterranean, passing as it did so through the heart of Constantinople, where its appearance was greeted with enthusiastic cheers from the city shores.

Back in Egypt, Napoleon remained ignorant of these developments, and in the absence of any concrete evidence he still refused to believe that the Porte had declared war on France. The presence of Hassan Bey and his warships amongst the blockading British squadron could easily be accounted for, not least because Hassan Bey consistently refused to give any of Napoleon's envoys an unequivocal message on paper confirming that the Porte had declared war. General Marmont insisted in his memoirs: "The certainty of any declaration of war by the Porte

Napoleon in 1796.

Pauline Fourès, Napoleon's "Cleopatra," by an unknown artist.

The Battle of the Pyramids, July 21, 1798.
To the left are the Nile and the village of Embaba; in the foreground is Dugua's division, from which Napoleon directed the battle, and on the far right can be seen Desaix's division.

(*Clockwise from top left*)

Andoche Junot.

Louis-Joseph Maximilie
Caffarelli.

Gaspard Monge.

Claude-Louis Berthollet.

Nicolas Jacques Conté.

Déodat de Dolomieu.

Joachim Murat.

Jacques-François Menou.

(*Clockwise from top left*)

Jean-Baptiste Kléber, Napoleon's difficult second-in-command.

Louis-Charles-Antoine Desaix.

Sheik El-Bekri.

Murad Bey.

Savants measuring the
Sphinx, from *Voyage en
Égypte* by Dominique
Vivant Denon.

The remains of the
temple at Edfu,
engraving after Denon.

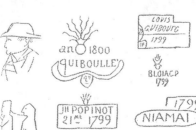

French graffiti
on the temples
of Upper Egypt.

Painting by the Romantic artist Gros of Napoleon
visiting the plague victims at Jaffa.

A romantic rendering
of Sir Sidney Smith
at the siege of Acre.

Napoleon on the retreat from Acre.

was not yet established."²⁵ This would seem to indicate that Napoleon was not alone in his belief that there was no rupture with Turkey. Indeed, this optimistic view appears to have been prevalent amongst the majority of the French Army of the Orient.

Less easy to explain away was the appearance in Egypt of a *firman*: an imperial decree issued by Sultan Selim III calling for a holy war against the French. This had been sent by the Porte to Djezzar, at Acre in Syria, who was still harboring the Mameluke leader Ibrahim Bey. Copies of the *firman* were then sent by messengers across the Sinai desert into Egypt, along with messages to the Egyptian people from Djezzar and Ibrahim Bey. These seem to have been read out after Friday prayers at the mosques in Cairo sometime during October. The *firman* may have been couched in poetic language, but its message was transparently clear:

In the name of God the merciful . . .

The French people (may God destroy their country from top to bottom and cover their flags in ignominy) are a faithless and obstinate nation whose wickedness knows no restraint. . . . They are sunk in a sea of vice and error, they are gathered together under the flag of the devil, and they are only happy amidst disorder, taking their inspiration from hell itself. . . . The lion does not care about the number of foxes who are thinking of attacking him, and the falcon is not afraid of a swarm of crows who croak at him. . . . With the power of the Prophet this army of atheists will be scattered before you and exterminated. . . .²⁶

It also included passages outlining French beliefs:

They mock all religions, they reject belief in another life, as well as its rewards and tortures, they do not believe in the resurrection of the body, nor in the last judgment, and they think that a blind chance presides over their life and death, that they owe their existence to pure matter, and that after this life their body returns to the earth. . . . Their aim is to spread disunity amongst rulers, trouble amongst emperors, and incite their subjects to revolt.

This perspicacious summary of French revolutionary principles also included the following:

The French think that men, being born equal, must be equally free; that all distinction between men is unjust, and that each ought to be the master of his own opinion and his manner of living. . . . They have the impudence to say: We are brothers and friends, the same interests unite us, and we have the same religious opinions.

This was a surprisingly accurate reflection of the ideas the French thought they were bringing to the Levant; such notions were the benefits of a progressive civilization, no less. Indeed, Napoleon himself could easily have written this last passage in his proclamation to the people of Egypt. The words would have been understood at once, and acted upon with zeal, had they been read out in public in many European countries of the period, and over the ensuing centuries many of these beliefs have come to be accepted throughout the Western world. Yet the Muslim authorities of the period were happy to broadcast them in mosques throughout the land, knowing that such ideas would not only be beyond the understanding of a people who had never known any freedom, but would also be rejected. The very core of what the French thought they were bringing to the Egyptians, and giving to their society, which appeared so backward, was not only incomprehensible but offensive to the people they were addressing. This was a situation which the French, in their turn, would soon begin to find incomprehensible and offensive.

There can be no doubt that Napoleon actually saw at least one verson of this *firman*. According to Nicolas Turc, "The general-in-chief [Napoleon] had a copy of this *firman* and it was equally known to the *ulema* of the Divan and the inhabitants of the provinces."[27] Napoleon himself, in his not always reliable memoirs, confirms this by describing a plausible incident: "Djezzar dispatched to Sheik El-Sadat the *firman* which contained the declaration of war from the Sultan against France. Napoleon went to dine with the sheik. When Napoleon found himself alone with the sheik, he commanded him peremptorily to hand over to him the original of the *firman*. El-Sadat denied having knowledge of it, hesitated, contradicted himself, and finally handed it over."[28]

Despite such evidence, Napoleon persisted in maintaining that this *firman* was the work of Djezzar and Ibrahim Bey, who were hell-bent on stirring up trouble for the French in Egypt. Whether at this late stage he actually believed this, or simply maintained it to suit his own purposes, is not known. Either way, as late as mid-November he wrote firmly to Djezzar, "I do not wish to make war with you if you are not my enemy, but it is time that you explained yourself. If you continue to give refuge to Ibrahim Bey on the borders of Egypt, I will recognize this as a mark of hostility and will march on Acre."[29]

The fearsome Djezzar was not used to being treated in this fashion, but instead of acting impulsively he chose to bide his time. Perhaps inevitably there were several versions of the sultan's *firman* in circulation, and one of these promised Djezzar: "Ships as tall as mountains will cover the surface of the seas. Cannons that produce lightning and thunder, heroes who despise death for the sake of victory in the cause of God . . . will arrive to chase out the French."[30] Djezzar was confident that victory would be sweet and certain when the time came.

Early in December, Napoleon decided to make a last concerted effort to resolve matters by sending to Constantinople Citizen Joseph Beauchamp, the French diplomatic representative at Muscat on the Persian Gulf, who had arrived in Cairo some weeks earlier. Beauchamp was a man of considerable intellect and experience. Besides being a noted astronomer, he had also explored throughout the Levant and the Black Sea region, and had resided in Constantinople for several years. To the grand vizier Napoleon wrote: "Beauchamp will make known to Your Excellency that the Porte has no more true friend than the French Republic."[31] Privately he instructed Beauchamp: "If ever you are asked the question: 'Would the French consent to leave Egypt?' reply, 'Why not?'"[32] Napoleon had no intention of acting upon this: it was simply a bargaining position, allowing him time to pursue other avenues. At the same time as offering to give in to Constantinople, he also had in mind the possibility of marching on the city! On December 11, the same day as he wrote to the grand vizier and gave his instructions to Beauchamp, he also wrote a note to Talleyrand, in the expectation that he must at last have arrived in Constantinople to open negotiations with the Porte: "I have sent to Constantinople Citizen Beauchamp, consul at Muscat, so that he can tell you of our situation here, which is extremely satisfactory, and also, so that he can insist, in concert with you, upon the release of all French citizens arrested in the ports of the Levant, and put an end to the intrigues of Russia and Britain. . . . Citizen Beauchamp will bring you by word of mouth all the details and all the news of interest to you."[33]

This is a telling statement. If Napoleon's intelligence had informed him that the French throughout the Ottoman Empire were being held in prison, and that both Britain and Russia were in league with the Porte, then he must have known that the *firman* declaring war on the

French was genuine, and came from the sultan himself. However, it is equally clear that he thought that Talleyrand, with his superlative diplomatic skills, would soon be able to resolve the situation. What he did not know, and had not yet guessed, was that Talleyrand had never had any intention of traveling to Constantinople. In doing so he would have placed himself in danger, and on top of this would doubtless have found himself deposed by his enemies in the Directory while he was away from Paris. Talleyrand would not risk anything for Napoleon if it meant risking his own position. But Napoleon was still unaware of this—and he would hear nothing from Constantinople to inform him otherwise, as the ship on which Beauchamp was traveling would be intercepted by the British off Rhodes.

Napoleon remained on his own, and in the dark, beset on land and sea by enemies—yet in his own mind many options still remained open.

XV

Insurrection

As if all this was not enough, Napoleon also found himself facing enemies within his own camp. From the outset, General Kléber had been dissatisfied with his appointment as governor of Alexandria. He saw himself as a field general, but the head wound he had sustained during the assault on the walls of Alexandria had left him unfit to command a division on the march to Cairo. As governor of Alexandria, he soon experienced difficulties with Sheik El-Koraïm, the local leader whom Napoleon had reappointed and put in charge of local administration and maintaining order. Kléber began to wonder if he could trust El-Koraïm, and was not long in discovering evidence to support his suspicions, which he passed on to Cairo. This was damning evidence indeed, as Nicolas Turc related: "There fell into the hands of the general-in-chief letters from El-Koraim addressed to Murad Bey calling upon him with insistence to come to Alexandria, with the promise that he would deliver the city over to him."[1]

Kléber placed El-Koraïm under arrest, and had him confined aboard a French warship in the harbor. He was then transferred under armed guard to Cairo, where he was charged with treason and sentenced to death, being allowed, as was the custom, the option of paying a fine, in this case set at the equivalent of 300,000 francs. This was a large and exemplary sum, though certainly within El-Koraïm's ability to pay, yet he showed no inclination to do so. Napoleon's secretary Bourrienne recorded how he had opportunity to speak alone with El-Koraïm, through an interpreter, and attempted to convince him that Napoleon would certainly carry out his sentence. He told El-Koraïm: "'You are rich, make the sacrifice.' El-Koraïm sneered and replied: 'If I am to die now, nothing can prevent this, and I give my money uselessly. If I am not to die, why give it?'"²

In refusing to pay this fine, El-Koraïm has been seen as obstinate, proud, inordinately miserly, or even imbued with a spiritual acceptance of his fate: his conversation with Bourrienne is open to all these interpretations. Yet Egyptian sources suggest otherwise. These claim that he would have understood the size of Napoleon's fine as the first move in a bargaining position, and that when he refused to pay, Napoleon should have lowered the figure. At that time in Egypt there was no Arabic word for *compromise*, in the sense of coming to an agreement by means of debate and climbdown. Instead there was only *faradin*, which involved the resolution of a problem with no loss of face on either side. In refusing Napoleon's offer, a move that was incomprehensible to Bourrienne, El-Koraïm was merely adhering to the only method he knew. This may have involved pride, or even obstinacy, but what the French did not understand was that for El-Koraïm there was no other way open.

On September 6 El-Koraïm was duly shot at the Citadel in Cairo. Afterwards his severed head was paraded through the streets of the city bearing the message: "El-Koraïm, sheriff of Alexandria, condemned to death for having betrayed the oath of loyalty that he had made to the French Republic, and for having continued relations with the Mamelukes, for whom he served as a spy. Thus will be punished all traitors and perjurers."³ According to Nicolas Turc: "His execution caused great bitterness amongst Egyptians, and after this a dreadful iciness stole over their hearts."

Kléber had no wish to be dealing with such matters. Again and again he wrote to Napoleon: "I will not cease, Citizen General, to beg you to send the order for me to rejoin my division. I do not know anything about administration."⁴ With the latter remark, Napoleon soon found himself agreeing: he was constantly chiding Kléber in letter after letter (on occasion, two a day) for his shortcomings, especially with regard to finance: "I do not approve, Citizen General, the measure you have taken to withhold the 15,000 livres that I intended for [Admiral] Ganteaume . . ."; "The administration of Alexandria has cost twice as much as that for the rest of the army"; "All the measures I have taken for the navy have been nullified by the money you have diverted to other services. . . ."

Napoleon had sent money to Alexandria for Ganteaume to provide for the 3,000 French prisoners taken at the Battle of the Nile, and subsequently returned to Alexandria on parole, i.e., on condition that they did not take up arms against the British. These men, many of them inexperienced sailors, and even jailbirds who had originally been pressganged into the navy just before the expedition sailed, soon became a source of indiscipline and general disorder in Alexandria. They even began deserting, until Napoleon finally ordered that they be rounded up and formed into a "naval brigade," which would be marched out to the remote fort at Aboukir Bay until ships could be found for them. At least three of these former prisoners would be unlucky enough to be taken on as crew members on a corvette that unsuccessfully attempted to elude the British blockade; after their identity was established, Commodore Hood felt obliged by the rules of war to have them shot.

When Kléber began to question some of Napoleon's commands, he was told by his commander-in-chief in no uncertain terms: "You will be so kind as not to upset the arrangements I am making. They are based on factors you cannot appreciate, since you are not at the center of things."[5] Kléber vented his almost incoherent rage in his pocketbook: "Never a fixed plan, everything goes by fits and starts. Each day influenced only by the events of that day. He claims to believe in fate"; "Is he loved? How could he be? He loves nobody. But he believes he can make up for this by influencing those around him with promotions and gifts." Yet Kléber could not help himself expressing admiration as well: "Always daring . . . an extraordinary man."[6]

Kléber was very much an army officer, especially in his dislike of politics; yet what he was reluctantly witnessing was the development of Napoleon the political administrator. Napoleon was beginning to emerge as Sultan El-Kebir, a man beholden to no superiors, the ruler of Egypt in every respect, giving the first intimations of the emperor he was to become: exuding power, charisma, and even charm. When Kléber finally resigned, "my health no longer permitting me, from this moment on, to remain in charge," and followed this with his demand "to obtain from you permission to return to France,"[7] Napoleon exercised all his authority and charm, inviting Kléber to come to Cairo and be at his side:

I am extremely angry about your indisposition, I hope that the Nile air will do you good, and leaving the sands of Alexandria behind you, perhaps you will find our Egypt not so bad as you imagined it at first. . . . You must believe the desire I have to see you promptly reestablished, as well as the high price that I attach to your esteem and friendship. I know that we have had our little misunderstandings, yet you will be unjust if you doubt the pain that these have caused me. The esteem that I have for you is at least equal to that which you have sometimes testified for me. I salute you and love you.*[8]

Kléber dutifully set off for Cairo, his armed convoy approaching the city on October 22—whereupon all his misgivings were immediately reinforced. As he rode up towards the city walls he could hear the sound of gunfire, and make out puffs of white smoke coming from the howitzers up on the Citadel, ranged along the battlements beneath the flying tricolor. The howitzers appeared to be firing down onto the rooftops of Cairo and in the direction of the Al-Azhar mosque. It was also noticeable that the open city gate had no uniformed guards on duty, and when Kléber's convoy entered the city streets they were astonished to find them in uproar: the local citizens were shouting and running in all directions, assembling makeshift barricades, and there was the sound of rifle and musket fire echoing in the alleyways. The voices of the muezzins were calling out from the minarets above the panic of the streets: the entire city seemed to be in a state of anarchy.

Discontent amongst the Arab population of Cairo had been building up over the previous months, and anti-French feelings had further been encouraged by the reading out of the sultan's *firman* in the mosques. Yet most sources seem to agree that what finally tipped the scales was a comparatively minor matter that only affected the wealthier merchants, a matter that had in fact been agreed by the general *divan* of assembled Egyptian dignitaries—notably, the tax on households. As we have seen, El-Djabarti recorded how the householders began "gathering together in groups muttering amongst themselves." In no time, "the groups began to swell, but there was no intelligent leader to guide them. They got out the arms they had hidden, and the revolt broke out."[9] This was early on October 21. As to precisely what happened next, eyewitness versions differ, but only in detail. According to Nicolas

---

* In French, this last sentence reads: "*Je vous salue et vous aime.*" Whilst *aime* here is intended in terms of fondness and deep friendship, the word *love* conveys something of the shock value this disarmingly sympathetic avowal must have had (and was intended to have). During this period Napoleon seldom signed off his letters with anything but a simple "Bonaparte"; even his one or two favored generals were lucky if they were greeted, "*Je vous salue.*"

Turc, "Someone . . . ran through the streets crying, 'All those who believe in the one God go to the Al-Azhar mosque. Today is the day we fight against the infidels!'"[10] El-Djabarti suggests that the mob initially made its way to the mansion of the *cadi*, the high judge, "who, seeing the crowd . . . shut the door of his mansion and directed his men to guard it to prevent the crowd from getting in. The rioters then began to throw all kinds of stones at the mansion. The Cadi was afraid and wanted to save himself but was not able to get out."[11]

There were two striking features of these events. First was the fact that they took the French completely by surprise. No one, from Napoleon down, appears to have been aware that Cairo had been building up, especially over the previous weeks, towards a serious revolt. Second, and this perhaps gives an element of vindication to the French state of unreadiness, was the wholly unforeseen way in which the revolt found such widespread and enthusiastic support amongst the poorest and most downtrodden citizens of Cairo. For as Nicolas Turc himself points out: "In reality, the French occupation improved the lot of the lower class—the stallholders, the street-porters, the craftsmen, the donkey-minders, the grooms, the pimps, the prostitutes— in a word, the dregs of the population had it easy because they had gained more liberty."[12] Most sources blame the imams, and extremists amongst the many religious students at the Al-Azhar mosque university, who knew how to appeal to the poorer people's deep-seated belief in Islam, as well as their fear of change, a fear which permeated a society that had seen virtually no change for centuries. Perhaps most telling of all was the fear, which affected the entire population, that the Mamelukes would soon be returning with a vengeance. The British blockade, the sultan's *firman*, the propaganda from Ibrahim Bey in Syria with Djezzar, and the knowledge that Murad Bey was still at large in Upper Egypt—all seemed to indicate that the French reign in Egypt would not last long. On the other hand, the artist-savant Denon and others would note that during the ensuing murderous disorders many middle-class Cairo families gave refuge to French soldiers, despite the fact that it was the middle classes, especially the merchants, who had suffered so severely from increased French taxes, and also from the British blockade on exports and imports.

Life begins in the early hours in a hot city such as Cairo, and the events of October 21 appear to have started some time before six A.M. Nicolas Turc recounts how these unfolded:

Now whilst most of the population knew what was going on in the city, the French remained unconcerned. In no time, the entire city rose up and news of this reached the governor General Dupuy, who was a very hard man. . . . He rode out immediately, accompanied only by five mounted guards. His aim was to find out what was going on and calm things down . . . he saw some citizens and working men who were putting up barricades. A Janissary suddenly came out from around a street corner and smashed him on the back of the neck with a club. The general fell from his horse, and his men carried him back to the old French quarter, but he died on the way.[13]

The city was soon in an uproar, with the muezzins calling from the minarets, summoning the faithful to action, and the streets descending into pandemonium, especially in the districts adjoining the Al-Azhar mosque and university.

Despite this, it was eight A.M. before the French garrison was placed on alert. This indicates that, at least at this stage, the disturbances must have been largely localized and had not spread to the northern edges of town around Ezbekiyah Square. Napoleon had already left early in the morning, along with his entourage and the engineer General Caffarelli, to inspect the fortifications being erected at Rodah Island. Not until ten A.M. did news reach him of the uprising and General Dupuy's death, whereupon he immediately set off back to Cairo.

Here he was in for a shock. When he arrived at the city walls he found the gates closed, and his entourage was greeted with a hail of stones. They skirted around the walls and eventually managed to get in through the Boulac Gate, whence they crossed the short distance to Ezbekiyah Square and Napoleon's headquarters in Elfi Bey's palace. By now most of the city was in an uproar. Muslims were attacking the Christian quarter, where houses were being ransacked and women raped. A hospital convoy of French soldiers from Bilbeis had been attacked and the patients slaughtered, and soon houses occupied by the French were being targeted. One French officer recalled: "The first house attacked was that occupied by General Caffarelli: it was entirely pillaged. Fortunately, the general had departed early with Napoleon to visit various military establishments, which saved his life. Two engineers, Thévenot and Duval, were in the house at the time: they gathered together all the servants in an attempt to resist the attacks of the angry fanatical crowd. Their efforts proved useless, for even after barricading themselves in the furthest rooms they were still torn to pieces."[14] In fact, all the household servants, three engineers and four savants, including Testeviude, who was in charge of the ordnance survey of Egypt, were slaughtered. El-Djabarti recorded: "In this house there were many precision instruments, such as telescopes and other astronomical and mathematical devices. There were no copies of these instruments, which were of great value to those who knew how to use them. The mob ran off with them and smashed a great many others. The French greatly regretted this loss. For a long time they made searches to recover some of them. They even gave rewards to those who brought any back."[15] Meanwhile the mob went on the rampage, encouraged by rumors that Djezzar was marching from Syria with a large army and had already reached Bilbeis, thirty miles northeast of Cairo.

Napoleon was furious, but remained levelheaded and quickly took stock of the situation. According to Major Detroye, an officer on his staff at the time, "The main positions occupied by the French were the Citadel, where we had a good supply of artillery, Place Birket-el-Fil, where most of our troops were garrisoned, and finally Ezbekiyah Square . . . which was defended by 15 artillery pieces. Communication was established, for better or for worse, between these different quarters."[16] General Bon succeeded Dupuy as governor of Cairo, and took charge of the beleaguered vantage point of the Citadel, which was now coming under musket fire from the minarets and the dome of the nearby historic Sultan Hassan mosque. At the same time General Dommartin was ordered to move his howitzers and mortars up onto the Moqattam hills which overlooked the east of the city.

The disturbances went on all day, but after sunset the city fell into silence, which continued through the hours of darkness, whilst both sides made their preparations for the next day's hostilities. Barricades now sealed off all approaches to the Al-Azhar mosque complex, and its large historic inner courtyard was filled with hundreds of armed rebels camping out for the night.

By next morning, Generals Bon and Dommartin were ready to implement Napoleon's orders. Bon was to break out of the Citadel, leading three columns and a squadron of cavalry towards the Al-Azhar quarters, smashing through the barricades and into the mosque itself. At the same time, Dommartin would open fire from the heights with his mortars and howitzers. Napoleon's orders were chillingly explicit: "Exterminate all who are in the mosque."[17] He went on to instruct Bon: "During the night pull down the grand mosque, by smashing several pillars, if that is possible." However, even at this late stage he wanted to avoid, if possible, any action that might lead to an irreversible breakdown in relations between the French and the Egyptians. Accordingly he sent a message to the sheiks and *ulema* of the Al-Azhar mosque indicating what military action he intended to take, and informing them that if they were prepared to surrender, thus avoiding considerable bloodshed, he was willing to be lenient. No reply was forthcoming, and Napoleon went ahead with his plans.

The bombardment began at noon, and continued throughout the afternoon, as El-Djabarti recalled:

The French directed their shells at the Al-Azhar mosque and the houses in the nearby quarters. . . . The bombardment was so terrible that the inhabitants of the city had never seen its like, and raising their faces they cried out in supplication to the heavens to save them from this misfortune. The rioters ceased shooting, but the French continued to fire down on the houses, the shops, the palaces, the inns, and they all collapsed. The people's ears were deafened by the detonations of the cannons. They abandoned the houses and the streets to hide themselves in holes. The sheiks resolved to go and beg the commander-in-chief to cease this rain of shells.[18]

Sources differ as to what precisely took place at this meeting. Most seem to agree that Napoleon took an unforgiving line, telling the sheiks: "You refused when I offered you clemency. Now is the time for vengeance. You should have surrendered earlier when you had the chance. What you have begun, is for me to finish!"[19] Even so, El-Djabarti claims, "he gave the order to cease the bombardment, just as the sun was on the point of setting."[20]

Yet this was far from being the end of the matter, for events had now taken on their own momentum. By late afternoon General Bon was advancing towards the Al-Azhar quarter with his three columns, under direct orders from Napoleon "that all houses which throw stones at you in the street are to be burnt to the ground, while the others are to be pardoned."[21] Bon was accompanied by a detachment of 300 cavalry, led by the mulatto giant General Dumas. The armed columns forced their way, with rifle fire and bayonets, up to the walls of the mosque complex, and General Dumas then led the cavalry as they charged into the historic courtyard, where they met with little resistance. Several hundred rebels were taken prisoner, and as night fell the French troops moved into the holy precincts of the mosque itself, at the same time securing the entire quarter. Yet despite Napoleon's orders, the Al-Azhar mosque was not razed to the ground, nor does there seem to have been the undisciplined slaughter that might have been expected from troops who had fought their way through the city streets under such dangerous conditions. However, El-Djabarti records the outrages that did take place:

In the night . . . they demolished all the barricades that they encountered and ensured the complete tranquility of the inhabitants. They then entered the mosque of Al-Azhar with their horses, which they tied up to the *kiblah*.* They smashed the lamps, the candles and the desks of the students, they pillaged all they could find in the cupboards, they cast to the ground the Koran and the holy books and trampled over them with their boots. They urinated and spat in the mosque, they drank wine in it, they broke their empty wine bottles by throwing them into the corners, and they stripped everyone they met in order to grab their clothes.²²

Some of the most precious items from the mosque's sacred collection— namely several centuries-old copies of the Koran and other ancient relics—were in fact "rescued" by a number of Orientalist savants who had been co-opted by General Bon, and followed the French troops into the Al-Azhar. These items were taken under escort to Ezbekiyah Square, where they remained for the time being under Napoleon's "protection."

Meanwhile, the savants had been trapped at the Institute in Kassim Bey's palace, out beyond the edge of the city, almost two miles from Ezbekiyah Square. Amidst the initial disorders, the military authorities appeared to forget about them, and during the morning of October 21 a small but increasing crowd gathered outside the palace, so that the situation looked as if it might become threatening. None of the savants was armed, and two engineers were dispatched on horseback to Ezbekiyah Square. It took till evening before a company of grenadiers arrived, whereupon forty rifles and 200 cartridges were distributed amongst the savants, many of whom had never used a gun before. After a tense night, orders came through that the grenadiers were to withdraw, as they were required for the assault on the Al-Azhar mosque. During the afternoon, when the assault began, groups of armed rebels retreating from the city soon began appearing amongst the crowd outside

* One of the holiest places in the mosque, marking the direction in which Muslims pray to Mecca.

the Institute, and it looked as if they might attempt to storm the building. Many of the savants were for evacuating the palace and escaping while there was still time, but Monge and Berthollet stood firm, Monge declaring: "How dare you think of abandoning the precious instruments which have been placed in our care?"[23]

In fact, much more than instruments was at stake: there were the laboratories and the library, both of which were irreplaceable under the circumstances, and there were also the burgeoning scientific collections of hitherto unknown plants and biological specimens, as well as the geological surveys and learned papers which the savants had been industriously assembling. What was at risk was the entire intellectual enterprise of the expedition, whose declared aim was to increase human knowledge as well as to disseminate it—the bringing to Egypt of Western civilization, no less, as well as the search for the origins of this very civilization. Such, in the eyes of Napoleon and many of his compatriots, was, and would later be seen to be, the crowning justification of the entire expedition. Other matters, such as the conquest of empire by force, and the establishment of commerce, were in a somewhat high-minded way seen as lesser enterprises than the cultural enlightenment of humanity. Setting an example, the fifty-two-year-old Monge took up his rifle and prepared to man a dangerous forward post, inviting anyone to join him if they wished for some stimulating intellectual conversation "to while away the boredom of the situation."[24] Meanwhile, in another house of the Institute complex, the remainder of the savants, including the artist Denon, the geologist Dolomieu and the biologist Geoffroy Saint-Hilaire, also took up their positions in characteristic intellectual fashion—as Denon recalled: "We had been supplied with arms, and nominated our leaders, but each of us had his own plan and saw no reason why he should obey anyone else."[25]

Each according to his own plan, the savants sporadically took potshots at the increasingly indignant crowd, whilst in the distance the detonations of the cannonade from the Moqattam hills continued through the sultry, overcast afternoon. The crowd, encouraged by the armed rebels, was becoming increasingly angry, and it appeared only a matter of time before they stormed the Institute. Ironically, it would be superstition that saved the day for these enlightened intellectuals. Thunder was rare in Cairo, and when the distant rumble of the guns was suddenly drowned out by a deafening crash and a long, heavy roll of thunder overhead, the crowd outside the Institute panicked and scattered in fright. Before they could reassemble, the situation was relieved by the opportune arrival of two columns of French soldiers.*

By the night of October 22 the insurrection was over. Most French sources support Napoleon in his claim that the French "suffered 300 casualities, amongst whom were 100 dead."[26] On the other hand, his claim that 1,000 citizens of Cairo died was a gross underestimate: a figure of 3,000, including Christians and Jews slaughtered by the mob, would seem to be closer to the truth. This was by any measure a massacre.

Napoleon recalled in his memoirs: "At dawn next morning 60 sheiks and imams of the El Azhar mosque presented themselves at my headquarters. They had not slept for three days. Their expressions were those of guilty men consumed with anxiety. However, I had no reproaches for them: they had been loyal, but they had not been able to struggle against the torrent of public opinion."[27] He assured them: "I know that many of you have been weak, but I like to believe that none of you have committed any criminal act." Upon being pardoned, the sheiks and imams fell to their knees. Napoleon then told them that they should set about the task of burying their dead, and promised that their holy books would be returned to Al-Azhar after the necessary purification of the desecrated mosque had been carried out.

Napoleon had decided to be magnanimous. He knew that he had little choice if he wished to continue ruling Egypt with the apparent consent of its leaders. This clemency was not popular amongst the members of the expedition. From the generals to the men, including the savants, all believed it to be a sign of weakness, which would certainly be seen as such by the Egyptians, and would only lead to further danger. But this leniency was only for public appearances. On that very same day, Napoleon sent word to General Berthier: "Please, Citizen General, give the order to the governor to cut off the heads of all the prisoners who were captured bearing arms. . . . Take them by night to the banks of the Nile and cast their headless bodies into the river."[28]

Napoleon was most intent upon discovering the ringleaders behind the insurrection: those who had dispatched the fanatical students from

* This sudden roll of violent thunder was also heard above the Al-Azhar mosque; despite some claims to the contrary, it did not intimidate the rebels inside, who appeared not to distinguish it from the exploding shells.

the Al-Azhar mosque to rouse the people, those who had made speeches inflaming the mob, and those who had encouraged the insurgents to continue with their resistance, thus ensuring a bloodbath. It was several days before his intelligence managed to identify these leaders and discover their whereabouts. He learned that after the insurrection had been put down, a number of sheiks had taken sanctuary under the protection of Sheik El-Bekri in his palace, where they had remained under virtual house arrest—amongst these were the ringleaders. Napoleon ordered that for their own protection these sheiks should be removed from El-Bekri's palace and taken to the Citadel. Here they were summarily tried, and those found guilty were condemned to death. Six of the leaders of the insurrection were beheaded on November 3, and Napoleon would later justify this action by declaring them to be "men of a violent and intractable character."[29]

Despite this, nine of the men identified as leading insurgents managed to escape. As Napoleon noted in his memoirs: "Almost 4,000 men fled, crossing the desert and taking refuge in Suez."[30] However, the accuracy of Napoleon's memory cannot always be trusted here, as is shown by his absurd assessment of the damage caused by the bombardment during the uprising: "Only three houses were consumed by the flames, twenty were damaged, and the Al-Azhar mosque suffered little." As it happened, the main structure of the historic mosque did miraculously remain intact, but this was only because General Bon disobeyed Napoleon's orders. As for the houses, the hours of howitzer bombardment from the Moqattam hills certainly hit more than two dozen of these—many of which were collapsible mud-brick constructions, while even the stone buildings were frequently in a ramshackle state.

To ensure that Napoleon's apparent leniency was not misinterpreted by the population, he ordered the sheiks and *ulema* to sign, and read out in the mosques, a warning against any further revolt, or any further incitement against the French: "Sedition has been put to sleep. Let him be accursed who destroys its slumber."[31] This seemingly innocuous spiritual threat was backed by distinctly secular force, in the form of chief of police Barthelemy and his unscrupulous band of retainers. El-Djabarti described their effect:

Barthelemy was charged with disarming the citizens of Cairo. He went all over the city with his men, and arrested whoever he wanted as well as whoever had been denounced to him by Christians. Barthelemy did what he wanted with these people; he imposed large fines on them and kept the money; he bound them and threw them in prison. There he tortured them to obtain confessions, or to discover the hiding places of looted goods and weapons. Many of these unfortunates denounced other people, who were then arrested and had to submit to the same treatment. In a word, this Barthelemy committed the same horrors as those condemned by the authorities. Many people had their throats slit and were thrown into the Nile. God alone knows how many people died during these few days. In this way the Christians avenged themselves on the Moslems.[32]

As part of Napoleon's continuing propaganda campaign, he announced that the sultan's *firman* declaring war on the French was a fake document issued by Djezzar as an act of treason. It could not possibly be true because the French remained friends of the sultan.

At the outset of the Cairo insurrection the general *divan* had dissolved of its own accord, an event which Napoleon had been content to let pass. But several weeks after the disturbances were over, he realized that he would have to restore the *divan* if he wished to continue with the pretense that Egypt was being ruled with Arab consent. The reopening of the *divan* would also provide him with the opportunity to address publicly the Egyptian leaders, outlining to them his wishes for the country and how he felt things were progressing. Napoleon certainly made full use of this occasion, yet once again it was about himself that he was most revealing. In a truly astonishing speech he warned against any repetition of the Cairo insurrection, promising:

Those who declare themselves my enemies will find refuge neither in this world nor the next. Is there here a man blind enough not to see that destiny itself directs all my operations? Is there here a man incredulous enough to doubt that everything, in this vast universe, is subject to the power of destiny?

Make known to the people that since the creation of the world, it is written that after destroying the enemies of Islam, and defeating the Christians, I would come to the heart of the Orient to fulfill the tasks which have been imposed upon me. Make the people see that in the holy book of the Koran, in more than twenty passages, what has come to pass has been prophesied, and what shall come to pass is set down equally clearly. . . . The day will come when all the world will bear evidence that I am guided by orders from above and that all human efforts are powerless to stop me.[33]

This was just the official French version. The Arabic translation which was read out to the general *divan* goes even further, including such claims as: "The power of God passes through me so that I defeat the enemies of Islam and crush the Christian cross. . . . All I have done was inspired by God . . . [it is] the design of God; no one can prevent the execution of his will, and it is I who have been charged with this execution."[34]

It would appear that El-Djabarti saw through all the rhetoric right away: "This speech had no other aim than to make a powerful impression on its audience. . . . It was full of pretension . . . inspired by a false imagination." But was this really the case? It would be easy to claim that Napoleon was merely trying to put the fear of God into his audience, that he did not believe a word of what he was saying, but circumstances and his character strongly suggest otherwise. As we shall see, he remained obsessed by his fantasy of establishing an Oriental empire; meanwhile, he was for the first time coming to a full realization of his exceptional powers. He was both beginning to exercise them, and beginning to believe in them, and their extent had begun to appear limitless—he could do anything he chose. It was in Italy that he first "saw the world recede beneath me, as if I was being borne up into the sky."[35] Now his excessive ambition, megalomania, sense of destiny, call it what you will, was entering a new stage of its evolution. Isolated in Egypt, his power unchecked and under no supervision at all, the twenty-nine-year-old general was beginning to believe that he could achieve whatever he wished. He could even rewrite religion, with himself in the leading role. Here in this address to the reconvened general *divan* of Egypt was the first public manifestation of the man who dreamt of "marching to Asia, mounted on an elephant . . . in my hand a new Koran that I would have composed to suit my needs."[36]

XVI

Love and Dreams

On November 21, 1798, Napoleon wrote yet another of his regular reports to the Directory—which needless to say never reached its destination. In it he blithely informed his masters: "We have had a pretty lively insurrection here, but all is now more peaceful than it has ever been."[1]

With this behind him, he decided to embark upon a program of modernization for Cairo. Ambitious ideas that he had discussed with General Caffarelli and his engineers were now to be put into practice. A number of wide boulevards would be driven through the city, in order to aid transport and the swift movement of troops in case of future troubles. One boulevard would run from Ezbekiyah Square down to the Nile at Boulac, another would run alongside the northern city wall to bolster the defenses of the city, and a third would pass directly through the teeming central Abdin quarter. Ramshackle dwellings, houses, mosques, nothing was to stand in the way of these essential first steps towards turning Cairo into a modern city. At the same time, a pontoon bridge was to be constructed across the Nile from Rodah Island to the Giza shore, the first to span the Nile in its long history. Conté's windmills on Rodah Island were to be extended, and more were to be built on the Moqattam hills, while Conté himself was set to work reconstructing as far as possible the scientific and surveying instruments that had been destroyed or pillaged from Caffarelli's house during the insurrection.

As Napoleon embarked upon this new bout of frenetic activity, he insisted that the reluctant Kléber should be at his side, at least for the more important meetings and inspections. He was determined that

Kléber should acquire firsthand some of his administrative skills, but he also insisted that Kléber should relax, encouraging him to visit the pyramids and the savants out at the Institute. Napoleon made every effort to be encouraging and friendly—showing his "love" for his fellow general—but the ebullient Kléber appeared uncharacteristically cool. Although he soon recovered from what appears to have been a mild nervous breakdown in Alexandria, beneath his surface equanimity he remained distinctly disgruntled. Watching Napoleon at work only increased his antipathy towards his commander, and he continued to jot down his private opinions in his pocketbook: "He knows nothing about organization or about administration, and yet, wanting to do everything himself he organizes and administers. Hence the chaos, the waste in every department, hence the absolute destitution, this lack of anything in the midst of plenty."[2] Yet once again he could not avoid grudgingly noting Napoleon's qualities: "Is he evil? No, but that is because vices come from stupidity, and he is not stupid." But what most irritated this most military of generals was Napoleon's ever-increasing pretentiousness, his growing sense of his own destiny. Kléber recorded with disgust how at one meeting Napoleon let drop the remark: "For my part, I am playing with history. . . ."

Kléber was not the only one to notice this expanding gap between dreams of glory and the chaos of administrative reality. Things were hardly running smoothly in Cairo, but in the other cities under French rule the situation was often dire. The normally tolerant Menou soon became so exasperated with Napoleon that he fired off to him an eight-page letter outlining his situation: "While I have been at Rosetta, devoid of everything, I have had no other way of supplying my troops than with daily requisitions."[3] After complaining at length about his complete lack of money and all other essentials, he continued, "As for wine, there's not so much as a couple of pints left in the entire place. I haven't even had a glimpse of any for two months." Menou had now simply had enough of the whole chaotic business. "If this is what is known as administration, then all the knowledge that I have acquired during a lifetime of military service amounts to nothing, and I must therefore implore you to relieve me of my post." Such was his disgust that his letter pointedly ended with no greeting, or even the common courtesy of his signature.

Menou and Kléber were not the only generals who had had enough. The cavalry general Alexandre Dumas had from the outset made no secret of his disapproval of Napoleon and his methods in Egypt. Despite playing a heroic role in the suppression of the Cairo insurrection, Dumas now decided that he too could no longer stomach the way the expedition was being run. He approached the chief medical officer, General Desgenettes, asking for a certificate of ill health, on the grounds that he could not tolerate the Egyptian climate. Desgenettes consequently approached Napoleon on this delicate matter: there could be no question of cowardice where Dumas was concerned, yet it was also difficult to believe that a man of his gargantuan prowess was less able to bear the climate than men not so physically endowed. To Desgenettes' surprise, Napoleon consented to Dumas' request, and at the same time issued the following general order: "It is not my intention . . . to keep men in the army who are insensitive to the honor of being my companions-in-arms. Let them go. I shall ease their departure. But I do not want them to conceal their real motives for refusing to share our labors and our danger under the pretext of feigned maladies."[4]

Although there is no doubt that many felt inclined to take up this offer, few in fact did so, realizing that they would be returning to France in disgrace, their military careers at an end. However, the forty-eight-year-old savant Dolomieu felt no such qualms; he was still outraged at how he had been used to negotiate with the Knights of Malta, and decided to accept Napoleon's offer.

The first ship bound for France carrying men from the Army of the Orient was a Genoese merchantman which left Alexandria on December 15. This contained only soldiers who had received severe wounds in action, or had been rendered permanently blind by ophthalmia. After eluding the British blockade, the ship made landfall three weeks later in Sicily, which was territory ruled by the King of Naples. What the captain had not known was that the King of Naples had now declared war on France, and as a result the sick and wounded passengers were carted off to prison. Such was the local fervor against the French that some days later the prison was stormed by the populace and the prisoners were stoned to death.

Unaware of what had happened, Dolomieu and General Dumas embarked upon the next ship to leave Alexandria. This also succeeded in eluding the British blockade, but was forced by a fierce storm to take refuge at Taranto on the heel of Italy, which was also part of the kingdom of Naples. Here Dolomieu's betrayal of the Knights of Malta finally caught up with him, for several former Knights now held influential posts in the Neapolitan court. As a result, Dolomieu was kept in solitary confinement in a dungeon for twenty-one months. Despite suffering from increasing ill health, he made use of pieces of burnt coal to write in the margins of a Bible a treatise entitled *The Philosophy of Mineralogy*. In time, this would come to be regarded as one of the major scientific works of its age, responsible for "raising mineralogy to the degree of precision that had previously been achieved . . . by chemistry."⁵ Dolomieu eventually returned to France with his annotated Bible intact, but he was by now a broken man. He died in 1801, shortly after the publication of his masterpiece.

The physically more robust General Dumas suffered much the same treatment, but it was two years before he was released. On his return to France, his illustrious military career in ruins, he was unable to bear the disgrace of having abandoned his comrades in Egypt, and sank into a deep depression. In 1802 he fathered a son who would become the celebrated author of *The Three Musketeers*, and died four years later.

By the end of 1798, seismic political transformations were taking place throughout Europe, with old alliances being broken and new ones being formed—but no news of this was reaching Napoleon in Egypt. On November 20 he wrote to Desaix in Upper Egypt: "We have got French and English gazettes to the 10 August, up till then there was no development in Europe."⁶ The newspapers had arrived on one of the few neutral merchantmen which had managed to elude the blockade. A day later, in his report to the Directory, Napoleon would claim a little disingenuously: "We have had no news of Europe . . . since 18 Messidor [July 7]. We are becoming a little curious about what is going on." He had nothing other than scraps of out-of-date news, and what he took to be misleading propaganda that the blockading British were trying to make him believe about an alliance between themselves and the Ottoman Empire. On the home front, Napoleon did his best to maintain the fiction that he was in regular contact with France and abreast of affairs taking place beyond the confines of Egypt. As this situation became more difficult to maintain, the "news" in *Le Courier* now passed from propaganda and whimsical omniscience ("revolution in Batavia," etc.) to wishful thinking and sheer fantasy: "The General-in-Chief has received news from France. The legislative body has declared that our

victorious army has served the Fatherland with honor. . . . The news
of the conquest of Egypt has caused great excitement and pride . . . a
large number of ships sent by the General-in-Chief have arrived in
France carrying letters from our army."[7]

Meanwhile life returned to normal in Cairo: the Institute resumed
its regular meetings, the French distillers and hatmakers reopened,
and *Le Courier* continued to come out with its fascinating tidbits
about the behavior of Egyptian women in the bathhouses. Even
Napoleon seems to have relaxed a little, if one believes his secretary
Bourrienne: "During this time of repose and almost inactivity, though
it was less so for him, Napoleon would go to bed early. There I would
read to him every evening. When I read him poetry, he fell asleep.
When he asked me to read to him from the life of Cromwell, I knew
I would not be going to sleep early."[8] It is revealing that Napoleon
should now be interested in the life of the military leader who became
ruler of the first large-scale revolutionary republic in Europe, and it
prompts the question of why he had chosen to bring a life of Cromwell
to Egypt in the first place. Cromwell had been much more than a
military governor of England: he had been ruler of a country in tran-
sition. Was this what Napoleon saw himself becoming in Egypt, or
in the great Oriental empire of his dreams? But Cromwell was no
real exemplar for the running of an Oriental empire—the lessons to
be learned from the Lord Protector of the English Commonwealth
would best be applied to the running of a European republic, such
as France had now become. Napoleon was not only anxious to hear
the news from Europe, he also wanted to know what was happening
to the corrupt and ramshackle rule of the Directory in France. One
of his options, admittedly a lesser one under the present circumstances, remained returning to France and taking over from the
Directory. The presence of Cromwell in his library would seem to
indicate that he had continued to bear in mind this option before
setting out for Egypt, despite his disavowal of it to Bourrienne ("tiny
Europe has not enough to offer," etc.).

A further indication that Napoleon still retained the option of focusing
his ambitions on France can be seen in the fact that in early November
he sent his favorite brother Louis back home, on one of the few ships
that did manage to elude the British blockade. Louis' health had
begun to deteriorate in Egypt, but this gesture was not out of consideration for his well-being. Louis was almost certainly sent to make

contact with Talleyrand and Barras, to find out which way the wind was blowing in France, and how Napoleon was now regarded.

Amidst the general effort to improve the morale of the increasingly homesick Army of the Orient in Egypt, one particular innovation stands out—namely Le Tivoli. Modeled on a popular entertainment spot in Paris, this was opened in early December by ex-Guards officer Dargevel, who had been a fellow pupil of the young Napoleon at the Brienne military college. Le Tivoli was housed in a former Mameluke bey's palace close to Ezbekiyah Square, and operated much like an officers' club. A large room was set aside for gaming, another for a library, with the latest copies of *Le Courier* and *La Décade*, and there was even a room with a makeshift billiards table. In the evenings, coffee and light refreshments were served in the garden beneath the orange and lemon trees hung with Chinese lanterns, to the gentle strains of a military band. The opening night was attended by Napoleon and his staff, and was marked by a full-dress ball in the ballroom, complete with an orchestra and uniformed batmen acting as footmen. The event was described in glowing terms in *Le Courier*, whose correspondent noted that the thing which "produced the most agreeable sensation . . . was the presence of fifteen or twenty women dressed with some splendor—an absolutely novel sight in Egypt."[9] However, this novelty seems to have soon worn off, for subsequent balls were not quite so entertaining. According to young Captain Vertray: "The big difficulty was in organizing a ball. The local women would not show up, while so many of the wives and lovers of our men had been left behind at Toulon [and] only a few had managed to make it to Egypt. They did come to Le Tivoli, but there were not enough of them, and thus these occasions were hardly brilliant."[10]

Nonetheless Dargevel remained optimistic about the opportunities provided by Le Tivoli: "This will perhaps be a way of attracting into our society the inhabitants of the country and their wives, and encouraging them imperceptibly to acquire French habits, tastes and fashions."[11] Such expectations might might have appeared reasonable with regard to the inhabitants of a French-occupied European country—the Italians had certainly attended the social functions put on by Napoleon and Josephine at their residence in Milan—but with regard to Egyptians such optimism was simply ludicrous. Egyptian society of the period had no place whatsoever for such social gatherings, which would have been anathema. The fact that Dargevel harbored such hopes only goes to demonstrate how little the French had even begun to understand the country they had now been occupying for almost half a year. No Egyptians, and certainly no Egyptian wives, attended the officers' balls at Le Tivoli, and there were simply not enough French women to go around—on any social occasion, let alone at the balls. The lack of available European women seems to have been a particular problem for many French officers, and those who had managed to smuggle their wives onto the expedition had to take good care to look after them. On the other hand, some gave every indication of being able to look after themselves, such as the spirited Mme. Tempié, who would reply to any suggestive proposal with her own riposte: "My husband, naval lieutenant Tempié, is in command of *l'Amour*, which is defended by 36 guns and copper-bottomed."

As part of the ongoing campaign to improve morale, a public festival was announced for 10 Frimaire (November 30). The fact that this took place just six weeks after the insurrection is indicative of how quickly Cairo had returned to normal. As ever, there was much playing of military bands, and this time there was a march-past of crack troops from General Bon's division. *Le Courier* commented on how the men were wearing "their new uniforms, all looking extremely well nourished and fighting fit, their weapons spick and span and in tip-top condition."[12] Although such words were intended to fill French hearts with pride, they are also open to other inferences: the French soldiers had evidently been short of rations and many of them had been sick, but now at least their finest fighting men were back to their formidable best. There is no doubt that elements of Napoleon's army in Egypt—from generals to private soldiers—became disaffected, but evidence such as this article, as well as many comments in firsthand memoirs, suggests that despite all the hardships this expedition remained for many soldiers an adventure in which they enthusiastically participated, inspired by their charismatic leader. Captain Vertray, in his journal, echoed many in his contentment: "Experiencing a great tranquility, feeding myself well, I was without a care. I was as happy as one can be on campaign. One is happy when material needs are satisfied and one enjoys good health."[13]

The centerpiece of the November 30 celebrations was to be the long-awaited balloon ascent by the intrepid aeronaut Conté, who along with Monge had played such a leading role in the development of the balloon for military purposes. The French were the acknowledged leaders in this latest technology, and as early as 1785 had made the first balloon crossing of the English Channel—a feat that would later inspire British fears of a balloon-led invasion.

With all the balloon equipment brought on the Egyptian expedition sunk, Conté had been unable to construct a hydrogen balloon and was forced to assemble a much lighter hot-air balloon. The finished result was a magnificent sight, reported *Le Courier*: "The machine was made of paper and had a spherical form, the tapering panels which formed its surface were patriotically colored red, white and blue, its diameter was 12 meters ... the sight of all this made the greatest impression on the local Egyptians, who refused to believe it would fly, a disbelief which lasted throughout the preparations for the flight. Yet when they saw the great globe rise of its own accord, those who were in its path ran away in fright."[14]

Reports differ as to precisely what happened next, but it seems that the balloon caught fire, and its basket fell from the sky, causing a panic amongst the great crowd that had gathered to watch in Ezbekiyah Square. El-Djabarti was less than impressed: "When the balloon fell to the ground, the French went red with shame, because this was not a ship in which one could travel through the air and go from one country to another, as they had pretended, it was just a kite like our little boys fly at weddings or festivals."[15]

Later, a second attempt would be made to impress the Egyptians with this example of superior French technology, and once again El-Djabarti came to Ezbekiyah Square to cast his eye on the proceedings: "At midday everyone was there and the balloon was launched. It rose and sailed towards the Barkiya Hills, where it fell out of the sky. If the wind had driven it just a bit further and out of sight, the ruse would have succeeded and the French would have maintained that the balloon had traveled to a faraway land, just as they pretended it could."[16] Others remarked on how this time many of the Egyptians in the square paid no attention to the large tricolored apparition floating through the sky above them. They simply continued going about their business "without even raising their eyes, such was their indifference to this spectacle that was meant to impress them as a miracle."[17] This lack of interest was apparently because the Egyptians believed that the multicolored spectacle floating in the sky was simply a commonplace manifestation of sorcery, which so excited the French because they had only just mastered this art, whereas for Egyptians it had long been an everyday part of their lives.

Whilst Napoleon was watching Conté supervise the preparations for the historic first French balloon ascent in Egypt, he happened to overhear his seventeen-year-old stepson Eugene Beauharnais remarking to one of his fellow aides about a strikingly pretty woman amongst the French spectators. In common with many of his officers and men, Napoleon appeared to have been without female company during the previous six months or so. Some have attributed this to his misogyny, never far below the surface, which had now been reinforced by his hatred and disgust for Josephine after learning of her infidelities. Bernoyer, in a letter home written at this time, reflects the general opinion amongst Napoleon's officers: "Since he has been in Egypt he has had no particular liaison with a woman, and we are all surprised that in such a hot country he has never shown any desire to have one."[18]

This perception may not have been strictly accurate. Soon after Napoleon's arrival in Cairo, Sheik El-Bekri had sought to ingratiate himself by offering him one of his daughters, a sixteen-year-old called Zenab, an offer Napoleon was said to have accepted. There is no actual evidence of this liaison, but Zenab's subsequent fate would seem to confirm it. El-Djabarti records that three years later, long after the alleged *affaire* was over and Napoleon had departed the country, "the daughter of Sheik El-Bekri was arrested. She had been debauched by the French. The representatives of the authorities presented themselves after sunset at her mother's house . . . and made her appear before them with her father. She was interrogated about her conduct, and replied that she repented of it. They asked the advice of her father, and he replied that he disowned his daughter. Then the unfortunate girl's head was cut off."[19] There is no actual proof that El-Bekri offered his daughter to Napoleon, yet it is unthinkable that she could have formed a liaison with him, or any Frenchman, under any other circumstances.

Napoleon's relationship with a sixteen-year-old girl who spoke no French was unlikely to have prospered, given his sensibilities. Indeed there remains another piece of unverifiable gossip that during this period he embarked upon his sole homosexual adventure.[20] He was seemingly encouraged in this by the exploits of Alexander the Great and Julius Caesar, both of whom were bisexual, but this Egyptian adventure—if it ever took place—was certainly not to his taste. More

likely the entire story was a reflection of the not uncommon homosexual practices amongst soldiers of all ranks in the Army of the Orient
during this long period of heterosexual deprivation. Several French
soldiers left on record how they found the available Egyptian women
unattractive, not to say downright repulsive—though such remarks
are not entirely trustworthy, for by the time these records came to be
published, many of their authors were well-established family men, and
wished to remain so.

There is also a plausible story in Bourrienne's often implausible
memoirs, where he claims: "Towards mid-September, Napoleon had
half a dozen Asiatic women brought to him at the palace of Elfi-Bey,
all of whom were acclaimed for their grace and beauty. But he did not
care for this sort of thing, and was repelled by their obesity, so he
immediately sent them back."[21] Napoleon was easily put off women,
particularly if he did not like their smell. Sophisticated French women
of this period, especially Josephine, took great care in bathing themselves, even in their comparatively mild climate. The combination of
Cairo's heat, voluptuous physique, and the less subtle perfumes used
by Egyptian women would have been enough to provoke Napoleon's
sensitive distaste.

The attractive young woman who came to Napoleon's notice on
November 30 at the first balloon launch in Ezbekiyah Square was Pauline
Fourès, the twenty-year-old bride of junior infantry officer Lieutenant
Fourès. A self-portrait of Pauline from around this period would indicate that she had a round face with rather insipid features, and tight
dark curls falling down over her forehead. This is almost certainly a
reflection of her meager artistic talents, rather than her actual appearance, which was said to be strikingly attractive. She was described by
General Paulin and several other sources as having long blond tresses
which when unloosed fell down to her waist, covering her entire upper
body like a cloak—though whether this information was the result
of sex-starved army gossip, or actual firsthand experience, is not
mentioned in the memoirs. At any rate, she was certainly a striking
woman, and evidence from her later life suggests that she was also a
spirited and independent character: in other words, a worthy potential replacement for Napoleon's errant wife.

Pauline had been born the illegitimate daughter of a cook, and had
ended up working in a milliner's shop at Carcassonne, in southern
France, where she came to the attention of dashing young Lieutenant

Fourès. They were married shortly before the Egyptian campaign, and he smuggled her aboard his ship at Toulon dressed in a cavalry uniform with her copious blond hair stuffed under a soldier's cap. In Egypt, her beauty had soon attracted attention, and not a little speculation, amongst Fourès' fellow officers. However, Napoleon appears to have been too busy to notice her, until the balloon launch at Ezbekiyah Square, whereupon he seems to have been smitten. That night, in the hope of seeing her again, he turned up at Le Tivoli, and according to those present could not take his eyes off her. Alas, this was not a euphemism for the lingering glances of a love-struck suitor. Despite his sensitivity about women, Napoleon had a tendency to boorishness in such matters, and on this occasion he simply stared at Pauline, and went on staring, a habit which many later objects of his attention would find rather more unsettling than romantic.

Having made his intentions plain, Napoleon took the same course as he had done with Josephine when she had delayed coming to Italy: he dispatched his loyal aide Junot to discreetly convey his master's feelings. But Junot proved not up to this sensitive task, and his indelicate proposal to Pauline Fourès, couched in somewhat military language, was angrily rebuffed. This blunder was eventually overcome by the dispatch of one of Napoleon's more diplomatic aides, in the form of General Duroc, together with the placatory gift of an expensive jewel-encrusted bracelet. This appears to have had the desired effect. Yet what to do about Pauline's husband? On December 17 Napoleon gave orders for Lieutenant Fourès to set out on an important mission to Malta. He was to convey a letter to Admiral Villeneuve, whom Napoleon assumed had sailed to Malta after fleeing from the Battle of the Nile. From Malta, Fourès was to take ship for Italy, where he was to travel by stagecoach to Paris carrying letters for the Directory. "You will remain eight to ten days in Paris, after which you will return post-haste [with their replies]. . . . I count on your initiative in overcoming all unforeseen events which might prevent you from accomplishing your mission."[22]

If previous experience was anything to go by, this would see Lieutenant Fourès out of Cairo for at least three months, possibly much longer, but when he put in a request for his wife to travel with him, he was told that this was out of the question. No sooner had Fourès left Cairo on his mission than Madame Fourès and several other officers' wives were invited to a dinner party at Elfi Bey's palace, ostensibly given by the governor of Cairo, General Bon. Pauline duly attended, while once again Napoleon stared and stared. When coffee was served after dinner, the officer sitting next to her happened to upset his cup over her dress. This was undoubtedly no accident. Napoleon at once sprang to her rescue, offered her his services, and escorted her upstairs to repair the damage. Neither guest returned to the party.

Within days, Pauline had been established in a house in the grounds of Elfi Bey's palace, and in the words of Bourrienne, "This liaison was soon known all over the headquarters, and became the subject of every conversation."[23] Such a choice piece of gossip quickly spread throughout the army in Cairo, and beyond: Pauline became known as Napoleon's Cleopatra.

Yet all did not go quite according to plan. After Lieutenant Fourès set sail from Alexandria aboard *Le Chasseur*, it was intercepted, on December 29, by the British warship *Lion*. As a result, Fourès was relieved of his messages and dispatched back to Alexandria on parole. According to some sources, the British knew about Napoleon's liaison with Fourès' wife and sent him back in the hope of embarrassing the French commander-in-chief. The British certainly had an efficient spy network operating in Egypt, yet it is all but impossible to see how this knowledge could have reached *Lion* before Fourès was intercepted. A more likely explanation is that they sent him back to Alexandria on parole because this was their standard practice with junior officers at the time.

At any rate, Fourès eventually arrived back in Cairo some time early in January, where he soon learned of Pauline's infidelity. In classic military fashion he then went in search of his wife with a horse whip. Bursting into her house in the palace grounds, he discovered her in the bath and began whipping her, drawing blood, until the servants rushed in and restrained him. As a result of this incident, Fourès would be reprimanded for conduct unbecoming an officer. Napoleon was almost certainly away at Suez when Fourès returned to Cairo, otherwise the lieutenant might have been dragged before his commander-in-chief and in the heat of the moment received a more severe and immediate punishment.

The feelings of Lieutenant Fourès are transparent, but those of Pauline are less clear. She appears simply to have lost her head in the face of Napoleon's attentions, though there are indications that her marriage to Fourès may have been in difficulties. General Paulin implied that his information concerning the length and cloak-like qualities of

Pauline's hair was gained firsthand, and other sources suggest that she was sexually sophisticated. Junot's wife, in her memoirs, insisted that before Fourès departed to Alexandria on his mission, Pauline went to bed with him "with one eye streaming tears and the other wet with laughter," and then "buttered the bun" by leaving for Napoleon's bed.[24] Laure Junot claimed that she was told this story by her husband, and such idiomatic language would certainly seem to be an authentic echo of Junot's voice.

Napoleon made no attempt to keep his liaison secret. From now on Pauline acted as hostess at his official dinners in Elfi Bey's palace, and would sit beside him when he rode about Cairo in his open carriage. He was well aware that word of this would get back to Josephine in Paris sooner or later, and this was doubtless what he intended. When Eugene Beauharnais was required to escort Napoleon and Pauline in their open carriage, the young aide pointed out the anomaly of his situation, and was excused these duties. The affair was a cause of painfully divided loyalties for the seventeen-year-old Beauharnais, who felt a deep admiration for his stepfather, but also loved his mother— only his feelings towards Pauline would have been unambiguous. As for Napoleon's feelings towards Pauline, these are more difficult to discern. At least to begin with, this appears to have been something more than just a fling, more than just revenge on Josephine over her affair with Hippolyte Charles. He certainly urged Pauline to divorce the disgraced Lieutenant Fourès, and according to Bourrienne:

Napoleon strongly wished to have a child with this beautiful woman. Often when just the two of us had dinner together, I would speak with him about it. "What's to be done," he would reply, "the silly girl . . . can't do it."

She, for her part, when I pointed out to her the advantage of having a child by Napoleon, replied to me: "Good God . . . it's not my fault."[25]

Pauline's remark could have meant any one of several things, but at this point Bourrienne tactfully leaves us to draw our own conclusions.

XVII

A Suez Adventure

NAPOLEON's initial idyll with Pauline can only have lasted for a week or so, as on December 24 he embarked upon a long-planned expedition to Suez, and did not take her with him.

Suez, lying some eighty miles across the desert east of Cairo and the Nile valley, had not initially been taken by the French, but on December 4, just days after their full-dress march-past in Ezbekiyah Square, General Bon and his men set off for the port. The expeditionary force consisted of 1,200 infantry and 200 cavalry, accompanied by a camel convoy carrying provisions, water, firewood and the wooden sections of four gunboats, to be reassembled and launched on the Red Sea. Three days later Suez was taken without a shot being fired.

The first consequence of opening up this gateway to the Orient was not long in coming. On December 17 Napoleon was able to write in his regular report to the Directory (in fact, the very one carried by Lieutenant Fourès): "A ship which has arrived at Suez had on board an Indian bringing a letter for the commander of the French forces in Egypt. On arrival it was found that he had lost this letter. It appears that our arrival in Egypt has produced a great impression of our power in India and has caused an unfavorable effect on the British. Fighting has broken out there."[1]

Such was Napoleon's first nonsensical contact with the distant Orient of his dreams. However, the Indian messenger may not have been quite so incompetent as he appeared: "losing" the letter could easily have been a precautionary measure. He was not to know that Suez had been captured by the French. If he had been apprehended by the Egyptian authorities, and been found to be carrying a letter to Napoleon, this could have resulted in death, or at least torture. He had also evidently taken the precaution of not reading the contents of the letter, so that he could not reveal them under torture and thus incriminate himself, though he was able to convey news of the "unfavorable effect" of the French invasion of Egypt on the British in India.

Indicatively, Napoleon in his report to the Directory does not mention who this lost letter was from, a fact that even the hapless messenger would surely have been able to convey. Presumably, this was in case Napoleon's report was intercepted by the British blockade, which indeed it was. Subsequent evidence suggests that the letter must have come from Tippoo Sahib, who was still fighting against the British in India, and would have learned through his spies that the British had received news of Napoleon's invasion of Egypt. As we shall see, Napoleon would later second-guess the contents of this lost letter as he prepared for his invasion of India: his journey to Suez was but the first step in these preparations.

When Napoleon set out for Suez on December 24, he left Kléber in charge—a chance for his second in command to put into practice some of the administrative skills he had picked up at Napoleon's side. Napoleon was accompanied by several savants, including the ever-faithful Monge and Berthollet,★ his friend the wooden-legged General Caffarelli, and Bourrienne, as well as a suitably large armed escort to ward off any Bedouin attacks. He also brought along an old-fashioned horse-drawn four-wheeled covered carriage, but he chose not to ride in this. The trip to Suez was to be no grand procession, as El-Djabarti makes clear: "[Napoleon] took with him neither servants, nor a cook, nor a tent, nor a mattress. As their provisions, they carried just three roast chickens wrapped in paper. The soldiers had bread which they carried on the ends of their bayonets and water in flasks which they carried around their necks."² Conditions were not easy, as Bourrienne remembered: "We had proof during the day of the great heat of the desert, but by 11 o'clock at night the cold made itself felt in equally fierce fashion."³

Napoleon and his party followed the ancient caravan route taken by pilgrims and merchants through the centuries, skirting to the north of the bare mountains and escarpments of the interior. The way through

★ Monge and Berthollet had by now appended their names to so many of Napoleon's administrative projects in Egypt that many in the army were convinced that "Monge-Berthollet" was a single person.

the vast wilderness was marked only by the bones and remains of previous caravans. Bourrienne paints a macabre picture of how they made fires at night in the desert: "In place of firewood, of which there was none, we gathered large quantities of human and animal debris of all sorts. Monge was made to sacrifice several of the extraordinary heads that he had noticed en route and placed in the commander-in-chief's carriage for safe keeping. The carriage carried [Napoleon's] papers and maps to Suez—as well as Monge, Berthollet, and I too, when fatigue caused us to clamber aboard."⁴

Napoleon arrived at Suez three days later on December 27, only to find that this once thriving port was now a shadow of its former self. Much of the harbor had been allowed to silt up, and at low tide a wide sandbank separated part of the quayside from the sea. The sleepy town and its customs house had a run-down air, and the shipbuilding yard was derelict. Suez now only came to life during the annual pilgrimage to Mecca, when boats sailed down the gulf and across the Red Sea to Jeddah. A few boats brought coffee from Yemen and merchandise from Muscat, with the occasional dhow from the Persian Gulf. Suez's decline had begun in the sixteenth century, after the Portuguese had opened up the route around the Cape of Good Hope, and since then the remnant trade across the isthmus to the Mediterranean had been further ruined by the greed of the Mamelukes, who had charged excessive customs levies, and the predations of the Bedouin tribes roaming the area. The port that had once flourished with trade from the Far East and East Africa being conducted by European merchants from Venice, Genoa and Portugal was now little more than an outpost.

Determined not to be disheartened, Napoleon harked back to history. The early Mamelukes, as well as the sixteenth-century Ottoman ruler Suleiman the Magnificent, had launched large fleets from here to sail on India. He would do the same. "It is my intention to have as many armed ships as possible on the Red Sea,"⁵ he had written from Cairo to Bon, as soon as Suez had been taken. Standing on the empty quayside, he elaborated his plans to his assembled entourage. He intended to reopen the shipbuilding yards, and at the same time light transport craft would be carried in prefabricated sections from the shipbuilders on the Nile at Boulac. There would be insufficient time to build an invasion fleet, but there might be time to assemble some frigates, which would be able to open a communications link with any army marching overland to India. His listeners are said to have remained in awkward silence as Napoleon stood looking out to sea, his eloquence soaring into the realms of fantasy. Bourrienne mentions how he "gave orders for the rebuilding of several fortifications and improvements to the marine facilities" in preparation for "the arrival of several divisions coming from [sic] India, which he planned to invade."[6]

Napoleon then went about the town meeting various merchants from Muscat and the Yemen, in the ever-optimistic belief that he could establish friendly contact with their rulers. Meanwhile Monge, Berthollet and their fellow savants set out along the shore towards the head of the gulf in search of remnants of ancient civilizations. The pharaohs, the ancient Greeks and the Romans had all at some point had settlements here, but the savants were unable to discover any ruins amidst the sands.

Yet there was at least one known ancient site several miles away, and with this in mind Napoleon and the savants set off for a day trip on horseback down the coast, crossing the gulf to the eastern Sinai shore by means of a sandbank which was exposed when the tide went out. The purpose of this trip was to visit the Wells of Moses (known locally as Ayoun Moussa). At the time these consisted of eight warm fresh-water springs at an oasis some six miles or so inland, where according to the Bible Moses had led the Israelites to slake their thirst on their flight from Egypt.[7] Bourrienne described how when Napoleon's group eventually reached the springs, they "used the water to make coffee, though its brackish taste rendered the coffee barely drinkable."[8] Nothing had changed since Moses' visit over 3,000 years previously: in the biblical story, the Israelites had also found the water undrinkable, until Moses threw a certain tree into the pool, which had the effect of miraculously sweetening the water.

The Israelites had arrived at the oasis just after Moses had parted the waters of the Red Sea, allowing them to escape from Egypt. The waters had then closed, carrying off the pursuing pharaoh and his army. Although there is some doubt that these events took place on this arm of the Red Sea, what now happened to Napoleon and his savants would seem to confirm this location for the biblical story. By the time the group had ridden back from the Wells of Moses to the seashore, the light was beginning to fade and the rising tide was covering the sandbank which led to the other shore. Rashly they decided to ride on into the sea; but as the tide swept in, their local guide lost his way in the dark. (Some sources claim that to amuse themselves the accompanying soldiers had encouraged him to drink alcohol, which had befuddled him.)[9] The entire party was soon in danger of being swept away like Pharaoh and his chariots, and at one stage the water became so deep that some of the horses were forced to swim with their riders clinging to their necks. In the commotion Caffarelli's horse was swept from under him, he lost his wooden leg, and had to be rescued. But eventually all made it safely to the African shore. Bourrienne plays down this incident: "We were not lost in quicksands, as has been said, there weren't any of those. We couldn't see, but we cried out, calling to each other."[10] Subsequent evidence suggests that they had indeed been in danger: Napoleon was so grateful to the soldier who saved his friend Caffarelli's life that he was promoted to corporal and awarded with a ceremonial saber inscribed: "General Bonaparte to the mounted guide Louis," and on the other side: "Crossing of the Red Sea."[11]

Such gestures were not rare, as Kléber had noted in his pocketbook, and despite his sneer they did much to establish Napoleon's popularity amongst his men. Napoleon was a young, charismatic and brilliant general who had led his men to victory in every battle he had ever fought, and whose aim was to lead France to ever greater glory—such was the image taking shape in the minds of many who served under him. He was already beginning to take on legendary status—he was well aware of this and did everything to encourage it.

After spending just over a fortnight in Suez, Napoleon started back for Cairo, bringing with him his aide Eugene Beauharnais, whom he had allowed to join General Bon's expeditionary force. The seventeen-year-old Eugene had acquitted himself well, riding in the vanguard of the force entering Suez. He was not to have known that their entry would be unopposed, with not a shot fired. Napoleon had been impressed with his bravery, but he wanted to make sure he did not lose this young man, whom he was more and more coming to regard as a son.

At the start of the return journey, Napoleon left the main party, taking with him just the surveyor Jacques-Marie Le Père, Monge and a few senior staff officers. They rode off in search of remnants of the ancient Ptolemaic canal which was said to have linked the Red Sea to the Nile, by way of the Bitter Lakes, over 2,000 years previously. Historical evidence certainly supported the existence of such a canal: Cleopatra and her fleet had attempted to flee to the Red Sea down this waterway after their defeat by the Romans at the Battle of Actium in

31 BC, but the Nile had not yet flooded and the water had been too low to allow her ships through.

Napoleon had read about the Ptolemaic canal in Volney's *Voyage en Égypte et en Syrie*, but Volney had been unable to find any remnant of this historic waterway: "From the tops of the terraces at Suez we could not make out, with our telescopes, a single object on the naked and barren plain . . . the canals which conveyed [the waters of the Nile to Suez] are destroyed, for in this shifting sand they are quickly covered over, by the action of the winds and the passing Bedouins."[12] But Napoleon was not to be discouraged, and he recalled in his memoirs how after a thorough search he "discovered, around half a mile from the town [east along the coast], the remains of several pieces of masonry."[13] This was evidently where the ancient canal had met the sea. Together with Le Père and the others, Napoleon now set about tracing the path of the ancient canal north for around fifteen miles, to the point where it entered the declivity towards the Bitter Lakes, which at the time consisted of a basin below sea level surrounded by salt flats. Napoleon would always be particularly proud of his discovery of the ancient canal, another achievement in his insatiable quest for immortal glory, and he would later insist that this feat was ascribed to him personally in the official history of the expedition to Egypt.

Napoleon instructed Le Père to carry out a survey of the entire area, and the feasibility of excavating a canal which would follow the course of the Ptolemaic canal as far as the lakes, and then progress directly north to the Mediterranean. If anything, this suggestion was even more worthy of note than his "discovery." Others, including Leibniz, had suggested such a route, but only as a result of looking at the map. Volney, who had actually visited Suez, had specifically ruled it out, reckoning it an engineering impossibility on account of the shifting desert sands and the lack of navigable channels along either coast. Napoleon was the first to take steps that might implement this route (the one which the present Suez canal follows). But he was to be thwarted. Le Père would undertake no fewer than four surveying expeditions, all of them carried out under the most difficult conditions. Apart from the extreme heat, and extreme cold at night, and the vicious dust storms which could blow up without warning, Le Père also had to contend with the fact this this stretch of the desert was very much Bedouin country, and anyone wandering into it was liable to attack. His survey of the route as far as the lakes would be accurate, but when he ventured further north into increasingly dangerous territory, his findings became compounded with errors. He eventually came to the conclusion that the Red Sea was almost thirty-three feet higher than the Mediterranean, and that any attempt to dig a canal north from the lakes was liable to flood the northern plain with seawater, extending its low-lying marshy areas so as to render the entire region impassable, by land or canal.

When Le Père read out his findings at a meeting of the Institute, it was realized that the immediate plan for a canal would have to be shelved. Only later was his error detected: the sea levels were in fact almost the same—a finding which made the digging of the first Suez Canal directly across the isthmus much easier, when it was begun just over fifty years later by the Frenchman Ferdinand de Lesseps. However, the modern inauguration of this project, and the French involvement in it, certainly originated with Napoleon.

By the time Napoleon, Le Père, Monge and the others had finished tracing the route of the Ptolemaic canal, it was dusk, and they found themselves in some danger. They realized that their presence in the desert had almost certainly been observed by the Bedouin. Napoleon had arranged to meet up with the main party at the village of Ageroud (Al Ajrud), a short distance outside Suez on the caravan route to Cairo, but this was some way off. In his memoirs he described what happened next:

With night approaching, and it being over 20 miles★ across the desert to the camp, he [Napoleon] set off at full gallop. After losing his way a few times he eventually reached the camp. By now only the three or four on the best horses remained with him, the others all being left behind. Large fires were lit on a mound and on the minaret of the mosque at Ageroud fort; as well as this a cannon was ordered to be fired every quarter of an hour, until 11 o'clock, by which time everyone had fortunately made it back. No one was lost.[14]

All the party may finally have made it back to camp, but for at least one of them it had been something of an ordeal. The fifty-two-year-old mathematician Monge was no rider at the best of times, and even on the easy stages of the journey had been forced to travel much of the time in the closed carriage. He had been considerably alarmed by the

---

★ In fact, a little over half this distance.

sight of his leader galloping off into the dark, abandoning him to make his own way, lost in the desert, through the Bedouin-infested night.

Later, on the journey back to Cairo, Napoleon spotted a group of Arabs in the distance. Some of his party rode off after them, and found that they were in fact from a friendly tribe. Captain Doguereau, who was one of the pursuit party, recalled in his journal how in their fright and haste to escape, the Arabs "had lost their weapons in the sand; we found them and gave them back. . . . Napoleon bought several camels from them, and they were greatly pleased to be no longer afraid and instead receive money."[15] Napoleon later encouraged Eugene Beauharnais to mount one of the camels whilst the others held it down, and all watched with much merriment as Eugene struggled to haul himself aboard. But there was more to this than fooling around. Napoleon now had in mind the formation of a French camel corps, which would initially be used for carrying wounded soldiers across the desert to hospital, and also for warfare against the elusive Bedouin. If this proved successful, he would adapt the camels for more ambitious military use: the long march to India was beginning to take shape in his mind.

At one point on their return from Suez, Napoleon's party and their armed escort made a detour to attack a Bedouin tribal encampment, whose inhabitants had been harassing the French line of communication across the desert between Cairo and Suez. The encampment was burnt to the ground, hostages were taken, and all the livestock was rounded up.

El-Djabarti described Napoleon's return to the city: "On Sunday evening the general-in-chief re-entered Cairo; he led in several Bedouin and sheiks whom he had taken hostage. . . . He had conquered [2 villages] and brought with him into the city all the livestock that he found there. The villagers—men, women and children—had followed their livestock all the way to Cairo."[16] Thus the conqueror of Egypt, the intrepid explorer who had discovered the route of the lost ancient Suez Canal, made his triumphal re-entry into Cairo accompanied by a large dust-cloud of bleating goats, some strings of mangy camels, a column of wailing refugees, and a traumatized mathematician, in the form of Monge prostrated in the darkened interior of his dust-encrusted carriage.

Napoleon now set about laying the plans for his future invasion of India. As he wrote in his memoirs: "It is as far from Cairo to the Indus as it is from Bayonne* to Moscow. An army of 60,000 men, mounted on 50,000 camels, carrying with them rations for 50 days and water for six days, would arrive in forty days at the Euphrates, and in four months at the Indus in the midst of the Sikhs, Mahrattas, and the people of Hindustan [India], all impatient to shake off the British yoke which oppresses them."[17] Here we see the full extent of his ambitions for his camel corps. The sheer volume of this army was equally ambitious, considering he had only arrived in Egypt with at most 40,000 personnel, whose ranks had already been diminished by death and injury. Initially he had counted on swelling the ranks of his army by recruiting disaffected Mamelukes, and even conscripting Egyptians. When such plans were seen to be no longer feasible, he had searched for new ways of increasing his military force in preparation for any invasion of India, eventually pinning his hopes on the slave trade: "It is necessary for us to procure, each year, several thousand blacks from Senaar, and from Darfur, and to incorporate them in the French regiments, at the rate of twenty per company."[18]

Interestingly, Napoleon planned to integrate these black slaves into his army, where they would have been trained by their fellow French soldiers and would have fought alongside them; they would not have been segregated, as were the sepoy regiments in British India, who fought under white officers. His intelligence concerning the slave trade was well informed: Senaar, on the Blue Nile, was a center of the slave trade from East Africa; while Darfur, in what is now western Sudan, was where the caravans bringing slaves from as far afield as West Africa and the Congo set out north for Egypt. A few months later Napoleon would begin putting this plan into action, writing to the Sultan of Darfur: "Please send me, by the first caravan, 2,000 strong and healthy sixteen-year-old black slaves . . . order your caravan to come direct, without stopping en route. I am giving orders for it to travel under our protection the whole way."[19] At around the same time he wrote to Desaix in Upper Egypt: "I would like, Citizen General, to buy two or three thousand black slaves, all older than sixteen, so as to be able to incorporate them a hundred a time to each battalion. See if there isn't a way to begin their recruitment from the moment they are purchased. I have no need to stress for you the importance of this

---

* The town in the southwest corner of France after which the bayonet takes its name.

undertaking."[20] Marching to India with a grand army may have been Napoleon's dream, but his preparations for it were very real.

Napoleon now set about writing to Tippoo Sahib, the sultan of Mysore, who had long been an enemy of the British in India. Tippoo Sahib was regarded by the British as nothing more than a Muslim fanatic; in fact, although he was a warrior he was also a man of considerable culture, whose library at his capital Seringapatam contained a priceless collection of some 2,000 Oriental manuscripts.* In his attempts to oppose encroaching British influence in India, he had cultivated the French, even going so far as to embrace some of their revolutionary ideals. A Tree of Liberty had been ceremoniously planted at Seringapatam, and a revolutionary Jacobin Club had been founded. Members pledged death to all tyrants, and the overthrow of all unelected rulers (with the exception of Tippoo Sahib). A delegation had been dispatched across the Indian Ocean to the Isle de France (Mauritius) in the hope of gaining French military assistance against the British. This had arrived in January 1798, and news of its arrival had reached Napoleon before he sailed from Toulon in May.

Napoleon's letter to Tippoo Sahib, dated January 25, 1799, was brief but supportive, promising much but committing himself to nothing:

You have already learned of my arrival on the banks of the Red Sea with an innumerable and invincible army, filled with the desire to deliver you from the iron yoke of the British.

I take this first opportunity to let you know that I desire you should send me, by way of Moka [Yemen] and Muscat, news of the political situation in which you find yourself. I should be pleased if you can dispatch, to Suez or to Cairo, some able and intelligent man, who has your confidence, with whom I can confer on these matters.[21]

This letter was duly dispatched, along with a covering note to the Imam of Muscat: "As you have always been our friend . . . I pray also that you will assist in the conveyance of this letter to Tippoo Sahib, by making sure that it reaches him in India as soon as possible."[22]

Despite this, Napoleon's letter would take over three months to reach India, and Tippoo Sahib would never receive it. The British

---

* This collection was to become the basis of the Oriental manuscript collection at the British Library.

authorities had got wind of Tippoo Sahib's attempt to link up with the French, and in February 1799 decided to launch a pre-emptive strike. By early May the British had surrounded him at Seringapatam, launching their final assault on May 4; in the ensuing massacre Tippoo Sahib was slaughtered. Amongst the officers leading this assault, which would result in the thwarting of Napoleon's ultimate dream, was the young Colonel Wellesley, who would later become the Duke of Wellington.

XVIII

Pursuit into Upper Egypt

BY now Lower Egypt was gradually becoming pacified by the French army. There were occasional insurrections in the delta which were savagely repressed, and unruly Bedouins continued to harass lines of communication that passed through their desert territory, but the extension of French rule to Suez marked a significant expansion of their power. This port controlled all the pilgrim routes that passed down the Red Sea to Mecca by way of Jeddah—including all those which traversed North Africa from as far afield as Morocco, and those which passed from Syria south across Sinai. Napoleon was keen to protect these pilgrim caravans: a show of French goodwill towards Islam which would demonstrate once and for all that his intentions were friendly.

Yet this was only Lower Egypt, whose fertile populous region stretched from Cairo in the south, fanning out across the Nile delta to the coast between Alexandria and Damietta. Besides extending to the Red Sea, French rule also reached into the western desert, where General Andréossy now led an exploratory expedition which reported back to the Institute on the centuries-old Coptic desert monasteries, and the Natron Lakes, whose soda-encrusted shores had been the historic source of embalming chemicals for the ancient Egyptians. In Upper Egypt the situation remained much more fluid. General Desaix had been dispatched south from Cairo as early as August in pursuit of Murad Bey and the Mamelukes who had fled after the Battle of the Pyramids. Napoleon had ordered Desaix to defeat Murad Bey and secure Upper Egypt, a task which was to prove no easy matter. First of all he had to find Murad Bey, who could have been anywhere between Cairo and

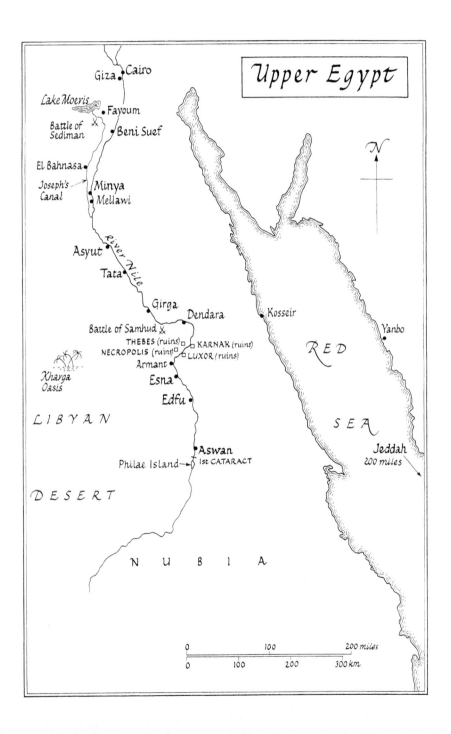

the Nubian hinterland beyond the First Cataract of the Nile, a territory roughly half the size of France. All Desaix would have at his disposal— even when reinforcements arrived—never amounted to more than 3,000 able-bodied men.

This was to be a campaign which would exploit to the uttermost the skills of its two protagonists. Desaix and Murad Bey were disparate characters, their supreme skills almost complementary, and their encounter would result in a brilliantly conducted campaign of cat and mouse. As we have seen, Desaix's meteoric rise in the French revolutionary army, as well as his military genius, was second only to that of Napoleon. He was also just as capable of inspiring deep loyalty in his men: witness their behavior on the Rhine when they defied the political commissioner sent by the Directory to arrest him. Such loyalty was curious, for Desaix was hardly a charismatic individual, cutting a distinctly unprepossessing figure in his grubby uniform and with his ugly saber-scarred face. Yet this short, scruffy character, with his straggly hair hanging down over his collar, and his long, drooping mustache, was capable of a certain aristocratic charm. This was used to the full in his womanizing, which was conducted with great and persistent enthusiasm—a side campaign which as we shall see he carried out on a heroic scale during his time in Upper Egypt. His military skills were to prove equally dogged on this campaign: no matter how far he had to go, he would never give up, as Murad Bey would discover to his chagrin. Yet there was so much more to Desaix's abilities than mere persistence. As no less than the president of the Institute, the great mathematician Fourier, exclaimed admiringly: "Desaix knows all the brilliant military actions down to the least detail. . . . He seems to have felt the need to become immersed in all that is great or useful."[1]

Murad Bey, on the other hand, remained a figure of some magnificence—despite his resounding defeat at the Battle of the Pyramids and the fact that he had been forced to flee in disarray from Cairo. Although he was by now probably in his fifties, well past his prime by the hard standards of the Mamelukes, his scarred Caucasian face, large staring eyes and bushy blond beard were still enough to instill fear in all who encountered him. These warrior's scars were one of the few things he had in common with Desaix. Both had fought in the thick of battle; both had survived as others were cut down at their side; both in their very different ways were soldiers through and through. But where Desaix's intellect sought to combine greatness and usefulness, Murad

Bey was an explosive mix of great contradictions: his immense bravery could be undercut by sudden cowardice; fierce loyalty could give way to unexpected betrayal; he ruled as a tyrant, yet the power behind him was his wife Setty-Nefissa, the former wife of his ruler Ali Bey.[2]

When Desaix set out down the Nile under cover of darkness on the night of August 25, 1798, he had just 2,861 infantrymen, and two field guns. He had no cavalry with which to oppose or give chase to Murad Bey's numerically superior mounted force. Between seven and eight thousand Mamelukes had fled the Battle of the Pyramids, and though Murad Bey had been unable to keep this entire force united, its main rump remained loyal to him in his time of need, and he knew he could call on further Bedouin support. On top of this, he had every tactical advantage. In Upper Egypt he was passing through the fiefdoms of local beys who were loyal to him, whereas Desaix was moving ever deeper into unknown territory. Desaix's local guides were often unreliable, as they had never guided such a force before, their previous experience being limited to river craft and camel trains. Yet fortunately he could also draw on assistance from the maps Napoleon had brought to Egypt amongst his library. The most authoritative and trustworthy of these were in the geographer D'Anville's atlas of Africa, published in 1749. This had been compiled from all manner of firsthand sources, mainly European travelers over recent centuries, but also some dating back to classical times. D'Anville's great strength as a cartographer had been his expert knowledge of disparate scales of measurement, including those used in classical times. When it came to distances, Desaix knew he could rely upon his maps, but the terrain was another matter. Worse still was his meager knowledge of the Nile itself, a distinct setback with much of his force traveling on a flotilla of craft ranging from *djermes* and *chebeks* (local sailing craft) to flat-bottomed gunboats adapted for carrying troops. When they started out, the Nile was in flood, with all manner of sandbanks, shoals and hidden hazards lurking beneath the swirls of its distinctive muddy waters.* At the same time, part of Desaix's division marched along the bank, accompanied by equipment and provisions carried on hired camel trains, which meant that liaison was a constant problem for their commander.

Desaix's aim was to head south as quickly as possible to try and

---

* The French would name the pastel greenish color of this muddy river water *eau de Nil*.

catch Murad Bey unawares. After traveling 125 miles up the Nile, he was informed by his spies that Murad Bey was encamped less than twenty miles to the west at El Bahnasa, on an ancient arm of the Nile known as Joseph's Canal (Bahr-el-Yusuf). The terrain between the Nile and the canal was flooded, and for the most part all that was visible above the water were the villages on their raised ground. Desaix's troops set out at once on foot, following in Indian file along the top of the little raised dykes that surrounded the fields, at times wading waist deep through the water holding their rifles above their heads. It took them just over three hours to reach within sight of El Bahnasa, but by then Murad Bey had got wind of what was happening, and the French arrived to see in the distance the last of his camel train fording the canal and heading off into the Libyan desert.

And so it went on, for days, then weeks. Desaix would receive intelligence about detachments of Mamelukes, or Murad's Nile flotilla, and travel post-haste down the Nile, or into the hinterland, only to discover that they had eluded him, often by less than twenty-four hours. Then, on September 24, he learned that Murad Bey had slipped behind him and was camped at Fayoum, close to the head of Joseph's Canal. Here Murad was less than sixty miles southwest of Cairo, in contact by courier with rebellious elements in the city. Moreover, his very proximity inhibited many citizens from cooperating with the French, for fear of his return, which now seemed a very real prospect for the first time since the Battle of the Nile.

Desaix made his way as best he could up the treacherous Joseph's Canal, whose waters were now beginning to silt up as the floods receded. After a week he disembarked, deciding to march the last half of the journey, and a week later, as he approached the village of Sediman at the edge of the desert beside the canal, he saw Murad Bey and his Mamelukes encamped on the heights above the valley some way ahead. Desaix focused his field glass on the Mameluke camp, and found that Murad Bey was "recognizable beside his tent, where we could see him sitting surrounded by his sheiks."[3] They were waiting for him: just as Desaix had calculated, in the end Murad Bey's pride had got the better of him—he would not flee forever.

Unlike at the Battle of the Pyramids, this time Murad Bey had numerical superiority. Desaix estimated that his adversary now had around 5,000 cavalry at his disposal, along with support troops, which meant that they outnumbered the French by about two to one. And to make matters worse, many of Desaix's troops were beginning to suffer from an outbreak of ophthalmia, their eyes smarting, their vision reduced in some cases to near blindness.

Following Napoleon's example at the Battle of the Pyramids, Desaix chose to fight in battle squares. But instead of a square made up of an entire division, he decided to form his men into two much smaller forward squares of just under 200 soldiers each, with the rest of his infantry, and his two artillery pieces, drawn up behind them in a larger square. That night, the men slept in their squares, their rifles between their legs. On the morning of October 8, the young officer Savary noticed that "the soldiers did everything that was necessary without being told. At daybreak, between two and three in the morning,* everyone was on their feet well before the sounding of the drums for reveille."[4]

The division moved forward in its squares towards Sediman, and an hour later, again in Savary's words: "In battle order we advanced up a hill in the desert with the aim of taking up a position at the top. . . . Suddenly we heard the sound of drums and saw a cloud of dust ahead, out of which emerged a swarm of Mameluke cavalry above us, their hooves pounding the sand as they swooped down on our squares."

The battle-hardened veterans of the Army of Italy and the Army of the Rhine stood their ground. Desaix had ordered his men not to fire until the Mameluke line was within twenty paces, but the overzealous officer in command of the leading small square on the left flank, one Captain Valette, was so convinced of the steadfast bravery of his men that he ordered them to withhold their fire until the enemy charge was within just ten paces. This proved a mistake, given the depth and size of his square. Many of the Mamelukes were mown down, but "their horses, although shot through with bullets, just continued their charge, passing through the square and out the other side before they finally fell to the ground a hundred feet away. In this way they made gaps in our ranks through which the Mamelukes followed them." This could have been fatal, but such experienced soldiers knew not to panic. They immediately threw themselves to the ground; meanwhile, in the words of Desaix, who was in the main square to the rear: "Our volleys and the fire of the division soon saved them from danger."[5] These hardy veterans knew their priorities, and as Desaix admiringly observed, "After

---

* Daybreak is not actually so early in Egypt during October. This discrepancy resulted from the fact that the French continued to observe Paris time.

having stripped their enemy of their valuables, they then made their way back to the division."

By this time the main body of Mamelukes had wheeled to attack the other leading square, but this managed to hold without being penetrated. The massed French infantry of the large divisional square, with its triple rank of firing men—one kneeling, one crouching, one standing—subjected the passing Mameluke warriors to heavy fire as they charged past.

Then Murad Bey sprang his surprise, producing four cannons which had been hidden behind a hillock, and now began to fire at the French squares. Desaix's battle plan had been thwarted, and he needed to make a quick decision. According to his aide General Friant, despite the battle raging around him Desaix was at all times "ten degrees colder than ice."[6] He ordered a charge of the Mameluke guns by his infantry with fixed bayonets. Such a move required extreme bravery from his men; and they would also be leaving behind their own wounded to face the savage vengeance of the Mameluke cavalry. One eyewitness image suffices to indicate the resolve that this involved: "A mortally wounded soldier, seeing the rest of the division departing, grabbed a comrade by his coat-tail and would not let him go. The other, realizing that he would be killed without any hope of saving his comrade, took out his knife, cut the coat-tail from his uniform, and left the unfortunate wounded man, who was finished off by the Mameluke sabers."[7]

Desaix's men charged the enemy guns with their bayonets, capturing two of them, which quickly caused those manning the other guns to flee. The Mameluke cavalry soon followed—but having no cavalry himself, Desaix was unable to pursue them. Even so, the Battle of Sediman had proved a resounding victory for the French: amongst their 3,000 troops there were just forty-four fatalities and 100 or so wounded, while the Mamelukes were estimated to have suffered some 400 casualties.

Desaix and his men now continued their advance. An officer recalled: "We ended up climbing the hill, from the summit of which we could see the green and rich province of Fayoum."[8] When they entered the nearby regional capital, which Murad Bey had simply deserted, Desaix set about establishing a new administration, at the same time requisitioning food and horses for his increasingly exhausted troops. But after a few days' rest, the main body of troops moved on once more as best they could. By now the soldiers, in their thick serge uniforms, were beginning to suffer from the growing heat. On top of this, the spread of ophthalmia and other diseases, as well as the wear and tear of marching, which was destroying their boots, were all beginning to take a heavy toll.

Napoleon was anxious to eliminate Murad Bey and secure Upper Egypt as quickly as possible. "I am impatient for news,"[9] he wrote to Desaix on October 4. In fact, by the time this message reached Desaix, the situation amongst his division had deteriorated drastically, to the point where he realized that his troops were no longer in any fit state to pursue the enemy. Although he was not one to complain, he felt it his duty to inform Napoleon of the true state of affairs, and writing on October 29 he told his commander-in-chief:

Sickness has reduced us to an embarrassing state. This eye disease is a terrible scourge. It has deprived me of more than 1,400 men. When I march I have to drag behind me a hundred of these poor unfortunates who have been rendered completely blind. And if you saw the men I've got left you'd be surprised. . . . We're stripped of even the basic necessities, without boots, without anything; to tell you the truth, the troops need a rest. Give us the provisions and the means to go on, and we'll go on. . . . What do you want me to do?[10]

This left Napoleon in a considerable dilemma: he had only just succeeded in putting down the Cairo uprising—should he risk sending Desaix further troops, or simply call off the entire Upper Egypt expedition until things improved?

Meanwhile, Desaix could only bide his time and continue as he saw best. By way of setting up his new administration, he now also set about collecting taxes from the local *fellahin*. But the trouble was, Murad Bey had already got there first, extracting for himself as much as he could. The *fellahin* found these new demands intolerable, and on November 8 they were encouraged into open revolt by the deposed local Mamelukes. By now most of Desaix's division had crossed back to the main course of the Nile, leaving a garrison inside the walls at Fayoum of just 500 men, almost a third of whom were suffering from ophthalmia.

Word of conditions amongst the French garrison at Fayoum soon reached the local Mamelukes, who roused the surrounding country-side with the intention of inflicting a savage revenge for the defeat of Murad Bey. According to a French officer who was present: "At eleven-thirty in the morning, a large crowd of Arabs, stamping their feet on the ground and beating tambourines, with some Mameluke chiefs at their head, began scaling the walls at the edge of the town."[11] In his subsequent report, Desaix would accept his officers' estimate that this crowd was around 3,000 men; these now began advancing on the French barracks in the Mameluke palace formerly occupied by the local chieftain Ali-Kachef. The French eyewitness continued: "The doors, passageways and terraces were defended entirely by our sick men; around the square and the courtyard were our reserve of 350 men." During the ensuing battle on the rooftops and in the surrounding streets, the French managed to hold off their attackers, before finally driving them from the town in disarray. During the course of this skirmish the French lost four dead and ten wounded, while losses amongst the *fellahin*, the Mamelukes and their supporting slaves were estimated at around 200. Upper Egypt was proving difficult to conquer, and even more difficult to govern.

On the very same day, Napoleon replied to Desaix's desperate plea by dispatching General Belliard from Cairo with reinforcements in the shape of an infantry battalion "forming in all 340 men,"[12] according to Belliard, while Napoleon recorded: "I have ordered General Belliard to leave with five or six hundred men."[13] Belliard's figure is more likely to represent the true number: Napoleon's order, as recorded in his *Correspondance*, was probably intended to put him in a more generous and obliging light. On the other hand, he may actually have given such an order, but by the time it filtered down the figure could have been reduced by commanders unwilling to give up the required number of men. Such instances illustrate the constant difficulty of arriving at the historical truth, even when relying upon firsthand accounts.

On his journey south along the Nile, Belliard recorded in his journal: "En route I learned that the French had chased the Mamelukes out of Fayoum province. I believed this had the support of the peasants, owing to the goodwill shown to us in the villages through which we passed."[14] Despite the initial difficulties encountered in Upper Egypt, the French remained optimistic: if they could only drive out the Mamelukes altogether, it might be possible to establish a stable administration. This would then have a knock-on effect in Cairo, the delta and the whole of Lower Egypt. Napoleon certainly believed this, and Desaix would do his best to implement his commander's wishes, though how far this belief extended throughout the Army of the Orient is difficult to tell. Curiously, despite all the suffering and discontent, the evidence suggests that it did indeed remain widespread—and not just amongst senior generals (with the notable exception of Kléber). Judging from the tone of the journals and letters they wrote, the majority of the officers amongst the Army of the Orient still appeared to believe that the Egyptian expedition would have a successful outcome. They remained loyal to their undefeated leader, and were willing to follow wherever he led.

In early November, Desaix's expedition was joined by the fifty-one-year-old artist-savant Vivant Denon, who had already lived through many adventures since his time as a young painter at the court of Louis XV at Versailles, not least of which had been his night-time arrival in Alexandria just four months previously. Even so, he was now embarking upon what would turn out to be the adventure of his life, the one for which he would achieve lasting fame. He was fascinated by the history of ancient Egypt, and had already sketched the pyramids: "The great distance from which they can be seen makes them appear diaphanous, of the same bluish tone as the sky, giving back to them the fineness and purity that has been worn away by the centuries."[15] He had also produced a memorable sketch of the savants using a ladder, plumb line and theodolite to measure the face of the Sphinx: "Although its proportions are colossal, those of its contours which have been preserved are as supple as they are pure. The expression on its face is gentle, gracious and tranquil, its character African—but the mouth, whose lips are thick, has a truly admirable harmony of execution and finesse of artistry. It is as if it is living flesh."[16] Like many others, he had heard rumors of the fabulous ruins that lay further up the Nile. Such was his desire to see for himself if these rumors were true, he had managed to persuade Napoleon to allow him to join Desaix's expedition, despite the seriousness of its military purpose.

Denon sailed from Cairo early in November on a *chebek* carrying ammunition and supplies for Desaix. He was immediately enchanted by what he saw. On the banks of the Nile the buffaloes circled beneath the blinding sun, pumping water into the irrigation ditches; laden donkeys and strings of camels passed along the pathways between the mud-hutted villages; and beyond the palm trees, across the flooded rice fields, were views of further pyramids, some dilapidated, others in ruins. Meanwhile, in the swollen river itself he could see "little islands covered with ducks, herons and pelicans."[17] But his view of life by the Nile was not entirely rose-tinted. When he went ashore, he found that the villages were invariably surrounded by piles of filth and rubble, which in the flat landscape were as good as mountains from which one could view the surrounding countryside. In the evenings the tops of these mounds were covered with groups of squatting villagers, taking the air, smoking their pipes, and watching to see that everything in the surrounding plain was peaceful. The disadvantage of these heaps of refuse is that they make the villages offensive, rendering them unhealthy by depriving them of fresh air, and the eyes of the inhabitants are made puffy by the mud-dust mixed with imperceptible bits of straw, which is one of the numerous causes of the eye infections with which Egypt is afflicted.[18]

Denon was evidently a sympathetic character, and General Belliard, who became Desaix's second-in-command, soon took the aging artist-savant under his wing. According to Denon, "General Belliard obligingly offered to divide up his living quarters with me. This involved a division of the infinitely small: our beds occupied the entire room. These had to be cleared out if we wanted to put in a table, and this in turn had to be cleared out when we wanted to wash or dress ourselves."[19] Unusually, the men also took to Denon, and soon became proud of their artist-in-residence, who despite his graying hair and unathletic figure sought no favors when they struck camp and set out on their daily march. Savary described the intrepid artist in his memoirs: "He carried on his shoulders a portfolio filled with papers and pencils, and had a little sack suspended from his neck, in which he put his writing case and some food."[20] If Denon stepped out of line to squat down and sketch some passing scene where there was no shelter, the soldiers would take turns to follow him and stand at his side, their shadows protecting him from the sun, while at the same time wondering at his artistic facility as the sketch took shape before their eyes.

In the last week of November, Desaix left Belliard in charge while he returned north, arriving in Cairo on December 1, to confront Napoleon in person. Their face-to-face encounter seems to have been grim, but Napoleon eventually agreed to provide suitable reinforcements to keep Desaix's infantry strength at over 3,000 men, as well as sending an additional 1,000 cavalry under General Davout. Finally, as a gesture of goodwill, he loaned Desaix his personal *djerme*, *L'Italie*, which had been outfitted in considerable luxury, to use as his shipboard headquarters during the campaign.

Despite this gesture, Desaix arrived back at his base at Beni Suef, seventy miles south of Cairo, in a foul temper. In the end he had fallen out with Napoleon over the use of a howitzer on his campaign. An argument between these two supreme tacticians had been inevitable: it was lucky that it had been over such a trivial matter. By now Desaix's men had been able to rest and recuperate, some for as long as four weeks. His staff had reorganized the division so as to make it better adapted to the task at hand, and a flotilla had arrived from Cairo bringing further provisions and vital supplies of marching boots, returning upstream with all those rendered *hors de combat* by disease.

Suitably refreshed, Desaix's division started south once more in pursuit of Murad Bey on December 16. Mornings began early, with reveille often at two A.M. (French time), and the entire division would be on the move within the hour, with its main body marching down the west bank of the Nile, while the flotilla, along with *L'Italie*, attempted to keep pace on the river. Desaix himself abandoned the luxury of life on *L'Italie* during the daytime, and only slept aboard when the flotilla managed to keep up with the marching columns. There were frequent skirmishes with small detachments of Mameluke cavalry, and Desaix would direct these operations in person. In the course of these, the French invariably inflicted heavy punishment, whilst suffering few casualties themselves.

In this way, Desaix's division made good progress down the Nile, passing through Minya and Mellawi before reaching Asyut. By now he knew he had Murad Bey on the run: all the indications were that his main group was just thirty miles ahead. During the last days of December Desaix reached Girga, the chief city of Upper Egypt, 250 miles up the Nile from Cairo. The green valley of the Nile had by now begun to narrow, with the river passing through the occasional gorge, and the fertile strip of land sometimes extending only five miles on either side before giving way to the desert. However, the land was more intensively cultivated here than in Lower Egypt, with well-irrigated fields amidst the citrus orchards and groves of date-palms, and the markets were plentifully supplied with local produce. In Asyut, the arrival of 3,000 French soldiers barely altered the price of pigeons, eggs and fruit, the most popular purchases amongst the men; yet after their diet of dried army biscuits, this rich cuisine soon resulted in a bad outbreak of dysentery. They were now approaching the tropics, and although it was midwinter the climate proved difficult for even the more hardened soldiers. Temperatures could rise above 30°C (into the nineties Fahrenheit) during the daytime, plunging to almost freezing at night. Many believed that it was this chill, more than the heat and dust of the daytime marches, that was responsible for the ophthalmia that continued to spread through the division. All took their own precautions against this disease, the most popular being to cover one's eyes at night. But still it spread through all ranks, and even the most senior officers were not immune: General Belliard himself succumbed at one stage.

Desaix's division was now entering unknown territory: no European army had penetrated this far south into Africa since the ancient Romans. Supply lines were becoming increasingly stretched and vulnerable to opportunist Bedouin raids; at the same time the continuous daily marching, often over sandstone, began taking its toll on the soldiers' boots, which now seldom lasted more than a month. When Desaix arrived at Girga, he discovered that Murad Bey had only left the city the previous night. According to Belliard: "The Mamelukes had their gunboats at Girga and we might have found them and taken possession of them if half an hour before our arrival there hadn't been a strong North wind, which carried them off [upstream]."[21]

The French had almost caught up with Murad Bey, but to Desaix's extreme frustration he was now forced to call a halt. He had lost contact with his flotilla, and when last heard of it was several days' sail downstream. Amongst other things it was carrying the division's supply of army biscuits and boots, without which it could go no further. Despite his annoyance, Desaix also knew that his men were in no fit state to continue: they needed a rest after their rapid march south.

Surprisingly, in spite of the skirmishes, the heat and the disease, Desaix's expedition seems to have been a fairly enjoyable experience for many of the French soldiers. The men were pleased to discover that prostitutes were readily available in all towns, and cost almost nothing, while the officers appear to have been more interested in the food. In Girga, Belliard noted: "I have never found a place where the food is so cheap: a duck sells for less than half a franc, one can buy six or seven eggs for three centimes, chickens sell at thirty-five centimes a pair, and a pair of pigeons for around fourteen centimes*. . . . When you arrive in a place where food costs so little, you'd think they live

---

* I have converted these prices, which are given by Belliard in the local currency, *médins*. To convey an idea of the worth of such prices for Belliard and his fellow diners, a senior savant such as Denon earned 500 francs a month. Even the *Courier*, a mere four-page weekly newspaper, cost twenty-one centimes—enough to buy a pair of pigeons and a dozen eggs, with change to spare!

in misery. But when four or five thousand soldiers arrive for ten days and the prices don't go up, then you can be sure there's enough for everybody."²² Girga was a town of around 10–12,000 inhabitants, and even though Belliard seems to have slightly exaggerated the number of soldiers, his point was real enough: this was indeed a land of plenty.

Girga was to prove a pleasant interlude. Belliard records how "every evening we met up at the general's house [Desaix's headquarters], and passed an agreeable couple of hours of our day discussing and debating topics great and small."²³ One evening they discussed the origins of ancient Egypt, and on December 31 they had a particularly memorable dinner: the great annual caravan from Darfur had just arrived in Girga, and Desaix invited the brother of its leader to be their guest. This black Nubian prince proved an exotic novelty to his European dining companions. Denon described him as "lively, happy, enthusiastic and intelligent,"²⁴ and he certainly seems to have played his part to the full, regaling his spellbound listeners with his travelers' tales about crossing the Sahara desert, "during which they only found water every eight days in underground wells." The prince "had just come back from a two-year voyage to Mecca and India. He claimed to have eighty brothers, who are like him all sons of the King of Darfur."²⁵ He explained to his French listeners that Darfur was "larger than Cairo, but not so well built." He also confirmed for them the existence of the legendary city of Timbuktu, which he said was a huge city on the banks of a great river, six months' journey from Darfur in the direction of the setting sun: "Its inhabitants are very small. They trade with Darfur, bringing gold and the teeth of elephantines [presumably ivory], which they exchange for camels and Egyptian cloth." His own convoy was even more colorful: this consisted of 2,000 camels, bringing with it "800 Nubians [slaves] from Senaar, and as many women, also elephantines' teeth and powdered gold . . . all merchandise bound for Cairo."²⁶ To the officers' questions, he replied that "when these female slaves were not captive, and they were bought, they cost one bad rifle each, the men two." Savary, who was present at this dinner, mentions that the caravan also carried "gum, ostrich plumes and tiger skins . . . also many children who were destined to be sold, the offspring of parents who had been too poor to feed them."²⁷ He adds that "we discussed this treatment of the blacks, and afterwards almost all of us were of the opinion that it was more philanthropic to permit it than to defend it." This enigmatic conclusion would seem to indicate that at least

among the officers there were distinct qualms about the slave trade—
which would be outlawed in the West Indies eight years later, and abolished by the French in 1848. The officers seem to have been unaware of
Napoleon's plan to import slaves to swell the ranks of the Army of
the Orient, and although Desaix certainly knew of this by now, it seems
he chose not to mention it.

Under Desaix, the behavior of the French soldiers towards the local
population was also more philanthropic. Adjudicating over disputes in
the region under his command, Desaix was already gaining the reputation which would lead to him being known by the Egyptians as Sultan
El-Adel (The Just Sultan). The invading French army in Upper Egypt
was beginning to attract support, especially amongst the Orthodox
Greek and Coptic minorities, which were numerous in the south. These
were useful allies, as the Copts had been employed by the Mamelukes
to gather the *miry*, and knew precisely how much tax was due from
each individual. Desaix's most notable new ally was the Copt leader
Moallam Jacob, formerly the chief tax collector for the whole of Upper
Egypt. His network of contacts throughout the region was to prove
invaluable, both for intelligence purposes and in preparing for the
arrival of French troops.

As Murad Bey journeyed south, he would order the immediate collection of the *miry*, to support his campaign, no matter whether the crops
had been gathered in yet or not. This may have deprived Desaix of
much-needed financial support, but it also turned some of the local
Egyptians into French allies, even if the majority of the population
remained hostile. Moallam Jacob's spies would inform him of who
might prove favorable to the advancing French, and from now on he
seldom left Desaix's side, even advising him on the terrain and which
were the best military tactics to adopt. Not for nothing did the French
soon become known amongst the local Egyptians as "Moallam Jacob's
army."

Not until January 19 did the flotilla finally make it to Girga, arriving
with due pomp: a military band playing on the deck of one of the
chebeks, as the soldiers on the riverbank cheered it in. Two days later,
Desaix and his division, accompanied by the flotilla, set off south
towards Samhud, sixteen miles upstream, where Moallam Jacob's spies
had informed him that Murad Bey's forces were massed, ready to
repulse the French.

Yet why had Murad Bey chosen once again to stand and fight? After the Battle of Sediman, his Mameluke beys and their cavalry, along with their supporting Bedouin, had simply scattered in all directions, some dispersing into the Libyan desert, others fleeing south along the Nile. Over half the beys had fled as far as Edfu, which was 120 miles south of Girga.

At this point Murad Bey had appealed to his great adversary Hassan Bey, the ruler of Esna province, south of Girga, to forget their differences and become his ally. Responding to this plea for Mameluke solidarity, Hassan Bey had joined forces with Murad Bey, bringing with him his entire cavalry. At the same time, Murad Bey had sent couriers across the eastern desert to the port of Kosseir, where they had crossed the Red Sea to Jeddah and Yanbo, bearing an appeal for Muslim warriors to join the fight against the infidels. He had even dispatched some of his beys south to Nubia, to bring black slaves to fight at his side. As a result, he now had an assembled force of 3,000 infantrymen, as well as 11,000 cavalry, consisting of 2,000 Mamelukes, 7,000 Arabs, and 2,000 "Meccans" from across the Red Sea. Meanwhile, Desaix was moving south with a force of just 3,000 infantry and 1,000 cavalry, but he remained confident: this was just the confrontation he had been waiting for.

On January 22 the two armies faced each other across the flat plain beside the Nile at Samhud. Desaix adopted the usual French tactics, forming his men into two infantry squares; but this time he had his cavalry, which was drawn up in three lines between them, with one line facing protectively to the rear. The Mamelukes too adopted their usual tactics, confident that this time their huge numerical superiority would win the day. Stretched out in a long glittering line, the array of Mameluke and Arab cavalry surged forward towards the French line, finally breaking into bloodcurdling shrieks as they charged towards the tight squares. Denon, who found himself in the middle of one of these squares, poetically evoked the scene: "The Mamelukes wheeled around us, their resplendent arms shining as they maneuvered their horses. They deployed all the splendor of the Orient, but our northern severity presented a harsh aspect which was no less imposing. The contrast was striking: it was iron defying gold—the plain glittered, the spectacle was superb."[28]

Once again the French squares held in the face of the determined Mameluke charge, and held again as they wheeled and charged once more, in search of weak points in the French ranks. To the Mamelukes, this was not fighting at all, and they soon rode off dispirited, leaving the "Meccan" cavalry, who had no experience of the French squares, to continue with their brave but futile charges. The Battle of Samhud was soon over, with seventy Arabs and thirty Mamelukes killed, many more wounded, and just one French guardsman killed. However, the French fighting was not without its valor. Captain Desvernois of the cavalry, who was amongst the advance platoon placed in front of the squares, recalled his youthful heroism in his memoirs: "I received 18 wounds of no importance, but the enemy then singled me out. A saber blow slashed the tendons of my right forearm, forcing me to grab my saber in my left. My position became perilous: I was disarmed, defense-less, in the midst of the fighting. I cried out to Savary to come to my aid. . . . He replied 'Look after yourself as best you can!' "[29] Exasperated, Desvernois made for his own lines. "Covered in blood, as too was my horse, I made it into the interior of General Friant's battle square. I had fourteen saber slashes through the gauntlet of my right arm, five through the left, with my index and middle fingers lightly wounded. My right arm, cut to the bone, which was itself broken, hung inert. Finally I had a severe bruise to the forehead: a blow which I had received from the shaft of a charging lance . . . my helmet had saved my life."

There is no mention of young Captain Desvernois' cry for help in Savary's own memoirs, which only recall how his cavalry under General Davout set off in pursuit of the fleeing Mamelukes, "but it was unable to engage the enemy, no matter how far it pursued them into the desert. In revenge, they [returned and] cut to pieces the unfortunate fanatics from Mecca."[30] Desaix, in his official report to Napoleon on the Battle of Samhud, describes how his entire division "came out of it virtually unscathed,"[31] though he does mention Captain Desvernois, who seems on closer medical inspection to have suffered only "his wrist sliced by a dagger, without any permanent damage."

Another extraordinary soldier's tale, though this time true, emerges from Savary's memoirs, in which he tells of a Mameluke who deserted to the French after the battle: "He was a Hungarian,* a former non-commissioned officer in the Wenschal regiment of the Austrian hussars, who had been taken prisoner in the war against the Turks in 1783 or 1784." He told the French that "even the officers of the Hungarian and

---

* Other sources, which confirm this story, claim he was a German, from Saxony.

Croat commandos who had been taken prisoner in the same war, had been taken off to Constantinople, then shipped to Egypt, where they were made Mamelukes. This did not displease them and they made no effort to return to their country, even though they had a consul in Egypt; yet it is fair to say that if their beys had even suspected them of entertaining such thoughts they would have had their heads cut off at once."[32]

Once again, Murad Bey and most of his Mamelukes had lived to fight another day. Although Desaix now had a substantial cavalry force at his disposal, he had been unable to prevent their flight. All he could do was pursue Murad Bey and his Mamelukes even further into Upper Egypt, with the aim of either catching them and eliminating them once and for all, or driving them from Egypt into the wastes of the Nubian desert.

XIX

Into the Unknown

As Desaix and his division marched further south along the Nile, they entered a world which few Europeans had penetrated. Soon they began coming across the fabulous remains of ancient Egypt: ruined cities, along with palaces and temples that had been no more than the chimera of travelers' tales. The legendary remains of a forgotten pre-history of Western civilization now became reality before the eyes of the amazed French soldiers. But Desaix was pressing south so fast in his pursuit of Murad Bey that there was no opportunity for sight-seeing. To Denon's immense frustration, he had little time for sketching. "We were constantly advancing,"[1] he complained, while Savary and others confirm that they only spent one night at each stop, and sometimes even marched through the night. Fortunately for Denon, both Desaix and his second-in-command Belliard took a sympathetic interest in what he was doing. As Denon recalled, "I found in General Desaix a scholar, curious for knowledge, a friend of the arts. I was obliged to him for all he allowed me to do despite the circumstances. . . . In General Belliard I found a kindred spirit, friendship and unfailing care."[2] Such protection was all too necessary. Denon recalled "that we were surrounded with Arabs and Mamelukes, and that, in all probability, I should be made prisoner, robbed, and very likely killed, if I had thought to venture only a hundred paces from the column."[3] Yet as one officer noticed, he did not always take heed of these dangers:

One day while the flotilla was traveling upriver, he saw some ruins and said he must do a drawing of them. Obliging his companions to set him down, he hurried out into the plain, ensconced himself in the sand, and began drawing. Just as he was finishing, a bullet whizzed past his piece of paper, and he looked up to see an Arab who, having missed his target the first time, was in the process of reloading. He snatched up his own gun, shot the Arab through the heart, shut his portfolio, and went back to the boat. In the evening when he was showing his drawings to the staff, General Desaix said: "Your horizon isn't straight." To which Denon replied: "Ah, that's the fault of that Arab. He fired too soon."

Ruins were not the only objects of interest the French encountered as they made their way south towards the tropics, leaving the cultivated green strip of the Nile valley to cut across the desert when there was a bend in the river. Denon describes one such occasion: "At last we entered the desert; where we saw not far away a wild beast that from its size and form we judged might be a hyena. We made after it, but our galloping horses were only able to follow it, without gaining on it."[4] Both officers and men now began to feel that they were approaching the limits of the known world. Everything was slowly changing before their eyes: as they crossed the desert, the distant Nile would ripple and then appear to evaporate in the heat haze; clusters of huts would suddenly appear and then disappear on the far shore of the mirage lakes which shimmered out in the desert. Even what was real appeared unreal. Denon recorded how they began coming across "date palms much larger than we had ever seen, gigantic tamarisks, villages stretching well over a mile along the bank of the river."[5]

Thirty miles upstream, Desaix's division reached Dendara (ancient Tentyra), where they came across a huge stone temple lying half buried in the sand with a number of makeshift Arab huts perched on its still intact roof. According to Denon: "Without any orders either having been given or received, every officer, every soldier left the road and rushed to Tentyra. Spontaneously, the whole army remained there for the rest of the day."[6] The ruins of the temple were unlike anything Denon had known from ancient Greece or Rome:

The Egyptians have borrowed nothing from others, they have added no foreign ornaments. . . . Order and simplicity have been their principles, and they have raised these to the sublime. . . . In the ruins of Tentyra the Egyptians appeared to me as giants. . . . We should refrain from thinking, as we are in the habit of doing in our derogatory fashion, that Egyptian architecture marks the birth of this art; on the contrary, we should regard it as the highest standard against which we measure this art.★7

Inside, the walls were inscribed with mysterious figures and indecipherable hieroglyphs, and in the ceiling of one of the inner rooms the French discovered a magnificent circular depiction of the zodiac.

Denon at once set to work sketching: "Pencil in hand, I passed from object to object, drawn from one by interest in the next, constantly enthralled, constantly distracted; my eyes, my hand, my mind were inadequate to the task of ordering and setting down all that overwhelmed me."8 Hours later the sun was setting, the soldiers had marched off, but Denon remained sketching, lost to the world, with Belliard standing protectively at his side. In the rapidly growing dusk they remounted their horses and galloped on after the marching columns, which were already more than two miles down the road. Denon recalled how that evening he encountered a soldier called Latournie, "an officer of great courage, intellect and refined taste, who sought me out and told me: 'During my time in Egypt, I have constantly felt overwhelmed by this country, reduced to a state of melancholy and illness. Tentyra has cured me of all that. What I have seen today has been worth all my previous misery. No matter what happens to me from now on in the expedition, I shall be eternally grateful for my memories of this day, which will remain with me for the rest of my life.'"9

Their next experience was not quite so inspiring, as Savary recalled:

The banks of the Nile began to be very dangerous, particularly at night, because of the enormous crocodiles which left the river to come and eat their fill of whatever they could find on the mud-banks. We often saw them, but we suffered no accidents. These animals, although monstrous, are very timid; the least sound makes them take flight, especially when they are away from the water, which they only leave at night.10

The French had never seen such beasts before. Denon described how "we saw something long and brown between a number of ducks. It was a crocodile, around fifteen or eighteen feet long, asleep. Someone fired a rifle at it, whereupon it slowly slid into the water, and then

★ Ironically, this temple does in fact date from the Greco-Roman period, having been built between 125 BC and AD 60. However, it was constructed in the ancient Egyptian style, so Denon's observations were not entirely spurious.

came out again a few minutes later."[11] Soon they came across even larger crocodiles: Denon saw one twenty-eight feet long, and records that "several trustworthy officers" even claimed to have seen one forty feet long, which must have been a truly massive beast.*[12]

By January 26, the French were approaching Thebes. According to Denon: "At nine o'clock in the morning, rounding the part of a range of mountains that formed a promontory, we suddenly saw spread out before us, in all its glory, the sight of ancient Thebes, the 'city of a hundred gates' described by Homer."[13] Desvernois describes what happened next: "At the sight of these gigantic ruins, at the vast sweep of ancient stones and remains which occupied such a great place in the history of antiquity, all the columns of the French division resounded with applause. The soldiers spontaneously lined themselves up in their ranks and presented arms to the sound of the drums and the playing of the military bands."[14] Denon was filled with patriotic pride at this demonstration: "The feelings which I experienced in the presence of such great monuments, and the electrifying sight of an army of soldiers of such civilized sensibility, made me overjoyed to be their companion, and rejoice in being French."[15] On the foreshore, ancient temples and colossal human figures rose amongst the stones, whilst across the river in the sunlight stood the magnificent temples of Karnak and Luxor, with two obelisks standing over seventy feet high, covered in hieroglyphics. It was sights such as these which led Denon to conclude, in awe: "The Greeks invented nothing."[16]

Besides recording these sights with pencil and sketchpad, Denon was also beginning to speculate about their significance. He became intrigued by the lines of hieroglyphs which adorned so many of the temples. The French officers had asked Moallam Jacob if he knew how to decipher them, but he was forced to plead ignorance: they bore no relation to any Coptic or Arabic script that he knew. Some of the more knowledgeable officers thought they bore a resemblance to Oriental pictograms, and speculated that the hieroglyphs might be an early form of Chinese. But in reality, the meaning of the language

---

* This latter sighting is usually dismissed as fantasy or exaggeration. However, recent sightings (and film evidence) of a giant crocodile of even larger proportions on the upper reaches of the Nile suggest that there may well have been some truth in what these French officers claimed to have seen.

of the hieroglyphs had by now been lost, forgotten for over one and a half millennia. During the centuries after the time of the pharaohs, several cults in Egypt had continued to worship the ancient gods in temples whose walls were covered in hieroglyphs. But in the fourth century AD the fanatical Christians of Alexandria had sacked most of these, and in 391 the Roman emperor Theodosius I decreed that all pagan temples should be closed. By now only a few temples dedicated to the ancient gods remained, but the closing of these meant that those who had been able to read the hieroglyphs no longer passed on their knowledge. Within just a few years a tradition that had lasted for over 3,000 years suddenly vanished into oblivion.

After sketching the temples at Thebes, Denon joined Desaix and they rode off to explore the hinterland, eventually coming to "the city of the dead," the Necropolis, where large galleries of ancient tombs were carved deep into the face of the rock: "I entered these on horseback with Desaix, believing that these dark recesses could only be a sanctuary of peace and silence; but scarcely had we entered into the shadow of the galleries than we were assailed with javelins and stones by an unseen enemy."[17] Denon and Desaix beat a hasty retreat: the tombs were the home of savage troglodytes who lived a fugitive existence beyond the law. Next morning, before they set off on their march once more, Denon found time to sketch the scattered stones of a large fallen statue, which he thought might have been Ozymandias—the ancient Greek name for Rameses II.

Despite being in charge of a full-scale military campaign, Desaix took a surprisingly deep interest in the ancient ruins along their way. In his report to Napoleon, written on the very day he arrived at Thebes, he described the site: "There are two obelisks, of incomparable size and workmanship. . . . Transported to Paris, they would cause a sensation!"*[18] The soldiers too took an interest in these ruins, and some carved their names into the walls of the temples. They were not the first to attempt this method of recording their passing presence, and were in fact inspired by the example of soldiers who had preceded them into this region some 1,500 years previously. As a result, one can now read on these temples

---

* Desaix would never live to see his suggestion realized, but twenty years later the viceroy of Egypt Mohammed Ali would give one of these obelisks to France, and it would later be erected in Paris at the center of the Place de la Concorde.

beside the Nile the names of French soldiers such as "A. Jacquet," "Louis Luneau" and "Louis Guibourg" carved alongside "Julius Tenax," "Valerius Priscus" and "'Quintus Viator," men of the Roman legion that penetrated into Upper Egypt in the first century AD.

Yet most of the French soldiers found better things to occupy their time during their all too brief halts. To begin with, only a few would venture into the Nile to bathe themselves and wash out their sweat-encrusted uniforms. But when it was realized that the crocodiles were not so fearsome as they appeared—as long as they were not disturbed or approached too closely—many of the men took advantage of the cool waters of the river after their long marches, which often covered as much as thirty-five miles in a day. Meanwhile others would go scavenging for wood and brush for fires to warm themselves against the chill of the night and to cook whatever food was available. In the manner of the times, Desaix's division lived off the land through which it passed, purchasing or simply requisitioning supplies at local markets and in the villages. The local population soon learned to flee, taking their livestock with them. Regiments would often march with strings of cattle and goats bringing up their rear, but with over 3,000 mouths to feed each day, provisions were frequently in short supply. As a result, the men sometimes went without food after a hard day's march, and were occasionally left starving. They would then take matters into their own hands, as in this harrowing scene described by Denon:

A soldier emerged from a hovel, leading after him a goat which he had taken; he was followed by an old man clutching two infants at his chest. He placed them on the ground, fell to his knees, and without uttering a word he revealed by his torrent of tears that the children were going to die if the goat was taken away from them. But blind and pressing need was not stopped by this heart-rending scene and the goat already had its throat slit.[19]

Others, however, showed mercy. Denon recorded how at the very same moment, another soldier came on the scene

carrying in his arms another child that a mother, in flight before us, had obviously abandoned in the desert. In spite of the weight with which he was loaded down, his rucksack, his rifle, his ammunition belt, and the exhaustion of four days' forced march, the need to save this unfortunate little creature had made him carefully pick it up and carry it for six miles in his arms. . . . While I had been horrified to see hunger reduce a fellow human being to the savagery of a wild beast, this other soldier soothed my distress, returning me to humanity.

By now Denon had begun to suffer from ophthalmia, his eyes stinging, oozing tears of pus. Yet unlike many of his fellow sufferers, he appears to have retained a certain clarity of vision, if his sketches are anything to judge by—though later travelers would point out that they contained a number of mistakes, particularly in his recording of hieroglyphics. Most have put this down to the speed at which he was forced to work, as well as the occasional cavalier disregard for detail, but if he was suffering from ophthalmia this may well account for some of his lapses.

Meanwhile Desaix's division continued on its rapid march south to the far limits of Egyptian territory, quickly making ground on Murad Bey. At Esna, Desaix discovered that Murad Bey had only left the previous night, and twenty miles upriver at Edfu, the French even caught sight of 200 Mamelukes and their baggage train disappearing into the hinterland across on the eastern shore of the Nile.

But beyond Edfu, conditions deteriorated as Desaix embarked upon a rapid march inland in a desperate attempt to cut off Murad Bey's retreat. Denon described how "on the 30th we departed at dawn. After marching for an hour through cultivated land we entered mountains composed of crumbling slate, sandstone, white and rose-colored quartz, brown pebbles and a few pieces of white coral. After five hours of marching through the desert, their boots torn to pieces, the soldiers wrapped around their feet whatever cloth they had; they were devoured by raging thirst."[20] Eventually Desaix was forced to return to the Nile, where they arrived at Taudi to find that "the Mamelukes had just abandoned the village, leaving their plates, dishes, even the soup they had prepared, which they were going to eat as soon as the sun had set, for this was the month of Ramadan, during which . . . even soldiers do not eat while the sun is above the horizon."

By this stage the plentiful verdant regions were behind them, and even the riverbanks themselves were becoming increasingly arid, with only the occasional wretched village containing a few dilapidated mud huts, some empty earthenware storage pots and a few chickens. This region had an entirely new feel to it, as Denon noticed:

The families of Arab-cultivators on the border of the desert . . . present an image of that tranquil monotony which is never disturbed by the shock of a single novelty, of that calm which leaves a length of time between each event of life, of that quiet, where every thing succeeds peaceably in the soul, where little by little an emotion becomes a sentiment, or a habitude of principle, where, in a word, the lightest impression is analyzed; and this to the degree, that, in conversing with this description of men one is altogether astonished to find in them the most nicest distinction [sic], and the most delicate sentiment, by the side of the most absolute ignorance.[21]

The French trudged forward beneath the relentless sun, their columns now accompanied by flocks of vultures which wheeled in the cloudless blue sky overhead. As they marched across the sandy valleys, almost the only signs of life on the ground were the occasional tracks of gazelles, which fed on what little vegetation there was by the river, and then hid in the vast silence of the desert. But as Denon grimly observed: "The tracks of these elegant and frail creatures were almost always followed by the footsteps of a beast of prey."[22]

As the French doggedly pressed on over the last stages of their march to the borders of Egypt, a number now began succumbing to the hideous heat: "It boiled our blood. . . . Nothing is as frightful as this death: the victim is suddenly surprised with a disorder of his heart and no assistance can save him from the faintings that succeed."[23] Finally, on February 1 they crossed to the eastern bank of the Nile to reach Aswan (ancient Syene), having covered over 250 miles of the most inhospitable terrain in just ten days. They were now almost 600 miles from Cairo, at the cataracts that marked the southern edge of Egypt. General Belliard stood high on the hillside above the river, watching his troops embarking:

Above the camp, on the promontory of the western mountains, is a view, from which one can see to the west an immense desert, and to the east the awe-inspiring spectacle of the steeply sloping rocks over which spill the waters of the Nile. They seem to indicate that here are the limits of the civilized world. Nature seems to be telling one: Stop, go no further. To the west is Elephantine Island, contrasting its greenery and clumps of palm trees against the arid mountains which surround it; to the east are the ruins of ancient Syene.[24]

Desvernois paints an equally vivid picture: "The famous cataracts of the Nile are simply whirlpools formed by the waters of the Nile flowing over rocks and producing a number of powerful small cascades scarcely a few inches high; this occurs when the course of the Nile is contained between the barren rocks of the rising mountains."[25] Only the pernickety Savary proved less impressed, finding Aswan "no more than a collection of little mud-brick houses . . . surrounded by sand . . . which would not exist if it had not been a halting post for the caravans passing up the Nile into Egypt and a military outpost of the Roman Empire."[26] And this was not all: "One of the inconveniences of such regions is that of being devoured by vermin, which even the greatest attention to personal hygiene does not always get rid of. We had been told that in the tropics they perished in the excessive heat; but this was just a fairy tale—here they multiplied to an intolerable degree, but the army just had to put up with this latest pestilence."

Below the cataracts the French discovered fifty river craft laden with baggage which the Mamelukes had abandoned. They had fled Aswan two days before Desaix's arrival and crossed into Sudan, dispersing into the Nubian desert. The French now set about establishing themselves in Aswan, where the inhabitants were largely Nubians, black Africans rather than lighter-skinned Egyptians. The new conquerors made themselves at home in this outpost in characteristic fashion. "An inscription of the French tricouleur was carved into the granite on the highest rock above the Cataracts and saluted by several rounds of musket-fire, marking our taking posssession of all of Upper Egypt, and its furthest point, where like the Romans the French had carried their arms to victory."[27] As ever, the soldiers were quick to follow suit, adding such inscriptions as: "Dupraville chaceur [sic] de la 21 [i.e. 21st Demibrigade, Belliard's command] 1799"; "J. N. Cuvillies. Chasseurs 21. Victory or Death."[28] Unfortunately, in this case it must have been the latter, for sometime afterward his colleagues carved a black cross beside his inscription.

Denon records his relief over his arrival at Aswan: "To undress, to sit down, to lie down and go to sleep seemed to me a truly voluptuous ease."[29] He was not alone in feeling this way, and making himself at home:

The soldiers were the same. Within two days of our arrival there had already sprouted up in the streets tailors' shops, boot-menders, trinket-stalls, French barbers with their signs, food stalls and restaurants with fixed-price menus . . . what particularly characterizes a French army is its ability to cater at the same time, and with the same care, for both the superfluous and the necessary; there were gardens set up, as well as cafés, and public gaming tables using cards the soldiers had made themselves in Aswan. The road north out of the village was a tree-lined avenue, and here the soldiers placed a military column inscribed: "Road to Paris No. 1,167,340." All this, just a few days after their daily rations had been down to only a few dates . . . Death alone can put an end to such bravado and gaiety; even the greatest unhappiness can never extinguish it.

French spies soon established that the Mamelukes were starving and had taken to marauding, preying on the few Sudanese villages they came across. It was only a matter of time before they would return to Egypt once more. In order to secure the southern border against Mameluke raids, Belliard led an expedition upriver to occupy the strategic island of Philae. As this was known to contain many ruins, including the spectacular Temple of Isis, Denon decided to join the expedition.* But this was to be no mere sightseeing tour, as the inhabitants of the island were known for their ferocity, having even resisted the Mamelukes. While the French craft approached, the islanders put up an intimidating display, the women screeeching and throwing dust into the air in their ritual battle chant. But they were not prepared for modern fighting tactics. When the first French soldiers landed, under cover of cannon fire, the islanders were terrified, as Denon recorded:

Men, women and children all threw themselves into the river to save themselves by swimming; in keeping with the ferocity of their character, we saw the mothers drowning the children they could not carry with them, and they mutilated the girls to preserve them from the ravaging of their conquerors. When I set foot on the island next day I found a little girl of seven or eight who had been brutally and cruelly sewn up in such a way as to prevent her even from relieving herself, which state had now reduced her to terrible convulsions. Only by making a counter-operation and giving her a bath did I manage to save the life of this unfortunate little creature, who was extremely beautiful. Other girls, of a more advanced age, showed a less puritan outlook and chose for themselves amongst their conquerors.[30]

This was the furthest south the French progressed, and they would leave behind them a large inscription carved into the grand gate of the

---

* The original island of Philae has now sunk beneath the waters of Lake Nasser, which was created by the construction of the New High Aswan Dam in 1970. The Temple of Isis was relocated and rebuilt on the nearby island of Aglika as part of the UNESCO project to preserve the ruins.

Temple of Isis, commemorating the arrival in Egypt of the French army under Bonaparte, and going on to describe how "Desaix, commander of the First Division, pursued [the Mamelukes] beyond the Cataracts where he arrived on 13th Ventôse Year 7, 3rd March 1799 AD, inscribed here by Castex, sculptor."*³¹

Desaix had left Aswan soon after his arrival, instructing Belliard to install himself and prevent any Mameluke incursions as best he could. Meanwhile Desaix set about securing the northern regions of Upper Egypt. This proved to be no mean task, as the Mamelukes soon began skirting around Belliard at Aswan, and launching raids north into the Nile valley. But Desaix was determined to establish order, and to this end he placed small garrisons in towns and villages at fifty-mile intervals along the Nile. This was intended to protect his supply lines, as well as to reassure the locals that they had no need to fear any reprisals from the Mamelukes, for the French were here to stay. But it did not have the desired effect, as the Mamelukes continued carrying out raids, and on more than one occasion actually wiped out an entire French garrison. They were still receiving support from the "Meccans," who continued to cross the Red Sea, arriving at Kosseir in their thousands and making their way across the eastern desert to join up with the Mameluke beys. Every time Desaix caught up with the reinforced Mameluke brigades, he continued to defeat them, inflicting heavy losses. Yet as he wrote to Napoleon: "I report to you, *mon général*, that the Mamelukes are beaten, but they are not defeated. They are like the mythical Hydra of ancient Greece, no sooner have you cut off one head than another one appears."³² But Desaix was a masterful commander, and he continued to pursue the Mamelukes wherever they went, constantly dogging them until they were worn out. He knew that he could rely on his troops: they respected him, but they also knew that there was good bounty to be had from the fallen Mamelukes, who continued to carry their treasure with them in the form of bracelets, pouches of gold coins and jewels. Like Napoleon, Desaix was a general who inspired his men, who were proud to follow him and proud of their unit—a

---

* This inscription can still be seen. However, the date is wrong, presumably because the artist-savant Castex was only commissioned to chisel his inscription some months later, by which time the actual date of the timeless event seems to have been forgotten.

loyalty that is reflected in their graffiti. Alongside their name some men would add the date, others the name of their home town in France, but by far the majority proudly added the name of their fighting unit: "le 21ᵐᵉ," "21," "Chasseur 21," etc.

Eventually Desaix and Belliard managed to drive the Mamelukes from the Nile valley in a pincer movement, inflicting heavy losses. While Desaix made sure there were no further incursions, Belliard led an expedition across the eastern desert to the Red Sea port of Kosseir, which he occupied without opposition, thus cutting off the Mamelukes' last hope of reinforcements from Arabia. Desaix's victory is generally recognized as one of the most brilliantly conducted military campaigns of its time, his generalship second only to that of his young commander-in-chief. With Upper Egypt now secured, the French became the rulers of all Egypt.

Desaix now set about establishing a permanent administration with the aim of winning over the people. Here "The Just Sultan" came into his own: trade along the Nile was re-established; the caravans to Cairo from Nubia and beyond were able to proceed unmolested; and with the aid of Moallam Jacob, the *miry* was soon being collected with the minimum of fuss. Even Nicolas Turc was full of praise: "General Desaix devoted himself to the pacification and organization of Upper Egypt with an intelligence, administrative good sense, tact, courage, zeal and magnanimity that were admirable—so much so that Upper Egypt was better governed than the Delta."[33]

Yet Desaix was no selfless administrator, and "The Just Sultan" proved as much of a sultan as he was just, as can be seen from this revealing letter he wrote to a woman friend back in France:

Let me tell you a word about my love life. I have loved the young Astiza, a nice Georgian girl, beautiful as Venus, blonde and sweet. She is fourteen years old, with two rosy budding breasts; she belonged to me by right of succession as governor of the city; her master was dead . . . I received as a present Sarah, a bright little scamp of an Abyssinian, aged fifteen. She was my traveling companion. I also had Mara, a naïve child from Tigray [northern Abyssinia]. As well as her I had Fatma [*sic*], large, beautiful, fine figure, who was very unhappy.[34]

He explains that she was unable "to share in my pleasures, my joys, my sensual delights" because in childhood she had undergone female circumcision. "Such is my harem," he wrote, "which also includes three black women ... a little black boy called Baquil, a little Mameluke boy called Ismaël, beautiful as an angel." He paints a vivid picture of himself at ease within his harem, "with myself reclining languidly on two cushions, attended by several of my wives, one now falling voluptuously asleep whilst tenderly rubbing my feet, another now undressing me, looking after me with a lightness of touch and care which is unknown in Europe." Even Desaix's biographer Armand Sauzet later felt the need to omit certain passages from this letter, suggesting that Desaix "was no doubt exaggerating ... because he wished to appear as a 'womanizer.' "³⁵ Sauzet goes on to make the interesting claim that by this stage in his career Desaix "had reached the pinnacle of his intellectual qualities and moral virtues."

The artist-savant Denon would reap considerable benefit from Desaix's lauded "intellectual qualities" during this period, to the extent that Denon's work in Upper Egypt gives him a strong claim to be the father of Egyptology. Desaix encouraged Denon to accompany him on his sorties up and down the Nile valley in pursuit of the Mamelukes, thus giving Denon an opportunity to sketch many of the sights he had been forced to rush past on his initial journey south. It was on one of these sorties that he stumbled upon the Valley of the Kings, which contained the hidden tombs of the New Kingdom pharaohs, adorned with many fabulous examples of ancient Egyptian art.

Despite the spectacular nature of Denon's discoveries, he was in fact not fully aware of the significance of what he saw. At this stage, ancient Egyptian history still remained lost in the mists of time. Even so, his arrival in Cairo with his portfolios full of sketches would mark the beginning of a new interest in ancient Egyptian history, as well as curiosity about the meaning of the strange hieroglyphs that adorned the walls of so many temples. There was a gradual realization that ancient Greece, and the founding of Western civilization, had been preceded by a vast history of what had become a lost civilization: the self-understanding of European culture was about to undergo a dramatic transformation. A good example was the zodiacal disc in the roof of the temple at Dendara, which Denon had sketched with great accuracy. When his drawing was later studied in detail, it became clear that the position of the constellations in the heavens which were depicted on this disc could only have been seen at a date which was much, much earlier than the date previously accepted for the origin of the world. The Dendara Zodiac was estimated to be 15,000 years old, whereas according to the Bible the world had only been created around 6,000 years previously. Desaix's expedition into Upper Egypt, though hardly a campaign of great historical significance, would in fact transform our understanding of human history.*

---

* Later, in the nineteenth century, the Dendara Zodiac would be the center of a great controversy between Egyptologists and the Church, which contested its estimated age. Ironically, in this instance the Church would eventually be proved right: the Dendara Zodiac did in fact date from the Greco-Roman era, but by then the biblical date for the origin of the world had been disproved by many of the Egyptologists' other findings.

XX

A Turn for the Worse

BACK in Cairo, the atmosphere of enforced calm established after the uprising showed no sign of being broken, and the French occupation continued as before into the New Year of 1799. A team of savants and engineers had completed a map of the city, and were now collating one of the whole of Lower Egypt, making use of local sketches and theodolite readings sent in by members of the engineering corps from the various garrisons along the coast and in the delta. Meanwhile *Le Courier* continued to regale its readers with its regular ration of gossip, propaganda and the private habits of Egyptian women, while every ten days *La Décade* would report on the meetings of the Institute, which were invariably attended by Napoleon himself. Papers presented at these meetings ran the entire gamut from the ingenious to the opaque. Costaz analyzed the composition of sand in the desert and identified "that alkaline substance which makes it scrunch underfoot like snow,"[1] while Fourier, who despite his onerous administrative duties still managed to continue doing original mathematics, described his early tentative work on algebraic series in a lecture that was comprehensible to himself alone.*

Of more general interest was General Andréossy's report on the expedition he had undertaken for the Institute, accompanied by the chemist Berthollet, to explore the Natron Lakes in the desert some fifty miles northwest of Cairo. The chemical crust formed around these lake-beds was composed of natron, a form of sodium carbonate crystals, which

---

* This would result in the Fourier series, as it came to be known: an infinite trigonometric series now important in harmonic analysis. In practical terms, it is used to measure the transference of heat between solid objects.

had been used in ancient times to embalm the dead. Andréossy and his expedition discovered that natron was still being collected from the lakes. "The men enter the water naked, breaking and digging up the natron with a piece of metal weighing around sixty pounds [*sic*], which ends in a sharp point . . . it is a strange sight to see these black or tanned Egyptians emerge white from the salt water."² In the basin of the lakes they came across the remains of trees long since crystallized by the natron, "and we found the vertebrae of a large fish which appeared transformed into mineral."

Berthollet observed how the natron salt (sesquicarbonate of soda) was formed by the combined action of the sun and the pressure caused by the weight of the crust, and this led him to an important insight into chemical processes. As a result, he would later propose the first modern theory to account for how chemicals reacted with one another, which took into account how pressure and heat could affect reactions. This, together with Fourier's work on his algebraic series, would be the major theoretical scientific advance to arise out of Napoleon's Egyptian expedition, the main practical advances being the foundation of modern Egyptology and the preliminary surveying of the Suez Canal. During the short period since its inception, the Institute had already established itself on a par with the finest similar institutions in the capitals of Europe.

Andréossy's report on his expedition to the lakes would also include a description of the nearby Coptic monasteries. The Copts were originally the early Christians of Egypt, who had been called by the Greek Christians "Aiguptoi" (i.e., Egyptians), of which the name Copt was a corruption. The Coptic monasteries of the Western Desert housed an ascetic community dating back to St. Anthony in the fourth century, though by the end of the eighteenth century these communities had become a shadow of their former selves, with the monks having lapsed into a life of sloth and grubbiness, utterly dependent on the work carried out by their serfs. As a result of the Institute, the history of Egypt was being opened up on all fronts, with many forgotten elements of the Western tradition, and its pre-history, coming to light for the first time.

But there were setbacks too. Egypt had long suffered from regular outbreaks of bubonic plague, although in a far less virulent form than the great plague epidemics which had swept Europe. Even so, the Egyptian version was highly contagious and largely fatal, causing considerable concern to the physician-in-chief General Desgenettes and his surgeon-in-chief General Larrey. In an attempt to regulate the spread of the disease, quarantine stations were set up at the Mediterranean ports, as well as at Cairo. All cases amongst the Egyptian population now had to be reported to the French medical authorities at once, on pain of serious punishment.

The plague appeared to strike on a seasonal basis, usually appearing at the onset of winter, and despite all the French army's precautions the last month of 1798 saw the usual outbreak in Alexandria, with another minor outbreak at Damietta. Inevitably, it was not long before the contagion spread to the French garrisons in these cities. It was not yet known that bubonic plague was spread by fleas from infected rats, but in the opinion of Desgenettes and his colleagues lack of contact with the diseased, as well as increased hygiene, were probably the best preventative measures. Napoleon sent orders to General Marchmont in Alexandria:

Put the battalion of the 85th out on the coast at Marabout, you can easily provision them by sea. . . . As for the unfortunate half-brigade of Light Infantry, make them strip off until they are completely naked, then make them take a good bath in the sea, so that they can rub themselves down from head to foot, and make them thoroughly wash out their uniforms. And watch out that they keep themselves clean. They are to have no more parades, no more mounting guard outside the camp. Make them dig a large ditch filled with quicklime where they can throw in the dead.[3]

Despite such preventative measures Private Millet, who was based at Damietta, caught the disease. He described its effect in his memoirs: "This sickness begins with a hot fever, and is followed by a severe headache accompanied by a bubo or gland, the size of an egg, which appears in the groin or another joint in one of the limbs. When that breaks out, the patient is as good as lost to the land of the living. If he lasts four days, there's real hope for him, but that rarely happens."[4]

Millet's son remembered the tale his father had told him about falling ill with the plague in Egypt: "The doctors discussed in his presence whether it was worth piercing his bubo before it suppurated; but believing my father was a fatal case they decided not to attempt this operation on him. When they had gone, Millet took out his pocket knife and used it to make the incision on himself which the doctors had not dared to make."[5] As a result, he survived to tell the tale.

Others were not so lucky. By early February 1799 some 200 French soldiers had died of the plague. Not unnaturally, an atmosphere of fear prevailed in the wards, amongst medical staff as well as patients. When some staff began refusing to treat plague patients, Napoleon issued an order that all personnel who avoided treating soldiers suffering from "contagious illness" were to be arrested, brought before a military tribunal, and dealt with under the articles concerning those who had fled in the face of the enemy. Indicatively, he refers only to "contagious illness": owing to the fear induced by the very mention of bubonic plague, this term was strictly avoided in all bulletins. Word was put out that this was not the plague, only a lesser fever which produced similar buboes. When a surgeon called Boyer refused to treat such patients, Napoleon was furious and decided to make an example of him, issuing the following order on January 8, 1799:

Citizen Boyer, surgeon attached to the hospital at Alexandria, has been so cowardly as to refuse to treat the wounded who have been in contact with sick people supposed to have caught a contagious disease. He is unworthy of being a French citizen. He will be dressed in women's clothing and paraded through the streets of Alexandria on a donkey, with a placard hung around his neck proclaiming "Unworthy to be a French citizen, he is afraid to die." After that he will be kept in prison and sent back to France on the first boat.[6]

In the event, Boyer proved innocent of this dereliction of duty. Nonetheless news spread of his intended punishment, which at least one woman recognized as nothing less than an insult to womanhood. Desgenettes recalled in his memoirs how Madame Tempié, the twenty-seven-year-old wife of a frigate captain,* "a woman of some beauty, stylish dress and forceful character, took great offense at the petticoats Boyer had been sentenced to wear as a sign of cowardice, and passion-ately declared that she would fight against Napoleon in a duel, if he would allow it, and that she would show him, pistol in hand, that she was not afraid, even of him."[7] Napoleon chose to ignore this challenge. His limited leisure time was already devoted to the passionate atten-tions of another woman—his new mistress, Pauline Fourès.

Although by early 1799 Napoleon's rule extended over most of Egypt, the external situation remained far from clear. Even after reading the

---

* This was the same Madame Tempié who had spiritedly proclaimed her honor to be "copper-bottomed." See page 257.

sultan's *firman*, which had played such a significant part in the Cairo uprising, Napoleon had clung to the belief that war against the Porte was not inevitable; he even felt that the threat closer at hand from Djezzar in Acre could still be avoided. Although he knew that Djezzar was harboring Ibrahim Bey, and he had received credible intelligence reports that he was assembling an army of 60,000 men, Napoleon had still been willing to write to him, "I do not wish to make war with you if you are not my enemy, but it is time that you explained yourself."[8] He had felt instinctively that it was Djezzar who was the aggressor, not the Porte, an opinion that had been confirmed when news reached him that Djezzar had simply beheaded the most recent French messenger. Djezzar was evidently a loose cannon, with no knowledge of diplomacy as it was practiced by a civilized government such as the Porte. (Napoleon had been unaware that the French representative in Constantinople had been flung into the dungeons.) Even when Napoleon had learned that Britain and Russia had signed a treaty with the Porte, forming an alliance against France, he had not seen this as final. Beauchamp had been dispatched to Constantinople with an appeasing note, whilst Napoleon had placed his faith in Talleyrand already being there, and rescuing the situation. But since then a decisive incident had taken place. Napoleon recalled in his memoirs how in January 1799, whilst on his way back from his brief expedition to Suez:

at four in the afternoon [Napoleon and his armed escort] reached the wells of Saba-Byat in the middle of the desert. The heat was extreme, there was hardly any water at the wells and what little there was tasted brackish. Whilst sharing out this foul water amongst themselves, they noticed a warrior approaching on a camel; only when he came closer did he notice the French troops at the well, and tried to make off, but too late. He was found to be a messenger taking dispatches from Ibrahim Bey and Djezzar to the Mamelukes in Upper Egypt. He brought news that hostilities had begun on the Syrian frontier and that the army of Djezzar had entered Egyptian territory, that his advance guard had already occupied the oasis of El Arish and that they were reinforcing the fort.[9]

Napoleon knew that he now had no alternative but to confront Djezzar's forces. On his way back to Cairo he reached his decision: instead of resisting Djezzar's intrusions into Egypt, he would mount a full-scale campaign into Syria which would eliminate him once and for all.

Even before setting out for Suez, Napoleon had taken the precaution of securing Egypt's northeastern border by dispatching General Lagrange to establish a strong frontier post at Katia (Qatiya), on the coastal caravan route from Syria. This was sixty miles from the distant outpost of El-Arish, which was itself some thirty miles from what was generally regarded as the desert border with Syria.

On January 17 Lagrange had reported that Katia was fully fortified, and Napoleon decided that this should be the rendezvous for all the units being assembled for his "Syrian campaign." A measure of the scale and seriousness of this campaign can be judged from the sheer size of this force, which seems to have consisted of more than half the active units he had in Lower Egypt, leaving less than 10,000 men to guard Cairo, Alexandria and the entire delta region. Napoleon's force for his Syrian campaign consisted of four infantry divisions, comprising in all nearly 10,000 men, commanded by the finest field generals remaining at his disposal, namely Kléber, Bon, Lannes and Reynier. Accompanying these were another 3,000 soldiers, including 1,400 artillery, 800 cavalry, and almost 100 men of the newly formed camel corps, the celebrated "*régiment des dromadaires.*"

Camels were also to be used for the transporting of supplies across the difficult terrain, but it was soon realized that the heavy siege artillery which would be needed for breaking down the walls of Acre, Djezzar's stronghold some hundred miles up the coast to the north, could not be transported across such terrain. Instead this was loaded onto a flotilla at Damietta, whence it would be shipped up the coast as required.

In the midst of these preparations, Napoleon received some important news. As he noted on February 5, "A trading ship out of Ragusa [Dubrovnik] carrying a cargo of wine has arrived at Alexandria bringing letters for me from Genoa and Ancona; this is the first news to arrive here from Europe for eight months."[10] In a dispatch to Kléber, he outlined the contents of these letters. First, just two courier ships from Egypt had managed to get through to France carrying news of the Egyptian expedition, "*La Marguerite*, sent after the taking of Alexandria, and *La Petite-Cesalpine*, sent from Rosetta a month after the naval battle at Aboukir." Concerning France's relations with Turkey, "Descorches [the new French ambassador] is on his way to Constantinople. [Meanwhile] at the beginning of November the Turkish ambassador in France was going about his business as usual." With regard to the British naval blockade: the allied Spanish fleet of twenty-one ships which might have been able to relieve the blockade was itself under blockade by a British squadron in its home port. As for the situation in France: "Measures have been taken to recruit for the army: it appears that all young men of eighteen are being requisitioned into the forces as conscripts. Internal affairs remain in absolutely the same state as when we departed. . . . [At the same time] the European nations are arming on all sides; yet at the moment they are doing no more than watch each other."

However, the Ragusan ship had also been carrying a French merchant called Hamelin, who was immediately sent to Cairo, where Napoleon questioned him closely. It quickly became apparent that the comparatively reassuring picture Napoleon had received in his dispatches from France was now out of date. The situation had taken a serious turn: war had broken out in Italy, and the Neapolitans had taken Rome from the French; the Porte had formally declared war on France, and formed an alliance with Russia; and an outbreak of hostilities across Europe appeared likely in the near future, with the probability that a powerful alliance would line up against France.

Napoleon could no longer pretend, even to himself, that the Porte could be won over to the French cause. In fact, he had already been made aware of some measures they had taken: as early as mid-November it had been intimated to Lieutenant Guibert at his meeting off Alexandria with the aged Turkish naval commander Hassan Bey that the Turks were assembling a fleet at Rhodes, while news reaching Cairo from Djezzar had suggested that forces were gathering in Syria prior to an invasion. These could no longer be regarded as separate and uncertain pieces of intelligence: Ottoman forces appeared to be planning a two-pronged attack.

What exactly Napoleon made of this latest news from Hamelin is uncertain. The indications are highly contradictory, yet these conflicts seem to have echoed those taking place in Napoleon's mind. According to his secretary Bourrienne, "The day before he left [on the Syrian campaign] he said that if in the course of March he received positive news of France being at war with a European coalition, he would return."[11] On the other hand, this news of international events seems to have woken Napoleon's latent megalomania. In his memoirs he described his aims for the campaign, and it is worth quoting from these truly astonishing plans at some length:

Napoleon resolved to take the offensive, to lead his forces across the desert, to defeat the army of Syria . . . to seize all the stores and all necessary equipment from El Arish, Gaza, Jaffa and Acre, to arm the Christians of Syria, to recruit the Druze and the Maronite Christians of Lebanon,* and then to take stock of the situation. He hoped that on hearing the news that Acre had fallen to the French, the Mamelukes and the Egyptian Arabs . . . would join forces with him; that by June he would be master of Damascus and Aleppo, and that his advanced guard would be at Mount Taurus [i.e., having penetrated well into southeastern Turkey]. By now he would have under his immediate command 26,000 French, 6,000 Mamelukes and Arab cavalry from Egypt, 18,000 Druze, Maronites and other Syrian troops; that Desaix would be in Egypt ready to reinforce him, leading 20,000 men, of whom 10,000 would be French and 10,000 recruited black slaves under French officers and NCOs. In this situation Napoleon would be in a position to dictate to the Porte, to force them to make peace, and oblige them to consent to his march on India. If fortune favored these projects, he could still arrive at the Indus by March 1800 with more than 40,000 men.[12]

Napoleon was convinced that all this could take place "regardless of the loss of his fleet," for it was to be an overland expedition in the footsteps of Alexander the Great; indeed, preparations for this "march on India" had already been set in motion. According to Napoleon, "He had intelligence from Persia, and was assured that the Shah would not oppose the passage of the French army through Basra, Shiraz and Mekran."†[13]

All this may appear to be little more than the grandiloquent dream of hindsight, but as we have seen (and shall see), there is a wealth of evidence to support the fact that Napoleon believed he could actually achieve this. Several of his generals mention in their memoirs his preparations for an invasion of India, echoing the figures and dates that appear above, and Bourrienne, although admittedly not always reliable, appears to confirm these preparations with his claim that even "before taking the decision to attack the avant-garde of the Turks in

---

* The Druze were members of a religious sect who took their teachings from their "Sacred Book"; its 200,000 or so members were scattered throughout what was then southwestern Syria, and although their faith bore strong resemblances to Islam, it was regarded as heretical by Muslims. The Maronites were Christians living in what is now Lebanon.

† The desert region bordering the Indian Ocean which straddles the southeast of modern-day Iran and southwestern Pakistan.

the valleys of Syria, he knew for a fact . . . through agents sent to the spot that the Shah of Persia would consent, in return for a payment made in advance, to let him establish at designated locations military depots of supplies and equipment."[14]

It now becomes clear why Napoleon was leaving behind so few forces to defend Egypt: he was gambling his all on this "Syrian campaign." Indeed, he was arguably playing for bigger stakes than he would ever play for in his entire life. All this would account for why he also brought with him so many members of the Institute, as well as a large number of lesser savants. These included the inevitable Monge and Berthollet (who would again be allowed to travel by carriage), along with mathematicians, physicists, biologists and Orientalists—so many, in fact, that a notice appeared in La Décade to the effect that for the time being there would be no further meetings of the Institute. Several of the savants were to undertake important tasks. The geographer Jacotin was to go to work "surveying on foot and by compass the distance covered on each day's march and the positions of the army's pitched camps, and in this way putting together a map of the invaded territory";[15] while the naturalist Savigny would be "employing his time collecting any insects he found in the desert." The indefatigable Geoffroy Saint-Hilaire, who had already completed his survey of the fauna of the delta, would seek to trap any lizards, snakes and quadrupeds he came across, and bring them back for the Institute's menagerie.

In this too, Napoleon's Syrian expedition would be following the example of Alexander the Great, who sent back to Aristotle in Greece examples of flora and fauna which his expedition found on the way to India. The main difference here was that Napoleon took his savants with him; besides describing and collecting what they found, they would also be purveyors of French culture, of European science and knowledge, as well as being founder members of further Institutes to be established in the Orient.

Other indications that the Syrian expedition was intended as the first step in a much grander project can be seen in the fact that Napoleon insisted upon bringing along a number of Egyptian notables. These included the Turkish official he had nominated as Emir el-Hadj in place of Murad Bey, as well as the cadi, the high judge of Cairo, and fifteen sheiks, "each of whom brought along three tents which were fitted out with every Asiatic luxury."[16] These notables were intended to show that Napoleon had the support of the Egyptian people, and was also a friend of Islam. They would prove useful as ambassadors, and might be helpful in any negotiations with Arabic or Islamic leaders. More important, they could be instrumental in the establishing of a French regime that took account of the religious susceptibilities of the local inhabitants, much as Napoleon liked to think he had done in Egypt. El-Djabarti too noticed that Napoleon's expedition seemed to be taking along more than was required for a simple punitive campaign against Djezzar. "The soldiers took with them a great deal of luggage, including beds, mattresses, carpets, as well as large tents for their wives and the White, Black and Abyssinian slaves they had taken from the mansions of the Mamelukes. All these women had adopted French costume."[17] Officers were evidently permitted to bring along their wives, or such mistresses as they had acquired in Egypt. There was however one notable exception: Pauline Fourès was left behind in her pavilion in the grounds of Elfi Bey's palace. Napoleon seemingly wished for no distraction whilst he set about fulfilling his great ambition. Far from being just a simple campaign, this looked much more like an entire expedition in itself.

XXI

The Syrian Campaign

LEAVING General Dugua in charge, Napoleon set off from Cairo with the divisions commanded by Bon and Lannes on February 10, 1799, intending to catch up with the divisions of Reynier and Kléber, which were already setting off from Katia for El-Arish. Kléber, once again in charge of a field division, was back to his formidable ebullient self, an indication of which can be judged from Nicholas Turc's description of him as "a man of high stature, an imposing presence and a voice of thunder."[1]

In Napoleon's latest report to the Directory, dictated to Bourrienne just an hour before he set off, he confidently predicted, "By the time you read this letter, it is possible I will be standing at the ruins of Solomon's Temple [i.e., in Jerusalem]"; but to begin with, he told them, "we must spend nine days crossing the desert devoid of water or vegetation."[2] Yet despite his divisions being accompanied by no fewer than 3,000 package camels and 3,000 laden mules, the expedition seems to have started out ill-prepared. Part of the blame for this doubtless lay with Napoleon's chief of staff, General Berthier, who was still pining for his beloved Countess Visconti back in Italy. Initially, this had been a source of some ribaldry to Napoleon and his staff, but of late the forty-five-year-old Berthier had gone into such a decline that Napoleon had given him permission to return to Europe on the first available boat. On arriving at Alexandria Berthier had been overcome by conscience and hurried to catch up with Napoleon, but by now the damage had been done: a full-scale military campaign is best not organized by a lovesick chief of staff.

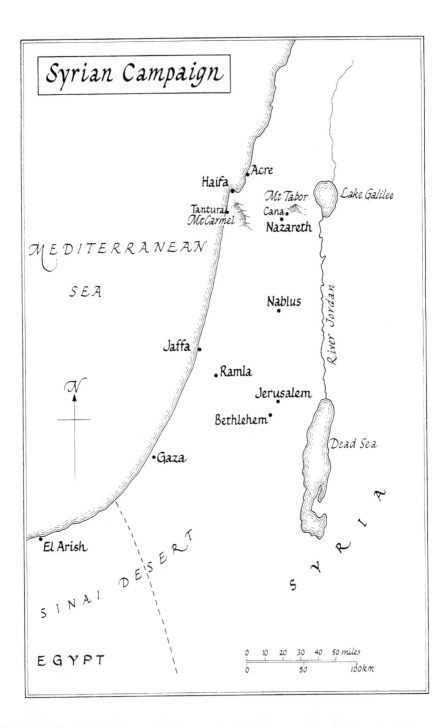

The crossing of the Sinai desert north to El-Arish proved a disorganized shambles. According to Bourrienne, who traveled at Napoleon's side: "The exhaustion of the desert and the lack of water provoked violent murmurings amongst the soldiers. When an officer passed beside the men on his horse they would give vent to their discontent . . . [with] the most bitter sarcasms . . . their more violent remarks being against the republic, and against the savants who were considered responsible for the [entire Egyptian] expedition in the first place."³ Those marching east from the coastal cities fared differently, but little better. Private Millet, who had recovered from the plague and was with the contingent marching from Damietta, recalled: "While we marched close to the sea, we had to weather it out through heavy rain. . . . The nights were very cold, the days were very hot."*⁴ General Damas noted in his journal:

The cold weather mixed with rain has lasted for 15–20 days, and according to the locals will last another month yet in this region, and will be worse in Syria. This holds out the prospect of some arduous marches across the desert and makes one fear that there will be outbreaks of sickness amongst the soldiers, who are badly equipped for the weather and the terrain; they are lightly dressed in tunics, trousers and cloaks, all of linen, which are insufficient to protect them against the cold nights and the frequent rain.⁵

In a classic military mix-up, the men had by now been issued with new lightweight uniforms, manufactured in Cairo and suitable for the Egyptian climate, but not for that prevailing along the Mediterranean coast in midwinter. The animals fared little better. Captain Doguereau of the cavalry was soon complaining: "Our horses went three days without eating anything but date palm leaves. . . . Our camels had to search for themselves for victuals. They were given nothing to eat and we feared we were going to see them perish without being able to replace them."⁶

All this would appear to be something more than the teething troubles that beset any large-scale logistic operation, and the blame should not be placed entirely on Berthier's shoulders. The root of the problem was almost certainly financial. By this stage Controller-General Poussielgue was finding it extremely difficult to balance the French

★ With regard to the hot days, Millet's memory seems to be mistaken. Other first-hand reports deny that it was hot during the day. In fact, the weather along this stretch of the Mediterranean coast during midwinter is usually cold and wet, with frequent storms.

administration's budget. Tax revenue was proving scarce, and in order not to let the soldiers' pay slip further into arrears, he had been forced to borrow against generous estimates of the tax receipts for next season's harvests, whose quantities were of course still uncertain.

The Syrian expedition had got off to an inauspicious start, and would show no signs of an early improvement. After Napoleon left Katia, he was annoyed to learn that El-Arish had not yet been taken. When Kléber and Reynier had arrived just a week previously, they had been surprised to discover that the reinforced garrison fort containing 1,800 Turks and Mamelukes had been further reinforced by 1,500 tough Albanian and Moroccan infantry swiftly dispatched from Acre by Djezzar. They had no alternative but to lay siege to it. According to Napoleon, after he heard this news, "he got on his camel, rode through the night, and arrived at El Arish at daybreak on 15 February."[7] During that very night, Reynier had launched a surprise attack on the enemy camp, catching most of its inmates asleep. Four hundred or so of the enemy had been killed and around 900 taken prisoner. According to Napoleon's report of the encounter: "Reynier lost 250 killed or wounded. The army grumbled about this, reproaching him for such losses. These reproaches were unjust; the general acted with initiative, just as the circumstances demanded."[8] The enemy camp may have fallen, but this was in fact outside the walls of the fort, so the siege continued.

The situation quickly descended into farce. The besieging French soon began running out of what little food they had, and the eyewitness Malus recalled: "We were eating camels, horses and donkeys. We were reduced to the last extremity."[9] A major woke up one morning to discover that during the night his men had eaten his horse. Meanwhile inside the fort the Turkish and Mameluke troops had all the food they needed, having recently been supplied by sea with a large quantity of provisions by a Greek merchant from Damietta, whose wares consisted largely of goods pilfered from French army stores and sold on the black market. However, the besieged garrison could not eat throughout the day, as the holy month of Ramadan had just begun and they were obliged to observe a fast between sunrise and sunset. No one now slept during the night, as those under siege cooked over their fires, and the mouth-watering smells wafted out over the vast number of starving besiegers.

After three days, Napoleon's patience was at an end. He sent in an emissary under a white flag to offer surrender terms, but the Turkish commandant proved obdurate and negotiations quickly broke down. The French artillery now formed a ring around the fort and began a heavy bombardment. Indeed, this was so heavy and the fort so small that several cannonballs flew right over it and landed amongst the French artillery on the far side. Unfortunately, this artillery consisted only of light field guns, as all the larger siege guns remained at Damietta, waiting to be shipped up the coast to Acre. In the end it took the French artillery all day before a small breach was opened in the walls at one of the towers. Under cover of darkness, the French sappers attempted to move in close and detonate a larger breach, but as Major Detroye noted: "The tower under attack was soon demolished to half its height. The enemy showed extraordinary bravery, working on repairs and firing from the tower in the midst of our cannon balls and shells."[10] The Syrian campaign was evidently going to involve a tougher enemy than the previous French battles against the Mamelukes.

At noon on the following day, Napoleon dispatched a further emissary, reminding the commandant that under the traditional rules of war, once the walls of a place under siege were breached those inside were required to surrender, or they could be slaughtered to the last man. This time the commandant decided to surrender. Most of the Mameluke prisoners were simply relieved of their valuables, disarmed and sent back to Egypt, but the other defenders received very different treatment. According to the official reports by Napoleon and his newly returned chief of staff Berthier, the surrendering garrison filed out, and were made to promise in the presence of the Koran that they would not take up arms against the French for the space of a year. They were then escorted almost twenty miles into the desert and ordered to march east to Baghdad. Malus gives the lie to this fairy tale: after the prisoners had sworn their oath and were permitted to march away on parole, "they were surrounded by Bon's division, then dispersed throughout the different divisions of the French army, where they were pressganged into serving with us." But he goes on to reveal, "They all deserted later, as soon as they found the opportunity."[11]

Napoleon knew that he had a problem where prisoners were concerned. As far as possible he was expecting his army to live off such supplies as it could gather, or capture, along the way. He barely had sufficient supplies for his own army, let alone additional hundreds or even thousands of prisoners. Nor could he spare all the men who would have to be left behind to guard these prisoners. He was left in a quandary, to which he had not yet found an answer.

But there was worse to come at El-Arish. When the French entered the fort they found "its interior in great disorder. The yard was filled with riderless horses on the loose, dead bodies and overturned equipment."[12] Several hundred had been killed inside the fort during the siege, and many more were wounded. But most ominous of all, the French found "an entire room was jammed full of people dying of the plague."

Napoleon was now eleven days behind the schedule he had drawn up for the campaign, and was already displaying signs of impatience. A skeleton French garrison was left at El-Arish, and the expeditionary army moved on up the coast with Kléber's division in the lead. Unfortunately his native guide mistook the way and they became lost in the desert, whereupon a furious Kléber had him shot on suspicion of treason. Meanwhile the other three divisions continued north, entering the plain of Gaza, where Napoleon reported on February 26: "There has been a terrible wind and for the last three days the shore has been battered by mountainous waves. We are soaked to the skin with mud up to our knees. It is as cold here as it is in Paris at this time of year."[13] But there had been some improvements, for they were now out of the Sinai desert: "The countryside is more beautiful than we expected: the citrus trees, olive groves and uneven terrain are almost exactly like the Languedoc." This resulted in a distinct improvement in morale. As Bernoyer remembered, "I experienced without doubt the same happiness as the Israelites arriving in the Promised Land."[14]

On February 24 the French advance party approached the town of Gaza, and as Bernoyer recalled: "We saw a sizable detachment of cavalry who made a show of wanting to attack us, and General Murat received the order to charge them. Afraid of combat, these bullshitters then took flight with such haste that they simply abandoned Gaza to us."[15]

Kléber and his exhausted division eventually caught up with Napoleon at Gaza, where Napoleon reported: "We have found here more supplies and ammunition than one would have believed possible. More than 30 thousand rounds of ammunition, and a great quantity of cannon balls capable of being used by our artillery."[16]

A few days later Napoleon's forces reached Ramla, some eight miles inland from the coast, whence the Arab population had fled, leaving the French to be welcomed by the numerous local Christians, who saw them as their saviors. By now scores of the French pack camels were succumbing to the cold and wet climate, and the army itself was faring little better. Napoleon ordered his physician-in-chief Desgenettes to set up a hospital in a nearby Greek Orthodox monastery, where he could treat the 700 soldiers who were now on the sick list. These included the wounded and those who had succumbed to the harsh conditions, but ominously, amongst them were also thirty-one soldiers who had developed the pus-filled buboes which signaled the onset of the plague.

On March 3 Napoleon arrived at Jaffa (by the site of modern Tel Aviv), which stood on a hill overlooking the sea, surrounded by a fortified wall. He laid siege to the city, and for the next three days his inadequate field guns ineffectually pounded the walls.

Napoleon was becoming increasingly irked by all these delays inflicted on him by an obstinate Turkish garrison commander, the appalling weather, the exhaustion and sickness of his men, and now another stubborn city governor. He was desperate to reach Acre, where the decisive action of the campaign would take place. With Djezzar defeated, and Acre taken, he could proceed—but to where? Constantinople? India? Or back to France? No one knew, and it is probable that he did not know himself. Years later, in his memoirs, he insisted that his aim had been to defeat Djezzar, thereby fomenting unrest throughout the Levant, "and then to decide what to do according to the circumstances."¹⁷ Once again he left his options open. As ever, he held firm to his profound belief in his "destiny," which "directs all my operations." In many ways, this was his substitute for self-knowledge.

The garrison troops at Jaffa defended bravely, despite the almost continuous French bombardment. The French sappers attempted to approach the city wall under cover of the orange orchard growing at its foot, so as to lay explosives and detonate a breach, but they were constantly repulsed by gunfire, and even by sorties from the besieged garrison. All this resulted in considerable French loss of life. When finally a breach was opened, Napoleon duly sent an emissary into the city under a flag of truce, making his usual offer according to the rules of war: if the garrison surrendered he would spare their lives, if not they could be slaughtered to the last man. According to Napoleon's subsequent report to the Directory, "At daybreak on 17 Ventôse [March 7] I sent a messenger to the governor: he cut off the head of my emissary and made no reply. At seven o'clock firing began. By one o'clock I judged we had a suitable breach."[18] The men took up their positions in the advance trenches, ready for the final assault. Above them on the walls they could see the head of the decapitated French emissary hanging from a pole at the top of the tower. But this only served to harden the hearts of the French soldiers, who were exasperated by the enemy's refusal to surrender, making it necessary for them to risk their lives in what they saw as a needless assault.

By now a number of soldiers from Bon's division had begun scouting around some of the city's defenses away from the main confrontation—with the aim of mounting a diversionary attack. According to Captain François, they "discovered a sort of breach in the wall beside the sea and took advantage of it to make a daring entry into the city. But they were repulsed by the inhabitants, and several had their throats slit. Those who had escaped with their lives ran to the division headquarters, yelling that their massacred comrades be avenged. This event took place just prior to the moment when Bonaparte ordered the assault."[19] Such news had a rousing effect on the soldiers preparing to charge the breach, although much more effect would certainly have been due to alcohol. The first wave of a charge into the breach in the wall of a besieged city invariably suffered heavy casualties—far more so than a charge in battle. For this reason men preparing to make such a charge would be issued with a copious amount of alcoholic spirits, to loosen their inhibitions and give them courage. Hence those taking part in this assault would have been drunk, their emotions roused beyond their conscious control, as they roared (literally) through the hail of bullets towards the walls.

The men charged in through the main breach, and the side breach, bayonets at the ready, their blood up for revenge. What happened next is best described by those who were there. In the words of Private Millet: "There was a terrible carnage, men, women and children were put to the bayonet. The massacre did not cease, even when the drummer sounded the order to assemble. It was a frightful spectacle to see so many innocent victims mixed up amongst the authors of this carnage, their dying cries ringing out in the streets and houses. All around was the spectacle of death. The French soldiers, with fury in their eyes, massacred everyone they could find."[20] Witness after aghast witness tells the same tale. This is Malus, but it could have been from any of a dozen French memoirs: "The soldiers went on the rampage all over the city, slitting the throats of men, women, old people, children, Christians, Turks, any in human form were victims of their fury."[21]

Seemingly, amidst the confusion many of the defending soldiers had tried to surrender, but the French continued slaughtering remorselessly, with their drunkenness prolonging the rape and rampage on into the night. In the course of this massacre some 2,000 Turkish soldiers lost their lives, but several thousand more managed to take refuge, barricading themselves in the citadel.

The following morning Napoleon dispatched two of his aides to discover what was going on, and to broadcast orders in his name calling a halt to the mayhem forthwith. Inexplicably he chose for this task two of his most junior aides—his seventeen-year-old stepson Beauharnais, and his equally young and inexperienced companion Crosier. When they entered the the city, both wearing the brightly colored official sashes that indicated that they were bearing Napoleon's orders, Beauharnais and Crosier came across a mob of bloodied, drunken French soldiers jeering and firing up at the windows of the citadel where the Turkish soldiers had taken refuge. Crosier bravely forced his way through the crowd and ordered them, in the name of their commander-in-chief, to cease firing. At the sight of his official sash, the soldiers took heed of his words and fell silent, whereupon the bey in charge of the Turkish soldiers, also recognizing the significance of the sashes, called down to the two young men. He promised to surrender on condition that he and his men were not maltreated like the other Turkish soldiers, and their lives were spared. On his own initiative, Crosier agreed to this proposal, and the Turkish soldiers all laid down their arms and filed silently out of the citadel. The French soldiers, now suitably sobered, formed a guard and escorted them through the carnage and squalor of the city streets to Napoleon's headquarters. Bourrienne described how Beauharnais and Crosier "led the prisoners to the camp in two troops, one of around 2,500 men, the other of around 1,500. I was walking with [Napoleon] in front of his tent when he caught sight of the mass of men arriving. . . . He said to me with a feeling of deep sorrow, 'What am I supposed to do? Have I any provisions to feed them? Or boats to transport them to Egypt or France? What the devil can I do with them all?'"[22] As Bourrienne went on to explain: "Beauharnais and Crosier were subjected to the strongest possible dressing-down. But the damage had been done. We had 4,000 men on our hands."

Napoleon now found himself faced with an all but impossible situation: he had 4,000 men whom he could not feed and did not know what to do with. To march them back to Egypt would require a guard of several hundred soldiers whom he could not afford to lose from his campaign force, and he certainly could not press them into his army and expect their loyalty after what had happened within the walls of Jaffa. In addition to this, as he revealed in his memoirs and other sources confirm: "Among the prisoners were found to be three Albanians from the garrison at Al-Arish, who revealed that all the garrison had turned up at Jaffa, violating the terms of their surrender and parole."[23] Of the 4,000 prisoners taken, as many as 1,000 of them were found to be former members of the garrison at El-Arish.

According to the rules of war all the prisoners taken at Jaffa could be slaughtered: their commander had dismissed Napoleon's offer of surrender. (What would he have done if they *had* all surrendered?) Thus Napoleon knew that he had a right to kill them. The safe conduct promised by Crosier and Beauharnais was irrelevant; armies did not run according to the word of junior aides. But could he really order the slaughter of 4,000 men in cold blood? The only real alternative would have been to abandon his march on Acre—and beyond. All Napoleon's dreams, his destiny, rested on this decision.

Of those who witnessed these days at Jaffa, it is Bourrienne's testimony that rings most true: "The prisoners were made to sit down en masse in front of our tents. Each had his hands tied behind his back by a cord. Their faces were set in a dull fury. They were given a little biscuit and unleavened bread from the already depleted provisions of our army."[24] Napoleon called a meeting of his divisional generals in his tent in order to decide what to do, but no decision was reached. According to Bourrienne, "The soldiers were complaining about their insufficient rations, at the same time there were murmurings and discontent at seeing their bread given to the enemy . . . the reports were alarming, especially that of General Bon. . . . He believed we were facing nothing less than a mutiny." Bourrienne was present at these meetings and took part in the discussions. After the first of these ended inconclusively, the entire camp was in a state of rising tension. "Another meeting was called, to which all the divisional generals were summoned. They discussed for several hours what steps should be taken. . . . [It was agreed that the prisoners] could not be released, for they would just go straight to Acre to reinforce Djezzar. . . . It was necessary to be there to appreciate fully the horrible necessity. . . . It is for posterity to judge our unanimous decision. . . . The order was given to shoot them." After a brief statement of the ensuing events, Bourrienne ends in anguished reticence. "I will add no further details of the horrible necessity of which I was an eyewitness." Others were to be less squeamish.

La Jonquière, the quasi-official historian of the Egyptian campaign, who had access to documents that remain unpublished, quotes from a long letter sent by the army paymaster Peyrusse to his mother in France:

By order of the commander-in-chief, the Egyptians, the Moroccans and the Turks were formed into separate groups.

Next day the Moroccans were all led down to the seashore, and two battalions began to shoot them. The only way they could try to save themselves was by throwing themselves into the sea; they did not wait, and all of them frantically attempted to swim away. There was easily time to shoot them and very soon the sea was red with blood and covered with corpses. A few were lucky enough to reach some rocks and save themselves; soldiers were sent after them in boats, to finish them off. . . . When this execution was finished, we fondly hoped that it would not be renewed, and that all the other prisoners would be spared. When the 800 Egyptians were sent off back to Cairo, our hopes were confirmed, but we were soon undeceived when next day 1,200 Turkish artillerymen, who had been kept in front of the commander-in-chief's tent for two days without food, were led off to be slaughtered. Our men had been told not to waste their ammunition and they worked up enough ferocity to run them through with their bayonets. Among the victims we found many children who had clung to their fathers as they were both killed.[25]

According to another eyewitness, Captain Krettly, on at least one occasion, "the first batch of prisoners were shot, the rest were charged by the cavalry, but the hearts of the French soldiers were overcome by horror, their limbs numbed . . . no one, or almost no one, could bring himself to strike them down . . . they were forced into the sea, where they attempted to swim, trying to reach the rocks a few hundred meters off shore . . . which saved our soldiers from the sad spectacle of seeing them massacred one by one without being able to defend themselves. But they were not saved in the end, since these poor unfortunates were overwhelmed by the waves."[26]

Other eyewitness sources also tell of unspeakable horrors—of prisoners being enticed to their death by French soldiers reassuring them, using "the Egyptian sign of reconciliation in use throughout these lands,"[27] of prisoners on the beach frantically piling up the corpses of their dead comrades in a vain attempt to hide from the bullets and bayonets of their murderers. The slaughter went on for three days—throughout March 8, 9 and 10.

Napoleon's responsibility for this massacre is undeniable. In a letter written on March 9 to his chief of staff, Berthier, he states plainly: "You will order the adjutant general to lead all the artillerymen and other Turks, who were captured bearing arms at Jaffa, to the seashore and to shoot them, taking such precautions as necessary to ensure that no one escapes."[28] In his memoirs, he simply records the taking of "2,500 prisoners, of whom 8 or 900 were from the garrison at El Arish. These latter thus . . . violated their parole: they were sent to the firing squad. The others were sent to Egypt."[29] In this way Napoleon suggests that the atrocity was within the rules of war, which strictly speaking it may have been, although the promise given by Crosier and Beauharnais could be seen as having compromised this. But he also suggests that fewer than a thousand prisoners perished, which is certainly not the case. Other firsthand accounts put the number of those massacred at anything from double this figure up to 4,000; some suggest even more.

Napoleon was well aware of what he was doing: this was terror tactics, intended to intimidate the enemy and have its effect on Djezzar's garrison at Acre. Even the paymaster Peyrusse knew this, but he could not help drawing another obvious conclusion, remarking at the end of his long letter to his mother: "This example will teach our enemies that they cannot count on our French decency; [but] sooner or later the blood of these 3,000 victims will be avenged on us."[30]

On the very same day that Napoleon issued his order to Berthier, he wrote to the sheiks and *ulema* of the surrounding region: "I have no intention of making war against your people, for I have only come to make war against the Mamelukes and Djezzar-Pasha, who I know is your enemy. I thus offer you, for the time being, the choice of peace or war."[31] He reinforced this message in God-like terms, promising "to strike my enemies like fire from heaven. It is best for you to understand that all human efforts against me are useless, because all that I undertake is bound to succeed. The example of what has happened at

Gaza and at Jaffa must make you realize that if I am terrible to my enemies I am good to my friends, and above all clement and merciful to the poor people."

On March 9 he also wrote to Djezzar at Acre:

The provinces of Gaza, Ramla and Jaffa are in my power. I have treated with generosity those of your troops who have submitted to my will. I have been severe with those who have violated the rules of war. In a few days I will march on Acre. . . . But what reason have I to deprive an old man who I do not know of a few years of his life? When God gives me victory I wish, by his example, to be clement and merciful not only to the people but also to their leaders. . . . Become my friend again [sic], be the enemy of the Mamelukes and the English. . . . Send your response with a man who is invested with your full powers and is aware of your intentions.

At the same time as Napoleon was in his tent dictating this letter to Bourrienne, others in the French camp had retired to their tents for different reasons. Bernoyer wrote: "During the barbaric executions I took to my tent in the attempt to blot out the noise of shrieking and grim cries of the dying who were being pitilessly slaughtered. Soon, the decomposition of this quantity of unburied bodies made itself felt in our camp. It poisoned the air with its stench, which threatened to endanger our lives."[32]

Yet the lives of Napoleon's troops were already in mortal danger. On March 10 Major Detroye recorded in his journal: "In General Bon's division men are suffering from an illness with buboes, which results in sudden death. The doctors assure everyone that it is not the plague."[33] But the rumors quickly spread, and two days later Detroye recorded: "Many soldiers have succumbed to . . . this disease which is believed to be the plague, and this belief has become so strongly held that four men, who caught the disease, have committed suicide."

Napoleon, together with his chief medical officer Desgenettes, took measures to halt the spread of the disease. Desgenettes knew that there had been cases of the plague in Jaffa, despite the denials by the Turkish prisoners: he had learned that during the night Turkish orderlies had thrown the victims over the walls. He rightly suspected that many of the new cases of plague amongst the French had been picked up during the overrunning of the city and the mayhem that had followed, which had inevitably brought the soldiers into close contact with the inhabitants. Consequently, he ordered that all clothes and precious fabrics pillaged from Jaffa were to be surrendered for immediate destruction. Those who succumbed to the disease were kept in wards isolated from other patients, and the cadavers were buried in sealed lime pits. Despite such measures, he and Napoleon did their best to avoid panic by maintaining the myth that this mystery disease was not in fact the plague, though in private they were forced to concede the truth.

Napoleon and Desgenettes responded in their own differing ways to the disease. Desgenettes insisted upon setting an example in the wards and treated many of the victims personally. In the interests of medical science, he went even further: "One day, in the middle of the plague ward, I plunged my lancet into the pus of the bubo of a convalescent . . . and made slight incisions with it in my groin and near one of my armpits, without taking any other precaution than to wash myself with water and soap."[34] Amazingly, this brave and dangerous experiment did not prove fatal; in fact, it served as a crude inoculation. (Jenner had published his pioneer work on vaccination in the previous year, but this referred to smallpox. Desgenettes evidently had a hunch that it applied equally to other contagious diseases, including the plague, but he must have known that he was gambling with his life.)

Napoleon adopted a characteristic view of the disease, which he would retain throughout his life: "It is one of the peculiar traits of the plague that it is most dangerous for those who are afraid of it; those who let themselves be overcome by fear almost always die of it."[35] This attitude may have been at variance with the orders and measures taken to combat the spread of this disease, but there can be no doubt that Napoleon believed what he said. On March 11 he even went so far as to pay a personal visit to the isolation wards where soldiers suffering from this bubo-inducing disease were laid out. He later recalled in his memoirs: "His presence brought great consolation; he made them treat several patients in front of him. They were piercing the buboes in order to induce the disease to its crisis. He touched those who seemed to be most discouraged, in order to prove to them that they only had an ordinary illness, not one that was contagious." Desgenettes, who was no friend of Napoleon, confirmed what happened, and went further, describing how "for more than an hour and a half, maintaining an attitude of complete calm, [Napoleon] witnessed every detail of the patients' treatment. Finding himself in a cramped ward which was over-filled with patients, he helped lift, or rather carry, the hideous corpse of a soldier whose tattered uniform was befouled by the spontaneous bursting of an enormous abscessed bubo."[36]

This may be seen as a typical act of hubris, or alternatively one of supreme bravery, aided by an erroneous belief in willpower and an overweening self-belief. Is it mere accident that this hazardous and self-less act should have come just a day after he had been responsible for the most cold-blooded atrocity he would ever commit? The coincidence would seem to be significant. Could his venture into the plague wards have been an act of superstition, some kind of compensation for his feelings over the massacre? Napoleon's notion of his own destiny was certainly superstitious: was his exposure of himself to the plague a tempting of fate which, if survived, would serve to confirm his sense of destiny?

All we can do is speculate here—though Napoleon himself was not concerned with such psychological self-unraveling. Similarly, he was never in any doubt as to the effect of his actions. Recalling in his memoirs his visit to the plague wards in Jaffa, he would pronounce: "As a result of what he did, the army were persuaded that it was not the plague." Although this is doubtful, Napoleon's actions amongst the plague victims would certainly have had a reassuring effect on the troops. This incident at Jaffa would later enter Napoleonic mythology when it was depicted in a highly dramatic (though entirely imaginary) painting by the romantic artist Gros, who would make his name by depicting illustrious events from Napoleon's life.

Not all those amongst the hospital staff reacted with their commander-in-chief's sangfroid. Before Napoleon moved on he appointed Adjutant General Grézieu to run the monastery plague-hospital. Grézieu was mortally afraid of the plague and immediately locked himself in the commandant's quarters, a house adjacent to the monastery, only venturing to issue his orders through a hole in the wall. Despite these precautions, he died within twenty-four hours of his appointment, and according to his assistant Malus: "His death had the effect of inducing in the men an oriental fatalism with regard to their survival."[37] Malus, who now had the unenviable task of taking charge of the hospital, has left a chilling picture of the situation:

For ten days I dutifully spent every morning there amidst the revolting stench of excrement, with the sick crammed into every corner. Not until the eleventh day did I myself begin to feel ill, when a raging fever and violent headaches forced me to my bed. . . . Half the garrison had already been struck down, and the men were dying at the rate of thirty a day. . . . Only one in twelve of those who caught the disease would manage to survive.[38]

Malus would be amongst these fortunate few.

Before leaving Jaffa and setting out for Acre, Napoleon established *divans* of sympathetic local sheiks in El-Arish, Gaza and Jaffa. These were men who had all suffered under the tyrannical Djezzar, and their loyalty was assured. The French could also rely upon the loyalty of the local Christian, Druze and Jewish populations, who formed sizable minorities in the region, and who now saw themselves as liberated from Muslim domination. Napoleon then summoned Menou from Rosetta to take on the post of overall governor of the entire Palestine region.*

Napoleon and his four divisions now moved north, often marching through driving rain, arriving sixty miles up the coast at Haifa on March 17. Here they found that Djezzar had evacuated the port, withdrawing his troops to the stronghold of Acre, where he evidently intended to make his final stand. Napoleon set up his headquarters on the slopes of the 1,500-foot Mount Carmel, from where he could look down over the entire sweep of the gulf towards Acre, which could be seen in the distance ten miles up the coast. Yet what now lay before him came as a distinct shock. Through his eyeglass he saw that the British battleship *Theseus* (a veteran of the Battle of the Nile), along with the battleship *Tigre*, a number of British gunboats and a Turkish flotilla, had taken up stations off Acre. He learned that they had arrived just two days previously.

Napoleon immediately dispatched instructions to Damietta, ordering that Captain Standelet should not put to sea with the flotilla carrying the French heavy siege guns which was to rendezvous with him at Acre. If Standelet had already left he was to be pursued with all haste and told to put in at Jaffa. But this order was too late: Standelet and his nine-ship flotilla were already approaching Mount Carmel. By now a sea mist had begun to form, and the French flotilla had already rounded Mount Carmel before they saw the British battleships and

---

* The Romans called the region Palaestina, and the earliest French reference to "Palestine" dates from 1793, although the word was probably not used during Napoleon's invasion, only coming into wider use some two or three decades later.

their escorts, which quickly put on sail and began converging upon the French. Napoleon watched from his vantage point as the naval maneuvers took place, as if in slow motion, far below him. In the nick of time, Captain Standelet managed to take evasive action and make his getaway, along with two of his escort ships, but the six unmaneuverable transport ships carrying the heavy siege guns were all captured and taken in tow towards Acre, where their cargo was unloaded in readiness for use against the French.

The following day, March 18, 1799, Napoleon and his army began taking up positions before the city walls of Acre.

XXII

The Siege of Acre

THE historic port of Acre (modern Akko) was first mentioned in an ancient Egyptian document dating from the nineteenth century BC; its natural harbor, overlooked by a fortified hill, made it one of the best-defended locations in all the Levant. Originally a Phoenician city, it was taken by Alexander the Great in 336 BC early on his march to India, and in the twelfth century AD it became the capital city of the Crusaders, who named it St. Jean d'Acre (the name still used by the French at the time of Napoleon's invasion).

Ahmed Pasha el-Djezzar, to give him his full title, had been governor of Acre and the surrounding *pashalik* (pasha's domain, or province) for almost twenty-five years, during which time he had reinforced the ancient walls to the point where they appeared all but impregnable. Djezzar was now an old man, judged to be somewhere in his late sixties or early seventies, but he still lived up to his title of "Butcher." He had been born with the name Ahmed, growing up in a remote mountain region of Bosnia at the western edge of the Ottoman Empire. During his youth he became involved in a murder, fled Bosnia and joined the Ottoman navy. But he proved unsuited to naval life, and deserted his ship after a quarrel, ending up on the streets of Constantinople, where he was soon penniless and starving. In order to survive, he took the drastic step of selling himself into slavery, and was shipped to Egypt to become a Mameluke, where he was taken into the service of the ruler Ali Bey. (His youthful service may well have coincided with that of the equally fearsome Murad Bey, who would later marry Ali Bey's wife Setty-Nefissa.) Ali Bey was still struggling to establish himself, and the young Bosnian played a leading role in the elimination of his rivals. His behavior towards those enemies unwise enough to fall into his hands alive soon led to him earning the nickname Djezzar ("The Butcher"), which was proudly incorporated into his name.

After the death of Ali Bey in 1773, Djezzar had fled from the powerful Mamelukes (among them Murad Bey and Ibrahim Bey) who fought to take over Egypt, eventually being taken into the service of the Bedouin sheik Dahr al-Omar, emir of Syria, who appointed him governor of Beirut. Djezzar repaid this generosity by overthrowing and murdering him. In characteristic fashion he then wreaked his vengeance on those who had supported Dahr al-Omar, notably the local Jewish, Druze and Greek Orthodox populations*—often cutting off their noses, ears or feet, gouging out their eyes, or having their feet shod with horseshoes. It was around this time, in 1777, that Baron de Tott visited the region, but as he recorded in his journal, "I did not choose to have any connection with [Djezzar]," citing as his reasons "the cruelties for which he was infamous, and the oppression which made him dreaded."[1] Even so, de Tott still saw chilling evidence of Djezzar's handiwork: "He had walled in alive a number of Greek Orthodox Christians, when he rebuilt the walls of Beirut to defend it from the invasion of the Russians. One could still see the heads of these unfortunate victims, which the Butcher had left exposed, in order the better to enjoy their torments."

Djezzar remained a loyal servant of the Ottoman Empire, promptly paying his *miry* in full to the sultan, an unusual generosity not displayed by all distant governors of this far-flung empire. Yet in reality he was virtually independent, and despite his growing years remained an energetic and fearsome character. According to an intrepid English visitor who was bold enough to accept his offer of hospitality:

Djezzar was at the same time his own chief minister, chancellor, treasurer and secretary, often even his own cook and gardener. . . . In his antechambers one encountered his servants, who were mutilated in all kinds of ways; one had lost an ear, another an arm, another an eye. We English were announced into his presence by a Jew, formerly his secretary, who had paid for an indiscretion with the loss of an ear and an eye. After a pilgrimage to Mecca [Djezzar] had killed with his own hands seven women from his harem whom he suspected of infidelity. He was sixty years old; but his vigour was still that of a man in the prime of life. We found him seated on a mat in a room without furnish-

* The Greek Orthodox Christians worshipped according to the Orthodox rite; often referred to simply as "Greeks," they were frequently of Armenian or local Syrian origin.

ings; he was wearing the clothes of a simple Arab and his white beard fell down over his chest; tucked into his waistband was a dagger encrusted with diamonds ... we had a long conversation with him, during which he cut all sorts of shapes in paper with some scissors; this was how he occupied himself all the time when foreigners were introduced to him. He presented to Captain Culverhouse a cannon which he had made out of paper, saying to him: "This is the symbol of your profession." All his conversation was in allegories, symbols and images.[2]

Djezzar had seemingly always had a particular hatred for the French, and when Napoleon invaded Egypt this blossomed into a fanatical obsession: he would crush the infidels who had the temerity to launch another crusade into the lands of Islam. But when Napoleon started his full-scale invasion of Syria, Djezzar was soon intimidated. His raging and threats against Napoleon had included a degree of bluff, and he watched warily as Napoleon advanced in apparently unstoppable fashion up the coast towards him. After losing Gaza, Djezzar had quickly withdrawn his troops from Haifa, and had been on the point of withdrawing from Acre when two more remarkable characters arrived on the scene, both of whom had previously had dealings with Napoleon.

One of the British ships arriving off Acre had put ashore a French engineer by the name of Louis-Edmond Phélippeaux, and it was he who had persuaded Djezzar to stay and resist the French, advising him on the best tactics to adopt against Napoleon, and how to build up the defenses of Acre. This was the very same Phélippeaux who had shared a desk with Napoleon at military school in Paris, topping the class and subjecting his neighbor to frequent kicks. When the Revolution broke out, the young Count Phélippeaux had gone into exile, later serving as a lieutenant-general under the Prince de Condé when he landed in the Vendée in 1793 at the time of the Royalist uprising. Sometime later he had been taken prisoner, but had managed to escape on the very night before he was due to be guillotined. His accomplices in this escape had been a male ballet dancer and the descendant of an English earl, and in 1797 the three of them returned clandestinely to Paris with the aim of rescuing prisoners of the Revolution. Eventually they hatched a plot to free three Englishmen from the Temple, the notorious prison where Louis XVI and Marie Antoinette had been held prior to their execution. After a series of adventures worthy of the Scarlet Pimpernel, the plot succeeded. One of the English escapees was the maverick naval captain Sir Sidney Smith, who consequently managed to get Phélippeaux commissioned into the British army as a colonel. He then took Phélippeaux on board when he was put in charge of the English battleship *Tigre*, which ended up off Acre when Napoleon arrived in March 1799.[3]

The life of Sir Sidney Smith was as remarkable as that of Djezzar and Phélippeaux. He too had had previous dealings with Napoleon, at the siege of Toulon in 1793 when the young Captain Bonaparte's artillery fire had forced the British to withdraw from the city. In the course of this withdrawal, Sir Sidney Smith had remained ashore until the last minutes, detonating the arsenal and setting fire to the remaining ships in an attempt to prevent them falling into French hands—one of many such acts of reckless bravery which he would display during his extraordinary naval career.

Sidney Smith had been born in 1764 in London, the son of a rakish naval captain and a disinherited heiress. He had joined the navy at the age of thirteen, soon experiencing a hurricane, a mutiny, and action in the Atlantic against the French. Distinguishing himself under fire, he rose to the rank of captain at the extraordinary age of nineteen. When peace was signed with France, he embarked upon a prolonged tour of the French ports and became friends with several of the naval officers against whom he had previously fought. Acting on his own initiative, he also became a spy for the British Admiralty, whilst at the same time conducting a number of love affairs ("I let the heart go as it will").[4] In 1790 he set off for Sweden, sailing up the Baltic in a seven-foot longboat with only a Portuguese cabin boy as crew, making a spectacular entry into the Swedish naval base at Karlskrona. King Gustav III was so impressed by the dashing young Englishman that he appointed him as his chief naval adviser, a post Smith gratefully accepted despite having been expressly forbidden to do so by the British Admiralty. During the Swedish war against the Russians, he showed extreme bravery under fire, on one occasion saving the king's life and preventing him from being captured, for which he was knighted by the grateful Gustav before he returned to England.

In 1792 Sir Sidney Smith, now dismissively nicknamed "the Swedish knight," was dispatched on a spying mission to Constantinople, where his brother was in charge of the British Embassy. Despite his undercover mission he cut such a conspicuous figure at court that he gained the friendship of Sultan Selim III, and then joined the Turkish navy as a volunteer. On hearing that Britain and France had declared war, he

bought a small lateen-rig at Smyrna, which he renamed *Swallow*, and
sailed across the Mediterranean to join Hood at the siege of Toulon,
where he was to thwart Captain Bonaparte and earn the enmity of the
French for his rearguard action. With some justification, the French
regarded Smith as a pirate, owing to the fact that when he turned up
at Toulon he was acting in a freelance capacity, and had not been
recommissioned by the British navy. On his return to Britain, he was
duly commissioned, given command of a ship, and led a series of flamboyant raids against enemy shipping along the French coast. During
one of these raids he was captured, taken to Paris to face a charge of
piracy, and incarcerated in the Temple prison. It was from here that
he was rescued by Phélippeaux.

Back in Britain, Smith was appointed to command the *Tigre*, an
eighty-gun battleship which had been captured from the French. He
was given orders to join the British fleet in the Mediterranean, and
given the diplomatic title "minister plenipotentiary," authorizing him to
deal with the Ottoman sultan on Britain's behalf. He sailed forthwith
for Constantinople, taking along his new friend Phélippeaux.
Surprisingly, considering that Smith was officially a deserter from the
Turkish navy, he received a warm welcome from Sultan Selim when
he arrived back at Constantinople in December 1798. This must at
least in part have been due to the expert diplomatic skills of his brother
Spencer Smith, who had recently negotiated the Treaty of Friendship
between Britain and the Porte.[5] In fact, the sultan proved so captivated
by the return of his friend that he gave Sidney Smith charge of the
entire Turkish land and sea forces which were being assembled with
the aim of driving the French out of the Levant, and appointed him a
member of his *divan*, an unprecedented honor for a foreigner. Smith
suggested that his friend Phélippeaux be made a colonel in the Turkish
army, a request which was generously granted, and in a characteristic
gesture he also requested the release of forty French galley slaves, in
recognition of the gentlemanly treatment he had received from the
prison governor of the Temple.

Calling himself Commodore Smith, a rank to which he was not entitled, Smith set sail in the *Tigre* for the Mediterranean. After making
contact with the British navy, he clashed with Nelson over who precisely
was in charge of Britain's Mediterranean fleet, and then sailed to
Alexandria, where in early March 1799 he took over command of the
blockading British squadron (thus officially qualifying for the rank of

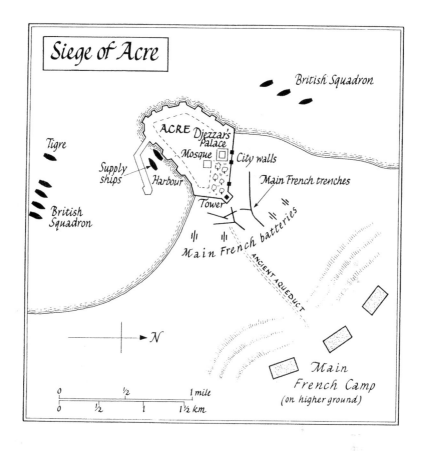

Siege of Acre

British Squadron

Tigre

ACRE Djezzar's
Palace

Mosque · City walls

Supply
ships

Harbour

Main French trenches

British
Squadron

Tower

Main French batteries

Main French

ANCIENT AQUEDUCT

N

Main
French Camp
(on higher ground)

0   ½   1 mile
0   ½   1   1½ km

commodore). Within days of his arrival he received an intelligence
report that Napoleon had taken Jaffa and was marching on Acre. He
immediately dispatched Phélippeaux on the *Theseus* to Acre, to liaise
with Djezzar. Phélippeaux used his aristocratic charm, reinforced by
his newly acquired commission in the Turkish army, to overcome
Djezzar's visceral hatred of the French. He managed to dissuade the
worried pasha from abandoning his stronghold, assuring him that help
was on the way in the shape of a British naval squadron, aided by
Turkish warships. After a tour of inspection of the city's defenses,
Phélippeaux made use of his considerable military talents to suggest
reinforcements and improvements.

Acre was built on a peninsula jutting out into the sea in such a way
as to protect the harbor below its southern walls. Facing the landward side was a crenellated wall incorporating a number of defensive
towers. From inside the walls rose the dome and minaret of the main

mosque, clumps of palm trees and the walls of Djezzar's palace, which emerged out of the cramped maze of narrow streets and ramshackle low rooftops. Along the defensive wall some 250 guns were positioned to fire on the enemy on the plain below.

With the arrival of Smith's squadron and the Turkish warships, Acre was now protected from the sea, and its walled harbor could receive reinforcements with little difficulty, even though it would soon come within range of the nearest French guns. Despite this, Smith had quickly begun to land further artillery, a vast supply of gunpowder and some 4,000 cannonballs, as well as several hundred British marines and trained naval gunnery units to assist the defenders. He also put ashore ample provisions for the 15,000 inhabitants of Acre and Djezzar's 4,000-man garrison of mixed Turkish, Albanian and Syrian soldiers. The morale of Djezzar and his defenders now underwent a transformation. Vowing to overcome once and for all the heretic Napoleon and his infidel army, Djezzar's troops manned the walls with renewed confidence, looking out at the ant-like figures of their besiegers taking up their positions amongst the olive groves and rolling countryside. The defensive walls on the landward side of Acre dated from the Crusader era, when they had been constructed by the Knights of St. John (hence the French name St. Jean d'Acre). Despite being reinforced by Djezzar, these walls were still continuing to crumble in parts, but they had been built so thick that such weaknesses were not deemed serious. After studying plans of the fortifications, Smith and Phélippeaux began working out with Djezzar how best to use the resources at their disposal in the defense of Acre.

Such was the city, and its three leading defenders, that now confronted the undefeated Napoleon in the most decisive engagement of his life so far—one upon which he knew his entire future plans depended. Smith too was well aware of Acre's vital strategic importance: if it could be defended, Napoleon would be unable to continue his advance through Syria, knowing that his lines of communication were threatened, and that an army could be landed in his rear. On the other hand, if Acre fell, the only fortified city of consequence which lay in Napoleon's path was Aleppo, 250 miles to the north. This was seventy miles inland, beyond the reach of British naval support, and stood at the crossroads leading either to Constantinople or to India.

The French forces were soon digging in, excavating a line of trenches across the neck of land facing the walls. Here they were camouflaged behind straw bales, as well as being hidden from view by the gardens and orchards, and the ancient ruined aqueduct. Under cover of darkness they began digging zigzag trenches forward towards the walls, which would enable the sappers to plant their devastating explosives and effect a breach. All this digging in would take at least a week, but to begin with it seems to have been undertaken hastily and made slow progress. As was so often the case, Kléber was not impressed with his commander-in-chief's methods, and was not afraid to say so. The tall Kléber, walking alongside the short figure of Napoleon as they inspected the trenches, could not refrain from remarking sardonically: "What the devil kind of trenches are they digging here, General? They may be fine for you, but they only come up as far as my stomach."[6]

Although Napoleon was as impatient as ever, the French could afford to take their time. They now had no shortage of supplies, as they were soon receiving ample provisions from the orchards, market gardens and herds of the friendly local Druze villages, who had promised Napoleon a further 15,000 men for his march north once Acre was taken. The main body of the French army was bivouacked out of range of the guns of Acre, on the heights to the north overlooking the plain before the city. Paymaster Peyrusse paints a vivid picture of life here: "Our camp becomes every day more like a great country fair. Wine, spirits, figs, discs of unleavened bread, grapes, butter, etc. . . . we have them all in abundance, even if we are charged ridiculously high prices; but when you're on campaign you don't care about money."[7]

Napoleon himself supervised the placing of the French light artillery. The loss of the flotilla bringing his heavy siege guns was a blow, but not an irreparable one. He had managed to breach the walls of El-Arish and Jaffa with these guns, and remained supremely confident that he could repeat this feat. And if not, he had already sent to Alexandria for replacement heavy artillery to be dispatched forthwith.

Before hostilities got under way, Napoleon sent word by sea to Smith, requesting an exchange of prisoners. He knew that the British squadron was holding a number of French prisoners taken from ships attempting to evade the blockade of Alexandria and the other northern ports. Similarly, on March 21 the French had captured a number of English sailors whom Smith had sent in on a daring but unsuccessful raid intended to capture several sloops which had fallen into French hands in Haifa harbor. Smith at once agreed to the exchange, but informed Napoleon that he would have to keep one badly beaten French officer called Delasalle, whom he had come across in the dungeons of Acre.

He told Napoleon that he had managed to persuade Djezzar to let him take Delasalle back to the *Tigre* for treatment, adding confidentially: "It would be much better not to complain to Djezzar about his mistreatment, for this would merely remind him of the matter, and make him wish to lay hands on him once more, given the present antagonism which Djezzar and the Turks now have towards the French. Monsieur Delasalle is at present my guest and will remain so until a suitable occasion arises for him to be sent back to France."[8] Napoleon conveyed his thanks to Smith in a similarly gracious reply: "Do not doubt, Commander, my desire to deal with you in a civilized fashion, hence my eagerness to seize the opportunity to be useful to men of your nation who have been unfortunate enough to suffer from the hazards of war."[9]

The French artillery barrage began just before dawn on March 28. It was immediately answered by heavy fire from the city walls, as well as a punishing crossfire from the British and Turkish ships anchored offshore. Within two hours the well-directed French fire had opened a breach in the city walls, but at considerable cost. Forty French artillerymen had been killed and many more wounded, while all but three of the French guns had been knocked out.

The breach was in the tower where the French had been concentrating their fire, and this opening in the walls was further extended by the detonation of a mine placed by French sappers. According to Captain François, who was in the front line, Napoleon and his staff were up with them in the trenches the whole time, assessing when to give the order to charge. Soon the trenches were filling up and almost overflowing as the support troops moved in behind those ready to go over the top, but still Napoleon hesitated, until the officers informed him that they could hold the men back no longer. François described what happened when the order was given:

[the men] charged towards the breach, the grenadiers at their head; but to their great surprise they were halted by the steep banks of the moat, which they had not realized was there. . . . The grenadiers were not going to let themselves be defeated by this unforeseen obstacle. With the aid of ladders which had been given to us by the Druze, they clambered down into the moat before the breach and prepared to mount into the tower, in spite of the terrible fire that the enemy was aiming down at them from the breach and from the ramparts above. Captain Mailly Châteaurenault of the general staff clambered up first, but he was felled by a burst of fire. If the grenadiers had been backed

up by the support troops, who were now separated from them by the fatal steep banks of the moat, they would have succeeded in scaling the tower. Nevertheless, they continued to advance; their ferocious bravery inspired such terror in the Turks that we saw them jump down from the breach into the moat and abandon the tower, but the pasha [Djezzar] forced more men into the breach, injuring some of them in the process, treating them as cowards, telling them that the French were fleeing. He threatened [the Turkish soldiers] with his vengeance and fired a couple of pistol shots at them.[10]

By now the support troops had come to a halt, realizing that without ladders they would not be able to get down into the moat and up the other side like the grenadiers. Finding themselves exposed to heavy fire from the ramparts, they retreated and sought cover back in the trenches:

Meanwhile the grenadiers, still at the foot of the tower, continued their efforts to clamber up the ten or twelve feet which separated them from the breach. By now all the fire of the Turks was directed at them. Most fell backwards, from the top of their ladders. . . . The besieged soldiers hurled a rain of stones, grenades, flaming blocks of tarred wood and boiling oil. The grenadiers fled and took cover in the trenches, leaving behind them a great number of their comrades. Then the Turks poured down into the moat and cut off the heads of the fallen soldiers, whether they were dead or wounded.

Djezzar had promised a large bounty for every infidel head brought before him, and that same evening the heads of the French soldiers were displayed on spikes along the city ramparts. Regarding all this as a minor setback, Napoleon wrote confidently next day to Dugua in Cairo, describing how "numerous deputations have arrived from all sides, even the Arab tribes have not been slow in showing their pleasure at our arrival; everyone wishes to be delivered from their oppressor who is boxed up in Acre. Our breach batteries are all in place, we have begun to pound the walls, and we hope to take the place pretty soon."[11] Meanwhile, Captain François noted in his diary: "Continued digging in. The soldiers putting in an incredible effort, despite being under enemy fire; they are filled with the desire to avenge what has happened. The besieged troops shout down menacing threats at us in Turkish, Arabic, in English and even in French."[12] Djezzar's actions had reinvigorated his troops, giving them new heart; they no longer feared the invincible French who had swept all before them in a tide of blood at Jaffa. At the same time, some of the French were becoming a little less optimistic than their commander-in-chief. As Doguereau noted in his journal: "From this moment on many amongst us came to the conclusion that we would not take the place."[13]

Djezzar's reaction to the initial French onslaught was in character. He ordered the slaughter of all Christians amongst the indigenous population of Acre, and had all French prisoners in his dungeons strangled. The victims of the massacre were thrown over the city walls into the sea, where their presence soon became evident: "The soldiers in the trenches of General Vial's division saw washed up on the seashore many bodies shoved into empty rice and coffee chests."[14] Bourrienne also recorded the grim scene, which evidently continued for some days: "The waves frequently washed up dead bodies on the beach, and we came across them when we bathed in the sea."[15] Napoleon held Sir Sidney Smith responsible for this massacre, blaming him for not restraining Djezzar, despite the fact that Smith had already warned him about Djezzar's uncontrollable behavior. At any rate, from now on Napoleon began to develop a deep hatred for Smith.

Once again, Napoleon became impatient. Despite his training as an artillery officer, he was never at ease whilst conducting a siege, whose brute force tactics gave little rein to his superlative military skills. Two heavy guns which had been captured at Haifa—a thirty-two-pounder and a twenty-four-pounder—finally arrived at Acre on April 1, having been dragged overland; but these remained unused as the French had no cannonballs of their caliber. Recognizing the French lack of any heavy artillery, the Ottoman defenders began to jeer at the French artillerymen, yelling through the night: "Sultan Selim boom, boom, boom. Bonaparte ping, ping, ping." Napoleon was irritated to observe that "the besieged forces lost no time in rendering the breach impenetrable, filling it with mines, explosives, charged grenades, barrels of pitch, bundles of sticks, wood wrapped with cloth soaked in inflammable sulphur and iron spikes."[16]

During the daytime the besieged Ottomans kept the French at bay with a constant artillery barrage from the ramparts. Now that they were being supplied by the British, they had all the ammunition they wanted, and soon the plain around the French trenches was littered with cannonballs of all sizes. Napoleon quickly turned this to his advantage, issuing the order on April 4: "All soldiers who during today and tomorrow find cannon balls on the plain and bring them to headquarters will be paid accordingly: 36 and 33 pounders 20 sous each, 12 pounders 15 sous each, 8 pounders 10 sous."[17] These were generous sums: a sou was a twentieth of a pound (livre), or five centimes. At this rate, a soldier heaving and hauling back a thirty-three-pound cannonball would get the best part of a day's wage for a junior savant, more than enough to buy a good supply of wine for him and his comrades, even at the inflated Druze prices.

Meanwhile the outbreak of plague amongst the French army was being brought under control. Desgenettes had issued some reassuring advice on the matter, which was distributed through all divisions: "The army is informed that it is very advantageous to health to wash at frequent intervals feet, hands and face with fresh water and even better to wash them with warm water, into which has been poured a few drops of vinegar or alcoholic spirit." He also recommended those who had caught the disease to take,

in order to sustain immediate hydration and strength, as a matter of urgency, a drink consisting of coffee and quinine, flavoured with fresh lemon or lemon juice. The swelling of the glands requires, in principle, a soothing poultice, and when the patient is weak, his tumors must immediately be opened by the application of one or several cauterizing lances. Experience has already shown the effectiveness of this treatment; experience has also proved, through close observation of a great number of cases, that this sickness is not contagious.[18]

To what extent Desgenettes actually believed this last claim is not clear. The disease certainly appears to have been contagious, yet not so much as in the more virulent strains of bubonic plague; his main aim remained the avoidance of panic. Either way, his methods were at least accompanied by a containment of the disease for the time being. On April 10 he set up a hospital on the slopes of Mount Carmel to deal with plague victims amongst the 9,000 men now engaged in the siege of Acre. On opening, the hospital had just over 150 patients, and during the following fortnight men were admitted at the rate of around twenty a day, with fatalities running at around four a day. This suggests that men in the besieging army were catching the plague at one or two per hundred per week. Although such figures were not alarming, there is no doubt that both Napoleon and Desgenettes viewed them with concern. Although Napoleon had in mind to attract volunteers and new recruits, as yet the Army of the Orient remained a limited, and decreasing, force.

With their replenished stock of cannonballs, the French guns were soon pounding the walls of Acre once more, this time with a little heavy artillery support. In an attempt to alleviate these barrages, the defenders began making a number of increasingly bold and powerful sorties into the French lines. The sortie on April 8 was a veritable infantry charge, but the French were ready for them. As Napoleon recalled in his memoirs: "800 Turks were killed, amongst whom were 60 Englishmen. The wounded Englishmen were looked after as if they were French, and these prisoners camped in the midst of our army as if they were from Normandy or Picardy; the rivalry of the two nations had disappeared at this great distance from their homeland amidst such barbaric people."[19] The French and English soldiers had instinctively understood the truth behind their presence here: in essence this was a war being waged by Europeans against the people of the Levant.

XXIII

The Battle of Mount Tabor

AT the outset of Napoleon's invasion of Syria, Djezzar had appealed to the governors of Aleppo and Damascus for support, and as Napoleon marched towards Acre he had continued to monitor the situation to the north, receiving intelligence through the network of Christian communities. According to his memoirs it was now, at the beginning of April, that "secret agents from the north announced the departure of an army from Damascus, adding that it was innumerably large."[1] Further intelligence reports soon indicated that this army was more than 30,000 strong, and had been joined by 7,000 men from the mountain tribes around Nablus, as well as attracting several thousand other Arab volunteers as it marched south.

Napoleon assessed his own situation: of the original army of 13,000 men who had set out from Egypt on the Syrian campaign, 1,000 had been killed, 1,000 were sick, 2,000 had been left behind to garrison El-Arish, Gaza and Jaffa, and 5,000 men would have to remain at Acre if the siege was to be maintained properly, with the artillery protected from enemy sorties. As he recorded in his memoirs: "This left only 4,000 at Napoleon's disposal to track down and fight the Army of Damascus and Nablus which was 40,000 strong."[2] He decided to dispatch three of his generals to investigate: General Vial's division was sent up the coast towards Tyre, while Murat and Junot were sent inland towards the River Jordan and Lake Galilee with much smaller forces.

Bernoyer recalled that: "Generals Murat and Vial returned several days later. In their reports they mentioned having seen nothing which would make them believe in the existence of large troop concentrations."[3] Napoleon was worried. He felt certain that the enemy was out there, stalking him, and he was caught in the one situation he abhorred: he and his troops in front of Acre were immobile, as well as being vulnerable from the rear. He ordered Junot and Murat back into the field, dispatching Junot towards Nazareth and Murat towards Lake Galilee. On April 8 Junot encountered the enemy. According to Napoleon's report: "General Junot with 300 men . . . has defeated 3 to 4,000 cavalry, inflicting 5–600 casualties. . . . This was one of the most brilliant military feats."[4] A day later Napoleon dispatched Kléber with his division of 1,500 infantry to support Junot, and on April 11 Kléber came across 5,000 enemy near Cana, quickly putting them to flight. Four days later Murat heard that a large force of enemy soldiers had crossed the River Jordan north of Lake Galilee. Racing overnight to the scene with just two infantry battalions at his disposal, he arrived at dawn to discover 5,000 enemy cavalry. The men were undaunted and formed up in two battalion squares. They had seen the tents of the enemy camp on the other side of the river, and sensed that victory was liable to result in a rich haul of booty. In the words of the commissary Miot, who was accompanying General Murat: "Soon our troops were no longer marching, they ran and tumbled down the slope." The enemy was caught completely by surprise: "As there was so little time between our appearance and our charge, this part of the Army of Damascus simply scarpered . . . not even having time to pack up their tents, their ammunition or their supplies." General Murat and a cavalry detachment set off in pursuit, leaving Miot in command, and telling him to seize everything in the enemy camp:

But the soldiers beat me to it. Filled with joy at their success they scattered throughout the camp to make, with their usual care, a meticulous search of the tents. They found there such quantities of Damascus sweets and cakes, renowned throughout the Orient, that they filled their pockets, their haversacks. . . . Instead of getting some rest they passed the night in celebration, dancing and singing and delivering the most heart-felt eulogies to the confectioners of Damascus as they gorged on their sweets. . . . At our headquarters we officers dined equally well and just as happily on pastries and delicacies of all kinds.[5]

Where raw alcohol had turned men into monsters at Jaffa, sweets turned them all into children.

Napoleon could now be certain that he faced no major threat from the north, but this meant that the main body of the Army of Damascus

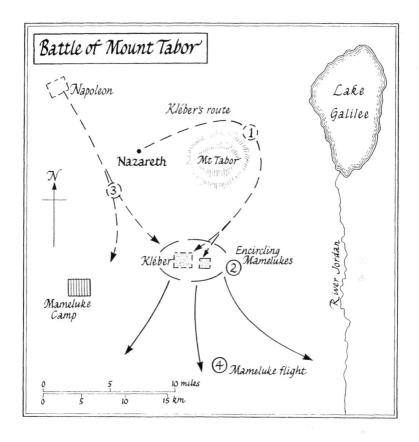

Battle of Mount Tabor

Napoleon

Kléber's route

Lake Galilee

Nazareth

Mt Tabor

N

① ② Encircling Mamelukes

③

Kléber

River Jordan

Mameluke Camp

④ Mameluke flight

| 0 | 5 | 10 miles |
| 0 | 5 | 10 | 15 km |

had now probably outflanked him and crossed the River Jordan south of Lake Galilee, aiming either to attack his positions at Acre from the rear or to reach the sea and cut him off.

Napoleon had been in constant contact with his generals in the field, daily sending them detailed instructions. Kléber in particular had begun to chafe under such close supervision, and now at last saw a chance to make a name for himself on the battlefield for the first time on the Egyptian expedition. The enemy were evidently easy to repulse, and no match for disciplined French troops, no matter how heavily the French were outnumbered. When Kléber reached Nazareth on April 15, he received intelligence that the main body of the Army of Damascus was encamped below Mount Tabor. Taking the precaution of informing his commander-in-chief what he intended to do, but too late for him to countermand this action, Kléber and his division set about making a rapid march under cover of darkness around Mount

Tabor, with the aim of launching a surprise attack on the rear of the enemy camp.

Unfortunately, Kléber underestimated both the distance and the terrain, and instead of surprising the enemy camp at two A.M., his tired troops did not reach the plain below Mount Tabor until six A.M., when the sun was already well risen. The element of surprise was lost, the enemy scouts had spotted his columns, and Kléber's division of 5,000 men found itself confronted by a vast army which was awaiting his arrival. This consisted of 10,000 infantry and 25,000 cavalry, including Djezzar's cavalry and the Mameluke warriors who had fled Egypt with Ibrahim Bey.

Kléber's men formed two defensive squares, which were soon being forced to defend themselves from wave after wave of Mameluke cavalry charges. The disciplined soldiers withstood these as best they could, cutting down swaths of Mamelukes in each charge, but for hour after hour the charges continued, and it soon became evident—to both sides—that the French could not last out like this indefinitely. As the sun rose in the sky and the heat intensified, Kléber's supplies and ammunition began to run low. He realized that his only hope was to hold out until nightfall, and then somehow effect a swift and orderly retreat before the Mamelukes could regroup and give chase. But it quickly became clear to him that they could not last till then, and he was forced to consider a more drastic tactic. It was just possible that he could launch a breakout directly across the plain and attempt to take refuge in Nazareth. But by now things were desperate, as Private Millet recalled:

We had been on the go since six in the morning, and were beginning to run out of ammunition for our rifles as well as ammunition for our stomachs. We had been given so little bread . . . but we had no time to eat even this. And even when we did have time, we were not able to take advantage of it because we were so strung out with thirst and exhaustion that we could not even speak. On top of this we were exposed to the heat of the sun at its height. . . . We were close to a lake, but we had no way to get to it. We had to put up with all this whilst we stood waiting for what seemed like inevitable death.[6]

Napoleon takes up the story in his memoirs: "Kléber was lost . . . he sustained and repulsed a great number of charges; but the Turks had taken all the foothills of Mount Tabor and occupied all the surrounding high ground. . . . His position was hopeless, when suddenly a number of soldiers called out: 'Look over there, it's the little corporal!'"* At first no one believed them. "But the old soldiers who had fought with Napoleon before, and were used to his tactics, took up their cries; they believed they could see in the distance the glint of bayonets." When word reached Kléber in the middle of his square, he "climbed to a vantage point and pointed his telescope at where they were indicating . . . but he could see nothing; the soldiers themselves believed it to be an illusion, and this glimmer of hope vanished."⁷

In desperation Kléber decided to abandon his artillery and wounded, form his men into a column, and attempt a breakout with every man for himself. Meanwhile it became evident that the enemy was massing for a final grand charge to overrun and slaughter the French. It was now that the miracle took place. Kléber's soldiers had not in fact been mistaken: Napoleon was indeed coming to their rescue, but for the moment his men were invisible as they moved forward across a slope covered with head-high wild wheat. Napoleon described how next "the commander-in-chief [himself] ordered a square to march up onto an embankment. The heads of these men and their bayonets were soon visible on the battlefield to friend and foe alike." At the same time he ordered a salvo from his artillery. The Turkish forces were momentarily disconcerted, but were soon reassured by the stirring sight of the advancing Mameluke cavalry of Ibrahim Bey and the tough regiments of the Nablus mountain tribesmen. The Army of Damascus still had the upper hand.

It was now that Napoleon played another master-stroke. Moving his three squares between the enemy forces and their camp, he simultaneously dispatched 300 men in amongst the enemy tents, with orders to set fire to them and make a great show of requisitioning their supplies and their camels. This was a purely psychological tactic, and had an immediate effect on the Turkish forces, who felt themselves cut off. Their ranks were overcome by panic and they began to flee, at first in their hundreds, and then, as the panic spread, in their thousands. Kléber needed no signal, and at once acted in instinctive cohesion with Napoleon, ordering his men to break out—this time in an aggressive charge, rather than a frantic flight for their lives. Their blood was up, and Millet, who took part in the charge, described what happened next:

* The soldiers' nickname for Napoleon.

Remember, we were dying of thirst. Well, our thirst for vengeance had extinguished our thirst for mere water, and instead kindled our thirst for blood. . . . Here we were, wading up to our waists through the water of that lake which only a short time previously we had been craving to drink from. But now we no longer even thought of drinking, only of killing and dyeing the lake red with the blood of those barbarians. Just a short time previously they had been longing to cut off our heads and drown our bodies in that very lake, in which they were now drowning and filling with their bodies.[8]

The vast Army of Damascus scattered in their tens of thousands. The cavalry headed into the mountains to the south, whilst the infantry scrambled towards the River Jordan, whose waters had risen due to the recent rains, and whose banks were a quagmire. Several thousand were drowned; French losses, on the other hand, were astonishingly light— if Napoleon is to be believed: "Kléber lost 250–300 men killed or wounded, while the columns of the commander-in-chief lost 3–4 men."[9]

In his memoirs, Napoleon described how after the battle he "ascended the mountain, which rises like a sugar loaf, dominating this part of Palestine. This was where the Devil had tempted Christ by offering him worldly power." He stood for a while contemplating the scene of his great victory, which he decided to call the Battle of Mount Tabor. The battle itself may not have burnished Napoleon's glory quite so brilliantly as he suggests in his memoirs (though his critics only disagree with him on minor points), but there is no denying that this was a victory which reflected his superlative military instincts. Back in Acre, he had sensed from Kléber's overconfident report that he was out of his depth, and had immediately set out at the head of Bon's division to march overnight and relieve the situation, arriving in the nick of time. Realizing that his men were too fatigued to fight a serious battle against overwhelming numbers after their thirty-mile forced march, he had maneuvered them cannily and struck at the enemy camp with the hope of gaining some respite—a move that had proved even more decisive than he had hoped.

After descending from the mountain, Napoleon followed his troops into Nazareth, where a community of monks known as the Fathers of the Holy Land invited him to set up his headquarters in their monastery, opening up their cloister as a hospital for the wounded and the dying, who were still being carried in from the battlefield. The following evening the monks celebrated a solemn *Te Deum* in honor of the French and their victory, which was attended by Napoleon and his senior officers, despite the fact that France was now officially "de-Christianized" and most of his officers were hardened disbelievers. Napoleon and his staff were also given a conducted tour of the site of the Annunciation, where the Angel Gabriel had announced to the Virgin Mary that she would give birth to Jesus. Napoleon's aide Captain Lavallette recalled how the prior, who was Spanish, showed them the famous black marble column beside the altar: "The prior told us with due solemnity that when the Angel Gabriel had come to announce to the Virgin Mary her glorious and holy destiny, he had brushed the column with his heel and broken it. Laughter broke out amongst us, but Napoleon gave us a stern look, forcing us to mask our derision with serious faces."[10]

The troops were equally disrespectful. Desgenettes relates how "a soldier had lost his finger in combat, but managed to pick it up and kept it. When he saw the cemetery, he made a little hole in the ground and buried it, telling his comrades: 'No matter where the rest of my body goes when I die, at least I'll always have a finger in the Holy Land.'"[11]

The following day Napoleon drew up his historic yet curiously little-known Proclamation to the Jews, in which he announced:

Bonaparte, Commander-in-Chief of the Armies of the French Republic, in Africa and Asia, to the rightful heirs of Palestine—the unique nation of the Jews, who have been deprived of the land of your fathers by thousands of years of lust for conquest and tyranny, which even so has never been able to destroy your name or your existence as a nation . . . Arise then, with gladness, ye exiled [and take unto yourselves] Israel's patrimony.

The young army, which Providence has called upon me to command, supported by justice and accompanied by victory, has made Jerusalem my headquarters and will, within a few days transfer them to Damascus, from whence David's city will feel no threat.

Rightful heirs of Palestine!

My great nation, which does not trade in human beings or in countries, as did those who sold your fathers into slavery in other nations, herewith calls upon you, not to conquer your inheritance, but to receive only that which has already been conquered, so that you can remain there as ruler, under our guarantee, and will defend it against all foreigners.[12]

This proclamation was headed: "General headquarters, Jerusalem 1 Floréal Year 7 of the French Republic, 20 April 1799." By an auspicious coincidence this also happened to be the first day of the Jewish celebration of Passover.

Napoleon's astonishing Proclamation to the Jews is of such import in the history of the region that it warrants a short digression from the main events of his Syrian campaign. This document is indeed historic: it was the first in which a leading international figure offered a homeland for the Jews. But the proclamation itself is fraught with controversies. Perhaps the least of these is the fact that it certainly could not have been issued in Jerusalem, which was never taken by Napoleon. On the day in question he was at Ramla, twenty-five miles from Jerusalem. However, such anticipation of events is not unknown in the writings of Napoleon. On the other hand, many serious historians have argued that he never in fact wrote such a document. In support of this claim they point out that no original of this proclamation has ever been discovered, nor even has a French copy of it come to light.

The only contemporary evidence of its existence comes in two references that appeared in the official French gazette *Le Moniteur*, published by the Directory. The first appeared on May 22, 1799, and stated: "Bonaparte has published a proclamation in which he invites the Jews of Asia and Africa to join his army in order to re-establish ancient Jerusalem. He has already armed a great number of them and their battalions are menacing Aleppo."[13] Even more intriguingly, the dateline given for this message is "Constantinople 28 Germinal," which is April 17—in other words, three days *before* Napoleon issued the proclamation 1,000 miles away near Jerusalem. Was this piece of news merely a propaganda ploy, with no message from Constantinople, and no basis whatsoever in fact? Were the Directory simply guessing, making use of tidbits of news they had received concerning Egypt and plans which Napoleon had outlined before he set out? This would seem to be the only, rather unconvincing, answer.

A few weeks later, on July 27, *Le Moniteur* reported: "Bonaparte has not conquered Syria simply to return their Jerusalem to the Jews; he has much wider plans . . . to march on Constantinople, in order to spread terror in Vienna and St. Petersburg." This coda to the previous message would seem to confirm the propaganda aspect, for France was now threatened by Austria and Russia. It would also accord with the ambitions that Napoleon had revealed to the Directory. So perhaps all this really was inspired guesswork by the Directory, after all. Such a view is confirmed by the absurd report which appeared in the May 24 edition of *Le Moniteur*, under the heading "Army of the Orient":

A courier has arrived with a message from Bonaparte in Jerusalem dated 22 Pluvôise [February 11]. The climate has had no effect on the general and very little on the army, which was in an excellent state and through local recruiting has increased its number up to 100,000 men. Berthier is cured of the deafness from which he has been suffering for the last three months. Our cavalry is now fully mounted on Arab steeds. Bonaparte is understood to have appointed to serve under him an ancient Mameluke chief named Barthelemy, and as a result has acquired great influence amongst the Eastern Greeks.

Such a mélange of fact, guesswork and pure imagination may appear laughable, but it does all point to one significant fact: Napoleon had certainly mentioned to the Directory before he set out that he planned to issue a Proclamation to the Jews. This suggests that he may well have prepared his proclamation in Cairo, before he set out on his Syrian campaign. In which case, he would almost certainly have consulted the rabbis of the Jewish community in Cairo, and intriguingly he may even have had it printed in Hebrew. (There has long been a rumor that the Jewish community of Cairo possessed a small Hebrew printing press prior to Napoleon's invasion.)

The existence of a copy of Napoleon's proclamation might have helped to clear up such questions, but for almost a century and a half no copy came to light, with the result that its very existence began to recede into the realms of mythology. Then in 1940 a sensational discovery was made in Vienna, when a copy in German on "strong old paper in a well-conserved handwriting" was found in the archives of a Viennese family with a rabbinical tradition. An eighteenth-century ancestor of this family was known to have been an authority to whom "questions of religious law were submitted for his ruling from remote parts of the world including Palestine and Morocco."[14] The discovery of such a document in Vienna, two years after the Nazis had taken over Austria and were persecuting the Jews, as well as destroying their property, was miraculous enough, but a copy was then somehow smuggled to wartime Britain, where it was translated into English and appeared in September 1940 in the now defunct magazine *New Judaea*.

Inevitably, all this was regarded with skepticism by some historians, who suspected that this German translation was either a forgery or a complete hoax. All the internal evidence in this document points against such a view. The somewhat bogus "Oriental style" of the proclamation precisely echoes that which Napoleon's orientalist savants used when putting together other proclamations that he made to the people of

Egypt and Syria. The 500-word proclamation, which incorporates several Biblical allusions—one to the Book of Isaiah, another to Maccabees, and two to Joel—bears many of the hallmarks of the fifty-six-year-old Orientalist Jean-Michel de Venture. He is known to have been one of the savants who accompanied Napoleon on the Syrian expedition, and in fact died on May 16, 1799, just a month after the proclamation was published, officially having succumbed to dysentery, but in fact almost certainly dying of the plague.

Others have pointed out that this German version of Napoleon's Proclamation to the Jews contains a number of glaring mistakes; but if anything these very mistakes would seem to confirm its authenticity. Why would any forger claim that it was written in Jerusalem, when this was so evidently impossible? This has the authentic ring of Napoleonic exaggeration. Lastly, and perhaps most convincingly, what would be the motive for such a forgery, which has brought neither money nor renown to its purported forger? Yet the unavoidable fact remains that no French (or Hebrew) version of this document has yet been found, either in the Middle East or in France, and even more damningly there is no reference whatsoever to such a proclamation in any of Napoleon's countless dispatches and voluminous memoirs. Despite this, I am inclined to believe that Napoleon did issue this Proclamation to the Jews, for at the same time he issued proclamations to the Christians, the Druze, and even various Arab leaders. He had high hopes of attracting all these people to his cause, and getting volunteers from amongst them to join him, thus swelling the dwindling ranks of French soldiers on his Syrian campaign—which we now know was intended to be just the beginning of a far greater enterprise.

XXIV

"That man made me lose my destiny"

Now that Napoleon had dispatched the Army of Damascus, the way ahead lay open, but although he certainly considered the option of marching north immediately to take Damascus and Aleppo, he resisted this temptation. Instead, he returned to Acre to complete the task at hand. By now word had reached him that Admiral Perrée had eluded the British naval blockade and landed at Tantura, fifteen miles south of Haifa, with three frigates bringing three twenty-four-pound cannons and four eighteen-pounders, as well as ammunition. These now had to be hauled twenty-five miles overland, but were expected at Acre within a matter of days.

The siege itself had by this stage become a succession of slogging artillery exchanges, which resulted in some heavy French casualties in the sappers' trenches, whose operations were directed in person by the indefatigable one-legged engineer Caffarelli. One night, whilst demonstrating his plans, Caffarelli inadvertently raised his arm above the parapet of the trench and it was shattered by a cannonball. He was quickly rushed to the field hospital, where Surgeon-in-Chief Larrey was forced to amputate in order to save his life. When the general's condition deteriorated, Napoleon ordered Bourrienne to remain at Caffarelli's side, though it soon became clear that he was dying: "A little before his final moments he said to me: 'My dear Bourrienne, please read to me that preface by Voltaire to [Montesquieu's] *The Spirit of Laws*.'" [1] Bourrienne told Napoleon about Caffarelli's request, and he guessed what this meant: for the atheist Caffarelli this great work of political theory was his Bible, and having it read to him was his equivalent of the last rites. Napoleon went to see him, but he had slipped into sleep;

later that night the forty-three-year-old Caffarelli died "with the utmost tranquility. His death was mourned by both the soldiers and the savants."★

Napoleon had lost the one general to whom he felt particularly close. At the same time, his confidant the aging mathematician Monge succumbed to dysentery, which he had caught whilst touring the hospital wards with Chief Medical Officer Desgenettes, whom he was assisting in a much-needed rationalization of the overstretched facilities. Monge quickly became delirious with the fever, and Napoleon had his camp bed moved into his commander-in-chief's tent, where he personally supervised Monge's treatment. On one particularly cold night, he even went so far as to get up and lay his own blankets over Monge's body as he lay shivering with fever. (He thought that Monge was asleep, but the savant would remember this incident with deep gratitude, even claiming that Napoleon had saved his life.)

Under cover of the artillery barrages, the French sappers were attempting to burrow up to the walls and mine the large central keep, the tower that appeared to be the linchpin of the city's defenses. According to Napoleon's intelligence, behind the tower lay open ground, the gardens of Djezzar's palace, with only a narrow wall between them and the streets of the city. The sappers finally succeeded in inserting a mine beneath the central tower, and Napoleon decided to launch his attack at once, without waiting for the heavy siege guns. On April 24 at nine A.M., the mine was exploded, but this merely blew a small hole in the side of the tower, causing one corner to crumble. Even so, the French were confident that the explosion had driven the enemy soldiers from the tower, and that there would be a way through the collapsed wall into the city. According to Paymaster Peyrusse, who witnessed the ensuing assault:

A column of grenadiers immediately charged the breach. Although it soon became clear that there was no hope of getting through, this did not deter the grenadiers, who bravely launched themselves into the breach. The enemy had in fact remained in the top of the tower and hidden behind the battlements; they began crushing our troops with rocks, shells and hand grenades. However,

★ Caffarelli was buried at Acre, and recent archaeological excavations here came across several graves dating from the period of Napoleon's campaign, one of which contained an unmistakable wooden leg. Caffarelli's body has since been shipped back to France and reburied with full military honors.

since nothing was able to repel our troops, the enemy resorted to throwing down on them 2 or 3 barrels of gunpowder whose ignition caused all our men to suffocate in the blast, although a few did manage to get out half-covered with flames.[2]

Despite such setbacks, Napoleon was still writing confidently back to Cairo: "I expect to take Acre by 5 or 6 May."[3]

As Napoleon had commented when he was a younger man, coincidentally in the same year as his previous encounter with Sidney Smith at the siege of Toulon: "It is axiomatic in the art of war that the side which remains behind its fortified line is always defeated. Experience and theory agree on that point."[4] It was evident that the tide was now turning against Djezzar's forces, which were suffering heavy casualties and would not be able to hold out much longer. Amongst these casualties was Napoleon's school bête noire Phélippeaux; Sir Sidney Smith wrote on May 2, the day after his friend's death: "Phélypeaux [sic] has fallen a sacrifice to his zeal for this service: want of rest and exposure to the sun having given him a fever, of which he died. Our grief for his loss is excessive on every account."[5] But Phélippeaux's influence lived on. He had instructed Djezzar to hang lanterns on the ramparts at night, and for the time being this successfully thwarted the French attempts to mine the walls under cover of darkness. Despite such measures, Djezzar was becoming increasingly pessimistic. Sidney Smith did his best to rouse him, but the old tyrant preferred to resort to his own time-honored devices, consulting his court astrologer, who cast chicken bones to read Napoleon's intentions. The bones predicted that Napoleon would attack the central tower—a safe bet, given that his artillery had focused on little else—and Djezzar pondered this revelation gloomily.

Four days later the siege passed into its fiftieth day, and on the following day Napoleon's heavy artillery arrived after its long haul overland. But as these guns were being maneuvered into position, the French received an unpleasant surprise. In the words of Bernoyer, there "appeared at sea a convoy of thirty sails. At first we thought it must be reinforcements arriving from France; but our hopes vanished when we made out the English and Turkish flags."[6] This fleet, under the command of Hassan Bey, had been dispatched from Rhodes and was bringing a division of Turkish troops, as well as large quantities of fresh supplies for the beleaguered garrison.

Napoleon immediately ordered an all-out artillery barrage, to be followed by an assault next morning before these reinforcements could be landed. Through the night, regardless of the lanterns, the French sappers moved along their trenches towards the walls, building up earthworks and mounds to protect themselves. Looking down from the ramparts, Smith grimly observed that these mounds were "composed of sand bags and *the bodies of their dead, built in with them* [his italics], their bayonets alone being visible above them."[7]

Before dawn the French launched their attack. The waves of bayonet-wielding grenadiers, their red uniforms and dark plumed helmets dimly illuminated in the lantern-glow, charged over the mounds of earth and cadavers that had now been pushed forward to fill in the moat. Smith recorded that "the enemy gained ground, made a lodgement on the second storey of the north-east tower, the upper part being completely battered down, and the ruins in the ditch forming the ascent by which they mounted. Daylight shewed us the French standard on the outer angle of the tower." He concluded that this was now "a most critical part of the conquest" and led the 800 British marines and naval gun crews down from the walls with the aim of defending the breach, which remained partially blocked, with only a few unarmed Turkish defenders tossing stones over the rubble onto the French heads. Smith and his men relieved them in a desperate last stand, with "the heaps of ruins between the two parties serving as a breastwork for both, the muzzles of their muskets touching and the spearheads of their standards locked." In a hectic last-ditch battle, the British and French soldiers continued shooting at each other at point-blank range amidst the rubble and smoke, with neither side willing to concede.

When Djezzar learned what Smith was doing, he was horrified. According to Smith: "Djezzar Pasha, hearing that the British were on the breach, quitted his station, where, according to ancient Turkish custom, he was sitting to reward such as should bring him the heads of the enemy and distributing musket cartridges with his own hands. The energetic old man, coming behind us, pulled us down with violence, saying if any harm happened to his English friends all was lost." Djezzar insisted that his own troops should defend the breach, knowing that this was how his soldiers fought at their best. Smith seems to have gambled on this response, and immediately evacuated his men to guard the landing of the Turkish troops and fresh supplies. By now the French heavy siege guns were beginning to have an effect, "every shot knocking down whole sheets of a wall, much less solid than that of the tower."

Through the morning the French artillery succeeded in opening a further breach in the walls adjoining the central tower, which Smith reckoned was "practicable for fifty men abreast."

Late that afternoon Smith mounted onto the battlements and scoured the enemy positions through his telescope. He noticed that "groups of generals and aides-de-camps . . . were now assembled on the [opposite hillside].

Bonaparte was distinguishable in the centre of the semi-circle; his gesticulation indicated a renewal of attack, and his despatching of an aide-de-camp to the camp shewed that he waited only for a reinforcement." Smith's reading of the situation was correct, and just before sunset the French launched a determined assault through the breach, with General Lannes leading his men in. According to Smith: "Djezzar Pasha's idea was not to defend the brink this time, but rather to let a certain number of the enemy in, and then close with them, according to the Turkish mode of war. The [French] column thus mounted the breach unmolested and descended from the ramparts into the Pasha's garden, where, in a very few minutes, the bravest and the most advanced among them lay headless corpses, the sabre, with the addition of a dagger in the other hand, proving more than a match for the bayonet."[8] The rest of Lannes' invaders defended themselves valiantly, eventually breaking through; but they were perturbed to notice that they were now cut off, with no support troops managing to make it into the garden after them. Despite this, they fought their way forward into the narrow streets of the town beside the main mosque and Djezzar's palace, where they encountered all kinds of obstructions, as well as fierce resistance from the crack Albanian troops that had disembarked from Hassan Bey's fleet. These men were encouraged in their resistance by the women of the town, who were letting out their traditional ululating shriek from the rooftops above the gunshots and cries of the men below. Chief of Staff Berthier recorded:

The firing from the buildings, from the barricades in the street, and from Djezzar's palace, caught the front and the rear of those who were descending the breach into the town, and those already in the town began to withdraw, as they were unable to hold out. . . . All the column inside the town was turned into a scrum of men trying to get out; General Lannes went forward in an effort to reverse this retreat and get the column moving forward again. . . . The effect of the initial charge through the breach was entirely dissipated; General Lannes was seriously wounded, General Rambaud was killed. . . . There was nothing else to do but sound the retreat, and the order was given.[9]

Amidst the chaos, the leading part of the column became cut off. Bernoyer describes their reaction:

Seeing they were not followed by their comrades, they lost hope of being rescued; these brave soldiers decided to stand their ground to the last man. They took possession of a mosque, where they barricaded themselves in and defended like lions against the efforts of the numerous opposing troops, who were enraged by the losses they had suffered in the course of the day's fighting.

Faced with such combat, which was to be a fight to the bitter end, the English Admiral Sidney Smith was moved by sentiments of humanity and generosity to intervene, and lost no time in coming to the rescue of our brave soldiers with a detachment of English soldiers. He called upon our grenadiers to surrender themselves and in return he promised them protection: they trusted him and this amiable officer saved the life of 200 men.*[10]

Eventually the French assault was abandoned. The fighting had now continued for over twenty-four hours, and there followed a lull, with "both parties being so fatigued as to be unable to move." Smith knew that this uncanny silence could not last. After supervising the landing of Hassan Bey's troops, at sunset he mounted the battlements once more. His assessment of the situation was grim: "The town is not, nor ever has been, defensible, according to the rules of art; but according to every other rule, it must and shall be defended." But this time it was not the French generals who stood on the heights, surveying the plain before Acre; through his eyeglass, Smith could make out crowds of tribesmen and villagers who had gathered from all around on the far hillsides to watch the final outcome of the siege. Smith fully understood the significance of this: "'Tis on the issue of this conflict that depends the opinion of the multitude of spectators on the surrounding hills, who wait only to see how it ends to join the victor, and with [a victory for Napoleon being] such a reinforcement for the execution of

★ Amiable though such sentiments may have been, this chivalrous treatment of the French soldiers by the British, and the complementary treatment of the British prisoners housed amidst the tents of the French army, exposes the unthinking racism of the period. Europeans saw themselves as superior; they were worthy of such treatment, and were capable of appreciating such marks of civilization amidst the carnage of war. No such sentiments were extended towards the Turkish army— or any of its Arab, Mameluke, Albanian, Levantine or Berber soldiers—in whose territory this conflict was taking place. (Nor, it must be said, did these scimitar-wielding warriors make, or expect, such gestures themselves.)

his known projects, Constantinople, and even Vienna, must feel the shock." Indicatively, Smith did not mention any effect, global or otherwise, that might result from Napoleon's defeat, and later confirmed his pessimism, admitting: "We may, and probably shall be overpowered." Such a judgment only makes his unceasing bravery even more admirable.

Meanwhile, in the opposing camp, not all the French generals were enthusiastic about their confident young commander-in-chief's tactics. According to a remark usually attributed to Junot: "The Turks have a medieval army inside and we Europeans with our modern army are on the outside, yet we're the ones using medieval methods, while they're defending European style."[11]

Throughout the next day, May 9, the eerie calm continued, while Napoleon prepared for his final all-out assault on Acre. That evening, as he walked on the beach out of range of the city's guns, with Bourrienne at his side, he confessed that "he was distressed to see the blood of so many brave men uselessly spilt." Then he outlined his plans: if he succeeded in overrunning Acre, as he was convinced he would, he expected to find Djezzar's treasures, which would be more than enough to finance an army, as well as

arms enough for 3,000 men. I will call to arms the whole of Syria. . . . I will march on Aleppo and Damascus. I will enlarge my army as I advance through the country attracting all those who are discontented. I will announce to the people the end of their servitude and of the tyrannous government of the pashas. I will arrive at Constantinople with massed armies. I will overthrow the Turkish empire. I will found in the Orient a great new empire which will write my name in history, and perhaps I will return to Paris by way of Adrianople [in European western Turkey] or through Vienna after having annihilated the House of Austria.[12]

Such a speech may sound like the exaggerated ranting of a man attempting to psych himself up on the eve of a decisive battle, but this does not mean that its contents can simply be dismissed. As we have seen, these grandiose dreams had been developing in Napoleon's mind throughout the Egyptian expedition. Bourrienne, for one, stresses that he was constantly referring to such schemes, and several generals' memoirs indicate that they too had heard, often firsthand, about Napoleon's "Oriental fantasy." The historian's need to refer to this, again and again, is in order to stress the actuality of this fantasy, and the primacy of its place in Napoleon's thinking. And it is possible that Napoleon's motive for repeating it involved very similar reasons. The self-conviction required for such an unprecedented ambition, in a sane mind very much in contact with reality, can only be imagined.

It was in a bid to appeal to this very sanity that Sidney Smith had written to Napoleon during the calm hours of May 9, in a letter revealing some information that had just reached him. Along with the Turkish reinforcements, Hassan Bey's fleet had also brought to Acre a young French Royalist officer, Major Charles de Trotté, who had been present when Beauchamp, Napoleon's final emissary to Constantinople, had been intercepted by the British. De Trotté had read Napoleon's letter to the grand vizier, as well as his secret instructions to Beauchamp about what to say if asked whether the French would leave Egypt, and he passed this information on to Smith. Mischievously, Smith decided to make use of this in his letter to Napoleon, quoting Beauchamp's secret instructions word for word (literally so, for he had the courtesy to write his letter in French):

Monsieur le Général,
    As your instructions to your emissary Beauchamp contained the words, "If you are asked whether the French would agree to leave Egypt" and your advice [was] that he should reply, "Why not?" . . . I did not wish to ask you the question, "Are the French willing to leave Syria?" before you had made an attempt to square up your forces against ours, since you could not be convinced, as I am, of the impracticability of your enterprise. But now that you have seen this place defended, as it can be, by virtue of its position, as well as its fortifications, and through the bravery of its garrison that is now no less numerous than its besiegers, and now that you can see that it becomes stronger day by day rather than being weakened by two months of siege, I ask you the following: "Are you willing to evacuate your troops from Ottoman territory before the arrival of the great allied army changes the nature of this question?"
    Believe me, Monsieur le Général, my only motive for suggesting this is my desire to avoid further bloodshed.[13]

This characteristically impudent letter would seem to have been a bold bluff by Smith, judging from the pessimism inadvertently revealed in his earlier report about the effects in Constantinople and Vienna of a French victory. Although Acre was certainly well supplied by now, his claim that it "becomes stronger day by day" was palpably untrue.

Likewise, his suggestion that a "great allied army" was on the way had no actual substance. The Turks were still taking an inordinate time assembling an army at Rhodes, and there was certainly no likelihood of this being joined by forces from its British and Russian allies. Yet Napoleon was not aware of this. He fully realized that the Turkish fleet would eventually bring an Ottoman army to Egypt, and he now had to contend with the possibility that the British or the Russians might have embarked upon similar plans. But by this stage he had more pressing concerns. Despite his professed distress to Bourrienne at seeing "the blood of so many brave men uselessly spilt," and Sir Sidney Smith's letter suggesting a means of avoiding further bloodshed, he was determined to go ahead with his final assault. To this end, Kléber had been ordered to march his division back from the Palestinian hinterland to join the besieging forces. Napoleon vowed that he himself would lead this assault in a do-or-die mission, an indication of how much importance he placed on the capture of Acre. Once again he would expose himself to death and put his destiny to the test. However, he was eventually dissuaded from this rash act by his generals. Instead, he decided that Kléber's grenadiers should lead the assault on the main breach, with Kléber himself ordered to keep to the rear, so that he could properly direct operations. (If Napoleon himself was not to lead the charge, no other general was going to steal his thunder.)

Early on the morning of May 10, Napoleon's final assault on Acre began. Inspired by stirring words from their general, and a generous issue of brandy, Kléber's men charged into the breach. Valiantly disobeying his orders, Kléber joined the leaders of the charge, encouraging them on with his saber-wielding example.

But now Hassan Bey's Turkish reinforcements sprang a surprise, launching a brave counterattack from the other, smaller breach, seizing the trenches before the battered central tower. General Bon's division, which was intended to support Kléber's in a two-pronged attack, was now forced to fight its way through the trenches in front of the walls, and during the course of this action Bon was killed. In the end, both prongs managed to penetrate the walls, only to be driven back by fierce fire from the reinforced defendants.

The French now regrouped in the heat of the day. By this stage the recaptured trenches before the walls had become a stinking morass of rotting flesh amongst the sandbags of the protective breastworks. To this were now added the unburied dead of the assault two days previously, as well as the dead and howling dying of the attack just abandoned. The battleground on either side of the walls had become a killing field piled with hundreds of French and thousands of Turkish bodies.

Napoleon stood at the forward siege battery, assessing the situation, with his telescope resting on the parapet of the trench. He was far from being out of danger himself, for according to his aide Lavallette, at one point "a bullet hit the upper parapet, the general-in-chief fell into the arms of General Berthier, and we thought him dead, but luckily he had not been hit." Lavallette described what happened next:

Kléber's grenadiers, who were back in their trenches, began demanding with loud shouts a renewal of the assault, but Napoleon hesitated, until he was finally persuaded by these brave men and gave the signal. It was a grand and terrific spectacle: the grenadiers rushed forward under a shower of cannon balls. General Kléber, with the gait of a giant, took his place on the bank of the breach, sword in hand, roaring his men on with a stentorian voice. The sight of all these men hurling themselves forward at the enemy, through the noise and smoke of the cannons, the yells of their fellow soldiers, and the howling of the Turks, made one's heart surge with a raging enthusiasm. There was no doubt that the city was ours at last, when suddenly the column stopped.[14]

According to Sir Sidney Smith, the French grenadiers "absolutely refused to mount the breach any more over the putrefied bodies of their unburied companions, sacrificed in former attacks by Bonaparte's impatience and precipitation, which led him to commit such palpable errors . . . He seemed to have no principle of action but that of pressing forward."[15]

Not surprisingly, Lavallette saw it somewhat differently: "Finally we learned what obstacle was preventing any more troops from advancing. During the interval between the two assaults the enemy had filled the ditch on the other side of the breach with all kinds of inflammable material [including a mine], and with furious and repeated barrages killed all who appeared before them . . . the ditch was vomiting out flames, a thick explosion of the materials with which the mine was charged . . . came out of the ground and overthrew every one. . . . Kléber, in a great rage, struck his thigh with his sword; but the General-in-Chief, judging the obstacle to be insurmountable, gave a gesture and ordered a retreat."[16]

This was to be Napoleon's last attempt to take Acre, although the siege was to persist for another ten days. On the evening after his last attack Napoleon outlined his immediate plans in his regular report to the Directory. The reason he would make no further attempt to overrun the city was because "it would cost more lives than I am willing to lose. In any case, the summer season is too advanced. The goal that I set myself is fulfilled: Egypt now calls me. I am setting up a battery of 24 pounders to raze to the ground Djezzar's palace and the principal buildings of the town. I am going to fire in around a thousand mortar shells, which will, in such a cramped space, cause a great deal of damage. Having reduced Acre to a heap of stones, I will come back across the desert ready to confront the European or Turkish army which will attempt to land in Egypt sometime in the months of Messidor or Thermidor [i.e., between mid-June and mid-August]."[17]

This was the first setback, the first hint of defeat, that Napoleon had suffered on the field of battle. His reaction was much as one might have predicted: a characteristic blend of vindictiveness and self-deception, which would gradually deepen as he attempted to overcome this blow to his superlative pride. Sir Sidney Smith, for his part, read the situation more realistically. He judged that morale in the French camp would now be at its lowest since the expedition began—lack of victory, the many dead and wounded, as well as the constant nagging fear of the plague and its continuing toll, would all be having their cumulative effect. In an effort to increase these debilitating factors, Smith now embarked on a propaganda campaign, having leaflets scattered from the battlements which were carried on the wind to the French camp. These contained a proclamation, purporting to come from the Sublime Porte, even carrying its official imprimatur, though it was almost certainly written by Smith himself. It was addressed "to the generals, officers and soldiers of the French army which has arrived in Egypt," and opened by blaming the Directory for "completely ignoring the rights of man" and sending the army to Egypt "in violation of the laws of war." It went on to warn the French that "at this very moment innumerable armies and immense fleets are already on their way across the sea" to attack them. There then followed an offer:

Those amongst you, of whatever rank, who wish to escape from this danger which threatens you, must, without the least delay, indicate your intentions to the commanders of the land and sea forces of the allied powers, who give safe guarantee that they will have them shipped wherever they desire to go, and will issue them with passports so that they will have free passage and need have nothing to fear from the allied fleets or any other battleships they encounter on their way.

This was undersigned by Smith, who described himself as "minister plenipotentiary of the King of England to the Ottoman Port and actual commander of the allied fleet at Acre."[18]

Some French memoirs of those present patriotically claim that this proclamation only had the effect of strengthening the resolve of the French soldiers, but Napoleon himself would later admit that Smith's proclamation "certainly shook some of [my troops], and I therefore published an order stating that he was mad, and forbidding all further communication with him."[19] Napoleon had already sent word to Admiral Perrée to prepare to sail up the coast and collect the wounded, and he now quickly began making preparations for his entire army to move on, but not before he had received an amazingly personal and provocative letter from Smith: "General, I am [aware] that for some days past you have been making to raise the siege; the preparations in hand to carry off your wounded, and to leave none behind you, do you credit."[20] The unspoken insinuation here is that, according to the rules of war, Napoleon would require Smith's permission if Perrée's ships were to land and collect the wounded without being fired upon. Smith now addressed himself intimately to Napoleon, uncannily selecting the very topic which to Napoleon was most sacred, and to which he was most susceptible— namely his destiny, which Smith had the effrontery to compare with his own. (His somewhat garbled style would seem to be a reflection of extreme exhaustion.)

I, who ought not to love you, to say nothing more: but circumstances remind me to wish that you would reflect on the instability of human affairs. In fact, could you have thought that a poor prisoner in a cell of the Temple prison— that an unfortunate for whom you refused, for a single moment, to give yourself any concern, being at the same time able to render him a signal service since you were then all-powerful—could you have thought, I say, that this same man would have become your antagonist and have compelled you in the midst of the sands of Syria to raise the siege of a miserable, almost defenseless town. Such events, you must admit, exceed all human calculations. Believe me, general, adopt sentiments more moderate; that a man will not be your

enemy who shall tell you that Asia is not a theatre made for your glory. This
letter is a little revenge that I give myself.

Smith was in the Temple at the time of Napoleon's triumphant return
to Paris from his Italian campaign, and now had the impudence to
suggest that Napoleon should have remembered the man—a pirate in
French eyes!—who had thwarted him so many years previously at the
siege of Toulon.* Napoleon was furious, and in order not to reveal
Smith's insults pretended to his officers (and later even convinced
himself) that Smith had had the impertinence to challenge him to a
duel. He claimed to have laughed at this, insisting that he could only
accept such a challenge from a "Marlborough" (a reference to the great
British general; in other words, only a military commander of the same
supreme rank as himself). Smith always denied that he had issued such
a challenge, but delighted in pointing out that he would have been
quite entitled to do so, for "at the time we were of equal rank—he,
General Bonaparte, commander-in-chief of the French army in Egypt,
and I, General [sic] Smith, commander-in-chief of the Turkish army, so
specially constituted by the Emperor Selim."²¹

From now on, Napoleon determined to have nothing further to do
with Smith. On May 21 the siege of Acre was called off, and the French
army began its long march back to Egypt. The siege had lasted sixty-
two days and had resulted in heavy losses all round. Inside Acre the
final toll amongst the citizens, the besieged army, and the division of
Turkish reinforcements has been estimated as high as 15,000—a huge
figure, accounting for almost 250 lives per day, to say nothing of the
wounded. Despite this, surrender had been out of the question for
Djezzar, and his troops had probably thought likewise—after seeing

---

* Curiously, Smith did in fact address a letter to Napoleon when he was in the
Temple, scratching it on the shutter of his cell in the hugely optimistic expectation that its contents would reach the man who was the toast of Paris. This expectation was unrequited, but the letter itself is astonishingly prescient, dealing as it
does with precisely the same topic as this letter to Napoleon at Acre just eighteen
months later: "One has to admit that Fortune's wheel makes strange revolutions
but, before it can be truly called a revolution, the turn of the wheel must be
complete. Today you are as high as you can be, but I do not envy you your happiness because I have a still greater happiness, and that is to be as low in Fortune's
wheel as I can go, so that as soon as that capricious lady turns her wheel again,
I shall rise for the same reason that you will fall" (Barrow, *Life and Correspondence
of Admiral Sir William Sidney Smith*, Vol. 1, pp. 216–17).

what had happened to their colleagues at Jaffa. French losses had also been heavy. Napoleon would later claim that his entire Syrian campaign resulted in 500 killed and 1,000 wounded. However, according to the historian La Jonquière, who had access to the Ministry of War archives, the French casualties on the Syrian campaign probably amounted to around 1,200 killed, another 1,000 dead of disease, and 2,300 wounded, which accounts for more than a third of the forces with which Napoleon had set out for Syria. These casualties were spread through all ranks: besides Caffarelli and Bon, five other generals lost their lives, as did half a dozen savants, the most distinguished being de Venture and Say. Amongst Napoleon's aides, Crosier was dead and Beauharnais wounded.[22]

Napoleon's defeat at Acre, for such it was, meant the end of his immediate dreams of overthrowing the Ottoman Empire, of following in the footsteps of Alexander to India, of establishing an Oriental empire. He had no doubts about the colossal extent of this setback to his destiny, nor who was responsible for it. Many years later he would confide to his brother Lucien: "I missed my fortune at Acre," and after he had got over his immediate denunciation of Smith as a "madman" and a "lunatic," he would finally admit, "That man made me lose my destiny."[23]

XXV

The Retreat from Acre

ON March 25, during the first week of the siege of Acre, the courier Wynand Mourveau had arrived at Napoleon's headquarters bringing a message from the Directory in Paris. Dated November 4, 1798, it had taken almost three months to reach its destination. In fact, it was the third copy of this message to have been dispatched. The first had left Paris in the first week of November carried by Brigadier Lucotte, who had traveled to Spain in the hope of finding a ship that would take him to Egypt, or at least part of the way there. But this quest had proved fruitless, and after three months he crossed Europe to Italy, arriving at the southeastern port of Ancona, only to find himself under siege before he could set sail. A second copy of the Directory's letter to Napoleon had been entrusted to a French businessman traveling to Tunis, but just two days after his arrival the Bey of Tunis had declared war on France, putting an end to this mission. Finally Wynand Mourveau had been dispatched from Paris in late January 1799, bearing the Directory's three-month-old message as well as some more up-to-date newspapers. On February 9 he had sailed from Genoa on a ship that had managed to beat the British naval blockade of Egypt and had arrived at Damietta on February 26, only to discover that Napoleon had left for Syria. It had then taken him a further month to reach Napoleon's headquarters outside Acre.

The message from the Directory was in the form of a lengthy letter, approved by the Directory, but for the most part written by Talleyrand. It opened by informing Napoleon that "since your departure from Malta, the Directory has only received one piece of news directly from you, that dated 2 Fructidor [August 20] which was brought to us on 23

Vendémiaire [October 14] by the courier Mothey. Any other couriers that you have been able to send have either been killed, or been taken prisoner."[1] The Directory's letter was intended to inform Napoleon of the latest developments in Europe and issue him with further instructions. On both counts it proved woefully inadequate. The description of the European political situation pre-dated the one Napoleon had received from the merchant Hamelin before setting out for Syria, and even the later newspapers gave him no significant further information. Russia, Turkey and Britain had formed a triple alliance and were at war with France; meanwhile the general European situation remained threatening but not too serious, in the view of the Directory. The letter ended with superfluous advice which can only have further convinced Napoleon of the Directory's ineptitude: "Not being able to give you any help, the Directory will refrain from giving you any orders, or even instructions. You will act according to your own assessment of your position and how strongly established you are in Egypt." Having admitted that it was incapable of shipping Napoleon's army back to France, it suggested:

This seems to leave you with three options amongst which you can choose. Either to sit it out in Egypt, setting yourself up so as to be protected from Turkish attacks ... or to march for India, where, if you arrive, there is no doubt you will find men ready to join up with you to destroy English domination. Or finally, to march on Constantinople and meet the enemy who is threatening you. It is up to you to choose, in accord with the elite of brave and distinguished men who surround you.

Talleyrand's motives were always difficult to fathom, but it appears from this message that he may have taken Napoleon's dreams of an Oriental empire seriously, even if the Directory had previously been somewhat less sure on this account. Or possibly he was simply using these dreams as a camouflage for the utter paucity of what he had to offer. Either way, this message boiled down to little more than a confession of complete impotence where Napoleon was concerned, and Napoleon would certainly have recognized this. He was in total command, and on his own: the fact had now been officially acknowledged. He took orders from no one.

Napoleon barely mentioned this message, beyond informing a few of his senior generals that little appeared to have changed in the international situation. There may have been no possibility of shipping his army back to Europe, but there can be no doubt that he still kept open the option that he himself might return. His inability to take Acre meant the end of his Oriental dreams, at least for the time being. The possibility of returning to France now became a more serious option—though indicatively it was not one of the options suggested by the Directory.

Napoleon was determined that the retreat from Acre should not have a further disillusioning effect upon the already low morale of his troops, and to this end he issued a proclamation:

Soldiers! You have crossed the desert which separates Africa from Asia faster than an army of Arabs.

The army which was marching towards Egypt has been destroyed; you have captured its general, its equipment, its waterskins and its camels. On the battle-field at Mount Tabor you put to flight a horde of men gathered from all over Asia intent on the pillage of Egypt.

The thirty ships which you saw anchored off Acre . . . brought an army . . . which is now destroyed. Its captured flags will accompany your triumph. Having captured forty guns and taken 6,000 prisoners, and reducing to rubble the fortifications of Gaza, Jaffa, Haifa and Acre, we shall return to Egypt. I must return because it is now the time of year when hostile landings can be expected.

Just a few days ago, you were on the point of taking Djezzar captive in his palace, but now the capture of Acre is not worth wasting time over. The brave men we might have lost here are needed for more important endeavors.

Soldiers! Hardship and danger lie ahead. . . . For you these will be new opportunities for glory. If, in the midst of so much combat, every day sees the death of a hero, then new heroes must rise up and take their place . . . and from such dangers seize victory.[2]

The French soldiers were surprised to learn that their Syrian campaign had been such a succession of glorious victories, and Bourrienne, to whom Napoleon would have dictated this proclamation, remarked in his memoirs: "This proclamation, from beginning to end, mutilated the truth."[3] Another document dictated to Bourrienne on this matter, which must have left him similarly unimpressed, was Napoleon's report to the Directory:

The occasion appeared favorable for taking Acre, but our spies, their deserters and our prisoners all indicated that the city was being ravaged by the plague, that more than sixty people per day were dying of the disease, all dying within 36 hours of catching the disease, amidst convulsions similar to rabies. As our men poured into the city it would have been impossible to prevent them from pillaging, and that night they would have brought back into our camp the germs of this terrible scourge, which is more formidable than any army in the world.[4]

This charade of glorious victory, and astute tactical holding back, was further encouraged by Napoleon's order to his retreating troops: "Every time the army passes through a village they will enter bearing the unfurled Turkish flags captured from the enemy, accompanied by a band playing."[5] Perhaps the locals could be convinced of French victory, even if the army itself could not.

In reality the French army crept away from Acre under cover of darkness. As Peyrusse recalled: "All that we could not take with us, which included cannons of all calibers, mortars, shells and bombs, and almost all the tools from the artillery depot, were buried in the fields and along the seashore. We blew up all the gunpowder that was left, and all the empty crates were stacked and burnt on the plain. Such was the fate of our entire artillery park."[6] But worst of all: "We had not time to lose: we were without any means of transport whatever and we had between a thousand and one thousand two hundred wounded or fever cases to carry, as well as forty pieces of artillery to drag, along with all their gear."

The sick and wounded presented a very real problem. Perrée had been ordered to put in at Tantura to pick up several hundred wounded, so that they could be shipped to Alexandria. However, he had felt certain that his flotilla would only be attacked by Smith's squadron, and had refused to take the risk. The problem of shipping the wounded back to hospitals in Egypt could have been resolved if Napoleon had been willing to ask Smith for safe conduct for French ships carrying the wounded, a request Smith would certainly have granted. Yet Napoleon stood on his pride, and still refused to have any further dealings with Smith, let alone ask him a favor. At this point, Perrée and his flotilla made for the safety of the open sea, and here he came to the extraordinary decision that his best course of action was simply to sail back to France.

Napoleon faced an impossible situation: no sick or wounded could be left behind, for the Turks would have beheaded them, or worse still subjected them to hideous tortures. (This was their custom with such victims of war, and after the massacre of their comrades at Jaffa it might even have appeared justified.) To make matters worse, the French were now joined by further sick and wounded from the outlying field hospitals, as well as patients from the plague hospital at Mount Carmel and other isolation centers.

This meant that Napoleon had the task of transporting 2,300 sick and wounded men the 500 miles overland to Egypt as best he could. To that end, he divided them into three categories: those who could walk (or could be assisted to do so by others), those who were able to ride on a horse or a donkey, and those who required to be carried on a makeshift stretcher. As for the army itself: every man, from the generals to the lowliest drummer boys, was ordered to walk. Horses, even Napoleon's own, were to be requisitioned for the second category of sick and wounded. Pack mules and donkeys which had previously been used for transporting water skins and supplies were also requisitioned for carrying those who could not walk. The aging Monge, who was still stricken with dysentery, was allowed to travel in Napoleon's carriage, along with Berthollet, who had also fallen ill, as well as the sick mathematician-savant Costaz, and an officer's wife who was breastfeeding a newly born child.

But this still left the problem of what to do with the plague victims. It was unlikely that many would volunteer to assist them back to Egypt, no matter how great the incentive. Desgenettes described in his memoirs what happened next:

Bonaparte summoned me to his tent, where he was alone with his chief of staff [Berthier]. After a brief chat about the general medical situation, he said to me: "If I was in your place, I would end at once the suffering of our plague patients, and would put an end to the dangers facing them by giving them [a lethal dose of] opium." I replied simply, "My duty, as I see it, is to preserve life." In consequence, the general began expounding his thoughts with great calmness, saying that he would not expect others to do anything that he would not do himself. He pointed out to me that he was, before anything else, charged with preserving the army, and *for that reason* to prevent our sick who cannot be taken with us from being left to the mercy of the Turkish scimitars. "I am not seeking to overcome your scruples," he added, "but I believe I can find people who will better appreciate my intentions."

General Berthier remained completely silent throughout this meeting, merely biting his nails; but afterwards he indicated to me that he approved of my refusal.[7]

Desgenettes, who had risked inoculating himself with the plague virus in order to fulfill his duties and encourage his patients, was not willing at this late stage to go back on his Hippocratic oath to save life. It seemed that he had called Napoleon's bluff, and for the time being the commander-in-chief decided against mass euthanasia for his men: the army left Acre carrying all its sick and wounded with them.

According to Desgenettes, "The retreat was undertaken in meticulous order." Lannes' division led the way, followed by the equipment; then came further long columns of trudging soldiers, with the sick and wounded protected in the midst of their divisions, which stretched back across the rolling countryside to Kléber's division, supported by Murat's cavalry, which guarded the rear. Many of the men had become unfit during the long siege, and the army made slow progress. Soon they were also being joined by streams of Christian refugees fleeing from the vengeance they knew Djezzar would wreak upon their communities. As the French army continued on its way, it burned villages, orchards and crops in its path, leaving a swath of scorched earth, so that if Djezzar's forces attempted to harass their retreat they would find it impossible to live off the land. Soon some of the sick and wounded proved too great a burden, and were simply abandoned by the wayside—those with the plague frequently being dumped at the first opportunity. Bourrienne tells of "dying figures cast by the roadside calling out in feeble voices: 'I have not got the plague, I am only wounded,' and in the effort to convince their passing comrades they would re-open their wounds or give themselves new ones."[8] Peyrusse described how

we continued quietly along our route beside the sea . . . we hoped we would not see before our eyes any more hideous sights of dead and dying men . . . when, upon entering Haifa that horrific night, we came across a hundred sick or wounded who had been left in the middle of a big square. These desperate wretches filled the air with their cries and curses. Some, convinced they had been abandoned, were tearing off their bandages and rolling in the dirt. This sight sent a chill through all the men, so we stopped for a moment and men from each company were detailed with the task of carrying them to Tantura; then we continued on our way.[9]

At Tantura, where the army had been waiting in vain for Perrée's flotilla, Peyrusse's retreating column stumbled in at three A.M. and came across "seven or eight hundred wounded or plague victims, together with twenty cannons and 1,200 bombs and no boat to transport them . . . The disorder was increased by the explosion of a crate of artillery shells which killed and wounded many people."[10]

As the long, straggling columns of French soldiers moved on through the burning countryside they were harassed by occasional raids from the tribesmen in the mountains around Nablus. At sea they made out the familiar sillhouette of the *Tigre*, along with Smith's squadron, following them down the coast, and soon the boom of cannons began sounding across the water, with cannonballs occasionally cutting swaths through their marching ranks.

By May 24 the first ragged columns were marching into Jaffa, some sixty miles south of Haifa, where Napoleon gave the order to rest for four days. Several vessels were in the harbor, and 1,200 of the sick and wounded were loaded on board for shipment to Damietta. According to Sir Sidney Smith: "I took care to be between Jaffa and Damietta. . . . The enemy's vessels being hurried to sea without seamen to navigate them, and the wounded being in want of every necessary, even water and provisions, they steered straight to His Majesty's ships, in full confidence of receiving the succours of humanity; in which they were not disappointed. . . . Their expressions of gratitude to us were mingled with execrations on the name of their general, who had, as they said, thus exposed them to perish."[11] Having given the French vessels water and provisions, Smith sent them on to Damietta where those on board could receive proper treatment.

But Napoleon still had some 800 or so sick and wounded left on his hands in Jaffa, many of whom were suffering from the plague. Most of these were transported with the advance parties as they left the town, many carried on stretchers or assisted by captured tribesmen and Turkish prisoners. Some had died in Jaffa, others had recovered, until according to Desgenettes all that were finally left were some thirty or so "without any hope of recovery." Though as we shall see, other eyewitnesses gave different figures.

Napoleon decided to assess the situation for himself, and visited the hospital. According to Bourrienne, who was with him:

Bonaparte strode rapidly through the wards, lightly rapping the top of his boot with his riding crop. . . . He addressed the patients: "We have to return to Egypt to save it from our enemies who are planning an invasion. In a few hours the Turks will be here, and all those who feel strong enough to rise can come with us; they will be carried on stretchers or on horseback." ... There were at least sixty plague patients ... their absolute silence, complete exhaustion and general apathy indicated that their end was approaching. To bring them with us, in the state that they were in, would have been tantamount to infecting the rest of the army with the disease."[12]

Napoleon suggested giving them fatal doses of opium, but once again Desgenettes refused to have anything to do with this, even to the point of denying that he had any left (which may well have been true). But Napoleon was determined, and brought in a Turkish physician from Constantinople called Hadj Mustafa, who had been aboard a ship which had inadvertently sailed into Jaffa without realizing the town had been taken by the French. He had with him sufficient laudanum (an opiate solution), and together with the French chief pharmacist Royer began administering this to the men. According to Desgenettes, who was present, lethal doses of laudanum were administered to twenty-five patients and "several of these rejected it by vomiting, felt relieved, were cured and lived to tell the tale."[13]

Two usually reliable sources—Napoleon's aide Lavallette and his surgeon-in-chief Larrey—strenuously denied that Napoleon did in fact poison dozens of his own soldiers at Jaffa. But it is difficult to disbelieve both Desgenettes and Bourrienne, and perhaps most indicative of all is a guilty note that Kléber scribbled in code in his private pocketbook at the time, which suggests that not only plague victims were involved. Decoded and translated, this note reads: "It was suggested that the health officers give opium to the fever patients and the seriously wounded."*[14]

Having left the last victims to die in peace, Napoleon evacuated Jaffa. Within a few hours Sir Sidney Smith sailed into the port and came ashore, where he found no sign of Turkish soldiers on the rampage. Instead, he was greeted by a ghoulish scene: "The heaps of unburied Frenchmen, lying on the bodies of those whom they massacred two months ago ... Seven poor wretches are left alive in the hospital; they are protected and shall be taken care of."[15]

From Jaffa the grim retreat continued south, reaching Gaza on May

---

* The precise note Kléber wrote in his pocketbook was: "*On propose aux o. d. s. d. d. d. l. aux f. et b. d.*," whose simple code was deciphered by his friend and colleague in Egypt, General Damas, as: "*On propose aux officiers de santé de donner de l'opium aux fièvreux et blessés dangereusement.*"

29. The temperature was now rising towards its debilitating summer zenith, and instead of the mud and cold rain they had to contend with on their way out, the French soldiers now faced the prospect of crossing the desert in temperatures of over 30° C (or the high eighties Fahrenheit). On top of this, they now had no pack mules carrying water skins. According to Napoleon's aide Lavallette, "When they saw before them the terrible desert, knowing from experience what they would have to suffer in crossing it without water, they began muttering amongst themselves, and after this they mutinied."[16] Such setbacks proved temporary, but Lavallette gives a good indication of the stress Napoleon was under. Despite his explicit order that horses should be strictly reserved for the sick and the wounded, "his chief stablemaster was foolish enough to ask if he was ready to mount his favorite mare, and this was the first time I saw him strike someone. Furious he went for him and thrashed him with his riding crop."

Bourrienne vividly evokes the effect of the desert on the men: "An all-consuming thirst, the total lack of water, the overwhelming heat, the tiring march through the burning sand dunes, made them lose all sense of compassion, so that they succumbed to the most cruel selfishness and were afflicted with a frightful indifference to their fellow humanity. I saw them throw men off their stretchers, officers who had amputated limbs whom they were ordered to carry, who had even given them money for their troubles."[17]

When the French soldiers made it across the desert to El-Arish, they knew that they were back in Egypt at last. Even so, there were still at least two long days' march before they reached the edge of the desert at Katia. According to Private Millet: "Having arrived at El Arish . . . we believed we would find provisions there; but there was very little, and this was under guard, reserved for the resident garrison and for the sick and wounded who were already there. So we had to go on to Katia without provisions, except for the little which remained from what we had received at Gaza."[18] Richardot records another scene:

Kléber's division, which continued to be the rearguard . . . halted around sunset. The troops, who were already exhausted, believed they had finished marching for the day and prepared to spend the night on the spot when, to their great surprise, the drums sounded for the continuation of the march. But either through spontaneous feeling, or by a prearranged plot, the troops would not budge, they refused to march on the command which was given, and you could hear the most violent swearing against the commander-in-chief

[Napoleon] coming from all units. One of Kléber's aides advanced quickly on the grenadiers who had ganged up together, and he commanded them in a threatening tone and gestures to start marching, but immediately he was greeted with fixed bayonets. The officer quickly ran to Kléber, who had already started, in order to inform him of what had happened. "Leave them be," said Kléber. "Let them please themselves and swear as much as they want—it's the only way they have of letting off steam. Just leave them. Let's not show that we know they've mutinied. They'll certainly come, you'll see. Let's march on." We followed the general's advice and a little later the division was on the march.[19]

During the afternoon of June 5 the French army finally reached Katia, where by this stage, according to Captain François, "the army was so strung out that it had just become one long queue, with many soldiers lost in the desert. It was necessary to sound several cannon shots by the wells where we had halted to give direction to those who were lost, many of whom did not arrive at the refreshing wells until well after nightfall."[20] As an example of how the soldiers coped crossing the desert, François recorded that: "My comrade Noel, who had both legs cut off at Acre, was saved by my care and by the twelve men charged with carrying him in turns on a stretcher; seven of our unit died crossing the desert. . . . As for me, in spite of the heat and the lack of a dressing, the wounds in my head healed into scars."

At Katia, tragedy momentarily gave way to comedy, when to his surprise Napoleon found himself encountering Menou, whom he had appointed governor of Palestine almost three months previously. Menou had been so reluctant to leave Rosetta, and his new wife, that he had only made it this far on his journey to Syria. Napoleon peremptorily informed General Abdullah Menou, as he now styled himself after his conversion to Islam, that his post no longer existed and he could return to Rosetta and his wife.

Napoleon now sent ahead to General Dugua in Cairo, informing him that owing to the great military success of the Syrian campaign, preparations were to be made for the army's triumphal entry into the city. He proposed to enter through the Bab-el-Nasr gate ("The Gate of Victory"), and he wished to be greeted by all the members of the *divan* and a full ceremonial guard of the resident French garrison.

Napoleon was determined that the victorious returning army should look at its best, and to this end the men would be provided with new uniforms and were to wear palm leaves in their caps as a mark of honor. Meanwhile the sick and wounded were to be dispatched north, where they would be dispersed through the hospitals of the coast and the delta. At the same time, the ragtag procession of refugees that had attached itself to the French army was to be sent to Damietta, with the promise of a parcel of fertile delta land for each family. After two days' rest and recuperation at Katia, the army set off on the road to Cairo, where they were eventually met by a supply convoy bringing their new uniforms. Smartly attired, they marched the last lap into Cairo on June 14. Here General Dugua had laid on a suitable welcome for the returning heroes, who paraded past lines of cheering crowds, accompanied by military bands playing rousing marches, each division bearing before it the many Turkish flags it had captured from the enemy during the course of the campaign. Napoleon himself was greeted by the *divan*, and Sheik El-Bekri presented him with a fine black Arab stallion, complete with a young Mameluke groom called Roustam Raza.*

Upon their return to barracks, the heroes of Napoleon's Syrian campaign were awarded a special "bounty" payment (which still did not make up for all the pay they were owed), and given three days' leave in the fleshpots of Cairo to spend it. Just as Napoleon hoped, news of his "glorious Syrian campaign" would eventually reach France, where its success was to be compared favorably with the failures of the increasingly inept Directory, making many long for the return of this hero to France.

---

* Roustam, who was of Armenian origin, would remain in Napoleon's service as his loyal bodyguard-cum-valet until 1814, when he retired and wrote his highly fanciful autobiography, *Souvenirs de Roustam: mamelouck de Napoleon Ier*, which was published posthumously in Paris in 1911.

XXVI

Sensational Discoveries

WHILE the heroic soldiers of the Syrian campaign celebrated in the stews of Cairo, Napoleon returned to his residence at Elfi Bey's palace and the waiting arms of his mistress Pauline Fourès. Yet as ever he found little time for relaxation: his arrival at his headquarters on Ezkebiyah Square prompted a flurry of orders, missives and dispatches. And just a week after his return, he sent word to Admiral Ganteaume in Alexandria that the fast frigates *La Muiron* and *La Carrère* should be put on a state of permanent readiness "so that they could sail at a moment's notice."[1] Although Ganteaume did not know it at the time, this order was given in case Napoleon should choose to return to France: there was no point in keeping his options open unless he made preparations to take them. Astonishingly, no one seems to have guessed at the motive behind this almost matter-of-fact order. Had anyone done so, the rumor would rapidly have spread throughout the army with catastrophic effect, but this was not the case.

Napoleon soon summoned a meeting of the Cairo *divan*, where his triumphant arrival carried an instructive message. According to Nicolas Turc, he began his opening speech to the assembled dignitaries: "I have learned, he declared, that enemies have spread rumors of my death. Take a good look at me, and assure yourselves that I really am Bonaparte."[2] He later issued instructions that this news should be posted in the streets of Cairo "so that all the city knows that Bonaparte is in good health, that he is not dead [and] that he has returned from conquering new countries bringing with him numerous victories."

General Dugua, assisted by Napoleon's chief financial officer Poussielgue, had maintained the French administration of Lower

Egypt as best he could. The financing of the Syrian expedition had left the exchequer all but empty, and Poussielgue had done his best to raise an early tax on the harvest estimates. This, combined with Napoleon's four-month absence, had led to a certain amount of grievance-airing and opportunistic unrest, which had resulted most notably in two uprisings. The first of these had been led by Mustafa, the Turk whom Napoleon had appointed Emir el-Hadj in place of the fugitive Murad Bey. Mustafa had been amongst the Cairo dignitaries whom Napoleon had ordered to accompany him into Syria, but he had lagged behind and finally slipped away on the pretext of organizing the annual pilgrimage to Mecca. In fact, he had remained in secret contact with Djezzar, and in late March a courier from Djezzar informed him that Napoleon had been killed at Acre and that his army was fleeing in disarray. Mustafa had immediately ridden through the eastern delta issuing a call to arms and distributing bribes, which had resulted in 2,000 Bedouin and other Mameluke supporters joining him. But significantly the local *fellahin* had not rallied to his cause, some doubtless through fear of the French, but others because their conditions had improved during French rule. This was a serious setback for Mustafa, who had planned to march on Cairo and overthrow French rule. Instead he now took to guerrilla tactics, ambushing French military convoys and attempting to pillage Napoleon's supply lines into Syria. With Mustafa's main objective aborted, the insurrection had turned into a scramble for booty, with greed over the distribution of the spoils causing infighting amongst the Bedouin. Dugua had dispatched General Lanusse from Cairo to put down the insurrection, and on April 3 Lanusse reported back to Cairo that "the emir hadj [Mustafa] was abandoned by all the Arabs whom he bribed, as well as his supporters, as soon as word spread that our troops were marching on the center of the uprising."[3] When Mustafa realized that the insurrection was sure to be defeated, he gave one of the Bedouin leaders a large bribe to escort him safely out of the country and across the Sinai desert. But no sooner had the Bedouin chief caught sight of the approaching French troops than he and his followers fled into the delta. "Mustafa had been abandoned, almost alone, and he had immediately ridden off towards Syria tearing at his beard in despair."

The other uprising had taken place to the west of the delta at Damanhur, and had been a rather more serious affair. This was inspired by a Libyan called Ahmed who claimed to be the Mahdi, the long-awaited Messiah whom the Koran promised would be sent by the Prophet to lead the faithful in a final destruction of the infidels. Part inspired holy man, part charlatan, Ahmed el-Mahdi, as he came to be known, was soon attracting huge crowds of *fellahin* to his cause with his

promises for this world and the next, his power over glory and religion, his solemn prophecies, ecstasies, revelations, miracles . . . He claimed that his body was immaterial . . . all he required in the way of food was to dip his fingers into a jug of milk and pass them lightly over his lips. Naked as a Muslim fakir, he declared that the heat had no effect on him, that the French bullets would bounce off his skin without harming him, that his breath would put out the fire of the cannons, that a grain of dust thrown from his hand would stop a cannon ball in its flight.[4]

Soon thousands of *fellahin* and Bedouin were flocking to his call—one contemporary estimate puts the number of his followers as high as 15,000 on foot and 4,000 on horseback. During the night of April 29–30 these all attacked the French garrison at Damanhur, which was forced to take refuge in a mosque. The Mahdi gave his blessing and the mosque was set on fire; no one escaped. Once again, General Lanusse was dispatched by Dugua from Cairo, and reached Damanhur on May 9. At the sight of the French troops the insurgents began to flee in terror, but the French soldiers were incensed at the burning to death of their comrades, and, according to Lanusse, "wreaked their vengeance on the town and the inhabitants of Damanhur. Around 200 or 300 of its inhabitants were killed as they fled; after that I abandoned this wretched town to the horrors of pillage and carnage. Damanhur no longer exists, and between 1,200 and 1,500 of its inhabitants have been burnt or shot."[5] Ahmed el-Mahdi was either killed or fled, and was never seen again.

Lower Egypt was pacified, but this was hardly the way to win friends. Despite this, when Napoleon returned to Cairo in the following month, his main concern remained external enemies. Writing to Desaix in Upper Egypt, he congratulated him on his success in driving out Murad Bey, but then went on to tell him: "Down here we are approaching the season when an invasion could well take place. I am losing no time in preparing for this." Though he added optimistically: "In all probability there will not be any enemy landing this year."[6] Even so, he told Desaix: "We are spending 2 to 300,000 francs each month building up our northern coastal defenses. You have sufficient money; be generous enough to send us 150,000 francs."

At the same time he wrote to the Directory: "We are masters of the entire eastern desert, and have foiled any invasion plans from that quarter for this year."[7] For the first time he made mention of the plague, giving details which were in fact not details at all: "The plague began six months ago in Alexandria, with the most severe symptoms. At Damietta it has been more benign. At Gaza and at Jaffa it made more ravages. It has not struck at Cairo or at Suez or in Upper Egypt." He used this as a partial excuse for his army having "lost 5,344 men since the beginning of the campaign." For this reason he was in need of reinforcements, but he promised: "If you could send us in excess of 15,000 men, we would be able to go anywhere, even Constantinople."

Owing to the British blockade, the French army was by this stage beginning to suffer from all kinds of shortages. With regard to the shortage of men, Napoleon instructed Dugua to "revise" the sentences of all French soldiers locked up in the Citadel on various charges, ranging from insubordination to murder. By now the Citadel also held a large number of Arab prisoners, many of whom were awaiting the death penalty, and Dugua wrote to Napoleon: "With the firing squads becoming more frequent at the Citadel, I suggest, *mon général*, that we replace these with a machine for cutting off heads.* This would save on our bullets and make much less noise."[8] The sound of gunfire echoing over the rooftops of Cairo at dawn was evidently not winning over the hearts and minds of the local population. In the margin of Dugua's report, Napoleon wrote simply "Agreed."

The Army of the Orient was by now running short on weapons and ammunition, despite the valiant efforts of Conté and his savant-engineers to manufacture replacements out of local materials. In an attempt to make good this deficiency, Napoleon now wrote to the commandant of the French island of Réunion in the Indian Ocean, asking him to send "3,000 rifles, 1,500 pairs of pistols and 1,000 sabers."[9] He assured the commandant that the Red Sea was under French control now that Suez was fortified and Desaix's forces in Upper Egypt had taken Kosseir, some 300 miles down the coast. Here he was

* Possibly owing to the guillotine's associations with the Terror, which had taken place just five years previously, General Dugua in fact uses the term "*un coupeur de têtes*," literally "a head-cutter," yet there is no doubting that he meant a guillotine.

being disingenuous. A few weeks earlier a British frigate and another vessel had arrived off Suez on an exploratory mission, but had been repelled by the French battery. There was no doubt that the British would be back. Indeed, writing on the same day to the French commandant of Mauritius, Napoleon asked him to try and keep a line of communication open between them "despite the battle cruisers which infest the Red Sea." Napoleon may well have been trying to deceive himself as much as the commandant of Réunion when assuring him of a safe passage for the shipment of weapons.

Under such circumstances, the morale of many of the French troops remained almost as low as it had been following the retreat from Acre. In an attempt to remedy this, Napoleon resorted to his customary round of promotions, dispatches singling out the exemplary conduct of particular soldiers, and rewards for bravery in the form of jewel-encrusted pistols, engraved sabers and the like. These rewards came from the booty seized after the flight of the Mamelukes at the Battle of Mount Tabor. And the increased wages bill resulting from the round of promotions made no difference to the exchequer, as the pay of the men was already in deep arrears. This distribution of carrots was reinforced by applications of the stick: senior officers were instructed to draw up lists of well-known troublemakers and barrack-room lawyers in their regiments, who were to be punished more severely than others when found guilty of misdemeanors.

French life in Cairo had quickly returned to normal, and just two weeks after Napoleon's return from Syria the Institute renewed its regular meetings, with the recovered Monge taking the presidential chair. The opening meeting was to witness an extraordinary scene between Napoleon and his chief medical officer Desgenettes. Relations between the two were already at a low ebb after their clashes during the Syrian campaign over giving opium to the plague victims, and matters were only made worse when Desgenettes discovered that Napoleon had written over his head to the Directory: "We need 18–20 physicians and 60–80 surgeons; many are dying out here. All the diseases prevalent in this country need to be studied, as they are all virtually unknown; but the more we know about them, the less dangerous they will become."[10] Desgenettes understandably saw this as a slight on the widespread researches he had already carried out into ophthalmia and the plague, and was outraged that Napoleon should have appealed to the Directory in this manner without consulting him.

The Institute meeting got off to a bad start when Napoleon proposed the setting up of a commission to report on the outbreak of bubonic plague which the army had suffered in Syria. Desgenettes was not given a seat on this commission, and quickly began to suspect that he was to be blamed for the severity with which the disease had taken hold in the army, which in turn would then be given as the reason for the failure of the entire Syrian campaign. In confirmation of his suspicions, during the ensuing discussion Napoleon "let slip a number of sarcastic remarks about medicine in general and the medical profession in particular. Desgenettes rose, and before the entire assembly, which was astonished at his anger, responded to the sarcasms of the general with a few rather more bitter and biting sarcasms of his own. He wished it to be known that he had honorably refused to take part in what he regarded as criminal acts [a reference to the poisoning of plague victims]."[11] He then launched into a long diatribe against the leadership of his commander-in-chief, making reference to the "mercenary adulation" of his subordinates, and his "oriental despotism." When Napoleon, and then Monge, tried to silence him, Desgenettes concluded, "I know, general—for when you attend these meetings you are more than just an ordinary member of the Institute, you insist upon being commander-in-chief even here—I know that I was carried away in the heat of the moment and said things that will have repercussions far from here, but I do not retract a single word. . . . I take refuge in the army's gratitude for what I have done."[12]

Desgenettes may have committed an unforgivable blunder in attacking Napoleon, but he knew that he was on firm ground with his final remark: the soldiers held him in high esteem, and he knew it. Word of this unprecedented row at the Institute quickly spread throughout the army, and when some days later Desgenettes happened to walk past several battalions which were being drilled outside the city gates, "the doctor was acclaimed by the soldiers with cheers and cries of support."[13] Napoleon, for his part, responded ambivalently to this man who had risked everything by standing up to his authority. Few men were brave enough to do this, and Napoleon could not help but admire Desgenettes, even if he did not like him. When Desgenettes honorably offered to resign and be sent back to France, Napoleon refused. He knew that such a move would have been widely construed as Desgenettes being sent home in disgrace.

Other business at the Institute meetings proved less stormy. During Napoleon's absence the engineer-savants had pressed ahead with implementing the new street plan, with its wide main thoroughfares passing through Cairo's maze of alleyways. They had also supervised the completion of the bridges crossing the Nile. The pontoon bridge linking Rodah Island and Giza was complete, with an additional pontoon linking Rodah to the Cairo shore in readiness for the Nile flooding. Even the citizens of Cairo seem to have been impressed by these advanced technological projects, which gave many employment. El-Djabarti remarked: "All this work was completed in a short time. There was no forced labor, and everyone was well paid; the instruments which the French used were of great assistance to them. For cutting stone and sawing wood they had tools which were much better made than those in Cairo."[14] Other engineers had been busy building the ring of forts which acted as the city's defenses; Napoleon decreed that these should be named after generals and leading officers of the Army of the Orient who had fallen in battle in Egypt and Syria.

Other savants had set up a topographical committee to collate all the maps being made of Lower Egypt, together with those being sent to Cairo by Desaix's engineers in Upper Egypt. This would result in a detailed atlas of the entire country, the first of its kind in the whole of Africa. Yet it would prove of little benefit to the world's geographers, as it was designated a state secret and would be kept under lock and key in Paris for many years to come.

Such work was matched by that of the indefatigable biologist Geoffroy Saint-Hilaire, who had moved on from his detailed study of the habits of the ostrich to similarly freakish occurrences throughout nature. In doing so, he opened up an entirely new science which specialized in the study of the natural monstrosities and abnormal formations which occur in the animal and plant worlds, to which he gave the name *teratology* (from the Greek *teras*, meaning a marvel, prodigy or monster). Many of his finds were now preserved in bottles and pressings in the basement of the Institute building, extending the studies of the great Swedish botanist Linnaeus, who just fifty years previously had laid the foundations of our understanding of different genera and species. Geoffroy Saint-Hilaire's studies marked an advance into previously uncharted science, and in time both Darwin's theory of evolution and later the study of genetics would gain insight from the new field of teratology founded in Egypt.

However, by far the most spectacular discovery of all was announced at the Institute meeting of July 19, 1799, in a report sent by the mathematician-savant Lancret. A few days earlier, during demolition work prior to the reconstruction of Fort Julien near Rosetta, a French soldier had unearthed a slab of black basalt, one side of which was carved with various inscriptions. The officer in charge, Lieutenant Bouchard, had shown the stone to Lancret, who had immediately recognized its significance. Lancret's report to the Institute described the stone as having three horizontal bands of inscriptions: "the first, at the bottom, contains several lines of Greek characters, which were inscribed in the reign of Ptolemy Philopater; the second inscription is written in unknown characters; and the third consists only of hieroglyphs."[15] This black basalt slab, just four feet high and weighing three quarters of a ton, would become known as the Rosetta Stone.

Lancret shipped it to Cairo, where its Greek inscription was found to be a decree, issued by the Temple priests at Memphis on a date equivalent to March 27, 196 BC. After inspecting the slab in some detail, the savants reached the opinion that each of the three different inscriptions probably contained the same message. The script of the middle inscription was at first thought to be an early form of Arabic, but this turned out not to be the case. Even so, it appeared that the stone contained two different versions which might prove the key to translating its ancient Egyptian hieroglyphs. Here was the instrument which might open up for the first time the closed book of ancient Egyptian history inscribed on so many of the country's ruins.

But the initial enthusiasm at this discovery soon lapsed into despair. It became clear that the hieroglyphs did not match in any simple word-for-word way with the ancient Greek. The mathematicians set to work with their code-breaking skills, and the Orientalists attempted to read the hieroglyphs as if they were Chinese-style ideograms—but all to no avail. The Institute ordered that rubbings, drawings and even plaster casts be taken of the Rosetta Stone, which they intended to distribute to scholars throughout Europe, whose knowledge might afford them a means of deciphering the hieroglyphic text. But for the time being the savants were thwarted: the Rosetta Stone remained a mystery.

Just a few weeks after this spectacular discovery, Vivant Denon arrived back in Cairo from Upper Egypt. His fellow savants were shocked at the fifty-two-year-old artist's appearance. With his straggly greying locks growing down to his shoulders, and looking emaciated and disheveled after the rigors of Desaix's relentless campaigning up and down the Nile, he seemed like a madman in his manic enthusiasm to tell of the wonders that he had seen. But when the members of the Institute saw what he had brought with him, they quickly began to share his excitement. Denon's notebooks and sketchpads contained hundreds of drawings of the temples and vast ruins that lay along the banks of the upper Nile. These drawings were accompanied by voluminous notes and diagrams explaining all that he had seen—from the Dendera Zodiac to the behavior of the troglodytes who lived amongst the tombs at Thebes, from the effects of a plague of locusts to the workings of the ancient Nilometer at Aswan. And of course there was page after page of transcribed hieroglyphs, copied from the walls, the temples and the columns of the ruins he had seen.

Napoleon immediately ordered that two commissions of savants should be established, and should make preparations to leave for Upper Egypt to catalog all that had been found there. Desaix had specifically requested that he be sent more engineers to back up his military endeavors and assist his administration, and the two commissions were soon well stocked with young engineer-savants keen to see for themselves the fabulous ruins of this lost civilization. When they finally arrived in Upper Egypt some months later, their enthusiasm would be the cause of some friction between them and Desaix's officers. The engineers were so keen to record the hieroglyphs and spectacular temples they saw that they became increasingly distracted from their military duties. Indeed, such was their enthusiasm that they quickly ran out of pencils. But several of these young engineer-savants had spent time in the workshops of the ingenious Conté, and they soon came up with a solution to their problems, melting down the lead from the soldiers' bullets, and using this to make lead pencils. Such resourcefulness may not have endeared them to the military officers, but it enabled them to make a comprehensive catalog of all that they had seen—a vast collection whose publication would one day stir the imagination of Europe.

Desaix had succeeded in chasing Murad Bey into Nubia, but the Mamelukes would soon begin circling back to attack his supply lines along the Nile. Yet eventually Desaix's constant pursuit had managed to wear down even Murad Bey and his 300 remaining warriors, who in March 1799 had taken refuge in the Kharga oasis. This was 150 miles west of Luxor in the vastness of the Libyan desert, out of reach even of Desaix, and here Murad Bey and his last warriors had remained, watching and waiting, for over four months. Despite this remote location, Murad Bey had managed to retain contact with some of his scattered Mameluke forces, even receiving the occasional message from as far afield as Djezzar in Syria. And around early July he had received a secret message which had prompted him and his warriors to ride north towards Lower Egypt.

Word eventually reached Napoleon in Cairo that Murad Bey and his men had been sighted out near the Natron Lakes some sixty miles northwest of Cairo. It looked as if he was intent upon making contact with Sir Sidney Smith and his blockading squadron, which was now back in place off Alexandria. Napoleon decided to adopt the same tactics as Desaix: "This is my urgent wish: it is vital that we kill Murad Bey or drive him until he drops dead of exhaustion, either way, so long as he dies."[16] He decided to let loose his finest cavalry commander to give chase. On July 12 General Murat and his cavalry column were ordered into the desert to seek out Murad Bey and attack him. Napoleon impressed upon Murat, "The general who has the pleasure of destroying Murad Bey will put the seal on the conquest of Egypt: I very much hope that fate has reserved this glory for you."[17]

But the elusive Murad Bey managed to give General Murat the slip, and the following day Napoleon's intelligence learned that he had doubled back towards Cairo. Just fifteen miles from the city he had paused to climb the Great Pyramid, where he had exchanged glinting mirror-signals with his wife, standing on the rooftop of her palace at Giza. There was no hint of what information these signals had contained, but Napoleon was not concerned about this. He now knew that Murad Bey was down to just "200 Mamelukes, half on horseback, half on camels, all in a bad way, as well as 50 to 60 Arabs." He at once set off himself in pursuit, leading his cavalry across the Nile's new pontoon bridges to Giza, where he camped for the night. Next day, as he wrote with almost childish enthusiasm to Kléber: "I have spent all day riding through the desert beyond the Pyramids, giving chase to Murad Bey."[18] Bourrienne described what happened after this exhilarating but ultimately fruitless day's hunting: "On the evening of 15 July we set out on a stroll into the desert in a northerly direction, when we noticed, on the route from Alexandria, an Arab riding towards us full tilt. He delivered to the general-in-chief a dispatch from General Marmont in Alexandria."[19] This news solved the riddle of the secret messages that Murad Bey had received: a Turkish fleet consisting of five battleships, three frigates and over fifty troop carriers had arrived and anchored off Aboukir Bay, where under the protection of Sir Sidney Smith and the British squadron it had already unloaded some 10,000 troops onto the beaches. The invasion had begun.

It was now that Napoleon once again demonstrated his supreme caliber, both as a man and as a military leader. Despite being exhausted after the long day's chase, as well as having Murat and his crack cavalry scattered through the desert, his response was immediate and decisive. This was the moment he had been waiting for. Orders were at once dispatched to Marmont on the coast, Kléber and his division in the eastern delta, Murat in the Western Desert and Desaix in Upper Egypt. Marmont was ordered to remain in Alexandria: it was essential that his 1,200 troops held the city's defenses and were not drawn out into combat with the vastly superior invasion force. This meant abandoning to their fate the thirty-five men of the garrison in the fort at Aboukir Point, as well as another 300 troops in the nearby camp. The 300 men were quickly overrun and slaughtered by the invading Turks, but the soldiers in the fort managed to hold out for three days before surrendering.

Kléber's division was ordered to make post-haste for Damanhur, forty miles southeast of Aboukir Bay, where Murat's cavalry was to regroup and meet up with him. Napoleon himself would join them with a large contingent of troops from Cairo, and together they would make ready to confront the advancing Turkish invading force. A measure of how serious Napoleon considered the situation can be seen from the fact that he withdrew virtually all his troops from Cairo, leaving the city's streets and defenses largely in the hands of the Greek Barthelemy and his notorious "police." Meanwhile Desaix was ordered to make his way back down the Nile as quickly as possible with as many of his division as he could spare, so that he could provide back-up in case the invaders broke past Napoleon and marched on Cairo.

In just over four days Napoleon had put affairs in order in Cairo and then covered the 100 miles north to Damanhur, where he was assembling 10,000 French troops, as well as Murat's 1,000 cavalry.

Kléber and his division were still on their way. But the intelligence Napoleon now received caused him to make a rapid reassessment of his plans. The Turkish force was led by the renowned white-bearded Sayd Mustafa-Pasha, who in previous campaigns had led the Turkish army to several victories against the Russians. He had already disembarked his entire force, which according to Napoleon's latest intelligence amounted to around 15,000 men. These had taken possession of the Aboukir peninsula and had dug in with three lines of defense across its flat half-mile-wide neck, with their positions protected from the sea by Turkish gunboats and the firepower from the British squadron anchored further out. Sayd Mustafa-Pasha was an experienced general, and had learned of Napoleon's strengths: the sensational speed with which he could maneuver his troops on the battlefield, and the imperviousness of the French battle squares to enemy charges. In order to neutralize these advantages, he had chosen initially to dig in and form an impenetrable beachhead, which could not be outmaneuvered and was not vulnerable to French defensive squares. The French would now have to attack him. Napoleon immediately saw the weakness of such tactics: the invasion was contained, and its defensive position was ultimately flawed, as it meant that the Turks had nowhere to fall back in retreat except the sea.

But this could only be the first stage of the Turkish invasion. Napoleon guessed that it would not be long before Mustafa-Pasha launched a mobile force from his well-established beachhead, one which could easily elude the gathered French forces and attack anywhere in Egypt at will. He decided to move at once. Without waiting for Kléber's division, he hastily marched for Aboukir Bay, which he reached on July 24. To his relief, he saw that the Turkish forces had not yet launched out of their beachhead, and he immediately began lining up his divisions, ready for battle the following day.

That night, as he was discussing his plans with Murat, he exclaimed: "This battle will decide the fate of the world."[20] The remark puzzled Murat; it has usually been interpreted, in the light of later experience, as an oblique reference confirming that Napoleon had already decided to return to France. However, it is worth pointing out that Napoleon here referred to "the world," rather than simply "Europe," the designation which he would probably have made if he had already decided to return to France. Thus it appears more likely that even at this late stage he still had in mind the possibility of marching on Constantinople

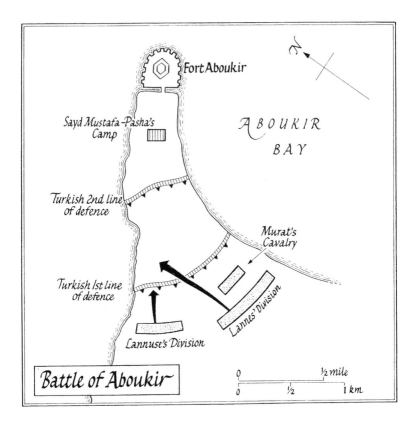

Battle of Aboukir

or India—an event which would certainly have involved "the fate of the world."

The Battle of Aboukir, as it came to be called, began at six A.M. on July 25, 1799. With Murat forming the vanguard in the center, General Lannes attacked the front line of Turkish defenses on the eastern flank, whilst General Lanusse simultaneously launched an attack on the western flank. The Turkish redoubts and trenches on the latter flank had not yet been completed, and after fierce fighting Lanusse finally achieved a breakthrough. On the opposite flank, Lannes took advantage of the enemy's confusion, broke through the center and circled to come round behind the enemy line on the western flank. This caused widespread panic amongst the Turkish troops in this sector, who fled where they could in disarray, eventually running for the sea. According to Napoleon: "The enemy threw themselves into the water in an attempt to reach the boats which were more than two miles out at sea; they all drowned, the most horrible sight that I have seen."[21] It must indeed have been a gruesome sight, even for a hardened soldier like Napoleon. Most estimates agree that thousands of Turks died in this stampede. However, the resistance in the second line of Turkish defenses proved much stronger, and as the heat of the day approached, the French found themselves being forced to withdraw by sheer weight of numbers. After the initial French retreat the Turkish soldiers began wandering over the battlefield, as was their custom, cutting off the heads of the dead and wounded.

Murat saw his opportunity and seized it, leading his troops in a furious cavalry charge through the scattered Turkish soldiers, who once again fled in confusion as he swept all before him. Such was the effectiveness of his breakthrough that within minutes he was charging into Mustafa-Pasha's camp. Captain François, who fought in the battle, tells what happened next: "General Murat burst into the tent of the enemy commander-in-chief, who, on seeing his adversary advancing, ran rapidly towards him. At the very moment when Murat ordered him to surrender he fired a pistol at [Murat], who was hit in the lower jaw by the bullet, but only lightly wounded. General Murat, with a blow of his saber, slashed off two fingers of [Mustafa-Pasha's] right hand, then had him seized by two soldiers of the 14th Dragoons."[*][22]

Outside, the battle was all but over. Lannes had taken advantage of the mayhem caused by Murat's charge, and the Turkish soldiers were now fleeing as the French mowed them down. Once again, thousands ran into the sea, this time on both sides of the peninsula, most of them drowning. Two thousand Turks are said to have been shot down, more thousands to have drowned. At the same time, several thousand managed to gain refuge with the garrison in the fort at the end of the peninsula.

The French victory had been as swift as it was complete. When Kléber finally arrived on the scene early in the afternoon, and saw what had happened, he was overwhelmed. According to Denon, who was present, "in a moment of enthusiasm," the tall burly Alsatian embraced his diminutive commander-in-chief, exclaiming, "General, your greatness is beyond all bounds, you are out of this world."[23] Napoleon had led the French to a fine victory, though he generously gave credit where it was due: "The winning of this battle, which will

---

[*] According to a widely retold story, the dashing Murat is said to have remarked of his bullet to the jaw: "The women of Paris have no need to worry, my lips are intact."

have so much influence on the glory of the Republic, is due properly to General Murat. His cavalry brigade achieved the impossible."[24]

Murat was promoted to the rank of divisional general, and Napoleon would describe the battle as "one of the most beautiful I have seen," although he admitted that afterwards "the shore [was] covered with enemy bodies; we have counted more than 6,000; 3,000 have been buried on the field of battle." In his dispatch to the Directory he reported 100 French dead and 500 wounded. This would seem to be accurate. However, the precise enemy death toll is not so clear. In other reports Napoleon claimed that 9,000 Turkish troops had been killed or drowned, and he revised his estimate of the entire Turkish force up to a total of 18,000 men. This would imply that he had won a victory over an enemy force almost twice the size of his own. Yet before the battle, Mustafa-Pasha claimed that he had only 7,000 men in a fit state to fight after the long sea voyage, a figure which concurs with Sir Sidney Smith's estimate. Other firsthand witnesses placed the Turkish fighting force at around 9,000, though many French historians continued to accept Napoleon's original intelligence estimate of 15,000 as being closer to the mark. Such exaggeration ensured Aboukir a permanent place in French history.*

But the invasion was not yet fully repulsed. The 5,000 or so Turkish troops who had taken refuge in Fort Aboukir continued to hold out under the command of Mustafa-Pasha's son, and their resolve was soon stiffened by a detachment of British marines dispatched from the *Tigre* by Sidney Smith. The French began subjecting the fort to artillery fire, and the Turkish officers eventually decided to surrender, yet their men mutinied, having heard what Napoleon had done to the Turkish prisoners at Jaffa. But in the end the continuous French artillery and mortar fire, which went on day and night, proved too much for them. After eight days there were only 3,000 left alive and these were starving, many half crazed from drinking seawater. Captain François vividly describes their surrender on August 2:

They came out to offer themselves up to the vengeance of their victors. The son of the pasha and his lieutenants came out at the head of the Turkish soldiers, who looked like ghosts. They threw down their arms that they no longer had the strength to carry, and all of them bowed down, asking for death. But our commanders and soldiers, forgetting their previous hatred of the enemy, felt for them all the compassion and care evoked by their deplorable

* The Paris metro station Aboukir is named after this victory.

state. We gave them food and drink, and in spite of the precautions taken to prevent the illness that comes from eating too much too quickly after having suffered from hunger, three-quarters of those 3,000 men died of indigestion.[25]

Napoleon would later claim that "of the enemy who came ashore not a single one escaped."[26] Like his exaggerated claims concerning the size of the invasion force, this too was not true, particularly in one important instance. Sir Sidney Smith sent longboats from the *Tigre* which managed to rescue a number of the Turkish soldiers who fled into the sea. Amongst those who were able to scramble through the waves, avoiding the French bullets and the desperate clutches of their drowning comrades, was a thirty-year-old regimental officer of Albanian descent called Mohammed Ali, who six years later would become ruler of Egypt.

After the victory, Napoleon issued a triumphant message to his troops: "The name of Aboukir has meant disaster to all Frenchmen; the day of 7 Thermidor [July 25] has now rendered it glorious. This is a victory that will hasten the army's return to France."[27] He then attempted to reinforce this fulsome promise with what can best be described as a fantasy about the European situation: "By invading Germany we have conquered Mainz and as far as the Rhine. This, along with our victory here, means that we can repossess our trading establishments in the Indies, as well as those of our allies. In one fell swoop we have put back in the hands of the government the power to force England, despite its naval triumphs, to sign a peace treaty which ensures glory for the Republic."

Was this perhaps "the fate of the world" to which Napoleon had referred on the eve of the battle? The regaining of a few trading posts in India hardly merited such a dramatic description. And as for the future peace treaty he mentioned, this relied upon French conquests in Europe which seemed highly unlikely in the light of the latest news he had received. It looks as if this triumphant declaration was nothing more than a piece of propaganda, designed to keep the troops happy: this was what they wanted to hear. However, its sheer mendacity points to Napoleon's indecisive state of mind. He did not know what to do next. He was dithering: for once in his life, keeping his options open had paralyzed his ability to decide. He could still march for Constantinople or India and "decide the fate of the world"; or he could return alone to France on one of Ganteaume's waiting frigates and take his chances in overthrowing the Directory. This cannot have been a strong possibility in his mind; he would hardly have suggested to his army that they would soon be going back to France if he was seriously thinking of doing so himself and simply abandoning them. This was no way to retain the loyalty of the army. On the other hand, he could remain in Egypt, laying down firm foundations for the establishment of his Oriental empire. At this point, he appears to have viewed none of these possibilities with much conviction. Were they even plausible? Or were they just dreams? It is possible that at this point Napoleon had stage fright before the enormity of his ambitions. For once, all the indications are that he had no particular strategy in mind. However, the events of the next few days would transform his entire strategic outlook, changing his life forever.

XXVII

The Decision of a Lifetime

NAPOLEON wished to send the many seriously wounded Turkish prisoners back to their ships, in exchange for the French soldiers who had surrendered after being besieged in Aboukir Fort during the first days of the Turkish invasion. With this in mind, he dispatched the young French officer Descorches from Alexandria harbor under a flag of truce to board the *Tigre* and negotiate with Sir Sidney Smith. During the course of these negotiations, Smith realized that the French had evidently not received any news for months about the situation in France and the general situation in Europe. He saw his chance to make mischief, and gave Descorches two of the latest newspapers he had received—*Gazette de Francfort* for June 6, and *Courrier Français de Londres* (an exile newspaper printed in Britain) for June 10—knowing that these would be passed on to Napoleon.

Descorches was handed these papers on August 6 and they would reach Napoleon a few days later as he was on his way back to Cairo. Napoleon spent the night in his tent reading the papers by candlelight from cover to cover. The situation in Europe had taken a dramatic turn for the worse: Austria, Britain and Russia had formed the Second Coalition, which was now at war with France. In southern Germany the French Army of the Rhine had been defeated by the Austrians and pushed back across the Rhine. As a result, the French had been forced to make a tactical withdrawal from most of Switzerland, in order to take up a defensive position around Geneva, almost on the French border. Meanwhile Malta was blockaded, and in Italy things had gone from bad to worse. The Austrians had invaded the French-occupied north, and then been joined by the Russians; Mantua and

Turin were under siege, and the French forces were being driven back towards Genoa. Most of the territory Napoleon had conquered in his Italian campaign was now lost, and France was threatened from all sides.

Meanwhile the French Atlantic fleet under Admiral Bruix, consisting of twenty-two battleships and eighteen frigates, had managed to break the British blockade of Brest and sailed into the Mediterranean. This fleet could have been used to ferry Napoleon and his army back from Egypt, but it had put in at Toulon, where once again it was blockaded by the British. The situation within France itself was perilous: the constitution was in danger of being overturned, there was another insurrection in the Vendée, and the Jacobins were calling for a second Terror. At the same time the Directory did little but dither, and the economy was failing fast.

When Napoleon had finished reading the newspaper, he exclaimed: "*So! . . . My presentiments were not wrong; Italy is lost!!! The wretches! All the fruits of our victories have disappeared! I must depart.*"[1] He came to an immediate decision: he would return to France at once. Only he could save the country. He would leave Kléber in charge in Egypt, and would take with him whoever he needed.

This meant abandoning the Army of the Orient in Egypt, a decision for which Napoleon has been severely condemned. In the eyes of his critics, this was the unprincipled act of a deserter who was intent only upon his own glory. He had received no orders to return to France, and should have been court-martialed for abandoning his post in the midst of a campaign. However, it is now known that this was precisely what the Directory wished him to do. In a letter sent on May 26, the Directory informed him that "the serious and almost alarming turn that the war has taken, requires the Republic to concentrate its forces."[2] In consequence, it had sent orders to Admiral Bruix in Toulon, in the pious hope

that he would employ all means in his power to make himself master of the Mediterranean and sail to Egypt to bring back the army under your command . . . You will be able to judge for yourself, citizen general, if it is safe to leave part of your army behind in Egypt; and the Directory authorizes you, in this case, to hand over your command to whomsoever you consider best suited to the task. The Directory will be pleased to see you return and take charge of the army of the Republic, which you have up to this time so gloriously commanded.

This letter had been entrusted to Bruix, who had found himself unable to leave Toulon. An attempt was then made to send a copy by another route, but this was intercepted by the British navy. As a result, well before August 1799 Nelson knew that the Directory wanted Napoleon back, and had passed on this news to Sir Sidney Smith. Indeed, Smith had gone so far as to convey the news verbally to Descorches as he was leaving the *Tigre* for Alexandria, confident that it would quickly be passed on to Napoleon. So Napoleon had in fact known that the Directory wished him to return to France, and cannot on this count be accused of desertion. Or can he? His defense would not have stood up in any court-martial. He had no proof of this letter, and in fact from his point of view it would have seemed almost certain that Smith was bluffing.

The indications are that the newspapers and Smith's suggestion of the Directory's wishes all triggered in Napoleon the decision that he unconsciously wished to take. His dream of an Oriental empire was beginning to look like just that—a dream. And the situation in Egypt was not getting any better, with his army running out of men and money. His only realistic hope of the glory he so craved lay in France: he would leave Egypt and take his chance with destiny.

Perceptively, Sidney Smith had predicted in a letter written on August 9 to Earl Spencer, head of the Admiralty, that this was precisely what Napoleon would do. Smith had learned—from the emissary he had sent ashore at Alexandria to facilitate the exchange of prisoners— that Admiral Ganteaume had two frigates standing ready to leave at a moment's notice, and had guessed that Napoleon would soon set sail for France. Furthermore, he had even predicted that Napoleon would leave Kléber in charge in Egypt, and that as Kléber had misgivings about the Egyptian expedition he would probably be open to negotiating a French evacuation. This was astonishingly perspicacious of Smith, which makes it all the more surprising that on August 12 he decided to set sail in the *Tigre* for Cyprus to replenish his stores and pick up salted provisions. He instructed his other battleship, the *Theseus*, to patrol to the west of Alexandria, ready to pounce if Ganteaume tried to make a run for it. Yet in a few days it too left its station, presumably under orders from Smith, setting sail for Rhodes, also to pick up stores and salted provisions. The explanation given for Smith's extraordinary conduct was that his squadron had exhausted all its salted provisions during the siege of Acre, which sounds perfectly credible. But there were no salted provisions available in either Cyprus or Rhodes. In the end, Smith would choose to remain in Cyprus for over two months, playing a characteristically dashing role in preventing a mutiny of Turkish soldiers, only returning to his station off Alexandria on October 18.

Napoleon and his victorious army made a triumphant entry into Cairo on August 11, whereupon he embarked upon a week of whirlwind activity in preparation for his departure. At this stage, only Bourrienne and Chief of Staff Berthier had been told of his plans. Astonishingly, no one else knew, or guessed, what was about to take place. Only at the very last moment did Napoleon inform those who were to embark with him on the momentous voyage back to France, and all of them were sworn to secrecy. Others were given their orders of the day and sent their dispatches much as usual. Napoleon had put out a cover story that he would be leaving the city on an expedition into the delta, followed by a visit to the Natron Lakes, and then south to Fayoum, all of which would keep him away from Cairo for some time. Only with hindsight is it possible to see that he was covertly bidding several of his loyal colleagues farewell. To Poussielgue he wrote: "I am leaving tomorrow morning before dawn [for the Delta]. . . . I recommend that you proceed vigorously with the collection of all land rents and taxes. . . . Finally, remain on friendly terms with the sheiks and maintain good order in Cairo. I recommend to General Dugua that he clamps down firmly at the first sign of any trouble: if necessary cut off six heads a day, but keep smiling."[3] He wrote angrily to Desaix in Upper Egypt, demanding to know why he had not obeyed orders and reported to Cairo. Napoleon admired Desaix and had wanted him to hand, for if he chose to go to France he wanted Desaix with him.* He ended his letter with the enigmatic words: "I tell you this for the future,"[4] the hidden implication being that Desaix would understand Napoleon's anger in the light of future events.

On August 17 Napoleon received a dispatch from Admiral Ganteaume, sent three days beforehand from Alexandria, which revealed

---

* Apart from his order to Ganteaume to stand by with two frigates, his letter ordering Desaix back from Upper Egypt is one of very few indications that Napoleon was considering returning to France. But he had not made up his mind as soon as he returned from Acre, as many claim. He had no intention of abandoning his army whilst there was the possibility of a Turkish invasion; and at the time he had no idea of the serious European situation.

that Sir Sidney Smith appeared to have temporarily lifted the blockade: "Seemingly the British and Turkish vessels which are absent have sailed for the island of Cyprus or the Archipelago [Aegean islands] to replenish their supplies, which had completely run out."[5] It looked as if the coast would be clear for a few days.

There was no time to lose. Napoleon decided to leave Cairo that night. The main figures he invited to accompany him on his voyage were Generals Murat, Marmont, Andréossy and Lannes, along with several aides including his stepson Beauharnais, and the savant-artist Denon, as well as his ever-faithful Monge and Berthollet. The latter pair, who were making preparations to leave on the expedition into the delta, were sent a secret note informing them of what was happening. This threw them into some confusion when their fellow savants began pressing them about the arrangements for the forthcoming expedition. And when Napoleon sent his carriage to the Institute at ten P.M. to collect Monge and Berthollet, Costaz and Fourier became particularly suspicious. They followed the two men to the carriage where their luggage was being loaded, demanding to know if there was any truth in the outrageous rumor sweeping the Institute that they were both going back to France. Monge, in some discomfort, blurted out incoherently: "My dear friends, if we are departing for France, I can assure you we knew nothing about it before noon today."[6]

Monge and Berthollet swept off in Napoleon's carriage, leaving the Institute in some disarray. The savants earnestly discussed what Monge could have meant by his last remark, but the poet-savant Parseval-Grandmaison had already made up his mind, and rushed upstairs to pack. If there was a group leaving for France, he was determined to be in it.

By midnight, Napoleon's headquarters at Elfi Bey's palace was a hive of activity, and a string of more than twenty camels was lined up in the front courtyard, seemingly in preparation for the expedition to the delta. Meanwhile the select members of the party leaving for France were assembling in the garden at the back of the palace. These included the generals and aides, as well as Napoleon's secretary Bourrienne, his cook and his new young Mameluke bodyguard Roustam. Napoleon himself was pacing up and down with Monge and Berthollet, affecting to discuss some scientific matter in an attempt to take his mind off what was happening. According to eyewitness reports, "Madame Fourès was strolling along an adjoining path, dressed in a tight-fitting hussar's uniform. . . . From time to time, as he often did on normal days when taking the air, he went over to Madame Fourès, giving her a few little friendly pats on the bottom, saying to her with such gaiety as to dispel any suspicions she might have: 'This looks like a little hussar who's spying on me!'"[7] Astonishingly, Pauline Fourès had no idea what was going on. She had not been let in on the secret, and was not being taken back to France. As far as she knew, Napoleon was leaving for the delta, and would be back in a week or two.

Shortly after midnight, Napoleon and his entourage set off for Boulac, where they boarded a river craft and embarked at three A.M. Next day, as they were sailing down the Nile, Napoleon dictated a message for Kléber: "Please report at once to Rosetta in person . . . on 7 Fructidor [August 24]. I have to confer with you on an extremely important matter."[8] At this meeting he planned to reveal to Kléber that he was leaving for France, and that Kléber was being left in command. Possibly because Napoleon did not wish to confront Kléber (he could easily predict his explosive reaction), or possibly because of the speed at which events unfolded, this meeting never took place. Bourrienne was in no doubt about which of these possibilities matched the truth, commenting in his memoirs, "Bonaparte gave [Kléber] a rendez-vous where he knew he would not be; he wished to avoid the reproaches and uncompromising frankness of Kléber."[9]

On the afternoon of August 23, Napoleon's party, now on horse-back, skirted Alexandria and reached the sea a couple of miles east of the city. Admiral Ganteaume and General Menou were on the beach to meet them, with the frigates *La Muiron* and *La Carrère* riding at anchor offshore. Napoleon led Menou to one side, informing him for the first time what was happening. Menou was given a package containing letters of instruction to Kléber, Dugua, Poussielgue and the Cairo *divan*. He was warned not to send the letters to Cairo until forty-eight hours after the sails of the two frigates, and their two accompanying courier ships, had disappeared over the horizon. By now the sun was setting and Ganteaume insisted that Napoleon should board ship immediately, in case Sir Sidney Smith and his warships returned. They waited for the sloops to pick them up, but night fell before they could reach the shore. Clouds obscured the moon and the stars, making it pitch dark, so they were forced to light a flare to guide the sloops to where they were on the beach, despite the risk of this being seen by any passing ship. It was eight o'clock before the sloops arrived, and a further hour before Napoleon reached *La Muiron*.

The sea was flat calm, the warm darkness utterly still. They would have to wait for the dawn breeze to carry them on their way. The long, tense hours of this vigil were almost over, with first light beginning to spread over the eastern horizon, when Napoleon and his entourage came on deck at five A.M. Bourrienne, who was aboard Ganteaume's *La Muiron* with Napoleon, recorded what happened next:

> Just as they were running up the sails, we saw coming towards us from the port of Alexandria a sloop with Monsieur Parseval-Grandmaison on board. This fine fellow, whom we all liked, had not been amongst those chosen by the commander-in-chief to accompany him back to France. Wishing to depart at once, Bonaparte did not want to hear about anyone else coming on board. . . . Parseval-Grandmaison implored and begged to be allowed on board, but in vain.[10]

Napoleon eventually relented, and Parseval-Grandmaison "was hoisted aboard with the wind already beginning to fill the sails."[11]

But this favorable breeze which started them on their way was to be a rarity. Trading ships were in the habit of sailing from Europe to Alexandria in the summer, following the prevailing winds, setting back on the return journey in winter when the wind was in the opposite direction. This meant that Napoleon's flotilla was sailing against the wind, and should have put out to sea in search of whatever breeze it was lucky enough to pick up in the opposite direction. But instead he ordered Ganteaume to hug the coast, in order to avoid any British naval vessels on patrol in the Mediterranean, and as a result they made little progess.

La Muiron and *La Carrère* both had 100 soldiers on board, but these could have offered no protection against the guns of the British navy. According to Bourrienne, Napoleon informed his shipboard colleagues: "If the English appear, I will have myself put ashore on the sand. I will set off overland with my troops for Oran, Tunis, or some other port, and there I will find a way of taking ship for France."[12] As Bourrienne put it: "Such was the irrevocable resolution fixed in his mind."

Yet what was the motive behind this "irrevocable resolution"? Why precisely was he so keen to get back to France? All the ambition he had once had for his Oriental empire was now channeled towards one aim—France. Of this there was never any doubt, from the moment he made his decision. In Egypt he had been much more than a soldier; he had been sole ruler, responsible to no one but himself. He was not returning to France to become just a soldier again, to place himself under orders. On the contrary: "If I have the luck to set foot in France again, the reign of these chatterers is over."[13] Before leaving Menou on the beach, he had promised him: "I will arrive in Paris. I will chase out that bunch of lawyers who are making a mockery of us and who are incapable of governing the Republic. I will install myself at the head of the government, and I will rally all parties in my support."[14] His intentions could not have been plainer. The Directory—the chatterers, the ditherers, the corrupt lawyers he so despised—had sent for him with the intention of putting him once more in charge of the army. Napoleon had not received this message, nor had he any intention of accepting such a post, which would have kept him away from Paris. France was in danger, it needed a powerful man to take charge of the Republic. There was no doubt in Napoleon's mind as to who this man should be.

Forty-seven days after setting out from Alexandria, Napoleon and his flotilla arrived off the coast of France. But he was not yet home and dry. At the very last moment, amidst a shifting mist, a British squadron caught sight of the French sails. Presuming that the only warships in this part of the Mediterranean were British, involved in the blockade of Toulon some fifty miles to the west down the coast, or allies of the British, the British naval squadron took no action and Napoleon was able to pass unmolested.

On October 9, 1799, he landed at Fréjus, where he was immediately acclaimed as the returning conqueror, the hero of whom France was in such need. Fortuitously, news of his great victory over the Turkish army at Aboukir had preceded him by just a few days. As he rapidly made his way north, he was received with acclaim at every city on his route. (Though an indication of the state into which France had sunk can be seen in the fact that his baggage train, which was following him, was attacked and robbed by brigands outside Aix-en-Provence.)

Napoleon arrived in Paris on October 16. His first meeting with Josephine was a predictably stormy affair, with promises of divorce, and her furniture being loaded onto carts and shipped out of Rue Victoire. It ended with Josephine pleading all night in tears outside his

locked bedroom door. But after the usual ructions, and her ritual humiliation, Napoleon and Josephine were reconciled. There is no doubt that
he still loved her; and besides, she remained part of the Parisian social
circle which included Barras and Talleyrand, as well as any others who
might be scheming against the Directory.

Ironically, by the time Napoleon arrived back in Paris the immediate war crisis was largely over. The German advance had been halted,
the situation in Switzerland had stabilized, and the Anglo-Russian expedition into the Netherlands was about to be thwarted. Only in Italy
had things remained much the same, with the gains of Napoleon's great
campaign having been lost.

Meanwhile the Directory continued with its corrupt machinations. For
some time Barras had been scheming to overthrow the government and
bring the exiled King Louis XVIII to power. In an attempt to forestall
this, one of the new members of the Directory, the fifty-one-year-old
former priest Sièyes, was plotting to bring about a coup, followed by the
installation of a military dictator, who would be in his pocket. For this
he needed a "sword" (a powerful military figurehead), but most of the
generals he approached turned him down, largely because they were
involved in plots of their own. It was at this stage that Napoleon turned
up in Paris, his arrival greeted by cheering crowds. Sièyes was initially
reluctant to approach him, rightly fearing that once installed he would
be a difficult man to control; but he was eventually persuaded by
Napoleon's brother Lucien, and Talleyrand, who had recently lost his post
as foreign minister. Amidst scenes of increasing civil turmoil, the coup
was finally staged on 18–19 Brumaire VIII (November 9–10, 1799). The
Directory was replaced by three consuls, with Napoleon as First Consul
quickly emerging as the dominant force.

Napoleon knew that his popularity depended upon France achieving
an honorable peace with her enemies, preferably by means of a spectacular military victory. After a rapid reorganization of the army, he
launched a surprise attack on Italy, marching across the snow-covered
St. Bernard pass in May with 40,000 men.* This led to his totally unexpected appearance behind the Austrian lines as they were besieging
Genoa. The Austrians had by this stage been deserted by their Russian

---

* This would be commemorated in the romantic portrait of Napoleon by David,
which shows Napoleon on horseback heroically urging his troops forward amidst the
snow. In reality, he had crossed the Alps on a mule, cursing his uncomfortable ride.

allies, but still remained a formidable force, with considerably more men at their disposal in Italy than the French.

On June 18 Napoleon and 22,000 of his troops were camped by the village of Marengo, near the Bormida River, some thirty miles northwest of Genoa. By now he had been joined by Desaix, who had traveled back from Egypt on his express command. The Austrians, with 30,000 men, supported by cavalry and over 100 cannon, crossed the river, taking Napoleon by surprise. After hours of fierce fighting, the French were finally driven into retreat. By mid-afternoon it was all over, and the Austrian commander Melas dispatched news of his victory to Vienna. His army marched from the field of battle, its bands playing and its soldiers singing. As Napoleon sat on his horse dejectedly looking down on the battlefield, he was joined by Desaix. He asked Desaix what he thought of the situation. Desaix pulled out his watch and said calmly: "It's three o'clock, the battle is lost. But there's still time to win another battle."[15] Spurred on by this reply, Napoleon ordered an artillery barrage, which was followed by a desperate charge led by Desaix. The enemy was caught by surprise, and the tired Austrian soldiers were eventually routed. Napoleon was jubilant—but his joy was tempered when he was informed that Desaix had been killed. Berthier heard his young commander-in-chief remark: "Why am I not permitted to weep?"[16] Napoleon was deeply moved by the death of his fellow "Egyptian," as he would sympathetically refer to his colleagues from this campaign. He had admired Desaix's military skill, recognizing it as second only to his own, and unusually amongst his generals he had come to regard Desaix as a friend. That night, a search of the battlefield was undertaken by lanternlight, and Desaix's body was discovered amongst the many fallen. A large musket ball had penetrated the left side of his chest, literally blasting his heart to pieces.

Meanwhile the plots continued in Paris, and those hoping for Napoleon's downfall awaited news of his defeat, ready to overthrow him. But his great victory at Marengo put an end to their schemes. This battle saw the triumph of the thirty-one-year-old Napoleon over his enemies both within and outside the country. From now on he would be the supreme ruler of France.

XXVIII

An Abandoned Army

WHEN Kléber learned that Napoleon had departed from Egypt, leaving him in command, without even having the decency to consult him in person, he was furious, exclaiming to his fellow officers: "That bugger has deserted us with his breeches full of shit. When we get back to Europe we'll rub his face in it."[1] Napoleon's letter informed him: "If by May you have not received any help or news, and if by this stage, despite all precautions, you have lost during the course of the year more than 1,500 men to the plague, you are authorized to make peace with the Ottoman Porte, even if they make the evacuation of Egypt their first condition."[2] But this was not really what he had in mind, for he immediately added: "All you have to do is play for time and put off actually complying with this condition, if possible, until a general [European] peace treaty is concluded." Then, with no European power in a position to oppose them, the French would be able to renege on their treaty with the Porte and hang on to Egypt.

Having transferred his powers to Kléber, Napoleon was in no position to "authorize" him to do anything. Despite this, his lengthy letter included pages of detailed instructions and advice, treating the veteran Kléber as if he was an inexperienced officer assuming command for the first time. One can but imagine Kléber's reaction when he was also helpfully informed: "I have already asked several times for a troupe of comedians to be sent out to Egypt, I will take particular care to make sure they reach you. This item is highly important for the army, and to begin to change the habits of the Egyptians."

When Kléber discovered the true state in which Napoleon had left the army, he vented his spleen by dictating a no-holds-barred letter to the Directory, informing them that the Army of the Orient was now reduced to half strength, with many of its soldiers dressed in rags and without boots. As for the exchequer: "Bonaparte, on his departure, left not a sou in the till, not even any bills of credit. On the contrary, he left a deficit of nearly 10 million francs; this is more than a year's revenue under the present circumstances. The back-pay owed to the whole army amounts to 4 million. . . . Due to the seasonal flooding of the Nile . . . we will not be able to restart collecting taxes until Frimaire [late November]."[3] This letter would be intercepted by the British navy, and sent to London. When it was read by the prime minister William Pitt he decided mischievously that it should be sent on to Paris, where the Directory had now been deposed by Napoleon, thus ensuring that it caused the maximum damage all round.

Kléber then turned his mind to other matters, and set about seducing Pauline Fourès (though he was not the first to comfort Napoleon's deserted mistress; this accolade fell to Napoleon's ever-resourceful aide Junot, who had not regained Napoleon's favor since enlightening him about Josephine's infidelity and had been left behind in Egypt).

Despite Napoleon's attempt to convince Kléber otherwise, the forthright Alsatian had continued to believe that the entire Egyptian expedition was a misguided enterprise, whose sole purpose was the aggrandizement of its commander-in-chief. Consequently, his first announcement to the troops suggested an early end to their present discomforts: "Soldiers, powerful help will soon be arriving, or if not we will negotiate a glorious peace, a peace with dignity which recognizes you and your efforts, and will return you to your homeland."[4] There was no doubt which option Kléber favored, and without waiting to hear from France he opened peace negotiations with the Turks and Sir Sidney Smith. These were held on board Smith's flagship the *Tigre*, anchored off El-Arish. An agreement was soon reached: the French would leave Egypt, taking their arms with them, and the Turkish army would occupy the country; honor was satisfied on all sides. The Convention of El-Arish, as it became known, was ratified on January 28, 1800.

Unfortunately, both Kléber and Smith had exceeded their authority in signing this agreement. Smith's role as plenipotentiary, with power to act on behalf of the British government, had now expired. He was by this stage nothing more than a naval commodore, and was due to return to the role of plain captain when he no longer commanded the squadron off Egypt. Kléber, for his part, was only the French governor of Egypt, a military and administrative command which gave him no authority to sign a peace treaty with a foreign power on behalf of the French government. When news of the El-Arish agreement reached London, Pitt immediately repudiated it, insisting that the French should submit to an unconditional surrender, after which they would be treated as prisoners of war and only be allowed to leave Egypt after giving up their arms. Britain and France were still at war, and there was no question of Britain allowing the fully armed Army of the Orient back to France to reinforce Napoleon. The well-meaning attempts of Smith and Kléber had come to nothing. Their superiors concurred that they had been out of their depth and had failed to take into account the overall situation.

By this stage, a Turkish army under the command of the grand vizier was advancing south through Syria towards Egypt, and despite Smith's appeals the advance continued. When the grand vizier's army reached the border fort at El-Arish, which contained a garrison of 250 French soldiers, the commander ordered the gates to be closed and told his soldiers to prepare to resist the Turkish invasion. But by now many of the soldiers had had enough of fighting. There was an immediate mutiny, during which the French flag was hauled down from the flagpole and soldiers broke into the stores, distributing barrels of liquor amongst their comrades. Amidst drunken scenes, the French soldiers lowered ropes over the walls, indicating that the enemy were welcome to join them, whereupon the Turkish soldiers began scaling the walls and the entire garrison was put to the sword.

Despite this, Kléber persisted in trying to negotiate with the Turks, and sent a representative to El-Arish. The French envoy found himself greeted by an extraordinary sight. The vast Turkish encampment was not guarded, but at its approaches were rows of putrefying heads on pikes—the remnants of the French garrison. The encampment itself stretched out over the surrounding wilderness and presented a spectacle of medieval exoticism and squalor. The army consisted of Turks, Arabs, Syrians, Albanians, Mamelukes, Moroccans and Nubians, each in their customary native dress. Their tents were equally diverse, ranging from primitive makeshift shelters made of skins to canopied pavilions whose interiors were hung with silken carpets. The soldiers squatted around their fires, roasting animal carcasses on spits, sharpening the glinting blades of their weapons. These fearsome warriors were accompanied by swarms of servants, stable boys, tailors, cooks, slaves, and an impoverished, filth-ridden rabble of hangers-on, many of whom appeared to be diseased. No provision was made for sanitation or medical treatment, and there was seemingly no collectivized order whatsoever. Each unit, with its national commander, appeared to decamp and move on as it saw fit. The camp seemed to stretch for miles, and each night various horsemen would set off from the grand vizier's compound, stopping at salient points to dismount and cry out the latest news and orders of the day. The wary French negotiators were courteously received by the grand vizier, but it soon became clear to them why the Turkish army had not heeded Kléber's appeals to halt, let alone retreat back to the border. It was explained to the French through interpreters that it was not the custom of the grand vizier to retreat, and they quickly came to the conclusion that his army was simply an unstoppable forward-moving force which appeared to advance by some collective will of its own.

Kléber remained uncertain what to do, until on March 18 he received a note from the British rejecting the peace treaty of El-Arish. This note was couched in the most insulting terms, and had the effect of clearing Kléber's mind. The inexperienced administrator, unsure of how to react, was transformed into the decisive and brilliant general. Express orders were issued to all units to halt plans for evacuation and prepare for battle, and at two A.M. on March 20, Kléber led 10,000 men from Cairo towards the advancing Turkish army of 40,000 men. The two armies met by the ruins of Heliopolis, just five miles northeast of Cairo, where Kléber won a brilliant victory and the grand vizier's army was put to flight, with the French in hot pursuit. Unfortunately for the French, the grand vizier's son Nassif Pasha managed to separate his forces from the general retreat, circled round Kléber's advance, and made for Cairo, which was only guarded by a skeleton force.

When Nassif Pasha entered the city and announced that the French had been defeated, Cairo was plunged into a bloody turmoil—more anarchy than uprising. By this stage many Mamelukes had joined up with the French, and Kléber had even sent out peace feelers to Murad

Bey, offering him the governorship of Upper Egypt if he supported French rule. Murad Bey had tired of life on the run, and soon sent word that he accepted Kléber's offer, his messenger arriving in the midst of the Cairo disturbances, which were still being orchestrated by Nassif Pasha. In the end it would take Kléber several weeks before he negotiated a peace, and order was fully returned to the streets of Cairo, with Nassif Pasha marching his men back to Syria.

Just two months later, on June 24, Kléber was walking on the terrace of his headquarters at Elfi Bey's palace when he was approached by an Arab who he thought was begging for alms. In fact, this was a twenty-four-year-old Syrian from Aleppo called Soliman, who according to El-Djabarti had been studying at the Al-Azhar mosque and had told one of the sheiks that he "wanted to fight for the glory of God, which signifies that he wanted to kill a Christian."[5] Soliman pulled out a knife from under his robes and stabbed Kléber to death. (By a grim coincidence, it was on the very same day that Desaix also met his death, 1,500 miles away on the battlefield at Marengo.)

Soliman was apprehended on the spot, and soon brought to trial, a nicety that astonished El-Djabarti, who recorded the proceedings as well as the final verdict: "The court sentenced Soliman of Aleppo to have his right hand burnt and then to be impaled. He must remain exposed on his spike until his corpse is devoured by the vultures."[6]

Precisely what this entailed was recorded by the newly promoted Sergeant François, who was present at Kléber's funeral, which took place in the Christian cemetery outside the walls of Cairo: "After the funeral ceremony the cortege set off back into the city, ending up at the esplanade outside the Institute building, which had been chosen as the spot for Soliman's execution. A great number of the city's inhabitants were gathered around and below the mound . . . awaiting the arrival of the condemned."[7] What happened next is described in gruesome detail by François, who was standing "five or six paces from the place where the execution took place." It involved a nine-foot spike, in a scene that is not for the faint-hearted:

The executioner laid the condemned man on the ground on his stomach, and with a knife made a large incision in his anus; shoving the tip of the spike into this incision he forced it into the body with heavy blows from a mallet. When he felt the spike reach as far as the breastbone, he bound the man's arms, raised him in the air and fixed the foot of the spike in a hole which had been dug in the ground. Throughout this frightful torture, the wretched Soliman made not a sound. One could only imagine the effort of will it required to conceal his torment. Once the spike was erected, Soliman cast his gaze over the spectators, and cried out, in Arabic, at the top of his voice, the Moslem profession of faith: "There is no other god but God, and Mahommed is his prophet."

François goes on to describe how at one stage a soldier was moved by Soliman's entreaties, and offered him some water. But the notorious Barthelemy—who was in charge of the execution—prevented him, telling the soldier that this would only interfere with the proceedings and thwart justice because it would kill Soliman instantly.

Kléber was succeeded as the French governor of Egypt by Menou, who quickly proceeded to make himself unpopular with both his fellow Muslims and his fellow officers. He began by insisting that Egypt should remain a French colony, and that all means of negotiating an end to this state of affairs should cease forthwith. He brought his young Arab bride to live with him in Elfi Bey's palace, where much to the annoyance of the savants he insisted upon sleeping with the Rosetta Stone beneath his bed for safekeeping. Previously, the eccentric fifty-one-year-old had been regarded by many of his young French colleagues as something of a joke, and he now succeeded Kléber only because his age ensured that he was the longest-serving, and thus the senior, general. As a commander-in-chief succeeding two highly charismatic commanders-in-chief, Menou cut an unprepossessing figure: he was pot-bellied, uninspiring in manner, and his appearance remained as scruffy as ever. The state of his uniform, his long, unwashed locks and his general lack of grooming had habitually irritated Napoleon, though he had overlooked this when Menou was safely out of sight as governor of Rosetta. Napoleon had positively warmed to him when he heard of his conversion to Islam and marriage to an Arab woman, holding him up as an example to his fellow officers and urging them to follow suit.

Menou had disliked Kléber, and considered his administration to have been hopelessly inefficient and corrupt. As a result, one of his first actions on taking office was to make a purge of all officers who had been close to Kléber. Anyone who had the temerity to disagree with him was instantly dismissed; in consequence, Kléber's former chief of staff Damas, the long-suffering financial supremo Poussielgue, as well as the savant and former politician Tallien, the financial commissioner Dauré, and many senior officers such as the adjutant-general Boyer, were all dismissed and ordered home to France to face court-martials and the ending of their careers in disgrace. Even so, Menou proved as competent an administrator as he had been in Rosetta, and the general running of the army soon improved, despite the growing scarcity of almost anything that an army required.

Kléber's victory at Heliopolis, and his suppression of the Cairo disturbances, had left the country largely pacified. But the international situation ensured that such a state of affairs could not last. The British were determined to eliminate any threat to their colony in India, and this meant ejecting the French from Egypt, a task which they realized could only be done by a well-equipped, well-armed and well-disciplined force, such as the British army. Large-scale plans were set in motion accordingly. Working in coordination with the Porte, a British expeditionary force of 17,000 men commanded by General Abercromby landed in March 1801 near Alexandria, followed by a Turkish landing further down the coast. Shortly afterwards a combined British and Indian force, commanded by General Baird, would land at Kosseir on the Red Sea.*

Menou's reaction—or lack of it—was disastrous: Abercromby was given days, and then weeks, to establish his bridgehead. When Menou finally marched north to confront the British, he left half his force behind to guard Cairo, thus ensuring that he faced the invading force with inferior numbers, rather than the superior force he had at his disposal. On March 21, 1801, a full three weeks after their landing, the 15,000-strong British expeditionary force was confronted by Menou's 12,000 men at Canopus, between Alexandria and Aboukir. The British eventually prevailed, but not until after heavy losses on both sides—as many as 4,000 French soldiers were captured, wounded or killed, and as many as half that number of British soldiers were

---

* This force was to have been commanded by General Wellesley, later Duke of Wellington, but he fell ill with "Malabar itch," a particularly virulent form of ringworm.

killed or wounded. Abercromby received a leg wound from which he died several days later, and on the French side General Lanusse was also fatally wounded. The latter was so disgusted with Menou's tactics that as he lay on his deathbed he famously informed his commander-in-chief that he was not even fit to be an onion-peeler in a Paris restaurant. This assessment had some truth: had Menou marched from Cairo immediately he heard of the British landing, taking all his troops with him, he would certainly have defeated Abercromby's force. He would then have had time to turn on the Turkish force, which consisted of the remnants of the army defeated at Heliopolis, once again under the command of the ineffectual grand vizier, and this time weakened by an outbreak of plague spreading through its ranks.

As it was, Menou moved from one calamity to the next. Having been defeated, he retreated with the remnants of his force to Alexandria, where he barricaded himself behind the city walls, leaving the British and Turkish armies free to take Rosetta and Damietta. British engineers then set about excavating a channel connecting the dried-up Lake Mareotis to the sea, thus flooding the lake and effectively cutting off Alexandria from the rest of Egypt, ensuring that the British needed only a marginal force to maintain a siege.

The British now advanced on Cairo, where General Belliard commanded a force of 12,000 men. Belliard considered the possibility of marching south to join up with Murad Bey, who was on his way with 15,000 Mamelukes. But this option was nullified when Murad Bey unexpectedly died and his successor chose to side with the British. Belliard was worried about the low morale of his men, and eventually decided to avoid further bloodshed by negotiating a surrender. On June 22 he dispatched an envoy to the British, and peace terms were eventually agreed. Ironically, these were almost exactly the same as those agreed by Kléber, Sir Sidney Smith and the Turkish representatives some eighteen months previously. Smith and Kléber may have been acting beyond their powers, but their vision of the larger picture appears to have been no less faulty than that of their superiors; and had the El-Arish Convention been implemented, thousands of French and Turkish lives—as well as hundreds of British lives—would have been saved.

By the night of July 4, a week after the peace agreement had been signed, the French preparations for leaving Cairo were well under way.

In the midst of this, a detachment of the camel corps arrived in Cairo from Alexandria, bearing from Menou "the order to defeat the British or die in the attempt."[8] The reaction of the French in Cairo is best summed up by Malus: "As General Menou knew that we were in no fit state to fight, that we could do nothing and that we were surrounded by vastly superior forces, this order could only have come from a man who had lost all reason."

Belliard ignored the order, and on July 6 the first detachment of French troops marched out of Cairo with full military honors, bearing the coffin containing the embalmed body of General Kléber, their bands playing solemn funeral music. They embarked upon river craft at Boulac, and proceeded down the Nile, with Kléber's coffin on the leading boat beneath a large black flag. Despite all this face-saving pomp, they were in fact a sorry crew: of the 13,000 French soldiers, savants, administrators, officers' wives and others who departed from Cairo, over a tenth were infected with diseases ranging from dysentery to syphilis. The last of the French were still leaving Cairo two weeks later when the contingent of 5,000 British and Indian troops under General Baird arrived from Kosseir, having traveled down the Nile.

Belliard and his men were transported to Rosetta, where they were embarked upon British ships, ready for the journey across the Mediterranean back to France. As part of the peace agreement, the savants were permitted to take with them all their voluminous research, rock and other samples, stuffed animals and so forth—but despite their vigorous protests they were not permitted to keep the Rosetta Stone.

Meanwhile Menou continued to hold out in Alexandria, where his 7,000 troops were quite easily contained by the surrounding water and a British encampment of 4,000 men. In fact he could easily have attacked this force, but he was now more concerned with fighting other battles, namely against the generals under his command, whom he blamed for his defeat at the Battle of Canopus. His second-in-command, General Reynier, a hero of the Syrian campaign, was eventually arrested for insubordination—i.e., venturing to criticize Menou—and would be deported, along with the likes of Poussielgue and Boyer, for court-martial in France. (Napoleon would personally intervene to have the case against Reynier dropped.)

So why on earth was Menou holding out in Alexandria? In fact, there was an element of method in his madness: he was awaiting the arrival of Admiral Ganteaume, who he felt sure would soon arrive with a fleet of ships bringing military reinforcements. This was a forlorn but not altogether misguided hope. Napoleon had ordered Ganteaume to sail back to Egypt almost as soon as he had been created First Consul. In February, Ganteaume and seven battle-ships containing 5,000 troops had succeeded in evading the British blockade of Toulon, only to return to port rather than risk losing the ships and men to the British, who now controlled the Mediterranean. The same procedure had taken place again a month later. By now Napoleon's fury knew no bounds, and Ganteaume was ordered to sea once more in May, with instructions to disembark in Libya and march overland along the coast to relieve the Army of the Orient in Egypt. In June Ganteaume finally arrived at Derna in Libya, where he was refused permission to land and disembark his force. He then set off for Crete, where his squadron managed to capture the British battleship *Swiftsure*, whereupon to Napoleon's further exasperation he returned to Toulon in July with his prize in tow. By coincidence, in that very same month another French flotilla arrived off Egypt. Instead of much-needed reinforcements and arms, this brought the contingent that Napoleon had promised to send to the Army of the Orient to improve its morale—a group of comedians, magicians and actresses. The British offered to allow the French flotilla to land at Alexandria, but Menou declined this generous gesture. On September 2 he finally agreed to a truce with the British, accepting much the same terms as those agreed by both Kléber and Belliard.

In October 1801 the last of the Army of the Orient left Egypt for France. What had begun with such high hopes just over three years previously had ended in barely concealed humiliation and farce. And of course there was tragedy too. Of the 40,000 Frenchmen who had set out, around 24,500 soldiers and nearly 2,000 sailors were repatriated by the British. Several thousand wounded had been shipped back to France prior to this. Official sources claimed the overall death toll at around 6,000; others put the figure at more than 20,000. It is impossible to assess an exact figure, but in all between 10,000 and 15,000 Frenchmen were probably killed or died of disease during the occupation of Egypt, as well as many times that number of

Muslim warriors and Mamelukes—all in the vain attempt to impose European civilization upon a backward people whose religion encouraged them to regard all change and all foreigners with the deepest suspicion.

After the French left Egypt, British and Ottoman forces continued to occupy the country, and Ibrahim Bey returned. There followed a period of more or less chaotic Mameluke rule, until in 1803 the British withdrew and the Albanian Mohammed Ali, who had swum to safety at the Battle of Aboukir, gradually took power, which he retained for over forty years. Mohammed Ali would maintain close links with France, which would play a major role in the archaeological expeditions that now began exploring the ruins of Upper Egypt. In 1869 the French engineer Ferdinand de Lesseps would fulfill Napoleon's dream by constructing the Suez Canal.

During Napoleon's last years in exile on St. Helena, he would often return to the theme of his "Oriental dream," insisting: "I would have done better to remain in Egypt; by now, I would have been emperor of all the East."[9] He would elaborate his plans: "If Acre had yielded to the French army, a great revolution would have taken place in the East. I would have founded an empire there, and the destiny of France would have been left to take another course."[10] He would even picture the future: "After ten years of French administration the fortification of Alexandria would have been complete; this city would be one of the most beautiful fortified spots in Europe [sic]; its population would be considerable . . . by way of the Ramaniyah canal, water from the Nile would arrive throughout the year . . . communication between the Red Sea and the Mediterranean would be open . . . shipyards would be established at Suez . . . sugar, cotton, rice, indigo would cover Upper Egypt . . . locks and pumps controlling the flooding of the Nile . . . a colony as powerful as this would not be long in declaring its independence. . . . After fifty years, civilization would have spread to the interior of Africa by way of Senaar, Abyssinia, Darfur, and Fezzan; several great nations would have come into being, and would be enjoying the benefits of Western culture, of science, and the religion of the true God—for it is through Egypt that the people of central Africa must receive enlightenment and happiness."[11] It is noticeable that even towards the end of his life he failed to understand the reason for his defeat in Egypt: the same reason why Egypt could not have ruled Africa in the nineteenth century—his underestimation of sea power. It seems that he had always regarded ruling France, and then Europe, as the less attractive option: "The smallest things can bring about the greatest events. If only Acre had fallen, I would have changed the face of the world."[12]

XXIX

Aftermath

THE Egyptian expedition resulted in failure, but Napoleon refused to see it as such, and since his arrival back in France in October 1799 coincided with news of his great victory at the Battle of Aboukir, this delusion would be shared by his fellow countrymen. By the time the Army of the Orient returned, and the truth became evident, Napoleon was on his way to declaring himself Emperor of France. The dream of one empire had given way to another.

Napoleon's experience in Egypt was in so many ways embryonic of his later rule in France. Here, at the meeting of Africa and Asia, his megalomania had been able to flourish, unrestricted by the everyday realities of Europe; his ambition thus nurtured, he returned to France with visions of a personal future such as no other sane man would have dared to contemplate. The man who sought to reform Egypt would end up by reforming France. The young general who attempted to bring modern civil justice to the ancient ways of Egypt would become the emperor who reformed France's medieval legal system and introduced the Napoleonic Code, whose principles remain to this day the foundation of legal systems throughout Europe. The ambitious ruler of Egypt who was willing to convert to Islam in order to receive the backing of the sheiks and *ulema* of Al-Azhar would be the ruler of "de-Christianized" France who in 1801 made a concordat with the pope. The warrior who dreamed of following in the footsteps of Alexander the Great and conquering Asia would instead settle for following his other classical hero Julius Caesar and conquering Europe. Napoleon's crowning of himself as emperor in 1804, and his dream of a continent-wide empire, would seem to have grown directly out of his dreams in Egypt.

Then there were the other less glorious parallels. The defeat by Nelson at the Battle of the Nile would be followed seven years later by Nelson's victory over the French fleet at Trafalgar, and Napoleon's reaction to both would be the same. Neither of these was a disaster at all: they would not prevent him from building his empire on land. His setback at Acre, and the consequent disastrous retreat of his army, would be uncannily paralleled in his setback at Moscow and his retreat across Europe; instead of desert, plague and death, there would be snow, typhoid and death. After Acre, Napoleon deserted the Army of the Orient, leaving Egypt to pursue his dreams of glory in France; thirteen years later he would similarly abandon the Grand Army after Moscow, heading for Paris to secure his position. Even his return from Egypt, and his rapturous reception in France as the savior of the Republic, would have its echo in his return from exile in Elba and the ecstatic welcome he received at the beginning of the "100 Days."

Those who had served Napoleon well in Egypt would also rise with him. Marmont, who had so ably governed Alexandria, would achieve the highest military honors, becoming a marshal of France, and consequently Napoleon's most trusted lieutenant—until finally, unable to accept Napoleon's despotism, he would turn against his master. The brave cavalry leader Murat would also become a marshal, and in 1808 Napoleon made him King of Naples. Another to achieve royal status was Napoleon's young aide and stepson Eugene Beauharnais, whom he made a prince in 1804; a year later Prince Eugene would be appointed Viceroy of Italy.

But not all of Napoleon's "Egyptians" would achieve such stellar status. His aide Junot, who had already fallen from favor after revealing Josephine's infidelity, would nonetheless pursue a valiant military career, capturing Lisbon in 1807, in recognition of which Napoleon made him Duke d'Abrantès. Later Napoleon would become exasperated by the crass and spendthrift behavior of Junot, and took a particular dislike to his wife (which, however, did not prevent him from attempting to seduce her). Junot himself developed the habit of eating 300 oysters of a morning to keep in shape; later such behavior developed into full-blown insanity, and he eventually committed suicide by leaping from a window in 1813.

The hapless Menou would return to France with his young wife Zobeida and their infant son, whereupon Napoleon made him governor of the province of Piedmont in northern Italy. Menou soon tired of his administrative duties, and when he left the post his desk was found to contain 900 unopened letters. Napoleon's faithful secretary Bourrienne also failed to live up to his promotion. In 1805 he was made envoy to Hamburg, but had to be dismissed five years later when he was found guilty of selling forged passports and embezzlement to the tune of two million francs. Napoleon eventually pardoned him his debts, and he settled down to write his memoirs. But after two volumes he asked a ghostwriter to piece together the rest from his scraps of notes; hence their unreliability. After these were published in 1829–31, Bourrienne too became insane and was confined to a lunatic asylum at Caen, where he died in 1834.

Napoleon was also to forgive his old enemy Sir Sidney Smith, of whom he would later say: "I am sorry I spoke ill of Smith. They tell me he is a good fellow. His government does not appreciate his services in Egypt and Syria."[1] Smith would continue to live up to his reputation as a larger-than-life character, again and again incurring the wrath of his superiors and the affectionate admiration of his men. In 1807 he succeeded once more in thwarting the French, this time at Lisbon, managing to rescue the entire Portuguese fleet, as well as all the gold in the treasury vaults, just as Junot's cavalry charged into the city. In 1815, he would on his own initiative turn up at the Battle of Waterloo, charging onto the battlefield in civilian clothes, commandeering a sword from a fallen officer and entering the fray. Later he would ride up to congratulate the Duke of Wellington, who was distinctly unimpressed by this civilian who had the temerity to shake his hand. Smith would die in his beloved Paris in 1840, being buried amongst the worthies in the Père Lachaise cemetery wrapped in a Union Jack.

Napoleon regarded the discoveries of the Egyptian expedition as its most lasting contribution, and was determined that these should be seen as one of his own great triumphs. He always had the highest regard for achievements of the intellect, and often insisted: "The real conquests, those that leave behind no regrets, are those made over ignorance."[2] To this end, he would in 1802 set up a commission which would include Monge, Conté and many of the savants from Egypt, to gather together the work of the Institute in Cairo, as well as all the explorations, drawings and discoveries of the other savants. These were to be published in a vast multi-volume work entitled *Description of Egypt*. It was to be consciously modeled upon the great French *Encyclopedia* of the previous century, the work that was seminal in spreading the knowledge, ideas and culture of the Enlightenment. The first volume of the *Description* would appear in 1809 and the entire work would not be completed until 1828, by which time it contained nine volumes of text and thirteen of plates, maps and engravings. As Fourier wrote in his introduction: "No other country has been subjected to researches so extended and so varied. No other was more worthy of being the object."[3] In fact, the *Description of Egypt* is now the sole source we have for several temples and ruins which have subsequently been destroyed. Even so, this work is far from being entirely accurate—many of the scenes are exaggerated, and in some cases the ruins have been imaginatively "reconstructed," showing how it was thought they might have appeared when they were built. Worst of all, some of the hieroglyphs recorded on the columns and temples were inaccurate, or simply invented, which would only add to the difficulties of those who later attempted to decipher this ancient script. Curiously, it was the artist-savants who tended to be guilty of this particular misdemeanor, rather than the engineer-savants, whose less accomplished drawings were invariably accurate in such details.

But it was Vivant Denon who would play the initial role of publicizing the discoveries of ancient Egypt, when in 1802 he published his *Travels in Lower and Upper Egypt*. This was illustrated with many of the drawings he had made, and quickly became a best-seller, being translated throughout Europe. Along with the *Description*, it would transform our knowledge of the origins of Western civilization, and even the age of the world itself.

On a more popular level, these works would also give rise to a fashionable craze for Egypt and all things Egyptian. When Napoleon moved into his palace at Malmaison in 1801, Josephine had many of the rooms decorated in the "Egyptian style," Damietta roses were planted in the garden, and the park contained Egyptian gazelles. This craze quickly spread from Parisian high society throughout the fashionable centers of Europe, where such things as Egyptian-style evening dress, pyramids, and the pastel shade *eau de Nil* became all the rage. This craze would penetrate to the very heart of the Republic. When Napoleon decided to dispense with the fleur-de-lis as the national symbol, on account of its Royalist associations, he asked Denon to design a new symbol, and the artist came up with a striking but simple design of a bee (intended to portray industry and sweetness, but with the power to sting). This was copied directly from the hieroglyph of an ancient Egyptian temple.*

But in many ways this was just the beginning. Despite the British claiming the Rosetta Stone as one of the spoils of war, and exhibiting it to the public in the British Museum (where it still remains), scholars all over Europe soon became intrigued by the mysterious ancient Egyptian hieroglyphs on this stone, which they were able to study on the plaster casts and rubbings which had been made and distributed by the French. These scholars soon agreed that the Rosetta Stone, with its three parallel texts, held the clue that could unlock the hidden secret of the ancient Egyptian language, but for the moment the task of deciphering these hieroglyphs proved beyond all who attempted it.

It was another of the savants who would play a decisive role in solving this mystery. The mathematician Fourier, former president of the Institute in Cairo, was rewarded by Napoleon on his return from Egypt with the post of governor of the Isère region in southeastern France. He would have preferred to continue with his mathematical researches, but reluctantly settled in Grenoble, where he proved an efficient and go-ahead administrator.† In the course of his work, he came across the eleven-year-old prodigy Jean-François Champollion, who exhibited an exceptional talent for languages. Fourier showed Champollion his collection of antiquities brought from Egypt, some of which contained ancient hieroglyphs, and the young genius was intrigued when he learned that they remained a mystery.

In the years to come Champollion became obsessed with the idea of deciphering these hieroglyphs, even going so far as to learn Coptic, which he correctly surmised was a late form of ancient Egyptian. By this time several scholars in Britain, Germany and France had begun to work on

---

* Although this Egyptomania spread to all advanced Western countries, it was not responsible for the pyramid design on the U.S. dollar bill, which pre-dates Napoleon's expedition and derives from Freemasonry.

† He was responsible for building the first road through the Mount Cenis pass linking Grenoble to Turin.

the hieroglyphs. Most suspected that they were like Chinese ideograms (some even thought that they might have been precursors of Chinese). Champollion's great insight was that the hieroglyphs were a complex mixture of ideograms and alphabet: some hieroglyphs stood for a letter, others for a syllable, others for an idea, and yet others for an object or entity. In the 1820s he began publishing his sensational discoveries, and his eventual solution to the mystery of the hieroglyphs. With this, the academic aspect of Egyptology was launched, and scholars were able to translate the many different texts. Far from being an indecipherable code, the hieroglyphs now became a window into the 6,000-year-old world of ancient Egypt—its history, its customs, its rulers all sprang vividly to life, and humanity began to understand for the first time the mysteries of one of the first great civilizations to emerge from prehistory.

Having set Champollion on his path, Fourier would go on to write the historical introduction to the *Description of Egypt*, but by this stage he had begun to suffer from a strange disease, whose main effect was to render him extremely sensitive to cold. This caused him to wrap up in many layers of heavy clothing, and live in a highly overheated room from which he seldom ventured forth, even during the midst of summer heatwaves. His colleagues mistook this behavior for hypochondria or eccentricity, but it is now thought that he must have contracted myxedema (a malfunction of the thyroid gland), or possibly malaria, during his time in Egypt with Napoleon. By a quirk of fate he would at the end of his life occupy a house in Paris on the Rue d'Enfer—Street of the Inferno, or Hell Street.

However, one "Egyptian" would outlive them all: Pauline Fourès, Napoleon's Cleopatra, would not die until the age of ninety in 1869 (precisely a hundred years after Napoleon's birth). After her adventure in Egypt, Pauline would blossom into a remarkable woman. On her arrival back in France in 1801 with the rest of the Army of the Orient, she was officially informed that Napoleon did not wish to see her again; instead she was quietly granted a pension and a country house outside Paris. Still an attractive young woman, she soon married Henri de Ranchoup, who had served as a major in the Ottoman army.* Through

---

* This was not unusual for French officers during the period prior to the invasion of Egypt, when France was allied to the Ottoman Empire; in fact, the young Napoleon himself had contemplated this option after the siege of Toulon, when he saw no outlet for his ambitions in the French army.

Pauline's influence, Ranchoup managed to obtain a number of minor diplomatic posts. Meanwhile his wife published a romantic historical novel, and then ran off to South America with another French officer, whom she soon dropped. In Brazil Pauline set up a successful business exporting rare woods to France, to which she returned some years later a changed woman, dressing in men's clothing, smoking a pipe, and living at home amongst her free-ranging menagerie of pet parrots and monkeys.

Pauline Fourès maintained that she never met Napoleon after her return from Egypt, but Napoleon claimed otherwise. During his exile in St. Helena he reminisced one day about encountering her at a masked ball in Paris. Although she was wearing a mask he recognized her, and suggested to her that she had once been "Cleopatra." According to Napoleon, she feigned not to remember such a thing, though she did recall having once had some affection for a "Caesar."

Napoleon may have put his Egyptian love out of his mind, but he never forgot his dream of an Oriental empire. Indeed, this persistent fantasy was even to play a role in his downfall. Having become emperor of France and ruler of much of mainland Europe from Spain to Poland, he wrote in 1808 to Tsar Alexander of Russia, proposing that they unite their armies and launch an overland attack on India. Napoleon had already written to the Shah of Persia, seeking his cooperation in such an enterprise. This plan would come to nothing, but it would not be forgotten. When Napoleon launched his invasion of Russia in 1812, many in his 600,000-strong Grand Army were convinced that Russia was not his ultimate aim. In the words of one officer: "Some said that Napoleon had made a secret alliance with Alexander, and that a combined Franco-Russian army was going to march against Turkey and take hold of its possessions in Europe and Asia; others said that the war would take us to the Great Indies, to chase out the English."[4] Such stories were current amongst all ranks: a fusilier wrote home that he was on his way to "the Great Indies" or perhaps to "Egippe."[5]

The echoes of Napoleon's Oriental dream would continue to haunt him to the end. After his defeat at Waterloo by Wellington, the man who had defeated Tippoo Sahib in India, Napoleon would be carried into exile aboard the *Bellerophon*, which had been part of Nelson's victorious fleet at the Battle of the Nile. As he sailed from France for the last time, Napoleon remarked to her captain: "But for you English, I would have been Emperor of the East."[6]

Notes

There is a vast literature on every aspect and period of Napoleon's life. In general, I have indicated only the firsthand or contemporary historical sources I have used when describing actual events.

Prologue: The Song of Departure

1. Different sources give Napoleon's height as anything between five foot two and five foot eight. At this time, the average height of a Frenchman was five foot six; many contemporaries made reference to Napoleon's short stature and several were unsympathetic towards him, such as his second-in-command on the Egyptian expedition, General Kléber, who used to refer to him privately as "that Corsican runt." I have favored this lower figure for Napoleon's height as it seems more likely given these circumstances.
2. Translated from a songsheet in *Le Départ du trompette de cuirassiers.*
3. Bourrienne, *Mémoires,* Vol. 1-2, p. 223. As many have noted, Napoleon's old schoolfriend and loyal secretary could be unreliable on details of fact, date and opinion; this is because these memoirs were at least in part written up by Maxime de Villemarest from scraps of notes. However, it is known that Bourrienne himself certainly wrote the first two volumes (those that cover the Egyptian campaign), which suffered only minor "editing"; here his memory of Napoleon's conversations, and the circumstances in which he held them, can often be vivid and revealing. I have tried to draw on Bourrienne's extensive *Mémoires* when the tenor and accuracy of his observations appear to be confirmed by other sources.
4. Arago, *Éloge de Monge,* delivered at the Académie des Sciences, May 1848. See Arago, *Biographie de Gaspard Monge,* p. 157; cited in Bell, *Men of Mathematics,* p. 223.
5. The following descriptive elements, as well as the debates and details of Caffarelli's speech, are assembled from several eyewitness accounts of these

discussions, most notably by the savant Antoine-Vincent Arnault in his *Souvenirs d'un sexagenaire* (Paris, 1833), Livre XIV, Ch. II, pp. 633–7; and by Bourrienne in his *Mémoires*, Vol. 2, pp. 231–2. There is also a suitably heroic painting by Charles Lucy, which draws on eyewitness reports and is reproduced in Aubry, *Monge*, opposite p. 234.

6. Napoleon, *Correspondance*, Vol. 4, pp. 191–2.
7. De Rémusat, *Mémoires*, Vol. 1, p. 274.

Chapter I: The Origins of the Egyptian Campaign

1. Herodotus, *Histories*, Book 2, p. 97.
2. See Napoleon, *Correspondance*, Vol. 8, p. 438.
3. François de Tott, *Mémoires sur les Turcs et les Tartares* (Maestricht, 1785), Part 4, pp. 11–12.
4. Details of this training regimen and various other facts concerning Volney's life appear in the opening pages of his *Oeuvres Complètes* under "Notice sur la vie . . ."
5. Ibid., Ch. 8, p. 157.
6. Ibid., Ch. 13, p. 169.
7. Cited in Charles-Roux, *Les Origines de l'Expédition d'Égypte*, p. 54.
8. For this and the preceding information see Archives du Ministère des Affaires Etrangères, lettres de consul Mure, 1776–7.
9. In keeping with the Revolution's aim to start afresh, France adopted a republican calendar in 1793. This began An I (Year One) on September 22, 1792, the day following the abolition of the monarchy and the establishment of the Republic. The new calendar attempted to "rationalize" the year, abolishing Christian and historical names. The year consisted of twelve months, each with thirty days; and instead of weeks, each month was divided into three "decades" (each lasting ten days). At the end of every year, five days (six in leap years) were added, to bring the new calendar into accord with the solar year. The months were evocatively named after the changing year: Vendémiaire (Vintage: Sept. 22–Oct. 21); Brumaire (Fog: Oct. 22–Nov. 20); Frimaire (Frost: Nov. 21–Dec. 20); Nivôse (Snow: Dec. 21–Jan. 19); Pluviôse (Rain: Jan 20–Feb. 18); Ventôse (Wind: Feb. 19–Mar. 20); Germinal (Blossom: Mar. 21–Apr. 19); Floréal (Flowers: Apr. 20–May 19); Prairial (Meadows: May 20–June 18); Messidor (Harvest: June 19–July 18); Thermidor (Heat: July 19–Aug. 17); Fructidor (Fruit: Aug. 18–Sept. 16).

    Instead of saints' days, each day of the year was named after a seed, tree, flower, fruit, animal or tool. The five (or six) extra days were called "Sansculottides," in honor of the sans-culottes, the name given to the revolutionaries, who wore trousers instead of the more aristocratic knee-breeches (culottes). This would be the official calendar in use throughout Napoleon's expedition to Egypt.
10. Talleyrand, *Essai sur les avantages à retirer des colonies nouvelles dans les circonstances présentes: lu à la séance publique [de l'Institut] du 15 messidor an V* (Paris, 1797).
11. Napoleon, *Correspondance*, Vol. 3, p. 294.

Chapter II: "The Liberator of Italy"

1. De Rémusat, *Mémoires*, Vol. 1, p. 267.
2. Volney, *Oeuvres Complètes*, "Notice sur la vie . . . ," p. 5.
3. Letter to his brother Joseph dated June 20, 1792, cited in Malraux, *Vie de Napoleon par lui-même*, p. 12.
4. Letter dated December 24, 1793; see Barrow, *The Life and Correspondence of Sir Sidney Smith*, Vol. 1, p. 153.
5. This quote appears in many of the biographies; e.g., McLynn, *Napoleon*, p. 74; Cronin, *Napoleon*, p. 75.
6. Doppet, *Mémoires politiques et militaires*, Book III, Ch. IV, Section 102, pp. 180–1.
7. Napoleon, *Correspondance*, Vol. 29, p. 84.
8. Throughout his life Napoleon frequently expressed variations on such sentiments to his confidants, especially Bourrienne; cf. this remark in September 1797: "Great events hang by a thread. The able man turns everything to profit, neglects nothing that may give him one chance more; the man of lesser ability, by overlooking just one thing, spoils the whole," cited in *Words of Napoleon*, ed. R. M. Johnston (London, 2002), p. 63.
9. This and the following quotes from Napoleon's letters to Josephine are from *Napoleon Lettres D'Amour à Josephine*, *présentées par Jean Tulard* (Paris, 1981); "the last two words were underlined . . ." cited in Christopher Hibbert, *Napoleon and His Women* (London, 2002), p. 49.
10. Gourgaud, *Journal de Sainte-Hélène 1815–1818*, Vol. 2, Ch. 10, p. 92.
11. Napoleon, *Correspondance*, Vol. 3, p. 235.
12. Bourrienne, *Mémoires*, Vol. 1–2, p. 226.
13. There are many references to this scene in contemporary sources. Those by two of the directors who were present are generally thought to be amongst the more reliable, despite their evident wish to justify themselves. These two sources are Barras, *Mémoires*, and the unpublished papers of Reubell, which came into the possession of Bernard Nabonne and were used by him in *La Diplomatie du Directoire et Bonaparte* (Paris, 1951).
14. Bourrienne, *Mémoires*, Vol. 1–2, p. 234.
15. Ibid., p. 223.

Chapter III: The Cream of France

1. March 30, 1821; cited in *Words of Napoleon*, ed. R. M. Johnston (London, 2002), p. 344.
2. See Kléber's unpublished pocketbook, which is in the *Archives historiques du ministère de la Guerre: Correspondance de l'armée d'Égypte: Mémoires historiques*, in Paris. This pocketbook contains jottings on Napoleon and the Egyptian campaign, some said to have been written down during staff meetings presided over by Napoleon.
3. *The Times*, London, April 25, 1798.
4. Bourrienne, *Mémoires*, Vol. 1–2, p. 231.
5. Napoleon, *Correspondance*, Vol. 4, p. 63.

6. Private correspondence between Earl Spencer, First Lord of the Admiralty, and Admiral St. Vincent, dated May 2, 1798.
7. Nelson, *Letters and Despatches*, p. 132.
8. Napoleon, *Correspondance*, Vol. 4, p. 96.
9. Nelson, *Letters and Despatches*, p. 133.

Chapter IV: Outward Bound

1. Napoleon, *Correspondance*, Vol. 4, p. 114.
2. Doublet, *Mémoires Historiques sur l'invasion et l'occupation de Malte en 1798*, p. 150.
3. Bourrienne, *Mémoires*, Vol. 1–2, p. 241.
4. Desvernois, *Mémoires*, p. 97.
5. Vertray, *Journal d'un officier de l'armée d'Égypte*, p. 29.
6. Bourrienne, *Mémoires*, Vol. 1–2, p. 243.
7. Denon, *Voyages dans la Basse et la Haute Égypte pendant les campagnes de Bonaparte*, Vol. 1, p. 7.
8. Bourrienne, *Mémoires*, Vol. 1–2, p. 242.
9. Ibid., p. 130.
10. Ibid., pp. 244–5.
11. Napoleon, *Correspondance*, Vol. 4, p. 120.
12. Nelson, *Letters and Despatches*, p. 136.
13. Ibid., p. 138.
14. Napoleon, *Correspondance*, Vol. 3, p. 459.
15. Nelson, *Letters and Despatches*, p. 143.
16. Pretyman MSS T 108/44, Suffolk Record Office, Ipswich.
17. Cited in Christopher Hibbert, *Nelson* (London, 1994), p. 138.

Chapter V: "A conquest which will change the world"

1. The source for these words is Turc, *Chronique d'Égypte 1798–1804*, p 8. Nicolas El-Turki (often known as Nicholas the Turk) was in fact a Druze poet, descended from Constantinople Greeks, who was living in Egypt at the time. His *Chronique* allows us to see Napoleon's invasion from a reasonably unpartisan local standpoint; Turc was neither an Arab nor a Muslim. When he himself is not present at the events he describes, he draws on local eyewitness reports, which although not always entirely reliable in the factual sense do tend to convey an authentic flavor of events seen from the Egyptian side.
2. Denon, *Voyages dans la Basse et la Haute Égypte pendant les campagnes de Bonaparte*, Vol. 1, p. 24.
3. Bourrienne, *Mémoires*, Vol. 1–2, p. 250.
4. Several sources mention this incident, and Napoleon's reaction, which would appear to be confirmed by the recorded arrival of *La Justice* off Alexandria on July 1. Bourrienne, *Mémoires*, Vol. 1–2, p. 251, alludes to the story, though he casts doubt on its veracity; this implies that *La Justice* might have been sighted later, *after* Napoleon boarded the Maltese galley, when Bourrienne would not have been present.
5. Vertray, *Journal d'un officier de l'armée d'Égypte*, p. 31.

6. Herold, *Bonaparte in Egypt*, p. 61.
7. Napoleon, *Correspondance*, Vol. 29, p. 432.
8. Ibid., p. 433.
9. Ibid.
10. Vertray, *Journal d'un officier de l'armée d'Égypte*, p. 28.
11. Napoleon, *Correspondance*, Vol. 29, p. 433.
12. Turc, *Chronique d'Égypte 1798–1804*, p. 9.
13. Ibid.
14. Marmont, Duc de Raguse, *Mémoires* (9 vols., published posthumously, Paris, 1857), Vol. 1, p. 367.
15. Napoleon, *Correspondance*, Vol. 4, p. 190.
16. Turc, *Chronique d'Égypte 1798–1804*, p. 24.
17. Napoleon, *Correspondance*, Vol. 29, p. 432.
18. El-Djabarti, *Merveilles biographiques et historiques, ou Chroniques*, Vol. 6, p. 7. Being both an educated Egyptian and a senior Muslim, El-Djabarti had a profound understanding of the Muslim reaction to the French invasion. He also had access to the workings of government. His views on the invasion are naturally trenchant, yet they are also often highly perceptive. Like Nicolas Turc, his descriptions of events are not always strictly accurate in a factual sense, but there is no doubting the accuracy of his description of Egyptian reactions to such events.
19. Desvernois, *Mémoires*, p. 100.
20. Napoleon, *Correspondance*, Vol. 4, p. 216.
21. Marmont, op. cit., Vol. 1, p. 366.
22. Thurman, *Bonaparte en Égypte: souvenirs*, p. 27.
23. Napoleon, *Correspondance*, Vol. 29, p. 434. As has been pointed out to me by Jon Latimer in his Internet review of *Napoleon in Egypt*, the "rifles" referred to in this instance, and indeed throughout the book, would in fact have been muskets. Napoleon, and almost all the firsthand sources I have referred to in this work, called the firearm used by the French soldiers (and their enemies) *fusil*, which translates as "rifle"—whereas the French for musket is *mousquet*. There is no doubt that Jon Latimer is technically correct on this point: rifles as we know them did not come into widespread military use until after the Egyptian expedition. However, in keeping with the usage by firsthand sources I have retained the word *rifle* throughout.
24. Ibid.
25. Ibid.
26. Ibid., Vol. 4, p. 218.
27. Ibid., p. 182.
28. Ibid.
29. Ibid.
30. Ibid., p. 184.
31. *Correspondance de l'armée française en Égypte*, p. 29. Remarkably, this is a French reprint of a work originally published in English and French in London earlier in the same year, under the self-explanatory title *Copies of Original Letters from the Army of General Buonaparte [sic] in Egypt, Intercepted by the Fleet under the Command of Admiral Lord Nelson*, which proved so popular that it went through three editions within eighteen months of its first publication.

32. Napoleon, *Correspondance*, Vol. 4, p. 189.
33. *Correspondance de l'armée française en Égypte*, p. 25.
34. Millet, *Souvenirs de la campagne d'Égypte*.
35. Vertray, *Journal d'un officier de l'armée d'Égypte*, p. 32.
36. Napoleon, *Correspondance*, Vol. 4, p. 195.
37. There are several extant versions of this proclamation, including the official French version in Napoleon's *Correspondance*, Vol. 4, pp. 191–2, and a slightly different French version which he gives in his memoirs of the Egyptian campaign in Vol. 29 of the *Correspondance*. The Arabic version mentioned by El-Djabarti and Nicolas Turc differed from these, as did the English version printed in the intercepted letters. I have given a shortened conflated variant which mentions the salient points and tends towards the Arabic version, this being the one which actually circulated. However, all the different versions had their own *raison d'être*: for example, the official French version intended for the eyes of the Directory referred to the French as "true friends of the Muslims," whereas the Arabic version claimed "the French are true Muslims."
38. Napoleon, *Correspondance*, Vol. 4, pp. 191–2; Turc, *Chronique d'Égypte 1798–1804*, pp. 10–12.
39. Napoleon, *Correspondance*, Vol. 29, p. 435.
40. Bourrienne, *Mémoires*, Vol. 1–2, p. 254.
41. Charles-Roux, *Bonaparte gouverneur d'Égypte*, pp. 130–1.
42. Denon, *Voyages dans la Basse et la Haute Égypte pendant les campagnes de Bonaparte*, Vol. 1, p. 28.
43. Ibid., p. 29.
44. Ibid., p. 36.
45. For full details of just one day's directives, see Napoleon, *Correspondance*, Vol. 4, p. 196.
46. Ibid., pp. 224–5.

Chapter VI: The March on Cairo

1. Napoleon, *Correspondance*, Vol. 4, p. 193.
2. Napoleon, *Correspondance inédite, officielle et confidentielle: Égypte*, Vol. 1, pp. 102–3.
3. This scene is recounted in Bourrienne, *Mémoires*, Vol. 1–2, p. 253.
4. Millet, *Souvenirs de la campagne d'Égypte*, p. 48.
5. De La Jonquière, *L'Expedition en Égypte 1798–1801*, Vol. 2, p. 135.
6. Ibid., p. 131.
7. Thurman, *Bonaparte en Égypte: Souvenirs*, p. 89.
8. Marmont, Duc de Raguse, *Mémoires* (9 Vols., published posthumously, Paris, 1857), Vol. 1, pp. 372–3.
9. Denon, *Voyages dans la Basse et la Haute Égypte pendant les campagnes de Bonaparte*, Vol. 1, p. 37.
10. Ibid.
11. Desvernois, *Mémoires*, p. 102.
12. Denon, *Voyages dans la Basse et la Haute Égypte pendant les campagnes de Bonaparte*, Vol. 1, p. 38.
13. Ibid. A strikingly similar encounter is described in Savary, *Mémoires*, pp. 42–3, and it appears that this was a previous encounter with the same woman.

14. Bourrienne, *Mémoires*, Vol. 1–2, p. 257.
15. Bernoyer, *Avec Bonaparte en Égypte*, pp. 51–2.
16. Denon, *Voyages dans la Basse et la Haute Égypte pendant les campagnes de Bonaparte*, Vol. 1, p. 39.
17. Desvernois, *Mémoires*, p. 110.
18. Cited in ibid., p. 111.
19. François, *Journal du Capitaine François, dit le Dromadaire d'Égypte*, Vol. 1, p. 195. During this period in Egypt François was only a corporal; he would be promoted to sergeant in November 1798, only later becoming an officer.
20. Ghorbal, *The Beginnings of the Egyptian Question*, p. 49.
21. Herold, *Bonaparte in Egypt*, p. 81.
22. Napoleon, *Correspondance*, Vol. 29, p. 438.
23. Ibid., Vol. 4, p. 223.
24. Elgood, *Bonaparte's Adventure in Egypt*, p. 103.
25. Las Cases, *Mémorial de Sainte-Hélène*, Vol. 1, p. 131.
26. Napoleon, *Correspondance*, Vol. 29, p. 446.
27. Las Cases, *Mémorial de Sainte-Hélène*, Vol. 1, p. 131.
28. Ibid., p. 132.
29. Desvernois, *Mémoires*, p. 108.
30. Napoleon, *Correspondance*, Vol. 4, p. 236.
31. Ibid., Vol. 29, p. 441.
32. Bernoyer, *Avec Bonaparte en Égypte*, p.54, and Vertray, *Journal d'un officier de l'armée d'Égypte*, p. 48.
33. Vertray, *Journal d'un officier de l'armée d'Égypte*, p. 49.
34. De La Jonquière, *L'Expédition en Égypte 1798–1801*, Vol. 2, p. 167.
35. This anecdote appears in one form or another in Elgood, *Bonaparte's Adventure in Egypt*, p. 113, and several other sources such as Herold, *Bonaparte in Egypt*, and a number of memoirs.
36. Desvernois, *Mémoires*, p. 118.
37. Napoleon, *Correspondance*, Vol. 29, p. 442.
38. Desvernois, *Mémoires*, p. 118.
39. Napoleon, *Correspondance*, Vol. 29, p. 442–3.
40. Grandjean, *Journaux sur l'Expédition de l'Égypte*, p. 75.
41. Ibid., p. 76.
42. Bourrienne, *Mémoires*, Vol. 1–2, p. 260.
43. Sadoun-Goupil, *Le Chimiste Claude-Louis Berthollet*, p. 255. This incident is confirmed by several sources, though this particular information comes from an unpublished letter written over twenty years after the event by Berthollet's fellow savant Geoffroy Saint-Hilaire to Cuvier, who was preparing a eulogy on the great chemist: *Bibliothèque d'Institut, Fonds Cuvier, liasse* 206. The behavior described was said to have been characteristic.
44. Bourrienne, *Mémoires*, Vol. 1–2, p. 260.
45. Turc, *Chronique d'Égypte 1798–1804*, p. 22.
46. *Correspondance de l'armée française en Égypte*, pp. 62–3.
47. Bourrienne, *Mémoires*, Vol. 1–2, p. 261.

Chapter VII: The Battle of the Pyramids

1. François, *Journal du Capitaine François, dit le Dromadaire d'Égypte*, Vol. 1, p. 202.
2. Cited in La Jonquière, *L'Expédition en Égypte 1798–1801*, Vol. 2, p. 162.
3. François, *Journal du Capitaine François, dit le Dromadaire d'Égypte*, Vol. 1, pp. 203–4.
4. Cited in Thiry, *Bonaparte en Égypte*, p. 145.
5. Denon, *Voyages dans la Basse et la Haute Égypte pendant les campagnes de Bonaparte*, Vol. 1, p. 40.
6. Napoleon, *Correspondance*, Vol. 29, p. 446.
7. El-Djabarti, *Merveilles biographiques et historiques, ou Chroniques*, Vol. 6, p. 318.
8. Ibid., p. 314.
9. Herold, *Bonaparte in Egypt*, p. 8.
10. Napoleon, *Correspondance*, Vol. 29, p. 440, cited and confirmed in Desvernois, *Mémoires*, note on p. 114. See also above, Ch. 5, n.14.
11. Details of Murad Bey's reaction, the conversations at the *divan* and the reactions in the streets appear in Turc, *L'Expédition des Français en Égypte*, pp. 25, 27–30. This does not match with the edition translated by Gaston Wiet published in Cairo in 1950. The two translations frequently differ, with some details appearing in one but not in the other. This suggests that there may have been more than one manuscript, as indeed there was more than one translator (I know of three, all of whom differ); any of the translators or copyists involved in these different versions could well have chosen to leave out details they considered too fanciful or historically irrelevant.
12. El-Djabarti, *Merveilles biographiques et historiques, ou Chroniques*, Vol. 6, p. 9.
13. Ibid., p. 13.
14. Napoleon, *Correspondance*, Vol. 29, p. 448.
15. These and the following figures appear in ibid., p. 448.
16. Cited in Herold, *Bonaparte in Egypt*, p. 89, note.
17. Napoleon, *Correspondance*, Vol. 29, p. 450.
18. Cited in La Jonquière, *L'Expédition en Égypte 1798–1801*, Vol. 2, p. 190.
19. See Napoleon, *Correspondance*, Vol. 29, p. 449, collated with Vol. 4, p. 249, which gives the figures.
20. Cited in La Jonquière, *L'Expédition en Égypte*, Vol. 2, p. 188.
21. François, *Journal du Capitaine François, dit le Dromadaire d'Égypte*, Vol. 1, p. 206.
22. Vertray, *Journal d'un officier de l'armée d' Égypte*, pp. 59–60.
23. Reynier's report to his commander-in-chief two days after the battle, cited in La Jonquiere, *L'Expédition en Égypte 1798–1801*, Vol. 2, p. 189.
24. Napoleon, *Correspondance*, Vol. 4, p. 251.
25. Desvernois, *Mémoires*, pp. 123–4.
26. Ibid., p. 124.
27. El-Djabarti, *Merveilles biographiques et historiques, ou Chroniques*, Vol. 6, p. 17.
28. Ibid.

29. Millet, *Souvenirs de la campagne d'Égypte*, pp. 51–2.
30. El-Djabarti, *Merveilles biographiques et historiques, ou Chroniques*, Vol. 6, p. 17.
31. Turc, *Chronique d'Égypte 1798–1804*, p. 24.
32. Ibid., pp. 23–4.
33. Napoleon, *Correspondance*, Vol. 29, p. 451.
34. Ibid.
35. Marmont, Duc de Raguse, *Mémoires* (9 vols., published posthumously, Paris, 1857), Vol. 1, p. 384.
36. El-Djabarti, *Merveilles biographiques et historiques, ou Chroniques*, Vol. 6, p. 20.
37. Napoleon, *Correspondance*, Vol. 4, p. 252.
38. Ibid., Vol. 29, p. 451.

Chapter VIII: Cairo

1. Napoleon, *Correspondance*, Vol. 4, p. 254.
2. Malus, *Souvenirs de l'Expédition de l'Égypte*, pp. 65–6.
3. François, *Journal du Capitaine François, dit le Dromadaire d'Égypte*, Vol. 1, p. 211.
4. Brigadier Detroye, *Journal* (unpublished), in *Archives Historiques du ministère de la Guerre: Correspondance de l'armée d'Égypte: Mémoires Historiques*, cited in Charles-Roux, *Bonaparte gouverneur d'Égypte*, p. 256.
5. Ibid.
6. Malus, *Souvenirs de l'Expédition de l'Égypte*, p. 68–9.
7. Denon, *Voyages dans la Basse et la Haute Égypte pendant les campagnes de Bonaparte*, Vol. 1, p. 82.
8. Ibid.
9. El-Djabarti, *Merveilles biographiques et historiques, ou Chroniques*, pp. 23, 26.
10. Turc, *L'Expédition des Français en Égypte*, p. 49.
11. Napoleon, *Correspondance*, Vol. 5, p. 574.
12. El-Djabarti, *Merveilles biographiques et historiques, ou Chroniques*, Vol. 6, p. 25.
13. Napoleon, *Correspondance*, Vol. 4, p. 254.
14. Ibid., p. 286.
15. Ibid., p. 420.
16. Ibid., Vol. 29, p. 478.
17. Ibid., p. 479.
18. Ibid., p. 481.
19. Ibid., pp. 480–1.
20. Ibid., Vol. 5, p. 572.
21. La Jonquière, *L'Expédition en Égypte 1798–1801*, Vol. 2, p. 293.
22. Turc, *L'Expédition des Français en Égypte*, p. 38.
23. El-Djabarti, *Merveilles biographiques et historiques, ou Chroniques*, Vol. 6, p. 29.
24. Napoleon, *Correspondance*, Vol. 29, p. 453.
25. Ibid., Vol. 4, p. 273.

26. Desvernois, *Mémoires*, p. 258.
27. Savary, *Lettres sur L'Égypte*, pp. 185–6.
28. Several sources mention this little trip, most notably Geoffroy Saint-Hilaire, *Lettres écrites d'Égypte*, pp. 236–7. Some sources say it took place later, on September 19, or even as late as the 24th according to Geoffroy Saint-Hilaire, though there does appear to have been an earlier trip. Indeed, it seems unlikely that Napoleon would have waited almost two months before visiting these historic monuments which had inspired his speech and given their name to his great battle. Whether his party camped at the foot of the Great Pyramid is also open to question, but there is no doubt that Berthier did erect a shrine in his tent to his *contessa*, and that Napoleon made a habit of ribbing him over this.

Chapter IX: "Josephine! . . . And I am 600 leagues away!"

1. The exact date is uncertain. Bourrienne, who was present and gives a vivid and seemingly reliable version of the scene, even places it well over six months later, but concrete evidence in the form of letters written by Napoleon about this revelation rules out such a late date. The weight of evidence points to Napoleon's fateful conversation with Junot taking place on July 19, 1798, two days before the Battle of the Pyramids.
2. This scene is largely reconstructed from Bourrienne, *Mémoires*, Vol. 1–2, pp. 314–5; many details, including Napoleon's words and reactions, are confirmed by memoirs of other eyewitnesses.
3. *Mémoires et Correspondance du Roi Joseph* [Bonaparte], ed. Du Casse (10 vols., Paris, 1855), Vol. 1, p. 189.
4. Ibid.
5. Napoleon, *Correspondance*, Vol. 4, p. 334.

Chapter X: The Battle of the Nile

1. BL Add. MSS 34974, cited in Brian Lavery, *Nelson and the Nile* (London, 1998), p. 134.
2. Nelson, *Letters and Despatches*, p. 145.
3. Ibid., p. 144.
4. National Maritime Museum, Greenwich, London: NMM AGC/W/2.
5. BL Add. MSS 30260.
6. Nicol, *The Life and Adventures of John Nicol* (Edinburgh, 1882), p. 187.
7. Ibid., p. 185.
8. Willyams, *A Voyage up the Mediterranean . . . with a Description of the Battle of the Nile* (London, 1802), p. 46.
9. The official sources and eyewitness accounts all generally agree here, with only minor differences of wording. The sequence of Nelson's orders can be seen in Captain Miller's narrative in Nelson, *Letters and Despatches*, pp. 155–6.
10. Ibid., p. 152.
11. Willyams, *A Voyage up the Mediterranean . . . with a Description of the Battle of the Nile*, p. 43.
12. Nicol, *The Life and Adventures of John Nicol*, p. 187.
13. Willyams, *A Voyage up the Mediterranean . . . with a Description of the Battle of the Nile*, p. 51.

14. Lee, *Memoirs*, p. 91. Doubt has been cast on Lee's veracity here, though he is supported by several patriotic French versions. Many otherwise credible eyewitness reports of the battle give differing versions of the events; even the official versions recorded in Nelson's *Letters and Despatches* and the records at the Greenwich Maritime Museum differ from each other. Indeed, it would be surprising if this were not the case, given the circumstances amidst the heat (and night) of such a battle. My intention has been to convey the feel of the battle, as well as its decisive events, adhering as far as possible to eyewitness reports that seem credible, or reports that were certainly drawn immediately afterwards from eyewitnesses. For instance, Nicol was manning a gun belowdecks, but much of his description has a vividness derived from the reports of fellow seamen above decks.

15. Willyams, *A Voyage up the Mediterranean . . . with a Description of the Battle of the Nile*, p. 54.

16. This and the following are from Nicol, *The Life and Adventures of John Nicol*, p. 187.

17. Lee, *Memoirs*, p. 92.

18. Ibid., p. 91.

19. La Jonquière, *L'Expédition en Égypte 1798–1801*, Vol. 2, p. 399.

20. Lee, *Memoirs*, p. 91.

21. This and the immediately following quotes are from Willyams, *A Voyage up the Mediterranean . . . with a Description of the Battle of the Nile*, pp. 53, 54.

22. Ibid., p. 55.

23. Lee, *Memoirs*, p. 93. Willyams described this as follows: "The tremulous motion, felt to the very bottom of each ship, was like that of an earthquake." His description was published in 1802, Lee's some thirty-four years later; there is no doubting that Lee read Willyams' words before writing his own. In my view, this prompted his memories, if not his words. This highlights one of so many difficulties facing any would-be historian: even authentic eyewitness accounts can contain inauthentic plagiarisms!

24. Nicol, *The Life and Adventures of John Nicol*, p. 187.

25. Nelson, *Letters and Despatches*, p. 153.

26. *Correspondance de l'armée française en Égypte*, pp. 221–2. According to the editor of this volume, Poussielgue's description was "shown to several of our officers who took part in the battle at Aboukir, and all unanimously agreed that it was an extraordinarily accurate document." See ibid., footnote, pp. 219–20.

27. This and the following relevant quotes are from Lee, *Memoirs*, p. 94.

28. Nicol, *The Life and Adventures of John Nicol*, pp. 187–8.

29. Napoleon, *Correspondance*, Vol. 29, pp. 469–70.

30. Lee, *Memoirs*, p. 105.

31. Denon, *Voyages dans la Basse et la Haute Égypte pendant les campagnes de Bonaparte*, Vol. 1, p. 63.

Chapter XI: "We are now obliged to accomplish great things"

1. Desvernois, *Mémoires*, p. 134.

2. Napoleon, *Correspondance*, Vol. 4, p. 195.

3. Quote from ibid., p. 360; mistakes listed in ibid., Vol. 29, p. 471.

4. Damas, *Journal*, cited in La Jonquière, *L'Expédition en Égypte 1798–1801*, Vol. 2, p. 425.
5. Nelson, *Letters and Despatches*, p. 164.
6. Napoleon, *Correspondance*, Vol. 29, p. 457.
7. Marmont, Duc de Raguse, *Mémoires* (9 Vols., published posthumously, Paris, 1857), Vol. 1, p. 390.
8. Desvernois, *Mémoires*, p. 134.
9. Napoleon, *Correspondance*, Vol. 29, p. 457.
10. Bourrienne, *Mémoires*, Vol. 1–2, p. 274.
11. This quote and the following, as told by Private Mourchon of the Dragoons to Colonel Laugier, are cited in La Jonquière, *L'Expédition en Égypte 1798–1801*, Vol. 2, p. 469.
12. Thurman, *Bonaparte en Égypte: souvenirs*, p. 270.
13. Napoleon, *Correspondance*, Vol. 4, p. 475.
14. Ibid., Vol. 29, pp. 484–5.
15. *Journal d'Abdurrahman Gabarti* [El-Djabarti] *pendant l'occupation française en Égypte*, p. 26.
16. El-Djabarti, *Merveilles biographiques et historiques, ou Chroniques*, Vol. 6, p. 307.
17. Details of the Egyptian economy, tax structure and economic figures from Napoleon, *Correspondance*; La Jonquière, *L'Expédition en Égypte 1798–1801*; Herold, *Bonaparte in Egypt*; Charles-Roux, *Bonaparte gouverneur d'Égypte*, etc.
18. Napoleon, *Correspondance*, Vol. 4, p. 391.
19. El-Djabarti, *Merveilles biographiques et historiques, ou Chroniques*, Vol. 6, p. 34.
20. Bourrienne, *Mémoires*, Vol. 1–2, p. 292.
21. Napoleon, *Correspondance*, Vol. 29, p. 486.
22. Brigadier Detroye's unpublished journal, cited in La Jonquière, *L'Expédition en Égypte 1798–1801*, Vol. 2, pp. 481–2 (see also above, Ch. 8, n.4.)
23. Malus, *Souvenirs de L'Expédition de l'Égypte*, p. 90.
24. *Rapport de la commission scientifique d'Égypte*, cited in ibid., p. 90, n.1.
25. Cited in Charles-Roux, *Bonaparte gouverneur d'Égypte*, pp. 92–3.
26. Napoleon, *Correspondance*, Vol. 4, pp. 399–400.
27. Turc, *L'Expédition des Français en Égypte*, p. 46.
28. Napoleon, *Correspondance*, Vol. 4, p. 380.
29. Turc, *L'Expédition des Français en Égypte*, p. 60.
30. Napoleon's reports to the Directory: *Correspondance*, Vol. 4, pp. 361, 436, 475.
31. Ibid., p. 475.
32. Desvernois, *Mémoires*, p. 139.
33. El-Djabarti, *Merveilles biographiques et historiques, ou Chroniques*, Vol. 6, p. 40.
34. Turc, *L'Expédition des Français en Égypte*, p. 52.
35. Desgenettes, *Souvenirs de la fin du XVIIIe. siècle*, Vol. 3, p. 165.
36. Bernoyer, *Avec Bonaparte en Égypte*, p. 80.
37. Details of New Year celebrations from *Le Courier de l'Égypte*, 6 Vendémiaire An VII, as well as La Jonquière, *l'Expédition en Égypte 1798–1801*, Vol. 3; El-Djabarti, *Merveilles biographiques et historiques, ou Chroniques*; Charles-

Roux, *Bonaparte gouverneur d'Égypte*; Bernoyer, *Avec Bonaparte en Égypte*, etc.

38. De Rémusat, *Mémoires*, Vol. 1, p. 274.
39. Napoleon, *Correspondance*, Vol. 29, pp. 429–30.

Chapter XII: The Institute of Egypt

1. For these and other details of the Institute's founding, see Napoleon, *Correspondance*, Vol. 4, pp. 383–6.
2. Ibid., p. 387.
3. Cited in several sources, most notably Charles-Roux, *Bonaparte gouverneur d'Égypte*, p. 219; this incident may well have taken place during the later proceedings of the Institute.
4. Napoleon, *Correspondance*, Vol. 4, pp. 390–1.
5. Jomard, *Souvenirs sur Gaspard Monge*, p. 47.
6. Geoffroy Saint-Hilaire, *Lettres écrites d'Égypte*, p. 53.
7. Ibid., p. 66.
8. Charles-Roux, *Bonaparte gouverneur d'Égypte*, p. 175.
9. *La Décade*, 1st issue, p. 6.
10. Ibid., 7th issue, p. 223.
11. This and the following quotes describing El-Djabarti's visits to the Institute are from El-Djabarti, *Merveilles biographiques et historiques, ou Chroniques*, Vol. 6, pp. 72–4.
12. This story comes from Arago, *Biographie de Gaspard Monge*, p. 116. Arago knew Monge personally, and for this work drew on conversations with him as well as recollections of his contemporaries and fellow members of the Egyptian expedition.

Chapter XIII: Life in Exile

1. *Le Courier de l'Égypte*, No. 1, p. 3.
2. Napoleon, *Correspondance*, Vol. 4, pp. 433–4.
3. La Jonquière, *L'Expédition en Égypte 1798–1801*, Vol. 3, p. 91.
4. *Le Courier de l'Égypte*, No. 76, pp. 2–3.
5. Ibid., No. 7, pp. 2–3.
6. These two notices appear in ibid., No. 16, p. 4, and No. 13, p. 4. Those following all appear in various issues of *Le Courier*, and are listed in Charles-Roux, *Bonaparte gouverneur d'Égypte*, p. 258.
7. Contemporary memoir, cited in ibid., p. 257.
8. Ibid., pp. 257–8.
9. La Jonquière, *L'Expédition en Égypte 1798–1801*, Vol. 3, p. 91.
10. El-Djabarti, *Merveilles biographiques et historiques, ou Chroniques*, Vol. 6, p. 26.
11. Ibid., p. 86.
12. Ibid., p. 305.
13. La Jonquière, *L'Expédition en Égypte 1798–1801*, Vol. 5, p. 15.
14. Ibid., p. 662.
15. Ibid., pp. 662–3.

16. El-Djabarti, *Merveilles biographiques et historiques, ou Chroniques*, Vol. 6, p. 306.
17. Ibid., p. 304.
18. Ibid., pp. 304–5.
19. Ibid., p. 306.
20. Ibid., pp. 305–6.
21. *Correspondance de l'armée française en Égypte*, pp. 137–8.
22. Herold, *Bonaparte in Egypt*, p. 158.
23. Turc, *L'Expédition des Français en Égypte*, p. 133.
24. This and the following order are cited in Charles-Roux, *Bonaparte gouverneur d'Égypte*, p. 304.
25. *Histoire scientifique et militaire de l'Expédition Française en Égypte*, Vol. 4, pp. 113–5. This ten-volume work compiled by X. Saintine and L. Reybaud drew on unpublished information provided by various members of Napoleon's expedition—ranging from Geoffroy Saint-Hilaire to Parseval-Grandmaison—but gives little or no indication of who were the sources for particular pieces of information. Herold, *Bonaparte in Egypt*, seems to suggest that the source for this incident was General Belliard, but this is unlikely as Belliard was at the time in Upper Egypt with Desaix's division. The following conversation also comes from this source, and seems to be an accurate reflection of Napoleon's manner and speech.
26. El-Djabarti, *Merveilles biographiques et historiques, ou Chroniques*, Vol. 6, p. 92.
27. François, *Journal du Capitaine François, dit le Dromadaire d'Égypte*, cited in Brégeon, *L'Égypte de Bonaparte*, p. 169.
28. See Regier, *Book of the Sphinx*, p. 62.
29. Napoleon, *Correspondance*, Vol. 29, p. 389.
30. Roustam Raza, *Souvenirs de Roustam, mamelouck de Napoleon Ier*, p. 57.
31. El-Djabarti, *Merveilles biographiques et historiques, ou Chroniques*, Vol. 6, p. 93.
32. Ibid., p. 90.

Chapter XIV: The Perils of Diplomacy

1. Napoleon, *Correspondance*, Vol. 5, p. 32.
2. El-Djabarti, *Merveilles biographiques et historiques, ou Chroniques*, Vol. 6, p. 50.
3. Ibid., pp. 52–4.
4. Ibid., p. 55.
5. This and the following quote are from a letter dated September 19 from Menou to Napoleon, cited in La Jonquière, *L'Expédition en Égypte 1798–1801*, Vol. 3, p. 114.
6. This and the following quote are from Marmont, Duc de Raguse, *Mémoires* (9 vols., published posthumously, Paris, 1857), Vol. 1, p. 394–5.
7. Devouges' firsthand account of this incident comes from La Jonquière, *L'Expédition en Égypte 1798–1801*, Vol. 3, pp. 61–2.
8. Napoleon, *Correspondance*, Vol. 4, p. 475.
9. Ibid., p. 361.
10. Ibid., p. 379.

11. This and the following quote are from Marmont, op. cit., Vol. 1, p. 419.
12. Napoleon, *Correspondance*, Vol. 4, p. 189.
13. Ibid., Vol. 5, p. 105.
14. Marmont, op. cit., Vol. 1, pp. 423–4.
15. Napoleon, *Correspondance*, Vol. 5, p. 143.
16. La Jonquière, *L'Expédition en Égypte 1798–1801*, Vol. 3, p. 397.
17. This quote and the following are from ibid., p. 399.
18. Ibid., Vol. 2, p. 600.
19. Ruffin's diplomatic report is cited in ibid., p. 602.
20. Several sources confirm this: the most significant being Talleyrand's letter written on November 4, 1798, which had not yet reached Napoleon. This is cited in ibid., Vol. 3, p. 267, and will be discussed in due course. It makes clear without any shadow of doubt that Napoleon had mentioned this alternative before he left France.
21. This and the following quote from Ruffin's diplomatic report are cited in ibid., p. 232.
22. Cited in ibid., p. 233.
23. Ibid.
24. Blanning, *The French Revolutionary Wars*, p. 230.
25. Marmont, op. cit., Vol. 1, p. 416.
26. This and the two following passages from the *firman* are taken from the full version, which appears in the book written by a former engineer-savant with Napoleon in Egypt: Martin, *Histoire de l'expédition française en Égypte*, Vol. 1, pp. 243–4.
27. Turc, *L'Expédition des Français en Égypte*, p. 136.
28. Napoleon, *Correspondance*, Vol. 29, p. 497.
29. Ibid., Vol. 5, p. 148.
30. Cited in Herold, *Bonaparte in Egypt*, p. 191.
31. Napoleon, *Correspondance*, Vol. 5, pp. 201–2.
32. Ibid., p. 203.
33. Ibid., pp. 203–4.

Chapter XV: Insurrection

1. Turc, *L'Expédition des Français en Égypte*, p. 55.
2. Bourrienne, *Mémoires*, Vol. 2, p. 288.
3. This and the following quote are from Turc, *L'Expédition des Français en Égypte*, p. 56.
4. For the full texts of letters between Kléber, Napoleon and various generals regarding these matters, see La Jonquière, *L'Expédition en Égypte 1798–1801*, Vol. 3, pp. 90–5.
5. Cited in Herold, *Bonaparte in Egypt*, p. 188.
6. For Kléber's pocketbook entries, see Charles-Roux, *Bonaparte gouverneur d'Égypte*, pp. 73–4.
7. La Jonquière, *L'Expédition en Égypte 1798–1801*, Vol. 3, pp. 93–4.
8. Napoleon, *Correspondance*, Vol. 5, p. 29.
9. El-Djabarti, *Merveilles biographiques et historiques, ou Chroniques*, Vol. 6, p. 55.
10. Turc, *Chronique d'Égypte 1798–1804*, p. 41.

11. El-Djabarti, *Merveilles biographiques et historiques, ou Chroniques*, Vol. 6, p. 55.
12. Turc, *Chronique d'Égypte 1798–1804*, p. 45.
13. Ibid., p. 54.
14. Bernoyer, *Avec Bonaparte en Égypte*, pp. 87–8.
15. El-Djabarti, *Merveilles biographiques et historiques, ou Chroniques*, Vol. 6, p. 66.
16. Cited in La Jonquière, *L'Expédition en Égypte 1798–1801*, Vol. 3, pp. 279–80.
17. This and the following quote are from Napoleon, *Correspondance*, Vol. 5, p. 88.
18. El-Djabarti, *Merveilles biographiques et historiques, ou Chroniques*, Vol. 6, pp. 56–7.
19. Bernoyer, *Avec Bonaparte en Égypte*, p. 90.
20. El-Djabarti, *Merveilles biographiques et historiques, ou Chroniques*, Vol. 6, p. 57.
21. Napoleon, *Correspondance*, Vol. 5, p. 88.
22. El-Djabarti, *Merveilles biographiques et historiques, ou Chroniques*, Vol. 6, p. 57.
23. Cited in Aubry, *Monge*, p. 257.
24. Cited in Charles-Roux, *Bonaparte gouverneur d'Égypte*, p. 215.
25. Denon, *Voyages dans la Basse et la Haute Égypte pendant les campagnes de Bonaparte*, Vol. 1, pp. 105–6.
26. Napoleon, *Correspondance*, Vol. 29, p. 502.
27. This and the following quote are from ibid., pp. 502–3.
28. Ibid., Vol. 5, pp. 89–90.
29. Ibid., Vol. 29, p. 502.
30. This and the following quote are from ibid.
31. Cited in Elgood, *Bonaparte's Adventure in Egypt*, p. 161.
32. El-Djabarti, *Merveilles biographiques et historiques, ou Chroniques*, Vol. 6, pp. 58–9.
33. Napoleon, *Correspondance*, Vol. 5, p. 221.
34. This and the following quote are from El-Djabarti, *Merveilles biographiques et historiques, ou Chroniques*, Vol. 6, pp. 79–80.
35. See Ch. II, n.10.
36. De Rémusat, *Mémoires*, Vol. 1, p. 274.

Chapter XVI: Love and Dreams

1. Napoleon, *Correspondance*, Vol. 5, p. 151.
2. This and the following quotes from Kléber's pocketbook are from Charles-Roux, *Bonaparte gouverneur d'Égypte*, pp. 73–4.
3. Quotes from Menou's letter are from Napoleon's *Correspondance inédite, officielle et confidentielle*. These volumes are confusingly numbered: Menou's letter is in the volume covering August 1798–August 1799, on pp. 83–90.
4. Cited in Herold, *Bonaparte in Egypt*, p. 214.
5. *Dictionary of Scientific Biography*, Vol. 4, p. 152.
6. Napoleon, *Correspondance*, Vol. 5, p. 151.
7. *Le Courier de L'Égypte*, No. 27, p. 4.
8. Bourrienne, *Mémoires*, Vol. 2, p. 294.

9. Cited in Herold, *Bonaparte in Egypt*, p. 163.
10. Vertray, *Journal d'un officier de l'armée d'Égypte*, p. 68.
11. Quotes from Dargevel and Mme. Tempié are cited in Charles-Roux, *Bonaparte gouverneur d'Égypte*, pp. 259–60.
12. *Le Courier de l'Égypte*, No. 20, pp. 2–3.
13. Vertray, *Journal d'un officier de l'armée d'Égypte*, p. 68. Admittedly, this passage also contains his relief after getting completely lost for three hours in the back alleyways of Cairo; however, there is no doubt that it also expressed his general state of mind at this period.
14. *Le Courier de l'Égypte*, No. 20, p. 2.
15. El-Djabarti, *Merveilles biographiques et historiques, ou Chroniques*, Vol. 6, pp. 68–9.
16. Ibid., p. 86.
17. Charles-Roux, *Bonaparte gouverneur d'Égypte*, p. 261.
18. Bernoyer, *Avec Bonaparte en Égypte*, p. 118.
19. El-Djabarti, *Merveilles biographiques et historiques, ou Chroniques*, Vol. 7, p. 44.
20. Several sources allude to this: see, for example, McLynn, *Napoleon*, p. 186.
21. Bourrienne, *Mémoires*, Vol. 2, p. 295.
22. Napoleon, *Correspondance*, Vol. 5, p. 216.
23. Bourrienne, *Mémoires*, Vol. 2, p. 296.
24. Junot, *Mémoires*, cited in McLynn, *Napoleon*, p. 187.
25. Bourrienne, *Mémoires*, Vol. 2, p. 296.

Chapter XVII: A Suez Adventure

1. Napoleon, *Correspondance*, Vol. 5, p. 213.
2. El-Djabarti, *Merveilles biographiques et historiques, ou Chroniques*, Vol. 6, p. 81.
3. Bourrienne, *Mémoires*, Vol. 2, p. 304.
4. Ibid.
5. Napoleon, *Correspondance*, Vol. 5, p. 206.
6. Bourrienne, *Mémoires*, Vol. 2, p. 305.
7. Exodus 15:22–25.
8. Bourrienne, *Mémoires*, Vol. 2, p. 305.
9. See for instance Herold, *Bonaparte in Egypt*, p. 222.
10. Bourrienne, *Mémoires*, Vol. 2, p. 306.
11. See Napoleon, *Correspondance*, Vol. 5, p. 240.
12. Volney, *Voyage en Égypte et en Syrie*, Vol. 1, pp. 192–3.
13. Napoleon, *Correspondance*, Vol. 29, p. 512.
14. Ibid.
15. Doguereau, *Journal de L'Expédition d'Égypte*, p. 114.
16. El-Djabarti, *Merveilles biographiques et historiques, ou Chroniques*, Vol. 6, p. 81.
17. Napoleon, *Correspondance*, Vol. 29, pp. 429–30.
18. Charles-Roux, *Bonaparte gouverneur d'Égypte*, p. 373.
19. Napoleon, *Correspondance*, Vol. 5, p. 490.
20. Ibid., p. 470.

21. Ibid., p. 278.
22. Ibid.

Chapter XVIII: Pursuit into Upper Egypt

1. Sauzet, *Desaix: le "sultan juste,"* p. 131.
2. El-Djabarti, *Merveilles biographiques et historiques, ou Chroniques*, Vol. 6, p. 318.
3. Desaix, cited in Sauzet, *Desaix: le "sultan juste,"* p. 214.
4. This and the following two descriptions are in Savary, *Mémoires*, Vol. 1, pp. 69–70.
5. This and the following are cited in Sauzet, *Desaix: le "sultan juste,"* p. 216.
6. Letter from General Friant cited in La Jonquière, *L'Expédition en Égypte 1798–1801*, Vol. 3, p. 218.
7. This eyewitness account in included in *Le Journal de Belliard*, cited in ibid., Vol. 3, p. 218. Although General Belliard himself was not actually present at this battle, other evidence strongly suggests that such a story was true.
8. Savary, *Mémoires*, Vol. 1, p. 70.
9. Napoleon, *Correspondance*, Vol. 5, p. 32.
10. La Jonquière, *L'Expédition en Égypte 1798–1801*, Vol. 3, p. 224.
11. This and the following eyewitness description are cited in ibid., p. 346.
12. Cited in ibid., p. 348.
13. Napoleon, *Correspondance*, Vol. 5, p. 118.
14. Cited in La Jonquière, *L'Expédition en Égypte 1798–1801*, Vol. 3, p. 348n.
15. Denon, *Voyages dans la Basse et la Haute Égypte pendant les campagnes de Bonaparte*, Vol. 1, p. 92.
16. Ibid., p. 98.
17. Ibid., p. 117.
18. Ibid., p. 120.
19. Ibid., p. 117. As well as his many drawings, Denon kept his own notes when he was with Desaix's expedition. Yet as Herold points out (*Bonaparte in Egypt*, p. 241n.), in places Denon's published account bears a strong resemblance to Belliard's journal, suggesting that he drew heavily upon this when writing up his own account. Conclusive evidence of this appears early on in Denon's account of Desaix's expedition, when he describes (using the first person plural) the Battle of Sediman, which took place a month before his arrival. Belliard was also not present at the battle, but his account of it appears to be reliable, drawing as it does on firsthand accounts by his fellow officers.
20. Savary, *Mémoires*, Vol. 1, p. 80.
21. *Le Journal de Belliard*, cited in La Jonquière, *L'Expédition en Égypte 1798–1801*, Vol. 3, p. 513.
22. Ibid.
23. Ibid., p. 517.
24. This and the following quote are from Denon, *Voyages dans la Basse et la Haute Égypte pendant les campagnes de Bonaparte*, Vol. 1, p. 163.
25. This and the following quotes are from *Le Journal de Belliard*, cited in La Jonquière, *L'Expédition en Égypte 1798–1801*, Vol. 3, pp. 515–6.

26. Denon, *Voyages dans la Basse et la Haute Égypte pendant les campagnes de Bonaparte*, Vol. 1, pp. 163-4.

27. This and the following quote are from Savary, *Mémoires*, Vol. 1, p. 82.

28. Denon, *Voyages dans la Basse et la Haute Égypte pendant les campagnes de Bonaparte*, Vol. 1, p. 174.

29. This and the following quote are from Desvernois, *Mémoires*, pp. 161, 162.

30. Savary, *Mémoires*, Vol. 1, p. 88.

31. This and the following quote are from Desaix's report, cited in La Jonquière, *L'Expédition en Égypte 1798-1801*, Vol. 3, p. 531.

32. Savary, *Mémoires*, Vol. 1, p. 89.

Chapter XIX: Into the Unknown

1. Denon, *Voyages dans la Basse et la Haute Égypte pendant les campagnes de Bonaparte*, Vol. 1, Preface.

2. Ibid.

3. This and the following are cited in Vercoutter, *The Search for Ancient Egypt*, p. 50.

4. Denon, *Voyages dans la Basse et la Haute Égypte pendant les campagnes de Bonaparte*, Vol. 1, p. 177.

5. Ibid., p. 184.

6. Cited in Herold, *Bonaparte in Egypt*, p. 249.

7. Denon, *Voyages dans la Basse et la Haute Égypte pendant les campagnes de Bonaparte*, Vol. 1, pp. 179-81.

8. Ibid., p. 183.

9. Ibid., p. 184.

10. Savary, *Mémoires*, Vol. 1, p. 89.

11. Denon, *Voyages dans la Basse et la Haute Égypte pendant les campagnes de Bonaparte*, Vol. 1, p. 184.

12. Cited in Herold, *Bonaparte in Egypt*, p. 250.

13. Denon, *Voyages dans la Basse et la Haute Égypte pendant les campagnes de Bonaparte*, Vol. 1, p. 185.

14. Desvernois, *Mémoires*, p. 164.

15. Denon, *Voyages dans la Basse et la Haute Égypte pendant les campagnes de Bonaparte*, Vol. 1, p. 186.

16. Cited in Charles-Roux, *Bonaparte gouverneur d'Égypte*, p. 235.

17. Denon, *Voyages dans la Basse et la Haute Égypte pendant les campagnes de Bonaparte*, Vol. 1, p. 187.

18. Cited in Tranié, *Bonaparte: la campagne d'Égypte*, p. 163.

19. This and the following two Denon quotes are in *Voyages dans la Basse et la Haute Égypte pendant les campagnes de Bonaparte*, Vol. 1, p. 200-1.

20. This and the following quote are in ibid., pp. 198, 215-6.

21. This does not appear in ibid., but does appear in an English translation taken from another edition: Denon, *Travels in Lower and Upper Egypt*, Vol. 1, pp. 231-2.

22. Denon, *Voyages dans la Basse et la Haute Égypte pendant les campagnes de Bonaparte*, Vol. 1, p. 201.

23. Cited in Moorehead, *The Blue Nile*, p. 120.

24. *Journal de Belliard*, cited in La Jonquière, *L'Expédition en Égypte 1798-1801*, Vol. 3, p. 539.

25. Desvernois, *Mémoires*, pp. 164–5.
26. This and the following two quotes are from Savary, *Mémoires*, Vol. 1, pp. 91–2.
27. Desvernois, *Mémoires*, p. 165.
28. See Brégeon, *L'Égypte de Bonaparte*, Annexe 2, p. 622.
29. This and the following quote are from Denon, *Voyages dans la Basse et la Haute Égypte pendant les campagnes de Bonaparte*, Vol. 1, p. 205.
30. Ibid., p. 219.
31. Brégeon, *L'Égypte de Bonaparte*, Annexe 2, p. 614.
32. Cited in La Jonquière, *L'Expédition en Égypte 1798–1801*, Vol. 3, p. 607.
33. Turc, *Chronique d'Égypte 1798–1804*, p. 48.
34. This and the following excerpt from Desaix's letter are cited in Sauzet, *Desaix: le "sultan juste,"* pp. 245–6.
35. This and the following quote are from ibid., p. 246.

Chapter XX: A Turn for the Worse

1. Cited in Charles-Roux, *Bonaparte gouverneur d'Égypte*, pp. 233–4.
2. This and the following quote are from Andréossy's article in *La Décade*, No. 4, Vol. 2, pp. 101–5.
3. Napoleon, *Correspondance*, Vol. 5, p. 282.
4. Millet, *Souvenirs de la campagne d'Égypte*, pp. 61–2.
5. Ibid., p. 62n.
6. Napoleon, *Correspondance*, Vol. 5, p. 239.
7. Cited in La Jonquière, *L'Expédition en Égypte 1798–1801*, Vol. 4, p. 28.
8. Napoleon, *Correspondance*, Vol. 5, p. 148.
9. Ibid., Vol. 29, p. 512.
10. This and the following quotes are from ibid., Vol. 5, p. 297–8.
11. Cited in Herold, *Bonaparte in Egypt*, p. 312.
12. Napoleon, *Correspondance*, Vol. 30, p. 14.
13. Ibid.
14. Bourrienne, *Mémoires*, Vol. 2, p. 302.
15. This and the following quote are cited in Charles-Roux, *Bonaparte gouverneur d'Égypte*, p. 330.
16. Napoleon, *Correspondance*, Vol. 30, p. 18.
17. El-Djabarti, *Merveilles biographiques et historiques, ou Chroniques*, Vol. 6, p. 94.

Chapter XXI: The Syrian Campaign

1. Turc, *Chronique d'Égypte 1798–1804*, p. 51.
2. Napoleon, *Correspondance*, Vol. 5, p. 310.
3. Bourrienne, *Mémoires*, Vol. 2, p. 316.
4. Millet, *Souvenirs de la campagne d'Égypte*, p. 72.
5. *Journal de Damas*, cited in La Jonquière, *L'Expédition en Égypte 1798–1801*, Vol. 4, p. 118.
6. Doguereau, *Journal de l'Expédition d'Égypte*, p. 143.
7. Napoleon, *Correspondance*, Vol. 30, p. 18.

8. This and the following quote are from ibid., p. 17.
9. Malus, *Souvenirs de l'Expédition de l'Égypte*, p. 119.
10. Cited in La Jonquière, *L'Expédition en Égypte 1798–1801*, Vol. 4, p. 195.
11. Malus, *Souvenirs de l'Expédition de l'Égypte*, p. 123.
12. This and the following quote are from ibid., pp. 123–4.
13. Compilation from letters written to General Marmont (in Alexandria) and General Dugua (in Cairo), cited in Napoleon, *Correspondance*, Vol. 5, p. 334.
14. Bernoyer, *Avec Bonaparte en Égypte*, p. 142.
15. Ibid.
16. Compilation cited in Napoleon, *Correspondance*, Vol. 5, p. 334.
17. Ibid., Vol. 30, p. 14.
18. Ibid., Vol. 5, p. 361.
19. François, *Journal du Capitaine François, dit le Dromadaire d'Égypte*, p. 273.
20. Millet, *Souvenirs de la campagne d'Égypte*, pp. 82–3.
21. Malus, *Souvenirs de l'Expédition de l'Égypte*, p. 135.
22. This and the following quote are from Bourrienne, *Mémoires*, Vol. 2, pp. 320–2.
23. Napoleon, *Correspondance*, Vol. 30, p. 26.
24. This and the following quotes are from Bourrienne, *Mémoires*, Vol. 2, pp. 320–2.
25. This extract from Peyrusse's letter is cited in La Jonquière, *L'Expédition en Égypte 1798–1801*, Vol. 4, p. 271.
26. Captain Krettly's *Souvenirs* are cited in Millet, *Souvenirs de la campagne d'Égypte*, p. 262.
27. Bourrienne, *Mémoires*, Vol. 2, p. 322.
28. Napoleon, *Correspondance*, Vol. 5, p. 348.
29. Ibid., Vol. 30, p. 27.
30. Cited in La Jonquière, *L'Expédition en Égypte 1798–1801*, Vol. 4, pp. 271–2.
31. This and Napoleon's following letters of March 9 collated from *Correspondance*, Vol. 5, pp. 351–2.
32. Bernoyer, *Avec Bonaparte en Égypte*, p. 146.
33. Excerpts from Detroye's journal cited in La Jonquière, *L'Expédition en Égypte 1798–1801*, Vol. 4, p. 284.
34. Desgenettes, *Histoire médicale de l'armée d'Orient*, Vol. 1, p. 88.
35. This and the following quotes are from Napoleon, *Correspondance*, Vol. 30, p. 29.
36. Desgenettes, *Souvenirs de la fin du XVIIIe. siècle*, Vol. 3, p. 221.
37. Malus, *Souvenirs de l'Expédition de l'Égypte*, p. 141.
38. Ibid., pp. 140–3.

Chapter XXII: The Siege of Acre

1. François de Tott, *Mémoires de baron de Tott sur les Turcs et les Tartares* (Paris, 1785), Vol. 2, Part 4, pp. 114–6.
2. Cited in *Biographie Universelle Ancienne et Moderne* (Paris, 1852), Vol. 11, p. 121, under entry for Djezzar.
3. Barrow, *Life and Correspondence of Admiral Sir William Sidney Smith*, Vol. 1, p. 17.
4. Letter to his brother Charles, dated June 1785, cited in ibid., pp. 21–3.

5. See *Thirst for Glory: The Life of Admiral Sir Sidney Smith*, p. 80.
6. Cited in La Jonquière, *L'Expédition en Égypte 1798–1801*, Vol. 4, p. 366.
7. Cited in ibid., p. 315.
8. Cited in ibid., p. 649.
9. Napoleon, *Correspondance*, Vol. 5, p. 373.
10. This and following quote are from François, *Journal du Capitaine François, dit le Dromadaire d'Égypte*, p. 295–6.
11. Napoleon, *Correspondance*, Vol. 5, p. 378.
12. François, *Journal du Capitaine François, dit le Dromadaire d'Égypte*, p. 297.
13. Doguereau, *Journal de l'Expédition d'Égypte*, p. 210.
14. Lavallette, *Mémoires*, Vol. 1, p. 307.
15. Bourrienne, *Mémoires*, Vol. 2, p. 324.
16. This and the following quote are from Napoleon, *Correspondance*, Vol. 30, pp. 43–4.
17. Ibid., Vol. 5, pp. 384–5.
18. Cited in La Jonquière, *L'Expédition en Égypte 1798–1801* Vol. 4, pp. 319–20.
19. Napoleon, *Correspondance*, Vol. 30, p. 44.

Chapter XXIII: The Battle of Mount Tabor

1. Napoleon, *Correspondance*, Vol. 30, p. 45.
2. Preceding figures and quote are from ibid.
3. Bernoyer, *Avec Bonaparte en Égypte*, pp. 154–5.
4. Napoleon, *Correspondance*, Vol. 5, pp. 399–400.
5. Miot, *Mémoires . . . des expéditions en Égypte et Syrie*, pp. 176–8.
6. Millet, *Souvenirs de la campagne d'Égypte*, pp. 104–5.
7. Napoleon, *Correspondance*, Vol. 30, pp. 48–9.
8. Millet, *Souvenirs de la campagne d'Égypte*, pp. 105–6.
9. This and the following quote are from Napoleon, *Correspondance*, Vol. 30, p. 49.
10. Lavallette, *Mémoires*, p. 313.
11. Desgenettes, *Souvenirs de la fin du XVIIIe. siècle*, Vol. 3, p. 237.
12. This has been collated from two sources: the extensive quotations in Schur, *Napoleon in the Holy Land*, p. 118, and the "complete" version which appears in Appendix 2 of Weider and Guigen, *Napoleon: The Man Who Shaped Europe*, pp. 212–3. These differ only slightly from the complete version in *New Judaea*, Vol. XVI, No. 12, p. 190, which is Franz Kobler's translation from the German.
13. Reports in *Le Moniteur* cited in original French in Guedalla, *Napoleon in Palestine*, p. 24, and *Réimpression de L'Ancien Moniteur* (Paris, 1847), Vol. 29, p. 686.
14. This and the previous quote are from *New Judaea*, Vol. XVII, Nos. 1–2, p. 18.

Chapter XXIV: "That man made me lose my destiny"

1. This and the following are from Bourrienne, *Mémoires*, Vol. 2, p. 326.
2. From a letter by Peyrusse to his mother in France, cited in La Jonquière, *L'Expédition en Égypte 1798–1801*, Vol. 4, p. 453.
3. Napoleon, *Correspondance*, Vol. 5, p. 405. This is just one of many such remarks.
4. Pamphlet of 1793, cited in Herold, *The Mind of Napoleon*, p. 217.
5. Barrow, *Life and Correspondence of Admiral Sir William Sidney Smith*, Vol. 1, p. 282.
6. Bernoyer, *Avec Bonaparte en Égypte*, p. 161.
7. This and all the following descriptions of the battle by Smith are from Barrow, *Life and Correspondence of Admiral Sir William Sidney Smith*, Vol. 1, pp. 288–91.
8. Cited in Schur, *Napoleon in the Holy Land*, pp. 145–6.
9. Berthier, *Relation des campagnes du général Bonaparte en Égypte et en Syrie*, p. 105.
10. Bernoyer, *Avec Bonaparte en Égypte*, p. 162.
11. Several sources mention this remark, giving different versions, and a few give different attributions. A typical reference comes in McLynn, *Napoleon*, p. 192.
12. Bourrienne, *Mémoires*, Vol. 2, pp. 330–1.
13. Cited in La Jonquière, *L'Expédition en Égypte 1798–1801*, Vol. 4, p. 527. The dating of the letters which Sir Sidney Smith wrote to Napoleon at this time is not altogether clear. I have ordered them in line with my own reading of the internal and external evidence. La Jonquière, Barrow, Hilbert, and Smith's biographer Pocock each date these letters differently, according to their own readings. Such differences do not drastically alter the overall picture.
14. This description is collated from Lavallette, *Mémoires*, Vol. 1, pp. 318–21, as well as from Barrow, *Life and Correspondence of Admiral Sir William Sidney Smith*, Vol. 1, pp. 305–7, which draws on a slightly different version by Lavallette (who told the story many times in different words). The two versions closely parallel each other, both giving many convincing details.
15. Cited in Schur, *Napoleon in the Holy Land*, p. 148, who names his source as Anon, *Siege of Acre*, a work that shows all the signs of having been written by one of Smith's British colleagues at Acre, or at least having been compiled from his words.
16. See note 14.
17. Napoleon, *Correspondance*, Vol. 5, p. 422.
18. Original French version cited in Berthier, *Relation des campagnes du général Bonaparte en Égypte et en Syrie*, pp. 75–6.
19. Napoleon calls Smith mad on several occasions. This comes from his most detailed and considered assessment of Smith, which was made in St. Helena, on November 9, 1816, cited in Malraux, *Vie de Napoléon par lui-même*, p. 357.
20. For all of Smith's letter, see Barrow, *Life and Correspondence of Admiral Sir William Sidney Smith*, Vol. 1, p. 292–4.
21. Ibid., p. 291.

22. La Jonquière, *L'Expédition en Égypte 1798–1801*, Vol. 4, pp. 632–3.
23. See note 19.

Chapter XXV: The Retreat from Acre

1. Quotes from Directory's letter are in La Jonquière, *L'Expédition en Égypte 1798–1801*, Vol. 3, pp. 261, 266–8.
2. Napoleon, *Correspondance*, Vol. 5, pp. 429–30.
3. Bourrienne, *Mémoires*, Vol. 2, p. 333.
4. Napoleon, *Correspondance*, Vol. 5, p. 440.
5. La Jonquière, *L'Expédition en Égypte 1798–1801*, Vol. 4, p. 539.
6. This and following quote are from ibid., pp. 543–4.
7. Cited in ibid., p. 556.
8. Bourrienne, *Mémoires*, Vol. 2, p. 323.
9. Cited in La Jonquière, *L'Expédition en Égypte 1798–1801*, Vol. 4, p. 548.
10. Ibid., p. 549.
11. Barrow, *Life and Correspondence of Admiral Sir William Sidney Smith*, Vol. 1, pp. 311–2.
12. Bourrienne, *Mémoires*, Vol. 2, pp. 337–8.
13. Cited in La Jonquière, *L'Expédition en Égypte 1798–1801*, Vol. 4, p. 577.
14. See Thiry, *Bonaparte en Égypte*, p. 379n.
15. Barrow, *Life and Correspondence of Admiral Sir William Sidney Smith*, Vol. 1, p. 313.
16. This and the following are from Lavallette, *Mémoires*, Vol. 1, p. 323.
17. Bourrienne, *Mémoires*, Vol. 2, p. 334.
18. Millet, *Souvenirs de la campagne d'Égypte*, p. 133.
19. Richardot, *Nouveaux mémoires sur l'armée française en Égypte et Syrie*, p. 178.
20. This and the following are from François, *Journal du Capitaine François, dit le Dromadaire d'Égypte*, Vol. 1, pp. 338–9.

Chapter XXVI: Sensational Discoveries

1. Napoleon, *Correspondance*, Vol. 5, p. 461.
2. This and the following quote are from Turc, *Chronique d'Égypte 1798–1804*, pp. 65–6.
3. This and the following quote are from Lanusse's report to Dugua, cited in La Jonquière, *L'Expédition en Égypte 1798–1801*, Vol. 5, p. 51.
4. Description of the Mahdi cited in Charles-Roux, *Bonaparte gouverneur d'Égypte*, p. 296.
5. Cited in La Jonquière, *L'Expédition en Égypte 1798–1801*, Vol. 5, p. 87.
6. This and the following are from a compilation from letters sent to Desaix on June 15 and 19: Napoleon, *Correspondance*, Vol. 5, pp. 454, 464.
7. This and the following are from a letter to the Directory: ibid., pp. 484–5.
8. Cited in La Jonquière, *L'Expédition en Égypte 1798–1801*, Vol. 5, p. 231.
9. This and the following are from Napoleon, *Correspondance*, Vol. 5, p. 491.
10. Ibid., p. 485.
11. This scene is described in some detail, complete with direct speech, using

various firsthand sources in *Victoires, conquêtes, désastres, revers et guerres civiles des Français de 1792 à 1815*, Vol. 10, pp. 313–4.

12. Ibid.
13. Cited in Charles-Roux, *Bonaparte gouverneur d'Égypte*, p. 345.
14. Cited in ibid., p. 248.
15. Cited in ibid., p. 346.
16. Napoleon, *Correspondance*, Vol. 5, p. 499.
17. This and the following quote are from ibid., pp. 508, 509.
18. Ibid., p. 517.
19. Bourrienne, *Mémoires*, Vol. 2, p. 361.
20. Cited in La Jonquière, *L'Expédition en Égypte 1798–1801*, Vol. 5, p. 405.
21. Napoleon, *Correspondance*, Vol. 5, p. 541.
22. François, *Journal du Capitaine François, dit le Dromadaire d'Égypte*, Vol. 1, p. 355.
23. Denon, *Voyages dans la Basse et la Haute Égypte pendant les campagnes de Bonaparte*, Vol. 1, p. 351.
24. This and the following are from Napoleon's dispatches: *Correspondance*, Vol. 5, pp. 537, 541–2.
25. François, *Journal du Capitaine François, dit le Dromadaire d'Égypte*, Vol. 1, p. 359.
26. Napoleon, *Correspondance*, Vol. 5, p. 537.
27. This and the following quote are from ibid., pp. 545–6.

Chapter XXVII: The Decision of a Lifetime

1. Exclamations and italics as in original, cited in Bourrienne, *Mémoires*, Vol. 2, p. 363.
2. This and the following quote are in La Jonquière, *L'Expédition en Égypte 1798–1801*, Vol. 5, pp. 166–7.
3. Cited in ibid., p. 576.
4. Napoleon, *Correspondance*, Vol. 5, p. 551.
5. La Jonquière, *L'Expédition en Égypte 1798–1801*, Vol. 5, p. 574.
6. Jomard, *Souvenirs sur Gaspard Monge*, p. 56.
7. Saintine and Reybaud, *Histoire scientifique et militaire de l'Expédition Française en Égypte*, Vol. 6, p. 284. (See Ch. XIII, n. 25 for the sources they used.)
8. Napoleon, *Correspondance*, Vol. 5, p. 569.
9. Bourrienne, *Mémoires*, Vol. 2, p. 367.
10. This and the following Bourrienne quote are from ibid., Vol. 3, p. 2.
11. Aubry, *Monge*, p. 275.
12. This and the following quote are from Bourrienne, *Mémoires*, Vol. 3, p. 3.
13. Cited in Malraux, *Vie de Napoleon par lui-même*, p. 78.
14. Napoleon, *Correspondance*, Vol. 30, p. 94.
15. Sauzet, *Desaix: le "sultan juste,"* pp. 289–90.
16. Chief of Staff Berthier mentions this in the report written by him in Napoleon, *Correspondance*, Vol. 6, p. 362.

Chapter XXVIII: An Abandoned Army

1. Larevellière-Lépaux, *Mémoires*, Vol. 2, p. 348.
2. This and the following quotes are from Napoleon's instructions: *Correspondance*, Vol. 5, pp. 573, 575.
3. *Kléber et Menou en Égypte depuis le départ de Bonaparte*, pp. 78–80.
4. Ibid., p. 8.
5. El-Djabarti, *Merveilles biographiques et historiques, ou Chroniques*, Vol. 6, p. 231.
6. Ibid., p. 250.
7. This and the following quotes are from François, *Journal du Capitaine François, dit le Dromadaire d'Égypte*, pp. 441–2.
8. This and the following quotes are from Malus, *Souvenirs de L'Expédition de l'Égypte*, p. 218.
9. Gourgaud, *Journal de Sainte-Hélène*, Vol. 1, p. 63.
10. Las Cases, *Mémorial de Sainte-Hélène*, Vol. 1, p. 131.
11. Napoleon, *Correspondance*, Vol. 29, pp. 429–30.
12. Bourrienne, *Mémoires*, Vol. 2, p. 330.

Chapter XXIX: Aftermath

1. Cited in Pocock, *Thirst for Glory: The Life of Admiral Sir Sidney Smith*, p. 237; source Las Cases, *Mémorial de Sainte-Hélène*.
2. Cited in Foreman, *Napoleon's Lost Fleet*, p. 156; also in Bourrienne, *Mémoires*, and others.
3. Cited in Russell, *The Discovery of Egypt*, p. 258.
4. Duverger, *Mes aventures dans la campagne du Russie*, p. 1. This and the following are cited by Zamoyski, *1812: Napoleon's Fatal March on Moscow*, p. 102.
5. Meerheimb, *Erlebnisse eines Veteranen der grossen Armee während des Feldzugs in Russland 1812*, p. 7.
6. Cited in Bainville, *Bonaparte*, p. 557.

Select Bibliography

There is a vast literature on almost every aspect and every period of Napoleon's life. As far as possible I have made use of firsthand or contemporary sources. Napoleon's Egyptian campaign was one of the first in history to produce a rash of memoirs from all sections of those who took part in it. This was encouraged by the exotic locale as well as the spread of education in post-revolutionary France. These first-hand reports range from the memoirs of generals to the recollections of sergeants and privates, from the journals of savants to the histories written by contemporary Egyptians. As ever, the reliability of such memoirs is subject to individual memory and motive.

There are certain comprehensive sources that promise a greater degree of reliability, though without always living up to such promise. Amongst these, the most obvious is Napoleon's *Correspondance*, whose thirty-two volumes were published in Paris between 1858 and 1870, i.e., around forty years after his death, on the orders of Napoleon III. Volumes 4–6 cover the period of the Egyptian expedition, and include everything from Napoleon's orders of the day and his correspondence, to his communications with his generals, the Egyptian authorities and the British fleet, his proclamations to his soldiers, the Egyptian people and others, official reports to the Directory, as well as his attempts to communicate with France, the sultan, the Porte and the French representative in Constantinople, and so forth. These give a day-to-day picture, and are largely accurate as they stand, though it is known that Napoleon removed certain documents during his time as ruler. Other obvious inaccuracies are indicated in my text, such as when his secretary Bourrienne states that Napoleon's proclamation to his troops after the siege of Acre "from beginning to end mutilated the truth." Less reliable are Napoleon's memoirs of the expedition, which occupy Volumes 29–30. For these he certainly draws on official documents and his own correspondence, and although his picture is fairly accurate it must be remembered that he was at the time on St. Helena and wished to paint a picture of history as he saw it. Any use of this source has to be measured against other firsthand sources.

Another comprehensive source is provided by C. de La Jonquière's excellent five-volume *L'Expédition en Égypte*, which makes wide use of firsthand sources in the official archives, a few of which remain unavailable to the public. Any historian of this campaign must remain indebted to La Jonquière. I also made use of X. Saintine and L. Reybaud's ten-volume *Histoire scientifique et militaire de l'Expédition Française en Égypte* (Paris, 1830–4), which includes work by several generals and savants. Anyone wishing to research the findings of the expedition must of course consult the sumptuous twenty-volume *Description de l'Égypte*, which was edited by the savant E. F. Jomard and was published between 1809 and 1828 under the auspices of Napoleon himself (the last volumes appeared posthumously).

What follows is a selected bibliography of the sources I consulted more fully during the course of writing this book:

Anon, *Siege of Acre* (London, 1801)
Dominique Arago, *Biographie de Gaspard Monge* (Paris, 1853)
Archives du Ministère des Affaires Etrangères, Paris: correspondance consulaire, Le Caire, lettres de consul Mure, 1776–7
Archives historiques du Ministère de la Guerre: correspondance de l'armée d'Égypte: mémoires historiques
Robert Asprey, *The Rise of Napoleon* (London, 2000)
Paul Aubry, *Monge* (Paris, 1954)
Jacques Bainville, *Bonaparte* (Paris, 1931)
Paul Barras, *Mémoires* (Paris, 1895–6)
John Barrow, *Life and Correspondence of Admiral Sir William Sidney Smith*, 2 vols. (London, 1848)
E. T. Bell, *Men of Mathematics* (London, 1937)
J. G. P. M. Benoist-Méchin, *Bonaparte en Égypte* (Lausanne, 1966)
François Bernoyer, *Avec Bonaparte en Égypte* (published posthumously, Abbeville, 1976)
Louis-Alexandre Berthier, *Relation des campagnes du général Bonaparte en Égypte et en Syrie* (Milan, Year 8, i.e., probably 1800)

Biographie Universelle Ancienne et Moderne (Paris, 1852)

T. C. W. Blanning, *The French Revolutionary Wars* (London, 1996)

Louis Antoine Fauvelet de Bourrienne, *Mémoires*, 10 vols. (Paris, 1831)

Jean-Joël Brégeon, *L'Égypte de Bonaparte* (Paris, 1991)

F. Charles-Roux, *Bonaparte gouverneur d'Égypte* (Paris, 1935)

F. Charles-Roux, *Les Origines de l'Expédition d'Égypte* (Paris, 1910)

A. Chuquet, *Dugommier* (Paris, 1904)

Copies of Original Letters from the Army of General Buonaparte [sic] *in Egypt, intercepted by the Fleet under the Command of Admiral Lord Nelson* (London, 1799)

Correspondance de l'armée française en Égypte (Paris, Year VII, i.e., 1799)

F. Coston, *Biographie des Premières Années de Napoléon Bonaparte* (Paris, 1840)

Le Courier de l'Égypte (Cairo, 1798–9)

Anthony Cronin, *Napoleon* (London, 1971)

La Décade (Cairo, 1798–9)

Vivant Denon, *Voyages dans la Basse et la Haute Égypte pendant les campagnes de Bonaparte*, 2 vols. (London, 1807)

Vivant Denon, *Travels in Lower and Upper Egypt* (trans. E. A. Kendal), 2 vols. (London, 1802; reprinted 1986)

Le Départ du trompette de cuirassiers: chanson militaire (Paris, 1825?)

René-Nicolas Desgenettes, *Souvenirs de la fin du XVIIIe. siècle* (published posthumously, Paris, 1835)

René-Nicolas Desgenettes, *Histoire médicale de l'armée d'Orient* (Paris, 1802)

Nicolas-Philibert Desvernois, *Mémoires* (published posthumously, Paris, 1898)

Dictionary of Scientific Biography, ed. C. C. Gillispie, 16 vols. (New York, 1970–80)

La Diplomatie du Directoire et Bonaparte (Paris, 1951)

Jean-Pierre Doguereau, *Journal de L'Expédition d'Égypte* (published posthumously, Paris, 1904)

F. Doppet, *Mémoires politiques et militaires* (Carouge, 1797)

Pierre-Jean Doublet, *Mémoires Historiques sur l'invasion et l'occupation de Malte en 1798* (published posthumously, Paris, 1883)

B. T. Duverger, *Mes aventures dans la campagne du Russie* (Paris, n.d.)

El-Djabarti, *Merveilles biographiques et historiques, ou Chroniques*, 9 vols., translated from the Arabic (Cairo, 1888–96)

Lt Col. P. G. Elgood, *Bonaparte's Adventure in Egypt* (London, 1936)

Laura Foreman, *Napoleon's Lost Fleet* (London, 1999)

C. François, *Journal du Capitaine François, dit le Dromadaire d'Égypte*, 2 vols. (published posthumously, Paris, 1903)

Etienne Geoffroy Saint-Hilaire, *Lettres écrites d'Égypte* (published posthumously, Paris, 1901)

Shafik Ghorbal, *The Beginnings of the Egyptian Question* (London, 1928)

Gaspard Gourgaud, *Journal de Sainte-Hélène, 1815–1818*, 2 vols. (Paris, 1899)

Lieutenant Laval Grandjean, *Journaux sur l'Expédition de l'Égypte* (published posthumously, 2000, Paris)

Philip Guedalla, *Napoleon in Palestine* (London, 1925)

Louis Hastier, *Le Grand Amour de Joséphine* (Paris, 1955)

J. Christopher Herold, *Bonaparte in Egypt* (London, 1962)

J. Christopher Herold, *The Mind of Napoleon* (New York, 1955)

Histoire de Saint Louis par Jean de Joinville (reprinted Paris, 1874)

E. E. Jomard, *Souvenirs sur Gaspard Monge* (Paris, 1853)

Journal d'Abdurrahman Gabarti [El-Djabarti] *pendant l'occupation française en Egypte* (trans. A. Cardin), (Paris, 1838)

Laure Junot, Duchesse d'Abrantès, *Mémoires*, 18 vols. (Paris, 1831–5)

Kléber et Menou en Egypte depuis le départ de Bonaparte (documents), ed. François Rousseau (Paris, 1900)

C. de La Jonquière, *L'Expédition en Égypte 1798–1801*, 5 vols. (Paris, 1899–1907)

Louise-Marie Larevellière-Lépaux, *Mémoires*, 3 vols. (Paris, 1873)

Emmanuel Las Cases, *Mémorial de Sainte-Hélène*, 2 vols. (corrected edition, Paris, 1935)

Count Lavallette, *Mémoires*, 2 vols. (published posthumously, Paris, 1831)

Sir John Theophilus Lee, *Memoirs* (London, 1836)

André Malraux, *Vie de Napoleon par lui-même* (Paris, 1930)

L'Agenda de Malus, *Souvenirs de l'Expédition de l'Égypte* (published posthumously, Paris, 1892)

P. Martin, *Histoire de l'expédition française en Égypte*, 2 vols. (Paris, 1815)

Frank McLynn, *Napoleon* (London, 1997)

Franz Meerheimb, *Erlebnisse eines Veteranen der grossen Armee während des Feldzugs in Russland 1812* (Dresden, 1860)

Mémoires de General Baron Thiébault, publiés sous les auspices de sa fille (Paris, 1893)

Mémoires et Correspondance du Roi Joseph [Bonaparte], ed. Du Casse, 10 vols. (Paris 1855)

Pierre Millet, *Souvenirs de la campagne d'Égypte* (published posthumously, Paris, 1903)

J.-F. Miot, *Mémoires . . . des expéditions en Égypte et Syrie* (Paris, 1814)

Alan Moorehead, *The Blue Nile* (London, 1962)

Napoleon Bonaparte, *Correspondance inédite, officielle et confidentielle: Égypte*, 3 vols. (Paris, 1819–20)

Napoleon Bonaparte, *Correspondance inédite, officielle et confidentielle*, 7 vols. (Paris, 1819–20)

Napoleon Lettres D'Amour à Josephine, présentées par Jean Tulard (Paris, 1981)

Horatio Nelson, *Letters and Despatches*, ed. J. K. Laughton (London, 1886)

Horatio Nelson, *Despatches and Letters 1798–1800 by Lord Nelson* (London, 1913)

John Nicol, *The Life and Adventures of John Nicol* (Edinburgh, 1822)

Barry O'Meara, *Napoleon in Exile*, 2 vols. (London, 1823)

Tom Pocock, *Thirst for Glory: The Life of Admiral Sir Sidney Smith* (London, 1996)

W. G. Regier, *Book of the Sphinx* (Nebraska, 2004)

Réimpression de L'Ancien Moniteur (Paris, 1847)

Claire de Rémusat, *Mémoires*, 3 vols. (Paris, 1880)

Charles Richardot, *Nouveaux mémoires sur l'armée française en Égypte et Syrie* (Paris, 1848)

Roustam Raza, *Souvenirs de Roustam, mamelouck de Napoleon 1er* (Paris, 1911?)

Jack Russell, *Nelson and the Hamiltons* (London, 1969)

Terence M. Russell, *The Discovery of Egypt* (Stroud, 2005)

Michelle Sadoun-Goupil, *Le Chimiste Claude-Louis Berthollet* (Paris, 1977)

Armand Sauzet, *Desaix: le "Sultan Juste"* (Paris, 1954)

A. Savary (Duc de Rovigo), *Mémoires*, 4 vols. (Paris 1828)

Claude Savary, *Lettres sur L'Égypte* (Paris, 1785)

Nathan Schur, *Napoleon in the Holy Land* (London, 1999)

J. Thiry, *Bonaparte en Égypte* (Paris, 1978)

Lieutenant Thurman, *Bonaparte en Égypte: souvenirs* (published posthumously, Paris, 1902)

Jean Tranié, *Bonaparte: la campagne d'Égypte* (Paris, 1988)

Nicolas Turc, *Chronique d'Égypte 1798–1804*, trans. Gaston Wiet (Cairo, 1950)

Nicolas Turc (Nakoula el-Turk), *L'Expédition des Français en Égypte*, trans. M. Desgranges (Paris, 1839)

Jean Vercoutter, *The Search for Ancient Egypt* (London, 1992)

M. Vertray, *Journal d'un officier de l'armeé d'Égypte* (published posthumously, Paris, 1883)

Victoires, conquêtes, désastres, revers et guerres civiles des Français de 1792 à 1815, 28 vols. (Paris, 1818–95)

Constantin Volney, *Oeuvres Complètes* (Paris, 1860)

Constantin Volney, *Voyage en Égypte et en Syrie*, 2 vols. (Paris, 1787)

Ben Weider and Émile Guigen, *Napoleon: The Man Who Shaped Europe* (Staplehurst, 2001)

Cooper Willyams, *A Voyage up the Mediterranean . . . with a Description of the Battle of the Nile* (London, 1802)

Adam Zamoyski, *1812: Napoleon's Fatal March on Moscow* (London, 2004)

Index

About the Author

PAUL STRATHERN studied philosophy at Trinity College, Dublin. He has lectured in philosophy and mathematics and is a Somerset Maugham Prize–winning novelist. He is the bestselling author of several books of nonfiction, including *The Artist, The Philosopher and the Warrior: The Intersecting Lives of da Vinci, Machiavelli, and Borgia and the World They Shaped, Philosophers in 90 Minutes,* and *The Big Idea: Scientists Who Changed the World.*

Printed in the United States
by Baker & Taylor Publisher Services